THE NEW TESTAMENT AND OTHER EARLY CHRISTIAN WRITINGS

THE NEW TESTAMENT AND OTHER EARLY CHRISTIAN WRITINGS

A READER

SECOND EDITION

Bart D. Ehrman

New York   Oxford
OXFORD UNIVERSITY PRESS
2004

Oxford University Press

Oxford   New York
Auckland   Bangkok   Buenos Aires   Cape Town   Chennai
Dar es Salaam   Delhi   Hong Kong   Istanbul   Karachi   Kolkata
Kuala Lumpur   Madrid   Melbourne   Mexico City   Mumbai
Nairobi   São Paulo   Shanghai   Taipei   Tokyo   Toronto

Published by Oxford University Press, Inc.
198 Madison Avenue, New York, New York 10016
http://www.oup-usa.org

Oxford is a registered trademark of Oxford University Press

Library of Congress Cataloging-in-Publication Data

Ehrman, Bart D.
  The New Testament and other early Christian writings : a reader / Bart D. Ehrman.—2nd ed.
    p.   cm.
  Includes bibliographical references.
  ISBN 978-0-19-515464-1
  1. Bible. N.T.—Introductions.   2. Christian literature, Early—History and criticism.
  3. Church history—Primitive and early church, ca. 30–600.   I. Title.
  BS2330.2 .E355   2003
  270.1—dc21   2002193003

Printed in the United States of America
on acid-free paper.

Contents

Preface to the Second Edition

I appreciate the encouragement and support I have received from readers of this collection of early Christian texts. In addition to some minor editing of the introductions, I have incorporated two major changes in the second edition. First, I have included an additional text, the Martyrdom of Polycarp, which does not fall within my strict chronological parameters but which makes sense in a collection of the earliest Christian writings. For reasons I spell out in its introduction, its addition should make the book more useful for the classes for which it was designed. Second, I have replaced a number of the older translations of non-canonical works with translations of my own. Most of these have been taken from my two-volume edition of the *Apostolic Fathers* in the Loeb Classical Library (Cambridge: Harvard University Press, 2003), used with permission: the *Martyrdom of Polycarp*, 1 Clement, the *Didache*, the letters of Ignatius, the Letter of Polycarp, the Letter of Barnabas, the Fragments of Papias, and *The Shepherd* of Hermas. For these I appreciate the help given by Margaret Fulton, General Editor for the Humanities at Harvard University Press, and by Jeffrey Hamilton, General Editor of the Loeb Classical Library. In addition, I have translated several other texts afresh for this edition: the *Gospel of Peter*, the *Infancy Gospel of Thomas*, the *Secret Gospel of Mark*, and *Papyrus Egerton 2*.

For this second edition I am grateful for the assistance rendered by my graduate student, Carl Cosaert, and by the editorial staff at Oxford University Press, especially my long-term editor and friend, Robert Miller.

Preface to the First Edition

The impetus for this collection of the earliest Christian writings came from my classroom experience. Even though my undergraduate class on the New Testament focuses, naturally enough, on the twenty-seven books that Christians eventually came to regard as canonical Scripture, it also considers other Christian books written at approximately the same time but not included, for a variety of reasons, in the Christian canon, books like the Gospels of *Peter* and *Thomas* and the letters of Ignatius and Barnabas. Many of these books were at one time or another considered Scripture by various Christians, and they are absolutely critical for any full understanding of the history and literature of early Christianity. But until now they have not been available in one volume, so that students wanting to own them have had to buy not only a New Testament, but also collections of the "Apostolic Fathers" (for such books as the letters of Ignatius and the *Epistle of Barnabas*), of the "New Testament Apocrypha" (e.g., for the *Gospel* and *Apocalypse of Peter*), and of the newly discovered "Nag Hammadi Library" (e.g., for the *Gospel of Thomas*).

It occurred to me, then, that it would make sense to have an inexpensive collection of *all* of the earliest Christian writings from the ancient world. Moreover, it seemed reasonable to assume that this collection would also appeal to readers outside the classroom setting, to anyone, in fact, interested in the earliest Christian church, its history, beliefs, practices, and literature. And so, as explained in the general introduction, this volume presents in clear and readable English translations every surviving document produced by a Christian during the first hundred years of the church, that is, from the time of Jesus' death (ca. 30 C.E.) through the first third of the second century (ca. 130 C.E.). Each document is provided with a brief introduction; the collection is preceded by a general introduction to the writings of the early Christians and to the question of how some of these writings came to be collected into the canon of Scripture.

Here I would like to acknowledge several people who assisted me in making this collection and, especially, in writing the introductions: Elizabeth Parker, my friend and former student, whose perspicacity exceeds her years; my good friends since graduate days, E. Elizabeth Johnson, Dale Martin, and Jeffrey Siker, themselves keen scholars and superb teachers; and Robert Miller, my exceptionally clearheaded editor at Oxford.

General Introduction

In the judgment of most scholars, the earliest New Testament book is 1 Thessalonians, written sometime around 50 C.E.; the latest is probably 2 Peter, written around 120 C.E. The seventy years separating these two works saw the appearance of scores of other Christian documents, some of them later canonized as parts of the New Testament, others of them not. Around 95 C.E., for example, a member of the Christian congregation in Rome produced the letter called 1 Clement. Some fifteen or twenty years later Ignatius of Antioch wrote his surviving seven letters. At about the same time, the *Gospel of Thomas* was in circulation, as was the church manual called the *Didache* and the apocalypse known as *The Shepherd* of Hermas. These other works were not included among the books of the New Testament when the canon came to be fixed in the fourth and fifth centuries. Yet they also represent writings of the early Christians. And many of them, at one time or another, were considered sacred Scripture.

The purpose of the present work is to collect all of the earliest surviving Christian writings in one volume. For purposes of convenience, the term "earliest" refers to the first century of Christianity, 30 C.E. (the approximate year of Jesus' death) to 130 C.E., or thereabouts. The volume includes every work thought to have been produced by a Christian from this period, books that made it into the New Testament and those that did not, books later judged to be orthodox and those condemned as heretical, books that survive complete and books that survive only in fragments.

The collection does not, of course, include all of the literature actually *produced* during Christianity's first hundred years. On the contrary, we know of numerous texts from the period that, for one reason or another, no longer survive. Just from the writings of the New Testament, for example, we learn of a letter that Paul sent to the Christians of Corinth *before* he wrote 1 Corinthians (1 Cor 5:9), a letter that some of the Corinthians had sent to him (1 Cor 7:1), a letter forged in Paul's name to the Thessalonians (2 Thess 2:2), and a letter sent in his name to the church of Laodicea (Col 4:16). Moreover, the author of the Gospel of Luke indicates that "many" authors before him had written accounts of Jesus' life (1:1). Scholars are reasonably sure that the Gospel of Mark was one of these predecessors, but what of the others? At least one of them, the source of Jesus' sayings that scholars have called Q (from the German *Quelle*, "source," which was also used by Matthew), can probably be reconstructed to some extent. But this is a hypothetical undertaking.

The historical reality is that most of the noncanonical books mentioned in our early surviving sources have been lost. Some were destroyed when Christian leaders found their teachings dangerous. Others simply disappeared out of general disinterest: no one bothered to reproduce them for posterity. The books that do survive were copied through the Middle Ages by Christian scribes intent on preserving their sacred texts, or they were hidden for one reason or another in antiquity, only to be turned up in modern times by professional archaeologists or rummaging bedouin. In any event, most of the writings that survive from early Christianity have come down to us in the New Testament itself.

THE CANON OF THE NEW TESTAMENT

One of the major breakthroughs in biblical scholarship over the past century—a break-through whose roots lie in the Reformation—is the recognition that even the twenty-seven books of the New Testament evidence a considerable degree of diversity among themselves. These writings were produced by at least seventeen different authors living in various countries. These authors addressed different audiences for different reasons; in some instances, they express fundamentally different perspectives on fundamentally significant issues. When the early literature that was *not* included in the New Testament is thrown into the mix, the rich and wide diversity of the early Christian movement becomes even more apparent.

This, then, raises the question of why some books were chosen to be included in the New Testament while others were excluded. Full-length studies of this question are readily available; for the purposes of this introduction, a basic sketch of the situation will suffice.[1]

From the very beginning, Christianity was deeply rooted both in oral traditions about its founder and in written texts that it had inherited from Judaism. Jesus himself, as a Jewish teacher and prophet, discussed, explained, and debated the Hebrew Scriptures; his followers eventually came to understand him to be the Messiah sent from God in fulfillment of these Scriptures. As the early Christians told stories about what he said and did, the Scriptures were never far removed from their thoughts; indeed the oral traditions about Jesus, especially in the formative period of the religion, were closely informed by Christian understandings of the Law, the Psalms, and the Prophets. Soon after Jesus' death, his followers interpreted his life in light of these writings; they eventually saw themselves as the true heirs of the traditions they contained, even when their own communities were comprised, by and large, of Gentiles rather than Jews.

We do not know which Christian was the first to write a book, but the earliest surviving works are by the apostle Paul, who some twenty years after Jesus' death began to write letters to churches that he had founded in the northeastern Mediterranean. Soon thereafter a flood of literature appeared: letters urging certain beliefs and lifestyles on their Christian addressees; accounts of the life, death, and resurrection of Jesus; apocalyptic portrayals of the end time. Eventually there appeared histories of the Christian church, sermons delivered to Christian congregations, manuals for conducting Christian rituals, and accounts of the deaths of early Christian martyrs.

Early Christianity became a remarkably literary movement. Apart from Judaism, there was nothing quite like it in the entire Greco-Roman world, where literary texts typically had very little to do with religion per se. In part, of course, the literary impulse came from the Jewish religion from which the Christian church emerged, but in part it came from the universalistic thrust of the new religion itself. Many Christians believed that in fulfillment of the promises made to the Jewish patriarchs, Jesus had come as a savior of the entire world, not just Israel. As different communities came to be established throughout the Roman Empire, Christians everywhere had a sense that they *belonged* together, that they were part of something larger

---

[1]For a brief sketch, see Bart D. Ehrman, *The New Testament: A Historical Introduction to the Early Christian Writings,* 3rd ed. (New York: Oxford, 2004), chap. 1. For a fuller, article-length discussion, see Harry Gamble, "Canon: New Testament," in the *Anchor Bible Dictionary,* vol. 1 (New York: Doubleday, 1992) pp. 852–61. A nice, concise, book-length treatment can be found in H. Gamble, *The New Testament Canon: Its Making and Meaning,* Guides to Biblical Scholarship (Philadelphia: Fortress, 1985). For a full and authoritative discussion, see Bruce M. Metzger, *The Canon of the New Testament* (New York: Oxford, 1987).

than their own small communities, that the church was not merely a local congregation but a worldwide movement through which God was bringing salvation to all people.

The literature that was produced by early Christians served to bind the various Christian communities together. Leaders and groups from one congregation wrote to others; books written in one place for one purpose were taken to another place, copied there, and read by Christians completely unknown to the author and his or her own community. This earliest Christian literature thus provided spiritual, intellectual, and emotional cohesion for communities that were geographically separated.

Already by the middle of the first century C.E., many Christians considered the words of Jesus to be as authoritative as the words of Scripture found in the Hebrew Bible; by the end of the century, some Christian writings were being granted comparable authority. The process is already evident in works that made it into the New Testament: 1 Timothy 5:18, for example, places a saying of Jesus on a par with the Jewish Bible, and 2 Peter 3:16 numbers Paul's letters among the Scriptures. Even at this relatively early stage, then, two kinds of Christian authority had begun to emerge: traditions about Jesus and writings by his apostles. The Christian canon that eventually developed reflects this bipartite structure, comprising Gospels and other apostolic books.

A good deal of the early Christian literature responded to the needs of the various local congregations. Leaders of the churches were concerned that their followers understood what to believe (doctrine), how to live (ethics), and how to engage in Christian worship and ritual (practice). As might be expected of congregations scattered throughout vast tracts of the Roman empire, individuals coming from richly varied backgrounds—in terms of cultural heritage, social class, economic position, religious upbringing, educational opportunity, and so forth—had widely diverse views about almost everything Christian. The written texts produced by these individuals reflect their range of opinions.

This kind of diversity soon became a problem for Christian leaders intent on the unity of the religion, who saw Christianity as *one* thing rather than lots of *different* things, who understood the gospel of Christ as having a single meaning to be professed and practiced by all Christians in the same way everywhere. The diversity of the movement came to be especially evident around the middle of the second century, just after the period covered in the present volume. Forceful and charismatic Christians came forward, advocating beliefs and practices that were seen by others as totally unacceptable. Battle lines were drawn, with each side claiming to represent the authentic Christian tradition passed down from Jesus himself to the disciples.

In the debates that ensued, nothing proved more important than the Christian literature that had been produced earlier. Christians of various stripe put forth their own "authoritative" texts, claiming that books written by apostles were normative for what Christians should believe and how they should live. The side that won these debates decided the contours of the canon that was to be passed down to Christian posterity. We have the results of this victory in the writings of the New Testament. Even for ancient readers, when these books were taken individually outside of their canonical contexts they could be thought to represent a wide range of Christian perspective; but when they were grouped together into *one* book, the New Testament canon, they were understood to present a unified theological and practical perspective that was acceptable to the majority of Christians involved in the selection process.

The decisions concerning which books should be considered Scripture did not come immediately to an end at the close of the second century. On the contrary, the debates continued for centuries. To be sure, already by 200 C.E. many churches accepted most of the books that eventually made it into the canon. But not all churches agreed. We know of some second- and third-century Christian communities, for example, that accepted only one of our canonical Gospels as authoritative (e.g., only Matthew or only Luke or only John); other communities that accepted none of the four individually, but used a much fuller Gospel created around 170 C.E., a harmonization of our four books into one megagospel (the so-called *Diatesseron,* which no longer survives intact); and other communities that had their own favorites, including Gospels that did not come to be included in the New Testament (e.g., the *Gospel of Peter* or the *Gospel of Thomas*). During this same period, some Christian communities saw the apostle Paul as the only final authority for faith and practice, while other communities saw him as an arch-heretic and enemy of God. There were some communities that accepted the Apocalypse of John as a divine revelation of the future course of events, and other communities that rejected the book as naive and nonapostolic. And there were some communities that accepted the *Letter of 1 Clement, The Shepherd* of Hermas, and the *Letter of Barnabas* as Scripture, while other communities did not.

Christians involved in the disputes over the canon of Scripture typically invoked several considerations. Generally it was thought that, to be included, a book needed to be ancient (close to the time of Jesus), apostolic (written by an apostle or one of their companions), orthodox (affirming the "right" belief, whatever that was judged to be), and catholic (widely used throughout the church). The debates were sometimes harsh; by all counts, they were long and drawn out. Strikingly enough, it was not until 367 C.E.—nearly 250 years after the last of the canonical books was actually written—that any Christian author listed the twenty-seven books of our New Testament, and only these books, as belonging to the Christian Scriptures. The author was Athanasius, the bishop of Alexandria, who penned his list precisely because so many people in his community and elsewhere disagreed.

In sum, it is important for modern readers to realize that the book we call the New Testament is actually a *collection* of books, put together by persons living much later than the actual authors. When "Matthew" wrote his Gospel, he had no idea that someone would eventually combine his book with three others that were more or less like it to form the first section of a canon of Scripture, a canon that was to include a history of the Christian movement, personal letters sent by other early Christians, and an apocalyptic narrative of the end time. The New Testament, in other words, is a historical construct, not a "given." It comprises twenty-seven diverse books brought together under one cover for particular religious reasons and under specific historical circumstances. And it is not fully representative of the views and writings of the early Christians.

On the other hand, and somewhat unfortunately, *no* collection of Christian books can be fully representative of these early Christians, precisely because so much of their literature has been lost. The present collection at least provides the best cross-sampling possible, in that it gives all of the earliest Christian literature that has come down to us, both the books that came to form part of the New Testament and those that did not.

By way of conclusion, it may be worthwhile to say a brief word concerning the collection itself.

LIMITATIONS OF THE COLLECTION

This collection includes the early Christian writings that appear to have been composed by the first third of the second century. These writings survive either in manuscript form (i.e., as copied by scribes) or in direct quotations by other authors. The collection does not include texts that do not actually survive, such as the Q source of Jesus' sayings that appears to lie behind Matthew and Luke. Nor does it include paraphrases of early Christian writings found in later sources. As a matter of convenience, several highly fragmentary texts have been excluded, such as the one-sentence statement drawn from the Apology of Quadratus by the fourth-century church father Eusebius (*Ecclesiastical History* 4.3).

There are some texts that other scholars would include among the literature of this period, such as the *Apocryphon of James* and the *Gospel of the Egyptians,* that have been excluded here simply because, in the opinion of the present editor, they cannot be reliably dated to the first hundred years of the Christian movement (30–130 C.E.). These two particular examples, in any event, happen to be gospel texts, of which enough other samples survive to provide a good sense of the materials that were being produced and read in the period.

The two exceptions to my self-imposed chronological boundaries, the Acts of Paul and Thecla and the *Martyrdom of Polycarp,* are explained in their introductions.

TEXTS

All of the texts are either given in previously published and well-established English translations, with full permission of their original publishers, or are my own. Translations have been chosen on the grounds of accuracy and, especially, readability. The New Revised Standard Version of the New Testament will be familiar to many readers; the other texts are also readily available. Alterations have been kept to a minimum and been made with permission; these involve such things as the standardization of spelling, capitalization, and punctuation and the occasional modernization of language (e.g., *thee's* and *thou's* and jarring instances of non-inclusive language).

Cross-references are provided for explicit or clear citations of the Hebrew Bible and other sacred texts (including earlier Christian writings cited by later authors; these earlier writings are themselves, of course, also presented in full). No attempt has been made to identify scriptural allusions or distant echoes.

The complete text of each book or surviving fragment has been included, except in the cases of *The Shepherd* of Hermas and the *Apocalypse of Peter.* These are unusually long documents; the selections provided here should give an adequate idea of their content and style.

STRUCTURE

There is no completely satisfactory way to arrange these materials. It is impossible to give them chronologically, since so many of them can be dated with only proximate accuracy. And because so many of them cover a variety of topics, a thematic arrangement is likewise out of the question. For the sake of convenience, therefore, the collection follows the structure provided by the New Testament itself, with books arranged more or less by genre: Gospels (written accounts of the words and/or deeds of Jesus), Acts (narratives of the history of the church and/or the activities of the apostles), Pauline epistles (letters sent by Paul and other early Christians in his name), other writings (a mixture of genres, including other letters, a sermon, a persuasive essay, a church manual, and a martyrology), and apocalypses (narrative visions of the heavenly realities that explain earthly existence).

INTRODUCTIONS

Each of the texts is provided with a concise introduction that highlights its important features and supplies essential background information. The collection as a whole has been designed to accompany the fuller introduction to this literature in Bart D. Ehrman, *The New Testament: A Historical Introduction to the Early Christian Writings*, 3rd ed. (New York: Oxford University Press, 2004). Anyone interested in learning more about these texts can turn to that volume or to any other historical introduction to the New Testament and other early Christian writings.

EARLY CHRISTIAN GOSPELS

The Gospel According to Matthew

Matthew was awarded pride of place as the first Gospel of the New Testament, not because it was the first to be written, but probably because it was the most widely used by early Christians interested in knowing about the birth, life, death, and resurrection of Jesus. Indeed, stories found in Matthew but in none of our other Gospels continue to be among the best known and most popular accounts for readers of the New Testament today. Only here do we read of the visit of the magi to the infant Jesus and of the flight to Egypt; here alone does Jesus deliver his Sermon on the Mount with its memorable form of the Beatitudes ("Blessed are the poor in spirit" . . .), Antitheses ("You have heard that it was said, 'An eye for an eye and a tooth for a tooth,' But I say to you . . ."), and other inspirational sayings ("Store up for yourselves treasures in heaven," "No one can serve two masters," "Do not worry about tomorrow, for tomorrow will bring worries of its own").

Christian writers of the second century ascribed the book to Matthew, the tax collector called by Jesus to be his disciple (see Matt 9:9). The actual author of the book, however, did not disclose his name. Scholars today generally think that he was a Greek-speaking Christian writing in the second half of the first century, perhaps around 80–85 C.E., probably outside of Palestine, possibly, in the opinion of some, in Antioch of Syria. The author's insistence that Jesus' followers adhere closely to the Jewish law (Matt 7:17–20) may suggest that he was himself a Jewish Christian; at the same time, his claim that Gentiles who accepted Jesus would enter into God's kingdom while many Jews would remain outside (8:10–12) may indicate that his own Christian community was comprised of both Jews and Gentiles.

It appears that Matthew's accounts were drawn from written and oral sources, including the Gospel of Mark and a collection of Jesus' sayings that scholars have designated Q (from the German word for "source," *Quelle*), a lost Gospel that was also available to the author of Luke. "Matthew" used these sources to create a distinctive portrayal of Jesus as a new Moses who provides the authoritative interpretation of the Jewish law (e.g., 5:1–48). His followers are to adhere to this law in all its particulars, and to do so even better than the Jewish leaders, the scribes and Pharisees who throughout this Gospel are condemned as self-serving hypocrites (see chap. 23).

These leaders fail to be convinced of Jesus' identity, despite his many miraculous deeds; as his opponents, they ultimately arrange to have him executed (chaps. 26–27). But this death is according to God's plan, for through it Jesus "saves his people from their sins" (1:21). On the third day, Jesus is raised from the dead and appears to his disciples, commissioning them to spread his "good news" throughout the entire world, teaching their converts to observe all that Jesus commanded, until he returns (28:19–20).

From the New Revised Standard Version Bible, © 1989.

1 An account of the genealogy[a] of Jesus the Messiah,[b] the son of David, the son of Abraham.

2 Abraham was the father of Isaac, and Isaac the father of Jacob, and Jacob the father of Judah and his brothers, 3 and Judah the father of Perez and Zerah by Tamar, and Perez the father of Hezron, and Hezron the father of Aram, 4 and Aram the father of Aminadab, and Aminadab the father of Nahshon, and Nahshon the father of Salmon, 5 and Salmon the father of Boaz by Rahab, and Boaz the father of Obed by Ruth, and Obed the father of Jesse, 6 and Jesse the father of King David.

And David was the father of Solomon by the wife of Uriah, 7 and Solomon the father of Rehoboam, and Rehoboam the father of Abijah, and Abijah the father of Asaph,[c] 8 and Asaph[c] the father of Jehoshaphat, and Jehoshaphat the father of Joram, and Joram the father of Uzziah, 9 and Uzziah the father of Jotham, and Jotham the father of Ahaz, and Ahaz the father of Hezekiah, 10 and Hezekiah the father of Manasseh, and Manasseh the father of Amos,[d] and Amos[d] the father of Josiah, 11 and Josiah the father of Jechoniah and his brothers, at the time of the deportation to Babylon.

12 And after the deportation to Babylon: Jechoniah was the father of Salathiel, and Salathiel the father of Zerubbabel, 13 and Zerubbabel the father of Abiud, and Abiud the father of Eliakim, and Eliakim the father of Azor, 14 and Azor the father of Zadok, and Zadok the father of Achim, and Achim the father of Eliud, 15 and Eliud the father of Eleazar, and Eleazar the father of Matthan, and Matthan the father of Jacob, 16 and Jacob the father of Joseph the husband of Mary, of whom Jesus was born, who is called the Messiah.[e]

17 So all the generations from Abraham to David are fourteen generations; and from David to the deportation to Babylon, fourteen generations; and from the deportation to Babylon to the Messiah,[e] fourteen generations.

18 Now the birth of Jesus the Messiah[b] took place in this way. When his mother Mary had been engaged to Joseph, but before they lived together, she was found to be with child from the Holy Spirit. 19 Her husband Joseph, being a righteous man and unwilling to expose her to public disgrace, planned to dismiss her quietly. 20 But just when he had resolved to do this, an angel of the Lord appeared to him in a dream and said, "Joseph, son of David, do not be afraid to take Mary as your wife, for the child conceived in her is from the Holy Spirit. 21 She will bear a son, and you are to name him Jesus, for he will save his people from their sins." 22 All this took place to fulfill what had been spoken by the Lord through the prophet:

23   "Look, the virgin shall conceive
                and bear a son,
           and they shall name him
                Emmanuel,"[1]

which means, "God is with us."[2] 24 When Joseph awoke from sleep, he did as the angel of the Lord commanded him; he took her as his wife, 25 but had no marital relations with her until she had borne a son;[f] and he named him Jesus.

2 In the time of King Herod, after Jesus was born in Bethlehem of Judea, wise men[g] from the East came to Jerusalem, 2 asking, "Where is the child who has been born king of the Jews? For we observed his star at its rising,[i] and have come to pay him homage." 3 When King Herod heard this, he was frightened, and all Jerusalem with him; 4 and calling together all the chief priests and scribes of the people, he inquired of them where the Messiah[e] was to be born. 5 They told him, "In Bethlehem of Judea; for so it has been written by the prophet:

6   'And you, Bethlehem, in the land
                of Judah,
           are by no means least among
                the rulers of Judah;
           for from you shall come a ruler
           who is to shepherd[j] my people
                Israel.'"[3]

7 Then Herod secretly called for the wise men[g] and learned from them the exact time when the star had appeared. 8 Then he sent them to Bethlehem, saying, "Go and search diligently for the child; and when you have found him, bring me word so

---

[a]Or *birth* [b]Or *Jesus Christ* [c]Other ancient authorities read *Asa* [d]Other ancient authorities read *Amon* [e]Or *the Christ* [f]Or *rule* [g]Or *astrologers*; Gk *magi* [h]Other ancient authorities read *her firstborn son* [i]Or *in the East* [j]Or *rule*

[1]Isa 7:14 [2]Isa 8:8, 10 [3]Mic 5:2; 2 Sam 5:2

that I may also go and pay him homage." 9 When they had heard the king, they set out; and there, ahead of them, went the star that they had seen at its rising,[k] until it stopped over the place where the child was. 10 When they saw that the star had stopped,[l] they were overwhelmed with joy. 11 On entering the house, they saw the child with Mary his mother; and they knelt down and paid him homage. Then, opening their treasure chests, they offered him gifts of gold, frankincense, and myrrh. 12 And having been warned in a dream not to return to Herod, they left for their own country by another road.

13 Now after they had left, an angel of the Lord appeared to Joseph in a dream and said, "Get up, take the child and his mother, and flee to Egypt, and remain there until I tell you; for Herod is about to search for the child, to destroy him." 14 Then Joseph[m] got up, took the child and his mother by night, and went to Egypt, 15 and remained there until the death of Herod. This was to fulfill what had been spoken by the Lord through the prophet, "Out of Egypt I have called my son."[4]

16 When Herod saw that he had been tricked by the wise men,[n] he was infuriated, and he sent and killed all the children in and around Bethlehem who were two years old or under, according to the time that he had learned from the wise men.[n] 17 Then was fulfilled what had been spoken through the prophet Jeremiah:

18   "A voice was heard in Ramah,
          wailing and loud lamentation,
        Rachel weeping for her children;
          she refused to be consoled,
            because they are no more."[5]

19 When Herod died, an angel of the Lord suddenly appeared in a dream to Joseph in Egypt and said, 20 "Get up, take the child and his mother, and go to the land of Israel, for those who were seeking the child's life are dead." 21 Then Joseph[m] got up, took the child and his mother, and went to the land of Israel. 22 But when he heard that Archelaus was ruling over Judea in place of his father Herod, he was afraid to go there. And after being warned in a dream, he went away to the district of Galilee. 23 There he made his home in a town called Nazareth, so that what had been spoken through the prophets might be fulfilled, "He will be called a Nazorean."[6]

3 In those days John the Baptist appeared in the wilderness of Judea, proclaiming, 2 "Repent, for the kingdom of heaven has come near."[o] 3 This is the one of whom the prophet Isaiah spoke when he said,

        "The voice of one crying out in
              the wilderness:
        'Prepare the way of the Lord,
            make his paths straight.'"[7]

4 Now John wore clothing of camel's hair with a leather belt around his waist, and his food was locusts and wild honey. 5 Then the people of Jerusalem and all Judea were going out to him, and all the region along the Jordan, 6 and they were baptized by him in the river Jordan, confessing their sins.

7 But when he saw many Pharisees and Sadducees coming for baptism, he said to them, "You brood of vipers! Who warned you to flee from the wrath to come? 8 Bear fruit worthy of repentance. 9 Do not presume to say to yourselves, 'We have Abraham as our ancestor'; for I tell you, God is able from these stones to raise up children to Abraham. 10 Even now the ax is lying at the root of the trees; every tree therefore that does not bear good fruit is cut down and thrown into the fire.

11 "I baptize you with[p] water for repentance, but one who is more powerful than I is coming after me; I am not worthy to carry his sandals. He will baptize you with[p] the Holy Spirit and fire. 12 His winnowing fork is in his hand, and he will clear his threshing floor and will gather his wheat into the granary; but the chaff he will burn with unquenchable fire."

13 Then Jesus came from Galilee to John at the Jordan, to be baptized by him. 14 John would have prevented him, saying, "I need to be baptized by you, and do you come to me?" 15 But Jesus answered him, "Let it be so now; for it is proper for us in this way to fulfill all righteousness." Then he consented. 16 And when Jesus had been baptized, just as he came up from the water, suddenly the heavens were opened to him and he saw the Spirit of God descending like a dove and alighting on

---

[k]Or in the East   [l]Gk saw the star   [m]Gk he   [n]Or astrologers; Gk magi   [o]Or is at hand   [p]Or in

---

[4]Hos 11:1   [5]Jer 31:15   [6]Isa 11:1(?)   [7]Isa 40:3

him. 17 And a voice from heaven said, "This is my Son, the Beloved,[q] with whom I am well pleased."

4 Then Jesus was led up by the Spirit into the wilderness to be tempted by the devil. 2 He fasted forty days and forty nights, and afterwards he was famished. 3 The tempter came and said to him, "If you are the Son of God, command these stones to become loaves of bread." 4 But he answered, "It is written,

'One does not live by bread alone,
but by every word that comes
from the mouth of God.'"[8]

5 Then the devil took him to the holy city and placed him on the pinnacle of the temple, 6 saying to him, "If you are the Son of God, throw yourself down; for it is written,

'He will command his angels
concerning you,'
and 'On their hands they will
bear you up,
so that you will not dash your
foot against a stone.'"[9]

7 Jesus said to him, "Again it is written, 'Do not put the Lord your God to the test.'"[10]

8 Again, the devil took him to a very high mountain and showed him all the kingdoms of the world and their splendor; 9 and he said to him, "All these I will give you, if you will fall down and worship me." 10 Jesus said to him, "Away with you, Satan! for it is written,

'Worship the Lord your God,
and serve only him.'"[11]

11 Then the devil left him, and suddenly angels came and waited on him.

12 Now when Jesus[r] heard that John had been arrested, he withdrew to Galilee. 13 He left Nazareth and made his home in Capernaum by the sea, in the territory of Zebulun and Naphtali, 14 so that what had been spoken through the prophet Isaiah might be fulfilled:

15   "Land of Zebulun, land of
            Naphtali,
        on the road by the sea, across
            the Jordan, Galilee of the
            Gentiles—

16   the people who sat in darkness
        have seen a great light,
        and for those who sat in

the region and shadow of death
    light has dawned."[12]

17 From that time Jesus began to proclaim, "Repent, for the kingdom of heaven has come near."[s]

18 As he walked by the Sea of Galilee, he saw two brothers, Simon, who is called Peter, and Andrew his brother, casting a net into the sea—for they were fishermen. 19 And he said to them, "Follow me, and I will make you fish for people." 20 Immediately they left their nets and followed him. 21 As he went from there, he saw two other brothers, James son of Zebedee and his brother John, in the boat with their father Zebedee, mending their nets, and he called them. 22 Immediately they left the boat and their father, and followed him.

23 Jesus[r] went throughout Galilee, teaching in their synagogues and proclaiming the good news[t] of the kingdom and curing every disease and every sickness among the people. 24 So his fame spread throughout all Syria, and they brought to him all the sick, those who were afflicted with various diseases and pains, demoniacs, epileptics, and paralytics, and he cured them. 25 And great crowds followed him from Galilee, the Decapolis, Jerusalem, Judea, and from beyond the Jordan.

5 When Jesus[r] saw the crowds, he went up the mountain; and after he sat down, his disciples came to him. 2 Then he began to speak, and taught them, saying:

3 "Blessed are the poor in spirit, for theirs is the kingdom of heaven.

4 "Blessed are those who mourn, for they will be comforted.

5 "Blessed are the meek, for they will inherit the earth.

6 "Blessed are those who hunger and thirst for righteousness, for they will be filled.

7 "Blessed are the merciful, for they will receive mercy.

8 "Blessed are the pure in heart, for they will see God.

9 "Blessed are the peacemakers, for they will be called children of God.

[q]Or *my beloved Son*   [r]Gk *he*   [s]Or *is at hand*   [t]Gk *gospel*

[8]Deut 8:3   [9]Ps 91:11–12   [10]Deut 6:16   [11]Deut 6:13   [12]Isa 9:1–2

10 "Blessed are those who are persecuted for righteousness' sake, for theirs is the kingdom of heaven.

11 "Blessed are you when people revile you and persecute you and utter all kinds of evil against you falsely[u] on my account. 12 Rejoice and be glad, for your reward is great in heaven, for in the same way they persecuted the prophets who were before you.

13 "You are the salt of the earth; but if salt has lost its taste, how can its saltiness be restored? It is no longer good for anything, but is thrown out and trampled under foot.

14 "You are the light of the world. A city built on a hill cannot be hid. 15 No one after lighting a lamp puts it under the bushel basket, but on the lampstand, and it gives light to all in the house. 16 In the same way, let your light shine before others, so that they may see your good works and give glory to your Father in heaven.

17 "Do not think that I have come to abolish the law or the prophets; I have come not to abolish but to fulfill. 18 For truly I tell you, until heaven and earth pass away, not one letter,[v] not one stroke of a letter, will pass from the law until all is accomplished. 19 Therefore, whoever breaks[w] one of the least of these commandments, and teaches others to do the same, will be called least in the kingdom of heaven; but whoever does them and teaches them will be called great in the kingdom of heaven. 20 For I tell you, unless your righteousness exceeds that of the scribes and Pharisees, you will never enter the kingdom of heaven.

21 "You have heard that it was said to those of ancient times, 'You shall not murder';[13] and 'whoever murders shall be liable to judgment.' 22 But I say to you that if you are angry with a brother or sister,[x] you will be liable to judgment; and if you insult[y] a brother or sister,[z] you will be liable to the council; and if you say, 'You fool,' you will be liable to the hell[a] of fire. 23 So when you are offering your gift at the altar, if you remember that your brother or sister[b] has something against you, 24 leave your gift there before the altar and go; first be reconciled to your brother or sister,[b] and then come and offer your gift. 25 Come to terms quickly with your accuser while you are on the way to court[c] with him, or your accuser may hand you over to the judge, and the judge to the guard,

and you will be thrown into prison. 26 Truly I tell you, you will never get out until you have paid the last penny.

27 "You have heard that it was said, 'You shall not commit adultery.'[14] 28 But I say to you that everyone who looks at a woman with lust has already committed adultery with her in his heart. 29 If your right eye causes you to sin, tear it out and throw it away; it is better for you to lose one of your members than for your whole body to be thrown into hell.[a] 30 And if your right hand causes you to sin, cut it off and throw it away; it is better for you to lose one of your members than for your whole body to go into hell.[a]

31 "It was also said, 'Whoever divorces his wife, let him give her a certificate of divorce.'[15] 32 But I say to you that anyone who divorces his wife, except on the ground of unchastity, causes her to commit adultery; and whoever marries a divorced woman commits adultery.

33 "Again, you have heard that it was said to those of ancient times, 'You shall not swear falsely, but carry out the vows you have made to the Lord.'[16] 34 But I say to you, Do not swear at all, either by heaven, for it is the throne of God, 35 or by the earth, for it is his footstool, or by Jerusalem, for it is the city of the great King. 36 And do not swear by your head, for you cannot make one hair white or black. 37 Let your word be 'Yes, Yes' or 'No, No'; anything more than this comes from the evil one.[d]

38 "You have heard that it was said, 'An eye for an eye and a tooth for a tooth.'[17] 39 But I say to you, Do not resist an evildoer. But if anyone strikes you on the right cheek, turn the other also; 40 and if anyone wants to sue you and take your coat, give your cloak as well; 41 and if anyone forces you to go one mile, go also the second mile. 42 Give to everyone who begs from you, and do not refuse anyone who wants to borrow from you.

43 "You have heard that it was said, 'You shall love your neighbor and hate your enemy.'[18]

---

[u]Other ancient authorities lack *falsely*   [v]Gk *one iota*   [w]Or *annuls*
[x]Gk *a brother*; other ancient authorities add *without cause*   [y]Gk *say Raca to* (an obscure term of abuse)   [z]Gk *a brother*   [a]Gk *Gehenna*
[b]Gk *your brother*   [c]Gk lacks *to court*   [d]Or *evil*

---

[13]Exod 20:13; Deut 5:17   [14]Exod 20:14; Deut 5:18   [15]Deut 24:1
[15]Exod 20:7; Lev 19:12; Num 30:2; Deut 23:21   [17]Exod 21:24; Lev 24:20; Deut 19:21   [18]Lev 19:18

44 But I say to you, Love your enemies and pray for those who persecute you, 45 so that you may be children of your Father in heaven; for he makes his sun rise on the evil and on the good, and sends rain on the righteous and on the unrighteous. 46 For if you love those who love you, what reward do you have? Do not even the tax collectors do the same? 47 And if you greet only your brothers and sisters,ᵉ what more are you doing than others? Do not even the Gentiles do the same? 48 Be perfect, therefore, as your heavenly Father is perfect.

6 "Beware of practicing your piety before others in order to be seen by them; for then you have no reward from your Father in heaven.

2 "So whenever you give alms, do not sound a trumpet before you, as the hypocrites do in the synagogues and in the streets, so that they may be praised by others. Truly I tell you, they have received their reward. 3 But when you give alms, do not let your left hand know what your right hand is doing, 4 so that your alms may be done in secret; and your Father who sees in secret will reward you.ᶠ

5 "And whenever you pray, do not be like the hypocrites; for they love to stand and pray in the synagogues and at the street corners, so that they may be seen by others. Truly I tell you, they have received their reward. 6 But whenever you pray, go into your room and shut the door and pray to your Father who is in secret; and your Father who sees in secret will reward you.ᶠ

7 "When you are praying, do not heap up empty phrases as the Gentiles do; for they think that they will be heard because of their many words. 8 Do not be like them, for your Father knows what you need before you ask him.

9 "Pray then in this way:
Our Father in heaven,
hallowed be your name.
10   Your kingdom come.
Your will be done,
on earth as it is in heaven.
11   Give us this day our daily
bread.ᵍ
12   And forgive us our debts,
as we also have forgiven our
debtors.

13   And do not bring us to the time
of trial,ʰ
but rescue us from the evil
one.ⁱ

14 For if you forgive others their trespasses, your heavenly Father will also forgive you; 15 but if you do not forgive others, neither will your Father forgive your trespasses.

16 "And whenever you fast, do not look dismal, like the hypocrites, for they disfigure their faces so as to show others that they are fasting. Truly I tell you, they have received their reward. 17 But when you fast, put oil on your head and wash your face, 18 so that your fasting may be seen not by others but by your Father who is in secret; and your Father who sees in secret will reward you.ᶠ

19 "Do not store up for yourselves treasures on earth, where moth and rustʲ consume and where thieves break in and steal; 20 but store up for yourselves treasures in heaven, where neither moth nor rustʲ consumes and where thieves do not break in and steal. 21 For where your treasure is, there your heart will be also.

22 "The eye is the lamp of the body. So, if your eye is healthy, your whole body will be full of light; 23 but if your eye is unhealthy, your whole body will be full of darkness. If then the light in you is darkness, how great is the darkness!

24 "No one can serve two masters; for a slave will either hate the one and love the other, or be devoted to the one and despise the other. You cannot serve God and wealth.ᵏ

25 "Therefore I tell you, do not worry about your life, what you will eat or what you will drink,ˡ or about your body, what you will wear. Is not life more than food, and the body more than clothing? 26 Look at the birds of the air; they neither sow nor reap nor gather into barns, and yet your heavenly Father feeds them. Are you not of more value than they? 27 And can any of you by worrying add a single hour to your span of life?ᵐ 28 And why do you worry about clothing? Consider the lilies of

ᵉGk your brothers ᶠOther ancient authorities add openly ᵍOr our bread for tomorrow ʰOr us into temptation ⁱOr from evil. Other ancient authorities add, in some form, For the kingdom and the power and the glory are yours forever. Amen. ʲGk eating ᵏGk mammon ˡOther ancient authorities lack or what you will drink ᵐOr add one cubit to your height

the field, how they grow; they neither toil nor spin, 29 yet I tell you, even Solomon in all his glory was not clothed like one of these. 30 But if God so clothes the grass of the field, which is alive today and tomorrow is thrown into the oven, will he not much more clothe you—you of little faith? 31 Therefore do not worry, saying, 'What will we eat?' or 'What will we drink?' or 'What will we wear?' 32 For it is the Gentiles who strive for all these things; and indeed your heavenly Father knows that you need all these things. 33 But strive first for the kingdom of God[n] and his[o] righteousness, and all these things will be given to you as well.

34 "So do not worry about tomorrow, for tomorrow will bring worries of its own. Today's trouble is enough for today.

7 "Do not judge, so that you may not be judged. 2 For with the judgment you make you will be judged, and the measure you give will be the measure you get. 3 Why do you see the speck in your neighbor's[p] eye, but do not notice the log in your own eye? 4 Or how can you say to your neighbor,[q] 'Let me take the speck out of your eye,' while the log is in your own eye? 5 You hypocrite, first take the log out of your own eye, and then you will see clearly to take the speck out of your neighbor's[p] eye.

6 "Do not give what is holy to dogs; and do not throw your pearls before swine, or they will trample them under foot and turn and maul you.

7 "Ask, and it will be given you; search, and you will find; knock, and the door will be opened for you. 8 For everyone who asks receives, and everyone who searches finds, and for everyone who knocks, the door will be opened. 9 Is there anyone among you who, if your child asks for bread, will give a stone? 10 Or if the child asks for a fish, will give a snake? 11 If you then, who are evil, know how to give good gifts to your children, how much more will your Father in heaven give good things to those who ask him!

12 "In everything do to others as you would have them do to you; for this is the law and the prophets.

13 "Enter through the narrow gate; for the gate is wide and the road is easy[r] that leads to destruction, and there are many who take it. 14 For the

gate is narrow and the road is hard that leads to life, and there are few who find it.

15 "Beware of false prophets, who come to you in sheep's clothing but inwardly are ravenous wolves. 16 You will know them by their fruits. Are grapes gathered from thorns, or figs from thistles? 17 In the same way, every good tree bears good fruit, but the bad tree bears bad fruit. 18 A good tree cannot bear bad fruit, nor can a bad tree bear good fruit. 19 Every tree that does not bear good fruit is cut down and thrown into the fire. 20 Thus you will know them by their fruits.

21 "Not everyone who says to me, 'Lord, Lord,' will enter the kingdom of heaven, but only the one who does the will of my Father in heaven. 22 On that day many will say to me, 'Lord, Lord, did we not prophesy in your name, and cast out demons in your name, and do many deeds of power in your name?' 23 Then I will declare to them, 'I never knew you; go away from me, you evildoers.'

24 "Everyone then who hears these words of mine and acts on them will be like a wise man who built his house on rock. 25 The rain fell, the floods came, and the winds blew and beat on that house, but it did not fall, because it had been founded on rock. 26 And everyone who hears these words of mine and does not act on them will be like a foolish man who built his house on sand. 27 The rain fell, and the floods came, and the winds blew and beat against that house, and it fell—and great was its fall!"

28 Now when Jesus had finished saying these things, the crowds were astounded at his teaching, 29 for he taught them as one having authority, and not as their scribes.

8 When Jesus[s] had come down from the mountain, great crowds followed him; 2 and there was a leper[t] who came to him and knelt before him, saying, "Lord, if you choose, you can make me clean." 3 He stretched out his hand and touched him, saying, "I do choose. Be made clean!" Immediately his leprosy[t] was cleansed. 4 Then Jesus said to him, "See that you say noth-

[n]Other ancient authorities lack *of God*   [o]Or *its*   [p]Gk *brother's*
[q]Gk *brother*   [r]Other ancient authorities read *for the road is wide and easy*   [s]Gk *he*   [t]The terms *leper* and *leprosy* can refer to several diseases

ing to anyone; but go, show yourself to the priest, and offer the gift that Moses commanded, as a testimony to them."

5 When he entered Capernaum, a centurion came to him, appealing to him 6 and saying, "Lord, my servant is lying at home paralyzed, in terrible distress." 7 And he said to him, "I will come and cure him." 8 The centurion answered, "Lord, I am not worthy to have you come under my roof; but only speak the word, and my servant will be healed. 9 For I also am a man under authority, with soldiers under me; and I say to one, 'Go,' and he goes, and to another, 'Come,' and he comes, and to my slave, 'Do this,' and the slave does it." 10 When Jesus heard him, he was amazed and said to those who followed him, "Truly I tell you, in no one[u] in Israel have I found such faith. 11 I tell you, many will come from east and west and will eat with Abraham and Isaac and Jacob in the kingdom of heaven, 12 while the heirs of the kingdom will be thrown into the outer darkness, where there will be weeping and gnashing of teeth." 13 And to the centurion Jesus said, "Go; let it be done for you according to your faith." And the servant was healed in that hour.

14 When Jesus entered Peter's house, he saw his mother-in-law lying in bed with a fever; 15 he touched her hand, and the fever left her, and she got up and began to serve him. 16 That evening they brought to him many who were possessed with demons; and he cast out the spirits with a word, and cured all who were sick. 17 This was to fulfill what had been spoken through the prophet Isaiah, "He took our infirmities and bore our diseases."[19]

18 Now when Jesus saw great crowds around him, he gave orders to go over to the other side. 19 A scribe then approached and said, "Teacher, I will follow you wherever you go." 20 And Jesus said to him, "Foxes have holes, and birds of the air have nests; but the Son of Man has nowhere to lay his head." 21 Another of his disciples said to him, "Lord, first let me go and bury my father." 22 But Jesus said to him, "Follow me, and let the dead bury their own dead."

23 And when he got into the boat, his disciples followed him. 24 A windstorm arose on the sea, so great that the boat was being swamped by the waves; but he was asleep. 25 And they went and

woke him up, saying, "Lord, save us! We are perishing!" 26 And he said to them, "Why are you afraid, you of little faith?" Then he got up and rebuked the winds and the sea; and there was a dead calm. 27 They were amazed, saying, "What sort of man is this, that even the winds and the sea obey him?"

28 When he came to the other side, to the country of the Gadarenes,[v] two demoniacs coming out of the tombs met him. They were so fierce that no one could pass that way. 29 Suddenly they shouted, "What have you to do with us, Son of God? Have you come here to torment us before the time?" 30 Now a large herd of swine was feeding at some distance from them. 31 The demons begged him, "If you cast us out, send us into the herd of swine." 32 And he said to them, "Go!" So they came out and entered the swine; and suddenly, the whole herd rushed down the steep bank into the sea and perished in the water. 33 The swineherds ran off, and on going into the town, they told the whole story about what had happened to the demoniacs. 34 Then the whole town came out to meet Jesus; and when they saw him, they begged him to leave their neighborhood.

9 And after getting into a boat he crossed the sea and came to his own town.

2 And just then some people were carrying a paralyzed man lying on a bed. When Jesus saw their faith, he said to the paralytic, "Take heart, son; your sins are forgiven." 3 Then some of the scribes said to themselves, "This man is blaspheming." 4 But Jesus, perceiving their thoughts, said, "Why do you think evil in your hearts? 5 For which is easier, to say, 'Your sins are forgiven,' or to say, 'Stand up and walk'? 6 But so that you may know that the Son of Man has authority on earth to forgive sins"—he then said to the paralytic—"Stand up, take your bed and go to your home." 7 And he stood up and went to his home. 8 When the crowds saw it, they were filled with awe, and they glorified God, who had given such authority to human beings.

9 As Jesus was walking along, he saw a man called Matthew sitting at the tax booth; and he said

[u]Other ancient authorities read *Truly I tell you, not even* [v]Other ancient authorities read *Gergesenes*; others, *Gerasenes*

[19]Isa 53:4

to him, "Follow me." And he got up and followed him.

10 And as he sat at dinner[w] in the house, many tax collectors and sinners came and were sitting[x] with him and his disciples. 11 When the Pharisees saw this, they said to his disciples, "Why does your teacher eat with tax collectors and sinners?" 12 But when he heard this, he said, "Those who are well have no need of a physician, but those who are sick. 13 Go and learn what this means, 'I desire mercy, not sacrifice.'[20] For I have come to call not the righteous but sinners."

14 Then the disciples of John came to him, saying, "Why do we and the Pharisees fast often,[y] but your disciples do not fast?" 15 And Jesus said to them, "The wedding guests cannot mourn as long as the bridegroom is with them, can they? The days will come when the bridegroom is taken away from them, and then they will fast. 16 No one sews a piece of unshrunk cloth on an old cloak, for the patch pulls away from the cloak, and a worse tear is made. 17 Neither is new wine put into old wineskins; otherwise, the skins burst, and the wine is spilled, and the skins are destroyed; but new wine is put into fresh wineskins, and so both are preserved."

18 While he was saying these things to them, suddenly a leader of the synagogue[z] came in and knelt before him, saying, "My daughter has just died; but come and lay your hand on her, and she will live." 19 And Jesus got up and followed him, with his disciples. 20 Then suddenly a woman who had been suffering from hemorrhages for twelve years came up behind him and touched the fringe of his cloak, 21 for she said to herself, "If I only touch his cloak, I will be made well." 22 Jesus turned, and seeing her he said, "Take heart, daughter; your faith has made you well." And instantly the woman was made well. 23 When Jesus came to the leader's house and saw the flute players and the crowd making a commotion, 24 he said, "Go away; for the girl is not dead but sleeping." And they laughed at him. 25 But when the crowd had been put outside, he went in and took her by the hand, and the girl got up. 26 And the report of this spread throughout that district.

27 As Jesus went on from there, two blind men followed him, crying loudly, "Have mercy on us, Son of David!" 28 When he entered the house, the blind men came to him; and Jesus said to them, "Do you believe that I am able to do this?" They said to him, "Yes, Lord." 29 Then he touched their eyes and said, "According to your faith let it be done to you." 30 And their eyes were opened. Then Jesus sternly ordered them, "See that no one knows of this." 31 But they went away and spread the news about him throughout that district.

32 After they had gone away, a demoniac who was mute was brought to him. 33 And when the demon had been cast out, the one who had been mute spoke; and the crowds were amazed and said, "Never has anything like this been seen in Israel." 34 But the Pharisees said, "By the ruler of the demons he casts out the demons."[a]

35 Then Jesus went about all the cities and villages, teaching in their synagogues, and proclaiming the good news of the kingdom, and curing every disease and every sickness. 36 When he saw the crowds, he had compassion for them, because they were harassed and helpless, like sheep without a shepherd. 37 Then he said to his disciples, "The harvest is plentiful, but the laborers are few; 38 therefore ask the Lord of the harvest to send out laborers into his harvest."

10 Then Jesus[b] summoned his twelve disciples and gave them authority over unclean spirits, to cast them out, and to cure every disease and every sickness. 2 These are the names of the twelve apostles: first, Simon, also known as Peter, and his brother Andrew; James son of Zebedee, and his brother John; 3 Philip and Bartholomew; Thomas and Matthew the tax collector; James son of Alphaeus, and Thaddaeus;[c] 4 Simon the Cananaean, and Judas Iscariot, the one who betrayed him.

5 These twelve Jesus sent out with the following instructions: "Go nowhere among the Gentiles, and enter no town of the Samaritans, 6 but go rather to the lost sheep of the house of Israel. 7 As you go, proclaim the good news, 'The kingdom of heaven has come near.'[d] 8 Cure the sick,

---

[w]Gk reclined [x]Gk were reclining [y]Other ancient authorities lack often [z]Gk lacks of the synagogue [a]Other ancient authorities lack this verse [b]Gk he [c]Other ancient authorities read Lebbaeus, or Lebbaeus called Thaddaeus [d]Or is at hand

[20]Hos 6:6

raise the dead, cleanse the lepers,[e] cast out demons. You received without payment; give without payment. 9 Take no gold, or silver, or copper in your belts, 10 no bag for your journey, or two tunics, or sandals, or a staff; for laborers deserve their food. 11 Whatever town or village you enter, find out who in it is worthy, and stay there until you leave. 12 As you enter the house, greet it. 13 If the house is worthy, let your peace come upon it; but if it is not worthy, let your peace return to you. 14 If anyone will not welcome you or listen to your words, shake off the dust from your feet as you leave that house or town. 15 Truly I tell you, it will be more tolerable for the land of Sodom and Gomorrah on the day of judgment than for that town.

16 "See, I am sending you out like sheep into the midst of wolves; so be wise as serpents and innocent as doves. 17 Beware of them, for they will hand you over to councils and flog you in their synagogues; 18 and you will be dragged before governors and kings because of me, as a testimony to them and the Gentiles. 19 When they hand you over, do not worry about how you are to speak or what you are to say; for what you are to say will be given to you at that time; 20 for it is not you who speak, but the Spirit of your Father speaking through you. 21 Brother will betray brother to death, and a father his child, and children will rise against parents and have them put to death; 22 and you will be hated by all because of my name. But the one who endures to the end will be saved. 23 When they persecute you in one town, flee to the next; for truly I tell you, you will not have gone through all the towns of Israel before the Son of Man comes.

24 "A disciple is not above the teacher, nor a slave above the master; 25 it is enough for the disciple to be like the teacher, and the slave like the master. If they have called the master of the house Beelzebul, how much more will they malign those of his household!

26 "So have no fear of them; for nothing is covered up that will not be uncovered, and nothing secret that will not become known. 27 What I say to you in the dark, tell in the light; and what you hear whispered, proclaim from the housetops. 28 Do not fear those who kill the body but cannot kill the soul; rather fear him who can destroy both soul and body in hell.[f] 29 Are not two sparrows sold for a penny? Yet not one of them will fall to the ground apart from your Father. 30 And even the hairs of your head are all counted. 31 So do not be afraid; you are of more value than many sparrows.

32 "Everyone therefore who acknowledges me before others, I also will acknowledge before my Father in heaven; 33 but whoever denies me before others, I also will deny before my Father in heaven.

34 "Do not think that I have come to bring peace to the earth; I have not come to bring peace, but a sword.

| 35 | For I have come to set a man against his father, and a daughter against her mother, and a daughter-in-law against her mother-in-law; |
| 36 | and one's foes will be members of one's own household.[21] |

37 Whoever loves father or mother more than me is not worthy of me; and whoever loves son or daughter more than me is not worthy of me; 38 and whoever does not take up the cross and follow me is not worthy of me. 39 Those who find their life will lose it, and those who lose their life for my sake will find it.

40 "Whoever welcomes you welcomes me, and whoever welcomes me welcomes the one who sent me. 41 Whoever welcomes a prophet in the name of a prophet will receive a prophet's reward; and whoever welcomes a righteous person in the name of a righteous person will receive the reward of the righteous; 42 and whoever gives even a cup of cold water to one of these little ones in the name of a disciple—truly I tell you, none of these will lose their reward."

11 Now when Jesus had finished instructing his twelve disciples, he went on from there to teach and proclaim his message in their cities.

2 When John heard in prison what the Messiah[g] was doing, he sent word by his[h] disciples 3 and

---

[e]The terms *leper* and *leprosy* can refer to several diseases [f]Gk *Gehenna* [g]Or *the Christ* [h]Other ancient authorities read *two of his*

---

[21]Mic 7:6

said to him, "Are you the one who is to come, or are we to wait for another?" 4 Jesus answered them, "Go and tell John what you hear and see: 5 the blind receive their sight, the lame walk, the lepers[i] are cleansed, the deaf hear, the dead are raised, and the poor have good news brought to them. 6 And blessed is anyone who takes no offense at me."

7 As they went away, Jesus began to speak to the crowds about John: "What did you go out into the wilderness to look at? A reed shaken by the wind? 8 What then did you go out to see? Someone[j] dressed in soft robes? Look, those who wear soft robes are in royal palaces. 9 What then did you go out to see? A prophet?[k] Yes, I tell you, and more than a prophet. 10 This is the one about whom it is written,

'See, I am sending my messenger
      ahead of you,
   who will prepare your way
      before you.'[22]

11 Truly I tell you, among those born of women no one has arisen greater than John the Baptist; yet the least in the kingdom of heaven is greater than he. 12 From the days of John the Baptist until now the kingdom of heaven has suffered violence,[l] and the violent take it by force. 13 For all the prophets and the law prophesied until John came; 14 and if you are willing to accept it, he is Elijah who is to come. 15 Let anyone with ears[m] listen!

16 "But to what will I compare this generation? It is like children sitting in the marketplaces and calling to one another,

17   'We played the flute for you, and
            you did not dance;
         we wailed, and you did not
            mourn.'

18 For John came neither eating nor drinking, and they say, 'He has a demon'; 19 the Son of Man came eating and drinking, and they say, 'Look, a glutton and a drunkard, a friend of tax collectors and sinners!' Yet wisdom is vindicated by her deeds."[n]

20 Then he began to reproach the cities in which most of his deeds of power had been done, because they did not repent. 21 "Woe to you, Chorazin! Woe to you, Bethsaida! For if the deeds of power done in you had been done in Tyre and Sidon, they would have repented long ago in sackcloth and ashes. 22 But I tell you, on the day of judgment it will be more tolerable for Tyre and Sidon than for you. 23 And you, Capernaum,

   will you be exalted to heaven?
      No, you will be brought down
         to Hades.

For if the deeds of power done in you had been done in Sodom, it would have remained until this day. 24 But I tell you that on the day of judgment it will be more tolerable for the land of Sodom than for you."

25 At that time Jesus said, "I thank[o] you, Father, Lord of heaven and earth, because you have hidden these things from the wise and the intelligent and have revealed them to infants; 26 yes, Father, for such was your gracious will.[p] 27 All things have been handed over to me by my Father; and no one knows the Son except the Father, and no one knows the Father except the Son and anyone to whom the Son chooses to reveal him.

28 "Come to me, all you that are weary and are carrying heavy burdens, and I will give you rest. 29 Take my yoke upon you, and learn from me; for I am gentle and humble in heart, and you will find rest for your souls. 30 For my yoke is easy, and my burden is light."

12 At that time Jesus went through the grainfields on the sabbath; his disciples were hungry, and they began to pluck heads of grain and to eat. 2 When the Pharisees saw it, they said to him, "Look, your disciples are doing what is not lawful to do on the sabbath." 3 He said to them, "Have you not read what David did when he and his companions were hungry? 4 He entered the house of God and ate the bread of the Presence, which it was not lawful for him or his companions to eat, but only for the priests. 5 Or have you not read in the law that on the sabbath the priests in the temple break the sabbath and yet are guiltless? 6 I tell you, something greater than the temple is here. 7 But if you had known what this means, 'I desire mercy and not sacrifice,'[23] you would not have

[i]The terms *leper* and *leprosy* can refer to several diseases   [j]Or *Why then did you go out? To see someone*   [k]Other ancient authorities read *Why then did you go out? To see a prophet?*   [l]Or *has been coming violently*   [m]Other ancient authorities add *to hear*   [n]Other ancient authorities read *children*   [o]Or *praise*   [p]Or *for so it was well-pleasing in your sight*

[22]Mal 3:1   [23]Hos 6:6

condemned the guiltless. 8 For the Son of Man is lord of the sabbath."

9 He left that place and entered their synagogue; 10 a man was there with a withered hand, and they asked him, "Is it lawful to cure on the sabbath?" so that they might accuse him. 11 He said to them, "Suppose one of you has only one sheep and it falls into a pit on the sabbath; will you not lay hold of it and lift it out? 12 How much more valuable is a human being than a sheep! So it is lawful to do good on the sabbath." 13 Then he said to the man, "Stretch out your hand." He stretched it out, and it was restored, as sound as the other. 14 But the Pharisees went out and conspired against him, how to destroy him.

15 When Jesus became aware of this, he departed. Many crowds[q] followed him, and he cured all of them, 16 and he ordered them not to make him known. 17 This was to fulfill what had been spoken through the prophet Isaiah:

18   "Here is my servant, whom I have
                   chosen,
             my beloved, with whom my soul
                   is well pleased.
       I will put my Spirit upon him,
             and he will proclaim justice to
                   the Gentiles.
19   He will not wrangle or cry aloud,
             nor will anyone hear his voice
                   in the streets.
20   He will not break a bruised reed
             or quench a smoldering wick
       until he brings justice to victory.
21   And in his name the Gentiles
             will hope."[24]

22 Then they brought to him a demoniac who was blind and mute; and he cured him, so that the one who had been mute could speak and see. 23 All the crowds were amazed and said, "Can this be the Son of David?" 24 But when the Pharisees heard it, they said, "It is only by Beelzebul, the ruler of the demons, that this fellow casts out the demons." 25 He knew what they were thinking and said to them, "Every kingdom divided against itself is laid waste, and no city or house divided against itself will stand. 26 If Satan casts out Satan, he is divided against himself; how then will his kingdom stand? 27 If I cast out demons by Beelzebul, by whom do your own exorcists[r] cast

them out? Therefore they will be your judges. 28 But if it is by the Spirit of God that I cast out demons, then the kingdom of God has come to you. 29 Or how can one enter a strong man's house and plunder his property, without first tying up the strong man? Then indeed the house can be plundered. 30 Whoever is not with me is against me, and whoever does not gather with me scatters. 31 Therefore I tell you, people will be forgiven for every sin and blasphemy, but blasphemy against the Spirit will not be forgiven. 32 Whoever speaks a word against the Son of Man will be forgiven, but whoever speaks against the Holy Spirit will not be forgiven, either in this age or in the age to come.

33 "Either make the tree good, and its fruit good; or make the tree bad, and its fruit bad; for the tree is known by its fruit. 34 You brood of vipers! How can you speak good things, when you are evil? For out of the abundance of the heart the mouth speaks. 35 The good person brings good things out of a good treasure, and the evil person brings evil things out of an evil treasure. 36 I tell you, on the day of judgment you will have to give an account for every careless word you utter; 37 for by your words you will be justified, and by your words you will be condemned."

38 Then some of the scribes and Pharisees said to him, "Teacher, we wish to see a sign from you." 39 But he answered them, "An evil and adulterous generation asks for a sign, but no sign will be given to it except the sign of the prophet Jonah. 40 For just as Jonah was three days and three nights in the belly of the sea monster, so for three days and three nights the Son of Man will be in the heart of the earth. 41 The people of Nineveh will rise up at the judgment with this generation and condemn it, because they repented at the proclamation of Jonah, and see, something greater than Jonah is here! 42 The queen of the South will rise up at the judgment with this generation and condemn it, because she came from the ends of the earth to listen to the wisdom of Solomon, and see, something greater than Solomon is here!

43 "When the unclean spirit has gone out of a person, it wanders through waterless regions look-

---

[q]Other ancient authorities lack *crowds*   [r]Gk *sons*

---

[24]Isa 42:1–4

ing for a resting place, but it finds none. 44 Then it says, 'I will return to my house from which I came.' When it comes. it finds it empty, swept, and put in order. 45 Then it goes and brings along seven other spirits more evil than itself, and they enter and live there; and the last state of that person is worse than the first. So will it be also with this evil generation."

46 While he was still speaking to the crowds, his mother and his brothers were standing outside, wanting to speak to him. 47 Someone told him, "Look, your mother and your brothers are standing outside, wanting to speak to you."[s] 48 But to the one who had told him this, Jesus[t] replied, "Who is my mother, and who are my brothers?" 49 And pointing to his disciples, he said, "Here are my mother and my brothers! 50 For whoever does the will of my Father in heaven is my brother and sister and mother."

13 That same day Jesus went out of the house and sat beside the sea. 2 Such great crowds gathered around him that he got into a boat and sat there, while the whole crowd stood on the beach. 3 And he told them many things in parables, saying: "Listen! A sower went out to sow. 4 And as he sowed, some seeds fell on the path, and the birds came and ate them up. 5 Other seeds fell on rocky ground, where they did not have much soil, and they sprang up quickly, since they had no depth of soil. 6 But when the sun rose, they were scorched; and since they had no root, they withered away. 7 Other seeds fell among thorns, and the thorns grew up and choked them. 8 Other seeds fell on good soil and brought forth grain, some a hundredfold, some sixty, some thirty. 9 Let anyone with ears[u] listen!"

10 Then the disciples came and asked him, "Why do you speak to them in parables?" 11 He answered, "To you it has been given to know the secrets[v] of the kingdom of heaven, but to them it has not been given. 12 For to those who have, more will be given, and they will have an abundance; but from those who have nothing, even what they have will be taken away. 13 The reason I speak to them in parables is that 'seeing they do not perceive, and hearing they do not listen, nor do they understand.' 14 With them indeed is fulfilled the prophecy of Isaiah that says:

'You will indeed listen, but never understand,
and you will indeed look, but never perceive.
15 For this people's heart has grown dull,
and their ears are hard of hearing,
and they have shut their eyes;
so that they might not look with their eyes,
and listen with their ears,
and understand with their heart and turn—
and I would heal them.'[25]

16 But blessed are your eyes, for they see, and your ears, for they hear. 17 Truly I tell you, many prophets and righteous people longed to see what you see, but did not see it, and to hear what you hear, but did not hear it.

18 "Hear then the parable of the sower. 19 When anyone hears the word of the kingdom and does not understand it, the evil one comes and snatches away what is sown in the heart; this is what was sown on the path. 20 As for what was sown on rocky ground, this is the one who hears the word and immediately receives it with joy; 21 yet such a person has no root, but endures only for a while, and when trouble or persecution arises on account of the word, that person immediately falls away.[w] 22 As for what was sown among thorns, this is the one who hears the word, but the cares of the world and the lure of wealth choke the word, and it yields nothing. 23 But as for what was sown on good soil, this is the one who hears the word and understands it, who indeed bears fruit and yields, in one case a hundredfold, in another sixty, and in another thirty."

24 He put before them another parable: "The kingdom of heaven may be compared to someone who sowed good seed in his field; 25 but while everybody was asleep, an enemy came and sowed weeds among the wheat, and then went away. 26 So when the plants came up and bore grain, then the weeds appeared as well. 27 And the

[s]Other ancient authorities lack verse 47 [t]Gk *he* [u]Other ancient authorities add *to hear* [v]Or *mysteries* [w]Gk *stumbles*

[25]Isa 6:9–10

slaves of the householder came and said to him, 'Master, did you not sow good seed in your field? Where, then, did these weeds come from?' 28 He answered, 'An enemy has done this.' The slaves said to him, 'Then do you want us to go and gather them?' 29 But he replied, 'No; for in gathering the weeds you would uproot the wheat along with them. 30 Let both of them grow together until the harvest; and at harvest time I will tell the reapers, Collect the weeds first and bind them in bundles to be burned, but gather the wheat into my barn.'"

31 He put before them another parable: "The kingdom of heaven is like a mustard seed that someone took and sowed in his field; 32 it is the smallest of all the seeds, but when it has grown it is the greatest of shrubs and becomes a tree, so that the birds of the air come and make nests in its branches."

33 He told them another parable: "The kingdom of heaven is like yeast that a woman took and mixed in with[x] three measures of flour until all of it was leavened."

34 Jesus told the crowds all these things in parables; without a parable he told them nothing. 35 This was to fulfill what had been spoken through the prophet:[y]

"I will open my mouth to speak
        in parables;
   I will proclaim what has been
        hidden from the foundation
        of the world."[z][26]

36 Then he left the crowds and went into the house. And his disciples approached him, saying, "Explain to us the parable of the weeds of the field." 37 He answered, "The one who sows the good seed is the Son of Man; 38 the field is the world, and the good seed are the children of the kingdom; the weeds are the children of the evil one, 39 and the enemy who sowed them is the devil; the harvest is the end of the age, and the reapers are angels. 40 Just as the weeds are collected and burned up with fire, so will it be at the end of the age. 41 The Son of Man will send his angels, and they will collect out of his kingdom all causes of sin and all evildoers, 42 and they will throw them into the furnace of fire, where there will be weeping and gnashing of teeth. 43 Then the righteous will shine like the sun in the kingdom of their Father. Let anyone with ears[a] listen!

44 "The kingdom of heaven is like treasure hidden in a field, which someone found and hid; then in his joy he goes and sells all that he has and buys that field.

45 "Again, the kingdom of heaven is like a merchant in search of fine pearls; 46 on finding one pearl of great value, he went and sold all that he had and bought it.

47 "Again, the kingdom of heaven is like a net that was thrown into the sea and caught fish of every kind; 48 when it was full, they drew it ashore, sat down, and put the good into baskets but threw out the bad. 49 So it will be at the end of the age. The angels will come out and separate the evil from the righteous 50 and throw them into the furnace of fire, where there will be weeping and gnashing of teeth.

51 "Have you understood all this?" They answered, "Yes." 52 And he said to them, "Therefore every scribe who has been trained for the kingdom of heaven is like the master of a household who brings out of his treasure what is new and what is old." 53 When Jesus had finished these parables, he left that place.

54 He came to his hometown and began to teach the people[b] in their synagogue, so that they were astounded and said, "Where did this man get this wisdom and these deeds of power? 55 Is not this the carpenter's son? Is not his mother called Mary? And are not his brothers James and Joseph and Simon and Judas? 56 And are not all his sisters with us? Where then did this man get all this?" 57 And they took offense at him. But Jesus said to them, "Prophets are not without honor except in their own country and in their own house." 58 And he did not do many deeds of power there, because of their unbelief.

14 At that time Herod the ruler[c] heard reports about Jesus; 2 and he said to his servants, "This is John the Baptist; he has been raised from the dead, and for this reason these powers are at work in him." 3 For Herod had arrested John, bound him, and put him in prison on account of Herodias, his brother Philip's wife,[d]

[x]Gk hid in [y]Other ancient authorities read the prophet Isaiah
[z]Other ancient authorities lack of the world [a]Other ancient
authorities add to hear [b]Gk them [c]Gk tetrarch [d]Other ancient
authorities read his brother's wife

[26]Ps 78:2

4 because John had been telling him, "It is not lawful for you to have her." 5 Though Herod[e] wanted to put him to death, he feared the crowd, because they regarded him as a prophet. 6 But when Herod's birthday came, the daughter of Herodias danced before the company, and she pleased Herod 7 so much that he promised on oath to grant her whatever she might ask. 8 Prompted by her mother, she said, "Give me the head of John the Baptist here on a platter." 9 The king was grieved, yet out of regard for his oaths and for the guests, he commanded it to be given; 10 he sent and had John beheaded in the prison. 11 The head was brought on a platter and given to the girl, who brought it to her mother. 12 His disciples came and took the body and buried it; then they went and told Jesus.

13 Now when Jesus heard this, he withdrew from there in a boat to a deserted place by himself. But when the crowds heard it, they followed him on foot from the towns. 14 When he went ashore, he saw a great crowd; and he had compassion for them and cured their sick. 15 When it was evening, the disciples came to him and said, "This is a deserted place, and the hour is now late; send the crowds away so that they may go into the villages and buy food for themselves." 16 Jesus said to them, "They need not go away; you give them something to eat." 17 They replied, "We have nothing here but five loaves and two fish." 18 And he said, "Bring them here to me." 19 Then he ordered the crowds to sit down on the grass. Taking the five loaves and the two fish, he looked up to heaven, and blessed and broke the loaves, and gave them to the disciples, and the disciples gave them to the crowds. 20 And all ate and were filled; and they took up what was left over of the broken pieces, twelve baskets full. 21 And those who ate were about five thousand men, besides women and children.

22 Immediately he made the disciples get into the boat and go on ahead to the other side, while he dismissed the crowds. 23 And after he had dismissed the crowds, he went up the mountain by himself to pray. When evening came, he was there alone, 24 but by this time the boat, battered by the waves, was far from the land,[f] for the wind was against them. 25 And early in the morning he came walking toward them on the sea. 26 But when the disciples saw him walking on the sea, they were terrified, saying, "It is a ghost!" And they cried out in fear. 27 But immediately Jesus spoke to them and said, "Take heart, it is I; do not be afraid."

28 Peter answered him, "Lord, if it is you, command me to come to you on the water." 29 He said, "Come." So Peter got out of the boat, started walking on the water, and came toward Jesus. 30 But when he noticed the strong wind,[g] he became frightened, and beginning to sink, he cried out, "Lord, save me!" 31 Jesus immediately reached out his hand and caught him, saying to him, "You of little faith, why did you doubt?" 32 When they got into the boat, the wind ceased. 33 And those in the boat worshiped him, saying, "Truly you are the Son of God."

34 When they had crossed over, they came to land at Gennesaret. 35 After the people of that place recognized him, they sent word throughout the region and brought all who were sick to him, 36 and begged him that they might touch even the fringe of his cloak; and all who touched it were healed.

15 Then Pharisees and scribes came to Jesus from Jerusalem and said, 2 "Why do your disciples break the tradition of the elders? For they do not wash their hands before they eat." 3 He answered them, "And why do you break the commandment of God for the sake of your tradition? 4 For God said,[h] 'Honor your father and your mother,'[27] and, 'Whoever speaks evil of father or mother must surely die.'[28] 5 But you say that whoever tells father or mother, 'Whatever support you might have had from me is given to God,'[i] then that person need not honor the father.[j] 6 So, for the sake of your tradition, you make void the word[k] of God. 7 You hypocrites! Isaiah prophesied rightly about you when he said:

8   'This people honors me with their
              lips,
       but their hearts are far from me;

---

[e]Gk *he*   [f]Other ancient authorities read *was out on the sea*   [g]Other ancient authorities read *the wind*   [h]Other ancient authorities read *commanded, saying*   [i]Or *is an offering*   [j]Other ancient authorities add *or the mother*   [k]Other ancient authorities read *law*; others, *commandment*

---

[27]Exod 20:12; Deut 5:16   [28]Exod 21:17; Lev 20:9

9   in vain do they worship me,
              teaching human precepts as
              doctrines.'"[29]

10 Then he called the crowd to him and said to them, "Listen and understand: 11 it is not what goes into the mouth that defiles a person, but it is what comes out of the mouth that defiles." 12 Then the disciples approached and said to him, "Do you know that the Pharisees took offense when they heard what you said?" 13 He answered, "Every plant that my heavenly Father has not planted will be uprooted. 14 Let them alone; they are blind guides of the blind.[l] And if one blind person guides another, both will fall into a pit." 15 But Peter said to him, "Explain this parable to us." 16 Then he said, "Are you also still without understanding? 17 Do you not see that whatever goes into the mouth enters the stomach, and goes out into the sewer? 18 But what comes out of the mouth proceeds from the heart, and this is what defiles. 19 For out of the heart come evil intentions, murder, adultery, fornication, theft, false witness, slander. 20 These are what defile a person, but to eat with unwashed hands does not defile."

21 Jesus left that place and went away to the district of Tyre and Sidon. 22 Just then a Canaanite woman from that region came out and started shouting, "Have mercy on me, Lord, Son of David; my daughter is tormented by a demon." 23 But he did not answer her at all. And his disciples came and urged him, saying, "Send her away, for she keeps shouting after us." 24 He answered, "I was sent only to the lost sheep of the house of Israel." 25 But she came and knelt before him, saying, "Lord, help me." 26 He answered, "It is not fair to take the children's food and throw it to the dogs." 27 She said, "Yes, Lord, yet even the dogs eat the crumbs that fall from their masters' table." 28 Then Jesus answered her, "Woman, great is your faith! Let it be done for you as you wish." And her daughter was healed instantly.

29 After Jesus had left that place, he passed along the Sea of Galilee, and he went up the mountain, where he sat down. 30 Great crowds came to him, bringing with them the lame, the maimed, the blind, the mute, and many others. They put them at his feet, and he cured them, 31 so that the crowd was amazed when they saw the mute speaking, the maimed whole, the lame walking, and the blind seeing. And they praised the God of Israel.

32 Then Jesus called his disciples to him and said, "I have compassion for the crowd, because they have been with me now for three days and have nothing to eat; and I do not want to send them away hungry, for they might faint on the way." 33 The disciples said to him, "Where are we to get enough bread in the desert to feed so great a crowd?" 34 Jesus asked them, "How many loaves have you?" They said, "Seven, and a few small fish." 35 Then ordering the crowd to sit down on the ground, 36 he took the seven loaves and the fish; and after giving thanks he broke them and gave them to the disciples, and the disciples gave them to the crowds. 37 And all of them ate and were filled; and they took up the broken pieces left over, seven baskets full. 38 Those who had eaten were four thousand men, besides women and children. 39 After sending away the crowds, he got into the boat and went to the region of Magadan.[m]

16 The Pharisees and Sadducees came, and to test Jesus[n] they asked him to show them a sign from heaven. 2 He answered them, "When it is evening, you say, 'It will be fair weather, for the sky is red.' 3 And in the morning, 'It will be stormy today, for the sky is red and threatening.' You know how to interpret the appearance of the sky, but you cannot interpret the signs of the times.[o] 4 An evil and adulterous generation asks for a sign, but no sign will be given to it except the sign of Jonah." Then he left them and went away.

5 When the disciples reached the other side, they had forgotten to bring any bread. 6 Jesus said to them, "Watch out, and beware of the yeast of the Pharisees and Sadducees." 7 They said to one another, "It is because we have brought no bread." 8 And becoming aware of it, Jesus said, "You of little faith, why are you talking about having no bread? 9 Do you still not perceive? Do you not remember the five loaves for the five thousand, and how many baskets you gathered? 10 Or the seven loaves for the four thousand, and how many bas-

---

[l]Other ancient authorities lack *of the blind*   [m]Other ancient authorities read *Magdala* or *Magdalan*   [n]Gk *him*   [o]Other ancient authorities lack [2]*When it is . . . of the times*

[29]Isa 29:13

kets you gathered? 11 How could you fail to perceive that I was not speaking about bread? Beware of the yeast of the Pharisees and Sadducees!" 12 Then they understood that he had not told them to beware of the yeast of bread, but of the teaching of the Pharisees and Sadducees.

13 Now when Jesus came into the district of Caesarea Philippi, he asked his disciples, "Who do people say that the Son of Man is?" 14 And they said, "Some say John the Baptist, but others Elijah, and still others Jeremiah or one of the prophets." 15 He said to them, "But who do you say that I am?" 16 Simon Peter answered, "You are the Messiah,[p] the Son of the living God." 17 And Jesus answered him, "Blessed are you, Simon son of Jonah! For flesh and blood has not revealed this to you, but my Father in heaven. 18 And I tell you, you are Peter,[q] and on this rock[r] I will build my church, and the gates of Hades will not prevail against it. 19 I will give you the keys of the kingdom of heaven, and whatever you bind on earth will be bound in heaven, and whatever you loose on earth will be loosed in heaven." 20 Then he sternly ordered the disciples not to tell anyone that he was[s] the Messiah.[p]

21 From that time on, Jesus began to show his disciples that he must go to Jerusalem and undergo great suffering at the hands of the elders and chief priests and scribes, and be killed, and on the third day be raised. 22 And Peter took him aside and began to rebuke him, saying, "God forbid it, Lord! This must never happen to you." 23 But he turned and said to Peter, "Get behind me, Satan! You are a stumbling block to me; for you are setting your mind not on divine things but on human things."

24 Then Jesus told his disciples, "If any want to become my followers, let them deny themselves and take up their cross and follow me. 25 For those who want to save their life will lose it, and those who lose their life for my sake will find it. 26 For what will it profit them if they gain the whole world but forfeit their life? Or what will they give in return for their life?

27 "For the Son of Man is to come with his angels in the glory of his Father, and then he will repay everyone for what has been done. 28 Truly I tell you, there are some standing here who will not taste death before they see the Son of Man coming in his kingdom."

17 Six days later, Jesus took with him Peter and James and his brother John and led them up a high mountain, by themselves. 2 And he was transfigured before them, and his face shone like the sun, and his clothes became dazzling white. 3 Suddenly there appeared to them Moses and Elijah, talking with him. 4 Then Peter said to Jesus, "Lord, it is good for us to be here; if you wish, I[t] will make three dwellings[u] here, one for you, one for Moses, and one for Elijah." 5 While he was still speaking, suddenly a bright cloud overshadowed them, and from the cloud a voice said, "This is my Son, the Beloved;[v] with him I am well pleased; listen to him!" 6 When the disciples heard this, they fell to the ground and were overcome by fear. 7 But Jesus came and touched them, saying, "Get up and do not be afraid." 8 And when they looked up, they saw no one except Jesus himself alone.

9 As they were coming down the mountain, Jesus ordered them, "Tell no one about the vision until after the Son of Man has been raised from the dead." 10 And the disciples asked him, "Why, then, do the scribes say that Elijah must come first?" 11 He replied, "Elijah is indeed coming and will restore all things; 12 but I tell you that Elijah has already come, and they did not recognize him, but they did to him whatever they pleased. So also the Son of Man is about to suffer at their hands." 13 Then the disciples understood that he was speaking to them about John the Baptist.

14 When they came to the crowd, a man came to him, knelt before him, 15 and said, "Lord, have mercy on my son, for he is an epileptic and he suffers terribly; he often falls into the fire and often into the water. 16 And I brought him to your disciples, but they could not cure him." 17 Jesus answered, "You faithless and perverse generation, how much longer must I be with you? How much longer must I put up with you? Bring him here to me." 18 And Jesus rebuked the demon,[w] and it[x] came out of him, and the boy was cured instantly. 19 Then the disciples came to Jesus privately and

[p]Or the Christ   [q]Gk Petros   [r]Gk petra   [s]Other ancient authorities add Jesus   [t]Other ancient authorities read we   [u]Or tents   [v]Or my beloved Son   [w]Gk it or him   [x]Gk the demon

said, "Why could we not cast it out?" 20 He said to them, "Because of your little faith. For truly I tell you, if you have faith the size of a[y] mustard seed, you will say to this mountain, 'Move from here to there,' and it will move; and nothing will be impossible for you."[z]

22 As they were gathering[a] in Galilee, Jesus said to them, "The Son of Man is going to be betrayed into human hands, 23 and they will kill him, and on the third day he will be raised." And they were greatly distressed.

24 When they reached Capernaum, the collectors of the temple tax[b] came to Peter and said, "Does your teacher not pay the temple tax?"[b] 25 He said, "Yes, he does." And when he came home, Jesus spoke of it first, asking, "What do you think, Simon? From whom do kings of the earth take toll or tribute? From their children or from others?" 26 When Peter[c] said, "From others," Jesus said to him, "Then the children are free. 27 However, so that we do not give offense to them, go to the sea and cast a hook; take the first fish that comes up; and when you open its mouth, you will find a coin;[d] take that and give it to them for you and me."

18

At that time the disciples came to Jesus and asked, "Who is the greatest in the kingdom of heaven?" 2 He called a child, whom he put among them, 3 and said, "Truly I tell you, unless you change and become like children, you will never enter the kingdom of heaven. 4 Whoever becomes humble like this child is the greatest in the kingdom of heaven. 5 Whoever welcomes one such child in my name welcomes me.

6 "If any of you put a stumbling block before one of these little ones who believe in me, it would be better for you if a great millstone were fastened around your neck and you were drowned in the depth of the sea. 7 Woe to the world because of stumbling blocks! Occasions for stumbling are bound to come, but woe to the one by whom the stumbling block comes!

8 "If your hand or your foot causes you to stumble, cut it off and throw it away; it is better for you to enter life maimed or lame than to have two hands or two feet and to be thrown into the eternal fire. 9 And if your eye causes you to stumble, tear it out and throw it away; it is better for you to en-

ter life with one eye than to have two eyes and to be thrown into the hell[e] of fire.

10 "Take care that you do not despise one of these little ones; for, I tell you, in heaven their angels continually see the face of my Father in heaven.[f] 12 What do you think? If a shepherd has a hundred sheep, and one of them has gone astray, does he not leave the ninety-nine on the mountains and go in search of the one that went astray? 13 And if he finds it, truly I tell you, he rejoices over it more than over the ninety-nine that never went astray. 14 So it is not the will of your[g] Father in heaven that one of these little ones should be lost.

15 "If another member of the church[h] sins against you,[i] go and point out the fault when the two of you are alone. If the member listens to you, you have regained that one.[j] 16 But if you are not listened to, take one or two others along with you, so that every word may be confirmed by the evidence of two or three witnesses. 17 If the member refuses to listen to them, tell it to the church; and if the offender refuses to listen even to the church, let such a one be to you as a Gentile and a tax collector. 18 Truly I tell you, whatever you bind on earth will be bound in heaven, and whatever you loose on earth will be loosed in heaven. 19 Again, truly I tell you, if two of you agree on earth about anything you ask, it will be done for you by my Father in heaven. 20 For where two or three are gathered in my name, I am there among them."

21 Then Peter came and said to him, "Lord, if another member of the church[k] sins against me, how often should I forgive? As many as seven times?" 22 Jesus said to him, "Not seven times, but, I tell you, seventy-seven[l] times.

23 "For this reason the kingdom of heaven may be compared to a king who wished to settle accounts with his slaves. 24 When he began the reckoning, one who owed him ten thousand talents[m] was brought to him; 25 and, as he could not

[y]Gk faith as a grain of [z]Other ancient authorities add verse 21, But this kind does not come out except by prayer and fasting [a]Other ancient authorities read living [b]Gk didrachma [c]Gk he [d]Gk stater; the stater was worth two didrachmas [e]Gk Gehenna [f]Other ancient authorities add verse 11, For the Son of Man came to save the lost [g]Other ancient authorities read my [h]Gk If your brother [i]Other ancient authorities lack against you [j]Gk the brother [k]Gk if my brother [l]Or seventy times seven [m]A talent was worth more than fifteen years' wages of a laborer

pay, his lord ordered him to be sold, together with his wife and children and all his possessions, and payment to be made. 26 So the slave fell on his knees before him, saying, 'Have patience with me, and I will pay you everything.' 27 And out of pity for him, the lord of that slave released him and forgave him the debt. 28 But that same slave, as he went out, came upon one of his fellow slaves who owed him a hundred denarii;[n] and seizing him by the throat, he said, 'Pay what you owe.' 29 Then his fellow slave fell down and pleaded with him, 'Have patience with me, and I will pay you.' 30 But he refused; then he went and threw him into prison until he would pay the debt. 31 When his fellow slaves saw what had happened, they were greatly distressed, and they went and reported to their lord all that had taken place. 32 Then his lord summoned him and said to him, 'You wicked slave! I forgave you all that debt because you pleaded with me. 33 Should you not have had mercy on your fellow slave, as I had mercy on you?' 34 And in anger his lord handed him over to be tortured until he would pay his entire debt. 35 So my heavenly Father will also do to every one of you, if you do not forgive your brother or sister[o] from your heart."

19 When Jesus had finished saying these things, he left Galilee and went to the region of Judea beyond the Jordan. 2 Large crowds followed him, and he cured them there.

3 Some Pharisees came to him, and to test him they asked, "Is it lawful for a man to divorce his wife for any cause?" 4 He answered, "Have you not read that the one who made them at the beginning 'made them male and female,'[30] 5 and said, 'For this reason a man shall leave his father and mother and be joined to his wife, and the two shall become one flesh'?[31] 6 So they are no longer two, but one flesh. Therefore what God has joined together, let no one separate." 7 They said to him, "Why then did Moses command us to give a certificate of dismissal and to divorce her?"[32] 8 He said to them, "It was because you were so hardhearted that Moses allowed you to divorce your wives, but from the beginning it was not so. 9 And I say to you, whoever divorces his wife, except for unchastity, and marries another commits adultery."[p]

10 His disciples said to him, "If such is the case of a man with his wife, it is better not to marry." 11 But he said to them, "Not everyone can accept this teaching, but only those to whom it is given. 12 For there are eunuchs who have been so from birth, and there are eunuchs who have been made eunuchs by others, and there are eunuchs who have made themselves eunuchs for the sake of the kingdom of heaven. Let anyone accept this who can."

13 Then little children were being brought to him in order that he might lay his hands on them and pray. The disciples spoke sternly to those who brought them; 14 but Jesus said, "Let the little children come to me, and do not stop them; for it is to such as these that the kingdom of heaven belongs." 15 And he laid his hands on them and went on his way.

16 Then someone came to him and said, "Teacher, what good deed must I do to have eternal life?" 17 And he said to him, "Why do you ask me about what is good? There is only one who is good. If you wish to enter into life, keep the commandments." 18 He said to him, "Which ones?" And Jesus said, "You shall not murder; You shall not commit adultery; You shall not steal; You shall not bear false witness; 19 Honor your father and mother;[33] also, You shall love your neighbor as yourself."[34] 20 The young man said to him, "I have kept all these;[q] what do I still lack?" 21 Jesus said to him, "If you wish to be perfect, go, sell your possessions, and give the money[r] to the poor, and you will have treasure in heaven; then come, follow me." 22 When the young man heard this word, he went away grieving, for he had many possessions.

23 Then Jesus said to his disciples, "Truly I tell you, it will be hard for a rich person to enter the kingdom of heaven. 24 Again I tell you, it is easier for a camel to go through the eye of a needle than for someone who is rich to enter the kingdom of God." 25 When the disciples heard this, they

---

[n]The denarius was the usual day's wage for a laborer   [o]Gk *brother* [p]Other ancient authorities read *except on the ground of unchastity, causes her to commit adultery*; others add at the end of the verse *and he who marries a divorced woman commits adultery*   [q]Other ancient authorities add *from my youth*   [r]Gk lacks *the money*

[30]Gen 1:27   [31]Gen 2:24   [32]Deut 24:1   [33]Exod 20:12–16; Deut 5:16–20   [34]Lev 19:18

were greatly astounded and said, "Then who can be saved?" 26 But Jesus looked at them and said, "For mortals it is impossible, but for God all things are possible."

27 Then Peter said in reply, "Look, we have left everything and followed you. What then will we have?" 28 Jesus said to them, "Truly I tell you, at the renewal of all things, when the Son of Man is seated on the throne of his glory, you who have followed me will also sit on twelve thrones, judging the twelve tribes of Israel. 29 And everyone who has left houses or brothers or sisters or father or mother or children or fields, for my name's sake, will receive a hundredfold,ˢ and will inherit eternal life. 30 But many who are first will be last, and the last will be first.

20 "For the kingdom of heaven is like a landowner who went out early in the morning to hire laborers for his vineyard. 2 After agreeing with the laborers for the usual daily wage,ᵗ he sent them into his vineyard. 3 When he went out about nine o'clock, he saw others standing idle in the marketplace; 4 and he said to them, 'You also go into the vineyard, and I will pay you whatever is right.' So they went. 5 When he went out again about noon and about three o'clock, he did the same. 6 And about five o'clock he went out and found others standing around; and he said to them, 'Why are you standing here idle all day?' 7 They said to him, 'Because no one has hired us.' He said to them, 'You also go into the vineyard.' 8 When evening came, the owner of the vineyard said to his manager, 'Call the laborers and give them their pay, beginning with the last and then going to the first.' 9 When those hired about five o'clock came, each of them received the usual daily wage.ᵗ 10 Now when the first came, they thought they would receive more; but each of them also received the usual daily wage.ᵗ 11 And when they received it, they grumbled against the landowner, 12 saying, 'These last worked only one hour, and you have made them equal to us who have borne the burden of the day and the scorching heat.' 13 But he replied to one of them, 'Friend, I am doing you no wrong; did you not agree with me for the usual daily wage?ᵗ 14 Take what belongs to you and go; I choose to give to this last the same as I give to you. 15 Am I not allowed to do what I choose with what

belongs to me? Or are you envious because I am generous?'ᵘ 16 So the last will be first, and the first will be last."ᵛ

17 While Jesus was going up to Jerusalem, he took the twelve disciples aside by themselves, and said to them on the way, 18 "See, we are going up to Jerusalem, and the Son of Man will be handed over to the chief priests and scribes, and they will condemn him to death; 19 then they will hand him over to the Gentiles to be mocked and flogged and crucified; and on the third day he will be raised."

20 Then the mother of the sons of Zebedee came to him with her sons, and kneeling before him, she asked a favor of him. 21 And he said to her, "What do you want?" She said to him, "Declare that these two sons of mine will sit, one at your right hand and one at your left, in your kingdom." 22 But Jesus answered, "You do not know what you are asking. Are you able to drink the cup that I am about to drink?"ʷ They said to him, "We are able." 23 He said to them, "You will indeed drink my cup, but to sit at my right hand and at my left, this is not mine to grant, but it is for those for whom it has been prepared by my Father."

24 When the ten heard it, they were angry with the two brothers. 25 But Jesus called them to him and said, "You know that the rulers of the Gentiles lord it over them, and their great ones are tyrants over them. 26 It will not be so among you; but whoever wishes to be great among you must be your servant, 27 and whoever wishes to be first among you must be your slave; 28 just as the Son of Man came not to be served but to serve, and to give his life a ransom for many."

29 As they were leaving Jericho, a large crowd followed him. 30 There were two blind men sitting by the roadside. When they heard that Jesus was passing by, they shouted, "Lord,ˣ have mercy on us, Son of David!" 31 The crowd sternly ordered them to be quiet; but they shouted even more loudly, "Have mercy on us, Lord, Son of David!" 32 Jesus stood still and called them, saying, "What do you want me to do for you?" 33 They said to

ˢOther ancient authorities read *manifold* ᵗGk *a denarius* ᵘGk *is your eye evil because I am good?* ᵛOther ancient authorities add *for many are called but few are chosen* ʷOther ancient authorities add *or to be baptized with the baptism that I am baptized with?* ˣOther ancient authorities lack *Lord*

him, "Lord, let our eyes be opened." 34 Moved with compassion, Jesus touched their eyes. Immediately they regained their sight and followed him.

21 When they had come near Jerusalem and had reached Bethphage, at the Mount of Olives, Jesus sent two disciples, 2 saying to them, "Go into the village ahead of you, and immediately you will find a donkey tied, and a colt with her; untie them and bring them to me. 3 If anyone says anything to you, just say this, 'The Lord needs them.' And he will send them immediately.ʸ" 4 This took place to fulfill what had been spoken through the prophet, saying,

5 "Tell the daughter of Zion,
Look, your king is coming to
you,
humble, and mounted on a
donkey,
and on a colt, the foal of a
donkey."³⁵

6 The disciples went and did as Jesus had directed them; 7 they brought the donkey and the colt, and put their cloaks on them, and he sat on them. 8 A very large crowdᶻ spread their cloaks on the road, and others cut branches from the trees and spread them on the road. 9 The crowds that went ahead of him and that followed were shouting,

"Hosanna to the Son of David!
Blessed is the one who comes in
the name of the Lord!³⁶
Hosanna in the highest heaven!"

10 When he entered Jerusalem, the whole city was in turmoil, asking, "Who is this?" 11 The crowds were saying, "This is the prophet Jesus from Nazareth in Galilee."

12 Then Jesus entered the templeᵃ and drove out all who were selling and buying in the temple, and he overturned the tables of the money changers and the seats of those who sold doves. 13 He said to them, "It is written,

'My house shall be called a house
of prayer';
but you are making it a den of
robbers."³⁷

14 The blind and the lame came to him in the temple, and he cured them. 15 But when the chief priests and the scribes saw the amazing things that he did, and heardᵇ the children crying out in the

temple, "Hosanna to the Son of David," they became angry 16 and said to him, "Do you hear what these are saying?" Jesus said to them, "Yes; have you never read,

'Out of the mouths of infants and
nursing babies
you have prepared praise for
yourself'?"³⁸

17 He left them, went out of the city to Bethany, and spent the night there.

18 In the morning, when he returned to the city, he was hungry. 19 And seeing a fig tree by the side of the road, he went to it and found nothing at all on it but leaves. Then he said to it, "May no fruit ever come from you again!" And the fig tree withered at once. 20 When the disciples saw it, they were amazed, saying, "How did the fig tree wither at once?" 21 Jesus answered them, "Truly I tell you, if you have faith and do not doubt, not only will you do what has been done to the fig tree, but even if you say to this mountain, 'Be lifted up and thrown into the sea,' it will be done. 22 Whatever you ask for in prayer with faith, you will receive."

23 When he entered the temple, the chief priests and the elders of the people came to him as he was teaching, and said, "By what authority are you doing these things, and who gave you this authority?" 24 Jesus said to them, "I will also ask you one question; if you tell me the answer, then I will also tell you by what authority I do these things. 25 Did the baptism of John come from heaven, or was it of human origin?" And they argued with one another, "If we say, 'From heaven,' he will say to us, 'Why then did you not believe him?' 26 But if we say, 'Of human origin,' we are afraid of the crowd; for all regard John as a prophet." 27 So they answered Jesus, "We do not know." And he said to them, "Neither will I tell you by what authority I am doing these things.

28 "What do you think? A man had two sons; he went to the first and said, 'Son, go and work in the vineyard today.' 29 He answered, 'I will not'; but later he changed his mind and went. 30 The fatherᶜ went to the second and said the same; and he

ʸOr 'The Lord needs them and will send them back immediately.'
ᶻOr Most of the crowd ᵃOther ancient authorities add of God
ᵇGk lacks heard ᶜGk He

³⁵Isa 62:11; Zech 9:9 ³⁶Ps 118:25–26 ³⁷Isa 56:7; Jer 7:11 ³⁸Ps 8:3

answered, 'I go, sir'; but he did not go. 31 Which of the two did the will of his father?" They said, "The first." Jesus said to them, "Truly I tell you, the tax collectors and the prostitutes are going into the kingdom of God ahead of you. 32 For John came to you in the way of righteousness and you did not believe him, but the tax collectors and the prostitutes believed him; and even after you saw it, you did not change your minds and believe him.

33 "Listen to another parable. There was a landowner who planted a vineyard, put a fence around it, dug a wine press in it, and built a watchtower. Then he leased it to tenants and went to another country. 34 When the harvest time had come, he sent his slaves to the tenants to collect his produce. 35 But the tenants seized his slaves and beat one, killed another, and stoned another. 36 Again he sent other slaves, more than the first; and they treated them in the same way. 37 Finally he sent his son to them, saying, 'They will respect my son.' 38 But when the tenants saw the son, they said to themselves, 'This is the heir; come, let us kill him and get his inheritance.' 39 So they seized him, threw him out of the vineyard, and killed him. 40 Now when the owner of the vineyard comes, what will he do to those tenants?" 41 They said to him, "He will put those wretches to a miserable death, and lease the vineyard to other tenants who will give him the produce at the harvest time."

42 Jesus said to them, "Have you never read in the scriptures:

'The stone that the builders
    rejected
  has become the cornerstone;[d]
this was the Lord's doing,
    and it is amazing in our eyes'?[39]

43 Therefore I tell you, the kingdom of God will be taken away from you and given to a people that produces the fruits of the kingdom.[e] 44 The one who falls on this stone will be broken to pieces; and it will crush anyone on whom it falls."[f]

45 When the chief priests and the Pharisees heard his parables, they realized that he was speaking about them. 46 They wanted to arrest him, but they feared the crowds, because they regarded him as a prophet.

22 Once more Jesus spoke to them in parables, saying: 2 "The kingdom of heaven may be compared to a king who gave a wedding banquet for his son. 3 He sent his slaves to call those who had been invited to the wedding banquet, but they would not come. 4 Again he sent other slaves, saying, 'Tell those who have been invited: Look, I have prepared my dinner, my oxen and my fat calves have been slaughtered, and everything is ready; come to the wedding banquet.' 5 But they made light of it and went away, one to his farm, another to his business, 6 while the rest seized his slaves, mistreated them, and killed them. 7 The king was enraged. He sent his troops, destroyed those murderers, and burned their city. 8 Then he said to his slaves, 'The wedding is ready, but those invited were not worthy. 9 Go therefore into the main streets, and invite everyone you find to the wedding banquet.' 10 Those slaves went out into the streets and gathered all whom they found, both good and bad; so the wedding hall was filled with guests.

11 "But when the king came in to see the guests, he noticed a man there who was not wearing a wedding robe, 12 and he said to him, 'Friend, how did you get in here without a wedding robe?' And he was speechless. 13 Then the king said to the attendants, 'Bind him hand and foot, and throw him into the outer darkness, where there will be weeping and gnashing of teeth.' 14 For many are called, but few are chosen."

15 Then the Pharisees went and plotted to entrap him in what he said. 16 So they sent their disciples to him, along with the Herodians, saying, "Teacher, we know that you are sincere, and teach the way of God in accordance with truth, and show deference to no one; for you do not regard people with partiality. 17 Tell us, then, what you think. Is it lawful to pay taxes to the emperor, or not?" 18 But Jesus, aware of their malice, said, "Why are you putting me to the test, you hypocrites? 19 Show me the coin used for the tax." And they brought him a denarius. 20 Then he said to them, "Whose head is this, and whose title?" 21 They answered, "The emperor's." Then he said to them, "Give therefore to the emperor the things that are the emperor's, and to God the things that are

---

[d]Or *keystone*   [e]Gk *the fruits of it*   [f]Other ancient authorities lack verse 44

---

[39]Ps 118:22–23

God's." 22 When they heard this, they were amazed; and they left him and went away.

23 The same day some Sadducees came to him, saying there is no resurrection;[g] and they asked him a question, saying, 24 "Teacher, Moses said, 'If a man dies childless, his brother shall marry the widow, and raise up children for his brother.'[40] 25 Now there were seven brothers among us; the first married, and died childless, leaving the widow to his brother. 26 The second did the same, so also the third, down to the seventh. 27 Last of all, the woman herself died. 28 In the resurrection, then, whose wife of the seven will she be? For all of them had married her."

29 Jesus answered them, "You are wrong, because you know neither the scriptures nor the power of God. 30 For in the resurrection they neither marry nor are given in marriage, but are like angels[h] in heaven. 31 And as for the resurrection of the dead, have you not read what was said to you by God, 32 'I am the God of Abraham, the God of Isaac, and the God of Jacob'? He is God not of the dead, but of the living."[41] 33 And when the crowd heard it, they were astounded at his teaching.

34 When the Pharisees heard that he had silenced the Sadducees, they gathered together, 35 and one of them, a lawyer, asked him a question to test him. 36 "Teacher, which commandment in the law is the greatest?" 37 He said to him, "'You shall love the Lord your God with all your heart, and with all your soul, and with all your mind.'[42] 38 This is the greatest and first commandment. 39 And a second is like it: 'You shall love your neighbor as yourself.'[43] 40 On these two commandments hang all the law and the prophets."

41 Now while the Pharisees were gathered together, Jesus asked them this question: 42 "What do you think of the Messiah?[i] Whose son is he?" They said to him, "The son of David." 43 He said to them, "How is it then that David by the Spirit[j] calls him Lord, saying,

44   'The Lord said to my Lord,
      "Sit at my right hand,
         until I put your enemies under
            your feet"'?[44]

45 If David thus calls him Lord, how can he be his son?" 46 No one was able to give him an answer, nor from that day did anyone dare to ask him any more questions.

23 Then Jesus said to the crowds and to his disciples, 2 "The scribes and the Pharisees sit on Moses' seat; 3 therefore, do whatever they teach you and follow it; but do not do as they do, for they do not practice what they teach. 4 They tie up heavy burdens, hard to bear,[k] and lay them on the shoulders of others; but they themselves are unwilling to lift a finger to move them. 5 They do all their deeds to be seen by others; for they make their phylacteries broad and their fringes long. 6 They love to have the place of honor at banquets and the best seats in the synagogues, 7 and to be greeted with respect in the marketplaces, and to have people call them rabbi. 8 But you are not to be called rabbi, for you have one teacher, and you are all students.[l] 9 And call no one your father on earth, for you have one Father—the one in heaven. 10 Nor are you to be called instructors, for you have one instructor, the Messiah.[m] 11 The greatest among you will be your servant. 12 All who exalt themselves will be humbled, and all who humble themselves will be exalted.

13 "But woe to you, scribes and Pharisees, hypocrites! For you lock people out of the kingdom of heaven. For you do not go in yourselves, and when others are going in, you stop them.[n] 15 Woe to you, scribes and Pharisees, hypocrites! For you cross sea and land to make a single convert, and you make the new convert twice as much a child of hell[o] as yourselves.

16 "Woe to you, blind guides, who say, 'Whoever swears by the sanctuary is bound by nothing, but whoever swears by the gold of the sanctuary is bound by the oath.' 17 You blind fools! For which is greater, the gold or the sanctuary that has made the gold sacred? 18 And you say, 'Whoever swears by the altar is bound by nothing, but whoever swears by the gift that is on the altar is bound by the oath.' 19 How blind you are! For which is

---

[g]Other ancient authorities read *who say that there is no resurrection* [h]Other ancient authorities add *of God* [i]Or *Christ* [j]Gk *in spirit* [k]Other ancient authorities lack *hard to bear* [l]Gk *brothers* [m]Or *the Christ* [n]Other authorities add here (or after verse 12) verse 14, *Woe to you, scribes and Pharisees, hypocrites! For you devour widows' houses and for the sake of appearance you make long prayers; therefore you will receive the greater condemnation* [o]Gk *Gehenna*

---

[40]Deut 25:5; Gen 38:8   [41]Exod 3:6,15   [42]Deut 6:5   [43]Lev 19:18   [44]Ps 110:1

greater, the gift or the altar that makes the gift sacred? 20 So whoever swears by the altar, swears by it and by everything on it; 21 and whoever swears by the sanctuary, swears by it and by the one who dwells in it; 22 and whoever swears by heaven, swears by the throne of God and by the one who is seated upon it.

23 "Woe to you, scribes and Pharisees, hypocrites! For you tithe mint, dill, and cummin, and have neglected the weightier matters of the law: justice and mercy and faith. It is these you ought to have practiced without neglecting the others. 24 You blind guides! You strain out a gnat but swallow a camel!

25 "Woe to you, scribes and Pharisees, hypocrites! For you clean the outside of the cup and of the plate, but inside they are full of greed and self-indulgence. 26 You blind Pharisee! First clean the inside of the cup,[p] so that the outside also may become clean.

27 "Woe to you, scribes and Pharisees, hypocrites! For you are like whitewashed tombs, which on the outside look beautiful, but inside they are full of the bones of the dead and of all kinds of filth. 28 So you also on the outside look righteous to others, but inside you are full of hypocrisy and lawlessness.

29 "Woe to you, scribes and Pharisees, hypocrites! For you build the tombs of the prophets and decorate the graves of the righteous, 30 and you say, 'If we had lived in the days of our ancestors, we would not have taken part with them in shedding the blood of the prophets.' 31 Thus you testify against yourselves that you are descendants of those who murdered the prophets. 32 Fill up, then, the measure of your ancestors. 33 You snakes, you brood of vipers! How can you escape being sentenced to hell?[q] 34 Therefore I send you prophets, sages, and scribes, some of whom you will kill and crucify, and some you will flog in your synagogues and pursue from town to town, 35 so that upon you may come all the righteous blood shed on earth, from the blood of righteous Abel to the blood of Zechariah son of Barachiah, whom you murdered between the sanctuary and the altar. 36 Truly I tell you, all this will come upon this generation.

37 "Jerusalem, Jerusalem, the city that kills the prophets and stones those who are sent to it! How often have I desired to gather your children together as a hen gathers her brood under her wings, and you were not willing! 38 See, your house is left to you, desolate.[r] 39 For I tell you, you will not see me again until you say, 'Blessed is the one who comes in the name of the Lord.'"[45]

24

As Jesus came out of the temple and was going away, his disciples came to point out to him the buildings of the temple. 2 Then he asked them, "You see all these, do you not? Truly I tell you, not one stone will be left here upon another; all will be thrown down."

3 When he was sitting on the Mount of Olives, the disciples came to him privately, saying, "Tell us, when will this be, and what will be the sign of your coming and of the end of the age?" 4 Jesus answered them, "Beware that no one leads you astray. 5 For many will come in my name, saying, 'I am the Messiah!'[s] and they will lead many astray. 6 And you will hear of wars and rumors of wars; see that you are not alarmed; for this must take place, but the end is not yet. 7 For nation will rise against nation, and kingdom against kingdom, and there will be famines[t] and earthquakes in various places: 8 all this is but the beginning of the birth pangs.

9 "Then they will hand you over to be tortured and will put you to death, and you will be hated by all nations because of my name. 10 Then many will fall away,[u] and they will betray one another and hate one another. 11 And many false prophets will arise and lead many astray. 12 And because of the increase of lawlessness, the love of many will grow cold. 13 But the one who endures to the end will be saved. 14 And this good news[v] of the kingdom will be proclaimed throughout the world, as a testimony to all the nations; and then the end will come.

15 "So when you see the desolating sacrilege standing in the holy place, as was spoken of by the prophet Daniel (let the reader understand), 16 then those in Judea must flee to the mountains; 17 the one on the housetop must not go down to

[p]Other ancient authorities add *and of the plate* [q]Gk *Gehenna* [r]Other ancient authorities lack *desolate* [s]Or *the Christ* [t]Other ancient authorities add *and pestilences* [u]Or *stumble* [v]Or *gospel*

[45]Ps 118:26

take what is in the house; 18 the one in the field must not turn back to get a coat. 19 Woe to those who are pregnant and to those who are nursing infants in those days! 20 Pray that your flight may not be in winter or on a sabbath. 21 For at that time there will be great suffering, such as has not been from the beginning of the world until now, no, and never will be. 22 And if those days had not been cut short, no one would be saved; but for the sake of the elect those days will be cut short. 23 Then if anyone says to you, 'Look! Here is the Messiah!'[w] or 'There he is!'—do not believe it. 24 For false messiahs[x] and false prophets will appear and produce great signs and omens, to lead astray, if possible, even the elect. 25 Take note, I have told you beforehand. 26 So, if they say to you, 'Look! He is in the wilderness,' do not go out. If they say, 'Look! He is in the inner rooms,' do not believe it. 27 For as the lightning comes from the east and flashes as far as the west, so will be the coming of the Son of Man. 28 Wherever the corpse is, there the vultures will gather.

29 "Immediately after the suffering of those days
the sun will be darkened,
and the moon will not give its
light;
the stars will fall from heaven,
and the powers of heaven will
be shaken.

30 Then the sign of the Son of Man will appear in heaven, and then all the tribes of the earth will mourn, and they will see 'the Son of Man coming on the clouds of heaven'[46] with power and great glory. 31 And he will send out his angels with a loud trumpet call, and they will gather his elect from the four winds, from one end of heaven to the other.

32 "From the fig tree learn its lesson: as soon as its branch becomes tender and puts forth its leaves, you know that summer is near. 33 So also, when you see all these things, you know that he[y] is near, at the very gates. 34 Truly I tell you, this generation will not pass away until all these things have taken place. 35 Heaven and earth will pass away, but my words will not pass away.

36 "But about that day and hour no one knows, neither the angels of heaven, nor the Son,[z] but only the Father. 37 For as the days of Noah were, so will be the coming of the Son of Man. 38 For as

in those days before the flood they were eating and drinking, marrying and giving in marriage, until the day Noah entered the ark, 39 and they knew nothing until the flood came and swept them all away, so too will be the coming of the Son of Man. 40 Then two will be in the field; one will be taken and one will be left. 41 Two women will be grinding meal together; one will be taken and one will be left. 42 Keep awake therefore, for you do not know on what day[a] your Lord is coming. 43 But understand this: if the owner of the house had known in what part of the night the thief was coming, he would have stayed awake and would not have let his house be broken into. 44 Therefore you also must be ready, for the Son of Man is coming at an unexpected hour.

45 "Who then is the faithful and wise slave, whom his master has put in charge of his household, to give the other slaves[b] their allowance of food at the proper time? 46 Blessed is that slave whom his master will find at work when he arrives. 47 Truly I tell you, he will put that one in charge of all his possessions. 48 But if that wicked slave says to himself, 'My master is delayed,' 49 and he begins to beat his fellow slaves, and eats and drinks with drunkards, 50 the master of that slave will come on a day when he does not expect him and at an hour that he does not know. 51 He will cut him in pieces[c] and put him with the hypocrites, where there will be weeping and gnashing of teeth.

25 "Then the kingdom of heaven will be like this. Ten bridesmaids[d] took their lamps and went to meet the bridegroom.[e] 2 Five of them were foolish, and five were wise. 3 When the foolish took their lamps, they took no oil with them; 4 but the wise took flasks of oil with their lamps. 5 As the bridegroom was delayed, all of them became drowsy and slept. 6 But at midnight there was a shout, 'Look! Here is the bridegroom! Come out to meet him.' 7 Then all those bridesmaids[d] got up and trimmed their lamps. 8 The foolish said to the wise, 'Give us some of your oil,

---

[w]Or the Christ [x]Or christs [y]Or it [z]Other ancient authorities lack nor the Son [a]Other ancient authorities read at what hour [b]Gk to give them [c]Or cut him off [d]Gk virgins [e]Other ancient authorities add and the bride

[46]Dan 7:13

for our lamps are going out.' 9 But the wise replied, 'No! there will not be enough for you and for us; you had better go to the dealers and buy some for yourselves.' 10 And while they went to buy it, the bridegroom came, and those who were ready went with him into the wedding banquet; and the door was shut. 11 Later the other bridesmaids[f] came also, saying, 'Lord, lord, open to us.' 12 But he replied, 'Truly I tell you, I do not know you.' 13 Keep awake therefore, for you know neither the day nor the hour.[g]

14 "For it is as if a man, going on a journey, summoned his slaves and entrusted his property to them; 15 to one he gave five talents,[h] to another two, to another one, to each according to his ability. Then he went away. 16 The one who had received the five talents went off at once and traded with them, and made five more talents. 17 In the same way, the one who had the two talents made two more talents. 18 But the one who had received the one talent went off and dug a hole in the ground and hid his master's money. 19 After a long time the master of those slaves came and settled accounts with them. 20 Then the one who had received the five talents came forward, bringing five more talents, saying, 'Master, you handed over to me five talents; see, I have made five more talents.' 21 His master said to him, 'Well done, good and trustworthy slave; you have been trustworthy in a few things, I will put you in charge of many things; enter into the joy of your master.' 22 And the one with the two talents also came forward, saying, 'Master, you handed over to me two talents; see, I have made two more talents.' 23 His master said to him, 'Well done, good and trustworthy slave; you have been trustworthy in a few things, I will put you in charge of many things; enter into the joy of your master.' 24 Then the one who had received the one talent also came forward, saying, 'Master, I knew that you were a harsh man, reaping where you did not sow, and gathering where you did not scatter seed; 25 so I was afraid, and I went and hid your talent in the ground. Here you have what is yours.' 26 But his master replied, 'You wicked and lazy slave! You knew, did you, that I reap where I did not sow, and gather where I did not scatter? 27 Then you ought to have invested my money with the bankers, and on my return I would have received what was my

own with interest. 28 So take the talent from him, and give it to the one with the ten talents. 29 For to all those who have, more will be given, and they will have an abundance; but from those who have nothing, even what they have will be taken away. 30 As for this worthless slave, throw him into the outer darkness, where there will be weeping and gnashing of teeth.'

31 "When the Son of Man comes in his glory, and all the angels with him, then he will sit on the throne of his glory. 32 All the nations will be gathered before him, and he will separate people one from another as a shepherd separates the sheep from the goats, 33 and he will put the sheep at his right hand and the goats at the left. 34 Then the king will say to those at his right hand, 'Come, you that are blessed by my Father, inherit the kingdom prepared for you from the foundation of the world; 35 for I was hungry and you gave me food, I was thirsty and you gave me something to drink, I was a stranger and you welcomed me, 36 I was naked and you gave me clothing, I was sick and you took care of me, I was in prison and you visited me.' 37 Then the righteous will answer him, 'Lord, when was it that we saw you hungry and gave you food, or thirsty and gave you something to drink? 38 And when was it that we saw you a stranger and welcomed you, or naked and gave you clothing? 39 And when was it that we saw you sick or in prison and visited you?' 40 And the king will answer them, 'Truly I tell you, just as you did it to one of the least of these who are members of my family,[i] you did it to me.' 41 Then he will say to those at his left hand, 'You that are accursed, depart from me into the eternal fire prepared for the devil and his angels; 42 for I was hungry and you gave me no food, I was thirsty and you gave me nothing to drink, 43 I was a stranger and you did not welcome me, naked and you did not give me clothing, sick and in prison and you did not visit me.' 44 Then they also will answer, 'Lord, when was it that we saw you hungry or thirsty or a stranger or naked or sick or in prison, and did not take care of you?' 45 Then he will answer them, 'Truly I tell you, just as you did not do it to one of the least of these, you did not do it to me.' 46 And

[f]Gk *virgins*   [g]Other ancient authorities add *in which the Son of Man is coming*   [h]A talent was worth more than fifteen years' wages of a laborer   [i]Gk *these my brothers*

these will go away into eternal punishment, but the righteous into eternal life."

26 When Jesus had finished saying all these things, he said to his disciples, 2 "You know that after two days the Passover is coming, and the Son of Man will be handed over to be crucified."

3 Then the chief priests and the elders of the people gathered in the palace of the high priest, who was called Caiaphas, 4 and they conspired to arrest Jesus by stealth and kill him. 5 But they said, "Not during the festival, or there may be a riot among the people."

6 Now while Jesus was at Bethany in the house of Simon the leper,ʲ 7 a woman came to him with an alabaster jar of very costly ointment, and she poured it on his head as he sat at the table. 8 But when the disciples saw it, they were angry and said, "Why this waste? 9 For this ointment could have been sold for a large sum, and the money given to the poor." 10 But Jesus, aware of this, said to them, "Why do you trouble the woman? She has performed a good service for me. 11 For you always have the poor with you, but you will not always have me. 12 By pouring this ointment on my body she has prepared me for burial. 13 Truly I tell you, wherever this good newsᵏ is proclaimed in the whole world, what she has done will be told in remembrance of her."

14 Then one of the twelve, who was called Judas Iscariot, went to the chief priests 15 and said, "What will you give me if I betray him to you?" They paid him thirty pieces of silver. 16 And from that moment he began to look for an opportunity to betray him.

17 On the first day of Unleavened Bread the disciples came to Jesus, saying, "Where do you want us to make the preparations for you to eat the Passover?" 18 He said, "Go into the city to a certain man, and say to him, 'The Teacher says, My time is near; I will keep the Passover at your house with my disciples.'" 19 So the disciples did as Jesus had directed them, and they prepared the Passover meal.

20 When it was evening, he took his place with the twelve;ˡ 21 and while they were eating, he said, "Truly I tell you, one of you will betray me." 22 And they became greatly distressed and began to say to him one after another, "Surely not I, Lord?" 23 He answered, "The one who has dipped his hand into the bowl with me will betray me. 24 The Son of Man goes as it is written of him, but woe to that one by whom the Son of Man is betrayed! It would have been better for that one not to have been born." 25 Judas, who betrayed him, said, "Surely not I, Rabbi?" He replied, "You have said so."

26 While they were eating, Jesus took a loaf of bread, and after blessing it he broke it, gave it to the disciples, and said, "Take, eat; this is my body." 27 Then he took a cup, and after giving thanks he gave it to them, saying, "Drink from it, all of you; 28 for this is my blood of theᵐ covenant, which is poured out for many for the forgiveness of sins. 29 I tell you, I will never again drink of this fruit of the vine until that day when I drink it new with you in my Father's kingdom."

30 When they had sung the hymn, they went out to the Mount of Olives.

31 Then Jesus said to them, "You will all become deserters because of me this night; for it is written,

'I will strike the shepherd,
        and the sheep of the flock will
                be scattered.'⁴⁷

32 But after I am raised up, I will go ahead of you to Galilee." 33 Peter said to him, "Though all become deserters because of you, I will never desert you." 34 Jesus said to him, "Truly I tell you, this very night, before the cock crows, you will deny me three times." 35 Peter said to him, "Even though I must die with you, I will not deny you." And so said all the disciples.

36 Then Jesus went with them to a place called Gethsemane; and he said to his disciples, "Sit here while I go over there and pray." 37 He took with him Peter and the two sons of Zebedee, and began to be grieved and agitated. 38 Then he said to them, "I am deeply grieved, even to death; remain here, and stay awake with me." 39 And going a little farther, he threw himself on the ground and

ʲThe terms *leper* and *leprosy* can refer to several diseases   ᵏOr *gospel*
ˡOther ancient authorities add *disciples*   ᵐOther ancient authorities add *new*

⁴⁷Zech 13:7

prayed, "My Father, if it is possible, let this cup pass from me; yet not what I want but what you want." 40 Then he came to the disciples and found them sleeping; and he said to Peter, "So, could you not stay awake with me one hour? 41 Stay awake and pray that you may not come into the time of trial;[n] the spirit indeed is willing, but the flesh is weak." 42 Again he went away for the second time and prayed, "My Father, if this cannot pass unless I drink it, your will be done." 43 Again he came and found them sleeping, for their eyes were heavy. 44 So leaving them again, he went away and prayed for the third time, saying the same words. 45 Then he came to the disciples and said to them, "Are you still sleeping and taking your rest? See, the hour is at hand, and the Son of Man is betrayed into the hands of sinners. 46 Get up, let us be going. See, my betrayer is at hand."

47 While he was still speaking, Judas, one of the twelve, arrived; with him was a large crowd with swords and clubs, from the chief priests and the elders of the people. 48 Now the betrayer had given them a sign, saying, "The one I will kiss is the man; arrest him." 49 At once he came up to Jesus and said, "Greetings, Rabbi!" and kissed him. 50 Jesus said to him, "Friend, do what you are here to do." Then they came and laid hands on Jesus and arrested him. 51 Suddenly, one of those with Jesus put his hand on his sword, drew it, and struck the slave of the high priest, cutting off his ear. 52 Then Jesus said to him, "Put your sword back into its place; for all who take the sword will perish by the sword. 53 Do you think that I cannot appeal to my Father, and he will at once send me more than twelve legions of angels? 54 But how then would the scriptures be fulfilled, which say it must happen in this way?" 55 At that hour Jesus said to the crowds, "Have you come out with swords and clubs to arrest me as though I were a bandit? Day after day I sat in the temple teaching, and you did not arrest me. 56 But all this has taken place, so that the scriptures of the prophets may be fulfilled." Then all the disciples deserted him and fled.

57 Those who had arrested Jesus took him to Caiaphas the high priest, in whose house the scribes and the elders had gathered. 58 But Peter was following him at a distance, as far as the courtyard of the high priest; and going inside, he sat with the guards in order to see how this would end. 59 Now the chief priests and the whole council were looking for false testimony against Jesus so that they might put him to death, 60 but they found none, though many false witnesses came forward. At last two came forward 61 and said, "This fellow said, 'I am able to destroy the temple of God and to build it in three days.'" 62 The high priest stood up and said, "Have you no answer? What is it that they testify against you?" 63 But Jesus was silent. Then the high priest said to him, "I put you under oath before the living God, tell us if you are the Messiah,[o] the Son of God." 64 Jesus said to him, "You have said so. But I tell you,

> From now on you will see
> the Son of Man
> seated at the right hand of
> Power
> and coming on the clouds of
> heaven."[48]

65 Then the high priest tore his clothes and said, "He has blasphemed! Why do we still need witnesses? You have now heard his blasphemy. 66 What is your verdict?" They answered, "He deserves death." 67 Then they spat in his face and struck him; and some slapped him, 68 saying, "Prophesy to us, you Messiah![o] Who is it that struck you?"

69 Now Peter was sitting outside in the courtyard. A servant-girl came to him and said, "You also were with Jesus the Galilean." 70 But he denied it before all of them, saying, "I do not know what you are talking about." 71 When he went out to the porch, another servant-girl saw him, and she said to the bystanders, "This man was with Jesus of Nazareth."[p] 72 Again he denied it with an oath, "I do not know the man." 73 After a little while the bystanders came up and said to Peter, "Certainly you are also one of them, for your accent betrays you." 74 Then he began to curse, and he swore an oath, "I do not know the man!" At that moment the cock crowed. 75 Then Peter remembered what Jesus had said: "Before the cock crows, you will deny me three times." And he went out and wept bitterly.

[n]Or *into temptation*   [o]Or *Christ*   [p]Gk *the Nazorean*

[48]Ps 110:1; Dan 7:13

27

When morning came, all the chief priests and the elders of the people conferred together against Jesus in order to bring about his death. 2 They bound him, led him away, and handed him over to Pilate the governor.

3 When Judas, his betrayer, saw that Jesus[q] was condemned, he repented and brought back the thirty pieces of silver to the chief priests and the elders. 4 He said, "I have sinned by betraying innocent[r] blood." But they said, "What is that to us? See to it yourself." 5 Throwing down the pieces of silver in the temple, he departed; and he went and hanged himself. 6 But the chief priests, taking the pieces of silver, said, "It is not lawful to put them into the treasury, since they are blood money." 7 After conferring together, they used them to buy the potter's field as a place to bury foreigners. 8 For this reason that field has been called the Field of Blood to this day. 9 Then was fulfilled what had been spoken through the prophet Jeremiah,[s] "And they took[t] the thirty pieces of silver, the price of the one on whom a price had been set,[u] on whom some of the people of Israel had set a price, 10 and they gave[v] them for the potter's field, as the Lord commanded me."[49]

11 Now Jesus stood before the governor; and the governor asked him, "Are you the King of the Jews?" Jesus said, "You say so." 12 But when he was accused by the chief priests and elders, he did not answer. 13 Then Pilate said to him, "Do you not hear how many accusations they make against you?" 14 But he gave him no answer, not even to a single charge, so that the governor was greatly amazed.

15 Now at the festival the governor was accustomed to release a prisoner for the crowd, anyone whom they wanted. 16 At that time they had a notorious prisoner, called Jesus[w] Barabbas. 17 So after they had gathered, Pilate said to them, "Whom do you want me to release for you, Jesus[w] Barabbas or Jesus who is called the Messiah?"[x] 18 For he realized that it was out of jealousy that they had handed him over. 19 While he was sitting on the judgment seat, his wife sent word to him, "Have nothing to do with that innocent man, for today I have suffered a great deal because of a dream about him." 20 Now the chief priests and the elders persuaded the crowds to ask for Barabbas and to have Jesus killed. 21 The governor again said to them, "Which of the two do you want me to release for you?" And they said, "Barabbas." 22 Pilate said to them, "Then what should I do with Jesus who is called the Messiah?"[x] All of them said, "Let him be crucified!" 23 Then he asked, "Why, what evil has he done?" But they shouted all the more, "Let him be crucified!"

24 So when Pilate saw that he could do nothing, but rather that a riot was beginning, he took some water and washed his hands before the crowd, saying, "I am innocent of this man's blood;[y] see to it yourselves." 25 Then the people as a whole answered, "His blood be on us and on our children!" 26 So he released Barabbas for them; and after flogging Jesus, he handed him over to be crucified.

27 Then the soldiers of the governor took Jesus into the governor's headquarters,[z] and they gathered the whole cohort around him. 28 They stripped him and put a scarlet robe on him, 29 and after twisting some thorns into a crown, they put it on his head. They put a reed in his right hand and knelt before him and mocked him, saying, "Hail, King of the Jews!" 30 They spat on him, and took the reed and struck him on the head. 31 After mocking him, they stripped him of the robe and put his own clothes on him. Then they led him away to crucify him.

32 As they went out, they came upon a man from Cyrene named Simon; they compelled this man to carry his cross. 33 And when they came to a place called Golgotha (which means Place of a Skull), 34 they offered him wine to drink, mixed with gall; but when he tasted it, he would not drink it. 35 And when they had crucified him, they divided his clothes among themselves by casting lots;[a] 36 then they sat down there and kept watch over him. 37 Over his head they put the charge against him, which read, "This is Jesus, the King of the Jews."

38 Then two bandits were crucified with him,

---

[q]Gk he [r]Other ancient authorities read *righteous* [s]Other ancient authorities read *Zechariah* or *Isaiah* [t]Or *I took* [u]Or *the price of the precious One* [v]Other ancient authorities read *I gave* [w]Other ancient authorities lack *Jesus* [x]Or *the Christ* [y]Other ancient authorities read *this righteous blood*, or *this righteous man's blood* [z]Gk the *praetorium* [a]Other ancient authorities add *in order that what had been spoken through the prophet might be fulfilled, "They divided my clothes among themselves, and for my clothing they cast lots."*

[49]Zech 11:12–13; Jer 32:5–9

one on his right and one on his left. 39 Those who passed by derided[b] him, shaking their heads 40 and saying, "You who would destroy the temple and build it in three days, save yourself! If you are the Son of God, come down from the cross." 41 In the same way the chief priests also, along with the scribes and elders, were mocking him, saying, 42 "He saved others; he cannot save himself.[c] He is the King of Israel; let him come down from the cross now, and we will believe in him. 43 He trusts in God; let God deliver him now, if he wants to; for he said, 'I am God's Son.'" 44 The bandits who were crucified with him also taunted him in the same way.

45 From noon on, darkness came over the whole land[d] until three in the afternoon. 46 And about three o'clock Jesus cried with a loud voice, "Eli, Eli, lema sabachthani?" that is, "My God, my God, why have you forsaken me?"[50] 47 When some of the bystanders heard it, they said, "This man is calling for Elijah." 48 At once one of them ran and got a sponge, filled it with sour wine, put it on a stick, and gave it to him to drink. 49 But the others said, "Wait, let us see whether Elijah will come to save him."[e] 50 Then Jesus cried again with a loud voice and breathed his last.[f] 51 At that moment the curtain of the temple was torn in two, from top to bottom. The earth shook, and the rocks were split. 52 The tombs also were opened, and many bodies of the saints who had fallen asleep were raised. 53 After his resurrection they came out of the tombs and entered the holy city and appeared to many. 54 Now when the centurion and those with him, who were keeping watch over Jesus, saw the earthquake and what took place, they were terrified and said, "Truly this man was God's Son!"[g]

55 Many women were also there, looking on from a distance; they had followed Jesus from Galilee and had provided for him. 56 Among them were Mary Magdalene, and Mary the mother of James and Joseph, and the mother of the sons of Zebedee.

57 When it was evening, there came a rich man from Arimathea, named Joseph, who was also a disciple of Jesus. 58 He went to Pilate and asked for the body of Jesus; then Pilate ordered it to be given to him. 59 So Joseph took the body and wrapped it in a clean linen cloth 60 and laid it in his own new tomb, which he had hewn in the rock.

He then rolled a great stone to the door of the tomb and went away. 61 Mary Magdalene and the other Mary were there, sitting opposite the tomb.

62 The next day, that is, after the day of Preparation, the chief priests and the Pharisees gathered before Pilate 63 and said, "Sir, we remember what that impostor said while he was still alive, 'After three days I will rise again.' 64 Therefore command the tomb to be made secure until the third day; otherwise his disciples may go and steal him away, and tell the people, 'He has been raised from the dead,' and the last deception would be worse than the first." 65 Pilate said to them, "You have a guard[h] of soldiers; go, make it as secure as you can."[i] 66 So they went with the guard and made the tomb secure by sealing the stone.

28 After the sabbath, as the first day of the week was dawning, Mary Magdalene and the other Mary went to see the tomb. 2 And suddenly there was a great earthquake; for an angel of the Lord, descending from heaven, came and rolled back the stone and sat on it. 3 His appearance was like lightning, and his clothing white as snow. 4 For fear of him the guards shook and became like dead men. 5 But the angel said to the women, "Do not be afraid; I know that you are looking for Jesus who was crucified. 6 He is not here; for he has been raised, as he said. Come, see the place where he[j] lay. 7 Then go quickly and tell his disciples, 'He has been raised from the dead,[k] and indeed he is going ahead of you to Galilee; there you will see him.' This is my message for you." 8 So they left the tomb quickly with fear and great joy, and ran to tell his disciples. 9 Suddenly Jesus met them and said, "Greetings!" And they came to him, took hold of his feet, and worshiped him. 10 Then Jesus said to them, "Do not be afraid; go and tell my brothers to go to Galilee; there they will see me."

11 While they were going, some of the guard went into the city and told the chief priests everything that had happened. 12 After the priests[l]

---

[b]Or *blasphemed*   [c]Or *is he unable to save himself?*   [d]Or *earth*
[e]Other ancient authorities add *And another took a spear and pierced his side, and out came water and blood*   [f]Or *gave up his spirit*
[g]Or *a son of God*   [h]Or *Take a guard*   [i]Gk *you know how*   [j]Other ancient authorities read *the Lord*   [k]Other ancient authorities lack *from the dead*   [l]Gk *they*

[50]Ps 22:1

had assembled with the elders, they devised a plan to give a large sum of money to the soldiers, 13 telling them, "You must say, 'His disciples came by night and stole him away while we were asleep.' 14 If this comes to the governor's ears, we will satisfy him and keep you out of trouble." 15 So they took the money and did as they were directed. And this story is still told among the Jews to this day.

16 Now the eleven disciples went to Galilee, to the mountain to which Jesus had directed them. 17 When they saw him, they worshiped him; but some doubted. 18 And Jesus came and said to them, "All authority in heaven and on earth has been given to me. 19 Go therefore and make disciples of all nations, baptizing them in the name of the Father and of the Son and of the Holy Spirit, 20 and teaching them to obey everything that I have commanded you. And remember, I am with you always, to the end of the age."m

mOther ancient authorities add *Amen*

The Gospel According to Mark

Mark is the shortest of the New Testament Gospels, and, in the opinion of most scholars, it was the first to be written. Although traditionally ascribed to John Mark, the companion of the apostle Peter, its author chose to remain anonymous. Most scholars think that the book was composed thirty or forty years after Jesus' death, possibly during the early years of the Jewish uprising against Rome that culminated in the destruction of the Jerusalem Temple in 70 C.E. Its author was a Greek-speaking Christian who had heard, and possibly read, accounts of Jesus' life and death and created a kind of biographical account of his own in order to proclaim the "good news of Jesus, the Christ, the Son of God." (1:1).

Jesus is declared to be the Son of God by God himself at the outset of the narrative (1:11) and is proclaimed the Son of God during his ministry by the evil spirits that he casts out (3:11). One of the striking features of this Gospel, however, is that no one else seems to understand who Jesus is. Despite the fact that his teachings astound his listeners (1:22) and that his miracles cause his fame to spread far and wide (1:28, 45), his family thinks that he has gone out of his mind (3:21), the Jewish leaders claim that he is inspired by the devil (3:22), the people from his hometown do not accept him (6:1–5), and, worst of all, his own disciples do not understand who he is (6:51–52; 8:21).

It is not until halfway through the Gospel that the disciples begin to have an inkling of Jesus' identity (8:27–30). Even then, their understanding is partial at best (8:31–33). They recognize that he is the Messiah, but appear to share the traditional Jewish notion that the Messiah would be a great and powerful figure who would bring salvation through his mighty deeds against God's enemies. They do not understand that Jesus, as God's Son, must suffer humiliation and death (9:30–31; 10:32–34).

For this author, however, this is precisely Jesus' destiny. At the end of his life Jesus makes a pilgrimage to Jerusalem for Passover, where he is betrayed, arrested, tried, and executed (chaps. 11–15). For Mark, this death is not a simple miscarriage of justice; it is a death for the sake of others in fulfillment of God's will (10:45). God's definitive vindication of Jesus on the one hand and his followers' continuing inability to understand on the other are decisively shown in the concluding scene of the narrative. For on the third day, three women go to Jesus' tomb to anoint his body, only to find that he is not there but has been raised from the dead. They flee the tomb, not saying anything to anybody, "for they were afraid" (16:1–8).

From the New Revised Standard Version Bible, © 1989.

1 The beginning of the good news[a] of Jesus Christ, the Son of God.[b]

2 As it is written in the prophet Isaiah,[c]

> "See, I am sending my messenger
> ahead of you,[d]
> who will prepare your way;[1]

3
> the voice of one crying out in the wilderness:
> 'Prepare the way of the Lord,
> make his paths straight,'"[2]

4 John the baptizer appeared[e] in the wilderness, proclaiming a baptism of repentance for the forgiveness of sins. 5 And people from the whole Judean countryside and all the people of Jerusalem were going out to him, and were baptized by him in the river Jordan, confessing their sins. 6 Now John was clothed with camel's hair, with a leather belt around his waist, and he ate locusts and wild honey. 7 He proclaimed, "The one who is more powerful than I is coming after me; I am not worthy to stoop down and untie the thong of his sandals. 8 I have baptized you with[f] water; but he will baptize you with[f] the Holy Spirit."

9 In those days Jesus came from Nazareth of Galilee and was baptized by John in the Jordan. 10 And just as he was coming up out of the water, he saw the heavens torn apart and the Spirit descending like a dove on him. 11 And a voice came from heaven, "You are my Son, the Beloved;[g] with you I am well pleased."

12 And the Spirit immediately drove him out into the wilderness. 13 He was in the wilderness forty days, tempted by Satan; and he was with the wild beasts; and the angels waited on him.

14 Now after John was arrested, Jesus came to Galilee, proclaiming the good news[a] of God,[h] 15 and saying, "The time is fulfilled, and the kingdom of God has come near;[i] repent, and believe in the good news."[a]

16 As Jesus passed along the Sea of Galilee, he saw Simon and his brother Andrew casting a net into the sea—for they were fishermen. 17 And Jesus said to them, "Follow me and I will make you fish for people." 18 And immediately they left their nets and followed him. 19 As he went a little farther, he saw James son of Zebedee and his brother John, who were in their boat mending the nets. 20 Immediately he called them; and they left their father Zebedee in the boat with the hired men, and followed him.

21 They went to Capernaum; and when the sabbath came, he entered the synagogue and taught. 22 They were astounded at his teaching, for he taught them as one having authority, and not as the scribes. 23 Just then there was in their synagogue a man with an unclean spirit, 24 and he cried out, "What have you to do with us, Jesus of Nazareth? Have you come to destroy us? I know who you are, the Holy One of God." 25 But Jesus rebuked him, saying, "Be silent, and come out of him!" 26 And the unclean spirit, convulsing him and crying with a loud voice, came out of him. 27 They were all amazed, and they kept on asking one another, "What is this? A new teaching—with authority! He[j] commands even the unclean spirits, and they obey him." 28 At once his fame began to spread throughout the surrounding region of Galilee.

29 As soon as they[k] left the synagogue, they entered the house of Simon and Andrew, with James and John. 30 Now Simon's mother-in-law was in bed with a fever, and they told him about her at once. 31 He came and took her by the hand and lifted her up. Then the fever left her, and she began to serve them.

32 That evening, at sundown, they brought to him all who were sick or possessed with demons. 33 And the whole city was gathered around the door. 34 And he cured many who were sick with various diseases, and cast out many demons; and he would not permit the demons to speak, because they knew him.

35 In the morning, while it was still very dark, he got up and went out to a deserted place, and there he prayed. 36 And Simon and his companions hunted for him. 37 When they found him, they said to him, "Everyone is searching for you." 38 He answered, "Let us go on to the neighboring towns, so that I may proclaim the message there also; for that is what I came out to do." 39 And he went throughout Galilee, proclaiming the message in their synagogues and casting out demons.

40 A leper[l] came to him begging him, and

---

[j]Or *A new teaching! With authority he*   [k]Other ancient authorities read *he*   [l]The terms *leper* and *leprosy* can refer to several diseases

---

[1]Mal 3:1   [2]Isa 40:3

kneeling[m] he said to him, "If you choose, you can make me clean." 41 Moved with pity,[n] Jesus[o] stretched out his hand and touched him, and said to him, "I do choose. Be made clean!" 42 Immediately the leprosy[p] left him, and he was made clean. 43 After sternly warning him he sent him away at once, 44 saying to him, "See that you say nothing to anyone; but go, show yourself to the priest, and offer for your cleansing what Moses commanded, as a testimony to them." 45 But he went out and began to proclaim it freely, and to spread the word, so that Jesus[o] could no longer go into a town openly, but stayed out in the country; and people came to him from every quarter.

2 When he returned to Capernaum after some days, it was reported that he was at home. 2 So many gathered around that there was no longer room for them, not even in front of the door; and he was speaking the word to them. 3 Then some people[q] came, bringing to him a paralyzed man, carried by four of them. 4 And when they could not bring him to Jesus because of the crowd, they removed the roof above him; and after having dug through it, they let down the mat on which the paralytic lay. 5 When Jesus saw their faith, he said to the paralytic, "Son, your sins are forgiven." 6 Now some of the scribes were sitting there, questioning in their hearts, 7 "Why does this fellow speak in this way? It is blasphemy! Who can forgive sins but God alone?" 8 At once Jesus perceived in his spirit that they were discussing these questions among themselves; and he said to them, "Why do you raise such questions in your hearts? 9 Which is easier, to say to the paralytic, 'Your sins are forgiven,' or to say, 'Stand up and take your mat and walk'? 10 But so that you may know that the Son of Man has authority on earth to forgive sins"—he said to the paralytic— 11 "I say to you, stand up, take your mat and go to your home." 12 And he stood up, and immediately took the mat and went out before all of them; so that they were all amazed and glorified God, saying, "We have never seen anything like this!"

13 Jesus[r] went out again beside the sea; the whole crowd gathered around him, and he taught them. 14 As he was walking along, he saw Levi son of Alphaeus sitting at the tax booth, and he said to him, "Follow me." And he got up and followed him.

15 And as he sat at dinner[s] in Levi's[t] house, many tax collectors and sinners were also sitting[u] with Jesus and his disciples—for there were many who followed him. 16 When the scribes of[v] the Pharisees saw that he was eating with sinners and tax collectors, they said to his disciples, "Why does he eat[w] with tax collectors and sinners?" 17 When Jesus heard this, he said to them, "Those who are well have no need of a physician, but those who are sick; I have come to call not the righteous but sinners."

18 Now John's disciples and the Pharisees were fasting; and people[x] came and said to him, "Why do John's disciples and the disciples of the Pharisees fast, but your disciples do not fast?" 19 Jesus said to them, "The wedding guests cannot fast while the bridegroom is with them, can they? As long as they have the bridegroom with them, they cannot fast. 20 The days will come when the bridegroom is taken away from them, and then they will fast on that day.

21 "No one sews a piece of unshrunk cloth on an old cloak; otherwise, the patch pulls away from it, the new from the old, and a worse tear is made. 22 And no one puts new wine into old wineskins; otherwise, the wine will burst the skins, and the wine is lost, and so are the skins; but one puts new wine into fresh wineskins."[y]

23 One sabbath he was going through the grainfields; and as they made their way his disciples began to pluck heads of grain. 24 The Pharisees said to him, "Look, why are they doing what is not lawful on the sabbath?" 25 And he said to them, "Have you never read what David did when he and his companions were hungry and in need of food? 26 He entered the house of God, when Abiathar was high priest, and ate the bread of the Presence, which it is not lawful for any but the priests to eat, and he gave some to his companions." 27 Then he said to them, "The sabbath was made for humankind, and not humankind for the sabbath; 28 so the Son of Man is lord even of the sabbath."

[m]Other ancient authorities lack *kneeling*   [n]Other ancient authorities read *anger*   [o]Gk *he*   [p]The terms *leper* and *leprosy* can refer to several diseases   [q]Gk *they*   [r]Gk *He*   [s]Gk *reclined*   [t]Gk *his*   [u]Gk *reclining*   [v]Other ancient authorities read *and*   [w]Other ancient authorities add *and drink*   [x]Gk *they*   [y]Other ancient authorities lack *but one puts new wine into fresh wineskins*

3 Again he entered the synagogue, and a man was there who had a withered hand. 2 They watched him to see whether he would cure him on the sabbath, so that they might accuse him. 3 And he said to the man who had the withered hand, "Come forward." 4 Then he said to them, "Is it lawful to do good or to do harm on the sabbath, to save life or to kill?" But they were silent. 5 He looked around at them with anger; he was grieved at their hardness of heart and said to the man, "Stretch out your hand." He stretched it out, and his hand was restored. 6 The Pharisees went out and immediately conspired with the Herodians against him, how to destroy him.

7 Jesus departed with his disciples to the sea, and a great multitude from Galilee followed him; 8 hearing all that he was doing, they came to him in great numbers from Judea, Jerusalem, Idumea, beyond the Jordan, and the region around Tyre and Sidon. 9 He told his disciples to have a boat ready for him because of the crowd, so that they would not crush him; 10 for he had cured many, so that all who had diseases pressed upon him to touch him. 11 Whenever the unclean spirits saw him, they fell down before him and shouted, "You are the Son of God!" 12 But he sternly ordered them not to make him known.

13 He went up the mountain and called to him those whom he wanted, and they came to him. 14 And he appointed twelve, whom he also named apostles,[z] to be with him, and to be sent out to proclaim the message, 15 and to have authority to cast out demons. 16 So he appointed the twelve:[a] Simon (to whom he gave the name Peter); 17 James son of Zebedee and John the brother of James (to whom he gave the name Boanerges, that is, Sons of Thunder); 18 and Andrew, and Philip, and Bartholomew, and Matthew, and Thomas, and James son of Alphaeus, and Thaddaeus, and Simon the Cananaean, 19 and Judas Iscariot, who betrayed him.

Then he went home; 20 and the crowd came together again, so that they could not even eat. 21 When his family heard it, they went out to restrain him, for people were saying, "He has gone out of his mind." 22 And the scribes who came down from Jerusalem said, "He has Beelzebul, and by the ruler of the demons he casts out demons." 23 And he called them to him, and spoke to them in parables, "How can Satan cast out Satan? 24 If a kingdom is divided against itself, that kingdom cannot stand. 25 And if a house is divided against itself, that house will not be able to stand. 26 And if Satan has risen up against himself and is divided, he cannot stand, but his end has come. 27 But no one can enter a strong man's house and plunder his property without first tying up the strong man; then indeed the house can be plundered.

28 "Truly I tell you, people will be forgiven for their sins and whatever blasphemies they utter; 29 but whoever blasphemes against the Holy Spirit can never have forgiveness, but is guilty of an eternal sin"— 30 for they had said, "He has an unclean spirit."

31 Then his mother and his brothers came; and standing outside, they sent to him and called him. 32 A crowd was sitting around him; and they said to him, "Your mother and your brothers and sisters[b] are outside, asking for you." 33 And he replied, "Who are my mother and my brothers?" 34 And looking at those who sat around him, he said, "Here are my mother and my brothers! 35 Whoever does the will of God is my brother and sister and mother."

4 Again he began to teach beside the sea. Such a very large crowd gathered around him that he got into a boat on the sea and sat there, while the whole crowd was beside the sea on the land. 2 He began to teach them many things in parables, and in his teaching he said to them: 3 "Listen! A sower went out to sow. 4 And as he sowed, some seed fell on the path, and the birds came and ate it up. 5 Other seed fell on rocky ground, where it did not have much soil, and it sprang up quickly, since it had no depth of soil. 6 And when the sun rose, it was scorched; and since it had no root, it withered away. 7 Other seed fell among thorns, and the thorns grew up and choked it, and it yielded no grain. 8 Other seed fell into good soil and brought forth grain, growing up and increasing and yielding thirty and sixty and a hundredfold." 9 And he said, "Let anyone with ears to hear listen!"

[z]Other ancient authorities lack *whom he also named apostles*   [a]Other ancient authorities lack *So he appointed the twelve*   [b]Other ancient authorities lack *and sisters*

10 When he was alone, those who were around him along with the twelve asked him about the parables. 11 And he said to them, "To you has been given the secret[c] of the kingdom of God, but for those outside, everything comes in parables; 12 in order that

'they may indeed look, but not
        perceive,
  and may indeed listen, but not
        understand;
  so that they may not turn again
        and be forgiven.'"[3]

13 And he said to them, "Do you not understand this parable? Then how will you understand all the parables? 14 The sower sows the word. 15 These are the ones on the path where the word is sown: when they hear, Satan immediately comes and takes away the word that is sown in them. 16 And these are the ones sown on rocky ground: when they hear the word, they immediately receive it with joy. 17 But they have no root, and endure only for a while; then, when trouble or persecution arises on account of the word, immediately they fall away.[d] 18 And others are those sown among the thorns: these are the ones who hear the word, 19 but the cares of the world, and the lure of wealth, and the desire for other things come in and choke the word, and it yields nothing. 20 And these are the ones sown on the good soil: they hear the word and accept it and bear fruit, thirty and sixty and a hundredfold."

21 He said to them, "Is a lamp brought in to be put under the bushel basket, or under the bed, and not on the lampstand? 22 For there is nothing hidden, except to be disclosed; nor is anything secret, except to come to light. 23 Let anyone with ears to hear listen!" 24 And he said to them, "Pay attention to what you hear; the measure you give will be the measure you get, and still more will be given you. 25 For to those who have, more will be given; and from those who have nothing, even what they have will be taken away."

26 He also said, "The kingdom of God is as if someone would scatter seed on the ground, 27 and would sleep and rise night and day, and the seed would sprout and grow, he does not know how. 28 The earth produces of itself, first the stalk, then the head, then the full grain in the head. 29 But when the grain is ripe, at once he goes in with his sickle, because the harvest has come."

30 He also said, "With what can we compare the kingdom of God, or what parable will we use for it? 31 It is like a mustard seed, which, when sown upon the ground, is the smallest of all the seeds on earth; 32 yet when it is sown it grows up and becomes the greatest of all shrubs, and puts forth large branches, so that the birds of the air can make nests in its shade."

33 With many such parables he spoke the word to them, as they were able to hear it; 34 he did not speak to them except in parables, but he explained everything in private to his disciples.

35 On that day, when evening had come, he said to them, "Let us go across to the other side." 36 And leaving the crowd behind, they took him with them in the boat, just as he was. Other boats were with him. 37 A great windstorm arose, and the waves beat into the boat, so that the boat was already being swamped. 38 But he was in the stern, asleep on the cushion; and they woke him up and said to him, "Teacher, do you not care that we are perishing?" 39 He woke up and rebuked the wind, and said to the sea, "Peace! Be still!" Then the wind ceased, and there was a dead calm. 40 He said to them, "Why are you afraid? Have you still no faith?" 41 And they were filled with great awe and said to one another, "Who then is this, that even the wind and the sea obey him?"

5 They came to the other side of the sea, to the country of the Gerasenes.[e] 2 And when he had stepped out of the boat, immediately a man out of the tombs with an unclean spirit met him. 3 He lived among the tombs; and no one could restrain him any more, even with a chain; 4 for he had often been restrained with shackles and chains, but the chains he wrenched apart, and the shackles he broke in pieces; and no one had the strength to subdue him. 5 Night and day among the tombs and on the mountains he was always howling and bruising himself with stones. 6 When he saw Jesus from a distance, he ran and bowed down before him; 7 and he shouted at the top of his voice,

---

[c]Or *mystery* [d]Or *stumble* [e]Other ancient authorities read *Gergesenes*; others, *Gadarenes*

[3]Isa 6:9–10

"What have you to do with me, Jesus, Son of the Most High God? I adjure you by God, do not torment me." 8 For he had said to him, "Come out of the man, you unclean spirit!" 9 Then Jesus[f] asked him, "What is your name?" He replied, "My name is Legion; for we are many." 10 He begged him earnestly not to send them out of the country. 11 Now there on the hillside a great herd of swine was feeding; 12 and the unclean spirits[g] begged him, "Send us into the swine; let us enter them." 13 So he gave them permission. And the unclean spirits came out and entered the swine; and the herd, numbering about two thousand, rushed down the steep bank into the sea, and were drowned in the sea.

14 The swineherds ran off and told it in the city and in the country. Then people came to see what it was that had happened. 15 They came to Jesus and saw the demoniac sitting there, clothed and in his right mind, the very man who had had the legion; and they were afraid. 16 Those who had seen what had happened to the demoniac and to the swine reported it. 17 Then they began to beg Jesus[h] to leave their neighborhood. 18 As he was getting into the boat, the man who had been possessed by demons begged him that he might be with him. 19 But Jesus[f] refused, and said to him, "Go home to your friends, and tell them how much the Lord has done for you, and what mercy he has shown you." 20 And he went away and began to proclaim in the Decapolis how much Jesus had done for him; and everyone was amazed.

21 When Jesus had crossed again in the boat[i] to the other side, a great crowd gathered around him; and he was by the sea. 22 Then one of the leaders of the synagogue named Jairus came and, when he saw him, fell at his feet 23 and begged him repeatedly, "My little daughter is at the point of death. Come and lay your hands on her, so that she may be made well, and live." 24 So he went with him.

And a large crowd followed him and pressed in on him. 25 Now there was a woman who had been suffering from hemorrhages for twelve years. 26 She had endured much under many physicians, and had spent all that she had; and she was no better, but rather grew worse. 27 She had heard about Jesus, and came up behind him in the crowd and touched his cloak, 28 for she said, "If I but touch his clothes, I will be made well." 29 Immediately her hemorrhage stopped; and she felt in her body that she was healed of her disease. 30 Immediately aware that power had gone forth from him, Jesus turned about in the crowd and said, "Who touched my clothes?" 31 And his disciples said to him, "You see the crowd pressing in on you; how can you say, 'Who touched me?'" 32 He looked all around to see who had done it. 33 But the woman, knowing what had happened to her, came in fear and trembling, fell down before him, and told him the whole truth. 34 He said to her, "Daughter, your faith has made you well; go in peace, and be healed of your disease."

35 While he was still speaking, some people came from the leader's house to say, "Your daughter is dead. Why trouble the teacher any further?" 36 But overhearing[j] what they said, Jesus said to the leader of the synagogue, "Do not fear, only believe." 37 He allowed no one to follow him except Peter, James, and John, the brother of James. 38 When they came to the house of the leader of the synagogue, he saw a commotion, people weeping and wailing loudly. 39 When he had entered, he said to them, "Why do you make a commotion and weep? The child is not dead but sleeping." 40 And they laughed at him. Then he put them all outside, and took the child's father and mother and those who were with him, and went in where the child was. 41 He took her by the hand and said to her, "Talitha cum," which means, "Little girl, get up!" 42 And immediately the girl got up and began to walk about (she was twelve years of age). At this they were overcome with amazement. 43 He strictly ordered them that no one should know this, and told them to give her something to eat.

6 He left that place and came to his hometown, and his disciples followed him. 2 On the sabbath he began to teach in the synagogue, and many who heard him were astounded. They said, "Where did this man get all this? What is this wisdom that has been given to him? What deeds of power are being done by his hands! 3 Is not this the carpenter, the son of Mary[k] and brother of James and Joses and Judas and Simon, and are not

[f]Gk *he* [g]Gk *they* [h]Gk *him* [i]Other ancient authorities lack *in the boat* [j]Or *ignoring*; other ancient authorities read *hearing* [k]Other ancient authorities read *son of the carpenter and of Mary*

his sisters here with us?" And they took offense[l] at him. 4 Then Jesus said to them, "Prophets are not without honor, except in their hometown, and among their own kin, and in their own house." 5 And he could do no deed of power there, except that he laid his hands on a few sick people and cured them. 6 And he was amazed at their unbelief.

Then he went about among the villages teaching. 7 He called the twelve and began to send them out two by two, and gave them authority over the unclean spirits. 8 He ordered them to take nothing for their journey except a staff; no bread, no bag, no money in their belts; 9 but to wear sandals and not to put on two tunics. 10 He said to them, "Wherever you enter a house, stay there until you leave the place. 11 If any place will not welcome you and they refuse to hear you, as you leave, shake off the dust that is on your feet as a testimony against them." 12 So they went out and proclaimed that all should repent. 13 They cast out many demons, and anointed with oil many who were sick and cured them.

14 King Herod heard of it, for Jesus'[m] name had become known. Some were[n] saying, "John the baptizer has been raised from the dead; and for this reason these powers are at work in him." 15 But others said, "It is Elijah." And others said, "It is a prophet, like one of the prophets of old." 16 But when Herod heard of it, he said, "John, whom I beheaded, has been raised."

17 For Herod himself had sent men who arrested John, bound him, and put him in prison on account of Herodias, his brother Philip's wife, because Herod[o] had married her. 18 For John had been telling Herod, "It is not lawful for you to have your brother's wife." 19 And Herodias had a grudge against him, and wanted to kill him. But she could not, 20 for Herod feared John, knowing that he was a righteous and holy man, and he protected him. When he heard him, he was greatly perplexed;[p] and yet he liked to listen to him. 21 But an opportunity came when Herod on his birthday gave a banquet for his courtiers and officers and for the leaders of Galilee. 22 When his daughter Herodias[q] came in and danced, she pleased Herod and his guests; and the king said to the girl, "Ask me for whatever you wish, and I will

give it." 23 And he solemnly swore to her, "Whatever you ask me, I will give you, even half of my kingdom." 24 She went out and said to her mother, "What should I ask for?" She replied, "The head of John the baptizer." 25 Immediately she rushed back to the king and requested, "I want you to give me at once the head of John the Baptist on a platter." 26 The king was deeply grieved; yet out of regard for his oaths and for the guests, he did not want to refuse her. 27 Immediately the king sent a soldier of the guard with orders to bring John's[m] head. He went and beheaded him in the prison, 28 brought his head on a platter, and gave it to the girl. Then the girl gave it to her mother. 29 When his disciples heard about it, they came and took his body, and laid it in a tomb.

30 The apostles gathered around Jesus, and told him all that they had done and taught. 31 He said to them, "Come away to a deserted place all by yourselves and rest a while." For many were coming and going, and they had no leisure even to eat. 32 And they went away in the boat to a deserted place by themselves. 33 Now many saw them going and recognized them, and they hurried there on foot from all the towns and arrived ahead of them. 34 As he went ashore, he saw a great crowd; and he had compassion for them, because they were like sheep without a shepherd; and he began to teach them many things. 35 When it grew late, his disciples came to him and said, "This is a deserted place, and the hour is now very late; 36 send them away so that they may go into the surrounding country and villages and buy something for themselves to eat." 37 But he answered them, "You give them something to eat." They said to him, "Are we to go and buy two hundred denarii[r] worth of bread, and give it to them to eat?" 38 And he said to them, "How many loaves have you? Go and see." When they had found out, they said, "Five, and two fish." 39 Then he ordered them to get all the people to sit down in groups on the green grass. 40 So they sat down in groups of hundreds and of fifties. 41 Taking the five loaves and the two fish, he looked up to heaven, and

[l]Or *stumbled*   [m]Gk *his*   [n]Other ancient authorities read *He was* [o]Gk *he*   [p]Other ancient authorities read *he did many things*   [q]Other ancient authorities read *the daughter of Herodias herself* [r]The denarius was the usual day's wage for a laborer

blessed and broke the loaves, and gave them to his disciples to set before the people; and he divided the two fish among them all. 42 And all ate and were filled; 43 and they took up twelve baskets full of broken pieces and of the fish. 44 Those who had eaten the loaves numbered five thousand men.

45 Immediately he made his disciples get into the boat and go on ahead to the other side, to Bethsaida, while he dismissed the crowd. 46 After saying farewell to them, he went up on the mountain to pray.

47 When evening came, the boat was out on the sea, and he was alone on the land. 48 When he saw that they were straining at the oars against an adverse wind, he came towards them early in the morning, walking on the sea. He intended to pass them by. 49 But when they saw him walking on the sea, they thought it was a ghost and cried out; 50 for they all saw him and were terrified. But immediately he spoke to them and said, "Take heart, it is I; do not be afraid." 51 Then he got into the boat with them and the wind ceased. And they were utterly astounded, 52 for they did not understand about the loaves, but their hearts were hardened.

53 When they had crossed over, they came to land at Gennesaret and moored the boat. 54 When they got out of the boat, people at once recognized him, 55 and rushed about that whole region and began to bring the sick on mats to wherever they heard he was. 56 And wherever he went, into villages or cities or farms, they laid the sick in the marketplaces, and begged him that they might touch even the fringe of his cloak; and all who touched it were healed.

7 Now when the Pharisees and some of the scribes who had come from Jerusalem gathered around him, 2 they noticed that some of his disciples were eating with defiled hands, that is, without washing them. 3 (For the Pharisees, and all the Jews, do not eat unless they thoroughly wash their hands,^{s} thus observing the tradition of the elders; 4 and they do not eat anything from the market unless they wash it;^{t} and there are also many other traditions that they observe, the washing of cups, pots, and bronze kettles.^{u}) 5 So the Pharisees and the scribes asked him, "Why do your disciples not live^v according to the tradition of the elders, but eat with defiled hands?" 6 He

said to them, "Isaiah prophesied rightly about you hypocrites, as it is written,

'This people honors me with their
         lips,
   but their hearts are far from me;
7   in vain do they worship me,
      teaching human precepts as
         doctrines.'^{4}

8 You abandon the commandment of God and hold to human tradition."

9 Then he said to them, "You have a fine way of rejecting the commandment of God in order to keep your tradition! 10 For Moses said, 'Honor your father and your mother';^{5} and, 'Whoever speaks evil of father or mother must surely die.'^{6} 11 But you say that if anyone tells father or mother, 'Whatever support you might have had from me is Corban' (that is, an offering to God^w)— 12 then you no longer permit doing anything for a father or mother, 13 thus making void the word of God through your tradition that you have handed on. And you do many things like this."

14 Then he called the crowd again and said to them, "Listen to me, all of you, and understand: 15 there is nothing outside a person that by going in can defile, but the things that come out are what defile."^{x}

17 When he had left the crowd and entered the house, his disciples asked him about the parable. 18 He said to them, "Then do you also fail to understand? Do you not see that whatever goes into a person from outside cannot defile, 19 since it enters, not the heart but the stomach, and goes out into the sewer?" (Thus he declared all foods clean.) 20 And he said, "It is what comes out of a person that defiles. 21 For it is from within, from the human heart, that evil intentions come: fornication, theft, murder, 22 adultery, avarice, wickedness, deceit, licentiousness, envy, slander, pride, folly. 23 All these evil things come from within, and they defile a person."

24 From there he set out and went away to the region of Tyre.^{y} He entered a house and did not

^{w}Gk lacks *to God* ^{x}Other ancient authorities add verse 16, *"Let anyone with ears to hear listen"* ^{y}Other ancient authorities add *and Sidon*

^{4}Isa 29:13 ^{5}Exod 20:12; Deut 5:16 ^{6}Exod 21:17; Lev 20:9

want anyone to know he was there. Yet he could not escape notice, 25 but a woman whose little daughter had an unclean spirit immediately heard about him, and she came and bowed down at his feet. 26 Now the woman was a Gentile, of Syrophoenician origin. She begged him to cast the demon out of her daughter. 27 He said to her, "Let the children be fed first, for it is not fair to take the children's food and throw it to the dogs." 28 But she answered him, "Sir,ᶻ even the dogs under the table eat the children's crumbs." 29 Then he said to her, "For saying that, you may go—the demon has left your daughter." 30 So she went home, found the child lying on the bed, and the demon gone.

31 Then he returned from the region of Tyre, and went by way of Sidon towards the Sea of Galilee, in the region of the Decapolis. 32 They brought to him a deaf man who had an impediment in his speech; and they begged him to lay his hand on him. 33 He took him aside in private, away from the crowd, and put his fingers into his ears, and he spat and touched his tongue. 34 Then looking up to heaven, he sighed and said to him, "Ephphatha," that is, "Be opened." 35 And immediately his ears were opened, his tongue was released, and he spoke plainly. 36 Then Jesusᵃ ordered them to tell no one; but the more he ordered them, the more zealously they proclaimed it. 37 They were astounded beyond measure, saying, "He has done everything well; he even makes the deaf to hear and the mute to speak."

8 In those days when there was again a great crowd without anything to eat, he called his disciples and said to them, 2 "I have compassion for the crowd, because they have been with me now for three days and have nothing to eat. 3 If I send them away hungry to their homes, they will faint on the way—and some of them have come from a great distance." 4 His disciples replied, "How can one feed these people with bread here in the desert?" 5 He asked them, "How many loaves do you have?" They said, "Seven." 6 Then he ordered the crowd to sit down on the ground; and he took the seven loaves, and after giving thanks he broke them and gave them to his disciples to distribute; and they distributed them to the crowd. 7 They had also a few small fish; and after blessing them, he ordered that these too should be distributed. 8 They ate and were filled; and

they took up the broken pieces left over, seven baskets full. 9 Now there were about four thousand people. And he sent them away. 10 And immediately he got into the boat with his disciples and went to the district of Dalmanutha.ᵇ

11 The Pharisees came and began to argue with him, asking him for a sign from heaven, to test him. 12 And he sighed deeply in his spirit and said, "Why does this generation ask for a sign? Truly I tell you, no sign will be given to this generation." 13 And he left them, and getting into the boat again, he went across to the other side.

14 Now the disciplesᶜ had forgotten to bring any bread; and they had only one loaf with them in the boat. 15 And he cautioned them, saying, "Watch out—beware of the yeast of the Pharisees and the yeast of Herod."ᵈ 16 They said to one another, "It is because we have no bread." 17 And becoming aware of it, Jesus said to them, "Why are you talking about having no bread? Do you still not perceive or understand? Are your hearts hardened? 18 Do you have eyes, and fail to see? Do you have ears, and fail to hear? And do you not remember? 19 When I broke the five loaves for the five thousand, how many baskets full of broken pieces did you collect?" They said to him, "Twelve." 20 "And the seven for the four thousand, how many baskets full of broken pieces did you collect?" And they said to him, "Seven." 21 Then he said to them, "Do you not yet understand?"

22 They came to Bethsaida. Some peopleᵉ brought a blind man to him and begged him to touch him. 23 He took the blind man by the hand and led him out of the village; and when he had put saliva on his eyes and laid his hands on him, he asked him, "Can you see anything?" 24 And the manᵃ looked up and said, "I can see people, but they look like trees, walking." 25 Then Jesusᵃ laid his hands on his eyes again; and he looked intently and his sight was restored, and he saw everything clearly. 26 Then he sent him away to his home, saying, "Do not even go into the village."ᶠ

ᶻOr Lord; other ancient authorities prefix Yes   ᵃGk he   ᵇOther ancient authorities read Mageda or Magdala   ᶜGk they   ᵈOther ancient authorities read the Herodians   ᵉGk They   ᶠOther ancient authorities add or tell anyone in the village

27 Jesus went on with his disciples to the villages of Caesarea Philippi; and on the way he asked his disciples, "Who do people say that I am?" 28 And they answered him, "John the Baptist; and others, Elijah; and still others, one of the prophets." 29 He asked them, "But who do you say that I am?" Peter answered him, "You are the Messiah."g 30 And he sternly ordered them not to tell anyone about him.

31 Then he began to teach them that the Son of Man must undergo great suffering, and be rejected by the elders, the chief priests, and the scribes, and be killed, and after three days rise again. 32 He said all this quite openly. And Peter took him aside and began to rebuke him. 33 But turning and looking at his disciples, he rebuked Peter and said, "Get behind me, Satan! For you are setting your mind not on divine things but on human things."

34 He called the crowd with his disciples, and said to them, "If any want to become my followers, let them deny themselves and take up their cross and follow me. 35 For those who want to save their life will lose it, and those who lose their life for my sake, and for the sake of the gospel,h will save it. 36 For what will it profit them to gain the whole world and forfeit their life? 37 Indeed, what can they give in return for their life? 38 Those who are ashamed of me and of my wordsi in this adulterous and sinful generation, of them the Son of Man will also be ashamed when he comes in the glory of his Father with the holy angels."

9 And he said to them, "Truly I tell you, there are some standing here who will not taste death until they see that the kingdom of God has come withj power."

2 Six days later, Jesus took with him Peter and James and John, and led them up a high mountain apart, by themselves. And he was transfigured before them, 3 and his clothes became dazzling white, such as no onek on earth could bleach them. 4 And there appeared to them Elijah with Moses, who were talking with Jesus. 5 Then Peter said to Jesus, "Rabbi, it is good for us to be here; let us make three dwellings,l one for you, one for Moses, and one for Elijah." 6 He did not know what to say, for they were terrified. 7 Then a cloud overshadowed them, and from the cloud there came a voice, "This is my Son, the Beloved;m listen to him!" 8 Suddenly when they looked around, they saw no one with them any more, but only Jesus.

9 As they were coming down the mountain, he ordered them to tell no one about what they had seen, until after the Son of Man had risen from the dead. 10 So they kept the matter to themselves, questioning what this rising from the dead could mean. 11 Then they asked him, "Why do the scribes say that Elijah must come first?" 12 He said to them, "Elijah is indeed coming first to restore all things. How then is it written about the Son of Man, that he is to go through many sufferings and be treated with contempt? 13 But I tell you that Elijah has come, and they did to him whatever they pleased, as it is written about him."

14 When they came to the disciples, they saw a great crowd around them, and some scribes arguing with them. 15 When the whole crowd saw him, they were immediately overcome with awe, and they ran forward to greet him. 16 He asked them, "What are you arguing about with them?" 17 Someone from the crowd answered him, "Teacher, I brought you my son; he has a spirit that makes him unable to speak; 18 and whenever it seizes him, it dashes him down; and he foams and grinds his teeth and becomes rigid; and I asked your disciples to cast it out, but they could not do so." 19 He answered them, "You faithless generation, how much longer must I be among you? How much longer must I put up with you? Bring him to me." 20 And they brought the boyn to him. When the spirit saw him, immediately it convulsed the boy,n and he fell on the ground and rolled about, foaming at the mouth. 21 Jesuso asked the father, "How long has this been happening to him?" And he said, "From childhood. 22 It has often cast him into the fire and into the water, to destroy him; but if you are able to do anything, have pity on us and help us." 23 Jesus said to him, "If you are able!—All things can be done for the one who believes." 24 Immediately the father of the child cried out,p "I believe; help my unbelief!" 25 When Jesus saw that a crowd came running together, he rebuked the unclean spirit, saying to it,

gOr the Christ hOther ancient authorities read lose their life for the sake of the gospel iOther ancient authorities read and of mine jOr in kGk no fuller lOr tents mOr my beloved Son nGk him oGk He pOther ancient authorities add with tears

"You spirit that keeps this boy from speaking and hearing, I command you, come out of him, and never enter him again!" 26 After crying out and convulsing him terribly, it came out, and the boy was like a corpse, so that most of them said, "He is dead." 27 But Jesus took him by the hand and lifted him up, and he was able to stand. 28 When he had entered the house, his disciples asked him privately, "Why could we not cast it out?" 29 He said to them, "This kind can come out only through prayer."[q]

30 They went on from there and passed through Galilee. He did not want anyone to know it; 31 for he was teaching his disciples, saying to them, "The Son of Man is to be betrayed into human hands, and they will kill him, and three days after being killed, he will rise again." 32 But they did not understand what he was saying and were afraid to ask him.

33 Then they came to Capernaum; and when he was in the house he asked them, "What were you arguing about on the way?" 34 But they were silent, for on the way they had argued with one another who was the greatest. 35 He sat down, called the twelve, and said to them, "Whoever wants to be first must be last of all and servant of all." 36 Then he took a little child and put it among them; and taking it in his arms, he said to them, 37 "Whoever welcomes one such child in my name welcomes me, and whoever welcomes me welcomes not me but the one who sent me."

38 John said to him, "Teacher, we saw someone[r] casting out demons in your name, and we tried to stop him, because he was not following us." 39 But Jesus said, "Do not stop him; for no one who does a deed of power in my name will be able soon afterward to speak evil of me. 40 Whoever is not against us is for us. 41 For truly I tell you, whoever gives you a cup of water to drink because you bear the name of Christ will by no means lose the reward.

42 "If any of you put a stumbling block before one of these little ones who believe in me,[s] it would be better for you if a great millstone were hung around your neck and you were thrown into the sea. 43 If your hand causes you to stumble, cut it off; it is better for you to enter life maimed than to have two hands and to go to hell,[t] to the unquenchable fire.[u] 45 And if your foot causes you to stumble, cut it off; it is better for you to enter life lame than to have two feet and to be thrown into hell.[t, u] 47 And if your eye causes you to stumble, tear it out; it is better for you to enter the kingdom of God with one eye than to have two eyes and to be thrown into hell,[t] 48 where their worm never dies, and the fire is never quenched.

49 "For everyone will be salted with fire.[v] 50 Salt is good; but if salt has lost its saltiness, how can you season it?[w] Have salt in yourselves, and be at peace with one another."

10 He left that place and went to the region of Judea and[x] beyond the Jordan. And crowds again gathered around him; and, as was his custom, he again taught them.

2 Some Pharisees came, and to test him they asked, "Is it lawful for a man to divorce his wife?" 3 He answered them, "What did Moses command you?" 4 They said, "Moses allowed a man to write a certificate of dismissal and to divorce her."[7] 5 But Jesus said to them, "Because of your hardness of heart he wrote this commandment for you. 6 But from the beginning of creation, 'God made them male and female.'[8] 7 'For this reason a man shall leave his father and mother and be joined to his wife,[y] 8 and the two shall become one flesh.'[9] So they are no longer two, but one flesh. 9 Therefore what God has joined together, let no one separate."

10 Then in the house the disciples asked him again about this matter. 11 He said to them, "Whoever divorces his wife and marries another commits adultery against her; 12 and if she divorces her husband and marries another, she commits adultery."

13 People were bringing little children to him in order that he might touch them; and the disciples spoke sternly to them. 14 But when Jesus saw this, he was indignant and said to them, "Let the little children come to me; do not stop them; for it

[q]Other ancient authorities add *and fasting* [r]Other ancient authorities add *who does not follow us* [s]Other ancient authorities lack *in me* [t]Gk *Gehenna* [u]Verses 44 and 46 (which are identical with verse 48) are lacking in the best ancient authorities [v]Other ancient authorities either add or substitute *and every sacrifice will be salted with salt* [w]Or *how can you restore its saltiness?* [x]Other ancient authorities lack *and* [y]Other ancient authorities lack *and be joined to his wife*

---

[7]Deut 24:1 [8]Gen 1:27 [9]Gen 2:24

is to such as these that the kingdom of God belongs. 15 Truly I tell you, whoever does not receive the kingdom of God as a little child will never enter it." 16 And he took them up in his arms, laid his hands on them, and blessed them.

17 As he was setting out on a journey, a man ran up and knelt before him, and asked him, "Good Teacher, what must I do to inherit eternal life?" 18 Jesus said to him, "Why do you call me good? No one is good but God alone. 19 You know the commandments: 'You shall not murder; You shall not commit adultery; You shall not steal; You shall not bear false witness; You shall not defraud; Honor your father and mother.'"[10] 20 He said to him, "Teacher, I have kept all these since my youth." 21 Jesus, looking at him, loved him and said, "You lack one thing; go, sell what you own, and give the money[z] to the poor, and you will have treasure in heaven; then come, follow me." 22 When he heard this, he was shocked and went away grieving, for he had many possessions.

23 Then Jesus looked around and said to his disciples, "How hard it will be for those who have wealth to enter the kingdom of God!" 24 And the disciples were perplexed at these words. But Jesus said to them again, "Children, how hard it is[a] to enter the kingdom of God! 25 It is easier for a camel to go through the eye of a needle than for someone who is rich to enter the kingdom of God." 26 They were greatly astounded and said to one another,[b] "Then who can be saved?" 27 Jesus looked at them and said, "For mortals it is impossible, but not for God; for God all things are possible."

28 Peter began to say to him, "Look, we have left everything and followed you." 29 Jesus said, "Truly I tell you, there is no one who has left house or brothers or sisters or mother or father or children or fields, for my sake and for the sake of the good news,[c] 30 who will not receive a hundredfold now in this age—houses, brothers and sisters, mothers and children, and fields, with persecutions—and in the age to come eternal life. 31 But many who are first will be last, and the last will be first."

32 They were on the road, going up to Jerusalem, and Jesus was walking ahead of them; they were amazed, and those who followed were afraid.

He took the twelve aside again and began to tell them what was to happen to him, 33 saying, "See, we are going up to Jerusalem, and the Son of Man will be handed over to the chief priests and the scribes, and they will condemn him to death; then they will hand him over to the Gentiles; 34 they will mock him, and spit upon him, and flog him, and kill him; and after three days he will rise again."

35 James and John, the sons of Zebedee, came forward to him and said to him, "Teacher, we want you to do for us whatever we ask of you." 36 And he said to them, "What is it you want me to do for you?" 37 And they said to him, "Grant us to sit, one at your right hand and one at your left, in your glory." 38 But Jesus said to them, "You do not know what you are asking. Are you able to drink the cup that I drink, or be baptized with the baptism that I am baptized with?" 39 They replied, "We are able." Then Jesus said to them, "The cup that I drink you will drink; and with the baptism with which I am baptized, you will be baptized; 40 but to sit at my right hand or at my left is not mine to grant, but it is for those for whom it has been prepared."

41 When the ten heard this, they began to be angry with James and John. 42 So Jesus called them and said to them, "You know that among the Gentiles those whom they recognize as their rulers lord it over them, and their great ones are tyrants over them. 43 But it is not so among you; but whoever wishes to become great among you must be your servant, 44 and whoever wishes to be first among you must be slave of all. 45 For the Son of Man came not to be served but to serve, and to give his life a ransom for many."

46 They came to Jericho. As he and his disciples and a large crowd were leaving Jericho, Bartimaeus son of Timaeus, a blind beggar, was sitting by the roadside. 47 When he heard that it was Jesus of Nazareth, he began to shout out and say, "Jesus, Son of David, have mercy on me!" 48 Many sternly ordered him to be quiet, but he cried out even more loudly, "Son of David, have mercy on

---

[z]Gk lacks the money [a]Other ancient authorities add for those who trust in riches [b]Other ancient authorities read to him [c]Or gospel

[10]Exod 20:12–16; Deut 5:16–20

me!" 49 Jesus stood still and said, "Call him here." And they called the blind man, saying to him, "Take heart; get up, he is calling you." 50 So throwing off his cloak, he sprang up and came to Jesus. 51 Then Jesus said to him, "What do you want me to do for you?" The blind man said to him, "My teacher,[d] let me see again." 52 Jesus said to him, "Go; your faith has made you well." Immediately he regained his sight and followed him on the way.

11 When they were approaching Jerusalem, at Bethphage and Bethany, near the Mount of Olives, he sent two of his disciples 2 and said to them, "Go into the village ahead of you, and immediately as you enter it, you will find tied there a colt that has never been ridden; untie it and bring it. 3 If anyone says to you, 'Why are you doing this?' just say this, 'The Lord needs it and will send it back here immediately.'" 4 They went away and found a colt tied near a door, outside in the street. As they were untying it, 5 some of the bystanders said to them, "What are you doing, untying the colt?" 6 They told them what Jesus had said; and they allowed them to take it. 7 Then they brought the colt to Jesus and threw their cloaks on it; and he sat on it. 8 Many people spread their cloaks on the road, and others spread leafy branches that they had cut in the fields. 9 Then those who went ahead and those who followed were shouting,

> "Hosanna!
>   Blessed is the one who comes in
>   the name of the Lord![11]
> 10   Blessed is the coming kingdom
>   of our ancestor David!
>   Hosanna in the highest heaven!"

11 Then he entered Jerusalem and went into the temple; and when he had looked around at everything, as it was already late, he went out to Bethany with the twelve.

12 On the following day, when they came from Bethany, he was hungry. 13 Seeing in the distance a fig tree in leaf, he went to see whether perhaps he would find anything on it. When he came to it, he found nothing but leaves, for it was not the season for figs. 14 He said to it, "May no one ever eat fruit from you again." And his disciples heard it.

15 Then they came to Jerusalem. And he entered the temple and began to drive out those who were selling and those who were buying in the temple, and he overturned the tables of the money changers and the seats of those who sold doves; 16 and he would not allow anyone to carry anything through the temple. 17 He was teaching and saying, "Is it not written,

> 'My house shall be called a house
>   of prayer for all the
>   nations'?
> But you have made it a den of
>   robbers.'"[12]

18 And when the chief priests and the scribes heard it, they kept looking for a way to kill him; for they were afraid of him, because the whole crowd was spellbound by his teaching. 19 And when evening came, Jesus and his disciples[e] went out of the city.

20 In the morning as they passed by, they saw the fig tree withered away to its roots. 21 Then Peter remembered and said to him, "Rabbi, look! The fig tree that you cursed has withered." 22 Jesus answered them, "Have[f] faith in God. 23 Truly I tell you, if you say to this mountain, 'Be taken up and thrown into the sea,' and if you do not doubt in your heart, but believe that what you say will come to pass, it will be done for you. 24 So I tell you, whatever you ask for in prayer, believe that you have received[g] it, and it will be yours.

25 "Whenever you stand praying, forgive, if you have anything against anyone; so that your Father in heaven may also forgive you your trespasses."[h]

27 Again they came to Jerusalem. As he was walking in the temple, the chief priests, the scribes, and the elders came to him 28 and said, "By what authority are you doing these things? Who gave you this authority to do them?" 29 Jesus said to them, "I will ask you one question; answer me, and I will tell you by what authority I do these things. 30 Did the baptism of John come from heaven, or was it of human origin? Answer

---

[d]Aramaic *Rabbouni*   [e]Gk *they*: other ancient authorities read *he*   [f]Other ancient authorities read "*If you have*   [g]Other ancient authorities read *are receiving*   [h]Other ancient authorities add verse 26, "*But if you do not forgive, neither will your Father in heaven forgive your trespasses.*"

[11]Ps 118:25–26   [12]Isa 56:7; Jer 7:11

me." 31 They argued with one another, "If we say, 'From heaven,' he will say, 'Why then did you not believe him?' 32 But shall we say, 'Of human origin'?"—they were afraid of the crowd, for all regarded John as truly a prophet. 33 So they answered Jesus, "We do not know." And Jesus said to them, "Neither will I tell you by what authority I am doing these things."

12 Then he began to speak to them in parables. "A man planted a vineyard, put a fence around it, dug a pit for the wine press, and built a watchtower; then he leased it to tenants and went to another country. 2 When the season came, he sent a slave to the tenants to collect from them his share of the produce of the vineyard. 3 But they seized him, and beat him, and sent him away empty-handed. 4 And again he sent another slave to them; this one they beat over the head and insulted. 5 Then he sent another, and that one they killed. And so it was with many others; some they beat, and others they killed. 6 He had still one other, a beloved son. Finally he sent him to them, saying, 'They will respect my son.' 7 But those tenants said to one another, 'This is the heir; come, let us kill him, and the inheritance will be ours.' 8 So they seized him, killed him, and threw him out of the vineyard. 9 What then will the owner of the vineyard do? He will come and destroy the tenants and give the vineyard to others. 10 Have you not read this scripture:

'The stone that the builders
       rejected
   has become the cornerstone;[i]
11   this was the Lord's doing,
       and it is amazing in our eyes'?"[13]

12 When they realized that he had told this parable against them, they wanted to arrest him, but they feared the crowd. So they left him and went away.

13 Then they sent to him some Pharisees and some Herodians to trap him in what he said. 14 And they came and said to him, "Teacher, we know that you are sincere, and show deference to no one; for you do not regard people with partiality, but teach the way of God in accordance with truth. Is it lawful to pay taxes to the emperor, or not? 15 Should we pay them, or should we not?" But knowing their hypocrisy, he said to them, "Why are you putting me to the test? Bring me a denarius and let me see it." 16 And they brought one. Then he said to them, "Whose head is this, and whose title?" They answered, "The emperor's." 17 Jesus said to them, "Give to the emperor the things that are the emperor's, and to God the things that are God's." And they were utterly amazed at him.

18 Some Sadducees, who say there is no resurrection, came to him and asked him a question, saying, 19 "Teacher, Moses wrote for us that if a man's brother dies, leaving a wife but no child, the man[j] shall marry the widow and raise up children for his brother.[14] 20 There were seven brothers; the first married and, when he died, left no children; 21 and the second married her and died, leaving no children; and the third likewise; 22 none of the seven left children. Last of all the woman herself died. 23 In the resurrection[k] whose wife will she be? For the seven had married her."

24 Jesus said to them, "Is not this the reason you are wrong, that you know neither the scriptures nor the power of God? 25 For when they rise from the dead, they neither marry nor are given in marriage, but are like angels in heaven. 26 And as for the dead being raised, have you not read in the book of Moses, in the story about the bush, how God said to him, 'I am the God of Abraham, the God of Isaac, and the God of Jacob'?[15] 27 He is God not of the dead, but of the living; you are quite wrong."

28 One of the scribes came near and heard them disputing with one another, and seeing that he answered them well, he asked him, "Which commandment is the first of all?" 29 Jesus answered, "The first is, 'Hear, O Israel: the Lord our God, the Lord is one; 30 you shall love the Lord your God with all your heart, and with all your soul, and with all your mind, and with all your strength.'[16] 31 The second is this, 'You shall love your neighbor as yourself.'[17] There is no other commandment greater than these." 32 Then the scribe said to him, "You are right, Teacher; you have truly said that 'he is one, and besides him there is no

---

[i]Or keystone   [j]Gk his brother   [k]Other ancient authorities add when they rise

---

[13]Ps 118:22–23   [14]Deut 25:5; Gen 38:8   [15]Exod 3:6, 15   [16]Deut 6:4–5   [17]Lev 19:18

other';[18] 33 and 'to love him with all the heart, and with all the understanding, and with all the strength,'[19] and 'to love one's neighbor as oneself,'[20]—this is much more important than all whole burnt offerings and sacrifices." 34 When Jesus saw that he answered wisely, he said to him, "You are not far from the kingdom of God." After that no one dared to ask him any question.

35 While Jesus was teaching in the temple, he said, "How can the scribes say that the Messiah[l] is the son of David? 36 David himself, by the Holy Spirit, declared,

'The Lord said to my Lord,
"Sit at my right hand,
     until I put your enemies under
          your feet."'[21]

37 David himself calls him Lord; so how can he be his son?" And the large crowd was listening to him with delight.

38 As he taught, he said, "Beware of the scribes, who like to walk around in long robes, and to be greeted with respect in the marketplaces, 39 and to have the best seats in the synagogues and places of honor at banquets! 40 They devour widows' houses and for the sake of appearance say long prayers. They will receive the greater condemnation."

41 He sat down opposite the treasury, and watched the crowd putting money into the treasury. Many rich people put in large sums. 42 A poor widow came and put in two small copper coins, which are worth a penny. 43 Then he called his disciples and said to them, "Truly I tell you, this poor widow has put in more than all those who are contributing to the treasury. 44 For all of them have contributed out of their abundance; but she out of her poverty has put in everything she had, all she had to live on."

13 As he came out of the temple, one of his disciples said to him, "Look, Teacher, what large stones and what large buildings!" 2 Then Jesus asked him, "Do you see these great buildings? Not one stone will be left here upon another; all will be thrown down."

3 When he was sitting on the Mount of Olives opposite the temple, Peter, James, John, and Andrew asked him privately, 4 "Tell us, when will this be, and what will be the sign that all these things are about to be accomplished?" 5 Then Jesus began to say to them, "Beware that no one leads you astray. 6 Many will come in my name and say, 'I am he!'[m] and they will lead many astray. 7 When you hear of wars and rumors of wars, do not be alarmed; this must take place, but the end is still to come. 8 For nation will rise against nation, and kingdom against kingdom; there will be earthquakes in various places; there will be famines. This is but the beginning of the birth pangs.

9 "As for yourselves, beware; for they will hand you over to councils; and you will be beaten in synagogues; and you will stand before governors and kings because of me, as a testimony to them. 10 And the good news[n] must first be proclaimed to all nations. 11 When they bring you to trial and hand you over, do not worry beforehand about what you are to say; but say whatever is given you at that time, for it is not you who speak, but the Holy Spirit. 12 Brother will betray brother to death, and a father his child, and children will rise against parents and have them put to death; 13 and you will be hated by all because of my name. But the one who endures to the end will be saved.

14 "But when you see the desolating sacrilege set up where it ought not to be (let the reader understand), then those in Judea must flee to the mountains; 15 the one on the housetop must not go down or enter the house to take anything away; 16 the one in the field must not turn back to get a coat. 17 Woe to those who are pregnant and to those who are nursing infants in those days! 18 Pray that it may not be in winter. 19 For in those days there will be suffering, such as has not been from the beginning of the creation that God created until now, no, and never will be. 20 And if the Lord had not cut short those days, no one would be saved; but for the sake of the elect, whom he chose, he has cut short those days. 21 And if anyone says to you at that time, 'Look! Here is the Messiah!'[o] or 'Look! There he is!'— do not believe it. 22 False messiahs[p] and false prophets will appear and produce signs and omens, to lead astray, if possible, the elect. 23 But be alert; I have already told you everything.

---

[l]Or *the Christ*   [m]Gk *I am*   [n]Gk *gospel*   [o]Or *the Christ*   [p]Or *christs*

[18]Deut 4:35; Isa 45:21   [19]Deut 6:5   [20]Lev 19:18   [21]Ps 110:1

24 "But in those days, after that suffering,
        the sun will be darkened,
            and the moon will not give its
                light,
25   and the stars will be falling from
                heaven,
            and the powers in the heavens
                will be shaken.

26 Then they will see 'the Son of Man coming in clouds'[22] with great power and glory. 27 Then he will send out the angels, and gather his elect from the four winds, from the ends of the earth to the ends of heaven.

28 "From the fig tree learn its lesson: as soon as its branch becomes tender and puts forth its leaves, you know that summer is near. 29 So also, when you see these things taking place, you know that he[q] is near, at the very gates. 30 Truly I tell you, this generation will not pass away until all these things have taken place. 31 Heaven and earth will pass away, but my words will not pass away.

32 "But about that day or hour no one knows, neither the angels in heaven, nor the Son, but only the Father. 33 Beware, keep alert;[r] for you do not know when the time will come. 34 It is like a man going on a journey, when he leaves home and puts his slaves in charge, each with his work, and commands the doorkeeper to be on the watch. 35 Therefore, keep awake—for you do not know when the master of the house will come, in the evening, or at midnight, or at cockcrow, or at dawn, 36 or else he may find you asleep when he comes suddenly. 37 And what I say to you I say to all: Keep awake."

14 It was two days before the Passover and the festival of Unleavened Bread. The chief priests and the scribes were looking for a way to arrest Jesus[s] by stealth and kill him; 2 for they said, "Not during the festival, or there may be a riot among the people."

3 While he was at Bethany in the house of Simon the leper,[t] as he sat at the table, a woman came with an alabaster jar of very costly ointment of nard, and she broke open the jar and poured the ointment on his head. 4 But some were there who said to one another in anger, "Why was the ointment wasted in this way? 5 For this ointment could have been sold for more than three hundred

denarii,[u] and the money given to the poor." And they scolded her. 6 But Jesus said, "Let her alone; why do you trouble her? She has performed a good service for me. 7 For you always have the poor with you, and you can show kindness to them whenever you wish; but you will not always have me. 8 She has done what she could; she has anointed my body beforehand for its burial. 9 Truly I tell you, wherever the good news[v] is proclaimed in the whole world, what she has done will be told in remembrance of her."

10 Then Judas Iscariot, who was one of the twelve, went to the chief priests in order to betray him to them. 11 When they heard it, they were greatly pleased, and promised to give him money. So he began to look for an opportunity to betray him.

12 On the first day of Unleavened Bread, when the Passover lamb is sacrificed, his disciples said to him, "Where do you want us to go and make the preparations for you to eat the Passover?" 13 So he sent two of his disciples, saying to them, "Go into the city, and a man carrying a jar of water will meet you; follow him, 14 and wherever he enters, say to the owner of the house, 'The Teacher asks, Where is my guest room where I may eat the Passover with my disciples?' 15 He will show you a large room upstairs, furnished and ready. Make preparations for us there." 16 So the disciples set out and went to the city, and found everything as he had told them; and they prepared the Passover meal.

17 When it was evening, he came with the twelve. 18 And when they had taken their places and were eating, Jesus said, "Truly I tell you, one of you will betray me, one who is eating with me." 19 They began to be distressed and to say to him one after another, "Surely, not I?" 20 He said to them, "It is one of the twelve, one who is dipping bread[w] into the bowl[x] with me. 21 For the Son of Man goes as it is written of him, but woe to that one by whom the Son of Man is betrayed! It would have been better for that one not to have been born."

[q]Or it   [r]Other ancient authorities add *and pray*   [s]Gk *him*
[t]The terms *leper* and *leprosy* can refer to several diseases
[u]The denarius was the usual day's wage for a laborer   [v]Or *gospel*
[w]Gk lacks *bread*   [x]Other ancient authorities read *same bowl*

[22]Dan 7:13

22 While they were eating, he took a loaf of bread, and after blessing it he broke it, gave it to them, and said, "Take; this is my body." 23 Then he took a cup, and after giving thanks he gave it to them, and all of them drank from it. 24 He said to them, "This is my blood of the[y] covenant, which is poured out for many. 25 Truly I tell you, I will never again drink of the fruit of the vine until that day when I drink it new in the kingdom of God."

26 When they had sung the hymn, they went out to the Mount of Olives. 27 And Jesus said to them, "You will all become deserters; for it is written,

'I will strike the shepherd,
    and the sheep will be scattered.'[23]

28 But after I am raised up, I will go before you to Galilee." 29 Peter said to him, "Even though all become deserters, I will not." 30 Jesus said to him, "Truly I tell you, this day, this very night, before the cock crows twice, you will deny me three times." 31 But he said vehemently, "Even though I must die with you, I will not deny you." And all of them said the same.

32 They went to a place called Gethsemane; and he said to his disciples, "Sit here while I pray." 33 He took with him Peter and James and John, and began to be distressed and agitated. 34 And he said to them, "I am deeply grieved, even to death; remain here, and keep awake." 35 And going a little farther, he threw himself on the ground and prayed that, if it were possible, the hour might pass from him. 36 He said, "Abba,[z] Father, for you all things are possible; remove this cup from me; yet, not what I want, but what you want." 37 He came and found them sleeping; and he said to Peter, "Simon, are you asleep? Could you not keep awake one hour? 38 Keep awake and pray that you may not come into the time of trial;[a] the spirit indeed is willing, but the flesh is weak." 39 And again he went away and prayed, saying the same words. 40 And once more he came and found them sleeping, for their eyes were very heavy; and they did not know what to say to him. 41 He came a third time and said to them, "Are you still sleeping and taking your rest? Enough! The hour has come; the Son of Man is betrayed into the hands of sinners. 42 Get up, let us be going. See, my betrayer is at hand."

43 Immediately, while he was still speaking, Judas, one of the twelve, arrived; and with him there was a crowd with swords and clubs, from the chief priests, the scribes, and the elders. 44 Now the betrayer had given them a sign, saying, "The one I will kiss is the man; arrest him and lead him away under guard." 45 So when he came, he went up to him at once and said, "Rabbi!" and kissed him. 46 Then they laid hands on him and arrested him. 47 But one of those who stood near drew his sword and struck the slave of the high priest, cutting off his ear. 48 Then Jesus said to them, "Have you come out with swords and clubs to arrest me as though I were a bandit? 49 Day after day I was with you in the temple teaching, and you did not arrest me. But let the scriptures be fulfilled." 50 All of them deserted him and fled.

51 A certain young man was following him, wearing nothing but a linen cloth. They caught hold of him, 52 but he left the linen cloth and ran off naked.

53 They took Jesus to the high priest; and all the chief priests, the elders, and the scribes were assembled. 54 Peter had followed him at a distance, right into the courtyard of the high priest; and he was sitting with the guards, warming himself at the fire. 55 Now the chief priests and the whole council were looking for testimony against Jesus to put him to death; but they found none. 56 For many gave false testimony against him, and their testimony did not agree. 57 Some stood up and gave false testimony against him, saying, 58 "We heard him say, 'I will destroy this temple that is made with hands, and in three days I will build another, not made with hands.'" 59 But even on this point their testimony did not agree. 60 Then the high priest stood up before them and asked Jesus, "Have you no answer? What is it that they testify against you?" 61 But he was silent and did not answer. Again the high priest asked him, "Are you the Messiah,[b] the Son of the Blessed One?" 62 Jesus said, "I am; and

'you will see the Son of Man
    seated at the right hand of the
        Power,'
and 'coming with the clouds of
        heaven.'"[24]

[y]Other ancient authorities add *new*   [z]Aramaic for *Father*   [a]Or *into temptation*   [b]Or *the Christ*

[23]Zech 13:7   [24]Ps 110:1; Dan 7:13

63 Then the high priest tore his clothes and said, "Why do we still need witnesses? 64 You have heard his blasphemy! What is your decision?" All of them condemned him as deserving death. 65 Some began to spit on him, to blindfold him, and to strike him, saying to him, "Prophesy!" The guards also took him over and beat him.

66 While Peter was below in the courtyard, one of the servant-girls of the high priest came by. 67 When she saw Peter warming himself, she stared at him and said, "You also were with Jesus, the man from Nazareth." 68 But he denied it, saying, "I do not know or understand what you are talking about." And he went out into the forecourt.[c] Then the cock crowed.[d] 69 And the servant-girl, on seeing him, began again to say to the bystanders, "This man is one of them." 70 But again he denied it. Then after a little while the bystanders again said to Peter, "Certainly you are one of them; for you are a Galilean." 71 But he began to curse, and he swore an oath, "I do not know this man you are talking about." 72 At that moment the cock crowed for the second time. Then Peter remembered that Jesus had said to him, "Before the cock crows twice, you will deny me three times." And he broke down and wept.

15 As soon as it was morning, the chief priests held a consultation with the elders and scribes and the whole council. They bound Jesus, led him away, and handed him over to Pilate. 2 Pilate asked him, "Are you the King of the Jews?" He answered him, "You say so." 3 Then the chief priests accused him of many things. 4 Pilate asked him again, "Have you no answer? See how many charges they bring against you." 5 But Jesus made no further reply, so that Pilate was amazed.

6 Now at the festival he used to release a prisoner for them, anyone for whom they asked. 7 Now a man called Barabbas was in prison with the rebels who had committed murder during the insurrection. 8 So the crowd came and began to ask Pilate to do for them according to his custom. 9 Then he answered them, "Do you want me to release for you the King of the Jews?" 10 For he realized that it was out of jealousy that the chief priests had handed him over. 11 But the chief priests stirred up the crowd to have him release Barabbas for them instead. 12 Pilate spoke to them again, "Then what do you wish me to do[e] with the man you call[f] the King of the Jews?" 13 They shouted back, "Crucify him!" 14 Pilate asked them, "Why, what evil has he done?" But they shouted all the more, "Crucify him!" 15 So Pilate, wishing to satisfy the crowd, released Barabbas for them; and after flogging Jesus, he handed him over to be crucified.

16 Then the soldiers led him into the courtyard of the palace (that is, the governor's headquarters[g]); and they called together the whole cohort. 17 And they clothed him in a purple cloak; and after twisting some thorns into a crown, they put it on him. 18 And they began saluting him, "Hail, King of the Jews!" 19 They struck his head with a reed, spat upon him, and knelt down in homage to him. 20 After mocking him, they stripped him of the purple cloak and put his own clothes on him. Then they led him out to crucify him.

21 They compelled a passer-by, who was coming in from the country, to carry his cross; it was Simon of Cyrene, the father of Alexander and Rufus. 22 Then they brought Jesus[h] to the place called Golgotha (which means the place of a skull). 23 And they offered him wine mixed with myrrh; but he did not take it. 24 And they crucified him, and divided his clothes among them, casting lots to decide what each should take.

25 It was nine o'clock in the morning when they crucified him. 26 The inscription of the charge against him read, "The King of the Jews." 27 And with him they crucified two bandits, one on his right and one on his left.[i] 29 Those who passed by derided[j] him, shaking their heads and saying, "Aha! You who would destroy the temple and build it in three days, 30 save yourself, and come down from the cross!" 31 In the same way the chief priests, along with the scribes, were also mocking him among themselves and saying, "He saved others; he cannot save himself. 32 Let the Messiah,[k] the King of Israel, come down from the cross now, so that we may see and believe." Those who were crucified with him also taunted him.

33 When it was noon, darkness came over the

[c]Or gateway　[d]Other ancient authorities lack Then the cock crowed　[e]Other ancient authorities read what should I do　[f]Other ancient authorities lack the man you call　[g]Gk the praetorium　[h]Gk him　[i]Other ancient authorities add verse 28, And the scripture was fulfilled that says, "And he was counted among the lawless."　[j]Or blasphemed　[k]Or the Christ

Jesus inside accused by High Priest confessing blasphemy fulfilling prophecy
Peter outside ID'd by maid denying blasphemy fulfilling Jesus' promise

whole land[l] until three in the afternoon. 34 At three o'clock Jesus cried out with a loud voice, "Eloi, Eloi, lema sabachthani?" which means, "My God, my God, why have you forsaken me?"[m][25] 35 When some of the bystanders heard it, they said, "Listen, he is calling for Elijah." 36 And someone ran, filled a sponge with sour wine, put it on a stick, and gave it to him to drink, saying, "Wait, let us see whether Elijah will come to take him down." 37 Then Jesus gave a loud cry and breathed his last. 38 And the curtain of the temple was torn in two, from top to bottom. 39 Now when the centurion, who stood facing him, saw that in this way he[n] breathed his last, he said, "Truly this man was God's Son!"[o]

40 There were also women looking on from a distance; among them were Mary Magdalene, and Mary the mother of James the younger and of Joses, and Salome. 41 These used to follow him and provided for him when he was in Galilee; and there were many other women who had come up with him to Jerusalem.

42 When evening had come, and since it was the day of Preparation, that is, the day before the sabbath, 43 Joseph of Arimathea, a respected member of the council, who was also himself waiting expectantly for the kingdom of God, went boldly to Pilate and asked for the body of Jesus. 44 Then Pilate wondered if he were already dead; and summoning the centurion, he asked him whether he had been dead for some time. 45 When he learned from the centurion that he was dead, he granted the body to Joseph. 46 Then Joseph[p] bought a linen cloth, and taking down the body,[q] wrapped it in the linen cloth, and laid it in a tomb that had been hewn out of the rock. He then rolled a stone against the door of the tomb. 47 Mary Magdalene and Mary the mother of Joses saw where the body[q] was laid.

16 When the sabbath was over, Mary Magdalene, and Mary the mother of James, and Salome bought spices, so that they might go and anoint him. 2 And very early on the first day of the week, when the sun had risen, they went to the tomb. 3 They had been saying to one another, "Who will roll away the stone for us from the entrance to the tomb?" 4 When they looked up, they saw that the stone, which was very large, had al-

ready been rolled back. 5 As they entered the tomb, they saw a young man, dressed in a white robe, sitting on the right side; and they were alarmed. 6 But he said to them, "Do not be alarmed; you are looking for Jesus of Nazareth, who was crucified. He has been raised; he is not here. Look, there is the place they laid him. 7 But go, tell his disciples and Peter that he is going ahead of you to Galilee; there you will see him, just as he told you." 8 So they went out and fled from the tomb, for terror and amazement had seized them; and they said nothing to anyone, for they were afraid.[r]

THE SHORTER ENDING OF MARK

[And all that had been commanded them they told briefly to those around Peter. And afterward Jesus himself sent out through them, from east to west, the sacred and imperishable proclamation of eternal salvation.[s]]

THE LONGER ENDING OF MARK

9 [Now after he rose early on the first day of the week, he appeared first to Mary Magdalene, from whom he had cast out seven demons. 10 She went out and told those who had been with him, while they were mourning and weeping. 11 But when they heard that he was alive and had been seen by her, they would not believe it.

12 After this he appeared in another form to two of them, as they were walking into the country. 13 And they went back and told the rest, but they did not believe them.

14 Later he appeared to the eleven themselves as they were sitting at the table; and he upbraided them for their lack of faith and stubbornness, because they had not believed those who saw him af-

---

[l]Or *earth*   [m]Other ancient authorities read *made me a reproach*   [n]Other ancient authorities add *cried out and*   [o]Or *a son of God*   [p]Gk *he*   [q]Gk *it*   [r]Some of the most ancient authorities bring the book to a close at the end of verse 8. One authority concludes the book with the shorter ending; others include the shorter ending and then continue with verses 9-20. In most authorities verses 9-20 follow immediately after verse 8, though in some of these authorities the passage is marked as being doubtful.   [s]Other ancient authorities add *Amen*

[25]Ps 22:1

ter he had risen.ᵗ 15 And he said to them, "Go into all the world and proclaim the good newsᵘ to the whole creation. 16 The one who believes and is baptized will be saved; but the one who does not believe will be condemned. 17 And these signs will accompany those who believe: by using my name they will cast out demons; they will speak in new tongues; 18 they will pick up snakes in their hands,ᵛ and if they drink any deadly thing, it will not hurt them; they will lay their hands on the sick, and they will recover."

19 So then the Lord Jesus, after he had spoken to them, was taken up into heaven and sat down at the right hand of God. 20 And they went out and proclaimed the good news everywhere, while the Lord worked with them and confirmed the message by the signs that accompanied it.ʷ]

ᵗOther ancient authorities add, in whole or in part, *And they excused themselves, saying, "This age of lawlessness and unbelief is under Satan, who does not allow the truth and power of God to prevail over the unclean things of the spirits. Therefore reveal your righteousness now"—thus they spoke to Christ. And Christ replied to them, "The term of years of Satan's power has been fulfilled, but other terrible things draw near. And for those who have sinned I was handed over to death, that they may return to the truth and sin no more, that they may inherit the spiritual and imperishable glory of righteousness that is in heaven."* ᵘOr *gospel* ᵛOther ancient authorities lack *in their hands* ʷOther ancient authorities add *Amen*

The Gospel According to Luke

Luke is the only surviving Gospel whose author also produced a sequel, the Book of Acts. Whereas the Gospel records the birth, life, death, and resurrection of Jesus, the Book of Acts records the spread of Christianity after Jesus' resurrection and ascension to heaven. Taken together, these two books comprise over one-fourth of the entire New Testament.

Traditionally the author has been identified as Luke, the Gentile traveling companion of Paul; but as is the case with the other Gospels, the author does not actually disclose his identity. Whoever he was, he appears to have been writing in the final quarter of the first century, possibly around 80 or 85 C.E. He addresses his book to someone called "most excellent Theophilus" (1:3), whom some scholars take to be a non-Christian Roman official. If they are right, then Luke may have written his books to persuade Theophilus that Jesus and the religion he founded were morally admirable and socially innocuous (see, e.g., 23:47). Other scholars, however, think that the addressee's name is symbolic: it literally means "beloved of God" and may simply refer to the Christian community that the author addresses.

Like the author of Matthew, "Luke" appears to have had access to both the Gospel of Mark and the lost collection of sayings designated Q (from the German for "source," *Quelle*); from these and other sources (see 1:1–4) he constructed his own distinctive portrayal of Jesus. The basic story line of this Gospel is similar to those of Matthew and Mark; here, too, Jesus is the Son of God, who delivers inspired teachings and does astounding miracles; he is rejected by the leaders of his people and executed by the Romans for claiming to be the king of the Jews; but he is then raised by God from the dead.

More than the other Gospels, however, Luke is intent on showing that Jesus is God's special "prophet," or spokesperson, sent to his people. Thus, in stories found only in Luke, Jesus' birth is reminiscent of the prophet Samuel's (compare 1:46–56 with 1 Sam 2:1–10); he is anointed as a prophet (4:18), preaches as a prophet (4:20–30), does miracles as a prophet (7:11–17), and dies as a prophet (13:33–34). As God's prophet, Jesus not only proclaims God's will, but his entire life and the outcome of his death also conform to God's will, as found in the writings of the Jewish Scriptures (24:44).

As God's prophet, Jesus is rejected by his own people (13:33–34). This too, however, is according to the plan of God. For Jesus' rejection in Jerusalem allows his message to be taken outside of Israel, to the nations of the Gentiles (24:44–49). The spread of the good news of Jesus' salvation will then be recounted in Luke's second volume, the Book of Acts.

1 Since many have undertaken to set down an orderly account of the events that have been fulfilled among us, 2 just as they were handed on to us by those who from the beginning were eyewitnesses and servants of the word, 3 I too decided, after investigating everything carefully from the very first,[a] to write an orderly account for you, most excellent Theophilus, 4 so that you may

[a]Or *for a long time*

know the truth concerning the things about which you have been instructed.

5 In the days of King Herod of Judea, there was a priest named Zechariah, who belonged to the priestly order of Abijah. His wife was a descendant of Aaron, and her name was Elizabeth. 6 Both of them were righteous before God, living blamelessly according to all the commandments and regulations of the Lord. 7 But they had no children, because Elizabeth was barren, and both were getting on in years.

8 Once when he was serving as priest before God and his section was on duty, 9 he was chosen by lot, according to the custom of the priesthood, to enter the sanctuary of the Lord and offer incense. 10 Now at the time of the incense offering, the whole assembly of the people was praying outside. 11 Then there appeared to him an angel of the Lord, standing at the right side of the altar of incense. 12 When Zechariah saw him, he was terrified; and fear overwhelmed him. 13 But the angel said to him, "Do not be afraid, Zechariah, for your prayer has been heard. Your wife Elizabeth will bear you a son, and you will name him John. 14 You will have joy and gladness, and many will rejoice at his birth, 15 for he will be great in the sight of the Lord. He must never drink wine or strong drink; even before his birth he will be filled with the Holy Spirit. 16 He will turn many of the people of Israel to the Lord their God. 17 With the spirit and power of Elijah he will go before him, to turn the hearts of parents to their children, and the disobedient to the wisdom of the righteous, to make ready a people prepared for the Lord." 18 Zechariah said to the angel, "How will I know that this is so? For I am an old man, and my wife is getting on in years." 19 The angel replied, "I am Gabriel. I stand in the presence of God, and I have been sent to speak to you and to bring you this good news. 20 But now, because you did not believe my words, which will be fulfilled in their time, you will become mute, unable to speak, until the day these things occur."

21 Meanwhile the people were waiting for Zechariah, and wondered at his delay in the sanctuary. 22 When he did come out, he could not speak to them, and they realized that he had seen a vision in the sanctuary. He kept motioning to them and remained unable to speak. 23 When his time of service was ended, he went to his home.

24 After those days his wife Elizabeth conceived, and for five months she remained in seclusion. She said, 25 "This is what the Lord has done for me when he looked favorably on me and took away the disgrace I have endured among my people."

26 In the sixth month the angel Gabriel was sent by God to a town in Galilee called Nazareth, 27 to a virgin engaged to a man whose name was Joseph, of the house of David. The virgin's name was Mary. 28 And he came to her and said, "Greetings, favored one! The Lord is with you."[b] 29 But she was much perplexed by his words and pondered what sort of greeting this might be. 30 The angel said to her, "Do not be afraid, Mary, for you have found favor with God. 31 And now, you will conceive in your womb and bear a son, and you will name him Jesus. 32 He will be great, and will be called the Son of the Most High, and the Lord God will give to him the throne of his ancestor David. 33 He will reign over the house of Jacob forever, and of his kingdom there will be no end." 34 Mary said to the angel, "How can this be, since I am a virgin?"[c] 35 The angel said to her, "The Holy Spirit will come upon you, and the power of the Most High will overshadow you; therefore the child to be born[d] will be holy; he will be called Son of God. 36 And now, your relative Elizabeth in her old age has also conceived a son; and this is the sixth month for her who was said to be barren. 37 For nothing will be impossible with God." 38 Then Mary said, "Here am I, the servant of the Lord; let it be with me according to your word." Then the angel departed from her.

39 In those days Mary set out and went with haste to a Judean town in the hill country, 40 where she entered the house of Zechariah and greeted Elizabeth. 41 When Elizabeth heard Mary's greeting, the child leaped in her womb. And Elizabeth was filled with the Holy Spirit 42 and exclaimed with a loud cry, "Blessed are you among women, and blessed is the fruit of your womb. 43 And why has this happened to me, that

---

[b]Other ancient authorities add *Blessed are you among women*   [c]Gk *I do not know a man*   [d]Other ancient authorities add *of you*

the mother of my Lord comes to me? 44 For as soon as I heard the sound of your greeting, the child in my womb leaped for joy. 45 And blessed is she who believed that there would be[c] a fulfillment of what was spoken to her by the Lord."

46 And Mary[f] said,

"My soul magnifies the Lord,
47   and my spirit rejoices in God
       my Savior,
48   for he has looked with favor on
       the lowliness of his servant.
       Surely, from now on all
       generations will call me
       blessed;
49   for the Mighty One has done
       great things for me,
       and holy is his name.
50   His mercy is for those who fear
       him
       from generation to generation.
51   He has shown strength with his
       arm;
       he has scattered the proud in the
       thoughts of their hearts.
52   He has brought down the
       powerful from their
       thrones,
       and lifted up the lowly;
53   he has filled the hungry with good
       things,
       and sent the rich away empty.
54   He has helped his servant Israel,
       in remembrance of his mercy,
55   according to the promise he made
       to our ancestors,
       to Abraham and to his
       descendants forever."

56 And Mary remained with her about three months and then returned to her home.

57 Now the time came for Elizabeth to give birth, and she bore a son. 58 Her neighbors and relatives heard that the Lord had shown his great mercy to her, and they rejoiced with her. 59 On the eighth day they came to circumcise the child, and they were going to name him Zechariah after his father. 60 But his mother said, "No; he is to be called John." 61 They said to her, "None of your relatives has this name." 62 Then they began motioning to his father to find out what

name he wanted to give him. 63 He asked for a writing tablet and wrote, "His name is John." And all of them were amazed. 64 Immediately his mouth was opened and his tongue freed, and he began to speak, praising God. 65 Fear came over all their neighbors, and all these things were talked about throughout the entire hill country of Judea. 66 All who heard them pondered them and said, "What then will this child become?" For, indeed, the hand of the Lord was with him.

67 Then his father Zechariah was filled with the Holy Spirit and spoke this prophecy:

68   "Blessed be the Lord God of
       Israel,
       for he has looked favorably on
       his people and redeemed
       them.
69   He has raised up a mighty savior[g]
       for us
       in the house of his servant
       David,
70   as he spoke through the mouth of
       his holy prophets from of
       old,
71   that we would be saved from
       our enemies and from the
       hand of all who hate us.
72   Thus he has shown the mercy
       promised to our ancestors,
       and has remembered his holy
       covenant,
73   the oath that he swore to our
       ancestor Abraham,
       to grant us 74 that we, being
       rescued from the hands of
       our enemies,
       might serve him without fear, 75 in
       holiness and righteousness
       before him all our days.
76   And you, child, will be called the
       prophet of the Most High;
       for you will go before the Lord
       to prepare his ways,
77   to give knowledge of salvation to
       his people
       by the forgiveness of their sins.

---

[c]Or believed, for there will be   [f]Other ancient authorities read Elizabeth   [g]Gk a horn of salvation

78   By the tender mercy of our God,
            the dawn from on high will
                break upon[h] us,
79   to give light to those who sit in
                darkness and in the shadow
                of death,
            to guide our feet into the way
                of peace."
80 The child grew and became strong in spirit, and he was in the wilderness until the day he appeared publicly to Israel.

2 In those days a decree went out from Emperor Augustus that all the world should be registered. 2 This was the first registration and was taken while Quirinius was governor of Syria. 3 All went to their own towns to be registered. 4 Joseph also went from the town of Nazareth in Galilee to Judea, to the city of David called Bethlehem, because he was descended from the house and family of David. 5 He went to be registered with Mary, to whom he was engaged and who was expecting a child. 6 While they were there, the time came for her to deliver her child. 7 And she gave birth to her firstborn son and wrapped him in bands of cloth, and laid him in a manger, because there was no place for them in the inn.

8 In that region there were shepherds living in the fields, keeping watch over their flock by night. 9 Then an angel of the Lord stood before them, and the glory of the Lord shone around them, and they were terrified. 10 But the angel said to them, "Do not be afraid; for see—I am bringing you good news of great joy for all the people: 11 to you is born this day in the city of David a Savior, who is the Messiah,[i] the Lord. 12 This will be a sign for you: you will find a child wrapped in bands of cloth and lying in a manger." 13 And suddenly there was with the angel a multitude of the heavenly host,[j] praising God and saying,
14   "Glory to God in the highest
                heaven,
            and on earth peace among those
                whom he favors!"[k]

15 When the angels had left them and gone into heaven, the shepherds said to one another, "Let us go now to Bethlehem and see this thing that has taken place, which the Lord has made known to us." 16 So they went with haste and found Mary and Joseph, and the child lying in the manger. 17 When they saw this, they made known what had been told them about this child; 18 and all who heard it were amazed at what the shepherds told them. 19 But Mary treasured all these words and pondered them in her heart. 20 The shepherds returned, glorifying and praising God for all they had heard and seen, as it had been told them.

21 After eight days had passed, it was time to circumcise the child; and he was called Jesus, the name given by the angel before he was conceived in the womb.

22 When the time came for their purification according to the law of Moses, they brought him up to Jerusalem to present him to the Lord 23 (as it is written in the law of the Lord, "Every firstborn male shall be designated as holy to the Lord"[1]), 24 and they offered a sacrifice according to what is stated in the law of the Lord, "a pair of turtledoves or two young pigeons."[2]

25 Now there was a man in Jerusalem whose name was Simeon;[l] this man was righteous and devout, looking forward to the consolation of Israel, and the Holy Spirit rested on him. 26 It had been revealed to him by the Holy Spirit that he would not see death before he had seen the Lord's Messiah.[m] 27 Guided by the Spirit, Simeon[n] came into the temple; and when the parents brought in the child Jesus, to do for him what was customary under the law, 28 Simeon[o] took him in his arms and praised God, saying,
29   "Master, now you are dismissing
                your servant[p] in peace,
                according to your word;
30   for my eyes have seen your
                salvation,
31   which you have prepared in the
                presence of all peoples,
32   a light for revelation to the
                Gentiles
            and for glory to your people
                Israel."

33 And the child's father and mother were

[h]Other ancient authorities read *has broken upon*   [i]Or *the Christ*
[j]Gk *army*   [k]Other ancient authorities read *peace, goodwill among people*   [l]Gk *Symeon*   [m]Or *the Lord's Christ*   [n]Gk *In the Spirit, he*
[o]Gk *he*   [p]Gk *slave*

[1]Exod 13:2   [2]Lev 12:8

amazed at what was being said about him. 34 Then Simeon[q] blessed them and said to his mother Mary, "This child is destined for the falling and the rising of many in Israel, and to be a sign that will be opposed 35 so that the inner thoughts of many will be revealed—and a sword will pierce your own soul too."

36 There was also a prophet, Anna[r] the daughter of Phanuel, of the tribe of Asher. She was of a great age, having lived with her husband seven years after her marriage, 37 then as a widow to the age of eighty-four. She never left the temple but worshiped there with fasting and prayer night and day. 38 At that moment she came, and began to praise God and to speak about the child[s] to all who were looking for the redemption of Jerusalem.

39 When they had finished everything required by the law of the Lord, they returned to Galilee, to their own town of Nazareth. 40 The child grew and became strong, filled with wisdom; and the favor of God was upon him.

41 Now every year his parents went to Jerusalem for the festival of the Passover. 42 And when he was twelve years old, they went up as usual for the festival. 43 When the festival was ended and they started to return, the boy Jesus stayed behind in Jerusalem, but his parents did not know it. 44 Assuming that he was in the group of travelers, they went a day's journey. Then they started to look for him among their relatives and friends. 45 When they did not find him, they returned to Jerusalem to search for him. 46 After three days they found him in the temple, sitting among the teachers, listening to them and asking them questions. 47 And all who heard him were amazed at his understanding and his answers. 48 When his parents[t] saw him they were astonished; and his mother said to him, "Child, why have you treated us like this? Look, your father and I have been searching for you in great anxiety." 49 He said to them, "Why were you searching for me? Did you not know that I must be in my Father's house?"[u] 50 But they did not understand what he said to them. 51 Then he went down with them and came to Nazareth, and was obedient to them. His mother treasured all these things in her heart.

52 And Jesus increased in wisdom and in years,[v] and in divine and human favor.

3 In the fifteenth year of the reign of Emperor Tiberius, when Pontius Pilate was governor of Judea, and Herod was ruler[w] of Galilee, and his brother Philip ruler[w] of the region of Ituraea and Trachonitis, and Lysanias ruler[w] of Abilene, 2 during the high priesthood of Annas and Caiaphas, the word of God came to John son of Zechariah in the wilderness. 3 He went into all the region around the Jordan, proclaiming a baptism of repentance for the forgiveness of sins, 4 as it is written in the book of the words of the prophet Isaiah,

> "The voice of one crying out in
>   the wilderness:
> 'Prepare the way of the Lord,
>   make his paths straight.
> 5   Every valley shall be filled,
>   and every mountain and hill
>   shall be made low,
> and the crooked shall be made
>   straight,
>   and the rough ways made
>   smooth;
> 6   and all flesh shall see the salvation
>   of God.'"[3]

7 John said to the crowds that came out to be baptized by him, "You brood of vipers! Who warned you to flee from the wrath to come? 8 Bear fruits worthy of repentance. Do not begin to say to yourselves, 'We have Abraham as our ancestor'; for I tell you, God is able from these stones to raise up children to Abraham. 9 Even now the ax is lying at the root of the trees; every tree therefore that does not bear good fruit is cut down and thrown into the fire."

10 And the crowds asked him, "What then should we do?" 11 In reply he said to them, "Whoever has two coats must share with anyone who has none; and whoever has food must do likewise." 12 Even tax collectors came to be baptized, and they asked him, "Teacher, what should we do?" 13 He said to them, "Collect no more than the amount prescribed for you." 14 Soldiers also asked him, "And we, what should we do?" He said to them, "Do not extort money from anyone by

---

[q]Gk *Symeon*   [r]Gk *Hanna*   [s]Gk *him*   [t]Gk *they*   [u]Or *be about my Father's interests?*   [v]Or *in stature*   [w]Gk *tetrarch*

[3]Isa 40:3–5

threats or false accusation, and be satisfied with your wages."

15 As the people were filled with expectation, and all were questioning in their hearts concerning John, whether he might be the Messiah,[x] 16 John answered all of them by saying "I baptize you with water; but one who is more powerful than I is coming; I am not worthy to untie the thong of his sandals. He will baptize you with[y] the Holy Spirit and fire. 17 His winnowing fork is in his hand, to clear his threshing floor and to gather the wheat into his granary; but the chaff he will burn with unquenchable fire."

18 So, with many other exhortations, he proclaimed the good news to the people. 19 But Herod the ruler,[z] who had been rebuked by him because of Herodias, his brother's wife, and because of all the evil things that Herod had done, 20 added to them all by shutting up John in prison.

21 Now when all the people were baptized, and when Jesus also had been baptized and was praying, the heaven was opened, 22 and the Holy Spirit descended upon him in bodily form like a dove. And a voice came from heaven, "You are my Son, the Beloved;[a] with you I am well pleased."[b]

23 Jesus was about thirty years old when he began his work. He was the son (as was thought) of Joseph son of Heli, 24 son of Matthat, son of Levi, son of Melchi, son of Jannai, son of Joseph, 25 son of Mattathias, son of Amos, son of Nahum, son of Esli, son of Naggai, 26 son of Maath, son of Mattathias, son of Semein, son of Josech, son of Joda, 27 son of Joanan, son of Rhesa, son of Zerubbabel, son of Shealtiel,[c] son of Neri, 28 son of Melchi, son of Addi, son of Cosam, son of Elmadam, son of Er, 29 son of Joshua, son of Eliezer, son of Jorim, son of Matthat, son of Levi, 30 son of Simeon, son of Judah, son of Joseph, son of Jonam, son of Eliakim, 31 son of Melea, son of Menna, son of Mattatha, son of Nathan, son of David, 32 son of Jesse, son of Obed, son of Boaz, son of Sala,[d] son of Nahshon, 33 son of Amminadab, son of Admin, son of Arni,[e] son of Hezron, son of Perez, son of Judah, 34 son of Jacob, son of Isaac, son of Abraham, son of Terah, son of Nahor, 35 son of Serug, son of Reu, son of Peleg, son of Eber, son of Shelah, 36 son of Cainan, son of Arphaxad, son of Shem, son of Noah, son of Lamech, 37 son of Methuselah, son of Enoch, son of Jared, son of Mahalaleel, son of Cainan, 38 son of Enos, son of Seth, son of Adam, son of God.

4 Jesus, full of the Holy Spirit, returned from the Jordan and was led by the Spirit in the wilderness, 2 where for forty days he was tempted by the devil. He ate nothing at all during those days, and when they were over, he was famished. 3 The devil said to him, "If you are the Son of God, command this stone to become a loaf of bread." 4 Jesus answered him, "It is written, 'One does not live by bread alone.'"[4]

5 Then the devil[f] led him up and showed him in an instant all the kingdoms of the world. 6 And the devil[f] said to him, "To you I will give their glory and all this authority; for it has been given over to me, and I give it to anyone I please. 7 If you, then, will worship me, it will all be yours." 8 Jesus answered him, "It is written,

'Worship the Lord your God,
    and serve only him.'"[5]

9 Then the devil[f] took him to Jerusalem, and placed him on the pinnacle of the temple, saying to him, "If you are the Son of God, throw yourself down from here, 10 for it is written,

'He will command his angels
        concerning you,
    to protect you,'

11 and

'On their hands they will bear you
        up,
    so that you will not dash your
        foot against a stone.'"[6]

12 Jesus answered him, "It is said, 'Do not put the Lord your God to the test.'"[7] 13 When the devil had finished every test, he departed from him until an opportune time.

14 Then Jesus, filled with the power of the Spirit, returned to Galilee, and a report about him spread through all the surrounding country. 15 He

[x]Or the Christ [y]Or in [z]Gk tetrarch [a]Or my beloved Son [b]Other ancient authorities read You are my Son, today I have begotten you [c]Gk Salathiel [d]Other ancient authorities read Salmon [e]Other ancient authorities read Amminadab, son of Aram; others vary widely [f]Gk he

[4]Deut 8:3 [5]Deut 6:13 [6]Ps 91:11–12 [7]Deut 6:16

began to teach in their synagogues and was praised by everyone.

16 When he came to Nazareth, where he had been brought up, he went to the synagogue on the sabbath day, as was his custom. He stood up to read, 17 and the scroll of the prophet Isaiah was given to him. He unrolled the scroll and found the place where it was written:

18   "The Spirit of the Lord is upon
                    me,
            because he has anointed me
                  to bring good news to the
                        poor.
            He has sent me to proclaim release
                  to the captives
            and recovery of sight to the
                  blind,
                  to let the oppressed go
                        free,
19   to proclaim the year of the Lord's
                  favor."[8]

20 And he rolled up the scroll, gave it back to the attendant, and sat down. The eyes of all in the synagogue were fixed on him. 21 Then he began to say to them, "Today this scripture has been fulfilled in your hearing." 22 All spoke well of him and were amazed at the gracious words that came from his mouth. They said, "Is not this Joseph's son?" 23 He said to them, "Doubtless you will quote to me this proverb, 'Doctor, cure yourself!' And you will say, 'Do here also in your hometown the things that we have heard you did at Capernaum.'" 24 And he said, "Truly I tell you, no prophet is accepted in the prophet's hometown. 25 But the truth is, there were many widows in Israel in the time of Elijah, when the heaven was shut up three years and six months, and there was a severe famine over all the land; 26 yet Elijah was sent to none of them except to a widow at Zarephath in Sidon. 27 There were also many lepers[g] in Israel in the time of the prophet Elisha, and none of them was cleansed except Naaman the Syrian." 28 When they heard this, all in the synagogue were filled with rage. 29 They got up, drove him out of the town, and led him to the brow of the hill on which their town was built, so that they might hurl him off the cliff. 30 But he passed through the midst of them and went on his way.

31 He went down to Capernaum, a city in Galilee, and was teaching them on the sabbath. 32 They were astounded at his teaching, because he spoke with authority. 33 In the synagogue there was a man who had the spirit of an unclean demon, and he cried out with a loud voice, 34 "Let us alone! What have you to do with us, Jesus of Nazareth? Have you come to destroy us? I know who you are, the Holy One of God." 35 But Jesus rebuked him, saying, "Be silent, and come out of him!" When the demon had thrown him down before them, he came out of him without having done him any harm. 36 They were all amazed and kept saying to one another, "What kind of utterance is this? For with authority and power he commands the unclean spirits, and out they come!" 37 And a report about him began to reach every place in the region.

38 After leaving the synagogue he entered Simon's house. Now Simon's mother-in-law was suffering from a high fever, and they asked him about her. 39 Then he stood over her and rebuked the fever, and it left her. Immediately she got up and began to serve them.

40 As the sun was setting, all those who had any who were sick with various kinds of diseases brought them to him; and he laid his hands on each of them and cured them. 41 Demons also came out of many, shouting, "You are the Son of God!" But he rebuked them and would not allow them to speak, because they knew that he was the Messiah.[h]

42 At daybreak he departed and went into a deserted place. And the crowds were looking for him; and when they reached him, they wanted to prevent him from leaving them. 43 But he said to them, "I must proclaim the good news of the kingdom of God to the other cities also; for I was sent for this purpose." 44 So he continued proclaiming the message in the synagogues of Judea.[i]

5 Once while Jesus[j] was standing beside the lake of Gennesaret, and the crowd was pressing in on him to hear the word of God, 2 he saw two boats there at the shore of the lake; the fishermen had gone out of them and were washing their nets. 3 He got into one of the boats, the one

---

[g]The terms *leper* and *leprosy* can refer to several diseases   [h]Or *the Christ*   [i]Other ancient authorities read *Galilee*   [j]Gk *he*

[8]Isa 61:1–2; 58:6

belonging to Simon, and asked him to put out a little way from the shore. Then he sat down and taught the crowds from the boat. 4 When he had finished speaking, he said to Simon, "Put out into the deep water and let down your nets for a catch." 5 Simon answered, "Master, we have worked all night long but have caught nothing. Yet if you say so, I will let down the nets." 6 When they had done this, they caught so many fish that their nets were beginning to break. 7 So they signaled their partners in the other boat to come and help them. And they came and filled both boats, so that they began to sink. 8 But when Simon Peter saw it, he fell down at Jesus' knees, saying, "Go away from me, Lord, for I am a sinful man!" 9 For he and all who were with him were amazed at the catch of fish that they had taken; 10 and so also were James and John, sons of Zebedee, who were partners with Simon. Then Jesus said to Simon, "Do not be afraid; from now on you will be catching people." 11 When they had brought their boats to shore, they left everything and followed him.

12 Once, when he was in one of the cities, there was a man covered with leprosy.[k] When he saw Jesus, he bowed with his face to the ground and begged him, "Lord, if you choose, you can make me clean." 13 Then Jesus[l] stretched out his hand, touched him, and said, "I do choose. Be made clean." Immediately the leprosy[k] left him. 14 And he ordered him to tell no one. "Go," he said, "and show yourself to the priest, and, as Moses commanded, make an offering for your cleansing, for a testimony to them." 15 But now more than ever the word about Jesus[m] spread abroad; many crowds would gather to hear him and to be cured of their diseases. 16 But he would withdraw to deserted places and pray.

17 One day, while he was teaching, Pharisees and teachers of the law were sitting near by (they had come from every village of Galilee and Judea and from Jerusalem); and the power of the Lord was with him to heal.[n] 18 Just then some men came, carrying a paralyzed man on a bed. They were trying to bring him in and lay him before Jesus;[m] 19 but finding no way to bring him in because of the crowd, they went up on the roof and let him down with his bed through the tiles into the middle of the crowd[o] in front of Jesus. 20 When he saw their faith, he said, "Friend,[p] your sins are forgiven you." 21 Then the scribes and the Pharisees began to question, "Who is this who is speaking blasphemies? Who can forgive sins but God alone?" 22 When Jesus perceived their questionings, he answered them, "Why do you raise such questions in your hearts? 23 Which is easier, to say, 'Your sins are forgiven you,' or to say, 'Stand up and walk'? 24 But so that you may know that the Son of Man has authority on earth to forgive sins"—he said to the one who was paralyzed—"I say to you, stand up and take your bed and go to your home." 25 Immediately he stood up before them, took what he had been lying on, and went to his home, glorifying God. 26 Amazement seized all of them, and they glorified God and were filled with awe, saying, "We have seen strange things today."

27 After this he went out and saw a tax collector named Levi, sitting at the tax booth; and he said to him, "Follow me." 28 And he got up, left everything, and followed him.

29 Then Levi gave a great banquet for him in his house; and there was a large crowd of tax collectors and others sitting at the table[q] with them. 30 The Pharisees and their scribes were complaining to his disciples, saying, "Why do you eat and drink with tax collectors and sinners?" 31 Jesus answered, "Those who are well have no need of a physician, but those who are sick; 32 I have come to call not the righteous but sinners to repentance."

33 Then they said to him, "John's disciples, like the disciples of the Pharisees, frequently fast and pray, but your disciples eat and drink." 34 Jesus said to them, "You cannot make wedding guests fast while the bridegroom is with them, can you? 35 The days will come when the bridegroom will be taken away from them, and then they will fast in those days." 36 He also told them a parable: "No one tears a piece from a new garment and sews it on an old garment; otherwise the new will be torn, and the piece from the new will not match the old. 37 And no one puts new wine into old wineskins; otherwise the new wine will burst the skins and will be spilled, and the skins will be destroyed. 38 But new wine must be put into fresh wineskins. 39 And no one after drink-

---

[k]The terms *leper* and *leprosy* can refer to several diseases   [l]Gk *he*
[m]Gk *him*   [n]Other ancient authorities read *was present to heal them*
[o]Gk *into the midst*   [p]Gk *Man*   [q]Gk *reclining*

ing old wine desires new wine, but says, 'The old is good.'"ʳ

6 One sabbathˢ while Jesusᵗ was going through the grainfields, his disciples plucked some heads of grain, rubbed them in their hands, and ate them. 2 But some of the Pharisees said, "Why are you doing what is not lawfulᵘ on the sabbath?" 3 Jesus answered, "Have you not read what David did when he and his companions were hungry? 4 He entered the house of God and took and ate the bread of the Presence, which it is not lawful for any but the priests to eat, and gave some to his companions?" 5 Then he said to them, "The Son of Man is lord of the sabbath."

6 On another sabbath he entered the synagogue and taught, and there was a man there whose right hand was withered. 7 The scribes and the Pharisees watched him to see whether he would cure on the sabbath, so that they might find an accusation against him. 8 Even though he knew what they were thinking, he said to the man who had the withered hand, "Come and stand here." He got up and stood there. 9 Then Jesus said to them, "I ask you, is it lawful to do good or to do harm on the sabbath, to save life or to destroy it?" 10 After looking around at all of them, he said to him, "Stretch out your hand." He did so, and his hand was restored. 11 But they were filled with fury and discussed with one another what they might do to Jesus.

12 Now during those days he went out to the mountain to pray; and he spent the night in prayer to God. 13 And when day came, he called his disciples and chose twelve of them, whom he also named apostles: 14 Simon, whom he named Peter, and his brother Andrew, and James, and John, and Philip, and Bartholomew, 15 and Matthew, and Thomas, and James son of Alphaeus, and Simon, who was called the Zealot, 16 and Judas son of James, and Judas Iscariot, who became a traitor.

17 He came down with them and stood on a level place, with a great crowd of his disciples and a great multitude of people from all Judea, Jerusalem, and the coast of Tyre and Sidon. 18 They had come to hear him and to be healed of their diseases; and those who were troubled with unclean spirits were cured. 19 And all in the crowd were trying to touch him, for power came out from him and healed all of them.

20 Then he looked up at his disciples and said:
"Blessed are you who are poor,
for yours is the kingdom of
God.
21
"Blessed are you who are hungry
now,
for you will be filled.
"Blessed are you who weep now,
for you will laugh.

22 "Blessed are you when people hate you, and when they exclude you, revile you, and defame youᵛ on account of the Son of Man. 23 Rejoice in that day and leap for joy, for surely your reward is great in heaven; for that is what their ancestors did to the prophets.
24
"But woe to you who are rich,
for you have received your
consolation.
25
"Woe to you who are full now,
for you will be hungry.
"Woe to you who are laughing
now,
for you will mourn and weep.

26 "Woe to you when all speak well of you, for that is what their ancestors did to the false prophets.

27 "But I say to you that listen, Love your enemies, do good to those who hate you, 28 bless those who curse you, pray for those who abuse you. 29 If anyone strikes you on the cheek, offer the other also; and from anyone who takes away your coat do not withhold even your shirt. 30 Give to everyone who begs from you; and if anyone takes away your goods, do not ask for them again. 31 Do to others as you would have them do to you.

32 "If you love those who love you, what credit is that to you? For even sinners love those who love them. 33 If you do good to those who do good to you, what credit is that to you? For even sinners do the same. 34 If you lend to those from whom you hope to receive, what credit is that to you? Even sinners lend to sinners, to receive as much again. 35 But love your enemies, do good, and lend, expecting nothing in return.ʷ Your re-

ʳOther ancient authorities read *better*; others lack verse 39   ˢOther ancient authorities read *On the second first sabbath*   ᵗGk *he*   ᵘOther ancient authorities add *to do*   ᵛGk *cast out your name as evil*   ʷOther ancient authorities read *despairing of no one*

ward will be great, and you will be children of the Most High; for he is kind to the ungrateful and the wicked. 36 Be merciful, just as your Father is merciful.

37 "Do not judge, and you will not be judged; do not condemn, and you will not be condemned. Forgive, and you will be forgiven; 38 give, and it will be given to you. A good measure, pressed down, shaken together, running over, will be put into your lap; for the measure you give will be the measure you get back."

39 He also told them a parable: "Can a blind person guide a blind person? Will not both fall into a pit? 40 A disciple is not above the teacher, but everyone who is fully qualified will be like the teacher. 41 Why do you see the speck in your neighbor's[x] eye, but do not notice the log in your own eye? 42 Or how can you say to your neighbor,[y] 'Friend,[y] let me take out the speck in your eye,' when you yourself do not see the log in your own eye? You hypocrite, first take the log out of your own eye, and then you will see clearly to take the speck out of your neighbor's[x] eye.

43 "No good tree bears bad fruit, nor again does a bad tree bear good fruit; 44 for each tree is known by its own fruit. Figs are not gathered from thorns, nor are grapes picked from a bramble bush. 45 The good person out of the good treasure of the heart produces good, and the evil person out of evil treasure produces evil; for it is out of the abundance of the heart that the mouth speaks.

46 "Why do you call me 'Lord, Lord,' and do not do what I tell you? 47 I will show you what someone is like who comes to me, hears my words, and acts on them. 48 That one is like a man building a house, who dug deeply and laid the foundation on rock; when a flood arose, the river burst against that house but could not shake it, because it had been well built.[z] 49 But the one who hears and does not act is like a man who built a house on the ground without a foundation. When the river burst against it, immediately it fell, and great was the ruin of that house."

7 After Jesus[a] had finished all his sayings in the hearing of the people, he entered Capernaum. 2 A centurion there had a slave whom he valued highly, and who was ill and close to death. 3 When he heard about Jesus, he sent some Jewish elders to him, asking him to come and heal his slave. 4 When they came to Jesus, they appealed to him earnestly, saying, "He is worthy of having you do this for him, 5 for he loves our people, and it is he who built our synagogue for us." 6 And Jesus went with them, but when he was not far from the house, the centurion sent friends to say to him, "Lord, do not trouble yourself, for I am not worthy to have you come under my roof; 7 therefore I did not presume to come to you. But only speak the word, and let my servant be healed. 8 For I also am a man set under authority, with soldiers under me; and I say to one, 'Go,' and he goes, and to another, 'Come,' and he comes, and to my slave, 'Do this,' and the slave does it." 9 When Jesus heard this he was amazed at him, and turning to the crowd that followed him, he said, "I tell you, not even in Israel have I found such faith." 10 When those who had been sent returned to the house, they found the slave in good health.

11 Soon afterwards[b] he went to a town called Nain, and his disciples and a large crowd went with him. 12 As he approached the gate of the town, a man who had died was being carried out. He was his mother's only son, and she was a widow; and with her was a large crowd from the town. 13 When the Lord saw her, he had compassion for her and said to her, "Do not weep." 14 Then he came forward and touched the bier, and the bearers stood still. And he said, "Young man, I say to you, rise!" 15 The dead man sat up and began to speak, and Jesus[a] gave him to his mother. 16 Fear seized all of them; and they glorified God, saying, "A great prophet has risen among us!" and "God has looked favorably on his people!" 17 This word about him spread throughout Judea and all the surrounding country.

18 The disciples of John reported all these things to him. So John summoned two of his disciples 19 and sent them to the Lord to ask, "Are you the one who is to come, or are we to wait for another?" 20 When the men had come to him, they said, "John the Baptist has sent us to you to ask, 'Are you the one who is to come, or are we to wait for another?'" 21 Jesus[c] had just then cured many people of diseases, plagues, and evil spirits,

[x] Gk brother's [y] Gk brother [z] Other ancient authorities read founded upon the rock [a] Gk he [b] Other ancient authorities read Next day [c] Gk He

and had given sight to many who were blind. 22 And he answered them, "Go and tell John what you have seen and heard: the blind receive their sight, the lame walk, the lepers[d] are cleansed, the deaf hear, the dead are raised, the poor have good news brought to them. 23 And blessed is anyone who takes no offense at me."

24 When John's messengers had gone, Jesus[e] began to speak to the crowds about John:[f] "What did you go out into the wilderness to look at? A reed shaken by the wind? 25 What then did you go out to see? Someone[g] dressed in soft robes? Look, those who put on fine clothing and live in luxury are in royal palaces. 26 What then did you go out to see? A prophet? Yes, I tell you, and more than a prophet. 27 This is the one about whom it is written,

> 'See, I am sending my messenger
> ahead of you,
> who will prepare your way
> before you.'[9]

28 I tell you, among those born of women no one is greater than John; yet the least in the kingdom of God is greater than he." 29 (And all the people who heard this, including the tax collectors, acknowledged the justice of God,[h] because they had been baptized with John's baptism. 30 But by refusing to be baptized by him, the Pharisees and the lawyers rejected God's purpose for themselves.)

31 "To what then will I compare the people of this generation, and what are they like? 32 They are like children sitting in the marketplace and calling to one another,

> 'We played the flute for you, and
> you did not dance;
> we wailed, and you did not
> weep.'

33 For John the Baptist has come eating no bread and drinking no wine, and you say, 'He has a demon'; 34 the Son of Man has come eating and drinking, and you say, 'Look, a glutton and a drunkard, a friend of tax collectors and sinners!' 35 Nevertheless, wisdom is vindicated by all her children."

36 One of the Pharisees asked Jesus[i] to eat with him, and he went into the Pharisee's house and took his place at the table. 37 And a woman in the city, who was a sinner, having learned that he was eating in the Pharisee's house, brought an alabaster jar of ointment. 38 She stood behind him at his feet, weeping, and began to bathe his feet with her tears and to dry them with her hair. Then she continued kissing his feet and anointing them with the ointment. 39 Now when the Pharisee who had invited him saw it, he said to himself, "If this man were a prophet, he would have known who and what kind of woman this is who is touching him—that she is a sinner." 40 Jesus spoke up and said to him, "Simon, I have something to say to you." "Teacher," he replied, "speak." 41 "A certain creditor had two debtors; one owed five hundred denarii,[j] and the other fifty. 42 When they could not pay, he canceled the debts for both of them. Now which of them will love him more?" 43 Simon answered, "I suppose the one for whom he canceled the greater debt." And Jesus[e] said to him, "You have judged rightly." 44 Then turning toward the woman, he said to Simon, "Do you see this woman? I entered your house; you gave me no water for my feet, but she has bathed my feet with her tears and dried them with her hair. 45 You gave me no kiss, but from the time I came in she has not stopped kissing my feet. 46 You did not anoint my head with oil, but she has anointed my feet with ointment. 47 Therefore, I tell you, her sins, which were many, have been forgiven; hence she has shown great love. But the one to whom little is forgiven, loves little." 48 Then he said to her, "Your sins are forgiven." 49 But those who were at the table with him began to say among themselves, "Who is this who even forgives sins?" 50 And he said to the woman, "Your faith has saved you; go in peace."

8 Soon afterwards he went on through cities and villages, proclaiming and bringing the good news of the kingdom of God. The twelve were with him, 2 as well as some women who had been cured of evil spirits and infirmities: Mary, called Magdalene, from whom seven demons had gone out, 3 and Joanna, the wife of Herod's steward Chuza, and Susanna, and many others, who provided for them[k] out of their resources.

---

[d]The terms *leper* and *leprosy* can refer to several diseases   [e]Gk *he*
[f]Gk *him*   [g]Or *Why then did you go out? To see someone*
[h]Or *praised God*   [i]Gk *him*   [j]The denarius was the usual day's wage for a laborer   [k]Other ancient authorities read *him*

---

[9]Mal 3:1

4 When a great crowd gathered and people from town after town came to him, he said in a parable: 5 "A sower went out to sow his seed; and as he sowed, some fell on the path and was trampled on, and the birds of the air ate it up. 6 Some fell on the rock; and as it grew up, it withered for lack of moisture. 7 Some fell among thorns, and the thorns grew with it and choked it. 8 Some fell into good soil, and when it grew, it produced a hundredfold." As he said this, he called out, "Let anyone with ears to hear listen!"

9 Then his disciples asked him what this parable meant. 10 He said, "To you it has been given to know the secrets[l] of the kingdom of God; but to others I speak[m] in parables, so that

'looking they may not perceive,
and listening they may not
understand.'[10]

11 "Now the parable is this: The seed is the word of God. 12 The ones on the path are those who have heard; then the devil comes and takes away the word from their hearts, so that they may not believe and be saved. 13 The ones on the rock are those who, when they hear the word, receive it with joy. But these have no root; they believe only for a while and in a time of testing fall away. 14 As for what fell among the thorns, these are the ones who hear; but as they go on their way, they are choked by the cares and riches and pleasures of life, and their fruit does not mature. 15 But as for that in the good soil, these are the ones who, when they hear the word, hold it fast in an honest and good heart, and bear fruit with patient endurance.

16 "No one after lighting a lamp hides it under a jar, or puts it under a bed, but puts it on a lampstand, so that those who enter may see the light. 17 For nothing is hidden that will not be disclosed, nor is anything secret that will not become known and come to light. 18 Then pay attention to how you listen; for to those who have, more will be given; and from those who do not have, even what they seem to have will be taken away."

19 Then his mother and his brothers came to him, but they could not reach him because of the crowd. 20 And he was told, "Your mother and your brothers are standing outside, wanting to see you." 21 But he said to them, "My mother and my brothers are those who hear the word of God and do it."

22 One day he got into a boat with his disciples, and he said to them, "Let us go across to the other side of the lake." So they put out, 23 and while they were sailing he fell asleep. A windstorm swept down on the lake, and the boat was filling with water, and they were in danger. 24 They went to him and woke him up, shouting, "Master, Master, we are perishing!" And he woke up and rebuked the wind and the raging waves; they ceased, and there was a calm. 25 He said to them, "Where is your faith?" They were afraid and amazed, and said to one another, "Who then is this, that he commands even the winds and the water, and they obey him?"

26 Then they arrived at the country of the Gerasenes,[n] which is opposite Galilee. 27 As he stepped out on land, a man of the city who had demons met him. For a long time he had worn[o] no clothes, and he did not live in a house but in the tombs. 28 When he saw Jesus, he fell down before him and shouted at the top of his voice, "What have you to do with me, Jesus, Son of the Most High God? I beg you, do not torment me"— 29 for Jesus[p] had commanded the unclean spirit to come out of the man. (For many times it had seized him; he was kept under guard and bound with chains and shackles, but he would break the bonds and be driven by the demon into the wilds.) 30 Jesus then asked him, "What is your name?" He said, "Legion"; for many demons had entered him. 31 They begged him not to order them to go back into the abyss.

32 Now there on the hillside a large herd of swine was feeding; and the demons[q] begged Jesus[r] to let them enter these. So he gave them permission. 33 Then the demons came out of the man and entered the swine, and the herd rushed down the steep bank into the lake and was drowned.

34 When the swineherds saw what had happened, they ran off and told it in the city and in the country. 35 Then people came out to see what had happened, and when they came to Jesus, they found the man from whom the demons had gone

---

[l]Or mysteries [m]Gk lacks I speak [n]Other ancient authorities read Gadarenes; others, Gergesenes [o]Other ancient authorities read a man of the city who had had demons for a long time met him. He wore [p]Gk he [q]Gk they [r]Gk him

[10]Isa 6:9

sitting at the feet of Jesus, clothed and in his right mind. And they were afraid. 36 Those who had seen it told them how the one who had been possessed by demons had been healed. 37 Then all the people of the surrounding country of the Gerasenes[s] asked Jesus[t] to leave them; for they were seized with great fear. So he got into the boat and returned. 38 The man from whom the demons had gone begged that he might be with him; but Jesus[u] sent him away, saying, 39 "Return to your home, and declare how much God has done for you." So he went away, proclaiming throughout the city how much Jesus had done for him.

40 Now when Jesus returned, the crowd welcomed him, for they were all waiting for him. 41 Just then there came a man named Jairus, a leader of the synagogue. He fell at Jesus' feet and begged him to come to his house, 42 for he had an only daughter, about twelve years old, who was dying.

As he went, the crowds pressed in on him. 43 Now there was a woman who had been suffering from hemorrhages for twelve years; and though she had spent all she had on physicians,[v] no one could cure her. 44 She came up behind him and touched the fringe of his clothes, and immediately her hemorrhage stopped. 45 Then Jesus asked, "Who touched me?" When all denied it, Peter[w] said, "Master, the crowds surround you and press in on you." 46 But Jesus said, "Someone touched me; for I noticed that power had gone out from me." 47 When the woman saw that she could not remain hidden, she came trembling; and falling down before him, she declared in the presence of all the people why she had touched him, and how she had been immediately healed. 48 He said to her, "Daughter, your faith has made you well; go in peace."

49 While he was still speaking, someone came from the leader's house to say, "Your daughter is dead; do not trouble the teacher any longer." 50 When Jesus heard this, he replied, "Do not fear. Only believe, and she will be saved." 51 When he came to the house, he did not allow anyone to enter with him, except Peter, John, and James, and the child's father and mother. 52 They were all weeping and wailing for her; but he said, "Do not weep; for she is not dead but sleeping." 53 And they laughed at him, knowing that she was dead.

54 But he took her by the hand and called out, "Child, get up!" 55 Her spirit returned, and she got up at once. Then he directed them to give her something to eat. 56 Her parents were astounded; but he ordered them to tell no one what had happened.

9 Then Jesus[u] called the twelve together and gave them power and authority over all demons and to cure diseases, 2 and he sent them out to proclaim the kingdom of God and to heal. 3 He said to them, "Take nothing for your journey, no staff, nor bag, nor bread, nor money—not even an extra tunic. 4 Whatever house you enter, stay there, and leave from there. 5 Wherever they do not welcome you, as you are leaving that town shake the dust off your feet as a testimony against them." 6 They departed and went through the villages, bringing the good news and curing diseases everywhere.

7 Now Herod the ruler[x] heard about all that had taken place, and he was perplexed, because it was said by some that John had been raised from the dead, 8 by some that Elijah had appeared, and by others that one of the ancient prophets had arisen. 9 Herod said, "John I beheaded; but who is this about whom I hear such things?" And he tried to see him.

10 On their return the apostles told Jesus[t] all they had done. He took them with him and withdrew privately to a city called Bethsaida. 11 When the crowds found out about it, they followed him; and he welcomed them, and spoke to them about the kingdom of God, and healed those who needed to be cured.

12 The day was drawing to a close, and the twelve came to him and said, "Send the crowd away, so that they may go into the surrounding villages and countryside, to lodge and get provisions; for we are here in a deserted place." 13 But he said to them, "You give them something to eat." They said, "We have no more than five loaves and two fish—unless we are to go and buy food for all these people." 14 For there were about five thousand men. And he said to his disciples, "Make

---

[s]Other ancient authorities read *Gadarenes*; others, *Gergesenes*
[t]Gk *him* [u]Gk *he* [v]Other ancient authorities lack *and though she had spent all she had on physicians* [w]Other ancient authorities add *and those who were with him* [x]Gk *tetrarch*

them sit down in groups of about fifty each."
15 They did so and made them all sit down.
16 And taking the five loaves and the two fish, he
looked up to heaven, and blessed and broke them,
and gave them to the disciples to set before the
crowd. 17 And all ate and were filled. What was
left over was gathered up, twelve baskets of broken
pieces.

18 Once when Jesus[y] was praying alone, with
only the disciples near him, he asked them, "Who
do the crowds say that I am?" 19 They answered,
"John the Baptist; but others, Elijah; and still others,
that one of the ancient prophets has arisen."
20 He said to them, "But who do you say that I
am?" Peter answered, "The Messiah[z] of God."

21 He sternly ordered and commanded them not
to tell anyone, 22 saying, "The Son of Man must
undergo great suffering, and be rejected by the elders,
chief priests, and scribes, and be killed, and
on the third day be raised."

23 Then he said to them all, "If any want to become
my followers, let them deny themselves and
take up their cross daily and follow me. 24 For
those who want to save their life will lose it, and
those who lose their life for my sake will save it.
25 What does it profit them if they gain the whole
world, but lose or forfeit themselves? 26 Those
who are ashamed of me and of my words, of them
the Son of Man will be ashamed when he comes
in his glory and the glory of the Father and of the
holy angels. 27 But truly I tell you, there are some
standing here who will not taste death before they
see the kingdom of God."

28 Now about eight days after these sayings Jesus[y]
took with him Peter and John and James, and
went up on the mountain to pray. 29 And while he
was praying, the appearance of his face changed,
and his clothes became dazzling white. 30 Suddenly
they saw two men, Moses and Elijah, talking
to him. 31 They appeared in glory and were
speaking of his departure, which he was about to
accomplish at Jerusalem. 32 Now Peter and his
companions were weighed down with sleep; but
since they had stayed awake,[a] they saw his glory
and the two men who stood with him. 33 Just as
they were leaving him, Peter said to Jesus, "Master,
it is good for us to be here; let us make three
dwellings,[b] one for you, one for Moses, and one
for Elijah"—not knowing what he said. 34 While

he was saying this, a cloud came and overshadowed
them; and they were terrified as they entered
the cloud. 35 Then from the cloud came a voice
that said, "This is my Son, my Chosen;[c] listen to
him!" 36 When the voice had spoken, Jesus was
found alone. And they kept silent and in those days
told no one any of the things they had seen.

37 On the next day, when they had come down
from the mountain, a great crowd met him. 38 Just
then a man from the crowd shouted, "Teacher, I
beg you to look at my son; he is my only child.
39 Suddenly a spirit seizes him, and all at once he[d]
shrieks. It convulses him until he foams at the
mouth; it mauls him and will scarcely leave him.
40 I begged your disciples to cast it out, but they
could not." 41 Jesus answered, "You faithless and
perverse generation, how much longer must I be
with you and bear with you? Bring your son here."
42 While he was coming, the demon dashed him
to the ground in convulsions. But Jesus rebuked
the unclean spirit, healed the boy, and gave him
back to his father. 43 And all were astounded at
the greatness of God.

While everyone was amazed at all that he was
doing, he said to his disciples, 44 "Let these
words sink into your ears: The Son of Man is going
to be betrayed into human hands." 45 But they
did not understand this saying; its meaning was
concealed from them, so that they could not perceive
it. And they were afraid to ask him about this
saying.

46 An argument arose among them as to which
one of them was the greatest. 47 But Jesus, aware
of their inner thoughts, took a little child and put it
by his side, 48 and said to them, "Whoever welcomes
this child in my name welcomes me, and
whoever welcomes me welcomes the one who sent
me; for the least among all of you is the greatest."

49 John answered, "Master, we saw someone
casting out demons in your name, and we tried to
stop him, because he does not follow with us."
50 But Jesus said to him, "Do not stop him; for
whoever is not against you is for you."

51 When the days drew near for him to be taken
up, he set his face to go to Jerusalem. 52 And

---

[y]Gk he   [z]Or The Christ   [a]Or but when they were fully awake
[b]Or tents   [c]Other ancient authorities read my Beloved   [d]Or it

he sent messengers ahead of him. On their way they entered a village of the Samaritans to make ready for him; 53 but they did not receive him, because his face was set toward Jerusalem. 54 When his disciples James and John saw it, they said, "Lord, do you want us to command fire to come down from heaven and consume them?"[c] 55 But he turned and rebuked them. 56 Then[f] they went on to another village.

57 As they were going along the road, someone said to him, "I will follow you wherever you go." 58 And Jesus said to him, "Foxes have holes, and birds of the air have nests; but the Son of Man has nowhere to lay his head." 59 To another he said, "Follow me." But he said, "Lord, first let me go and bury my father." 60 But Jesus[g] said to him, "Let the dead bury their own dead; but as for you, go and proclaim the kingdom of God." 61 Another said, "I will follow you, Lord; but let me first say farewell to those at my home." 62 Jesus said to him, "No one who puts a hand to the plow and looks back is fit for the kingdom of God."

10 After this the Lord appointed seventy[h] others and sent them on ahead of him in pairs to every town and place where he himself intended to go. 2 He said to them, "The harvest is plentiful, but the laborers are few; therefore ask the Lord of the harvest to send out laborers into his harvest. 3 Go on your way. See, I am sending you out like lambs into the midst of wolves. 4 Carry no purse, no bag, no sandals; and greet no one on the road. 5 Whatever house you enter, first say, 'Peace to this house!' 6 And if anyone is there who shares in peace, your peace will rest on that person; but if not, it will return to you. 7 Remain in the same house, eating and drinking whatever they provide, for the laborer deserves to be paid. Do not move about from house to house. 8 Whenever you enter a town and its people welcome you, eat what is set before you; 9 cure the sick who are there, and say to them, 'The kingdom of God has come near to you.'[i] 10 But whenever you enter a town and they do not welcome you, go out into its streets and say, 11 'Even the dust of your town that clings to our feet, we wipe off in protest against you. Yet know this: the kingdom of God has come near.'[j] 12 I tell you, on that day it will be more tolerable for Sodom than for that town. 13 "Woe to you, Chorazin! Woe to you, Beth-

saida! For if the deeds of power done in you had been done in Tyre and Sidon, they would have repented long ago, sitting in sackcloth and ashes. 14 But at the judgment it will be more tolerable for Tyre and Sidon than for you. 15 And you, Capernaum,

> will you be exalted to heaven?
> No, you will be brought down
>   to Hades.

16 "Whoever listens to you listens to me, and whoever rejects you rejects me, and whoever rejects me rejects the one who sent me."

17 The seventy[k] returned with joy, saying, "Lord, in your name even the demons submit to us!" 18 He said to them, "I watched Satan fall from heaven like a flash of lightning. 19 See, I have given you authority to tread on snakes and scorpions, and over all the power of the enemy; and nothing will hurt you. 20 Nevertheless, do not rejoice at this, that the spirits submit to you, but rejoice that your names are written in heaven."

21 At that same hour Jesus[l] rejoiced in the Holy Spirit[m] and said, "I thank[n] you, Father, Lord of heaven and earth, because you have hidden these things from the wise and the intelligent and have revealed them to infants; yes, Father, for such was your gracious will.[o] 22 All things have been handed over to me by my Father; and no one knows who the Son is except the Father, or who the Father is except the Son and anyone to whom the Son chooses to reveal him."

23 Then turning to the disciples, Jesus[p] said to them privately, "Blessed are the eyes that see what you see! 24 For I tell you that many prophets and kings desired to see what you see, but did not see it, and to hear what you hear, but did not hear it."

25 Just then a lawyer stood up to test Jesus.[q] "Teacher," he said, "what must I do to inherit eternal life?" 26 He said to him, "What is written in the law? What do you read there?" 27 He answered, "You shall love the Lord your God with all your heart, and with all your soul, and with all

---

[c]Other ancient authorities add *as Elijah did*   [f]Other ancient authorities read *rebuked them, and said, "You do not know what spirit you are of, 56for the Son of Man has not come to destroy the lives of human beings but to save them." Then*   [g]Gk *he*   [h]Other ancient authorities read *seventy-two*   [i]Or *is at hand for you*   [j]Or *is at hand*   [k]Other ancient authorities read *seventy-two*   [l]Gk *he*   [m]Other authorities read *in the spirit*   [n]Or *praise*   [o]Or *for so it was well-pleasing in your sight*   [p]Gk *he*   [q]Gk *him*

your strength, and with all your mind; and your neighbor as yourself."[11] 28 And he said to him, "You have given the right answer; do this, and you will live."

29 But wanting to justify himself, he asked Jesus, "And who is my neighbor?" 30 Jesus replied, "A man was going down from Jerusalem to Jericho, and fell into the hands of robbers, who stripped him, beat him, and went away, leaving him half dead. 31 Now by chance a priest was going down that road; and when he saw him, he passed by on the other side. 32 So likewise a Levite, when he came to the place and saw him, passed by on the other side. 33 But a Samaritan while traveling came near him; and when he saw him, he was moved with pity. 34 He went to him and bandaged his wounds, having poured oil and wine on them. Then he put him on his own animal, brought him to an inn, and took care of him. 35 The next day he took out two denarii,[r] gave them to the innkeeper, and said, 'Take care of him; and when I come back, I will repay you whatever more you spend.' 36 Which of these three, do you think, was a neighbor to the man who fell into the hands of the robbers?" 37 He said, "The one who showed him mercy." Jesus said to him, "Go and do likewise."

38 Now as they went on their way, he entered a certain village, where a woman named Martha welcomed him into her home. 39 She had a sister named Mary, who sat at the Lord's feet and listened to what he was saying. 40 But Martha was distracted by her many tasks; so she came to him and asked, "Lord, do you not care that my sister has left me to do all the work by myself? Tell her then to help me." 41 But the Lord answered her, "Martha, Martha, you are worried and distracted by many things; 42 there is need of only one thing.[s] Mary has chosen the better part, which will not be taken away from her."

11 He was praying in a certain place, and after he had finished, one of his disciples said to him, "Lord, teach us to pray, as John taught his disciples." 2 He said to them, "When you pray, say:

Father,[t] hallowed be your name.
　Your kingdom come.[u]
3　　Give us each day our daily
　　　bread.[v]

4　And forgive us our sins,
　　　for we ourselves forgive
　　　　everyone indebted to us.
　　And do not bring us to the time
　　　of trial.'"[w]

5 And he said to them, "Suppose one of you has a friend, and you go to him at midnight and say to him, 'Friend, lend me three loaves of bread; 6 for a friend of mine has arrived, and I have nothing to set before him.' 7 And he answers from within, 'Do not bother me; the door has already been locked, and my children are with me in bed; I cannot get up and give you anything.' 8 I tell you, even though he will not get up and give him anything because he is his friend, at least because of his persistence he will get up and give him whatever he needs.

9 "So I say to you, Ask, and it will be given you; search, and you will find; knock, and the door will be opened for you. 10 For everyone who asks receives, and everyone who searches finds, and for everyone who knocks, the door will be opened. 11 Is there anyone among you who, if your child asks for[x] a fish, will give a snake instead of a fish? 12 Or if the child asks for an egg, will give a scorpion? 13 If you then, who are evil, know how to give good gifts to your children, how much more will the heavenly Father give the Holy Spirit[y] to those who ask him!"

14 Now he was casting out a demon that was mute; when the demon had gone out, the one who had been mute spoke, and the crowds were amazed. 15 But some of them said, "He casts out demons by Beelzebul, the ruler of the demons." 16 Others, to test him, kept demanding from him a sign from heaven. 17 But he knew what they were thinking and said to them, "Every kingdom divided against itself becomes a desert, and house falls on house. 18 If Satan also is divided against himself, how will his kingdom stand? —for you say

[r]The denarius was the usual day's wage for a laborer　[s]Other ancient authorities read *few things are necessary, or only one*　[t]Other ancient authorities read *Our Father in heaven*　[u]Other ancient authorities read *Our Father in heaven*　[v]Or *our bread for tomorrow*　[w]Or *us into temptation*. Other ancient authorities add *but rescue us from the evil one* (or *from evil*)　[x]Other ancient authorities add *bread, will give a stone; or if your child asks for*　[y]Other ancient authorities read *the Father give the Holy Spirit from heaven*

[11]Deut 6:5; Lev 19:18

that I cast out the demons by Beelzebul. 19 Now if I cast out the demons by Beelzebul, by whom do your exorcists^z cast them out? Therefore they will be your judges. 20 But if it is by the finger of God that I cast out the demons, then the kingdom of God has come to you. 21 When a strong man, fully armed, guards his castle, his property is safe. 22 But when one stronger than he attacks him and overpowers him, he takes away his armor in which he trusted and divides his plunder. 23 Whoever is not with me is against me, and whoever does not gather with me scatters.

24 "When the unclean spirit has gone out of a person, it wanders through waterless regions looking for a resting place, but not finding any, it says, 'I will return to my house from which I came.' 25 When it comes, it finds it swept and put in order. 26 Then it goes and brings seven other spirits more evil than itself, and they enter and live there; and the last state of that person is worse than the first."

27 While he was saying this, a woman in the crowd raised her voice and said to him, "Blessed is the womb that bore you and the breasts that nursed you!" 28 But he said, "Blessed rather are those who hear the word of God and obey it!"

29 When the crowds were increasing, he began to say, "This generation is an evil generation; it asks for a sign, but no sign will be given to it except the sign of Jonah. 30 For just as Jonah became a sign to the people of Nineveh, so the Son of Man will be to this generation. 31 The queen of the South will rise at the judgment with the people of this generation and condemn them, because she came from the ends of the earth to listen to the wisdom of Solomon, and see, something greater than Solomon is here! 32 The people of Nineveh will rise up at the judgment with this generation and condemn it, because they repented at the proclamation of Jonah, and see, something greater than Jonah is here!

33 "No one after lighting a lamp puts it in a cellar,^a but on the lampstand so that those who enter may see the light. 34 Your eye is the lamp of your body. If your eye is healthy, your whole body is full of light; but if it is not healthy, your body is full of darkness. 35 Therefore consider whether the light in you is not darkness. 36 If then your whole body is full of light, with no part of it in darkness, it will be as full of light as when a lamp gives you light with its rays."

37 While he was speaking, a Pharisee invited him to dine with him; so he went in and took his place at the table. 38 The Pharisee was amazed to see that he did not first wash before dinner. 39 Then the Lord said to him, "Now you Pharisees clean the outside of the cup and of the dish, but inside you are full of greed and wickedness. 40 You fools! Did not the one who made the outside make the inside also? 41 So give for alms those things that are within; and see, everything will be clean for you.

42 "But woe to you Pharisees! For you tithe mint and rue and herbs of all kinds, and neglect justice and the love of God; it is these you ought to have practiced, without neglecting the others. 43 Woe to you Pharisees! For you love to have the seat of honor in the synagogues and to be greeted with respect in the marketplaces. 44 Woe to you! For you are like unmarked graves, and people walk over them without realizing it."

45 One of the lawyers answered him, "Teacher, when you say these things, you insult us too." 46 And he said, "Woe also to you lawyers! For you load people with burdens hard to bear, and you yourselves do not lift a finger to ease them. 47 Woe to you! For you build the tombs of the prophets whom your ancestors killed. 48 So you are witnesses and approve of the deeds of your ancestors; for they killed them, and you build their tombs. 49 Therefore also the Wisdom of God said, 'I will send them prophets and apostles, some of whom they will kill and persecute,' 50 so that this generation may be charged with the blood of all the prophets shed since the foundation of the world, 51 from the blood of Abel to the blood of Zechariah, who perished between the altar and the sanctuary. Yes, I tell you, it will be charged against this generation. 52 Woe to you lawyers! For you have taken away the key of knowledge; you did not enter yourselves, and you hindered those who were entering."

53 When he went outside, the scribes and the Pharisees began to be very hostile toward him and to cross-examine him about many things, 54 lying in wait for him, to catch him in something he might say.

---

^zGk *sons*   ^aOther ancient authorities add *or under the bushel basket*

12

Meanwhile, when the crowd gathered by the thousands, so that they trampled on one another, he began to speak first to his disciples, "Beware of the yeast of the Pharisees, that is, their hypocrisy. 2 Nothing is covered up that will not be uncovered, and nothing secret that will not become known. 3 Therefore whatever you have said in the dark will be heard in the light, and what you have whispered behind closed doors will be proclaimed from the housetops.

4 "I tell you, my friends, do not fear those who kill the body, and after that can do nothing more. 5 But I will warn you whom to fear: fear him who, after he has killed, has authority[b] to cast into hell.[c] Yes, I tell you, fear him! 6 Are not five sparrows sold for two pennies? Yet not one of them is forgotten in God's sight. 7 But even the hairs of your head are all counted. Do not be afraid; you are of more value than many sparrows.

8 "And I tell you, everyone who acknowledges me before others, the Son of Man also will acknowledge before the angels of God; 9 but whoever denies me before others will be denied before the angels of God. 10 And everyone who speaks a word against the Son of Man will be forgiven; but whoever blasphemes against the Holy Spirit will not be forgiven. 11 When they bring you before the synagogues, the rulers, and the authorities, do not worry about how[d] you are to defend yourselves or what you are to say; 12 for the Holy Spirit will teach you at that very hour what you ought to say."

13 Someone in the crowd said to him, "Teacher, tell my brother to divide the family inheritance with me." 14 But he said to him, "Friend, who set me to be a judge or arbitrator over you?" 15 And he said to them, "Take care! Be on your guard against all kinds of greed; for one's life does not consist in the abundance of possessions." 16 Then he told them a parable: "The land of a rich man produced abundantly. 17 And he thought to himself, 'What should I do, for I have no place to store my crops?' 18 Then he said, 'I will do this: I will pull down my barns and build larger ones, and there I will store all my grain and my goods. 19 And I will say to my soul, Soul, you have ample goods laid up for many years; relax, eat, drink, be merry.' 20 But God said to him, 'You fool! This very night your life is being demanded of

you. And the things you have prepared, whose will they be?' 21 So it is with those who store up treasures for themselves but are not rich toward God."

22 He said to his disciples, "Therefore I tell you, do not worry about your life, what you will eat, or about your body, what you will wear. 23 For life is more than food, and the body more than clothing. 24 Consider the ravens: they neither sow nor reap, they have neither storehouse nor barn, and yet God feeds them. Of how much more value are you than the birds! 25 And can any of you by worrying add a single hour to your span of life?[e] 26 If then you are not able to do so small a thing as that, why do you worry about the rest? 27 Consider the lilies, how they grow: they neither toil nor spin;[f] yet I tell you, even Solomon in all his glory was not clothed like one of these. 28 But if God so clothes the grass of the field, which is alive today and tomorrow is thrown into the oven, how much more will he clothe you—you of little faith! 29 And do not keep striving for what you are to eat and what you are to drink, and do not keep worrying. 30 For it is the nations of the world that strive after all these things, and your Father knows that you need them. 31 Instead, strive for his[g] kingdom, and these things will be given to you as well.

32 "Do not be afraid, little flock, for it is your Father's good pleasure to give you the kingdom. 33 Sell your possessions, and give alms. Make purses for yourselves that do not wear out, an unfailing treasure in heaven, where no thief comes near and no moth destroys. 34 For where your treasure is, there your heart will be also.

35 "Be dressed for action and have your lamps lit; 36 be like those who are waiting for their master to return from the wedding banquet, so that they may open the door for him as soon as he comes and knocks. 37 Blessed are those slaves whom the master finds alert when he comes; truly I tell you, he will fasten his belt and have them sit down to eat, and he will come and serve them. 38 If he comes during the middle of the night, or near dawn, and finds them so, blessed are those slaves.

39 "But know this: if the owner of the house had

[b]Or *power* [c]Gk *Gehenna* [d]Other ancient authorities add *or what* [e]Or *add a cubit to your stature* [f]Other ancient authorities read *Consider the lilies; they neither spin nor weave* [g]Other ancient authorities read *God's*

known at what hour the thief was coming, he[h] would not have let his house be broken into. 40 You also must be ready, for the Son of Man is coming at an unexpected hour."

41 Peter said, "Lord, are you telling this parable for us or for everyone?" 42 And the Lord said, "Who then is the faithful and prudent manager whom his master will put in charge of his slaves, to give them their allowance of food at the proper time? 43 Blessed is that slave whom his master will find at work when he arrives. 44 Truly I tell you, he will put that one in charge of all his possessions. 45 But if that slave says to himself, 'My master is delayed in coming,' and if he begins to beat the other slaves, men and women, and to eat and drink and get drunk, 46 the master of that slave will come on a day when he does not expect him and at an hour that he does not know, and will cut him in pieces,[i] and put him with the unfaithful. 47 That slave who knew what his master wanted, but did not prepare himself or do what was wanted, will receive a severe beating. 48 But the one who did not know and did what deserved a beating will receive a light beating. From everyone to whom much has been given, much will be required; and from the one to whom much has been entrusted, even more will be demanded.

49 "I came to bring fire to the earth, and how I wish it were already kindled! 50 I have a baptism with which to be baptized, and what stress I am under until it is completed! 51 Do you think that I have come to bring peace to the earth? No, I tell you, but rather division! 52 From now on five in one household will be divided, three against two and two against three; 53 they will be divided:

> father against son
> and son against father,
> mother against daughter
> and daughter against mother,
> mother-in-law against her
> daughter-in-law
> and daughter-in-law against
> mother-in-law."

54 He also said to the crowds, "When you see a cloud rising in the west, you immediately say, 'It is going to rain'; and so it happens. 55 And when you see the south wind blowing, you say, 'There will be scorching heat'; and it happens. 56 You hypocrites! You know how to interpret the ap-

pearance of earth and sky, but why do you not know how to interpret the present time?

57 "And why do you not judge for yourselves what is right? 58 Thus, when you go with your accuser before a magistrate, on the way make an effort to settle the case,[j] or you may be dragged before the judge, and the judge hand you over to the officer, and the officer throw you in prison. 59 I tell you, you will never get out until you have paid the very last penny."

13 At that very time there were some present who told him about the Galileans whose blood Pilate had mingled with their sacrifices. 2 He asked them, "Do you think that because these Galileans suffered in this way they were worse sinners than all other Galileans? 3 No, I tell you; but unless you repent, you will all perish as they did. 4 Or those eighteen who were killed when the tower of Siloam fell on them—do you think that they were worse offenders than all the others living in Jerusalem? 5 No, I tell you; but unless you repent, you will all perish just as they did."

6 Then he told this parable: "A man had a fig tree planted in his vineyard; and he came looking for fruit on it and found none. 7 So he said to the gardener, 'See here! For three years I have come looking for fruit on this fig tree, and still I find none. Cut it down! Why should it be wasting the soil?' 8 He replied, 'Sir, let it alone for one more year, until I dig around it and put manure on it. 9 If it bears fruit next year, well and good; but if not, you can cut it down.'"

10 Now he was teaching in one of the synagogues on the sabbath. 11 And just then there appeared a woman with a spirit that had crippled her for eighteen years. She was bent over and was quite unable to stand up straight. 12 When Jesus saw her, he called her over and said, "Woman, you are set free from your ailment." 13 When he laid his hands on her, immediately she stood up straight and began praising God. 14 But the leader of the synagogue, indignant because Jesus had cured on the sabbath, kept saying to the crowd, "There are six days on which work ought to be done; come on those days and be cured, and not on the sabbath day." 15 But the Lord answered him

[h]Other ancient authorities add *would have watched and*   [i]Or *cut him off*   [j]Gk *settle with him*

and said, "You hypocrites! Does not each of you on the sabbath untie his ox or his donkey from the manger, and lead it away to give it water? 16 And ought not this woman, a daughter of Abraham whom Satan bound for eighteen long years, be set free from this bondage on the sabbath day?" 17 When he said this, all his opponents were put to shame; and the entire crowd was rejoicing at all the wonderful things that he was doing.

18 He said therefore, "What is the kingdom of God like? And to what should I compare it? 19 It is like a mustard seed that someone took and sowed in the garden; it grew and became a tree, and the birds of the air made nests in its branches."

20 And again he said, "To what should I compare the kingdom of God? 21 It is like yeast that a woman took and mixed in with[k] three measures of flour until all of it was leavened."

22 Jesus[l] went through one town and village after another, teaching as he made his way to Jerusalem. 23 Someone asked him, "Lord, will only a few be saved?" He said to them, 24 "Strive to enter through the narrow door; for many, I tell you, will try to enter and will not be able. 25 When once the owner of the house has got up and shut the door, and you begin to stand outside and to knock at the door, saying, 'Lord, open to us,' then in reply he will say to you, 'I do not know where you come from.' 26 Then you will begin to say, 'We ate and drank with you, and you taught in our streets.' 27 But he will say, 'I do not know where you come from; go away from me, all you evildoers!' 28 There will be weeping and gnashing of teeth when you see Abraham and Isaac and Jacob and all the prophets in the kingdom of God, and you yourselves thrown out. 29 Then people will come from east and west, from north and south, and will eat in the kingdom of God. 30 Indeed, some are last who will be first, and some are first who will be last."

31 At that very hour some Pharisees came and said to him, "Get away from here, for Herod wants to kill you." 32 He said to them, "Go and tell that fox for me,[m] 'Listen, I am casting out demons and performing cures today and tomorrow, and on the third day I finish my work. 33 Yet today, tomorrow, and the next day I must be on my way, because it is impossible for a prophet to be killed outside of Jerusalem.' 34 Jerusalem, Jerusalem, the

city that kills the prophets and stones those who are sent to it! How often have I desired to gather your children together as a hen gathers her brood under her wings, and you were not willing! 35 See, your house is left to you. And I tell you, you will not see me until the time comes when[n] you say, 'Blessed is the one who comes in the name of the Lord.'"[12]

14 On one occasion when Jesus[o] was going to the house of a leader of the Pharisees to eat a meal on the sabbath, they were watching him closely. 2 Just then, in front of him, there was a man who had dropsy. 3 And Jesus asked the lawyers and Pharisees, "Is it lawful to cure people on the sabbath, or not?" 4 But they were silent. So Jesus[o] took him and healed him, and sent him away. 5 Then he said to them, "If one of you has a child[p] or an ox that has fallen into a well, will you not immediately pull it out on a sabbath day?" 6 And they could not reply to this.

7 When he noticed how the guests chose the places of honor, he told them a parable. 8 "When you are invited by someone to a wedding banquet, do not sit down at the place of honor, in case someone more distinguished than you has been invited by your host; 9 and the host who invited both of you may come and say to you, 'Give this person your place,' and then in disgrace you would start to take the lowest place. 10 But when you are invited, go and sit down at the lowest place, so that when your host comes, he may say to you, 'Friend, move up higher'; then you will be honored in the presence of all who sit at the table with you. 11 For all who exalt themselves will be humbled, and those who humble themselves will be exalted."

12 He said also to the one who had invited him, "When you give a luncheon or a dinner, do not invite your friends or your brothers or your relatives or rich neighbors, in case they may invite you in return, and you would be repaid. 13 But when you give a banquet, invite the poor, the crippled, the lame, and the blind. 14 And you will be blessed, because they cannot repay you, for you will be repaid at the resurrection of the righteous."

[k]Gk *hid in* [l]Gk *He* [m]Gk lacks *for me* [n]Other ancient authorities lack *the time comes when* [o]Gk *he* [p]Other ancient authorities read *a donkey*

[12]Ps 118:26

15 One of the dinner guests, on hearing this, said to him, "Blessed is anyone who will eat bread in the kingdom of God!" 16 Then Jesus[q] said to him, "Someone gave a great dinner and invited many. 17 At the time for the dinner he sent his slave to say to those who had been invited, 'Come; for everything is ready now.' 18 But they all alike began to make excuses. The first said to him, 'I have bought a piece of land, and I must go out and see it; please accept my regrets.' 19 Another said, 'I have bought five yoke of oxen, and I am going to try them out; please accept my regrets.' 20 Another said, 'I have just been married, and therefore I cannot come.' 21 So the slave returned and reported this to his master. Then the owner of the house became angry and said to his slave, 'Go out at once into the streets and lanes of the town and bring in the poor, the crippled, the blind, and the lame.' 22 And the slave said, 'Sir, what you ordered has been done, and there is still room.' 23 Then the master said to the slave, 'Go out into the roads and lanes, and compel people to come in, so that my house may be filled. 24 For I tell you,[r] none of those who were invited will taste my dinner.'"

25 Now large crowds were traveling with him; and he turned and said to them, 26 "Whoever comes to me and does not hate father and mother, wife and children, brothers and sisters, yes, and even life itself, cannot be my disciple. 27 Whoever does not carry the cross and follow me cannot be my disciple. 28 For which of you, intending to build a tower, does not first sit down and estimate the cost, to see whether he has enough to complete it? 29 Otherwise, when he has laid a foundation and is not able to finish, all who see it will begin to ridicule him, 30 saying, 'This fellow began to build and was not able to finish.' 31 Or what king, going out to wage war against another king, will not sit down first and consider whether he is able with ten thousand to oppose the one who comes against him with twenty thousand? 32 If he cannot, then, while the other is still far away, he sends a delegation and asks for the terms of peace. 33 So therefore, none of you can become my disciple if you do not give up all your possessions.

34 "Salt is good; but if salt has lost its taste, how can its saltiness be restored?[s] 35 It is fit neither for the soil nor for the manure pile; they throw it away. Let anyone with ears to hear listen!"

15 Now all the tax collectors and sinners were coming near to listen to him. 2 And the Pharisees and the scribes were grumbling and saying, "This fellow welcomes sinners and eats with them."

3 So he told them this parable: 4 "Which one of you, having a hundred sheep and losing one of them, does not leave the ninety-nine in the wilderness and go after the one that is lost until he finds it? 5 When he has found it, he lays it on his shoulders and rejoices. 6 And when he comes home, he calls together his friends and neighbors, saying to them, 'Rejoice with me, for I have found my sheep that was lost.' 7 Just so, I tell you, there will be more joy in heaven over one sinner who repents than over ninety-nine righteous persons who need no repentance.

8 "Or what woman having ten silver coins,[t] if she loses one of them, does not light a lamp, sweep the house, and search carefully until she finds it? 9 When she has found it, she calls together her friends and neighbors, saying, 'Rejoice with me, for I have found the coin that I had lost.' 10 Just so, I tell you, there is joy in the presence of the angels of God over one sinner who repents."

11 Then Jesus[u] said, "There was a man who had two sons. 12 The younger of them said to his father, 'Father, give me the share of the property that will belong to me.' So he divided his property between them. 13 A few days later the younger son gathered all he had and traveled to a distant country, and there he squandered his property in dissolute living. 14 When he had spent everything, a severe famine took place throughout that country, and he began to be in need. 15 So he went and hired himself out to one of the citizens of that country, who sent him to his fields to feed the pigs. 16 He would gladly have filled himself with[v] the pods that the pigs were eating; and no one gave him anything. 17 But when he came to himself he said, 'How many of my father's hired hands have bread enough and to spare, but here I am dying of

---

[q]Gk *he*   [r]The Greek word for *you* here is plural   [s]Or *how can it be used for seasoning?*   [t]Gk *drachmas*, each worth about a day's wage for a laborer   [u]Gk *he*   [v]Other ancient authorities read *filled his stomach with*

hunger! 18 I will get up and go o my father, and I will say to him, "Father, I have sinned against heaven and before you; 19 I am no longer worthy to be called your son; treat me like one of your hired hands."' 20 So he set off and went to his father. But while he was still far off, his father saw him and was filled with compassion; he ran and put his arms around him and kissed him. 21 Then the son said to him, 'Father, I have sinned against heaven and before you; I am no onger worthy to be called your son.'ʷ 22 But the father said to his slaves, 'Quickly, bring out a robe—the best one— and put it on him; put a ring on his finger and san- dals on his feet. 23 And get the fatted calf and kill it, and let us eat and celebrate; 24 for this son of mine was dead and is alive again he was lost and is found!' And they began to celebrate.

25 "Now his elder son was in the field; and when he came and approached the house, he heard music and dancing. 26 He called one of the slaves and asked what was going on. 27 He replied, 'Your brother has come, and your father has killed the fatted calf, because he has got him back safe and sound.' 28 Then he became angry and refused to go in. His father came out and began to plead with him. 29 But he answered his father, 'Listen! For all these years I have been working like a slave for you, and I have never disobeyed your com- mand; yet you have never given me even a young goat so that I might celebrate with my friends. 30 But when this son of yours came back, who has devoured your property with prostitutes, you killed the fatted calf for him!' 31 Then the fatherˣ said to him, 'Son, you are always with me, and all that is mine is yours. 32 But we had to celebrate and rejoice, because this brother of yours was dead and has come to life; he was lost and has been found.'"

16 Then Jesusˣ said to the disciples, "There was a rich man who had a manager, and charges were brought to him that this man was squandering his property. 2 So he summoned him and said to him, 'What is this that I hear about you? Give me an accounting of your management, because you cannot be my manager any longer.' 3 Then the manager said to himself, 'What will I do, now that my master is taking the position away from me? I am not strong enough to dig, and I am

ashamed to beg. 4 I have decided what to do so that, when I am dismissed as manager, people may welcome me into their homes.' 5 So, summoning his master's debtors one by one, he asked the first, 'How much do you owe my master?' 6 He an- swered, 'A hundred jugs of olive oil.' He said to him, 'Take your bill, sit down quickly, and make it fifty.' 7 Then he asked another, 'And how much do you owe?' He replied, 'A hundred containers of wheat.' He said to him, 'Take your bill and make it eighty.' 8 And his master commended the dis- honest manager because he had acted shrewdly; for the children of this age are more shrewd in dealing with their own generation than are the children of light. 9 And I tell you, make friends for yourselves by means of dishonest wealthᵛ so that when it is gone, they may welcome you into the eternal homes.ᶻ

10 "Whoever is faithful in a very little is faithful also in much; and whoever is dishonest in a very little is dishonest also in much. 11 If then you have not been faithful with the dishonest wealth,ᵛ who will entrust to you the true riches? 12 And if you have not been faithful with what belongs to an- other, who will give you what is your own? 13 No slave can serve two masters; for a slave will either hate the one and love the other, or be devoted to the one and despise the other. You cannot serve God and wealth."ᵛ

14 The Pharisees, who were lovers of money, heard all this, and they ridiculed him. 15 So he said to them, "You are those who justify your- selves in the sight of others; but God knows your hearts; for what is prized by human beings is an abomination in the sight of God.

16 "The law and the prophets were in effect un- til John came; since then the good news of the kingdom of God is proclaimed, and everyone tries to enter it by force.ᵃ 17 But it is easier for heaven and earth to pass away, than for one stroke of a let- ter in the law to be dropped.

18 "Anyone who divorces his wife and marries another commits adultery, and whoever marries a woman divorced from her husband commits adultery.

ʷOther ancient authorities add *Treat me like one of your hired servants* ˣGk *he* ʸGk *mammon* ᶻGk *tents* ᵃOr *everyone is strongly urged to enter it*

19 "There was a rich man who was dressed in purple and fine linen and who feasted sumptuously every day. 20 And at his gate lay a poor man named Lazarus, covered with sores, 21 who longed to satisfy his hunger with what fell from the rich man's table; even the dogs would come and lick his sores. 22 The poor man died and was carried away by the angels to be with Abraham.[b] The rich man also died and was buried. 23 In Hades, where he was being tormented, he looked up and saw Abraham far away with Lazarus by his side.[c] 24 He called out, 'Father Abraham, have mercy on me, and send Lazarus to dip the tip of his finger in water and cool my tongue; for I am in agony in these flames.' 25 But Abraham said, 'Child, remember that during your lifetime you received your good things, and Lazarus in like manner evil things; but now he is comforted here, and you are in agony. 26 Besides all this, between you and us a great chasm has been fixed, so that those who might want to pass from here to you cannot do so, and no one can cross from there to us.' 27 He said, 'Then, father, I beg you to send him to my father's house— 28 for I have five brothers—that he may warn them, so that they will not also come into this place of torment.' 29 Abraham replied, 'They have Moses and the prophets; they should listen to them.' 30 He said, 'No, father Abraham; but if someone goes to them from the dead, they will repent.' 31 He said to him, 'If they do not listen to Moses and the prophets, neither will they be convinced even if someone rises from the dead.'"

17 Jesus[d] said to his disciples, "Occasions for stumbling are bound to come, but woe to anyone by whom they come! 2 It would be better for you if a millstone were hung around your neck and you were thrown into the sea than for you to cause one of these little ones to stumble. 3 Be on your guard! If another disciple[e] sins, you must rebuke the offender, and if there is repentance, you must forgive. 4 And if the same person sins against you seven times a day, and turns back to you seven times and says, 'I repent,' you must forgive."

5 The apostles said to the Lord, "Increase our faith!" 6 The Lord replied, "If you had faith the size of a[f] mustard seed, you could say to this mulberry tree, 'Be uprooted and planted in the sea,' and it would obey you.

7 "Who among you would say to your slave who has just come in from plowing or tending sheep in the field, 'Come here at once and take your place at the table'? 8 Would you not rather say to him, 'Prepare supper for me, put on your apron and serve me while I eat and drink; later you may eat and drink'? 9 Do you thank the slave for doing what was commanded? 10 So you also, when you have done all that you were ordered to do, say, 'We are worthless slaves; we have done only what we ought to have done!'"

11 On the way to Jerusalem Jesus[g] was going through the region between Samaria and Galilee. 12 As he entered a village, ten lepers[h] approached him. Keeping their distance, 13 they called out, saying, "Jesus, Master, have mercy on us!" 14 When he saw them, he said to them, "Go and show yourselves to the priests." And as they went, they were made clean. 15 Then one of them, when he saw that he was healed, turned back, praising God with a loud voice. 16 He prostrated himself at Jesus'[i] feet and thanked him. And he was a Samaritan. 17 Then Jesus asked, "Were not ten made clean? But the other nine, where are they? 18 Was none of them found to return and give praise to God except this foreigner?" 19 Then he said to him, "Get up and go on your way; your faith has made you well."

20 Once Jesus[g] was asked by the Pharisees when the kingdom of God was coming, and he answered, "The kingdom of God is not coming with things that can be observed; 21 nor will they say, 'Look, here it is!' or 'There it is!' For, in fact, the kingdom of God is among[j] you."

22 Then he said to the disciples, "The days are coming when you will long to see one of the days of the Son of Man, and you will not see it. 23 They will say to you, 'Look there!' or 'Look here!' Do not go, do not set off in pursuit. 24 For as the lightning flashes and lights up the sky from one side to the other, so will the Son of Man be in his day.[k] 25 But first he must endure much suffering and be rejected by this generation. 26 Just as it was in the days of Noah, so too it will be in the days of the Son of Man. 27 They were eating and drinking,

[b]Gk *to Abraham's bosom* [c]Gk *in his bosom* [d]Gk *He* [e]Gk *your brother* [f]Gk *faith as a grain of* [g]Gk *he* [h]The terms *leper* and *leprosy* can refer to several diseases [i]Gk *his* [j]Or *within* [k]Other ancient authorities lack *in his day*

and marrying and being given in marriage, until the day Noah entered the ark, and the flood came and destroyed all of them. 28 Likewise, just as it was in the days of Lot: they were eating and drinking, buying and selling, planting and building, 29 but on the day that Lot left Sodom, it rained fire and sulfur from heaven and destroyed all of them 30 —it will be like that on the day that the Son of Man is revealed. 31 On that day, anyone on the housetop who has belongings in the house must not come down to take them away; and likewise anyone in the field must not turn back. 32 Remember Lot's wife. 33 Those who try to make their life secure will lose it, but those who lose their life will keep it. 34 I tell you, on that night there will be two in one bed; one will be taken and the other left. 35 There will be two women grinding meal together; one will be taken and the other left."[l] 37 Then they asked him, "Where, Lord?" He said to them, "Where the corpse is, there the vultures will gather."

18 Then Jesus[m] told them a parable about their need to pray always and not to lose heart. 2 He said, "In a certain city there was a judge who neither feared God nor had respect for people. 3 In that city there was a widow who kept coming to him and saying, 'Grant me justice against my opponent.' 4 For a while he refused; but later he said to himself, 'Though I have no fear of God and no respect for anyone, 5 yet because this widow keeps bothering me, I will grant her justice, so that she may not wear me out by continually coming.'"[n] 6 And the Lord said, "Listen to what the unjust judge says. 7 And will not God grant justice to his chosen ones who cry to him day and night? Will he delay long in helping them? 8 I tell you, he will quickly grant justice to them. And yet, when the Son of Man comes, will he find faith on earth?"

9 He also told this parable to some who trusted in themselves that they were righteous and regarded others with contempt: 10 "Two men went up to the temple to pray, one a Pharisee and the other a tax collector. 11 The Pharisee, standing by himself, was praying thus, 'God, I thank you that I am not like other people: thieves, rogues, adulterers, or even like this tax collector. 12 I fast twice a week; I give a tenth of all my income.' 13 But the tax collector, standing far off, would not

even look up to heaven, but was beating his breast and saying, 'God, be merciful to me, a sinner!' 14 I tell you, this man went down to his home justified rather than the other; for all who exalt themselves will be humbled, but all who humble themselves will be exalted."

15 People were bringing even infants to him that he might touch them; and when the disciples saw it, they sternly ordered them not to do it. 16 But Jesus called for them and said, "Let the little children come to me, and do not stop them; for it is to such as these that the kingdom of God belongs. 17 Truly I tell you, whoever does not receive the kingdom of God as a little child will never enter it."

18 A certain ruler asked him, "Good Teacher, what must I do to inherit eternal life?" 19 Jesus said to him, "Why do you call me good? No one is good but God alone. 20 You know the commandments: 'You shall not commit adultery; You shall not murder; You shall not steal; You shall not bear false witness; Honor your father and mother.'"[13] 21 He replied, "I have kept all these since my youth." 22 When Jesus heard this, he said to him, "There is still one thing lacking. Sell all that you own and distribute the money[o] to the poor, and you will have treasure in heaven; then come, follow me." 23 But when he heard this, he became sad; for he was very rich. 24 Jesus looked at him and said, "How hard it is for those who have wealth to enter the kingdom of God! 25 Indeed, it is easier for a camel to go through the eye of a needle than for someone who is rich to enter the kingdom of God."

26 Those who heard it said, "Then who can be saved?" 27 He replied, "What is impossible for mortals is possible for God."

28 Then Peter said, "Look, we have left our homes and followed you." 29 And he said to them, "Truly I tell you, there is no one who has left house or wife or brothers or parents or children, for the sake of the kingdom of God, 30 who will not get back very much more in this age, and in the age to come eternal life."

[l]Other ancient authorities add verse 36, *"Two will be in the field; one will be taken and the other left."* [m]Gk *he* [n]Or *so that she may not finally come and slap me in the face* [o]Gk lacks *the money*

[13]Exod 20:12–16; Deut 5:16–20

31 Then he took the twelve aside and said to them, "See, we are going up to Jerusalem, and everything that is written about the Son of Man by the prophets will be accomplished. 32 For he will be handed over to the Gentiles; and he will be mocked and insulted and spat upon. 33 After they have flogged him, they will kill him, and on the third day he will rise again." 34 But they understood nothing about all these things; in fact, what he said was hidden from them, and they did not grasp what was said.

35 As he approached Jericho, a blind man was sitting by the roadside begging. 36 When he heard a crowd going by, he asked what was happening. 37 They told him, "Jesus of Nazareth[p] is passing by." 38 Then he shouted, "Jesus, Son of David, have mercy on me!" 39 Those who were in front sternly ordered him to be quiet; but he shouted even more loudly, "Son of David, have mercy on me!" 40 Jesus stood still and ordered the man to be brought to him; and when he came near, he asked him, 41 "What do you want me to do for you?" He said, "Lord, let me see again." 42 Jesus said to him, "Receive your sight; your faith has saved you." 43 Immediately he regained his sight and followed him, glorifying God; and all the people, when they saw it, praised God.

19 He entered Jericho and was passing through it. 2 A man was there named Zacchaeus; he was a chief tax collector and was rich. 3 He was trying to see who Jesus was, but on account of the crowd he could not, because he was short in stature. 4 So he ran ahead and climbed a sycamore tree to see him, because he was going to pass that way. 5 When Jesus came to the place, he looked up and said to him, "Zacchaeus, hurry and come down; for I must stay at your house today." 6 So he hurried down and was happy to welcome him. 7 All who saw it began to grumble and said, "He has gone to be the guest of one who is a sinner." 8 Zacchaeus stood there and said to the Lord, "Look, half of my possessions, Lord, I will give to the poor; and if I have defrauded anyone of anything, I will pay back four times as much." 9 Then Jesus said to him, "Today salvation has come to this house, because he too is a son of Abraham. 10 For the Son of Man came to seek out and to save the lost."

11 As they were listening to this, he went on to tell a parable, because he was near Jerusalem, and because they supposed that the kingdom of God was to appear immediately. 12 So he said, "A nobleman went to a distant country to get royal power for himself and then return. 13 He summoned ten of his slaves, and gave them ten pounds,[q] and said to them, 'Do business with these until I come back.' 14 But the citizens of his country hated him and sent a delegation after him, saying, 'We do not want this man to rule over us.' 15 When he returned, having received royal power, he ordered these slaves, to whom he had given the money, to be summoned so that he might find out what they had gained by trading. 16 The first came forward and said, 'Lord, your pound has made ten more pounds.' 17 He said to him, 'Well done, good slave! Because you have been trustworthy in a very small thing, take charge of ten cities.' 18 Then the second came, saying, 'Lord, your pound has made five pounds.' 19 He said to him, 'And you, rule over five cities.' 20 Then the other came, saying, 'Lord, here is your pound. I wrapped it up in a piece of cloth, 21 for I was afraid of you, because you are a harsh man; you take what you did not deposit, and reap what you did not sow.' 22 He said to him, 'I will judge you by your own words, you wicked slave! You knew, did you, that I was a harsh man, taking what I did not deposit and reaping what I did not sow? 23 Why then did you not put my money into the bank? Then when I returned, I could have collected it with interest.' 24 He said to the bystanders, 'Take the pound from him and give it to the one who has ten pounds.' 25 (And they said to him, 'Lord, he has ten pounds!') 26 'I tell you, to all those who have, more will be given; but from those who have nothing, even what they have will be taken away. 27 But as for these enemies of mine who did not want me to be king over them— bring them here and slaughter them in my presence.'"

28 After he had said this, he went on ahead, going up to Jerusalem.

29 When he had come near Bethphage and Bethany, at the place called the Mount of Olives, he sent two of the disciples, 30 saying, "Go into

[p]Gk the Nazorean   [q]The mina, rendered here by pound, was about three months' wages for a laborer

the village ahead of you, and as you enter it you will find tied there a colt that has never been ridden. Untie it and bring it here. 31 If anyone asks you, 'Why are you untying it?' just say this, 'The Lord needs it.'" 32 So those who were sent departed and found it as he had told them. 33 As they were untying the colt, its owners asked them, "Why are you untying the colt?" 34 They said, "The Lord needs it." 35 Then they brought it to Jesus; and after throwing their cloaks on the colt, they set Jesus on it. 36 As he rode along, people kept spreading their cloaks on the road. 37 As he was now approaching the path down from the Mount of Olives, the whole multitude of the disciples began to praise God joyfully with a loud voice for all the deeds of power that they had seen, 38 saying,

"Blessed is the king
who comes in the name of the
Lord!"[14]
Peace in heaven,
and glory in the highest
heaven!"

39 Some of the Pharisees in the crowd said to him, "Teacher, order your disciples to stop." 40 He answered, "I tell you, if these were silent, the stones would shout out."

41 As he came near and saw the city, he wept over it, 42 saying, "If you, even you, had only recognized on this day the things that make for peace! But now they are hidden from your eyes. 43 Indeed, the days will come upon you, when your enemies will set up ramparts around you and surround you, and hem you in on every side. 44 They will crush you to the ground, you and your children within you, and they will not leave within you one stone upon another; because you did not recognize the time of your visitation from God."[r]

45 Then he entered the temple and began to drive out those who were selling things there; 46 and he said, "It is written,

'My house shall be a house of
prayer';
but you have made it a den of
robbers."[15]

47 Every day he was teaching in the temple. The chief priests, the scribes, and the leaders of the people kept looking for a way to kill him; 48 but they did not find anything they could do,

for all the people were spellbound by what they heard.

20 One day, as he was teaching the people in the temple and telling the good news, the chief priests and the scribes came with the elders 2 and said to him, "Tell us, by what authority are you doing these things? Who is it who gave you this authority?" 3 He answered them, "I will also ask you a question, and you tell me: 4 Did the baptism of John come from heaven, or was it of human origin?" 5 They discussed it with one another, saying, "If we say, 'From heaven,' he will say, 'Why did you not believe him?' 6 But if we say, 'Of human origin,' all the people will stone us; for they are convinced that John was a prophet." 7 So they answered that they did not know where it came from. 8 Then Jesus said to them, "Neither will I tell you by what authority I am doing these things."

9 He began to tell the people this parable: "A man planted a vineyard, and leased it to tenants, and went to another country for a long time. 10 When the season came, he sent a slave to the tenants in order that they might give him his share of the produce of the vineyard; but the tenants beat him and sent him away empty-handed. 11 Next he sent another slave; that one also they beat and insulted and sent away empty-handed. 12 And he sent still a third; this one also they wounded and threw out. 13 Then the owner of the vineyard said, 'What shall I do? I will send my beloved son; perhaps they will respect him.' 14 But when the tenants saw him, they discussed it among themselves and said, 'This is the heir; let us kill him so that the inheritance may be ours.' 15 So they threw him out of the vineyard and killed him. What then will the owner of the vineyard do to them? 16 He will come and destroy those tenants and give the vineyard to others." When they heard this, they said, "Heaven forbid!" 17 But he looked at them and said, "What then does this text mean:

'The stone that the builders
rejected
has become the cornerstone'?[s][16]

18 Everyone who falls on that stone will be broken to pieces; and it will crush anyone on whom it

[r]Gk lacks *from God*   [s]Or *keystone*

[14]Ps 118:26   [15]Isa 56:7; Jer 7:11   [16]Ps 118:22

falls." 19 When the scribes and chief priests realized that he had told this parable against them, they wanted to lay hands on him at that very hour, but they feared the people.

20 So they watched him and sent spies who pretended to be honest, in order to trap him by what he said, so as to hand him over to the jurisdiction and authority of the governor. 21 So they asked him, "Teacher, we know that you are right in what you say and teach, and you show deference to no one, but teach the way of God in accordance with truth. 22 Is it lawful for us to pay taxes to the emperor, or not?" 23 But he perceived their craftiness and said to them, 24 "Show me a denarius. Whose head and whose title does it bear?" They said, "The emperor's." 25 He said to them, "Then give to the emperor the things that are the emperor's, and to God the things that are God's." 26 And they were not able in the presence of the people to trap him by what he said; and being amazed by his answer, they became silent.

27 Some Sadducees, those who say there is no resurrection, came to him 28 and asked him a question, "Teacher, Moses wrote for us that if a man's brother dies, leaving a wife but no children, the man[t] shall marry the widow and raise up children for his brother.[17] 29 Now there were seven brothers; the first married, and died childless; 30 then the second 31 and the third married her, and so in the same way all seven died childless. 32 Finally the woman also died. 33 In the resurrection, therefore, whose wife will the woman be? For the seven had married her."

34 Jesus said to them, "Those who belong to this age marry and are given in marriage; 35 but those who are considered worthy of a place in that age and in the resurrection from the dead neither marry nor are given in marriage. 36 Indeed they cannot die anymore, because they are like angels and are children of God, being children of the resurrection. 37 And the fact that the dead are raised Moses himself showed, in the story about the bush, where he speaks of the Lord as the God of Abraham, the God of Isaac, and the God of Jacob.[18] 38 Now he is God not of the dead, but of the living; for to him all of them are alive." 39 Then some of the scribes answered, "Teacher, you have spoken well." 40 For they no longer dared to ask him another question.

41 Then he said to them, "How can they say that the Messiah[u] is David's son? 42 For David himself says in the book of Psalms,

'The Lord said to my Lord,
"Sit at my right hand,
43   until I make your enemies your
footstool."'[19]

44 David thus calls him Lord; so how can he be his son?"

45 In the hearing of all the people he said to the[v] disciples, 46 "Beware of the scribes, who like to walk around in long robes, and love to be greeted with respect in the marketplaces, and to have the best seats in the synagogues and places of honor at banquets. 47 They devour widows' houses and for the sake of appearance say long prayers. They will receive the greater condemnation."

21 He looked up and saw rich people putting their gifts into the treasury; 2 he also saw a poor widow put in two small copper coins. 3 He said, "Truly I tell you, this poor widow has put in more than all of them; 4 for all of them have contributed out of their abundance, but she out of her poverty has put in all she had to live on."

5 When some were speaking about the temple, how it was adorned with beautiful stones and gifts dedicated to God, he said, 6 "As for these things that you see, the days will come when not one stone will be left upon another; all will be thrown down."

7 They asked him, "Teacher, when will this be, and what will be the sign that this is about to take place?" 8 And he said, "Beware that you are not led astray; for many will come in my name and say, 'I am he!'[w] and, 'The time is near!'[x] Do not go after them.

9 "When you hear of wars and insurrections, do not be terrified; for these things must take place first, but the end will not follow immediately." 10 Then he said to them, "Nation will rise against nation, and kingdom against kingdom; 11 there will be great earthquakes, and in various places famines and plagues; and there will be dreadful portents and great signs from heaven.

12 "But before all this occurs, they will arrest you and persecute you; they will hand you over to

---

[t]Gk his brother   [u]Or the Christ   [v]Other ancient authorities read his
[w]Gk I am   [x]Or at hand

---

[17]Deut 25:5; Gen 38:8   [18]Exod 3:6, 15   [19]Ps 110:1

synagogues and prisons, and you will be brought before kings and governors because of my name. 13 This will give you an opportunity to testify. 14 So make up your minds not to prepare your defense in advance; 15 for I will give you words[y] and a wisdom that none of your opponents will be able to withstand or contradict. 16 You will be betrayed even by parents and brothers, by relatives and friends; and they will put some of you to death. 17 You will be hated by all because of my name. 18 But not a hair of your head will perish. 19 By your endurance you will gain your souls.

20 "When you see Jerusalem surrounded by armies, then know that its desolation has come near.[z] 21 Then those in Judea must flee to the mountains, and those inside the city must leave it, and those out in the country must not enter it; 22 for these are days of vengeance as a fulfillment of all that is written. 23 Woe to those who are pregnant and to those who are nursing infants in those days! For there will be great distress on the earth and wrath against this people; 24 they will fall by the edge of the sword and be taken away as captives among all nations; and Jerusalem will be trampled on by the Gentiles, until the times of the Gentiles are fulfilled.

25 "There will be signs in the sun, the moon, and the stars, and on the earth distress among nations confused by the roaring of the sea and the waves. 26 People will faint from fear and foreboding of what is coming upon the world, for the powers of the heavens will be shaken. 27 Then they will see 'the Son of Man coming in a cloud' with power and great glory. 28 Now when these things begin to take place, stand up and raise your heads, because your redemption is drawing near."

29 Then he told them a parable: "Look at the fig tree and all the trees; 30 as soon as they sprout leaves you can see for yourselves and know that summer is already near. 31 So also, when you see these things taking place, you know that the kingdom of God is near. 32 Truly I tell you, this generation will not pass away until all things have taken place. 33 Heaven and earth will pass away, but my words will not pass away.

34 "Be on guard so that your hearts are not weighed down with dissipation and drunkenness and the worries of this life, and that day does not catch you unexpectedly, 35 like a trap. For it will come upon all who live on the face of the whole earth. 36 Be alert at all times, praying that you may have the strength to escape all these things that will take place, and to stand before the Son of Man."

37 Every day he was teaching in the temple, and at night he would go out and spend the night on the Mount of Olives, as it was called. 38 And all the people would get up early in the morning to listen to him in the temple.

22 Now the festival of Unleavened Bread, which is called the Passover, was near. 2 The chief priests and the scribes were looking for a way to put Jesus[a] to death, for they were afraid of the people.

3 Then Satan entered into Judas called Iscariot, who was one of the twelve; 4 he went away and conferred with the chief priests and officers of the temple police about how he might betray him to them. 5 They were greatly pleased and agreed to give him money. 6 So he consented and began to look for an opportunity to betray him to them when no crowd was present.

7 Then came the day of Unleavened Bread, on which the Passover lamb had to be sacrificed. 8 So Jesus[b] sent Peter and John, saying, "Go and prepare the Passover meal for us that we may eat it." 9 They asked him, "Where do you want us to make preparations for it?" 10 "Listen," he said to them, "when you have entered the city, a man carrying a jar of water will meet you; follow him into the house he enters 11 and say to the owner of the house, 'The teacher asks you, "Where is the guest room, where I may eat the Passover with my disciples?"' 12 He will show you a large room upstairs, already furnished. Make preparations for us there." 13 So they went and found everything as he had told them; and they prepared the Passover meal.

14 When the hour came, he took his place at the table, and the apostles with him. 15 He said to them, "I have eagerly desired to eat this Passover with you before I suffer; 16 for I tell you, I will not eat it[c] until it is fulfilled in the kingdom of God." 17 Then he took a cup, and after giving thanks he

[y] Gk a mouth [z] Or is at hand [a] Gk him [b] Gk he [c] Other ancient authorities read never eat it again

said, "Take this and divide it among yourselves; 18 for I tell you that from now on I will not drink of the fruit of the vine until the kingdom of God comes." 19 Then he took a loaf of bread, and when he had given thanks, he broke it and gave it to them, saying, "This is my body, which is given for you. Do this in remembrance of me." 20 And he did the same with the cup after supper, saying, "This cup that is poured out for you is the new covenant in my blood.^{d} 21 But see, the one who betrays me is with me, and his hand is on the table. 22 For the Son of Man is going as it has been determined, but woe to that one by whom he is betrayed!" 23 Then they began to ask one another which one of them it could be who would do this.

24 A dispute also arose among them as to which one of them was to be regarded as the greatest. 25 But he said to them, "The kings of the Gentiles lord it over them; and those in authority over them are called benefactors. 26 But not so with you; rather the greatest among you must become like the youngest, and the leader like one who serves. 27 For who is greater, the one who is at the table or the one who serves? Is it not the one at the table? But I am among you as one who serves.

28 "You are those who have stood by me in my trials; 29 and I confer on you, just as my Father has conferred on me, a kingdom, 30 so that you may eat and drink at my table in my kingdom, and you will sit on thrones judging the twelve tribes of Israel.

31 "Simon, Simon, listen! Satan has demanded^e to sift all of you like wheat, 32 but I have prayed for you that your own faith may not fail; and you, when once you have turned back, strengthen your brothers." 33 And he said to him, "Lord, I am ready to go with you to prison and to death!" 34 Jesus^f said, "I tell you, Peter, the cock will not crow this day, until you have denied three times that you know me."

35 He said to them, "When I sent you out without a purse, bag, or sandals, did you lack anything?" They said, "No, not a thing." 36 He said to them, "But now, the one who has a purse must take it, and likewise a bag. And the one who has no sword must sell his cloak and buy one. 37 For I tell you, this scripture must be fulfilled in me, 'And he was counted among the lawless';^{20} and indeed what is written about me is being fulfilled."

38 They said, "Lord, look, here are two swords." He replied, "It is enough."

39 He came out and went, as was his custom, to the Mount of Olives; and the disciples followed him. 40 When he reached the place, he said to them, "Pray that you may not come into the time of trial."^{g} 41 Then he withdrew from them about a stone's throw, knelt down, and prayed, 42 "Father, if you are willing, remove this cup from me; yet, not my will but yours be done." [43 Then an angel from heaven appeared to him and gave him strength. 44 In his anguish he prayed more earnestly, and his sweat became like great drops of blood falling down on the ground.]^h 45 When he got up from prayer, he came to the disciples and found them sleeping because of grief, 46 and he said to them, "Why are you sleeping? Get up and pray that you may not come into the time of trial."^{g}

47 While he was still speaking, suddenly a crowd came, and the one called Judas, one of the twelve, was leading them. He approached Jesus to kiss him; 48 but Jesus said to him, "Judas, is it with a kiss that you are betraying the Son of Man?" 49 When those who were around him saw what was coming, they asked, "Lord, should we strike with the sword?" 50 Then one of them struck the slave of the high priest and cut off his right ear. 51 But Jesus said, "No more of this!" And he touched his ear and healed him. 52 Then Jesus said to the chief priests, the officers of the temple police, and the elders who had come for him, "Have you come out with swords and clubs as if I were a bandit? 53 When I was with you day after day in the temple, you did not lay hands on me. But this is your hour, and the power of darkness!"

54 Then they seized him and led him away, bringing him into the high priest's house. But Peter was following at a distance. 55 When they had kindled a fire in the middle of the courtyard and sat down together, Peter sat among them. 56 Then a servant-girl, seeing him in the firelight, stared at him and said, "This man also was with him." 57 But he denied it, saying, "Woman, I do not

---

^{d}Other ancient authorities lack, in whole or in part, verses 19b-20 (*which is given . . . in my blood*) ^{e}Or *has obtained permission* ^{f}Gk *He* ^{g}Or *into temptation* ^{h}Other ancient authorities lack verses 43 and 44

---

^{20}Isa 53:12

know him." 58 A little later someone else, on see-ing him, said, "You also are one of them." But Pe-ter said, "Man, I am not!" 59 Then about an hour later still another kept insisting, "Surely this man also was with him; for he is a Galilean." 60 But Peter said, "Man, I do not know what you are talk-ing about!" At that moment, while he was still speaking, the cock crowed. 61 The Lord turned and looked at Peter. Then Peter remembered the word of the Lord, how he had said to him, "Before the cock crows today, you will deny me three times." 62 And he went out and wept bitterly.

63 Now the men who were holding Jesus began to mock him and beat him; 64 they also blind-folded him and kept asking him, "Prophesy! Who is it that struck you?" 65 They kept heaping many other insults on him.

66 When day came, the assembly of the elders of the people, both chief priests and scribes, gath-ered together, and they brought him to their coun-cil. 67 They said, "If you are the Messiah,ⁱ tell us." He replied, "If I tell you, you will not believe; 68 and if I question you, you will not answer. 69 But from now on the Son of Man will be seat-ed at the right hand of the power of God."²¹ 70 All of them asked, "Are you, then, the Son of God?" He said to them, "You say that I am." 71 Then they said, "What further testimony do we need? We have heard it ourselves from his own lips!"

23 Then the assembly rose as a body and brought Jesusʲ before Pilate. 2 They be-gan to accuse him, saying, "We found this man perverting our nation, forbidding us to pay taxes to the emperor, and saying that he himself is the Messiah, a king."ᵏ 3 Then Pilate asked him, "Are you the king of the Jews?" He answered, "You say so." 4 Then Pilate said to the chief priests and the crowds, "I find no basis for an accusation against this man." 5 But they were insistent and said, "He stirs up the people by teaching throughout all Judea, from Galilee where he began even to this place."

6 When Pilate heard this, he asked whether the man was a Galilean. 7 And when he learned that he was under Herod's jurisdiction, he sent him off to Herod, who was himself in Jerusalem at that time. 8 When Herod saw Jesus, he was very glad, for he had been wanting to see him for a long time, because he had heard about him and was hoping

to see him perform some sign. 9 He questioned himˡ at some length, but Jesusˡ gave him no answer. 10 The chief priests and the scribes stood by, vehemently accusing him. 11 Even Herod with his soldiers treated him with contempt and mocked him; then he put an elegant robe on him, and sent him back to Pilate. 12 That same day Herod and Pilate became friends with each other; before this they had been enemies.

13 Pilate then called together the chief priests, the leaders, and the people, 14 and said to them, "You brought me this man as one who was per-verting the people; and here I have examined him in your presence and have not found this man guilty of any of your charges against him. 15 Nei-ther has Herod, for he sent him back to us. Indeed, he has done nothing to deserve death. 16 I will therefore have him flogged and release him."ᵐ

18 Then they all shouted out together, "Away with this fellow! Release Barabbas for us!" 19 (This was a man who had been put in prison for an insurrection that had taken place in the city, and for murder.) 20 Pilate, wanting to release Jesus, addressed them again; 21 but they kept shouting, "Crucify, crucify him!" 22 A third time he said to them, "Why, what evil has he done? I have found in him no ground for the sentence of death; I will therefore have him flogged and then release him." 23 But they kept urgently demanding with loud shouts that he should be crucified; and their voices prevailed. 24 So Pilate gave his verdict that their demand should be granted. 25 He re-leased the man they asked for, the one who had been put in prison for insurrection and murder, and he handed Jesus over as they wished.

26 As they led him away, they seized a man, Si-mon of Cyrene, who was coming from the coun-try, and they laid the cross on him, and made him carry it behind Jesus. 27 A great number of the people followed him, and among them were women who were beating their breasts and wail-ing for him. 28 But Jesus turned to them and said, "Daughters of Jerusalem, do not weep for me, but weep for yourselves and for your children. 29 For

---

ⁱOr *the Christ* ʲGk *him* ᵏOr *is an anointed king* ˡGk *he* ᵐHere, or after verse 19, other ancient authorities add verse 17, *Now he was obliged to release someone for them at the festival*

---

²¹Ps 110:1; Dan 7:13

the days are surely coming when they will say, 'Blessed are the barren, and the wombs that never bore, and the breasts that never nursed.' 30 Then they will begin to say to the mountains, 'Fall on us'; and to the hills, 'Cover us.'[22] 31 For if they do this when the wood is green, what will happen when it is dry?"

32 Two others also, who were criminals, were led away to be put to death with him. 33 When they came to the place that is called The Skull, they crucified Jesus[n] there with the criminals, one on his right and one on his left. [34 Then Jesus said, "Father, forgive them; for they do not know what they are doing."][o] And they cast lots to divide his clothing. 35 And the people stood by, watching; but the leaders scoffed at him, saying, "He saved others; let him save himself if he is the Messiah[p] of God, his chosen one!" 36 The soldiers also mocked him, coming up and offering him sour wine, 37 and saying, "If you are the King of the Jews, save yourself!" 38 There was also an inscription over him,[q] "This is the King of the Jews."

39 One of the criminals who were hanged there kept deriding[r] him and saying, "Are you not the Messiah?[s] Save yourself and us!" 40 But the other rebuked him, saying, "Do you not fear God, since you are under the same sentence of condemnation? 41 And we indeed have been condemned justly, for we are getting what we deserve for our deeds, but this man has done nothing wrong." 42 Then he said, "Jesus, remember me when you come into[t] your kingdom." 43 He replied, "Truly I tell you, today you will be with me in Paradise."

44 It was now about noon, and darkness came over the whole land[u] until three in the afternoon, 45 while the sun's light failed;[v] and the curtain of the temple was torn in two. 46 Then Jesus, crying with a loud voice, said, "Father, into your hands I commend my spirit."[23] Having said this, he breathed his last. 47 When the centurion saw what had taken place, he praised God and said, "Certainly this man was innocent."[w] 48 And when all the crowds who had gathered there for this spectacle saw what had taken place, they returned home, beating their breasts. 49 But all his acquaintances, including the women who had followed him from Galilee, stood at a distance, watching these things.

50 Now there was a good and righteous man named Joseph, who, though a member of the council, 51 had not agreed to their plan and action. He came from the Jewish town of Arimathea, and he was waiting expectantly for the kingdom of God. 52 This man went to Pilate and asked for the body of Jesus. 53 Then he took it down, wrapped it in a linen cloth, and laid it in a rock-hewn tomb where no one had ever been laid. 54 It was the day of Preparation, and the sabbath was beginning.[x] 55 The women who had come with him from Galilee followed, and they saw the tomb and how his body was laid. 56 Then they returned, and prepared spices and ointments.

On the sabbath they rested according to the commandment.

24 But on the first day of the week, at early dawn, they came to the tomb, taking the spices that they had prepared. 2 They found the stone rolled away from the tomb, 3 but when they went in, they did not find the body.[y] 4 While they were perplexed about this, suddenly two men in dazzling clothes stood beside them. 5 The women[z] were terrified and bowed their faces to the ground, but the men[a] said to them, "Why do you look for the living among the dead? He is not here, but has risen.[b] 6 Remember how he told you, while he was still in Galilee, 7 that the Son of Man must be handed over to sinners, and be crucified, and on the third day rise again." 8 Then they remembered his words, 9 and returning from the tomb, they told all this to the eleven and to all the rest. 10 Now it was Mary Magdalene, Joanna, Mary the mother of James, and the other women with them who told this to the apostles. 11 But these words seemed to them an idle tale, and they did not believe them. 12 But Peter got up and ran to the tomb; stooping and looking in, he saw the linen cloths by themselves; then he went home, amazed at what had happened.[c]

13 Now on that same day two of them were go-

[n]Gk him   [o]Other ancient authorities lack the sentence *Then Jesus . . . what they are doing*   [p]Or *the Christ*   [q]Other ancient authorities add *written in Greek and Latin and Hebrew* (that is, *Aramaic*)
[r]Or *blaspheming*   [s]Or *the Christ*   [t]Other ancient authorities read *in*
[u]Or *earth*   [v]Or *the sun was eclipsed.* Other ancient authorities read *the sun was darkened*   [w]Or *righteous*   [x]Gk *was dawning*   [y]Other ancient authorities add *of the Lord Jesus*   [z]Gk *They*   [a]Gk *but they*
[b]Other ancient authorities lack *He is not here, but has risen*   [c]Other ancient authorities lack verse 12

[22]Hos 10:8   [23]Ps 31:5

ing to a village called Emmaus, about seven miles[d] from Jerusalem, 14 and talking with each other about all these things that had happened. 15 While they were talking and discussing, Jesus himself came near and went with them, 16 but their eyes were kept from recognizing him. 17 And he said to them, "What are you discussing with each other while you walk along?" They stood still, looking sad.[e] 18 Then one of them, whose name was Cleopas, answered him, "Are you the only stranger in Jerusalem who does not know the things that have taken place there in these days?" 19 He asked them, "What things?" They replied, "The things about Jesus of Nazareth,[f] who was a prophet mighty in deed and word before God and all the people, 20 and how our chief priests and leaders handed him over to be condemned to death and crucified him. 21 But we had hoped that he was the one to redeem Israel.[g] Yes, and besides all this, it is now the third day since these things took place. 22 Moreover, some women of our group astounded us. They were at the tomb early this morning, 23 and when they did not find his body there, they came back and told us that they had indeed seen a vision of angels who said that he was alive. 24 Some of those who were with us went to the tomb and found it just as the women had said; but they did not see him." 25 Then he said to them, "Oh, how foolish you are, and how slow of heart to believe all that the prophets have declared! 26 Was it not necessary that the Messiah[h] should suffer these things and then enter into his glory?" 27 Then beginning with Moses and all the prophets, he interpreted to them the things about himself in all the scriptures.

28 As they came near the village to which they were going, he walked ahead as if he were going on. 29 But they urged him strongly, saying, "Stay with us, because it is almost evening and the day is now nearly over." So he went in to stay with them. 30 When he was at the table with them, he took bread, blessed and broke it, and gave it to them. 31 Then their eyes were opened, and they recognized him; and he vanished from their sight. 32 They said to each other, "Were not our hearts burning within us[i] while he was talking to us on the road, while he was opening the scriptures to us?" 33 That same hour they got up and returned to Jerusalem; and they found the eleven and their

companions gathered together. 34 They were saying, "The Lord has risen indeed, and he has appeared to Simon!" 35 Then they told what had happened on the road, and how he had been made known to them in the breaking of the bread.

36 While they were talking about this, Jesus himself stood among them and said to them, "Peace be with you."[j] 37 They were startled and terrified, and thought that they were seeing a ghost. 38 He said to them, "Why are you frightened, and why do doubts arise in your hearts? 39 Look at my hands and my feet; see that it is I myself. Touch me and see; for a ghost does not have flesh and bones as you see that I have." 40 And when he had said this, he showed them his hands and his feet.[k] 41 While in their joy they were disbelieving and still wondering, he said to them, "Have you anything here to eat?" 42 They gave him a piece of broiled fish, 43 and he took it and ate in their presence.

44 Then he said to them, "These are my words that I spoke to you while I was still with you—that everything written about me in the law of Moses, the prophets, and the psalms must be fulfilled." 45 Then he opened their minds to understand the scriptures, 46 and he said to them, "Thus it is written, that the Messiah[h] is to suffer and to rise from the dead on the third day, 47 and that repentance and forgiveness of sins is to be proclaimed in his name to all nations, beginning from Jerusalem. 48 You are witnesses[l] of these things. 49 And see, I am sending upon you what my Father promised; so stay here in the city until you have been clothed with power from on high."

50 Then he led them out as far as Bethany, and, lifting up his hands, he blessed them. 51 While he was blessing them, he withdrew from them and was carried up into heaven.[m] 52 And they worshiped him, and[n] returned to Jerusalem with great joy; 53 and they were continually in the temple blessing God.[o]

---

[d]Gk *sixty stadia;* other ancient authorities read *a hundred sixty stadia* [e]Other ancient authorities read *walk along, looking sad?"* [f]Other ancient authorities read *Jesus the Nazorean* [g]Or *to set Israel free* [h]Or *the Christ* [i]Other ancient authorities lack *within us* [j]Other ancient authorities lack *and said to them, "Peace be with you."* [k]Other ancient authorities lack verse 40 [l]Or *nations. Beginning from Jerusalem* [48]*you are witnesses* [m]Other ancient authorities lack *and was carried up into heaven* [n]Other ancient authorities lack *worshiped him, and* [o]Other ancient authorities add *Amen*

The Gospel According to John

Perennially one of the most beloved writings of the New Testament, the Gospel of John has always been recognized for its distinctive portrayal of Jesus. Here alone do we find Jesus turning the water into wine, raising Lazarus from the dead, and washing his disciples' feet. Here alone do we hear Jesus proclaim "I am the Light of the World," "I am the Bread of Life," "Before Abraham was, I am," and "I and the Father are one." Whereas in the other New Testament Gospels Jesus refuses to prove his identity by performing miraculous signs, here that is precisely what he does: his signs are performed and narrated to reveal his identity so that others might believe (cf. 2:10; 4:48; 20:30–31). Similarly, whereas in the other Gospels Jesus proclaims the coming kingdom of God but rarely speaks about himself, in this Gospel he proclaims almost nothing but himself and scarcely mentions the kingdom.

The Gospel has been traditionally ascribed to John, the son of Zebedee (a person never named in the narrative); as with the other New Testament Gospels, however, the book itself is anonymous. The author was clearly a Greek-speaking Christian; he evidently lived outside of Palestine. As one of his sources, he claims to have used the testimony of one of Jesus' closest followers (19:35; 21:24), whom he never names but calls the "disciple whom Jesus loved" (21:7).

Scholars today widely recognize that the author utilized several written sources, including (a) a written account of Jesus' signs that may have been composed, originally, to convince Jews that Jesus was the Messiah (see, e.g., 2:1–10; 20:30–31); (b) one or more collections of Jesus' long speeches, including the "Farewell Discourse" that comprises all of chapters 13–17; and (c) the introductory hymn to Christ that serves as the Gospel's prologue (1:1–18).

These various sources arose within the author's own community, which evidently began as a group of Jews who came to believe in Jesus as the Messiah and eventually were expelled from their synagogue as a result of their belief, leading them to form a worshipping community of their own (see 9:22; 16:2). The community's various conflicts stimulated their theological reflections about the meaning and importance of Jesus, reflections that came to be embodied within the Gospel when it was written sometime near the end of the first century (ca. 90–95 C.E.).

As in the other Gospels, here Jesus continues to be portrayed as a Jewish rabbi, a great prophet, and a messiah sent from God to die for the sins of the world. But he is also far more. For here Jesus is said to be the one who reveals God; he is the embodiment of God's very Word, through which the world was made and by which all things have life (1:1–18). Those who see Jesus have seen the Father, those who believe in him have eternal life, those who reject him are subject to the wrathful judgment of God (3:36; 14:9). In short, for this Gospel, Jesus is God's very presence on earth, the one who came from the Father to reveal his identity and who at his death and exaltation returned to heaven to prepare a place for his people (14:2).

1 In the beginning was the Word, and the Word was with God, and the Word was God. 2 He was in the beginning with God. 3 All things came into being through him, and without him not one thing came into being. What has come into being 4 in him was life,[a] and the life was the light of all people. 5 The light shines in the darkness, and the darkness did not overcome it.

6 There was a man sent from God, whose name was John. 7 He came as a witness to testify to the light, so that all might believe through him. 8 He himself was not the light, but he came to testify to the light. 9 The true light, which enlightens everyone, was coming into the world.[b]

10 He was in the world, and the world came into being through him; yet the world did not know him. 11 He came to what was his own,[c] and his own people did not accept him. 12 But to all who received him, who believed in his name, he gave power to become children of God, 13 who were born, not of blood or of the will of the flesh or of the will of man, but of God.

14 And the Word became flesh and lived among us, and we have seen his glory, the glory as of a father's only son,[d] full of grace and truth. 15 (John testified to him and cried out, "This was he of whom I said, 'He who comes after me ranks ahead of me because he was before me.'") 16 From his fullness we have all received, grace upon grace. 17 The law indeed was given through Moses; grace and truth came through Jesus Christ. 18 No one has ever seen God. It is God the only Son,[e] who is close to the Father's heart,[f] who has made him known.

19 This is the testimony given by John when the Jews sent priests and Levites from Jerusalem to ask him, "Who are you?" 20 He confessed and did not deny it, but confessed, "I am not the Messiah."[g] 21 And they asked him, "What then? Are you Elijah?" He said, "I am not." "Are you the prophet?" He answered, "No." 22 Then they said to him, "Who are you? Let us have an answer for those who sent us. What do you say about yourself?" 23 He said,

"I am the voice of one crying out
      in the wilderness,
   'Make straight the way of the
            Lord,'"[1]

as the prophet Isaiah said.

24 Now they had been sent from the Pharisees. 25 They asked him, "Why then are you baptizing if you are neither the Messiah,[g] nor Elijah, nor the prophet?" 26 John answered them, "I baptize with water. Among you stands one whom you do not know, 27 the one who is coming after me; I am not worthy to untie the thong of his sandal." 28 This took place in Bethany across the Jordan where John was baptizing.

29 The next day he saw Jesus coming toward him and declared, "Here is the Lamb of God who takes away the sin of the world! 30 This is he of whom I said, 'After me comes a man who ranks ahead of me because he was before me.' 31 I myself did not know him; but I came baptizing with water for this reason, that he might be revealed to Israel." 32 And John testified, "I saw the Spirit descending from heaven like a dove, and it remained on him. 33 I myself did not know him, but the one who sent me to baptize with water said to me, 'He on whom you see the Spirit descend and remain is the one who baptizes with the Holy Spirit.' 34 And I myself have seen and have testified that this is the Son of God."[h]

35 The next day John again was standing with two of his disciples, 36 and as he watched Jesus walk by, he exclaimed, "Look, here is the Lamb of God!" 37 The two disciples heard him say this, and they followed Jesus. 38 When Jesus turned and saw them following, he said to them, "What are you looking for?" They said to him, "Rabbi" (which translated means Teacher), "where are you staying?" 39 He said to them, "Come and see." They came and saw where he was staying, and they remained with him that day. It was about four o'clock in the afternoon. 40 One of the two who heard John speak and followed him was Andrew, Simon Peter's brother. 41 He first found his brother Simon and said to him, "We have found the Messiah" (which is translated Anointed[i]). 42 He brought Simon[j] to Jesus, who looked at him and

[a]Or [3]through him. And without him not one thing came into being that has come into being. [4]In him was life   [b]Or He was the true light that enlightens everyone coming into the world   [c]Or to his own home   [d]Or the Father's only Son   [e]Other ancient authorities read It is an only Son, God, or It is the only Son   [f]Gk bosom   [g]Or the Christ   [h]Other ancient authorities read is God's chosen one   [i]Or Christ   [j]Gk him

[1]Isa 40:3

said, "You are Simon son of John. You are to be called Cephas" (which is translated Peter[k]).

43 The next day Jesus decided to go to Galilee. He found Philip and said to him, "Follow me." 44 Now Philip was from Bethsaida, the city of Andrew and Peter. 45 Philip found Nathanael and said to him, "We have found him about whom Moses in the law and also the prophets wrote, Jesus son of Joseph from Nazareth." 46 Nathanael said to him, "Can anything good come out of Nazareth?" Philip said to him, "Come and see." 47 When Jesus saw Nathanael coming toward him, he said of him, "Here is truly an Israelite in whom there is no deceit!" 48 Nathanael asked him, "Where did you get to know me?" Jesus answered, "I saw you under the fig tree before Philip called you." 49 Nathanael replied, "Rabbi, you are the Son of God! You are the King of Israel!" 50 Jesus answered, "Do you believe because I told you that I saw you under the fig tree? You will see greater things than these." 51 And he said to him, "Very truly, I tell you,[l] you will see heaven opened and the angels of God ascending and descending upon the Son of Man."

2 On the third day there was a wedding in Cana of Galilee, and the mother of Jesus was there. 2 Jesus and his disciples had also been invited to the wedding. 3 When the wine gave out, the mother of Jesus said to him, "They have no wine." 4 And Jesus said to her, "Woman, what concern is that to you and to me? My hour has not yet come." 5 His mother said to the servants, "Do whatever he tells you." 6 Now standing there were six stone water jars for the Jewish rites of purification, each holding twenty or thirty gallons. 7 Jesus said to them, "Fill the jars with water." And they filled them up to the brim. 8 He said to them, "Now draw some out, and take it to the chief steward." So they took it. 9 When the steward tasted the water that had become wine, and did not know where it came from (though the servants who had drawn the water knew), the steward called the bridegroom 10 and said to him, "Everyone serves the good wine first, and then the inferior wine after the guests have become drunk. But you have kept the good wine until now." 11 Jesus did this, the first of his signs, in Cana of Galilee, and revealed his glory; and his disciples believed in him.

12 After this he went down to Capernaum with his mother, his brothers, and his disciples; and they remained there a few days.

13 The Passover of the Jews was near, and Jesus went up to Jerusalem. 14 In the temple he found people selling cattle, sheep, and doves, and the money changers seated at their tables. 15 Making a whip of cords, he drove all of them out of the temple, both the sheep and the cattle. He also poured out the coins of the money changers and overturned their tables. 16 He told those who were selling the doves, "Take these things out of here! Stop making my Father's house a marketplace!" 17 His disciples remembered that it was written, "Zeal for your house will consume me."[2] 18 The Jews then said to him, "What sign can you show us for doing this?" 19 Jesus answered them, "Destroy this temple, and in three days I will raise it up." 20 The Jews then said, "This temple has been under construction for forty-six years, and will you raise it up in three days?" 21 But he was speaking of the temple of his body. 22 After he was raised from the dead, his disciples remembered that he had said this; and they believed the scripture and the word that Jesus had spoken.

23 When he was in Jerusalem during the Passover festival, many believed in his name because they saw the signs that he was doing. 24 But Jesus on his part would not entrust himself to them, because he knew all people 25 and needed no one to testify about anyone; for he himself knew what was in everyone.

3 Now there was a Pharisee named Nicodemus, a leader of the Jews. 2 He came to Jesus[m] by night and said to him, "Rabbi, we know that you are a teacher who has come from God; for no one can do these signs that you do apart from the presence of God." 3 Jesus answered him, "Very truly, I tell you, no one can see the kingdom of God without being born from above."[n] 4 Nicodemus said to him, "How can anyone be born after having grown old? Can one enter a second time into the mother's womb and be born?" 5 Jesus answered, "Very truly, I tell you, no one can enter the kingdom of God without being born

[k]From the word for *rock* in Aramaic (*kepha*) and Greek (*petra*), respectively [l]Both instances of the Greek word for *you* in this verse are plural [m]Gk *him* [n]Or *born anew*

[2]Ps 69:9

of water and Spirit. 6 What is born of the flesh is flesh, and what is born of the Spirit is spirit.[o] 7 Do not be astonished that I said to you, 'You[p] must be born from above.'[q] 8 The wind[o] blows where it chooses, and you hear the sound of it, but you do not know where it comes from or where it goes. So it is with everyone who is born of the Spirit." 9 Nicodemus said to him, "How can these things be?" 10 Jesus answered him, "Are you a teacher of Israel, and yet you do not understand these things?

11 "Very truly, I tell you, we speak of what we know and testify to what we have seen; yet you[r] do not receive our testimony. 12 If I have told you about earthly things and you do not believe, how can you believe if I tell you about heavenly things? 13 No one has ascended into heaven except the one who descended from heaven, the Son of Man.[s] 14 And just as Moses lifted up the serpent in the wilderness, so must the Son of Man be lifted up, 15 that whoever believes in him may have eternal life.[t]

16 "For God so loved the world that he gave his only Son, so that everyone who believes in him may not perish but may have eternal life.

17 "Indeed, God did not send the Son into the world to condemn the world, but in order that the world might be saved through him. 18 Those who believe in him are not condemned; but those who do not believe are condemned already, because they have not believed in the name of the only Son of God. 19 And this is the judgment, that the light has come into the world, and people loved darkness rather than light because their deeds were evil. 20 For all who do evil hate the light and do not come to the light, so that their deeds may not be exposed. 21 But those who do what is true come to the light, so that it may be clearly seen that their deeds have been done in God."[t]

22 After this Jesus and his disciples went into the Judean countryside, and he spent some time there with them and baptized. 23 John also was baptizing at Aenon near Salim because water was abundant there; and people kept coming and were being baptized 24 —John, of course, had not yet been thrown into prison.

25 Now a discussion about purification arose between John's disciples and a Jew.[u] 26 They came to John and said to him, "Rabbi, the one who was with you across the Jordan, to whom you testified, here he is baptizing, and all are going to him." 27 John answered, "No one can receive anything except what has been given from heaven. 28 You yourselves are my witnesses that I said, 'I am not the Messiah,[v] but I have been sent ahead of him.' 29 He who has the bride is the bridegroom. The friend of the bridegroom, who stands and hears him, rejoices greatly at the bridegroom's voice. For this reason my joy has been fulfilled. 30 He must increase, but I must decrease."[w]

31 The one who comes from above is above all; the one who is of the earth belongs to the earth and speaks about earthly things. The one who comes from heaven is above all. 32 He testifies to what he has seen and heard, yet no one accepts his testimony. 33 Whoever has accepted his testimony has certified[x] this, that God is true. 34 He whom God has sent speaks the words of God, for he gives the Spirit without measure. 35 The Father loves the Son and has placed all things in his hands. 36 Whoever believes in the Son has eternal life; whoever disobeys the Son will not see life, but must endure God's wrath.

4 Now when Jesus[y] learned that the Pharisees had heard, "Jesus is making and baptizing more disciples than John" 2 —although it was not Jesus himself but his disciples who baptized— 3 he left Judea and started back to Galilee. 4 But he had to go through Samaria. 5 So he came to a Samaritan city called Sychar, near the plot of ground that Jacob had given to his son Joseph. 6 Jacob's well was there, and Jesus, tired out by his journey, was sitting by the well. It was about noon.

7 A Samaritan woman came to draw water, and Jesus said to her, "Give me a drink." 8 (His disciples had gone to the city to buy food.) 9 The Samaritan woman said to him, "How is it that you, a Jew, ask a drink of me, a woman of Samaria?" (Jews do not share things in common with Samaritans.)[z] 10 Jesus answered her, "If you knew the

[o]The same Greek word means both *wind* and *spirit* [p]The Greek word for *you* here is plural [q]Or *anew* [r]The Greek word for *you* here and in verse 12 is plural [s]Other ancient authorities add *who is in heaven* [t]Some interpreters hold that the quotation concludes with verse 15 [u]Other ancient authorities read *the Jews* [v]Or *the Christ* [w]Some interpreters hold that the quotation continues through verse 36 [x]Gk *set a seal to* [y]Other ancient authorities read *the Lord* [z]Other ancient authorities lack this sentence

gift of God, and who it is that is saying to you, 'Give me a drink,' you would have asked him, and he would have given you living water." 11 The woman said to him, "Sir, you have no bucket, and the well is deep. Where do you get that living water? 12 Are you greater than our ancestor Jacob, who gave us the well, and with his sons and his flocks drank from it?" 13 Jesus said to her, "Everyone who drinks of this water will be thirsty again, 14 but those who drink of the water that I will give them will never be thirsty. The water that I will give will become in them a spring of water gushing up to eternal life." 15 The woman said to him, "Sir, give me this water, so that I may never be thirsty or have to keep coming here to draw water."

16 Jesus said to her, "Go, call your husband, and come back." 17 The woman answered him, "I have no husband." Jesus said to her, "You are right in saying, 'I have no husband'; 18 for you have had five husbands, and the one you have now is not your husband. What you have said is true!" 19 The woman said to him, "Sir, I see that you are a prophet. 20 Our ancestors worshiped on this mountain, but you[a] say that the place where people must worship is in Jerusalem." 21 Jesus said to her, "Woman, believe me, the hour is coming when you will worship the Father neither on this mountain nor in Jerusalem. 22 You worship what you do not know; we worship what we know, for salvation is from the Jews. 23 But the hour is coming, and is now here, when the true worshipers will worship the Father in spirit and truth, for the Father seeks such as these to worship him. 24 God is spirit, and those who worship him must worship in spirit and truth." 25 The woman said to him, "I know that Messiah is coming" (who is called Christ). "When he comes, he will proclaim all things to us." 26 Jesus said to her, "I am he,[b] the one who is speaking to you."

27 Just then his disciples came. They were astonished that he was speaking with a woman, but no one said, "What do you want?" or, "Why are you speaking with her?" 28 Then the woman left her water jar and went back to the city. She said to the people, 29 "Come and see a man who told me everything I have ever done! He cannot be the Messiah,[c] can he?" 30 They left the city and were on their way to him.

31 Meanwhile the disciples were urging him, "Rabbi, eat something." 32 But he said to them, "I have food to eat that you do not know about." 33 So the disciples said to one another, "Surely no one has brought him something to eat?" 34 Jesus said to them, "My food is to do the will of him who sent me and to complete his work. 35 Do you not say, 'Four months more, then comes the harvest'? But I tell you, look around you, and see how the fields are ripe for harvesting. 36 The reaper is already receiving[d] wages and is gathering fruit for eternal life, so that sower and reaper may rejoice together. 37 For here the saying holds true, 'One sows and another reaps.' 38 I sent you to reap that for which you did not labor. Others have labored, and you have entered into their labor."

39 Many Samaritans from that city believed in him because of the woman's testimony, "He told me everything I have ever done." 40 So when the Samaritans came to him, they asked him to stay with them; and he stayed there two days. 41 And many more believed because of his word. 42 They said to the woman, "It is no longer because of what you said that we believe, for we have heard for ourselves, and we know that this is truly the Savior of the world."

43 When the two days were over, he went from that place to Galilee 44 (for Jesus himself had testified that a prophet has no honor in the prophet's own country). 45 When he came to Galilee, the Galileans welcomed him, since they had seen all that he had done in Jerusalem at the festival; for they too had gone to the festival.

46 Then he came again to Cana in Galilee where he had changed the water into wine. Now there was a royal official whose son lay ill in Capernaum. 47 When he heard that Jesus had come from Judea to Galilee, he went and begged him to come down and heal his son, for he was at the point of death. 48 Then Jesus said to him, "Unless you[e] see signs and wonders you will not believe." 49 The official said to him, "Sir, come down before my little boy dies." 50 Jesus said to him, "Go; your son will live." The man believed the word that Jesus spoke to him and started on his way.

[a]The Greek word for *you* here and in verses 21 and 22 is plural [b]Gk *I am* [c]Or *the Christ* [d]Or [35]. . . *the fields are already ripe for harvesting.* [36]*The reaper is receiving* [e]Both instances of the Greek word for *you* in this verse are plural

51 As he was going down, his slaves met him and told him that his child was alive. 52 So he asked them the hour when he began to recover, and they said to him, "Yesterday at one in the afternoon the fever left him." 53 The father realized that this was the hour when Jesus had said to him, "Your son will live." So he himself believed, along with his whole household. 54 Now this was the second sign that Jesus did after coming from Judea to Galilee.

5 After this there was a festival of the Jews, and Jesus went up to Jerusalem.

2 Now in Jerusalem by the Sheep Gate there is a pool, called in Hebrew[f] Beth-zatha,[g] which has five porticoes. 3 In these lay many invalids—blind, lame, and paralyzed.[h] 5 One man was there who had been ill for thirty-eight years. 6 When Jesus saw him lying there and knew that he had been there a long time, he said to him, "Do you want to be made well?" 7 The sick man answered him, "Sir, I have no one to put me into the pool when the water is stirred up; and while I am making my way, someone else steps down ahead of me." 8 Jesus said to him, "Stand up, take your mat and walk." 9 At once the man was made well, and he took up his mat and began to walk.

Now that day was a sabbath. 10 So the Jews said to the man who had been cured, "It is the sabbath; it is not lawful for you to carry your mat." 11 But he answered them, "The man who made me well said to me, 'Take up your mat and walk.'" 12 They asked him, "Who is the man who said to you, 'Take it up and walk'?" 13 Now the man who had been healed did not know who it was, for Jesus had disappeared in[i] the crowd that was there. 14 Later Jesus found him in the temple and said to him, "See, you have been made well! Do not sin any more, so that nothing worse happens to you." 15 The man went away and told the Jews that it was Jesus who had made him well. 16 Therefore the Jews started persecuting Jesus, because he was doing such things on the sabbath. 17 But Jesus answered them, "My Father is still working, and I also am working." 18 For this reason the Jews were seeking all the more to kill him, because he was not only breaking the sabbath, but was also calling God his own Father, thereby making himself equal to God.

19 Jesus said to them, "Very truly, I tell you, the Son can do nothing on his own, but only what he sees the Father doing; for whatever the Father[j] does, the Son does likewise. 20 The Father loves the Son and shows him all that he himself is doing; and he will show him greater works than these, so that you will be astonished. 21 Indeed, just as the Father raises the dead and gives them life, so also the Son gives life to whomever he wishes. 22 The Father judges no one but has given all judgment to the Son, 23 so that all may honor the Son just as they honor the Father. Anyone who does not honor the Son does not honor the Father who sent him. 24 Very truly, I tell you, anyone who hears my word and believes him who sent me has eternal life, and does not come under judgment, but has passed from death to life.

25 "Very truly, I tell you, the hour is coming, and is now here, when the dead will hear the voice of the Son of God, and those who hear will live. 26 For just as the Father has life in himself, so he has granted the Son also to have life in himself; 27 and he has given him authority to execute judgment, because he is the Son of Man. 28 Do not be astonished at this; for the hour is coming when all who are in their graves will hear his voice 29 and will come out—those who have done good, to the resurrection of life, and those who have done evil, to the resurrection of condemnation.

30 "I can do nothing on my own. As I hear, I judge; and my judgment is just, because I seek to do not my own will but the will of him who sent me.

31 "If I testify about myself, my testimony is not true. 32 There is another who testifies on my behalf, and I know that his testimony to me is true. 33 You sent messengers to John, and he testified to the truth. 34 Not that I accept such human testimony, but I say these things so that you may be saved. 35 He was a burning and shining lamp, and you were willing to rejoice for a while in his light. 36 But I have a testimony greater than John's. The works that the Father has given me to complete,

[f]That is, *Aramaic* [g]Other ancient authorities read *Bethesda*, others *Bethsaida* [h]Other ancient authorities add, wholly or in part, *waiting for the stirring of the water; [4]for an angel of the Lord went down at certain seasons into the pool, and stirred up the water; whoever stepped in first after the stirring of the water was made well from whatever disease that person had.* [i]Or had left because of [j]Gk *that one*

the very works that I am doing, testify on my behalf that the Father has sent me. 37 And the Father who sent me has himself testified on my behalf. You have never heard his voice or seen his form, 38 and you do not have his word abiding in you, because you do not believe him whom he has sent.

39 "You search the scriptures because you think that in them you have eternal life; and it is they that testify on my behalf. 40 Yet you refuse to come to me to have life. 41 I do not accept glory from human beings. 42 But I know that you do not have the love of God in [k] you. 43 I have come in my Father's name, and you do not accept me; if another comes in his own name, you will accept him. 44 How can you believe when you accept glory from one another and do not seek the glory that comes from the one who alone is God? 45 Do not think that I will accuse you before the Father; your accuser is Moses, on whom you have set your hope. 46 If you believed Moses, you would believe me, for he wrote about me. 47 But if you do not believe what he wrote, how will you believe what I say?"

6 After this Jesus went to the other side of the Sea of Galilee, also called the Sea of Tiberias.[l] 2 A large crowd kept following him, because they saw the signs that he was doing for the sick. 3 Jesus went up the mountain and sat down there with his disciples. 4 Now the Passover, the festival of the Jews, was near. 5 When he looked up and saw a large crowd coming toward him, Jesus said to Philip, "Where are we to buy bread for these people to eat?" 6 He said this to test him, for he himself knew what he was going to do. 7 Philip answered him, "Six months' wages[m] would not buy enough bread for each of them to get a little." 8 One of his disciples, Andrew, Simon Peter's brother, said to him, 9 "There is a boy here who has five barley loaves and two fish. But what are they among so many people?" 10 Jesus said, "Make the people sit down." Now there was a great deal of grass in the place; so they[n] sat down, about five thousand in all. 11 Then Jesus took the loaves, and when he had given thanks, he distributed them to those who were seated; so also the fish, as much as they wanted. 12 When they were satisfied, he told his disciples, "Gather up the fragments left over, so that

nothing may be lost." 13 So they gathered them up, and from the fragments of the five barley loaves, left by those who had eaten, they filled twelve baskets. 14 When the people saw the sign that he had done, they began to say, "This is indeed the prophet who is to come into the world."

15 When Jesus realized that they were about to come and take him by force to make him king, he withdrew again to the mountain by himself.

16 When evening came, his disciples went down to the sea, 17 got into a boat, and started across the sea to Capernaum. It was now dark, and Jesus had not yet come to them. 18 The sea became rough because a strong wind was blowing. 19 When they had rowed about three or four miles,[o] they saw Jesus walking on the sea and coming near the boat, and they were terrified. 20 But he said to them, "It is I;[p] do not be afraid." 21 Then they wanted to take him into the boat, and immediately the boat reached the land toward which they were going.

22 The next day the crowd that had stayed on the other side of the sea saw that there had been only one boat there. They also saw that Jesus had not got into the boat with his disciples, but that his disciples had gone away alone. 23 Then some boats from Tiberias came near the place where they had eaten the bread after the Lord had given thanks.[q] 24 So when the crowd saw that neither Jesus nor his disciples were there, they themselves got into the boats and went to Capernaum looking for Jesus.

25 When they found him on the other side of the sea, they said to him, "Rabbi, when did you come here?" 26 Jesus answered them, "Very truly, I tell you, you are looking for me, not because you saw signs, but because you ate your fill of the loaves. 27 Do not work for the food that perishes, but for the food that endures for eternal life, which the Son of Man will give you. For it is on him that God the Father has set his seal." 28 Then they said to him, "What must we do to perform the works of God?" 29 Jesus answered them, "This is the work of God, that you believe in him whom he has sent." 30 So they said to him, "What sign are you going to give us then, so that we may see it and believe

---

[k]Or *among*   [l]Gk *of Galilee of Tiberias*   [m]Gk *Two hundred denarii*; the denarius was the usual day's wage for a laborer   [n]Gk *the men*   [o]Gk *about twenty-five or thirty stadia*   [p]Gk *I am*   [q]Other ancient authorities lack *after the Lord had given thanks*

you? What work are you performing? 31 Our ancestors ate the manna in the wilderness; as it is written, 'He gave them bread from heaven to eat.'[3] 32 Then Jesus said to them, "Very truly I tell you, it was not Moses who gave you the bread from heaven, but it is my Father who gives you the true bread from heaven. 33 For the bread of God is that which[r] comes down from heaven and gives life to the world." 34 They said to him, "Sir, give us this bread always."

35 Jesus said to them, "I am the bread of life. Whoever comes to me will never be hungry, and whoever believes in me will never be thirsty. 36 But I said to you that you have seen me and yet do not believe. 37 Everything that the Father gives me will come to me, and anyone who comes to me I will never drive away; 38 for I have come down from heaven, not to do my own will, but the will of him who sent me. 39 And this is the will of him who sent me, that I should lose nothing of all that he has given me, but raise it up on the last day. 40 This is indeed the will of my Father, that all who see the Son and believe in him may have eternal life; and I will raise them up on the last day."

41 Then the Jews began to complain about him because he said, "I am the bread that came down from heaven." 42 They were saying, "Is not this Jesus, the son of Joseph, whose father and mother we know? How can he now say, 'I have come down from heaven'?" 43 Jesus answered them, "Do not complain among yourselves. 44 No one can come to me unless drawn by the Father who sent me; and I will raise that person up on the last day. 45 It is written in the prophets, 'And they shall all be taught by God.'[4] Everyone who has heard and learned from the Father comes to me. 46 Not that anyone has seen the Father except the one who is from God; he has seen the Father. 47 Very truly, I tell you, whoever believes has eternal life. 48 I am the bread of life. 49 Your ancestors ate the manna in the wilderness, and they died. 50 This is the bread that comes down from heaven, so that one may eat of it and not die. 51 I am the living bread that came down from heaven. Whoever eats of this bread will live forever; and the bread that I will give for the life of the world is my flesh."

52 The Jews then disputed among themselves, saying, "How can this man give us his flesh to eat?" 53 So Jesus said to them, "Very truly, I tell you, unless you eat the flesh of the Son of Man and drink his blood, you have no life in you. 54 Those who eat my flesh and drink my blood have eternal life, and I will raise them up on the last day; 55 for my flesh is true food and my blood is true drink. 56 Those who eat my flesh and drink my blood abide in me, and I in them. 57 Just as the living Father sent me, and I live because of the Father, so whoever eats me will live because of me. 58 This is the bread that came down from heaven, not like that which your ancestors ate, and they died. But the one who eats this bread will live forever." 59 He said these things while he was teaching in the synagogue at Capernaum.

60 When many of his disciples heard it, they said, "This teaching is difficult; who can accept it?" 61 But Jesus, being aware that his disciples were complaining about it, said to them, "Does this offend you? 62 Then what if you were to see the Son of Man ascending to where he was before? 63 It is the spirit that gives life; the flesh is useless. The words that I have spoken to you are spirit and life. 64 But among you there are some who do not believe." For Jesus knew from the first who were the ones that did not believe, and who was the one that would betray him. 65 And he said, "For this reason I have told you that no one can come to me unless it is granted by the Father."

66 Because of this many of his disciples turned back and no longer went about with him. 67 So Jesus asked the twelve, "Do you also wish to go away?" 68 Simon Peter answered him, "Lord, to whom can we go? You have the words of eternal life. 69 We have come to believe and know that you are the Holy One of God."[s] 70 Jesus answered them, "Did I not choose you, the twelve? Yet one of you is a devil." 71 He was speaking of Judas son of Simon Iscariot,[t] for he, though one of the twelve, was going to betray him.

7 After this Jesus went about in Galilee. He did not wish[u] to go about in Judea because

---

[r]Or *he who* [s]Other ancient authorities read *the Christ, the Son of the living God* [t]Other ancient authorities read *Judas Iscariot son of Simon;* others, *Judas son of Simon from Karyot* (Kerioth) [u]Other ancient authorities read *was not at liberty*

---

[3]Ps 78:24 [4]Isa 54:13

the Jews were looking for an opportunity to kill him. 2 Now the Jewish festival of Booths[v] was near. 3 So his brothers said to him, "Leave here and go to Judea so that your disciples also may see the works you are doing; 4 for no one who wants[w] to be widely known acts in secret. If you do these things, show yourself to the world." 5 (For not even his brothers believed in him.) 6 Jesus said to them, "My time has not yet come, but your time is always here. 7 The world cannot hate you, but it hates me because I testify against it that its works are evil. 8 Go to the festival yourselves. I am not[x] going to this festival, for my time has not yet fully come." 9 After saying this, he remained in Galilee.

10 But after his brothers had gone to the festival, then he also went, not publicly but as it were[y] in secret. 11 The Jews were looking for him at the festival and saying, "Where is he?" 12 And there was considerable complaining about him among the crowds. While some were saying, "He is a good man," others were saying, "No, he is deceiving the crowd." 13 Yet no one would speak openly about him for fear of the Jews.

14 About the middle of the festival Jesus went up into the temple and began to teach. 15 The Jews were astonished at it, saying, "How does this man have such learning,[z] when he has never been taught?" 16 Then Jesus answered them, "My teaching is not mine but his who sent me. 17 Anyone who resolves to do the will of God will know whether the teaching is from God or whether I am speaking on my own. 18 Those who speak on their own seek their own glory; but the one who seeks the glory of him who sent him is true, and there is nothing false in him.

19 "Did not Moses give you the law? Yet none of you keeps the law. Why are you looking for an opportunity to kill me?" 20 The crowd answered, "You have a demon! Who is trying to kill you?" 21 Jesus answered them, "I performed one work, and all of you are astonished. 22 Moses gave you circumcision (it is, of course, not from Moses, but from the patriarchs), and you circumcise a man on the sabbath. 23 If a man receives circumcision on the sabbath in order that the law of Moses may not be broken, are you angry with me because I healed a man's whole body on the sabbath? 24 Do

not judge by appearances, but judge with right judgment."

25 Now some of the people of Jerusalem were saying, "Is not this the man whom they are trying to kill? 26 And here he is, speaking openly, but they say nothing to him! Can it be that the authorities really know that this is the Messiah?[a] 27 Yet we know where this man is from; but when the Messiah[a] comes, no one will know where he is from." 28 Then Jesus cried out as he was teaching in the temple, "You know me, and you know where I am from. I have not come on my own. But the one who sent me is true, and you do not know him. 29 I know him, because I am from him, and he sent me." 30 Then they tried to arrest him, but no one laid hands on him, because his hour had not yet come. 31 Yet many in the crowd believed in him and were saying, "When the Messiah[a] comes, will he do more signs than this man has done?"[b]

32 The Pharisees heard the crowd muttering such things about him, and the chief priests and Pharisees sent temple police to arrest him. 33 Jesus then said, "I will be with you a little while longer, and then I am going to him who sent me. 34 You will search for me, but you will not find me; and where I am, you cannot come." 35 The Jews said to one another, "Where does this man intend to go that we will not find him? Does he intend to go to the Dispersion among the Greeks and teach the Greeks? 36 What does he mean by saying, 'You will search for me and you will not find me' and 'Where I am, you cannot come'?"

37 On the last day of the festival, the great day, while Jesus was standing there, he cried out, "Let anyone who is thirsty come to me, 38 and let the one who believes in me drink. As[c] the scripture has said, 'Out of the believer's heart[d] shall flow rivers of living water.'" 39 Now he said this about the Spirit, which believers in him were to receive; for as yet there was no Spirit,[e] because Jesus was not yet glorified.

40 When they heard these words, some in the

[v] Or *Tabernacles*   [w] Other ancient authorities read *wants i*   [x] Other ancient authorities add *yet*   [y] Other ancient authorities lack *as it were*   [z] Or *this man know his letters*   [a] Or *the Christ*   [b] Other ancient authorities read *is doing*   [c] Or *come to me and drink.* [38] *The one who believes in me, as*   [d] Gk *out of his belly*   [e] Other ancient authorities read *for as yet the Spirit* (others, *Holy Spirit*) *had not been given*

crowd said, "This is really the prophet." 41 Others said, "This is the Messiah."[f] But some asked, "Surely the Messiah[f] does not come from Galilee, does he? 42 Has not the scripture said that the Messiah[f] is descended from David and comes from Bethlehem, the village where David lived?" 43 So there was a division in the crowd because of him. 44 Some of them wanted to arrest him, but no one laid hands on him.

45 Then the temple police went back to the chief priests and Pharisees, who asked them, "Why did you not arrest him?" 46 The police answered, "Never has anyone spoken like this!" 47 Then the Pharisees replied, "Surely you have not been deceived too, have you? 48 Has any one of the authorities or of the Pharisees believed in him? 49 But this crowd, which does not know the law— they are accursed." 50 Nicodemus, who had gone to Jesus[g] before, and who was one of them, asked, 51 "Our law does not judge people without first giving them a hearing to find out what they are doing, does it?" 52 They replied, "Surely you are not also from Galilee, are you? Search and you will see that no prophet is to arise from Galilee."

8 [53 Then each of them went home, 1 while Jesus went to the Mount of Olives. 2 Early in the morning he came again to the temple. All the people came to him and he sat down and began to teach them. 3 The scribes and the Pharisees brought a woman who had been caught in adultery; and making her stand before all of them, 4 they said to him, "Teacher, this woman was caught in the very act of committing adultery. 5 Now in the law Moses commanded us to stone such women. Now what do you say?" 6 They said this to test him, so that they might have some charge to bring against him. Jesus bent down and wrote with his finger on the ground. 7 When they kept on questioning him, he straightened up and said to them, "Let anyone among you who is without sin be the first to throw a stone at her." 8 And once again he bent down and wrote on the ground.[h] 9 When they heard it, they went away, one by one, beginning with the elders; and Jesus was left alone with the woman standing before him. 10 Jesus straightened up and said to her, "Woman, where are they? Has no one condemned you?" 11 She said, "No one, sir."[i] And Jesus said, "Neither do I condemn you. Go your way, and from now on do not sin again."][j]

12 Again Jesus spoke to them, saying, "I am the light of the world. Whoever follows me will never walk in darkness but will have the light of life." 13 Then the Pharisees said to him, "You are testifying on your own behalf; your testimony is not valid." 14 Jesus answered, "Even if I testify on my own behalf, my testimony is valid because I know where I have come from and where I am going, but you do not know where I come from or where I am going. 15 You judge by human standards;[k] I judge no one. 16 Yet even if I do judge, my judgment is valid; for it is not I alone who judge, but I and the Father[l] who sent me. 17 In your law it is written that the testimony of two witnesses is valid. 18 I testify on my own behalf, and the Father who sent me testifies on my behalf." 19 Then they said to him, "Where is your Father?" Jesus answered, "You know neither me nor my Father. If you knew me, you would know my Father also." 20 He spoke these words while he was teaching in the treasury of the temple, but no one arrested him, because his hour had not yet come.

21 Again he said to them, "I am going away, and you will search for me, but you will die in your sin. Where I am going, you cannot come." 22 Then the Jews said, "Is he going to kill himself? Is that what he means by saying, 'Where I am going, you cannot come'?" 23 He said to them, "You are from below, I am from above; you are of this world, I am not of this world. 24 I told you that you would die in your sins, for you will die in your sins unless you believe that I am he."[m] 25 They said to him, "Who are you?" Jesus said to them, "Why do I speak to you at all?[n] 26 I have much to say about you and much to condemn; but the one who sent me is true, and I declare to the world what I have heard from him." 27 They did not understand that he was speaking to them about the Father. 28 So Jesus said, "When you have lifted up

[f]Or *the Christ* [g]Gk *him* [h]Other ancient authorities add *the sins of each of them* [i]Or *Lord* [j]The most ancient authorities lack 7.53— 8.11; other authorities add the passage here or after 7.36 or after 21.25 or after Luke 21.38, with variations of text; some mark the passage as doubtful. [k]Gk *according to the flesh* [l]Other ancient authorities read *he* [m]Gk *I am* [n]Or *What I have told you from the beginning*

the Son of Man, then you will realize that I am he,[o] and that I do nothing on my own, but I speak these things as the Father instructed me. 29 And the one who sent me is with me; he has not left me alone, for I always do what is pleasing to him." 30 As he was saying these things, many believed in him.

31 Then Jesus said to the Jews who had believed in him, "If you continue in my word, you are truly my disciples; 32 and you will know the truth, and the truth will make you free." 33 They answered him, "We are descendants of Abraham and have never been slaves to anyone. What do you mean by saying, 'You will be made free'?"

34 Jesus answered them, "Very truly, I tell you, everyone who commits sin is a slave to sin. 35 The slave does not have a permanent place in the household; the son has a place there forever. 36 So if the Son makes you free, you will be free indeed. 37 I know that you are descendants of Abraham; yet you look for an opportunity to kill me, because there is no place in you for my word. 38 I declare what I have seen in the Father's presence; as for you, you should do what you have heard from the Father."[p]

39 They answered him, "Abraham is our father." Jesus said to them, "If you were Abraham's children, you would be doing[q] what Abraham did, 40 but now you are trying to kill me, a man who has told you the truth that I heard from God. This is not what Abraham did. 41 You are indeed doing what your father does." They said to him, "We are not illegitimate children; we have one father, God himself." 42 Jesus said to them, "If God were your Father, you would love me, for I came from God and now I am here. I did not come on my own, but he sent me. 43 Why do you not understand what I say? It is because you cannot accept my word. 44 You are from your father the devil, and you choose to do your father's desires. He was a murderer from the beginning and does not stand in the truth, because there is no truth in him. When he lies, he speaks according to his own nature, for he is a liar and the father of lies. 45 But because I tell the truth, you do not believe me. 46 Which of you convicts me of sin? If I tell the truth, why do you not believe me? 47 Whoever is from God hears the words of God. The reason you do not hear them is that you are not from God."

48 The Jews answered him, "Are we not right in saying that you are a Samaritan and have a demon?" 49 Jesus answered, "I do not have a demon; but I honor my Father, and you dishonor me. 50 Yet I do not seek my own glory; there is one who seeks it and he is the judge. 51 Very truly, I tell you, whoever keeps my word will never see death." 52 The Jews said to him, "Now we know that you have a demon. Abraham died, and so did the prophets; yet you say, 'Whoever keeps my word will never taste death.' 53 Are you greater than our father Abraham, who died? The prophets also died. Who do you claim to be?" 54 Jesus answered, "If I glorify myself, my glory is nothing. It is my Father who glorifies me, he of whom you say, 'He is our God,' 55 though you do not know him. But I know him; if I would say that I do not know him, I would be a liar like you. But I do know him and I keep his word. 56 Your ancestor Abraham rejoiced that he would see my day; he saw it and was glad." 57 Then the Jews said to him, "You are not yet fifty years old, and have you seen Abraham?"[r] 58 Jesus said to them, "Very truly, I tell you, before Abraham was, I am." 59 So they picked up stones to throw at him, but Jesus hid himself and went out of the temple.

9 As he walked along, he saw a man blind from birth. 2 His disciples asked him, "Rabbi, who sinned, this man or his parents, that he was born blind?" 3 Jesus answered, "Neither this man nor his parents sinned; he was born blind so that God's works might be revealed in him. 4 We[s] must work the works of him who sent me[t] while it is day; night is coming when no one can work. 5 As long as I am in the world, I am the light of the world." 6 When he had said this, he spat on the ground and made mud with the saliva and spread the mud on the man's eyes, 7 saying to him, "Go, wash in the pool of Siloam" (which means Sent). Then he went and washed and came back able to see. 8 The neighbors and those who had seen him before as a beggar began to ask, "Is this not the man who used to sit and beg?" 9 Some were say-

[o]Gk I am   [p]Other ancient authorities read you do what you have heard from your father   [q]Other ancient authorities read If you are Abraham's children, then do   [r]Other ancient authorities read has Abraham seen you?   [s]Other ancient authorities read I   [t]Other ancient authorities read us

ing, "It is he." Others were saying, "No, but it is someone like him." He kept saying, "I am the man." 10 But they kept asking him, "Then how were your eyes opened?" 11 He answered, "The man called Jesus made mud, spread it on my eyes, and said to me, 'Go to Siloam and wash.' Then I went and washed and received my sight." 12 They said to him, "Where is he?" He said, "I do not know."

13 They brought to the Pharisees the man who had formerly been blind. 14 Now it was a sabbath day when Jesus made the mud and opened his eyes. 15 Then the Pharisees also began to ask him how he had received his sight. He said to them, "He put mud on my eyes. Then I washed, and now I see." 16 Some of the Pharisees said, "This man is not from God, for he does not observe the sabbath." But others said, "How can a man who is a sinner perform such signs?" And they were divided. 17 So they said again to the blind man, "What do you say about him? It was your eyes he opened." He said, "He is a prophet."

18 The Jews did not believe that he had been blind and had received his sight until they called the parents of the man who had received his sight 19 and asked them, "Is this your son, who you say was born blind? How then does he now see?" 20 His parents answered, "We know that this is our son, and that he was born blind; 21 but we do not know how it is that now he sees, nor do we know who opened his eyes. Ask him; he is of age. He will speak for himself." 22 His parents said this because they were afraid of the Jews; for the Jews had already agreed that anyone who confessed Jesus[u] to be the Messiah[v] would be put out of the synagogue. 23 Therefore his parents said, "He is of age; ask him."

24 So for the second time they called the man who had been blind, and they said to him, "Give glory to God! We know that this man is a sinner." 25 He answered, "I do not know whether he is a sinner. One thing I do know, that though I was blind, now I see." 26 They said to him, "What did he do to you? How did he open your eyes?" 27 He answered them, "I have told you already, and you would not listen. Why do you want to hear it again? Do you also want to become his disciples?" 28 Then they reviled him, saying, "You are his dis-

ciple, but we are disciples of Moses. 29 We know that God has spoken to Moses, but as for this man, we do not know where he comes from." 30 The man answered, "Here is an astonishing thing! You do not know where he comes from, and yet he opened my eyes. 31 We know that God does not listen to sinners, but he does listen to one who worships him and obeys his will. 32 Never since the world began has it been heard that anyone opened the eyes of a person born blind. 33 If this man were not from God, he could do nothing." 34 They answered him, "You were born entirely in sins, and are you trying to teach us?" And they drove him out.

35 Jesus heard that they had driven him out, and when he found him, he said, "Do you believe in the Son of Man?"[w] 36 He answered, "And who is he, sir?[x] Tell me, so that I may believe in him." 37 Jesus said to him, "You have seen him, and the one speaking with you is he." 38 He said, "Lord,[x] I believe." And he worshiped him. 39 Jesus said, "I came into this world for judgment so that those who do not see may see, and those who do see may become blind." 40 Some of the Pharisees near him heard this and said to him, "Surely we are not blind, are we?" 41 Jesus said to them, "If you were blind, you would not have sin. But now that you say, 'We see,' your sin remains.

10 "Very truly, I tell you, anyone who does not enter the sheepfold by the gate but climbs in by another way is a thief and a bandit. 2 The one who enters by the gate is the shepherd of the sheep. 3 The gatekeeper opens the gate for him, and the sheep hear his voice. He calls his own sheep by name and leads them out. 4 When he has brought out all his own, he goes ahead of them, and the sheep follow him because they know his voice. 5 They will not follow a stranger, but they will run from him because they do not know the voice of strangers." 6 Jesus used this figure of speech with them, but they did not understand what he was saying to them.

7 So again Jesus said to them, "Very truly, I tell you, I am the gate for the sheep. 8 All who came before me are thieves and bandits; but the sheep

---

[u] Gk him [v] Or the Christ [w] Other ancient authorities read the Son of God [x] Sir and Lord translate the same Greek word

did not listen to them. 9 I am the gate. Whoever enters by me will be saved, and will come in and go out and find pasture. 10 The thief comes only to steal and kill and destroy. I came that they may have life, and have it abundantly.

11 "I am the good shepherd. The good shepherd lays down his life for the sheep. 12 The hired hand, who is not the shepherd and does not own the sheep, sees the wolf coming and leaves the sheep and runs away—and the wolf snatches them and scatters them. 13 The hired hand runs away because a hired hand does not care for the sheep. 14 I am the good shepherd. I know my own and my own know me, 15 just as the Father knows me and I know the Father. And I lay down my life for the sheep. 16 I have other sheep that do not belong to this fold. I must bring them also, and they will listen to my voice. So there will be one flock, one shepherd. 17 For this reason the Father loves me, because I lay down my life in order to take it up again. 18 No one takesʸ it from me, but I lay it down of my own accord. I have power to lay it down, and I have power to take it up again. I have received this command from my Father."

19 Again the Jews were divided because of these words. 20 Many of them were saying, "He has a demon and is out of his mind. Why listen to him?" 21 Others were saying, "These are not the words of one who has a demon. Can a demon open the eyes of the blind?"

22 At that time the festival of the Dedication took place in Jerusalem. It was winter, 23 and Jesus was walking in the temple, in the portico of Solomon. 24 So the Jews gathered around him and said to him, "How long will you keep us in suspense? If you are the Messiah,ᶻ tell us plainly." 25 Jesus answered, "I have told you, and you do not believe. The works that I do in my Father's name testify to me; 26 but you do not believe, because you do not belong to my sheep. 27 My sheep hear my voice. I know them, and they follow me. 28 I give them eternal life, and they will never perish. No one will snatch them out of my hand. 29 What my Father has given me is greater than all else, and no one can snatch it out of the Father's hand.ᵃ 30 The Father and I are one."

31 The Jews took up stones again to stone him. 32 Jesus replied, "I have shown you many good works from the Father. For which of these are you going to stone me?" 33 The Jews answered, "It is not for a good work that we are going to stone you, but for blasphemy, because you, though only a human being, are making yourself God." 34 Jesus answered, "Is it not written in your law,ᵇ 'I said, you are gods'?⁵ 35 If those to whom the word of God came were called 'gods'—and the scripture cannot be annulled— 36 can you say that the one whom the Father has sanctified and sent into the world is blaspheming because I said, 'I am God's Son'? 37 If I am not doing the works of my Father, then do not believe me. 38 But if I do them, even though you do not believe me, believe the works, so that you may know and understandᶜ that the Father is in me and I am in the Father." 39 Then they tried to arrest him again, but he escaped from their hands.

40 He went away again across the Jordan to the place where John had been baptizing earlier, and he remained there. 41 Many came to him, and they were saying, "John performed no sign, but everything that John said about this man was true." 42 And many believed in him there.

11 Now a certain man was ill, Lazarus of Bethany, the village of Mary and her sister Martha. 2 Mary was the one who anointed the Lord with perfume and wiped his feet with her hair; her brother Lazarus was ill. 3 So the sisters sent a message to Jesus,ᵈ "Lord, he whom you love is ill." 4 But when Jesus heard it, he said, "This illness does not lead to death; rather it is for God's glory, so that the Son of God may be glorified through it." 5 Accordingly, though Jesus loved Martha and her sister and Lazarus, 6 after having heard that Lazarusᵉ was ill, he stayed two days longer in the place where he was.

7 Then after this he said to the disciples, "Let us go to Judea again." 8 The disciples said to him, "Rabbi, the Jews were just now trying to stone you, and are you going there again?" 9 Jesus answered, "Are there not twelve hours of daylight? Those who walk during the day do not stumble,

---

ʸOther ancient authorities read *has taken*   ᶻOr *the Christ*   ᵃOther ancient authorities read *My Father who has given them to me is greater than all, and no one can snatch them out of the Father's hand*   ᵇOther ancient authorities read *in the law*   ᶜOther ancient authorities lack *and understand*; others read *and believe*   ᵈGk *him*   ᵉGk *he*

⁵Ps 82:6

because they see the light of this world. 10 But those who walk at night stumble, because the light is not in them." 11 After saying this, he told them, "Our friend Lazarus has fallen asleep, but I am going there to awaken him." 12 The disciples said to him, "Lord, if he has fallen asleep, he will be all right." 13 Jesus, however, had been speaking about his death, but they thought that he was referring merely to sleep. 14 Then Jesus told them plainly, "Lazarus is dead. 15 For your sake I am glad I was not there, so that you may believe. But let us go to him." 16 Thomas, who was called the Twin,[f] said to his fellow disciples, "Let us also go, that we may die with him."

17 When Jesus arrived, he found that Lazarus[g]had already been in the tomb four days. 18 Now Bethany was near Jerusalem, some two miles[h] away, 19 and many of the Jews had come to Martha and Mary to console them about their brother. 20 When Martha heard that Jesus was coming, she went and met him, while Mary stayed at home. 21 Martha said to Jesus, "Lord, if you had been here, my brother would not have died. 22 But even now I know that God will give you whatever you ask of him." 23 Jesus said to her, "Your brother will rise again." 24 Martha said to him, "I know that he will rise again in the resurrection on the last day." 25 Jesus said to her, "I am the resurrection and the life.[i] Those who believe in me, even though they die, will live, 26 and everyone who lives and believes in me will never die. Do you believe this?" 27 She said to him, "Yes, Lord, I believe that you are the Messiah,[j] the Son of God, the one coming into the world."

28 When she had said this, she went back and called her sister Mary, and told her privately, "The Teacher is here and is calling for you." 29 And when she heard it, she got up quickly and went to him. 30 Now Jesus had not yet come to the village, but was still at the place where Martha had met him. 31 The Jews who were with her in the house, consoling her, saw Mary get up quickly and go out. They followed her because they thought that she was going to the tomb to weep there. 32 When Mary came where Jesus was and saw him, she knelt at his feet and said to him, "Lord, if you had been here, my brother would not have died." 33 When Jesus saw her weeping, and the Jews who came with her also weeping, he was

greatly disturbed in spirit and deeply moved. 34 He said, "Where have you laid him?" They said to him, "Lord, come and see." 35 Jesus began to weep. 36 So the Jews said, "See how he loved him!" 37 But some of them said, "Could not he who opened the eyes of the blind man have kept this man from dying?"

38 Then Jesus, again greatly disturbed, came to the tomb. It was a cave, and a stone was lying against it. 39 Jesus said, "Take away the stone." Martha, the sister of the dead man, said to him, "Lord, already there is a stench because he has been dead four days." 40 Jesus said to her, "Did I not tell you that if you believed, you would see the glory of God?" 41 So they took away the stone. And Jesus looked upward and said, "Father, I thank you for having heard me. 42 I knew that you always hear me, but I have said this for the sake of the crowd standing here, so that they may believe that you sent me." 43 When he had said this, he cried with a loud voice, "Lazarus, come out!" 44 The dead man came out, his hands and feet bound with strips of cloth, and his face wrapped in a cloth. Jesus said to them, "Unbind him, and let him go."

45 Many of the Jews therefore, who had come with Mary and had seen what Jesus did, believed in him. 46 But some of them went to the Pharisees and told them what he had done. 47 So the chief priests and the Pharisees called a meeting of the council, and said, "What are we to do? This man is performing many signs. 48 If we let him go on like this, everyone will believe in him, and the Romans will come and destroy both our holy place[k] and our nation." 49 But one of them, Caiaphas, who was high priest that year, said to them, "You know nothing at all! 50 You do not understand that it is better for you to have one man die for the people than to have the whole nation destroyed." 51 He did not say this on his own, but being high priest that year he prophesied that Jesus was about to die for the nation, 52 and not for the nation only, but to gather into one the dispersed children of God. 53 So from that day on they planned to put him to death.

54 Jesus therefore no longer walked about open-

[f]Gk *Didymus* [g]Gk *he* [h]Gk *fifteen stadia* [i]Other ancient authorities lack *and the life* [j]Or *the Christ* [k]Or *our temple*; Greek *our place*

ly among the Jews, but went from there to a town called Ephraim in the region near the wilderness; and he remained there with the disciples.

55 Now the Passover of the Jews was near, and many went up from the country to Jerusalem before the Passover to purify themselves. 56 They were looking for Jesus and were asking one another as they stood in the temple, "What do you think? Surely he will not come to the festival, will he?" 57 Now the chief priests and the Pharisees had given orders that anyone who knew where Jesus[l] was should let them know, so that they might arrest him.

12 Six days before the Passover Jesus came to Bethany, the home of Lazarus, whom he had raised from the dead. 2 There they gave a dinner for him. Martha served, and Lazarus was one of those at the table with him. 3 Mary took a pound of costly perfume made of pure nard, anointed Jesus' feet, and wiped them[m] with her hair. The house was filled with the fragrance of the perfume. 4 But Judas Iscariot, one of his disciples (the one who was about to betray him), said, 5 "Why was this perfume not sold for three hundred denarii[n] and the money given to the poor?" 6 (He said this not because he cared about the poor, but because he was a thief; he kept the common purse and used to steal what was put into it.) 7 Jesus said, "Leave her alone. She bought it[o] so that she might keep it for the day of my burial. 8 You always have the poor with you, but you do not always have me."

9 When the great crowd of the Jews learned that he was there, they came not only because of Jesus but also to see Lazarus, whom he had raised from the dead. 10 So the chief priests planned to put Lazarus to death as well, 11 since it was on account of him that many of the Jews were deserting and were believing in Jesus.

12 The next day the great crowd that had come to the festival heard that Jesus was coming to Jerusalem. 13 So they took branches of palm trees and went out to meet him, shouting,

"Hosanna!
Blessed is the one who comes in
    the name of the Lord—[6]
the King of Israel!"

14 Jesus found a young donkey and sat on it; as it is written:

15   "Do not be afraid, daughter of
            Zion.
        Look, your king is coming,
            sitting on a donkey's colt!"[7]

16 His disciples did not understand these things at first; but when Jesus was glorified, then they remembered that these things had been written of him and had been done to him. 17 So the crowd that had been with him when he called Lazarus out of the tomb and raised him from the dead continued to testify.[p] 18 It was also because they heard that he had performed this sign that the crowd went to meet him. 19 The Pharisees then said to one another, "You see, you can do nothing. Look, the world has gone after him!"

20 Now among those who went up to worship at the festival were some Greeks. 21 They came to Philip, who was from Bethsaida in Galilee, and said to him, "Sir, we wish to see Jesus." 22 Philip went and told Andrew; then Andrew and Philip went and told Jesus. 23 Jesus answered them, "The hour has come for the Son of Man to be glorified. 24 Very truly, I tell you, unless a grain of wheat falls into the earth and dies, it remains just a single grain; but if it dies, it bears much fruit. 25 Those who love their life lose it, and those who hate their life in this world will keep it for eternal life. 26 Whoever serves me must follow me, and where I am, there will my servant be also. Whoever serves me, the Father will honor.

27 "Now my soul is troubled. And what should I say—'Father, save me from this hour'? No, it is for this reason that I have come to this hour. 28 Father, glorify your name." Then a voice came from heaven, "I have glorified it, and I will glorify it again." 29 The crowd standing there heard it and said that it was thunder. Others said, "An angel has spoken to him." 30 Jesus answered, "This voice has come for your sake, not for mine. 31 Now is the judgment of this world; now the ruler of this world will be driven out. 32 And I, when I am lifted up from the earth, will draw all people[q] to myself." 33 He said this to indicate the

---

[l]Gk *he*   [m]Gk *his feet*   [n]Three hundred denarii would be nearly a year's wages for a laborer   [o]Gk lacks *She bought it*   [p]Other ancient authorities read *with him began to testify that he had called. . .from the dead*   [q]Other ancient authorities read *all things*

[6]Ps 118:26   [7]Zech 9:9

kind of death he was to die. 34 The crowd answered him, "We have heard from the law that the Messiah[r] remains forever. How can you say that the Son of Man must be lifted up? Who is this Son of Man?" 35 Jesus said to them, "The light is with you for a little longer. Walk while you have the light, so that the darkness may not overtake you. If you walk in the darkness, you do not know where you are going. 36 While you have the light, believe in the light, so that you may become children of light."

After Jesus had said this, he departed and hid from them. 37 Although he had performed so many signs in their presence, they did not believe in him. 38 This was to fulfill the word spoken by the prophet Isaiah:

"Lord, who has believed our
    message,
and to whom has the arm of the
    Lord been revealed?"[8]

39 And so they could not believe, because Isaiah also said,

40   "He has blinded their eyes
        and hardened their heart,
    so that they might not look with
        their eyes,
    and understand with their heart
        and turn—
    and I would heal them.'[9]

41 Isaiah said this because[s] he saw his glory and spoke about him. 42 Nevertheless many, even of the authorities, believed in him. But because of the Pharisees they did not confess it, for fear that they would be put out of the synagogue; 43 for they loved human glory more than the glory that comes from God.

44 Then Jesus cried aloud: "Whoever believes in me believes not in me but in him who sent me. 45 And whoever sees me sees him who sent me. 46 I have come as light into the world, so that everyone who believes in me should not remain in the darkness. 47 I do not judge anyone who hears my words and does not keep them, for I came not to judge the world, but to save the world. 48 The one who rejects me and does not receive my word has a judge; on the last day the word that I have spoken will serve as judge, 49 for I have not spoken on my own, but the Father who sent me has himself given me a commandment about what to say and what to speak. 50 And I know that his commandment is eternal life. What I speak, therefore, I speak just as the Father has told me."

13 Now before the festival of the Passover, Jesus knew that his hour had come to depart from this world and go to the Father. Having loved his own who were in the world, he loved them to the end. 2 The devil had already put it into the heart of Judas son of Simon Iscariot to betray him. And during supper 3 Jesus, knowing that the Father had given all things into his hands, and that he had come from God and was going to God, 4 got up from the table,[t] took off his outer robe, and tied a towel around himself. 5 Then he poured water into a basin and began to wash the disciples' feet and to wipe them with the towel that was tied around him. 6 He came to Simon Peter, who said to him, "Lord, are you going to wash my feet?" 7 Jesus answered, "You do not know now what I am doing, but later you will understand." 8 Peter said to him, "You will never wash my feet." Jesus answered, "Unless I wash you, you have no share with me." 9 Simon Peter said to him, "Lord, not my feet only but also my hands and my head!" 10 Jesus said to him, "One who has bathed does not need to wash, except for the feet,[u] but is entirely clean. And you[v] are clean, though not all of you." 11 For he knew who was to betray him; for this reason he said, "Not all of you are clean."

12 After he had washed their feet, had put on his robe, and had returned to the table, he said to them, "Do you know what I have done to you? 13 You call me Teacher and Lord—and you are right, for that is what I am. 14 So if I, your Lord and Teacher, have washed your feet, you also ought to wash one another's feet. 15 For I have set you an example, that you also should do as I have done to you. 16 Very truly, I tell you, servants[w] are not greater than their master, nor are messengers greater than the one who sent them. 17 If you know these things, you are blessed if you do them. 18 I am not speaking of all of you; I know whom I have chosen. But it is to fulfill the scripture, 'The

---

[r]Or the Christ   [s]Other ancient witnesses read when   [t]Gk from supper   [u]Other ancient authorities lack except for the feet   [v]The Greek word for you here is plural   [w]Gk slaves

---

[8]Isa 53:1   [9]Isa 6:10

one who ate my bread[x] has lifted his heel against me.'[10] 19 I tell you this now, before it occurs, so that when it does occur, you may believe that I am he.[y] 20 Very truly, I tell you, whoever receives one whom I send receives me; and whoever receives me receives him who sent me."

21 After saying this Jesus was troubled in spirit, and declared, "Very truly, I tell you, one of you will betray me." 22 The disciples looked at one another, uncertain of whom he was speaking. 23 One of his disciples—the one whom Jesus loved—was reclining next to him; 24 Simon Peter therefore motioned to him to ask Jesus of whom he was speaking. 25 So while reclining next to Jesus, he asked him, "Lord, who is it?" 26 Jesus answered, "It is the one to whom I give this piece of bread when I have dipped it in the dish."[z] So when he had dipped the piece of bread, he gave it to Judas son of Simon Iscariot.[a] 27 After he received the piece of bread,[b] Satan entered into him. Jesus said to him, "Do quickly what you are going to do." 28 Now no one at the table knew why he said this to him. 29 Some thought that, because Judas had the common purse, Jesus was telling him, "Buy what we need for the festival"; or, that he should give something to the poor. 30 So, after receiving the piece of bread, he immediately went out. And it was night.

31 When he had gone out, Jesus said, "Now the Son of Man has been glorified, and God has been glorified in him. 32 If God has been glorified in him,[c] God will also glorify him in himself and will glorify him at once. 33 Little children, I am with you only a little longer. You will look for me; and as I said to the Jews so now I say to you, 'Where I am going, you cannot come.' 34 I give you a new commandment, that you love one another. Just as I have loved you, you also should love one another. 35 By this everyone will know that you are my disciples, if you have love for one another."

36 Simon Peter said to him, "Lord, where are you going?" Jesus answered, "Where I am going, you cannot follow me now; but you will follow afterward." 37 Peter said to him, "Lord, why can I not follow you now? I will lay down my life for you." 38 Jesus answered, "Will you lay down your life for me? Very truly, I tell you, before the cock crows, you will have denied me three times.

14 "Do not let your hearts be troubled. Believe[d] in God, believe also in me. 2 In my Father's house there are many dwelling places. If it were not so, would I have told you that I go to prepare a place for you?[e] 3 And if I go and prepare a place for you, I will come again and will take you to myself, so that where I am, there you may be also. 4 And you know the way to the place where I am going."[f] 5 Thomas said to him, "Lord, we do not know where you are going. How can we know the way?" 6 Jesus said to him, "I am the way, and the truth, and the life. No one comes to the Father except through me. 7 If you know me, you will know[g] my Father also. From now on you do know him and have seen him."

8 Philip said to him, "Lord, show us the Father, and we will be satisfied." 9 Jesus said to him, "Have I been with you all this time, Philip, and you still do not know me? Whoever has seen me has seen the Father. How can you say, 'Show us the Father'? 10 Do you not believe that I am in the Father and the Father is in me? The words that I say to you I do not speak on my own; but the Father who dwells in me does his works. 11 Believe me that I am in the Father and the Father is in me; but if you do not, then believe me because of the works themselves. 12 Very truly, I tell you, the one who believes in me will also do the works that I do and, in fact, will do greater works than these, because I am going to the Father. 13 I will do whatever you ask in my name, so that the Father may be glorified in the Son. 14 If in my name you ask me[h] for anything, I will do it.

15 "If you love me, you will keep[i] my commandments. 16 And I will ask the Father, and he will give you another Advocate,[j] to be with you forever. 17 This is the Spirit of truth, whom the world cannot receive, because it neither sees him

---

[x]Other ancient authorities read *ate bread with me*   [y]Gk *I am*   [z]Gk *dipped it*   [a]Other ancient authorities read *Judas Iscariot son of Simon*; others, *Judas son of Simon from Karyot* (Kerioth)   [b]Gk *After the piece of bread*   [c]Other ancient authorities lack *If God has been glorified in him*   [d]Or *You believe*   [e]Or *If it were not so, I would have told you; for I go to prepare a place for you*   [f]Other ancient authorities read *Where I am going you know, and the way you know*   [g]Other ancient authorities read *If you had known me, you would have known*   [h]Other ancient authorities lack *me*   [i]Other ancient authorities read *me, keep*   [j]Or *Helper*

[10]Ps 41:9

nor knows him. You know him, because he abides with you, and he will be in[k] you.

18 "I will not leave you orphaned; I am coming to you. 19 In a little while the world will no longer see me, but you will see me; because I live, you also will live. 20 On that day you will know that I am in my Father, and you in me, and I in you. 21 They who have my commandments and keep them are those who love me; and those who love me will be loved by my Father, and I will love them and reveal myself to them." 22 Judas (not Iscariot) said to him, "Lord, how is it that you will reveal yourself to us, and not to the world?" 23 Jesus answered him, "Those who love me will keep my word, and my Father will love them, and we will come to them and make our home with them. 24 Whoever does not love me does not keep my words; and the word that you hear is not mine, but is from the Father who sent me.

25 "I have said these things to you while I am still with you. 26 But the Advocate,[l] the Holy Spirit, whom the Father will send in my name, will teach you everything, and remind you of all that I have said to you. 27 Peace I leave with you; my peace I give to you. I do not give to you as the world gives. Do not let your hearts be troubled, and do not let them be afraid. 28 You heard me say to you, 'I am going away, and I am coming to you.' If you loved me, you would rejoice that I am going to the Father, because the Father is greater than I. 29 And now I have told you this before it occurs, so that when it does occur, you may believe. 30 I will no longer talk much with you, for the ruler of this world is coming. He has no power over me; 31 but I do as the Father has commanded me, so that the world may know that I love the Father. Rise, let us be on our way.

15 "I am the true vine, and my Father is the vinegrower. 2 He removes every branch in me that bears no fruit. Every branch that bears fruit he prunes[m] to make it bear more fruit. 3 You have already been cleansed[m] by the word that I have spoken to you. 4 Abide in me as I abide in you. Just as the branch cannot bear fruit by itself unless it abides in the vine, neither can you unless you abide in me. 5 I am the vine, you are the branches. Those who abide in me and I in them bear much fruit, because apart from me you can

do nothing. 6 Whoever does not abide in me is thrown away like a branch and withers; such branches are gathered, thrown into the fire, and burned. 7 If you abide in me, and my words abide in you, ask for whatever you wish, and it will be done for you. 8 My Father is glorified by this, that you bear much fruit and become[n] my disciples. 9 As the Father has loved me, so I have loved you; abide in my love. 10 If you keep my commandments, you will abide in my love, just as I have kept my Father's commandments and abide in his love. 11 I have said these things to you so that my joy may be in you, and that your joy may be complete.

12 "This is my commandment, that you love one another as I have loved you. 13 No one has greater love than this, to lay down one's life for one's friends. 14 You are my friends if you do what I command you. 15 I do not call you servants[o] any longer, because the servant[p] does not know what the master is doing; but I have called you friends, because I have made known to you everything that I have heard from my Father. 16 You did not choose me but I chose you. And I appointed you to go and bear fruit, fruit that will last, so that the Father will give you whatever you ask him in my name. 17 I am giving you these commands so that you may love one another.

18 "If the world hates you, be aware that it hated me before it hated you. 19 If you belonged to the world,[q] the world would love you as its own. Because you do not belong to the world, but I have chosen you out of the world—therefore the world hates you. 20 Remember the word that I said to you, 'Servants[r] are not greater than their master.' If they persecuted me, they will persecute you; if they kept my word, they will keep yours also. 21 But they will do all these things to you on account of my name, because they do not know him who sent me. 22 If I had not come and spoken to them, they would not have sin; but now they have no excuse for their sin. 23 Whoever hates me hates my Father also. 24 If I had not done among them the works that no one else did, they would not have sin. But now they have seen and hated both me and my Father. 25 It was to fulfill the

[k]Or among [l]Or Helper [m]The same Greek root refers to pruning and cleansing [n]Or be [o]Gk slaves [p]Gk slave [q]Gk were of the world [r]Gk Slaves

word that is written in their law, 'They hated me without a cause.'[11]

26 "When the Advocate[s] comes, whom I will send to you from the Father, the Spirit of truth who comes from the Father, he will testify on my behalf. 27 You also are to testify because you have been with me from the beginning.

16 "I have said these things to you to keep you from stumbling. 2 They will put you out of the synagogues. Indeed, an hour is coming when those who kill you will think that by doing so they are offering worship to God. 3 And they will do this because they have not known the Father or me. 4 But I have said these things to you so that when their hour comes you may remember that I told you about them.

"I did not say these things to you from the beginning, because I was with you. 5 But now I am going to him who sent me; yet none of you asks me, 'Where are you going?' 6 But because I have said these things to you, sorrow has filled your hearts. 7 Nevertheless I tell you the truth: it is to your advantage that I go away, for if I do not go away, the Advocate[s] will not come to you; but if I go, I will send him to you. 8 And when he comes, he will prove the world wrong about[t] sin and righteousness and judgment: 9 about sin, because they do not believe in me; 10 about righteousness, because I am going to the Father and you will see me no longer; 11 about judgment, because the ruler of this world has been condemned.

12 "I still have many things to say to you, but you cannot bear them now. 13 When the Spirit of truth comes, he will guide you into all the truth; for he will not speak on his own, but will speak whatever he hears, and he will declare to you the things that are to come. 14 He will glorify me, because he will take what is mine and declare it to you. 15 All that the Father has is mine. For this reason I said that he will take what is mine and declare it to you.

16 "A little while, and you will no longer see me, and again a little while, and you will see me." 17 Then some of his disciples said to one another, "What does he mean by saying to us, 'A little while, and you will no longer see me, and again a little while, and you will see me'; and 'Because I am going to the Father'?" 18 They said, "What does he mean by this 'a little while'? We do not know what he is talking about." 19 Jesus knew

that they wanted to ask him, so he said to them, "Are you discussing among yourselves what I meant when I said, 'A little while, and you will no longer see me, and again a little while, and you will see me'? 20 Very truly, I tell you, you will weep and mourn, but the world will rejoice; you will have pain, but your pain will turn into joy. 21 When a woman is in labor, she has pain, because her hour has come. But when her child is born, she no longer remembers the anguish because of the joy of having brought a human being into the world. 22 So you have pain now; but I will see you again, and your hearts will rejoice, and no one will take your joy from you. 23 On that day you will ask nothing of me.[u] Very truly, I tell you, if you ask anything of the Father in my name, he will give it to you.[v] 24 Until now you have not asked for anything in my name. Ask and you will receive, so that your joy may be complete.

25 "I have said these things to you in figures of speech. The hour is coming when I will no longer speak to you in figures, but will tell you plainly of the Father. 26 On that day you will ask in my name. I do not say to you that I will ask the Father on your behalf; 27 for the Father himself loves you, because you have loved me and have believed that I came from God.[w] 28 I came from the Father and have come into the world; again, I am leaving the world and am going to the Father."

29 His disciples said, "Yes, now you are speaking plainly, not in any figure of speech! 30 Now we know that you know all things, and do not need to have anyone question you; by this we believe that you came from God." 31 Jesus answered them, "Do you now believe? 32 The hour is coming, indeed it has come, when you will be scattered, each one to his home, and you will leave me alone. Yet I am not alone because the Father is with me. 33 I have said this to you, so that in me you may have peace. In the world you face persecution. But take courage; I have conquered the world!"

17 After Jesus had spoken these words, he looked up to heaven and said, "Father, the hour has come; glorify your Son so that the Son

[s]Or *Helper* [t]Or *convict the world of* [u]Or *will ask me no question* [v]Other ancient authorities read *Father, he will give it to you in my name* [w]Other ancient authorities read *the Father*

[11]Ps 35:19; 69:4

may glorify you, 2 since you have given him authority over all people,ˣ to give eternal life to all whom you have given him. 3 And this is eternal life, that they may know you, the only true God, and Jesus Christ whom you have sent. 4 I glorified you on earth by finishing the work that you gave me to do. 5 So now, Father, glorify me in your own presence with the glory that I had in your presence before the world existed.

6 "I have made your name known to those whom you gave me from the world. They were yours, and you gave them to me, and they have kept your word. 7 Now they know that everything you have given me is from you; 8 for the words that you gave to me I have given to them, and they have received them and know in truth that I came from you; and they have believed that you sent me. 9 I am asking on their behalf; I am not asking on behalf of the world, but on behalf of those whom you gave me, because they are yours. 10 All mine are yours, and yours are mine; and I have been glorified in them. 11 And now I am no longer in the world, but they are in the world, and I am coming to you. Holy Father, protect them in your name that you have given me, so that they may be one, as we are one. 12 While I was with them, I protected them in your name thatʸ you have given me. I guarded them, and not one of them was lost except the one destined to be lost,ᶻ so that the scripture might be fulfilled. 13 But now I am coming to you, and I speak these things in the world so that they may have my joy made complete in themselves.ᵃ 14 I have given them your word, and the world has hated them because they do not belong to the world, just as I do not belong to the world. 15 I am not asking you to take them out of the world, but I ask you to protect them from the evil one.ᵇ 16 They do not belong to the world, just as I do not belong to the world. 17 Sanctify them in the truth; your word is truth. 18 As you have sent me into the world, so I have sent them into the world. 19 And for their sakes I sanctify myself, so that they also may be sanctified in truth.

20 "I ask not only on behalf of these, but also on behalf of those who will believe in me through their word, 21 that they may all be one. As you, Father, are in me and I am in you, may they also be in us,ᶜ so that the world may believe that you have sent me. 22 The glory that you have given

me I have given them, so that they may be one, as we are one, 23 I in them and you in me, that they may become completely one, so that the world may know that you have sent me and have loved them even as you have loved me. 24 Father, I desire that those also, whom you have given me, may be with me where I am, to see my glory, which you have given me because you loved me before the foundation of the world.

25 "Righteous Father, the world does not know you, but I know you; and these know that you have sent me. 26 I made your name known to them, and I will make it known, so that the love with which you have loved me may be in them, and I in them."

18 After Jesus had spoken these words, he went out with his disciples across the Kidron valley to a place where there was a garden, which he and his disciples entered. 2 Now Judas, who betrayed him, also knew the place, because Jesus often met there with his disciples. 3 So Judas brought a detachment of soldiers together with police from the chief priests and the Pharisees, and they came there with lanterns and torches and weapons. 4 Then Jesus, knowing all that was to happen to him, came forward and asked them, "Whom are you looking for?" 5 They answered, "Jesus of Nazareth."ᵈ Jesus replied, "I am he."ᵉ Judas, who betrayed him, was standing with them. 6 When Jesusᶠ said to them, "I am he,"ᵉ they stepped back and fell to the ground. 7 Again he asked them, "Whom are you looking for?" And they said, "Jesus of Nazareth."ᵈ 8 Jesus answered, "I told you that I am he.ᵉ So if you are looking for me, let these men go." 9 This was to fulfill the word that he had spoken, "I did not lose a single one of those whom you gave me." 10 Then Simon Peter, who had a sword, drew it, struck the high priest's slave, and cut off his right ear. The slave's name was Malchus. 11 Jesus said to Peter, "Put your sword back into its sheath. Am I not to drink the cup that the Father has given me?"

12 So the soldiers, their officer, and the Jewish police arrested Jesus and bound him. 13 First they took him to Annas, who was the father-in-law of

---

ˣGk flesh ʸOther ancient authorities read protected in your name those whom ᶻGk except the son of destruction ᵃOr among themselves ᵇOr from evil ᶜOther ancient authorities read be one in us ᵈGk the Nazorean ᵉGk I am ᶠGk he

Caiaphas, the high priest that year. 14 Caiaphas was the one who had advised the Jews that it was better to have one person die for the people.

15 Simon Peter and another disciple followed Jesus. Since that disciple was known to the high priest, he went with Jesus into the courtyard of the high priest, 16 but Peter was standing outside at the gate. So the other disciple, who was known to the high priest, went out, spoke to the woman who guarded the gate, and brought Peter in. 17 The woman said to Peter, "You are not also one of this man's disciples, are you?" He said, "I am not." 18 Now the slaves and the police had made a charcoal fire because it was cold, and they were standing around it and warming themselves. Peter also was standing with them and warming himself.

19 Then the high priest questioned Jesus about his disciples and about his teaching. 20 Jesus answered, "I have spoken openly to the world; I have always taught in synagogues and in the temple, where all the Jews come together. I have said nothing in secret. 21 Why do you ask me? Ask those who heard what I said to them; they know what I said." 22 When he had said this, one of the police standing nearby struck Jesus on the face, saying, "Is that how you answer the high priest?" 23 Jesus answered, "If I have spoken wrongly, testify to the wrong. But if I have spoken rightly, why do you strike me?" 24 Then Annas sent him bound to Caiaphas the high priest.

25 Now Simon Peter was standing and warming himself. They asked him, "You are not also one of his disciples, are you?" He denied it and said, "I am not." 26 One of the slaves of the high priest, a relative of the man whose ear Peter had cut off, asked, "Did I not see you in the garden with him?" 27 Again Peter denied it, and at that moment the cock crowed.

28 Then they took Jesus from Caiaphas to Pilate's headquarters.[g] It was early in the morning. They themselves did not enter the headquarters,[f] so as to avoid ritual defilement and to be able to eat the Passover. 29 So Pilate went out to them and said, "What accusation do you bring against this man?" 30 They answered, "If this man were not a criminal, we would not have handed him over to you." 31 Pilate said to them, "Take him yourselves and judge him according to your law." The Jews replied, "We are not permitted to put anyone to death." 32 (This was to fulfill what Jesus had said when he indicated the kind of death he was to die.)

33 Then Pilate entered the headquarters[g] again, summoned Jesus, and asked him, "Are you the King of the Jews?" 34 Jesus answered, "Do you ask this on your own, or did others tell you about me?" 35 Pilate replied, "I am not a Jew, am I? Your own nation and the chief priests have handed you over to me. What have you done?" 36 Jesus answered, "My kingdom is not from this world. If my kingdom were from this world, my followers would be fighting to keep me from being handed over to the Jews. But as it is, my kingdom is not from here." 37 Pilate asked him, "So you are a king?" Jesus answered, "You say that I am a king. For this I was born, and for this I came into the world, to testify to the truth. Everyone who belongs to the truth listens to my voice." 38 Pilate asked him, "What is truth?"

After he had said this, he went out to the Jews again and told them, "I find no case against him. 39 But you have a custom that I release someone for you at the Passover. Do you want me to release for you the King of the Jews?" 40 They shouted in reply, "Not this man, but Barabbas!" Now Barabbas was a bandit.

19 Then Pilate took Jesus and had him flogged. 2 And the soldiers wove a crown of thorns and put it on his head, and they dressed him in a purple robe. 3 They kept coming up to him, saying, "Hail, King of the Jews!" and striking him on the face. 4 Pilate went out again and said to them, "Look, I am bringing him out to you to let you know that I find no case against him." 5 So Jesus came out, wearing the crown of thorns and the purple robe. Pilate said to them, "Here is the man!" 6 When the chief priests and the police saw him, they shouted, "Crucify him! Crucify him!" Pilate said to them, "Take him yourselves and crucify him; I find no case against him." 7 The Jews answered him, "We have a law, and according to that law he ought to die because he has claimed to be the Son of God."

8 Now when Pilate heard this, he was more afraid than ever. 9 He entered his headquarters[g] again and asked Jesus, "Where are you from?" But

[g]Gk the praetorium

Jesus gave him no answer. 10 Pilate therefore said to him, "Do you refuse to speak to me? Do you not know that I have power to release you, and power to crucify you?" 11 Jesus answered him, "You would have no power over me unless it had been given you from above; therefore the one who handed me over to you is guilty of a greater sin." 12 From then on Pilate tried to release him, but the Jews cried out, "If you release this man, you are no friend of the emperor. Everyone who claims to be a king sets himself against the emperor."

13 When Pilate heard these words, he brought Jesus outside and sat[h] on the judge's bench at a place called The Stone Pavement, or in Hebrew[i] Gabbatha. 14 Now it was the day of Preparation for the Passover; and it was about noon. He said to the Jews, "Here is your King!" 15 They cried out, "Away with him! Away with him! Crucify him!" Pilate asked them, "Shall I crucify your King?" The chief priests answered, "We have no king but the emperor." 16 Then he handed him over to them to be crucified.

So they took Jesus; 17 and carrying the cross by himself, he went out to what is called The Place of the Skull, which in Hebrew[i] is called Golgotha. 18 There they crucified him, and with him two others, one on either side, with Jesus between them. 19 Pilate also had an inscription written and put on the cross. It read, "Jesus of Nazareth,[j] the King of the Jews." 20 Many of the Jews read this inscription, because the place where Jesus was crucified was near the city; and it was written in Hebrew,[i] in Latin, and in Greek. 21 Then the chief priests of the Jews said to Pilate, "Do not write, 'The King of the Jews,' but, 'This man said, I am King of the Jews.'" 22 Pilate answered, "What I have written I have written." 23 When the soldiers had crucified Jesus, they took his clothes and divided them into four parts, one for each soldier. They also took his tunic; now the tunic was seamless, woven in one piece from the top. 24 So they said to one another, "Let us not tear it, but cast lots for it to see who will get it." This was to fulfill what the scripture says,

"They divided my clothes among
themselves,
and for my clothing they cast
lots."[12]

25 And that is what the soldiers did.

Meanwhile, standing near the cross of Jesus were his mother, and his mother's sister, Mary the wife of Clopas, and Mary Magdalene. 26 When Jesus saw his mother and the disciple whom he loved standing beside her, he said to his mother, "Woman, here is your son." 27 Then he said to the disciple, "Here is your mother." And from that hour the disciple took her into his own home.

28 After this, when Jesus knew that all was now finished, he said (in order to fulfill the scripture), "I am thirsty." 29 A jar full of sour wine was standing there. So they put a sponge full of the wine on a branch of hyssop and held it to his mouth. 30 When Jesus had received the wine, he said, "It is finished." Then he bowed his head and gave up his spirit.

31 Since it was the day of Preparation, the Jews did not want the bodies left on the cross during the sabbath, especially because that sabbath was a day of great solemnity. So they asked Pilate to have the legs of the crucified men broken and the bodies removed. 32 Then the soldiers came and broke the legs of the first and of the other who had been crucified with him. 33 But when they came to Jesus and saw that he was already dead, they did not break his legs. 34 Instead, one of the soldiers pierced his side with a spear, and at once blood and water came out. 35 (He who saw this has testified so that you also may believe. His testimony is true, and he knows[k] that he tells the truth.) 36 These things occurred so that the scripture might be fulfilled, "None of his bones shall be broken."[13] 37 And again another passage of scripture says, "They will look on the one whom they have pierced."[14]

38 After these things, Joseph of Arimathea, who was a disciple of Jesus, though a secret one because of his fear of the Jews, asked Pilate to let him take away the body of Jesus. Pilate gave him permission; so he came and removed his body. 39 Nicodemus, who had at first come to Jesus by night, also came, bringing a mixture of myrrh and aloes, weighing about a hundred pounds. 40 They took the body of Jesus and wrapped it with the spices in linen cloths, according to the burial custom of the Jews. 41 Now there was a garden in the

---

[h]Or *seated him* [i]That is, *Aramaic* [j]Gk *the Nazorean* [k]Or *there is one who knows*

[12]Ps 22:18 [13]Ps 34:20; Exod 12:46; Num 9:12 [14]Zech 12:10

place where he was crucified, and in the garden there was a new tomb in which no one had ever been laid. 42 And so, because it was the Jewish day of Preparation, and the tomb was nearby, they laid Jesus there.

20 Early on the first day of the week, while it was still dark, Mary Magdalene came to the tomb and saw that the stone had been removed from the tomb. 2 So she ran and went to Simon Peter and the other disciple, the one whom Jesus loved, and said to them, "They have taken the Lord out of the tomb, and we do not know where they have laid him." 3 Then Peter and the other disciple set out and went toward the tomb. 4 The two were running together, but the other disciple outran Peter and reached the tomb first. 5 He bent down to look in and saw the linen wrappings lying there, but he did not go in. 6 Then Simon Peter came, following him, and went into the tomb. He saw the linen wrappings lying there, 7 and the cloth that had been on Jesus' head, not lying with the linen wrappings but rolled up in a place by itself. 8 Then the other disciple, who reached the tomb first, also went in, and he saw and believed; 9 for as yet they did not understand the scripture, that he must rise from the dead. 10 Then the disciples returned to their homes.

11 But Mary stood weeping outside the tomb. As she wept, she bent over to look[l] into the tomb; 12 and she saw two angels in white, sitting where the body of Jesus had been lying, one at the head and the other at the feet. 13 They said to her, "Woman, why are you weeping?" She said to them, "They have taken away my Lord, and I do not know where they have laid him." 14 When she had said this, she turned around and saw Jesus standing there, but she did not know that it was Jesus. 15 Jesus said to her, "Woman, why are you weeping? Whom are you looking for?" Supposing him to be the gardener, she said to him, "Sir, if you have carried him away, tell me where you have laid him, and I will take him away." 16 Jesus said to her, "Mary!" She turned and said to him in Hebrew,[m] "Rabbouni!" (which means Teacher). 17 Jesus said to her, "Do not hold on to me, because I have not yet ascended to the Father. But go to my brothers and say to them, 'I am ascending to my Father and your Father, to my God and your God.'" 18 Mary Magdalene went and announced

to the disciples, "I have seen the Lord"; and she told them that he had said these things to her.

19 When it was evening on that day, the first day of the week, and the doors of the house where the disciples had met were locked for fear of the Jews, Jesus came and stood among them and said, "Peace be with you." 20 After he said this, he showed them his hands and his side. Then the disciples rejoiced when they saw the Lord. 21 Jesus said to them again, "Peace be with you. As the Father has sent me, so I send you." 22 When he had said this, he breathed on them and said to them, "Receive the Holy Spirit. 23 If you forgive the sins of any, they are forgiven them; if you retain the sins of any, they are retained."

24 But Thomas (who was called the Twin[n]), one of the twelve, was not with them when Jesus came. 25 So the other disciples told him, "We have seen the Lord." But he said to them, "Unless I see the mark of the nails in his hands, and put my finger in the mark of the nails and my hand in his side, I will not believe."

26 A week later his disciples were again in the house, and Thomas was with them. Although the doors were shut, Jesus came and stood among them and said, "Peace be with you." 27 Then he said to Thomas, "Put your finger here and see my hands. Reach out your hand and put it in my side. Do not doubt but believe." 28 Thomas answered him, "My Lord and my God!" 29 Jesus said to him, "Have you believed because you have seen me? Blessed are those who have not seen and yet have come to believe."

30 Now Jesus did many other signs in the presence of his disciples, which are not written in this book. 31 But these are written so that you may come to believe[o] that Jesus is the Messiah,[p] the Son of God, and that through believing you may have life in his name.

21 After these things Jesus showed himself again to the disciples by the Sea of Tiberias; and he showed himself in this way. 2 Gathered there together were Simon Peter, Thomas called the Twin,[n] Nathanael of Cana in Galilee, the sons of Zebedee, and two others of his

---

[l]Gk lacks *to look*   [m]That is, *Aramaic*   [n]Gk *Didymus*   [o]Other ancient authorities read *may continue to believe*   [p]Or *the Christ*

disciples. 3 Simon Peter said to them, "I am going fishing." They said to him, "We will go with you." They went out and got into the boat, but that night they caught nothing.

4 Just after daybreak, Jesus stood on the beach; but the disciples did not know that it was Jesus. 5 Jesus said to them, "Children, you have no fish, have you?" They answered him, "No." 6 He said to them, "Cast the net to the right side of the boat, and you will find some." So they cast it, and now they were not able to haul it in because there were so many fish. 7 That disciple whom Jesus loved said to Peter, "It is the Lord!" When Simon Peter heard that it was the Lord, he put on some clothes, for he was naked, and jumped into the sea. 8 But the other disciples came in the boat, dragging the net full of fish, for they were not far from the land, only about a hundred yards⁹ off.

9 When they had gone ashore, they saw a charcoal fire there, with fish on it, and bread. 10 Jesus said to them, "Bring some of the fish that you have just caught." 11 So Simon Peter went aboard and hauled the net ashore, full of large fish, a hundred fifty-three of them; and though there were so many, the net was not torn. 12 Jesus said to them, "Come and have breakfast." Now none of the disciples dared to ask him, "Who are you?" because they knew it was the Lord. 13 Jesus came and took the bread and gave it to them, and did the same with the fish. 14 This was now the third time that Jesus appeared to the disciples after he was raised from the dead.

15 When they had finished breakfast, Jesus said to Simon Peter, "Simon son of John, do you love me more than these?" He said to him, "Yes, Lord; you know that I love you." Jesus said to him, "Feed my lambs." 16 A second time he said to him, "Simon son of John, do you love me?" He said to him, "Yes, Lord; you know that I love you." Jesus said to him, "Tend my sheep." 17 He said to him the third time, "Simon son of John, do you love me?" Peter felt hurt because he said to him the third time, "Do you love me?" And he said to him, "Lord, you know everything; you know that I love you." Jesus said to him, "Feed my sheep. 18 Very truly, I tell you, when you were younger, you used to fasten your own belt and to go wherever you wished. But when you grow old, you will stretch out your hands, and someone else will fasten a belt around you and take you where you do not wish to go." 19 (He said this to indicate the kind of death by which he would glorify God.) After this he said to him, "Follow me."

20 Peter turned and saw the disciple whom Jesus loved following them; he was the one who had reclined next to Jesus at the supper and had said, "Lord, who is it that is going to betray you?" 21 When Peter saw him, he said to Jesus, "Lord, what about him?" 22 Jesus said to him, "If it is my will that he remain until I come, what is that to you? Follow me!" 23 So the rumor spread in the communityʳ that this disciple would not die. Yet Jesus did not say to him that he would not die, but, "If it is my will that he remain until I come, what is that to you?"ˢ

24 This is the disciple who is testifying to these things and has written them, and we know that his testimony is true. 25 But there are also many other things that Jesus did; if every one of them were written down, I suppose that the world itself could not contain the books that would be written.

---

⁹Gk *two hundred cubits*   ʳGk *among the brothers*   ˢOther ancient authorities lack *what is that to you*

The Gospel of Thomas

The *Gospel of Thomas* was one of the most sensational archaeological discoveries of the twentieth century. The document was unknown except by name before 1945, when peasants digging for fertilizer near the village of Nag Hammadi, Egypt, accidentally uncovered a jar containing thirteen leather-bound manuscripts buried sometime in the late fourth century. When the manuscripts came to the attention of scholars of antiquity, their significance was almost immediately recognized: they contained fifty-two tractates that, by and large, represented "heretical" writings of Gnostic Christians. Although originally composed in Greek, the writings were in Coptic (ancient Egyptian) translation. Many of them had been previously known by title only.

None of the fifty-two tractates has attracted more attention than the *Gospel of Thomas*. For this is a book of Jesus' sayings that claims to have been written by Didymos Judas Thomas. According to some early Christian legends, Thomas was Jesus' twin brother.

The book records 114 "secret teachings" of Jesus. It includes no other material: no miracles, no passion narrative, no stories of any kind. In this it appears to resemble that lost collection of sayings that scholars have designated Q (from the German word *Quelle*, "source"), which was used by Matthew and Luke for their Gospels. What ultimately mattered for the author of Thomas was evidently not Jesus' death and resurrection (which he does not narrate or discuss), but the mysterious teachings that he delivered. Indeed, the Gospel begins by stating that anyone who learns the interpretation of these sayings will have eternal life.

Many of the sayings will sound familiar to readers already conversant with the Gospels of Matthew, Mark, and Luke. For example, here one finds, in slightly different wording, the warning against the "blind leading the blind" and the parables of the sower and of the mustard seed (sayings 9, 20, 34). Other sayings, however, are quite different and appear to presuppose a gnostic point of view, in which people are understood to be spirits who have fallen from the divine realm and become entrapped in matter (i.e., in the prisons of their material bodies). Salvation, according to this perspective, comes to those who learn the truth of their plight and so are enabled to escape this impoverished material existence by acquiring the knowledge necessary for salvation (e.g., sayings 11, 22, 29, 37, and 80). Jesus is the one who conveys this knowledge.

Some scholars have maintained that the sayings of Thomas may be closer to what Jesus actually taught than what we find in the New Testament; others, however, have pointed out that the theology implicit in the more gnostic teachings cannot be dated with confidence prior to the beginning of the second century. Thus, while some of these sayings may be quite old—may, in fact, go back to Jesus himself—the document as a whole probably came to be written sometime after the New Testament Gospels (possibly independently of them), perhaps in the early second century.

These are the secret sayings which the living Jesus spoke and which Didymos Judas Thomas wrote down.

1 And he said, "Whoever finds the interpretation of these sayings will not experience death."

2 Jesus said, "Let him who seeks continue seeking until he finds. When he finds, he will become troubled. When he becomes troubled, he will be astonished, and he will rule over the all."

3 Jesus said, "If those who lead you say to you, 'See the kingdom is in the sky,' then the birds of the sky will precede you. If they say to you, 'It is in the sea,' then the fish will precede you. Rather, the kingdom is inside of you, and it is outside of you. When you come to know yourselves, then you will become known, and you will realize that it is you who are the sons of the living father. But if you will not know yourselves, you dwell in poverty and it is you who are that poverty."

4 Jesus said, "The man old in days will not hesitate to ask a small child seven days old about the place of life, and he will live. For many who are first will become last, and they will become one and the same."

5 Jesus said, "Recognize what is in your (sing.) sight, and that which is hidden from you (sing.) will become plain to you (sing.). For there is nothing hidden which will not become manifest."

6 His disciples questioned him and said to him, "Do you want us to fast? How shall we pray? Shall we give alms? What diet shall we observe?"

Jesus said, "Do not tell lies,' and do not do what you hate, for all things are plain in the sight of heaven. For nothing hidden will not become manifest, and nothing covered will remain without being uncovered."

7 Jesus said, "Blessed is the lion which becomes man when consumed by man; and cursed is the man whom the lion consumes, and the lion becomes man."

8 And he said, "The man is like a wise fisherman who cast his net into the sea and drew it up from the sea full of small fish. Among them the wise fisherman found a fine large fish. He threw all the small fish back into the sea and chose the large fish without difficulty. Whoever has ears to hear, let him hear."

9 Jesus said, "Now the sower went out, took a handful (of seeds), and scattered them. Some fell on the road; the birds came and gathered them up. Others fell on rock, did not take root in the soil, and did not produce ears. And others fell on thorns; they choked the seed(s) and worms ate them. And others fell on the good soil and it produced good fruit: it bore sixty per measure and a hundred and twenty per measure."

10 Jesus said, "I have cast fire upon the world, and see, I am guarding it until it blazes."

11 Jesus said, "This heaven will pass away, and the one above it will pass away. The dead are not alive, and the living will not die. In the days when you consumed what is dead, you made it what is alive. When you come to dwell in the light, what will you do? On the day when you were one you became two. But when you become two, what will you do?"

12 The disciples said to Jesus, "We know that you will depart from us. Who is to be our leader?"

Jesus said to them, "Wherever you are, you are to go to James the righteous, for whose sake heaven and earth came into being."

13 Jesus said to his disciples, "Compare me to someone and tell me whom I am like."

Simon Peter said to him, "You are like a righteous angel."

Matthew said to him, "You are like a wise philosopher."

Thomas said to him, "Master, my mouth is wholly incapable of saying whom you are like."

Jesus said, "I am not your (sing.) master. Because you (sing.) have drunk, you (sing.) have become intoxicated from the bubbling spring which I have measured out."

And he took him and withdrew and told him three things. When Thomas returned to his companions, they asked him, "What did Jesus say to you?"

Thomas said to them, "If I tell you one of the things which he told me, you will pick up stones and throw them at me; a fire will come out of the stones and burn you up."

14 Jesus said to them, "If you fast, you will give rise to sin for yourselves; and if you pray, you will be condemned; and if you give alms, you will do harm to your spirits. When you go into any land and walk about in the districts, if they receive you, eat what they will set before you, and heal the sick among them. For what goes into your mouth will not defile you, but that which issues from your mouth—it is that which will defile you."

15 Jesus said, "When you see one who was not born of woman, prostrate yourselves on your faces and worship him. That one is your father."

16 Jesus said, "Men think, perhaps, that it is peace which I have come to cast upon the world. They do not know that it is dissension which I have come to cast upon the earth: fire, sword, and war. For there will be five in a house: three will be against two, and two against three, the father against the son, and the son against the father. And they will stand solitary."

17 Jesus said, "I shall give you what no eye has seen and what no ear has heard and what no hand has touched and what has never occurred to the human mind."

18 The disciples said to Jesus, "Tell us how our end will be."

Jesus said, "Have you discovered, then, the beginning, that you look for the end? For where the beginning is, there will the end be. Blessed is he who will take his place in the beginning; he will know the end and will not experience death."

19 Jesus said, "Blessed is he who came into being before he came into being. If you become my disciples and listen to my words, these stones will minister to you. For there are five trees for you in Paradise which remain undisturbed summer and winter and whose leaves do not fall. Whoever be-

comes acquainted with them will not experience death."

20 The disciples said to Jesus, "Tell us what the kingdom of heaven is like."

He said to them, "It is like a mustard seed. It is the smallest of all seeds. But when it falls on tilled soil, it produces a great plant and becomes a shelter for birds of the sky."

21 Mary said to Jesus, "Whom are your disciples like?"

He said, "They are like children who have settled in a field which is not theirs. When the owners of the field come, they will say, 'Let us have back our field.' They (will) undress in their presence in order to let them have back their field and to give it back to them. Therefore I say, if the owner of a house knows that the thief is coming, he will begin his vigil before he comes and will not let him dig through into his house of his domain to carry away his goods. You (pl.), then, be on your guard against the world. Arm yourselves with great strength lest the robbers find a way to come to you, for the difficulty which you expect will (surely) materialize. Let there be among you a man of understanding. When the grain ripened, he came quickly with his sickle in his hand and reaped it. Whoever has ears to hear, let him hear."

22 Jesus saw infants being suckled. He said to his disciples, "These infants being suckled are like those who enter the kingdom."

They said to him, "Shall we then, as children, enter the kingdom?"

Jesus said to them, "When you make the two one, and when you make the inside like the outside and the outside like the inside, and the above like the below, and when you make the male and the female one and the same, so that the male not be male nor the female female; and when you fashion eyes in place of an eye, and a hand in place of a hand, and a foot in place of a foot, and a likeness in place of a likeness; then will you enter [the kingdom]."

23 Jesus said, "I shall choose you, one out of a thousand, and two out of ten thousand, and they shall stand as a single one."

24 His disciples said to him, "Show us the place where you are, since it is necessary for us to seek it."

He said to them, "Whoever has ears, let him hear. There is light within a man of light, and he lights up the whole world. If he does not shine, he is darkness."

25 Jesus said, "Love your (sing.) brother like your soul, guard him like the pupil of your eye."

26 Jesus said, "You (sing.) see the mote in your brother's eye, but you do not see the beam in your own eye. When you cast the beam out of your own eye, then you will see clearly to cast the mote from your brother's eye."

27 [Jesus said,] "If you do not fast as regards the world, you will not find the kingdom. If you do not observe the Sabbath as a Sabbath, you will not see the father."

28 Jesus said, "I took my place in the midst of the world, and I appeared to them in flesh. I found all of them intoxicated; I found none of them thirsty. And my soul became afflicted for the sons of men, because they are blind in their hearts and do not have sight; for empty they came into the world, and empty too they seek to leave the world. But for the moment they are intoxicated. When they shake off their wine, then they will repent."

29 Jesus said, "If the flesh came into being because of spirit, it is a wonder. But if spirit came into being because of the body, it is a wonder of wonders. Indeed, I am amazed at how this great wealth has made its home in this poverty."

30 Jesus said, "Where there are three gods, they are gods. Where there are two or one, I am with him."

31 Jesus said, "No prophet is accepted in his own village; no physician heals those who know him."

32 Jesus said, "A city being built on a high mountain and fortified cannot fall, nor can it be hidden."

33 Jesus said, "Preach from your (pl.) housetops that which you (sing.) will hear in your (sing.) ear. For no one lights a lamp and puts it under a bushel, nor does he put it in a hidden place, but rather he sets it on a lampstand so that everyone who enters and leaves will see its light."

34 Jesus said, "If a blind man leads a blind man, they will both fall into a pit."

35 Jesus said, "It is not possible for anyone to enter the house of a strong man and take it by force unless he binds his hands; then he will (be able to) ransack his house."

36 Jesus said, "Do not be concerned from morning until evening and from evening until morning about what you will wear."

37 His disciples said, "When will you become revealed to us and when shall we see you?"

Jesus said, "When you disrobe without being ashamed and take up your garments and place them under your feet like little children and tread on them, then [will you see] the son of the living one, and you will not be afraid."

38 Jesus said, "Many times have you desired to hear these words which I am saying to you, and you have no one else to hear them from. There will be days when you will look for me and will not find me."

39 Jesus said, "The pharisees and the scribes have taken the keys of knowledge (gnosis) and hidden them. They themselves have not entered, nor have they allowed to enter those who wish to. You, however, be as wise as serpents and as innocent as doves."

40 Jesus said, "A grapevine has been planted outside of the father, but being unsound, it will be pulled up by its roots and destroyed."

41 Jesus said, "Whoever has something in his hand will receive more, and whoever has nothing will be deprived of even the little he has."

42 Jesus said, "Become passers-by."

43 His disciples said to him, "Who are you, that you should say these things to us?"

[Jesus said to them,] "You do not realize who I am from what I say to you, but you have become like the Jews, for they (either) love the tree and hate its fruit (or) love the fruit and hate the tree."

44 Jesus said, "Whoever blasphemes against the father will be forgiven, and whoever blasphemes against the son will be forgiven, but whoever blasphemes against the holy spirit will not be forgiven either on earth or in heaven."

45 Jesus said, "Grapes are not harvested from thorns, nor are figs gathered from thistles, for they do not produce fruit. A good man brings forth good from his storehouse; an evil man brings forth evil things from his evil storehouse, which is in his heart, and says evil things. For out

of the abundance of the heart he brings forth evil things."

46 Jesus said, "Among those born of women, from Adam until John the Baptist, there is no one so superior to John the Baptist that his eyes should not be lowered (before him). Yet I have said, whichever one of you comes to be a child will be acquainted with the kingdom and will become superior to John."

47 Jesus said, "It is impossible for a man to mount two horses or to stretch two bows. And it is impossible for a servant to serve two masters; otherwise, he will honor the one and treat the other contemptuously. No man drinks old wine and immediately desires to drink new wine. And new wine is not put into old wineskins, lest they burst; nor is old wine put into a new wineskin, lest it spoil it. An old patch is not sewn into a new garment, because a tear would result."

48 Jesus said, "If two make peace with each other in this one house, they will say to the mountain, 'Move away,' and it will move away."

49 Jesus said, "Blessed are the solitary and elect, for you will find the kingdom. For you are from it, and to it you will return."

50 Jesus said, "If they say to you, 'Where did you come from?', say to them, "We came from the light, the place where the light came into being on its own accord and established [itself] and became manifest through their image.' If they say to you, 'Is it you?', say, 'We are its children, and we are the elect of the living father.' If they ask you, 'What is the sign of your father in you?', say to them, 'It is movement and repose.'"

51 His disciples said to him, "When will the repose of the dead come about, and when will the new world come?"

He said to them, "What you look forward to has already come, but you do not recognize it."

52 His disciples said to him, "Twenty-four prophets spoke in Israel, and all of them spoke in you."

He said to them, "You have omitted the one living in your presence and have spoken (only) of the dead."

53 His disciples said to him, "Is circumcision beneficial or not?"

He said to them, "If it were beneficial, their father would beget them already circumcised from their mother. Rather, the true circumcision in spirit has become completely profitable."

54 Jesus said, "Blessed are the poor, for yours is the kingdom of heaven."

55 Jesus said, "Whoever does not hate his father and his mother cannot become a disciple to me. And whoever does not hate his brothers and sisters and take up his cross in my way will not be worthy of me."

56 Jesus said, "Whoever has come to understand the world has found (only) a corpse, and whoever has found a corpse is superior to the world."

57 Jesus said, "The kingdom of the father is like a man who had [good] seed. His enemy came by night and sowed weeds among the good seed. The man did not allow them to pull up the weeds; he said to them, 'I am afraid that you will go intending to pull up the weeds and pull up the wheat along with them.' For on the day of the harvest the weeds will be plainly visible, and they will be pulled up and burned."

58 Jesus said, "Blessed is the man who has suffered and found life."

59 Jesus said, "Take heed of the living one while you are alive, lest you die and seek to see him and be unable to do so."

60 [They saw] a Samaritan carrying a lamb on his way to Judea. He said to his disciples, "That man is round about the lamb."

They said to him, "So that he may kill it and eat it."

He said to them, "While it is alive, he will not eat it, but only when he has killed it and it has become a corpse."

They said to him, "He cannot do so otherwise."

He said to them, "You too, look for a place for yourselves within repose, lest you become a corpse and be eaten."

61 Jesus said, "Two will rest on a bed: the one will die, and the other will live."

Salome said, "Who are you, man, that you . . . have come up on my couch and eaten from my table?"

Jesus said to her, "I am he who exists from the undivided. I was given some of the things of my father."

[. . .] "I am your disciple."

[. . .] "Therefore I say, if he is destroyed he will

be filled with light, but if he is divided, he will be filled with darkness."

62 Jesus said, "It is to those [who are worthy of my] mysteries that I tell my mysteries. Do not let your (sing.) left hand know what your (sing.) right hand is doing."

63 Jesus said, There was a rich man who had much money. He said, 'I shall put my money to use so that I may sow, reap, plant, and fill my storehouse with produce, with the result that I shall lack nothing.' Such were his intentions, but that same night he died. Let him who has ears hear."

64 Jesus said, "A man had received visitors. And when he had prepared the dinner, he sent his servant to invite the guests. He went to the first one and said to him, 'My master invites you.' He said, 'I have claims against some merchants. They are coming to me this evening. I must go and give them my orders. I ask to be excused from the dinner.' He went to another and said to him, 'My master has invited you.' He said to him, 'I have just bought a house and am required for the day. I shall not have any spare time.' He went to another and said to him, 'My master invites you.' He said to him, 'My friend is going to get married, and I am to prepare the banquet. I shall not be able to come. I ask to be excused from the dinner.' He went to another and said to him, 'My master invites you.' He said to him, 'I have just bought a farm, and I am on my way to collect the rent. I shall not be able to come. I ask to be excused.' The servant returned and said to his master, 'Those whom you invited to the dinner have asked to be excused.' The master said to his servant, 'Go outside to the streets and bring back those whom you happen to meet, so that they may dine.' Businessmen and merchants [will] not enter the places of my father."

65 He said, "There was a good man who owned a vineyard. He leased it to tenant farmers so that they might work it and he might collect the produce from them. He sent his servant so that the tenants might give him the produce of the vineyard. They seized his servant and beat him, all but killing him. The servant went back and told his master. The master said, 'Perhaps he did not recognize them.' He sent another servant. The tenants beat this one as well. Then the owner sent his son and said, 'Perhaps they will show respect to my son.' Because the tenants knew that it was he who

was the heir to the vineyard, they seized him and killed him. Let him who has ears hear."

66 Jesus said, "Show me the stone which the builders have rejected. That one is the cornerstone."

67 Jesus said, "If one who knows the all still feels a personal deficiency, he is completely deficient."

68 Jesus said, "Blessed are you when you are hated and persecuted. Wherever you have been persecuted they will find no place."

69 Jesus said, "Blessed are they who have been persecuted within themselves. It is they who have truly come to know the father. Blessed are the hungry, for the belly of him who desires will be filled."

70 Jesus said, "That which you have will save you if you bring it forth from yourselves. That which you do not have within you [will] kill you if you do not have it within you."

71 Jesus said, "I shall [destroy this] house, and no one will be able to build it [. . .]"

72 [A man said] to him, "Tell my brothers to divide my father's possessions with me."

He said to him, "O man, who has made me a divider?"

He turned to his disciples and said to them, "I am not a divider, am I?"

73 Jesus said, "The harvest is great but the laborers are few. Beseech the lord, therefore, to send out laborers to the harvest."

74 He said, "O lord, there are many around the drinking trough, but there is nothing in the cistern."

75 Jesus said, "Many are standing at the door, but it is the solitary who will enter the bridal chamber."

76 Jesus said, "The kingdom of the father is like a merchant who had a consignment of merchandise and who discovered a pearl. That merchant was shrewd. He sold the merchandise and bought the pearl alone for himself. You too, seek his unfailing and enduring treasure where no moth comes near to devour and no worm destroys."

77 Jesus said, "It is I who am the light which is above them all. It is I who am the all. From me did the all come forth, and unto me did the all extend. Split a piece of wood, and I am there. Lift up the stone, and you will find me there."

78 Jesus said, "Why have you come out into the desert? To see a reed shaken by the wind? And to see a man clothed in fine garments [like your] kings and your great men? Upon them are the fine garments, and they are unable to discern the truth."

79 A woman from the crowd said to him, "Blessed are the womb which bore you and the breasts which nourished you."

He said to [her], "Blessed are those who have heard the word of the father and have truly kept it. For there will be days when you (pl.) will say, 'Blessed are the womb which has not conceived and the breasts which have not given milk.'"

80 Jesus said, "He who has recognized the world has found the body, but he who has found the body is superior to the world."

81 Jesus said, "Let him who has grown rich be king, and let him who possesses power renounce it."

82 Jesus said, "He who is near me is near the fire, and he who is far from me is far from the kingdom."

83 Jesus said, "The images are manifest to man, but the light in them remains concealed in the image of the light of the father. He will become manifest, but his image will remain concealed by his light."

84 Jesus said, "When you see your likeness, you rejoice. But when you see your images which came into being before you, and which neither die nor become manifest, how much you will have to bear!"

85 Jesus said, "Adam came into being from a great power and a great wealth, but he did not become worthy of you. For had he been worthy, [he would] not [have experienced] death."

86 Jesus said, "[The foxes have their holes] and the birds have their nests, but the son of man has no place to lay his head and rest."

87 Jesus said, "Wretched is the body that is dependent upon a body, and wretched is the soul that is dependent on these two."

88 Jesus said, "The angels and the prophets will come to you and give to you those things you (already) have. And you too, give them those things which you have, and say to yourselves, 'When will they come and take what is theirs?'"

89 Jesus said, "Why do you wash the outside of the cup? Do you not realize that he who made the inside is the same one who made the outside?"

90 Jesus said, "Come unto me, for my yoke is easy and my lordship is mild, and you will find repose for yourselves."

91 They said to him, "Tell us who you are so that we may believe in you."

He said to them, "You read the face of the sky and of the earth, but you have not recognized the one who is before you, and you do not know how to read this moment."

92 Jesus said, "Seek and you will find. Yet, what you asked me about in former times and which I did not tell you then, now I do desire to tell, but you do not inquire after it."

93 [Jesus said] "Do not give what is holy to dogs, lest they throw them on the dung heap. Do not throw the pearls [to] swine, lest they . . . it [. . .]."

94 Jesus [said], "He who seeks will find, and [he who knocks] will be let in."

95 [Jesus said], "If you have money, do not lend it at interest, but give [it] to one from whom you will not get it back."

96 Jesus said, "The kingdom of the father is like [a certain] woman. She took a little leaven, [concealed] it in some dough, and made it into large loaves. Let him who has ears hear."

97 Jesus said, "The kingdom of the [father] is like a certain woman who was carrying a [jar] full of meal. While she was walking [on the] road, still some distance from home, the handle of the jar broke and the meal emptied out behind her [on] the road. She did not realize it; she had noticed no accident. When she reached her house, she set the jar down and found it empty."

98 Jesus said, "The kingdom of the father is like a certain man who wanted to kill a powerful man. In his own house he drew his sword and stuck it into the wall in order to find out whether his hand could carry through. Then he slew the powerful man."

99 The disciples said to him, "Your brothers and your mother are standing outside."

He said to them, "Those here who do the will of my father are my brothers and my mother. It is they who will enter the kingdom of my father."

100 They showed Jesus a gold coin and said to him, "Caesar's men demand taxes from us."

He said to them, "Give Caesar what belongs to Caesar, give God what belongs to God, and give me what is mine."

101 [Jesus said] "Whoever does not hate his [father] and his mother as I do cannot become a [disciple] to me. And whoever does [not] love his [father and] his mother as I do cannot become a [disciple to] me. For my mother [. . .], but [my] true [mother] gave me life."

102 Jesus said, "Woe to the pharisees, for they are like a dog sleeping in the manger of oxen, for neither does he eat nor does he [let] the oxen eat."

103 Jesus said, "Fortunate is the man who knows where the brigands will enter, so that [he] may get up, muster his domain, and arm himself before they invade."

104 They said to Jesus, "Come, let us pray today and let us fast."

Jesus said, "What is the sin that I have committed, or wherein have I been defeated? But when the bridegroom leaves the bridal chamber then let them fast and pray."

105 Jesus said, "He who knows the father and the mother will be called the son of a harlot."

106 Jesus said, "When you make the two one, you will become the sons of man, and when you say, 'Mountain, move away,' it will move away."

107 Jesus said, "The kingdom is like a shepherd who had a hundred sheep. One of them, the largest, went astray. He left the ninety-nine and looked for that one until he found it. When he had gone to such trouble, he said to the sheep, 'I care for you more than the ninety-nine.'"

108 Jesus said, "He who will drink from my mouth will become like me. I myself shall become he, and the things that are hidden will be revealed to him."

109 Jesus said, "The kingdom is like a man who had a [hidden] treasure in his field without knowing it. And [after] he died, he left it to his [son]. The son [did] not know (about the treasure). He inherited the field and sold [it]. And the one who bought it went plowing and [found] the treasure. He began to lend money at interest to whomever he wished."

110 Jesus said, "Whoever finds the world and becomes rich, let him renounce the world."

111 Jesus said, "The heavens and the earth will be rolled up in your presence. And the one who lives from the living one will not see death." Does not Jesus say, "Whoever finds himself is superior to the world"?

112 Jesus said, "Woe to the flesh that depends on the soul; woe to the soul that depends on the flesh."

113 His disciples said to him, "When will the kingdom come?"

[Jesus said] "It will not come by waiting for it. It will not be a matter of saying 'here it is' or 'there it is'. Rather, the kingdom of the father is spread out upon the earth, and men do not see it."

114 Simon Peter said to them, "Let Mary leave us, for women are not worthy of life."

Jesus said, "I myself shall lead her in order to make her male, so that she too may become a living spirit resembling you males. For every woman who will make herself male will enter the kingdom of heaven."

The Gospel of Peter

The *Gospel of Peter* was known and used as Scripture in some parts of the Christian church in the second century. Its use was eventually disallowed by church leaders, however, who considered some of its teachings heretical and who claimed, as a consequence, that it could not have been written by its imputed author, Simon Peter. Having fallen out of circulation, it was practically forgotten in all but name until a fragment of its text was discovered near the end of the nineteenth century in the tomb of a Christian monk in Egypt.

The fragment narrates the events of Jesus' passion and resurrection; it begins in mid-sentence by describing Pilate's washing of his hands at Jesus' trial. The narrative that follows bears a close relationship with the accounts found in the New Testament Gospels, especially Matthew, including descriptions of Jesus' crucifixion, his burial, the posting of a guard, and the events surrounding the resurrection. Some of the details here, however, are strikingly different. During the crucifixion, for example, Jesus is said to have been "silent as if he had no pain" (v. 10). In addition, some of the stories found here occur nowhere else among our early Christian Gospels. Most significantly, the Gospel narrates an account of Jesus' emergence from his tomb. He is supported by two gigantic angels whose heads reach up to the sky; his own head reaches above the skies. Behind them emerges the cross. A voice then speaks from heaven, "Have you preached to those who are asleep?" The cross replies, "Yes" (vv. 39–42).

At the conclusion of the narrative the story breaks off in the middle of a sentence in which the author reveals his name: "But I, Simon Peter, and my brother Andrew, took our nets and went to the sea . . ." (v. 60).

It is impossible to know whether the complete *Gospel of Peter* contained only a passion narrative or, like the New Testament Gospels, simply ended with one. Some scholars maintain that its pseudonymous author (no one actually thinks it was Peter) derived his stories from the New Testament Gospels and modified them according to his own theological perspective; others think that he is depending on *other* sources than the canonical Gospels, or that all five Gospels derived their stories from the same sources, but independently of one another.

In any event, it is clear that one of this Gospel's principal concerns is to incriminate Jews for the death of Jesus. Here, for instance, after Jesus' crucifixion, the Jewish people bewail their guilt and lament the certain fate of their beloved sacred city Jerusalem, which God will now destroy as retribution for their disobedience (v. 25). This anti-Judaic slant can perhaps be used to help date the Gospel in its final form, for such themes became common among Christian authors in the second century. The author was possibly writing at the beginning of the century, utilizing traditions from oral and written sources that were themselves much older.

"The Gospel of Peter," translated by Bart D. Ehrman. All rights reserved. Based on the Greek text of PCair 10759, as found in Egbert Schlarb and Dieter Lührmann, *Fragmente apokryph gewordener Evangelien in Griechischer und Lateinischer Sprache* (MTS 59; Marburg: N. G. Elwert, 2000) 85–93.

1 . . . but none of the Jews washed his hands, nor did Herod or any of his judges. Since they did not wish to wash, Pilate stood up. 2 Then King Herod ordered the Lord to be taken away and said to them, "Do everything that I ordered you to do to him."

3 Standing there was Joseph, a friend of both Pilate and the Lord; when he knew that they were about to crucify him, he came to Pilate and asked for the Lord's body for burial. 4 Pilate sent word to Herod, asking for the body. 5 Herod said, "Brother Pilate, even if no one had asked for him we would have buried him, since the sabbath is dawning. For it is written in the Law that the sun must not set on one who has been killed."[1] And he delivered him over to the people the day before their Feast of Unleavened Bread.

6 Those who took the Lord began pushing him about, running up to him and saying, "Let us drag around the Son of God, since we have authority over him." 7 They clothed him in purple and sat him on a judge's seat, saying, "Give a righteous judgment, O King of Israel!" 8 One of them brought a crown made of thorns and placed it on the Lord's head. 9 Others standing there were spitting in his face; some slapped his cheeks; others were beating him with a reed; and some began to flog him, saying, "This is how we should honor the Son of God!"

10 They brought forward two evildoers and crucified the Lord between them. But he was silent, as if he had no pain. 11 When they had set the cross upright, they wrote an inscription: "This is the King of Israel." 12 Putting his clothes in front of him they divided them up and cast a lot for them. 13 But one of the evildoers reviled them, "We have suffered like this for the evil things we did; but this one, the Savior of the people—what wrong has he done you?" 14 They became angry at him and ordered his legs not be broken, so that he would die in torment.

15 It was noon and darkness came over all of Judea. They were disturbed and upset that the sun may have already set while he was still alive; for their Scripture says that the sun must not set on one who has been killed.[2] 16 One of them said, "Give him gall mixed with vinegar to drink." And they made the mixture and gave it to him to drink. 17 Thus they brought all things to fulfillment and completed all their sins on their heads.

18 But many were wandering around with torches, thinking that it was night; and they stumbled about. 19 And the Lord cried out, "My power, O power, you have left me behind!" When he said this, he[a] was taken up.

20 At that time, the curtain of the Temple in Jerusalem was ripped in half. 21 Then they pulled the nails from the Lord's hands and placed him on the ground. All the ground shook and everyone was terrified. 22 Then the sun shone and it was found to be three in the afternoon.

23 But the Jews were glad and gave his body to Joseph that he might bury him, since he had seen all the good things he did. 24 He took the Lord, washed him, wrapped him in a linen cloth, and brought him into his own tomb, called the Garden of Joseph. 25 Then the Jews, the elders, and the priests realized how much evil they had done to themselves and began beating their breasts, saying "Woe to us because of our sins. The judgment and the end of Jerusalem are near."

26 But I and my companions were grieving and went into hiding, wounded in heart. For we were being sought out by them as if we were evildoers who wanted to burn the Temple. 27 Because of these things we fasted and sat mourning and weeping, night and day, until the sabbath.

28 The scribes, Pharisees, and elders gathered together and heard all the people murmuring and beating their breasts, saying, "If such great signs happened when he died, you can see how righteous he was!" 29 The elders became fearful and went to Pilate and asked him, 30 "Give us some soldiers to guard his crypt for three days to keep his disciples from coming to steal him. Otherwise the people may assume he has been raised from the dead and then harm us."

31 So Pilate gave them the centurion Petronius and soldiers to guard the tomb. The elders and scribes came with them to the crypt. 32 Everyone who was there, along with the centurian and the soldiers, rolled a great stone and placed it there before the entrance of the crypt. 33 They smeared it with seven seals, pitched a tent there, and stood guard

[a]Or *it*

[1]Deut 21:22–23   [2]Deut 21:22–23

34 Early in the morning, as the sabbath dawned, a crowd came from Jerusalem and the surrounding area to see the sealed crypt. 35 But during the night on which the Lord's day dawned, while the soldiers stood guard two by two on their watch, a great voice came from the sky. 36 They saw the skies open and two men descend from there; they were very bright and drew near to the tomb. 37 The stone cast before the entrance rolled away by itself and moved to one side; the tomb was open and both young men entered.

38 When the solders saw these things, they woke up the centurion and the elders—for they were also there on guard. 39 As they were explaining what they had seen, they saw three men emerge from the tomb, two of them supporting the other, with a cross following behind them. 40 The heads of the two reached up to the sky, but the head of the one they were leading went up above the skies. 41 And they heard a voice from the skies, "Have you preached to those who are asleep?" 42 And a reply came from the cross, "Yes."

43 They then decided among themselves to go off to disclose what had happened to Pilate. 44 While they were still making their plans, the skies were again seen to open, and a person descended and entered the crypt. 45 Those who were with the centurion saw these things and hurried to Pilate at night, abandoning the tomb they had been guarding, and explained everything they had seen. Greatly agitated, they said, "He actually was the Son of God." 46 Pilate replied, "I am clean of the blood of the Son of God; you decided to do this."

47 Then everyone approached him to ask and urge him to order the centurion and the soldiers to say nothing about what they had seen. 48 "For it is better," they said, "for us to incur a great sin before God than to fall into the hands of the Jewish people and be stoned." 49 And so Pilate ordered the centurion and the soldiers not to say a word.

50 Now Mary Magdalene, a disciple of the Lord, had been afraid of the Jews, since they were inflamed with anger; and so she had not done at the Lord's crypt the things that women customarily do for loved ones who die. But early in the morning of the Lord's day 51 she took some of her women friends with her and came to the crypt where he had been buried. 52 They were afraid that the Jews might see them, and they said, "Even though we were not able to weep and beat our breasts on the day he was crucified, we should do these things now at his crypt. 53 But who will roll away for us the stone placed before the entrance of the crypt, that we can go in, sit beside him, and do what we should? 54 For it was a large stone, and we are afraid someone may see us. If we cannot move it, we should at least cast down the things we have brought at the entrance as a memorial to him; and we will weep and beat our breasts until we return home."

55 When they arrived they found the tomb opened. And when they came up to it they stooped down to look in, and they saw a beautiful young man dressed in a very bright garment, sitting in the middle of the tomb. He said to them, 56 "Why have you come? Whom are you seeking? Not the one who was crucified? He has risen and left. But if you do not believe it, stoop down to look, and see the place where he was laid, that he is not there. For he has risen and left for the place from which he was sent." 57 Then the women fled out of fear.

58 But it was the final day of the Feast of Unleavened Bread, and many left to return to their homes, now that the feast had ended. 59 But we, the twelve disciples of the Lord, wept and grieved; and each one returned to his home, grieving for what had happened. 60 But I, Simon Peter, and my brother Andrew, took our nets and went off to the sea. And with us was Levi, the son of Alphaeus, whom the Lord . . .

The Infancy Gospel of Thomas

Many early Christians were naturally curious to learn the details of Jesus' life. As stories circulated about the inspired teachings and miraculous deeds of Jesus' public ministry, some Christians began to speculate on what he said and did before it began. Only a couple of incidents involving Jesus prior to his baptism are found in the New Testament Gospels: the narratives of his birth and infancy in Matthew and Luke and the account, unique to Luke, of his pilgrimage to the Jerusalem Temple as a twelve-year-old (Luke 2:41–52). Other stories of Jesus as a youth, however, were soon in circulation. Behind many of these legends lay a fundamental question: if Jesus was a miracle-working Son of God as an adult, what was he like as a child?

The *Infancy Gospel of Thomas* (not to be confused with the Coptic *Gospel of Thomas* discovered near Nag Hammadi, Egypt) is one of the earliest accounts of these legends. The book was allegedly written by "Thomas, the Israelite." It is not clear whether or not the author intended his readers to recognize him as Judas Thomas, thought by some early Christians to have been Jesus' own brother. If this was his intent, then his accounts of Jesus as a youth, needless to say, would have been based on indisputable authority.

The narrative begins with Jesus as a five-year-old boy and relates a number of incidents, most of them miraculous, that betray a streak of the mischievous in Joseph and Mary's precocious son. Here are anecdotes of Jesus at play with his childhood companions (sometimes harming them with his divine power, sometimes healing them), in confrontation with his elders (usually bettering them), at school with his teachers (revealing their ignorance), and in the workshop with his father (miraculously correcting his mistakes). For modern readers it is difficult to decide whether such stories were meant as serious accounts of Jesus' early life or simply as speculative and entertaining stories of the youthful Son of God.

The text provides few clues to help us fix the time of its composition. Most scholars believe that such "infancy Gospels" began to circulate during the first half of the second century; some have dated the *Infancy Gospel of Thomas* itself as early as 125 C.E.

1 I, Thomas the Israelite, make this report to all of you, my brothers among the Gentiles, that you may know the magnificent childhood activities of our Lord Jesus Christ—all that he did after being born in our country. The beginning is as follows:

2 When this child Jesus was five years old, he was playing by the ford of a stream; and he gathered the flowing waters into pools and made them immediately pure. These things he ordered simply by speaking a word. 2 He then made some soft mud and fashioned twelve sparrows from it. It was the sabbath when he did this. A number of other children were also playing with him. 3 But when a certain Jew saw what Jesus had done while playing on the sabbath, he left right

away and reported to his father, Joseph, "Look, your child at the stream has taken mud and formed twelve sparrows. He has profaned the sabbath!" 4 When Joseph came to the place and saw what had happened, he cried out to him, "Why are you doing what is forbidden on the sabbath?" But Jesus clapped his hands and cried to the sparrows, "Be gone!" And the sparrows took flight and went off, chirping. 5 When the Jews saw this they were amazed; and they went away and reported to their leaders what they had seen Jesus do.

3 Now the son of Annas the scribe was standing there with Joseph; and he took a willow branch and scattered the water that Jesus had gathered. 2 Jesus was irritated when he saw what had happened, and he said to him: "You unrighteous, irreverent idiot! What did the pools of water do to harm you? See, now you also will be withered like a tree, and you will never bear leaves or root or fruit." 3 Immediately that child was completely withered. Jesus left and returned to Joseph's house. But the parents of the withered child carried him away, mourning his lost youth. They brought him to Joseph and began to accuse him, "What kind of child do you have who does such things?"

4 Somewhat later he was going through the village, and a child ran up and banged into his shoulder. Jesus was aggravated and said to him, "You will go no further on your way." And right away the child fell down and died. Some of those who saw what happened said, "Where was this child born? For everything he says is a deed accomplished." 2 The parents of the dead child came to Joseph and blamed him, saying "Since you have such a child you cannot live with us in the village. Or teach him to bless and not to curse—for he is killing our children!"

5 Joseph called to the child and admonished him privately, "Why are you doing such things? These people are suffering, they hate us and are persecuting us!" But Jesus replied, "I know these are not your words, and so I also will keep silent for your sake. But those others will bear their punishment." And immediately those who were accusing him were blinded. 2 Those who saw these things were frightened and disturbed; they began saying about him, "Everything he has said, whether good or bad, has become an amazing reality." When Joseph saw what Jesus had done, he rose up, grabbed his ear, and yanked it hard. 3 The child was irritated and said to him, "It is enough for you to seek and not find; you have not acted at all wisely. Do you not know that I am yours? Do not grieve me."

6 There was an instructor named Zachaeus standing off to the side who heard Jesus say these things to his father. And he was amazed that he was speaking such things, though just a child. 2 After a few days he approached Joseph and said to him, "You have a bright child with a good mind. Come, let me have him that he may learn to read, and through reading I will teach him everything, including how to greet all the elders and to honor them as his ancestors and fathers, and to love children his own age." 3 And he told him all the letters from Alpha to Omega, clearly and with great precision. But Jesus looked the instructor Zachaeus in the face and said to him, "Since you do not know the true nature of the Alpha, how can you teach anyone the Beta? You hypocrite! If you know it, first teach the Alpha, and then we will believe you about the Beta." Then he began to question the teacher sharply about the first letter, and he was not able to give him the answers. 4 And while many others were listening, the child said to Zachaeus, "Listen, teacher, to the arrangement of the first letter of the alphabet; observe here how it has set patterns, and middle strokes which you see collectively crossing, then coming together, and proceeding upward again till they reach the top, so that it is divided into three equal parts, each of them fundamental and foundational, of equal length. Now you have the set patterns of the Alpha."

7 When the teacher Zachaeus heard the child setting forth so many allegorical interpretations like this of the first letter, he was at a complete loss about this kind of explanation and teaching, and he said to those standing there, "Woe is me! I am wretched and at a complete loss; I have put myself to shame, taking on this child. 2 I beg of you, brother Joseph, take him away. I cannot bear his stern gaze or make sense of a single word. This child is not of this world; he can even tame fire. Maybe he was born before the world came into being. I cannot fathom what kind of uterus bore him or what kind of womb nourished him.

Woe is me, friend. He has befuddled me; I cannot follow his reasoning. I have fooled myself and am miserable three times over. I was struggling to have a student, and I have been found to have a teacher. 3 My friends, I know all too well my shame: though an old man, I have been defeated by a child. I may grow weak and die because of this child. For at this moment I cannot look him in the face. When everyone says that I have been defeated by a young child, what can I say? And how can I explain the things he told me about the set patterns of the first letter? I have no idea, my friends. For I do not know its[a] beginning or end. 4 And so I ask you, brother Joseph, take him back home. I do not know what kind of great thing he is—whether a divine being or angel; I do not know even what to say."

8 While the Jews were giving Zachaeus advice, the child laughed aloud and said, "Now let what is yours bear fruit. and let the blind in heart see. I have come from above to curse them and call them to the realm above, just as the one who sent me for your sake commanded." 2 When the child stopped speaking, immediately all those who had fallen under his curse were healed. No one dared to anger him from that time on, fearing that he might cripple them with a curse.

9 Some days later Jesus was playing on a flat rooftop of a house, and one of the children playing with him fell from the roof and died. When the other children saw what had happened, they ran away, so that Jesus stood there alone. 2 When the parents of the one who died arrived they accused him of throwing him down. But Jesus said, "I certainly did not throw him down." But they began to abuse him verbally. 3 Jesus leapt down from the roof and stood beside the child's corpse, and with a loud voice he cried out, "Zenon!" (for that was his name) "rise up and tell me: Did I throw you down?" And right away he rose up and said, "Not at all, Lord! You did not throw me down, but you have raised me up!" When they saw this they were astounded. The parents of the child glorified God for the sign that had occurred, and they worshiped Jesus.

10 A few days later there was a young man who was splitting wood in a secluded spot. The axe fell and split open the sole of his foot. He lost a lot of blood and was dying. 2 There

was a disturbance and a crowd started to gather, and the child Jesus also ran to the spot. Forcing his way through the crowd, he grabbed the young man's foot that had been struck, and immediately it was healed. And he said to the young man, "Rise now, split the wood, and remember me." When the crowd saw what had happened it worshiped the child, saying, "The Spirit of God certainly lives within this child."

11 When he was six years old, his mother gave him a water jug and sent him to draw some water to bring back home. But he was jostled by the crowd, and the water jug was shattered. 2 So Jesus unfolded the cloak he was wearing, filled it with water, and brought it back to his mother. When his mother saw the sign that had happened, she kissed him. And she kept to herself the mysterious deeds that she saw him do.

12 When it later became time for sowing, the child went out with his father to sow wheat in their field. And when his father sowed, the child Jesus also sowed a single grain of wheat. 2 When he harvested and threshed the grain, it produced a hundred large bushels. He called all the poor people of the village to the threshing floor and gave them the wheat; and Joseph took what was left of it. He was eight years old when he did this sign.

13 Now his father was a carpenter, and at that time he used to make plows and yokes. He received an order from a certain rich man to make a bed. But when the measurement for one of the beautiful crossbeams came out too short, he did not know what to do. The child Jesus said to his father Joseph, "Place the two pieces of wood on the floor and line them up from the middle to one end." 2 Joseph did just as the child said. Then Jesus stood at the other end, grabbed the shorter board, and stretched it out to make it the same length as the other. His father Joseph saw what he had done and was amazed. He embraced the child and gave him a kiss, saying "I am blessed that God has given me this child."

14 When Joseph observed the mind of the child and saw that he was starting to mature, he again did not want him to be unable to read, and so took him out to give him over to an-

---

[a]Or *his*

other teacher. The teacher said to Joseph, "First I will teach him to read Greek, and then Hebrew." For the teacher knew of the child's learning and was afraid of him. Nonetheless, he wrote out the alphabet and practiced it for him for a long time; but the child gave him no response. 2 Then Jesus said to him, "If you are really a teacher and know the letters well, tell me the power of the Alpha, and I will tell you the power of the Beta." The teacher was aggravated and struck him on the head. The child was hurt and cursed him; and immediately he fainted and fell to the ground on his face. 3 The child returned to Joseph's house. Joseph was smitten with grief and ordered his mother, "Do not let him out the door; for those who anger him die."

15 Some time later there was another instructor, a close friend of Joseph, who said to him, "Bring the child to me at the school. Maybe I can use flattery to teach him to read." Joseph said to him, "If you're that courageous, brother, take him along with you." He took him with great fear and much anxiety, but the child went along gladly. 2 He entered the school with confidence and found a book lying on the reading desk. He picked it up, but instead of reading the words in it, he opened his mouth and began to speak in the Holy Spirit, teaching the Law to those who were standing there. A great crowd gathered, standing there to hear him; and they were amazed at the great beauty of his teaching and his carefully crafted words—amazed that he could speak such things though still a babe. 3 But when Joseph heard about this he was frightened. He ran to the school, thinking that this instructor might also have proved ignorant. But the instructor said to Joseph, "You should know, brother, that I took the child as a pupil; but he is filled with great grace and wisdom. Now I ask you brother, take him home." 4 When the child heard these things, he immediately laughed at him and said, "Since you have rightly spoken and rightly borne witness, for your sake that other one who was struck down will be healed." And right away the other instructor was healed. Joseph took the child and returned home.

16 Now Joseph sent his son James to bundle some wood and bring it to the house. The child Jesus also followed him. While James was gathering the firewood, a snake bit his hand.

2 When he was stretched out on the ground dying, Jesus came up to him and breathed on the bite. The pain immediately stopped, the animal burst, and straight away James was returned to health.

17 After these things, an infant in Joseph's neighborhood became sick and died; and his mother was weeping loudly. When Jesus heard the outburst of sorrow and the disturbance, he ran up quickly and found the child dead. He touched its breast, saying "I say to you, young child, do not die but live, and be with your mother." Immediately the child opened its eyes and laughed. Jesus said to the woman, "Take him, give him milk, and remember me." 2 When the crowd standing there saw what had happened, it was amazed. The people said, "Truly this child is either God or an angel of God, for his every word is an accomplished deed." Jesus then left from there to play with the other children.

18 Some time later a house was being built and there was a great disturbance. Jesus got up and went out to the place. He saw a man lying down, dead; taking his hand he said, "I say to you, O man, rise up and do your work." Immediately he rose up and worshiped him. 2 When the crowd saw, it was amazed and said, "This child comes from heaven. For he has saved many souls from death—his entire life he is able to save them."

19 When he was twelve years old his parents made their customary trip to Jerusalem, in a caravan, for the Passover feast. After the Passover they returned home. While they were returning, the child Jesus went back up to Jerusalem. But his parents thought he was in the caravan. 2 After their first day of travel, they began looking for him among their relatives and were upset not to find him. They returned again to the city to look for him. And after the third day they found him sitting in the Temple in the midst of the teachers, both listening and asking them questions. Everyone was attending closely, amazed that though a child, he questioned the elders and teachers of the people sharply, explaining the chief points of the Law and the parables of the prophets. 3 When his mother Mary came up to him she said, "Why have you done this to us, child? See, we have been distressed, looking for you." Jesus replied to them, "Why are you looking for me?

THE INFANCY GOSPEL OF THOMAS

Don't you know that I must be with those who are my Father's?"[b] 4 The scribes and Pharisees said, "Are you the mother of this child?" She replied, "I am." They said to her, "You are most fortunate among women, because God has blessed the fruit of your womb. For we have never seen or heard of such glory, such virtue and wisdom. 5 Jesus got up from there and followed his mother, and he was obedient to his parents. But his mother kept to herself all these things that had happened. And Jesus grew in wisdom and stature and grace. To him be the glory forever and ever, amen.

[b]Or *be doing my Fathers' business;* or *be in my Father's house*

The Secret Gospel of Mark

The *Secret Gospel of Mark* is a longer edition of Mark's Gospel that has been known only since 1958. While cataloguing manuscripts in the library of the Greek Orthodox monastery of Mar Saba, located southeast of Jerusalem, an American scholar, Morton Smith, came upon a seventeenth-century edition of the letters of Ignatius. On the final blank pages of this volume, an eighteenth-century scribe had copied a portion of a letter allegedly from Clement of Alexandria, a church father who lived at the end of the second century and the beginning of the third. In this letter, Clement indicates that Mark had produced two versions of his Gospel, one for church members at large and the other for the spiritual elite who could grasp the full mysteries of the Kingdom. Clement indicates that this second expanded edition, the so-called *Secret Gospel,* had been entrusted to the Christians of Alexandria, his own city, but that it had come to be misused by members of the Carpocratian sect, a group of Gnostic Christians known for their illicit sexual rituals.

Clement then narrates two of the accounts found in the *Secret Gospel.* The contents of the stories, especially the first, show why this version of the Gospel could have seemed so dangerous in the hands of the uninitiated, and so interesting to the Carpocratians. Jesus raises a youth from the dead, who then loves Jesus and begs to be allowed to stay with him (the story is reminiscent of both the raising of Lazarus in John 11 and of the story of the "rich young man" of Matt 17:16–22 and Mark 10:17–31). After six days, the youth comes to Jesus in the evening, clothed with nothing but a linen garment over his naked body (cf. Mark 14:51). They spend the night together, with Jesus teaching the youth the mystery of the kingdom.

The highly unusual character of this story, in particular its homoerotic overtones, has led scholars to debate virtually every aspect of the *Secret Gospel.* Did Clement of Alexandria actually write this letter, preserved only in an eighteenth-century fragment that no one except Morton Smith has actually seen (Smith published photographs of the document, but the original is inaccessible). Is it a modern forgery? An ancient forgery? If the letter is actually by Clement, were the stories that it narrates known before the end of the second century? Do they actually come from a second edition of Mark's Gospel? Could they, instead, have originally been part of the *first* edition of the Gospel, only to be deleted by orthodox Christian scribes concerned with their ethical implications? Were these stories already widely known by Christians of the first century (such as the author of the Fourth Gospel)? Could they, in fact, have actually happened?

These and other questions have made the *Secret Gospel of Mark* one of the most hotly debated Christian texts to have been discovered in modern times.

The entire letter of Clement is not translated here, but only the quotations that relate to the *Secret Gospel*. Clement begins the letter by providing the account summarized above, indicating that the apostle Mark produced a second version of his Gospel for the spiritually enlightened in Alexandria, which was wrongfully procured and corrupted by the Carpocratians. He then goes on to indicate two passages that were in this second version, the *Secret Gospel*, along with one that was not in it, that he had been queried about.

Citation I (following Mark 10:34)

They came to Bethany, and a woman was there whose brother had died. She came and prostrated herself before Jesus, saying to him, "Son of David, have mercy on me." But his disciples rebuked her. Jesus became angry and went off with her to the garden where the tomb was.

Immediately a loud voice was heard from the tomb. Jesus approached and rolled the stone away from the entrance to the tomb. Immediately he went in where the young man was, stretched out his hand, and raised him by seizing his hand.

The young man looked at him intently and loved him; and he began pleading with him that he might be with him. When they came out of the tomb they went to the young man's house, for he was wealthy.

And after six days Jesus gave him a command. And when it was evening the young man came to him, wearing a linen cloth over his naked body. He stayed with him that night, for Jesus was teaching him the mystery of the Kingdom of God. When he got up from there, he returned to the other side of the Jordan.

The letter goes on to indicate a passage not found in the Secret Gospel:

Citation 2

"But the phrase 'naked man with naked man,' and the other matters you inquired about, are not found (in the text)."

Citation 3 (following Mark 10:46a)

"And the sister of the young man Jesus loved was there, along with his mother and Salome. And Jesus did not receive them."

The fragment of the letter concludes with a tantalizing statement that Clement now intends to provide "a true interpretation" of these matters, "in accordance with the true philosophy." But that is exactly where the letter breaks off.

Papyrus Egerton 2: The Unknown Gospel

The fragmentary manuscript known as *Papyrus Egerton 2* contains a noncanonical Gospel that was completely unknown until its publication in 1935. The fragments had been discovered among a collection of papyri purchased by the British Museum. They had come from Egypt and are usually dated to 150 C.E. or so. The so-called "Unknown Gospel" narrated in these papyri, however, must have been older. While some scholars have argued that it was written before the canonical Gospels, most have concluded that it was produced sometime during the first half of the second century. An additional small fragment was subsequently discovered in Cologne and published in 1987.

Since the *Unknown Gospel* is preserved only in fragments, it is impossible to judge its original length and contents. The surviving remains contain four separate stories: (1) an account of Jesus' controversy with Jewish leaders that is similar to the stories found in John 5:39–47 and 10:31–39; (2) the healing of a leper, reminiscent of Matthew 8:1–4, Mark 1:40–45, Luke 5:12–16, and 17:11–14; (3) a controversy over paying tribute to Caesar, comparable to Matthew 22:15–22, Mark 12:13–17, and Luke 20:20–26; and (4) a fragmentary account of a miracle by Jesus on the bank of the Jordan River, evidently performed to illustrate his parable about the miraculous growth of seeds. This final story has no parallel in the canonical Gospels.

Scholars continue to debate whether the author of this Gospel (a) used the four canonical Gospels as literary sources for his accounts, (b) quoted from memory stories that he knew from the canonical Gospels (changing them in the process), or (c) acquired his stories, not from the canonical Gospels, but from the oral traditions of Jesus in wide circulation in the first and second centuries.

1.

[And Jesus said]ᵃ to the lawyers: "[Punish] every wrongdoer and [transgressor], but not me. [For that one does not consider] how he does what he does.

Then he turned to the rulers of the people and spoke this word: "Search the Scriptures, for you think that in them you have life. They are the ones that testify concerning me. Do not think that I came to accuse you to my Father. The one who accuses you is Moses, in whom you have hoped."

They replied, "We know full well that God

ᵃLess certain restorations of the text are enclosed in square brackets spoke to Moses. But we do not know where you have come from."

Jesus answered them, "Now what stands accused is your failure to believe his testimonies. For if you had believed Moses, you would have believed me. For that one wrote to your fathers concerning me . . ."

2.

. . . to the crowd . . . stones together so that they might stone him. And the rulers were trying to lay their hands on him, that they might arrest him and deliver him over to the crowd. And they were unable to arrest him because the hour for him to be delivered over had not yet come. But the Lord himself went out through their midst and left them.

And behold, a leper approached him and said, "Teacher Jesus, while I was traveling with some lepers and eating with them at the inn, I myself contracted leprosy. If, then, you are willing, I will be made clean."

Then the Lord said to him, "I am willing: Be clean." And immediately the leprosy left him. And Jesus said to him, "Go, show yourself to the priests and make an offering for your cleansing as Moses commanded; and sin no more. . . ."

3.

. . . (They came) to him and began rigorously testing him, saying, "Teacher Jesus, we know that you have come from God. For the things you do give a testimony that is beyond all the prophets. And so, tell us: is it right to pay the kings the things that relate to their rule? Shall we pay them or not?"

But when Jesus understood their thought he became incensed and said to them, "Why do you call me teacher with your mouth, when you do not listen to what I say? Well did Isaiah prophecy about you, 'This people honors me with their lips, but their heart is far removed from me. In vain do they worship me, commandments. . . .'"[1]

4.

. . . hidden away in a secret place . . . placed underneath in secret . . . its weight beyond measure. . . . And while they were puzzling over his strange question, Jesus walked and stood on the banks of the Jordan river; he reached out his right hand, and filled it. . . . And he sowed it on the. . . . And then . . . water . . . and . . . before their eyes; and it brought forth fruit . . . many . . . for joy. . . .

---

[1]Isa 29:13

The Gospel of the Ebionites

The Ebionites were a group of Jewish Christians located in different regions of the Mediterranean from at least the second to the fourth centuries. The distinguishing characteristic of this group, at least in the eyes of their Christian opponents, was their attempt to combine Jewish views and lifestyles with the belief that Jesus was the Messiah. In particular, they were said to have emphasized their monotheistic belief in only one God to such an extreme that they denied, as a consequence, Jesus' own divinity. At the same time, the Ebionites differed from non-Christian Jews in asserting that Jesus was the sacrifice for the sins of the world and that all other sacrifices had therefore become meaningless. Among other things, this belief led them to embrace a vegetarian diet (since most meat was procured, in the ancient world, through the religious act of sacrificing an animal).

The *Gospel of the Ebionites* does not survive intact but only in quotations of an opponent of Jewish Christians, the fourth-century heresy hunter, Epiphanius of Salamis. These quotations, however, give us a good idea of what the entire Gospel must have looked like. It was written in Greek and represented a kind of harmony of the Gospels of Matthew, Mark, and Luke. This can be seen most clearly in the account of the voice at Jesus' baptism. In the three canonical accounts, the voice says slightly different things. These differences are harmonized, however, in the *Gospel of the Ebionites,* where the voice comes from heaven three times, saying something slightly different on each occasion (corresponding to the words found in each of the Synoptics).

Some of the Ebionites' distinctive concerns were embodied in their Gospel. This can be seen, for example, in the reference to the diet of John the Baptist, in which the canonical statement that he ate locusts (i.e., meat) and wild honey is modified by the change of simply one letter, so that now the Baptist, in anticipation of the Ebionites themselves, maintains a vegetarian cuisine: here he is said to have eaten *pancakes* and wild honey.

It is difficult to assign a date to this Gospel, but since it betrays a knowledge of Matthew, Mark, and Luke, and presupposes a thriving community of Jewish Christians, it is perhaps best to locate it sometime early in the second century.

Epiphanius, *adv. Haer.* 30.1–3

1.

And there was a man named Jesus, and he was about thirty years old; he has chosen us and he came into Capernaum and entered into the house of Simon, surnamed Peter, and he opened his mouth and said, "As I walked by the sea of Tiberias, I chose John and James, the sons of Zebedee, and Simon and Andrew and Thaddaeus and Simon Zelotes, and Judas Iscariot; you also, Matthew, when you were sitting at the receipt of custom, did I call and you followed me. According to my intention you shall be twelve apostles for a testimony to Israel."

2.

And it came to pass when John baptized, that the Pharisees came to him and were baptized, and all Jerusalem also. He had a garment of camels' hair, and a leathern girdle about his loins. And his meat was wild honey, which tasted like manna, formed like cakes of oil.[1]

3.

The beginning of their Gospel reads thus: "It came to pass in the days of Herod, King of Judaea, that John came and baptized with the baptism of repentance in the river Jordan; he is said to be from the tribe of Aaron and a son of Zacharias the priest and of Elizabeth, and all went out to him."

4.

And after many other words it goes on: "After the people had been baptized, Jesus came also, and was baptized by John. And as he came out of the water, the heavens opened, and he saw the Holy Spirit descending in the form of a dove and entering into him. And a voice was heard from heaven, "You are my beloved Son, and in you am I well pleased." And again, "This day have I begotten you." And suddenly a great light shone in that place. And John, seeing him, said, "Who are you, Lord?" Then a voice was heard from heaven, "This is my beloved Son, in whom I am well pleased." Thereat John fell at his feet and said, "I pray you, Lord, baptize me." But he would not, saying, "Suffer it, for thus it is fitting that all should be accomplished."[2]

Epiphanius *adv. Haer.* 30.14:

5.

They also deny that he is a man, basing their assertion on the word which he said when he was told: "Behold your mother and your brethren stand outside." "Who is my mother and who are my brethren?" And he stretched forth his hand toward his disciples and said, "My brethren and my mother and sisters are those who do the will of my Father."[3]

Epiphanius *adv. Haer.* 30.16:

6.

They say that he is not begotten by God the Father but created like one of the archangels, being greater than they. He rules over the angels and the beings created by God and he came and declared, as the gospel used by them records: "I have come to abolish the sacrifices: if you do not cease from sacrificing, the wrath [of God] will not cease from weighing upon you."

Epiphanius *adv. Haer.* 30.22:

7.

Those who reject meat have inconsiderately fallen into error and said, "I have no desire to eat the flesh of this Paschal Lamb with you." They leave the true order of words and distort the word which is clear to all from the connection of the words and make the disciples say: "Where do you want us to prepare for you to eat the Passover?"[4] To which he replied, "I have no desire to eat the flesh of this Paschal Lamb with you."

---

[1]Matt 3:4–5; Mark 1:5–6 [2]Matt 3:13–17; Mark 1:9–11; Luke 3:21–22 [3]Matt 12:46–50; Mark 3:31–35; Luke 8:19–21 [4]Matt 26:17; Mark 14:12

The Gospel of the Nazareans

Written in Aramaic, possibly near the end of the first century or at the beginning of the second, the *Gospel of the Nazareans* was popular among Jewish Christians (who were sometimes called "Nazareans") living in and around Palestine. Eventually the Gospel fell into disfavor with the Christian community at large, both because few Christians in later centuries could read Aramaic and because the Gospel's Jewish emphases were widely considered suspicious. We know of the work, therefore, only through quotations of its text (in Greek) by church fathers like Jerome, and by references to it in the margins of several Greek manuscripts of the Gospel according to Matthew.

According to some of the church fathers, this Gospel was in fact nothing other than an Aramaic revision of Matthew's Gospel. If these fathers are correct, then part of the revision may have involved the deletion of Matthew's first two chapters, which record the events surrounding Jesus' miraculous birth. According to many Jewish Christians, Jesus was not born of a virgin, but was a normal human being who was specially chosen to be the Messiah because God considered him to be more righteous than anyone else. Scholars debate, however, whether the church fathers were right in their assessment of the book: its author may simply have known traditions about Jesus similar to those also available to Matthew. The fragments of the Gospel that do survive, in any event, share with Matthew a concern for the Jewish Law and the question of whether the Jewish people are able to keep it.

Unlike other noncanonical Gospels, the *Gospel of the Nazareans* was similar in form and scope to those that were eventually included among the writings of the New Testament; it included, for example, stories of Jesus' baptism, public ministry, death, and resurrection. The following are among the longer fragments of the Gospel quoted in our surviving sources.

1. Pseudo-Origen *on Matt.* 15:14

It is written in a certain Gospel. . . . Another rich man said to him, "Master, what good thing shall I do to live?" He said to him, "O man, fulfil the law and the prophets." He replied, "I have done that." He said to him, "Go sell all that you possess and distribute it to the poor, and come, follow me." But the rich man began to scratch his head and it did not please him. And the Lord said to him, "How can you say, 'I have fulfilled the law and the prophets,' since it is written in the law: 'You shall love your neighbor as yourself,'[1] and lo! many of your brethren, sons of Abraham, are clothed in filth, dying of hunger, and your house is full of many goods, and nothing at all goes out of it to them?" And returning to Simon, his disciple, who was sitting by him, he said, "Simon, son of Jonas, it is easier for a camel to enter the eye of a needle than for a rich man (to enter) into the kingdom of heaven."[2]

2. Eusebius, *Theophania* 4:12

The cause therefore of the divisions of souls that take place in houses Christ himself taught, as we have found in a place in the Gospel existing among the Jews in the Hebrew language, in which it is said: "I will choose for myself the best which my Father in heaven has given me."

3. Jerome, on Matthew 6:11

In the Gospel . . . for the "supersubstantial bread" I found "Mahar" which signifies "tomorrow's," so that the meaning would be: "give us this day the bread for the morrow."[3]

4. Jerome, on Matthew 12:13

In the Gospel that the Nazarenes and Ebionites use, which I recently translated from the Hebrew into Greek and which most people designate as the authentic text of Matthew, we read that the man with the withered hand was a mason, who asked for help with these words: "I was a mason, working for my bread with my hands. I pray to you, Jesus, restore me to health so that I do not eat my bread in disgrace."

5. Jerome, on Matthew 23:35

In the Gospel which the Nazarenes use we find it written for "son of Barachias,"[4] "Son of Johoiada."

6. Jerome, on Matthew 27:16

In the so-called Gospel of the Hebrews, Barabbas who was condemned for sedition and murder is interpreted by "son of their teacher."[5]

7. Jerome, on Matthew 27:51

In the Gospel often mentioned we read that "the very great lintel of the Temple broke and fell into pieces."

8. Jerome, *on Isa.*, pref. to book 18

For when the apostles thought him to be a spirit or, in the words of the Gospel of the Hebrews which the Nazarenes read, "a bodiless demon" he said to them . . .

9. Jerome, *Dialogi contra Pelagianos* 3:2

In the Gospel of the Hebrews which is written in the Syro-Chaldaic tongue but in Hebrew characters, which the Nazarenes make use of at this day, and which is also called the "Gospel of the Apostles," or as many think, "that of Matthew," and which is in the library of Caesarea, the following narrative is given: "Behold, the mother of the Lord and his brothers said to him, 'John the Baptist baptizes for the remission of sins; let us go and be baptized by him.' But he said, 'What have I committed, that I should be baptized of him, unless it be that in saying this I am in ignorance?' " In the same volume (i.e. in the Gospel of the Hebrews) we read, "If your brother has sinned in word against you and has made satisfaction, forgive him up to seven times a day." Simon, his disciple, said to him, "Seven times?" The Lord answered saying, "Verily I say to you: until seventy times seven![6] For even in the prophets the word of sin is found after they have been anointed with the Holy Spirit."

---

[1]Lev 19:18   [2]Matt 19:24   [3]Matt 6:11; Luke 11:3   [4]Matt 23:35
[5]Matt 27:16   [6]Matt 18:21–22

10.

The following are "corrections" of the Gospel of Matthew made by scribes of several Greek manuscripts (= *MS,* as numbered below), who based their alterations on the text found in the Gospel of the Nazareans.

Matt 4:5. The Jewish copy has not "to the holy city" but "in Jerusalem." *MS* 566

Matt 5:22. The word "without cause" is not inserted in some copies, nor in the Jewish. *MS* 1424

Matt 7:5. The Jewish has here: "If you are in my bosom and do not do the will of my Father which is in heaven, out of my bosom will I cast you away." *MS* 1424

Matt 10:16. The Jewish has: "(wise) more than serpents" instead of "as serpents." *MS* 1424

Matt 11:12. (The kingdom of heaven suffers violence.) The Jewish has: "is ravished (or plundered)." *MS* 1424

Matt 12:40. The Jewish does not have: "three days and three nights (in the heart of the earth)." *MS* 899

Matt 15:5. The Jewish: "Corban, by which you shall be profited by us." *MS* 1424

Matt 16:2, 3. Omitted by the Jewish (as by many extant manuscripts). *MS* 1424

Matt 16:17. The Jewish: "[Simon] son of John." *MSS* 566, 1424.

Matt 18:22. The Jewish has, immediately after the seventy times seven: "For in the prophets, after they were anointed with the Holy Spirit, there was found in them a word (matter) of sin." *MSS* 566, 899

Matt 26:74. The Jewish: "and he denied and swore and cursed." *MSS* 4, 273, 566, 899, 1424

Matt 27:65. The Jewish: "And he delivered to them armed men, that they might sit opposite the cave and keep watch on it day and night." *MS* 1424.

The Gospel According to the Hebrews

The *Gospel according to the Hebrews* was evidently used by Jewish Christians in the city of Alexandria, Egypt, during the first half of the second century. As with the other distinctively Jewish–Christian Gospels of the Nazareans and of the Ebionites, the *Gospel according to the Hebrews* does not survive intact, but only in the quotations of church fathers like Clement of Alexandria and Origen.

The book was evidently given its name to differentiate it from another Gospel used extensively in Alexandria, but among the non-Jewish Christian population, the *Gospel of the Egyptians.* The *Gospel according to the Hebrews* was written in Greek and narrated important events of Jesus' life, including his baptism, temptation, and resurrection. It appears, however, that these stories were not simply taken over and modified from the Gospels that were later included in the New Testament. They were instead alternative forms of these traditions that had been passed along orally until the unknown author of this Gospel heard them and wrote them down.

Some of the quotations of this Gospel show that it embodied a distinctively gnostic slant, in which the goal of salvation is to discover the truth that will allow one to rise above the trappings of the material world to find rest in the realm of the spirit. Christ, then, is understood to be the one who comes down from that realm to bring the message that can lead to salvation.

1. Clement of Alexandria, *Strom.* 2.9.45

As it is also written in the Gospel of the Hebrews, "He who wonders shall reign, and he who reigns shall rest."

2. Origen, *on John* 2:12

If any should lend credence to the Gospel according to the Hebrews, where the Saviour himself says, "My mother, the Holy Spirit, took me just now by one of my hairs and carried me off to the great Mount Tabor," he will have difficulty in explaining how the Holy Spirit can be the mother of Christ.

3. Jerome, *on Eph.* 5:4

As we read in the Hebrew Gospel where the Lord says to his disciples, "Never be glad unless you are in charity with your brother."

4. Jerome, *de Vir. Ill.* 2

The Gospel also entitled "according to the Hebrews" which I lately translated into Greek and Latin, and which Origen often quotes, contains the following narrative after the Resurrection: "Now the Lord, when he had given the cloth to the servant of the priest, went to James and appeared to him." For James had taken an oath that he would not eat bread from that hour on which he had drunk the cup of the Lord till he saw him risen from the dead. Again a little later the Lord said, "Bring a table and bread," and forthwith it is added: "He took bread and blessed and broke it and gave to James the Just and said to him, 'My brother, eat your bread, for the Son of Man is risen from those who sleep.'"

5. Jerome, *on Ezek.* 18:7

In the Gospel of the Hebrews, which the Nazarenes are in the habit of reading, it belongs to the greatest sins when "one afflicts the spirit of his brother."

6. Jerome, *on Isa.* 11:2

But in the Gospel which is written in Hebrew and which the Nazarenes read, "the whole fountain of the Holy Spirit shall descend upon him." And the Lord is spirit, and where the Spirit of the Lord is, there is liberty. And in the Gospel referred to above I find this written: "And it came to pass, as the Lord came up out of the water, the whole fountain of the Holy Spirit descended upon him and rested upon him and said to him, 'My son, in all the prophets I expected that you might come and that I might rest upon you. You are my rest, you are my firstborn Son, who reigns in eternity.'"

EARLY CHRISTIAN ACTS

The Acts of the Apostles

The Book of Acts is the only historical account of the spread of Christianity that derives from the early church itself. It is self-consciously a sequel to the Gospel of Luke. Like its predecessor, it too is addressed to a person named "Theophilus," and it purports to continue the story that was started there (1:1–2). The book has been traditionally ascribed to Luke, the traveling companion of Paul, largely on the basis of several passages in which the author uses the first person plural (cf. 16:11–15). Some scholars have maintained, however, that the author is not directly referring to himself in these passages but has incorporated as a source a travelogue written by one of Paul's companions.

The narrative picks up where the Gospel ends, at the postresurrection appearances of Jesus to his disciples. In Acts he is said to have spent forty days with them, prior to commissioning them to spread the good news of his death and resurrection throughout the world (1:8) and then ascending into heaven (1:9–11). The book is principally about the fulfillment of this apostolic commission, as the apostles and their converts proclaim the gospel in Jerusalem, Judea and Samaria, and eventually in such predominantly Gentile regions as Asia Minor, Macedonia, Achaea, and Rome. The principal actors in the first portion of the narrative (chaps. 1–12) are the eleven apostles (joined by Matthias as the replacement for Judas Iscariot) and their converts. Much of this early narrative focuses on the apostle Peter. Just as Jesus received the Spirit in the Gospel of Luke, and so was empowered to preach and heal (see Luke 3:22; 4:18), so too his apostles receive the Spirit here (Acts 2:1–4) and, like Jesus, heal the sick (3:1–10), cast out demons (5:16; 8:6–7), raise the dead (9:36–41), and attract the multitudes by their proclamation. Also, like him, they are rejected and punished by the Jewish leadership in Jerusalem (4:1–3).

A key event occurs in chapter 9 with the conversion of Saul of Tarsus, also known as Paul. Most of the second part of the narrative, chapters 13–28, describes Paul's missionary journeys (chaps. 13–20), his trip to Jerusalem where he is arrested and several times put on trial (chaps. 20–26), and his final voyage to Rome (chaps. 27–28), where the book ends with him under house arrest preaching the gospel.

Far more than a disinterested historical sketch of the spread of the Christian church, the Book of Acts is intent to show that the Christian mission could not fail because God himself planned it (see 5:33–39). Even the rejection of the gospel by the Jewish leadership in Jerusalem and, subsequently, by most Jewish communities throughout the empire, occurs according to divine initiative. For this rejection moves the apostles to take the gospel to the Gentiles (see chaps. 10–11). When the question arises as to whether Gentiles must first become Jews prior to being admitted into the Christian church, the apostolic band shows remarkable unanimity in concluding that Gentile men do not need to be circumcised to be followers of Jesus (see chap. 15).

Along with its companion volume, then, the Book of Acts shows how the one true God has brought salvation through Christ, not just to the Jews, but to the entire world.

From the New Revised Standard Version Bible, © 1989.

1 In the first book, Theophilus, I wrote about all that Jesus did and taught from the beginning 2 until the day when he was taken up to heaven, after giving instructions through the Holy Spirit to the apostles whom he had chosen. 3 After his suffering he presented himself alive to them by many convincing proofs, appearing to them during forty days and speaking about the kingdom of God. 4 While staying[a] with them, he ordered them not to leave Jerusalem, but to wait there for the promise of the Father. "This," he said, "is what you have heard from me; 5 for John baptized with water, but you will be baptized with[b] the Holy Spirit not many days from now."

6 So when they had come together, they asked him, "Lord, is this the time when you will restore the kingdom to Israel?" 7 He replied, "It is not for you to know the times or periods that the Father has set by his own authority. 8 But you will receive power when the Holy Spirit has come upon you; and you will be my witnesses in Jerusalem, in all Judea and Samaria, and to the ends of the earth." 9 When he had said this, as they were watching, he was lifted up, and a cloud took him out of their sight. 10 While he was going and they were gazing up toward heaven, suddenly two men in white robes stood by them. 11 They said, "Men of Galilee, why do you stand looking up toward heaven? This Jesus, who has been taken up from you into heaven, will come in the same way as you saw him go into heaven."

12 Then they returned to Jerusalem from the mount called Olivet, which is near Jerusalem, a sabbath day's journey away. 13 When they had entered the city, they went to the room upstairs where they were staying, Peter, and John, and James, and Andrew, Philip and Thomas, Bartholomew and Matthew, James son of Alphaeus, and Simon the Zealot, and Judas son of[c] James. 14 All these were constantly devoting themselves to prayer, together with certain women, including Mary the mother of Jesus, as well as his brothers.

15 In those days Peter stood up among the believers[d] (together the crowd numbered about one hundred twenty persons) and said, 16 "Friends,[e] the scripture had to be fulfilled, which the Holy Spirit through David foretold concerning Judas, who became a guide for those who arrested Jesus— 17 for he was numbered among us and was allotted his share in this ministry." 18 (Now this man acquired a field with the reward of his wickedness; and falling headlong,[f] he burst open in the middle and all his bowels gushed out. 19 This became known to all the residents of Jerusalem, so that the field was called in their language Hakeldama, that is, Field of Blood.) 20 "For it is written in the book of Psalms,

'Let his homestead become
    desolate,
    and let there be no one to live
        in it';[1]

and

'Let another take his position of
    overseer.'[2]

21 So one of the men who have accompanied us during all the time that the Lord Jesus went in and out among us, 22 beginning from the baptism of John until the day when he was taken up from us— one of these must become a witness with us to his resurrection." 23 So they proposed two, Joseph called Barsabbas, who was also known as Justus, and Matthias. 24 Then they prayed and said, "Lord, you know everyone's heart. Show us which one of these two you have chosen 25 to take the place[g] in this ministry and apostleship from which Judas turned aside to go to his own place." 26 And they cast lots for them, and the lot fell on Matthias; and he was added to the eleven apostles.

2 When the day of Pentecost had come, they were all together in one place. 2 And suddenly from heaven there came a sound like the rush of a violent wind, and it filled the entire house where they were sitting. 3 Divided tongues, as of fire, appeared among them, and a tongue rested on each of them. 4 All of them were filled with the Holy Spirit and began to speak in other languages, as the Spirit gave them ability.

5 Now there were devout Jews from every nation under heaven living in Jerusalem. 6 And at this sound the crowd gathered and was bewildered, because each one heard them speaking in the native language of each. 7 Amazed and astonished, they asked, "Are not all these who are speaking Galileans? 8 And how is it that we hear,

---

[a]Or eating [b]Or by [c]Or the brother of [d]Gk brothers [e]Gk Men, brothers [f]Or swelling up [g]Other ancient authorities read the share

[1]Ps 69:25 [2]Ps 109:8

each of us, in our own native language? 9 Parthians, Medes, Elamites, and residents of Mesopotamia, Judea and Cappadocia, Pontus and Asia, 10 Phrygia and Pamphylia, Egypt and the parts of Libya belonging to Cyrene, and visitors from Rome, both Jews and proselytes, 11 Cretans and Arabs—in our own languages we hear them speaking about God's deeds of power." 12 All were amazed and perplexed, saying to one another, "What does this mean?" 13 But others sneered and said, "They are filled with new wine."

14 But Peter, standing with the eleven, raised his voice and addressed them, "Men of Judea and all who live in Jerusalem, let this be known to you, and listen to what I say. 15 Indeed, these are not drunk, as you suppose, for it is only nine o'clock in the morning. 16 No, this is what was spoken through the prophet Joel:

17   'In the last days it will be, God
            declares,
        that I will pour out my Spirit
            upon all flesh,
          and your sons and your
            daughters shall prophesy,
        and your young men shall see
            visions,
          and your old men shall dream
            dreams.
18   Even upon my slaves, both men
            and women,
          in those days I will pour out my
            Spirit;
          and they shall prophesy.
19   And I will show portents in the
            heaven above
          and signs on the earth below,
            blood, and fire, and smoky
            mist.
20   The sun shall be turned to
            darkness
          and the moon to blood,
            before the coming of the
            Lord's great and glorious
            day.
21   Then everyone who calls on the
            name of the Lord shall be
            saved.'[3]

22 "You that are Israelites,[h] listen to what I have to say: Jesus of Nazareth,[i] a man attested to you by God with deeds of power, wonders, and signs that God did through him among you, as you yourselves know— 23 this man, handed over to you according to the definite plan and foreknowledge of God, you crucified and killed by the hands of those outside the law. 24 But God raised him up, having freed him from death,[j] because it was impossible for him to be held in its power. 25 For David says concerning him,

        'I saw the Lord always before me,
            for he is at my right hand so
            that I will not be shaken;
26   therefore my heart was glad, and
            my tongue rejoiced;
          moreover my flesh will live in
            hope.
27   For you will not abandon my soul
            to Hades,
          or let your Holy One experience
            corruption.
28   You have made known to me the
            ways of life;
          you will make me full of
            gladness with your
            presence.'[4]

29 "Fellow Israelites,[k] I may say to you confidently of our ancestor David that he both died and was buried, and his tomb is with us to this day. 30 Since he was a prophet, he knew that God had sworn with an oath to him that he would put one of his descendants on his throne. 31 Foreseeing this, David[l] spoke of the resurrection of the Messiah,[m] saying,

        'He was not abandoned to Hades,
            nor did his flesh experience
            corruption.'[5]

32 This Jesus God raised up, and of that all of us are witnesses. 33 Being therefore exalted at[n] the right hand of God, and having received from the Father the promise of the Holy Spirit, he has poured out this that you both see and hear. 34 For David did not ascend into the heavens, but he himself says,

        'The Lord said to my Lord,
            "Sit at my right hand,

---

[h]Gk *Men, Israelites* [i]Gk *the Nazorean* [j]Gk *the pains of death* [k]Gk *Men, brothers* [l]Gk *he* [m]Or *the Christ* [n]Or *by*

[3]Joel 2:28–32   [4]Ps 16:8–11   [5]Ps 16:10

35   until I make your enemies your
                footstool.'"[6]

36 Therefore let the entire house of Israel know with certainty that God has made him both Lord and Messiah,[o] this Jesus whom you crucified."

37 Now when they heard this, they were cut to the heart and said to Peter and to the other apostles, "Brothers,[p] what should we do?" 38 Peter said to them, "Repent, and be baptized every one of you in the name of Jesus Christ so that your sins may be forgiven; and you will receive the gift of the Holy Spirit. 39 For the promise is for you, for your children, and for all who are far away, everyone whom the Lord our God calls to him." 40 And he testified with many other arguments and exhorted them, saying, "Save yourselves from this corrupt generation." 41 So those who welcomed his message were baptized, and that day about three thousand persons were added. 42 They devoted themselves to the apostles' teaching and fellowship, to the breaking of bread and the prayers.

43 Awe came upon everyone, because many wonders and signs were being done by the apostles. 44 All who believed were together and had all things in common; 45 they would sell their possessions and goods and distribute the proceeds[q] to all, as any had need. 46 Day by day, as they spent much time together in the temple, they broke bread at home[r] and ate their food with glad and generous[s] hearts, 47 praising God and having the goodwill of all the people. And day by day the Lord added to their number those who were being saved.

3 One day Peter and John were going up to the temple at the hour of prayer, at three o'clock in the afternoon. 2 And a man lame from birth was being carried in. People would lay him daily at the gate of the temple called the Beautiful Gate so that he could ask for alms from those entering the temple. 3 When he saw Peter and John about to go into the temple, he asked them for alms. 4 Peter looked intently at him, as did John, and said, "Look at us." 5 And he fixed his attention on them, expecting to receive something from them. 6 But Peter said, "I have no silver or gold, but what I have I give you; in the name of Jesus Christ of Nazareth,[t] stand up and walk." 7 And he took him by the right hand and raised him up; and immediately his feet and ankles were made strong.

8 Jumping up, he stood and began to walk, and he entered the temple with them, walking and leaping and praising God. 9 All the people saw him walking and praising God, 10 and they recognized him as the one who used to sit and ask for alms at the Beautiful Gate of the temple; and they were filled with wonder and amazement at what had happened to him.

11 While he clung to Peter and John, all the people ran together to them in the portico called Solomon's Portico, utterly astonished. 12 When Peter saw it, he addressed the people, "You Israelites,[u] why do you wonder at this, or why do you stare at us, as though by our own power or piety we had made him walk? 13 The God of Abraham, the God of Isaac, and the God of Jacob, the God of our ancestors has glorified his servant[v] Jesus, whom you handed over and rejected in the presence of Pilate, though he had decided to release him. 14 But you rejected the Holy and Righteous One and asked to have a murderer given to you, 15 and you killed the Author of life, whom God raised from the dead. To this we are witnesses. 16 And by faith in his name, his name itself has made this man strong, whom you see and know; and the faith that is through Jesus[w] has given him this perfect health in the presence of all of you.

17 "And now, friends,[x] I know that you acted in ignorance, as did also your rulers. 18 In this way God fulfilled what he had foretold through all the prophets, that his Messiah[y] would suffer. 19 Repent therefore, and turn to God so that your sins may be wiped out, 20 so that times of refreshing may come from the presence of the Lord, and that he may send the Messiah[z] appointed for you, that is, Jesus, 21 who must remain in heaven until the time of universal restoration that God announced long ago through his holy prophets. 22 Moses said, 'The Lord your God will raise up for you from your own people[x] a prophet like me. You must listen to whatever he tells you. 23 And it will be that everyone who does not listen to that prophet will be utterly rooted out of the people.'[7]

[o]Or *Christ*   [p]Gk *Men, brothers*   [q]Gk *them*   [r]Or *from house to house*
[s]Or *sincere*   [t]Gk *the Nazorean*   [u]Gk *Men, Israelites*   [v]Or *child*
[w]Gk *him*   [x]Gk *brothers*   [y]Or *his Christ*   [z]Or *the Christ*

[6]Ps 110:1   [7]Deut 18:15–19

24 And all the prophets, as many as have spoken, from Samuel and those after him, also predicted these days. 25 You are the descendants of the prophets and of the covenant that God gave to your ancestors, saying to Abraham, 'And in your descendants all the families of the earth shall be blessed.'[8] 26 When God raised up his servant,[a] he sent him first to you, to bless you by turning each of you from your wicked ways."

4 While Peter and John[b] were speaking to the people, the priests, the captain of the temple, and the Sadducees came to them, 2 much annoyed because they were teaching the people and proclaiming that in Jesus there is the resurrection of the dead. 3 So they arrested them and put them in custody until the next day, for it was already evening. 4 But many of those who heard the word believed; and they numbered about five thousand.

5 The next day their rulers, elders, and scribes assembled in Jerusalem, 6 with Annas the high priest, Caiaphas, John,[c] and Alexander, and all who were of the high-priestly family. 7 When they had made the prisoners[d] stand in their midst, they inquired, "By what power or by what name did you do this?" 8 Then Peter, filled with the Holy Spirit, said to them, "Rulers of the people and elders, 9 if we are questioned today because of a good deed done to someone who was sick and are asked how this man has been healed, 10 let it be known to all of you, and to all the people of Israel, that this man is standing before you in good health by the name of Jesus Christ of Nazareth,[e] whom you crucified, whom God raised from the dead. 11 This Jesus[f] is

'the stone that was rejected by
     you, the builders;
it has become the cornerstone.'[g][9]

12 There is salvation in no one else, for there is no other name under heaven given among mortals by which we must be saved."

13 Now when they saw the boldness of Peter and John and realized that they were uneducated and ordinary men, they were amazed and recognized them as companions of Jesus. 14 When they saw the man who had been cured standing beside them, they had nothing to say in opposition. 15 So they ordered them to leave the council while they discussed the matter with one another. 16 They said, "What will we do with them? For it is obvious to all who live in Jerusalem that a notable sign has been done through them; we cannot deny it. 17 But to keep it from spreading further among the people, let us warn them to speak no more to anyone in this name." 18 So they called them and ordered them not to speak or teach at all in the name of Jesus. 19 But Peter and John answered them, "Whether it is right in God's sight to listen to you rather than to God, you must judge; 20 for we cannot keep from speaking about what we have seen and heard." 21 After threatening them again, they let them go, finding no way to punish them because of the people, for all of them praised God for what had happened. 22 For the man on whom this sign of healing had been performed was more than forty years old.

23 After they were released, they went to their friends[h] and reported what the chief priests and the elders had said to them. 24 When they heard it, they raised their voices together to God and said, "Sovereign Lord, who made the heaven and the earth, the sea, and everything in them, 25 it is you who said by the Holy Spirit through our ancestor David, your servant:[a]

'Why did the Gentiles rage,
     and the peoples imagine vain
          things?
26   The kings of the earth took their
               stand,
          and the rulers have gathered
               together
          against the Lord and against
               his Messiah.'[i][10]

27 For in this city, in fact, both Herod and Pontius Pilate, with the Gentiles and the peoples of Israel, gathered together against your holy servant[a] Jesus, whom you anointed, 28 to do whatever your hand and your plan had predestined to take place. 29 And now, Lord, look at their threats, and grant to your servants[j] to speak your word with all boldness, 30 while you stretch out your hand to heal, and signs and wonders are performed through the name of your holy servant[a] Jesus." 31 When they had prayed, the place in which they were gathered

---

[a]Or child [b]Gk While they [c]Other ancient authorities read Jonathan [d]Gk them [e]Gk the Nazorean [f]Gk This [g]Or keystone [h]Gk their own [i]Or his Christ [j]Gk slaves

[8]Gen 22:18; 26:4   [9]Ps 118:22   [10]Ps 2:1–2

EARLY CHRISTIAN ACTS

together was shaken; and they were all filled with the Holy Spirit and spoke the word of God with boldness.

32 Now the whole group of those who believed were of one heart and soul, and no one claimed private ownership of any possessions, but everything they owned was held in common. 33 With great power the apostles gave their testimony to the resurrection of the Lord Jesus, and great grace was upon them all. 34 There was not a needy person among them, for as many as owned lands or houses sold them and brought the proceeds of what was sold. 35 They laid it at the apostles' feet, and it was distributed to each as any had need. 36 There was a Levite, a native of Cyprus, Joseph, to whom the apostles gave the name Barnabas (which means "son of encouragement"). 37 He sold a field that belonged to him, then brought the money, and laid it at the apostles' feet.

5 But a man named Ananias, with the consent of his wife Sapphira, sold a piece of property; 2 with his wife's knowledge, he kept back some of the proceeds, and brought only a part and laid it at the apostles' feet. 3 "Ananias," Peter asked, "why has Satan filled your heart to lie to the Holy Spirit and to keep back part of the proceeds of the land? 4 While it remained unsold, did it not remain your own? And after it was sold, were not the proceeds at your disposal? How is it that you have contrived this deed in your heart? You did not lie to us[k] but to God!" 5 Now when Ananias heard these words, he fell down and died. And great fear seized all who heard of it. 6 The young men came and wrapped up his body,[l] then carried him out and buried him.

7 After an interval of about three hours his wife came in, not knowing what had happened. 8 Peter said to her, "Tell me whether you and your husband sold the land for such and such a price." And she said, "Yes, that was the price." 9 Then Peter said to her, "How is it that you have agreed together to put the Spirit of the Lord to the test? Look, the feet of those who have buried your husband are at the door, and they will carry you out." 10 Immediately she fell down at his feet and died. When the young men came in they found her dead, so they carried her out and buried her beside her husband. 11 And great fear seized the whole church and all who heard of these things.

12 Now many signs and wonders were done among the people through the apostles. And they were all together in Solomon's Portico. 13 None of the rest dared to join them, but the people held them in high esteem. 14 Yet more than ever believers were added to the Lord, great numbers of both men and women, 15 so that they even carried out the sick into the streets, and laid them on cots and mats, in order that Peter's shadow might fall on some of them as he came by. 16 A great number of people would also gather from the towns around Jerusalem, bringing the sick and those tormented by unclean spirits, and they were all cured.

17 Then the high priest took action; he and all who were with him (that is, the sect of the Sadducees), being filled with jealousy, 18 arrested the apostles and put them in the public prison. 19 But during the night an angel of the Lord opened the prison doors, brought them out, and said, 20 "Go, stand in the temple and tell the people the whole message about this life." 21 When they heard this, they entered the temple at daybreak and went on with their teaching.

When the high priest and those with him arrived, they called together the council and the whole body of the elders of Israel, and sent to the prison to have them brought. 22 But when the temple police went there, they did not find them in the prison; so they returned and reported, 23 "We found the prison securely locked and the guards standing at the doors, but when we opened them, we found no one inside." 24 Now when the captain of the temple and the chief priests heard these words, they were perplexed about them, wondering what might be going on. 25 Then someone arrived and announced, "Look, the men whom you put in prison are standing in the temple and teaching the people!" 26 Then the captain went with the temple police and brought them, but without violence, for they were afraid of being stoned by the people.

27 When they had brought them, they had them stand before the council. The high priest questioned them, 28 saying, "We gave you strict orders not to teach in this name,[m] yet here you have filled Jerusalem with your teaching and you are

[k]Gk *to men*   [l]Meaning of Gk uncertain   [m]Other ancient authorities read *Did we not give you strict orders not to teach in this name?*

determined to bring this man's blood on us."
29 But Peter and the apostles answered, "We must
obey God rather than any human authority.[n]
30 The God of our ancestors raised up Jesus,
whom you had killed by hanging him on a tree.
31 God exalted him at his right hand as Leader and
Savior that he might give repentance to Israel and
forgiveness of sins. 32 And we are witnesses to
these things, and so is the Holy Spirit whom God
has given to those who obey him."

33 When they heard this, they were enraged and
wanted to kill them. 34 But a Pharisee in the council named Gamaliel, a teacher of the law, respected by all the people, stood up and ordered the men
to be put outside for a short time. 35 Then he said
to them, "Fellow Israelites,[o] consider carefully
what you propose to do to these men. 36 For sometime ago Theudas rose up, claiming to be some-
body, and a number of men, about four hundred,
joined him; but he was killed, and all who followed him were dispersed and disappeared.
37 After him Judas the Galilean rose up at the time
of the census and got people to follow him; he also
perished, and all who followed him were scattered. 38 So in the present case, I tell you, keep
away from these men and let them alone; because
if this plan or this undertaking is of human origin,
it will fail; 39 but if it is of God, you will not be
able to overthrow them—in that case you may
even be found fighting against God!"

They were convinced by him, 40 and when
they had called in the apostles, they had them
flogged. Then they ordered them not to speak in
the name of Jesus, and let them go. 41 As they left
the council, they rejoiced that they were considered worthy to suffer dishonor for the sake of the
name. 42 And every day in the temple and at
home[p] they did not cease to teach and proclaim Jesus as the Messiah.[q]

6 Now during those days, when the disciples
were increasing in number, the Hellenists
complained against the Hebrews because their
widows were being neglected in the daily distribution of food. 2 And the twelve called together
the whole community of the disciples and said,
"It is not right that we should neglect the word of
God in order to wait on tables.[r] 3 Therefore,
friends,[s] select from among yourselves seven men
of good standing, full of the Spirit and of wisdom,
whom we may appoint to this task, 4 while we, for
our part, will devote ourselves to prayer and to
serving the word." 5 What they said pleased the
whole community, and they chose Stephen, a man
full of faith and the Holy Spirit, together with
Philip, Prochorus, Nicanor, Timon, Parmenas, and
Nicolaus, a proselyte of Antioch. 6 They had
these men stand before the apostles, who prayed
and laid their hands on them.

7 The word of God continued to spread; the
number of the disciples increased greatly in
Jerusalem, and a great many of the priests became
obedient to the faith.

8 Stephen, full of grace and power, did great
wonders and signs among the people. 9 Then
some of those who belonged to the synagogue of
the Freedmen (as it was called), Cyrenians,
Alexandrians, and others of those from Cilicia and
Asia, stood up and argued with Stephen. 10 But
they could not withstand the wisdom and the
Spirit[t] with which he spoke. 11 Then they secretly instigated some men to say, "We have heard him
speak blasphemous words against Moses and
God." 12 They stirred up the people as well as the
elders and the scribes; then they suddenly con-
fronted him, seized him, and brought him before
the council. 13 They set up false witnesses who
said, "This man never stops saying things against
this holy place and the law; 14 for we have heard
him say that this Jesus of Nazareth[u] will destroy
this place and will change the customs that Moses
handed on to us." 15 And all who sat in the council looked intently at him, and they saw that his
face was like the face of an angel.

7 Then the high priest asked him, "Are these
things so?" 2 And Stephen replied:

"Brothers[v] and fathers, listen to me. The God of
glory appeared to our ancestor Abraham when he
was in Mesopotamia, before he lived in Haran,
3 and said to him, 'Leave your country and your
relatives and go to the land that I will show you.'[11]
4 Then he left the country of the Chaldeans and
settled in Haran. After his father died, God had

[n]Gk *than men* [o]Gk *Men, Israelites* [p]Or *from house to house*
[q]Or *the Christ* [r]Or *keep accounts* [s]Gk *brothers* [t]Or *spirit*
[u]Gk *the Nazorean* [v]Gk *Men, brothers*

[11]Gen 12:

him move from there to this country in which you are now living. 5 He did not give him any of it as a heritage, not even a foot's length, but promised to give it to him as his possession and to his descendants after him, even though he had no child. 6 And God spoke in these terms, that his descendants would be resident aliens in a country belonging to others, who would enslave them and mistreat them during four hundred years. 7 'But I will judge the nation that they serve,' said God, 'and after that they shall come out and worship me in this place.'[12] 8 Then he gave him the covenant of circumcision. And so Abraham[w] became the father of Isaac and circumcised him on the eighth day; and Isaac became the father of Jacob, and Jacob of the twelve patriarchs.

9 "The patriarchs, jealous of Joseph, sold him into Egypt; but God was with him, 10 and rescued him from all his afflictions, and enabled him to win favor and to show wisdom when he stood before Pharaoh, king of Egypt, who appointed him ruler over Egypt and over all his household. 11 Now there came a famine throughout Egypt and Canaan, and great suffering, and our ancestors could find no food. 12 But when Jacob heard that there was grain in Egypt, he sent our ances-tors there on their first visit. 13 On the second visit Joseph made himself known to his brothers, and Joseph's family became known to Pharaoh. 14 Then Joseph sent and invited his father Jacob and all his relatives to come to him, seventy-five in all; 15 so Jacob went down to Egypt. He himself died there as well as our ancestors, 16 and their bodies[x] were brought back to Shechem and laid in the tomb that Abraham had bought for a sum of silver from the sons of Hamor in Shechem.

17 "But as the time drew near for the fulfillment of the promise that God had made to Abraham, our people in Egypt increased and multiplied 18 until another king who had not known Joseph ruled over Egypt. 19 He dealt craftily with our race and forced our ancestors to abandon their infants so that they would die. 20 At this time Moses was born, and he was beautiful before God. For three months he was brought up in his father's house; 21 and when he was abandoned, Pharaoh's daughter adopted him and brought him up as her own son. 22 So Moses was instructed in all the wisdom of the Egyptians and was powerful in his words and deeds.

23 "When he was forty years old, it came into his heart to visit his relatives, the Israelites.[y] 24 When he saw one of them being wronged, he defended the oppressed man and avenged him by striking down the Egyptian. 25 He supposed that his kinsfolk would understand that God through him was rescuing them, but they did not understand. 26 The next day he came to some of them as they were quarreling and tried to reconcile them, saying, 'Men, you are brothers; why do you wrong each other?' 27 But the man who was wronging his neighbor pushed Moses[z] aside, saying, 'Who made you a ruler and a judge over us? 28 Do you want to kill me as you killed the Egyptian yesterday?'[13] 29 When he heard this, Moses fled and became a resident alien in the land of Midian. There he became the father of two sons.

30 "Now when forty years had passed, an angel appeared to him in the wilderness of Mount Sinai, in the flame of a burning bush. 31 When Moses saw it, he was amazed at the sight; and as he approached to look, there came the voice of the Lord: 32 'I am the God of your ancestors, the God of Abraham, Isaac, and Jacob.' Moses began to tremble and did not dare to look. 33 Then the Lord said to him, 'Take off the sandals from your feet, for the place where you are standing is holy ground. 34 I have surely seen the mistreatment of my people who are in Egypt and have heard their groaning, and I have come down to rescue them. Come now, I will send you to Egypt.'[14]

35 "It was this Moses whom they rejected when they said, 'Who made you a ruler and a judge?'[15] and whom God now sent as both ruler and liberator through the angel who appeared to him in the bush. 36 He led them out, having performed wonders and signs in Egypt, at the Red Sea, and in the wilderness for forty years. 37 This is the Moses who said to the Israelites, 'God will raise up a prophet for you from your own people[a] as he raised me up.'[16] 38 He is the one who was in the congregation in the wilderness with the angel who

---

[w]Gk *he*   [x]Gk *they*   [y]Gk *his brothers, the sons of Israel*   [z]Gk *him*
[a]Gk *your brothers*

---

[12]Gen 15:13–14; Exod 3:12   [13]Exod 2:14   [14]Exod 3:2–10   [15]Exod 2:14   [16]Deut 18:15

spoke to him at Mount Sinai, and with our ancestors; and he received living oracles to give to us. 39 Our ancestors were unwilling to obey him; instead, they pushed him aside, and in their hearts they turned back to Egypt, 40 saying to Aaron, 'Make gods for us who will lead the way for us; as for this Moses who led us out from the land of Egypt, we do not know what has happened to him.'[17] 41 At that time they made a calf, offered a sacrifice to the idol, and reveled in the works of their hands. 42 But God turned away from them and handed them over to worship the host of heaven, as it is written in the book of the prophets:

> 'Did you offer to me slain victims
>   and sacrifices
>   forty years in the wilderness,
>   O house of Israel?
> 43   No; you took along the tent of
>   Moloch,
>   and the star of your god
>   Rephan,
>   the images that you made to
>   worship;
> so I will remove you beyond
>   Babylon.'[18]

44 "Our ancestors had the tent of testimony in the wilderness, as God[b] directed when he spoke to Moses, ordering him to make it according to the pattern he had seen. 45 Our ancestors in turn brought it in with Joshua when they dispossessed the nations that God drove out before our ancestors. And it was there until the time of David, 46 who found favor with God and asked that he might find a dwelling place for the house of Jacob.[c] 47 But it was Solomon who built a house for him. 48 Yet the Most High does not dwell in houses made with human hands;[d] as the prophet says,

> 49   'Heaven is my throne,
>   and the earth is my footstool.
>   What kind of house will you build
>   for me, says the Lord,
>   or what is the place of my rest?
> 50   Did not my hand make all these
>   things?'[19]

51 "You stiff-necked people, uncircumcised in heart and ears, you are forever opposing the Holy Spirit, just as your ancestors used to do. 52 Which of the prophets did your ancestors not persecute? They killed those who foretold the coming of the Righteous One, and now you have become his betrayers and murderers. 53 You are the ones that received the law as ordained by angels, and yet you have not kept it."

54 When they heard these things, they became enraged and ground their teeth at Stephen.[e] 55 But filled with the Holy Spirit, he gazed into heaven and saw the glory of God and Jesus standing at the right hand of God. 56 "Look," he said, "I see the heavens opened and the Son of Man standing at the right hand of God!" 57 But they covered their ears, and with a loud shout all rushed together against him. 58 Then they dragged him out of the city and began to stone him; and the witnesses laid their coats at the feet of a young man named Saul. 59 While they were stoning Stephen, he prayed, "Lord Jesus, receive my spirit." 60 Then he knelt down and cried out in a loud voice, "Lord, do not hold this sin against them." When he had said this, he died.[f]

8 And Saul approved of their killing him.
That day a severe persecution began against the church in Jerusalem, and all except the apostles were scattered throughout the countryside of Judea and Samaria. 2 Devout men buried Stephen and made loud lamentation over him. 3 But Saul was ravaging the church by entering house after house; dragging off both men and women, he committed them to prison.

4 Now those who were scattered went from place to place, proclaiming the word. 5 Philip went down to the city[g] of Samaria and proclaimed the Messiah[h] to them. 6 The crowds with one accord listened eagerly to what was said by Philip, hearing and seeing the signs that he did, 7 for unclean spirits, crying with loud shrieks, came out of many who were possessed; and many others who were paralyzed or lame were cured. 8 So there was great joy in that city.

9 Now a certain man named Simon had previously practiced magic in the city and amazed the people of Samaria, saying that he was someone great. 10 All of them, from the least to the greatest, listened to him eagerly, saying, "This man is

[b]Gk *he*   [c]Other ancient authorities read *for the God of Jacob*
[d]Gk *with hands*   [e]Gk *him*   [f]Gk *fell asleep*   [g]Other ancient
authorities read *a city*   [h]Or *the Christ*

[17]Exod 32:1, 23   [18]Amos 5:25–27   [19]Isa 66:1–2

the power of God that is called Great." 11 And they listened eagerly to him because for a long time he had amazed them with his magic. 12 But when they believed Philip, who was proclaiming the good news about the kingdom of God and the name of Jesus Christ, they were baptized, both men and women. 13 Even Simon himself believed. After being baptized, he stayed constantly with Philip and was amazed when he saw the signs and great miracles that took place.

14 Now when the apostles at Jerusalem heard that Samaria had accepted the word of God, they sent Peter and John to them. 15 The two went down and prayed for them that they might receive the Holy Spirit 16 (for as yet the Spirit had not come[i] upon any of them; they had only been baptized in the name of the Lord Jesus). 17 Then Peter and John[j] laid their hands on them, and they received the Holy Spirit. 18 Now when Simon saw that the Spirit was given through the laying on of the apostles' hands, he offered them money, 19 saying, "Give me also this power so that anyone on whom I lay my hands may receive the Holy Spirit." 20 But Peter said to him, "May your silver perish with you, because you thought you could obtain God's gift with money! 21 You have no part or share in this, for your heart is not right before God. 22 Repent therefore of this wickedness of yours, and pray to the Lord that, if possible, the intent of your heart may be forgiven you. 23 For I see that you are in the gall of bitterness and the chains of wickedness." 24 Simon answered, "Pray for me to the Lord, that nothing of what you[k] have said may happen to me."

25 Now after Peter and John[l] had testified and spoken the word of the Lord, they returned to Jerusalem, proclaiming the good news to many villages of the Samaritans.

26 Then an angel of the Lord said to Philip, "Get up and go toward the south[m] to the road that goes down from Jerusalem to Gaza." (This is a wilderness road.) 27 So he got up and went. Now there was an Ethiopian eunuch, a court official of the Candace, queen of the Ethiopians, in charge of her entire treasury. He had come to Jerusalem to worship 28 and was returning home; seated in his chariot, he was reading the prophet Isaiah. 29 Then the Spirit said to Philip, "Go over to this chariot and join it." 30 So Philip ran up to it and heard him reading the prophet Isaiah. He asked, "Do you understand what you are reading?" 31 He replied, "How can I, unless someone guides me?" And he invited Philip to get in and sit beside him. 32 Now the passage of the scripture that he was reading was this:

> "Like a sheep he was led to the
> slaughter,
>   and like a lamb silent before its
>   shearer,
>   so he does not open his
>   mouth.
33   In his humiliation justice was
>   denied him.
>   Who can describe his
>   generation?
>   For his life is taken away
>   from the earth."[20]

34 The eunuch asked Philip, "About whom, may I ask you, does the prophet say this, about himself or about someone else?" 35 Then Philip began to speak, and starting with this scripture, he proclaimed to him the good news about Jesus. 36 As they were going along the road, they came to some water; and the eunuch said, "Look, here is water! What is to prevent me from being baptized?"[n] 38 He commanded the chariot to stop, and both of them, Philip and the eunuch, went down into the water, and Philip[o] baptized him. 39 When they came up out of the water, the Spirit of the Lord snatched Philip away; the eunuch saw him no more, and went on his way rejoicing. 40 But Philip found himself at Azotus, and as he was passing through the region, he proclaimed the good news to all the towns until he came to Caesarea.

9 Meanwhile Saul, still breathing threats and murder against the disciples of the Lord, went to the high priest 2 and asked him for letters to the synagogues at Damascus, so that if he found any who belonged to the Way, men or women, he

---

[i]Gk *fallen* [j]Gk *they* [k]The Greek word for *you* and the verb *pray* are plural [l]Gk *after they* [m]Or *go at noon* [n]Other ancient authorities add all or most of verse 37, *And Philip said, "If you believe with all your heart, you may." And he replied, "I believe that Jesus Christ is the Son of God."* [o]Gk *he*

---

[20]Isa 53:7–8

might bring them bound to Jerusalem. 3 Now as he was going along and approaching Damascus, suddenly a light from heaven flashed around him. 4 He fell to the ground and heard a voice saying to him, "Saul, Saul, why do you persecute me?" 5 He asked, "Who are you, Lord?" The reply came, "I am Jesus, whom you are persecuting. 6 But get up and enter the city, and you will be told what you are to do." 7 The men who were traveling with him stood speechless because they heard the voice but saw no one. 8 Saul got up from the ground, and though his eyes were open, he could see nothing; so they led him by the hand and brought him into Damascus. 9 For three days he was without sight, and neither ate nor drank.

10 Now there was a disciple in Damascus named Ananias. The Lord said to him in a vision, "Ananias." He answered, "Here I am, Lord." 11 The Lord said to him, "Get up and go to the street called Straight, and at the house of Judas look for a man of Tarsus named Saul. At this moment he is praying, 12 and he has seen in a vision[p] a man named Ananias come in and lay his hands on him so that he might regain his sight." 13 But Ananias answered, "Lord, I have heard from many about this man, how much evil he has done to your saints in Jerusalem; 14 and here he has authority from the chief priests to bind all who invoke your name." 15 But the Lord said to him, "Go, for he is an instrument whom I have chosen to bring my name before Gentiles and kings and before the people of Israel; 16 I myself will show him how much he must suffer for the sake of my name." 17 So Ananias went and entered the house. He laid his hands on Saul[q] and said, "Brother Saul, the Lord Jesus, who appeared to you on your way here, has sent me so that you may regain your sight and be filled with the Holy Spirit." 18 And immediately something like scales fell from his eyes, and his sight was restored. Then he got up and was baptized, 19 and after taking some food, he regained his strength.

For several days he was with the disciples in Damascus, 20 and immediately he began to proclaim Jesus in the synagogues, saying, "He is the Son of God." 21 All who heard him were amazed and said, "Is not this the man who made havoc in Jerusalem among those who invoked this name? And has he not come here for the purpose of bringing them bound before the chief priests?" 22 Saul became increasingly more powerful and confounded the Jews who lived in Damascus by proving that Jesus[r] was the Messiah.[s]

23 After some time had passed, the Jews plotted to kill him, 24 but their plot became known to Saul. They were watching the gates day and night so that they might kill him; 25 but his disciples took him by night and let him down through an opening in the wall,[t] lowering him in a basket.

26 When he had come to Jerusalem, he attempted to join the disciples; and they were all afraid of him, for they did not believe that he was a disciple. 27 But Barnabas took him, brought him to the apostles, and described for them how on the road he had seen the Lord, who had spoken to him, and how in Damascus he had spoken boldly in the name of Jesus. 28 So he went in and out among them in Jerusalem, speaking boldly in the name of the Lord. 29 He spoke and argued with the Hellenists; but they were attempting to kill him. 30 When the believers[u] learned of it, they brought him down to Caesarea and sent him off to Tarsus.

31 Meanwhile the church throughout Judea, Galilee, and Samaria had peace and was built up. Living in the fear of the Lord and in the comfort of the Holy Spirit, it increased in numbers.

32 Now as Peter went here and there among all the believers,[v] he came down also to the saints living in Lydda. 33 There he found a man named Aeneas, who had been bedridden for eight years, for he was paralyzed. 34 Peter said to him, "Aeneas, Jesus Christ heals you; get up and make your bed!" And immediately he got up. 35 And all the residents of Lydda and Sharon saw him and turned to the Lord.

36 Now in Joppa there was a disciple whose name was Tabitha, which in Greek is Dorcas.[w] She was devoted to good works and acts of charity. 37 At that time she became ill and died. When they had washed her, they laid her in a room upstairs. 38 Since Lydda was near Joppa, the disciples, who heard that Peter was there, sent two men to him with the request, "Please come to us without de-

---

[p]Other ancient authorities lack *in a vision*   [q]Gk *him*   [r]Gk *that this*
[s]Or *the Christ*   [t]Gk *through the wall*   [u]Gk *brothers*   [v]Gk *all of them*
[w]The name Tabitha in Aramaic and the name Dorcas in Greek mean *a gazelle*

lay." 39 So Peter got up and went with them; and when he arrived, they took him to the room upstairs. All the widows stood beside him, weeping and showing tunics and other clothing that Dorcas had made while she was with them. 40 Peter put all of them outside, and then he knelt down and prayed. He turned to the body and said, "Tabitha, get up." Then she opened her eyes, and seeing Peter, she sat up. 41 He gave her his hand and helped her up. Then calling the saints and widows, he showed her to be alive. 42 This became known throughout Joppa, and many believed in the Lord. 43 Meanwhile he stayed in Joppa for some time with a certain Simon, a tanner.

10 In Caesarea there was a man named Cornelius, a centurion of the Italian Cohort, as it was called. 2 He was a devout man who feared God with all his household; he gave alms generously to the people and prayed constantly to God. 3 One afternoon at about three o'clock he had a vision in which he clearly saw an angel of God coming in and saying to him, "Cornelius." 4 He stared at him in terror and said, "What is it, Lord?" He answered, "Your prayers and your alms have ascended as a memorial before God. 5 Now send men to Joppa for a certain Simon who is called Peter; 6 he is lodging with Simon, a tanner, whose house is by the seaside." 7 When the angel who spoke to him had left, he called two of his slaves and a devout soldier from the ranks of those who served him, 8 and after telling them everything, he sent them to Joppa.

9 About noon the next day, as they were on their journey and approaching the city, Peter went up on the roof to pray. 10 He became hungry and wanted something to eat; and while it was being prepared, he fell into a trance. 11 He saw the heaven opened and something like a large sheet coming down, being lowered to the ground by its four corners. 12 In it were all kinds of four-footed creatures and reptiles and birds of the air. 13 Then he heard a voice saying, "Get up, Peter; kill and eat." 14 But Peter said, "By no means, Lord; for I have never eaten anything that is profane or unclean." 15 The voice said to him again, a second time, "What God has made clean, you must not call profane." 16 This happened three times, and the thing was suddenly taken up to heaven.

17 Now while Peter was greatly puzzled about what to make of the vision that he had seen, suddenly the men sent by Cornelius appeared. They were asking for Simon's house and were standing by the gate. 18 They called out to ask whether Simon, who was called Peter, was staying there. 19 While Peter was still thinking about the vision, the Spirit said to him, "Look, three[x] men are searching for you. 20 Now get up, go down, and go with them without hesitation; for I have sent them." 21 So Peter went down to the men and said, "I am the one you are looking for; what is the reason for your coming?" 22 They answered, "Cornelius, a centurion, an upright and God-fearing man, who is well spoken of by the whole Jewish nation, was directed by a holy angel to send for you to come to his house and to hear what you have to say." 23 So Peter[y] invited them in and gave them lodging.

The next day he got up and went with them, and some of the believers[z] from Joppa accompanied him. 24 The following day they came to Caesarea. Cornelius was expecting them and had called together his relatives and close friends. 25 On Peter's arrival Cornelius met him, and falling at his feet, worshiped him. 26 But Peter made him get up, saying, "Stand up; I am only a mortal." 27 And as he talked with him, he went in and found that many had assembled; 28 and he said to them, "You yourselves know that it is unlawful for a Jew to associate with or to visit a Gentile; but God has shown me that I should not call anyone profane or unclean. 29 So when I was sent for, I came without objection. Now may I ask why you sent for me?"

30 Cornelius replied, "Four days ago at this very hour, at three o'clock, I was praying in my house when suddenly a man in dazzling clothes stood before me. 31 He said, 'Cornelius, your prayer has been heard and your alms have been remembered before God. 32 Send therefore to Joppa and ask for Simon, who is called Peter; he is staying in the home of Simon, a tanner, by the sea.' 33 Therefore I sent for you immediately, and you have been kind enough to come. So now all of us are here in the presence of God to listen to all that the Lord has commanded you to say."

---

[x]One ancient authority reads *two*; others lack the word   [y]Gk *he*
[z]Gk *brothers*

34 Then Peter began to speak to them: "I truly understand that God shows no partiality, 35 but in every nation anyone who fears him and does what is right is acceptable to him. 36 You know the message he sent to the people of Israel, preaching peace by Jesus Christ—he is Lord of all. 37 That message spread throughout Judea, beginning in Galilee after the baptism that John announced: 38 how God anointed Jesus of Nazareth with the Holy Spirit and with power; how he went about doing good and healing all who were oppressed by the devil, for God was with him. 39 We are witnesses to all that he did both in Judea and in Jerusalem. They put him to death by hanging him on a tree; 40 but God raised him on the third day and allowed him to appear, 41 not to all the people but to us who were chosen by God as witnesses, and who ate and drank with him after he rose from the dead. 42 He commanded us to preach to the people and to testify that he is the one ordained by God as judge of the living and the dead. 43 All the prophets testify about him that everyone who believes in him receives forgiveness of sins through his name."

44 While Peter was still speaking, the Holy Spirit fell upon all who heard the word. 45 The circumcised believers who had come with Peter were astounded that the gift of the Holy Spirit had been poured out even on the Gentiles, 46 for they heard them speaking in tongues and extolling God. Then Peter said, 47 "Can anyone withhold the water for baptizing these people who have received the Holy Spirit just as we have?" 48 So he ordered them to be baptized in the name of Jesus Christ. Then they invited him to stay for several days.

11 Now the apostles and the believers[a] who were in Judea heard that the Gentiles had also accepted the word of God. 2 So when Peter went up to Jerusalem, the circumcised believers[b] criticized him, 3 saying, "Why did you go to uncircumcised men and eat with them?" 4 Then Peter began to explain it to them, step by step, saying, 5 "I was in the city of Joppa praying, and in a trance I saw a vision. There was something like a large sheet coming down from heaven, being lowered by its four corners; and it came close to me. 6 As I looked at it closely I saw four-footed animals, beasts of prey, reptiles, and birds of the air. 7 I also heard a voice saying to me, 'Get up, Peter; kill and eat.' 8 But I replied, 'By no means, Lord; for nothing profane or unclean has ever entered my mouth.' 9 But a second time the voice answered from heaven, 'What God has made clean, you must not call profane.' 10 This happened three times; then everything was pulled up again to heaven. 11 At that very moment three men, sent to me from Caesarea, arrived at the house where we were. 12 The Spirit told me to go with them and not to make a distinction between them and us.[c] These six brothers also accompanied me, and we entered the man's house. 13 He told us how he had seen the angel standing in his house and saying, 'Send to Joppa and bring Simon, who is called Peter; 14 he will give you a message by which you and your entire household will be saved.' 15 And as I began to speak, the Holy Spirit fell upon them just as it had upon us at the beginning. 16 And I remembered the word of the Lord, how he had said, 'John baptized with water, but you will be baptized with the Holy Spirit.' 17 If then God gave them the same gift that he gave us when we believed in the Lord Jesus Christ, who was I that I could hinder God?" 18 When they heard this, they were silenced. And they praised God, saying, "Then God has given even to the Gentiles the repentance that leads to life."

19 Now those who were scattered because of the persecution that took place over Stephen traveled as far as Phoenicia, Cyprus, and Antioch, and they spoke the word to no one except Jews. 20 But among them were some men of Cyprus and Cyrene who, on coming to Antioch, spoke to the Hellenists[d] also, proclaiming the Lord Jesus. 21 The hand of the Lord was with them, and a great number became believers and turned to the Lord. 22 News of this came to the ears of the church in Jerusalem, and they sent Barnabas to Antioch. 23 When he came and saw the grace of God, he rejoiced, and he exhorted them all to remain faithful to the Lord with steadfast devotion; 24 for he was a good man, full of the Holy Spirit and of faith. And a great many people were brought to the Lord. 25 Then Barnabas went to Tarsus to look for

[a] Gk brothers [b] Gk lacks believers [c] Or not to hesitate [d] Other ancient authorities read Greeks

Saul, 26 and when he had found him, he brought him to Antioch. So it was that for an entire year they met with[c] the church and taught a great many people, and it was in Antioch that the disciples were first called "Christians."

27 At that time prophets came down from Jerusalem to Antioch. 28 One of them named Agabus stood up and predicted by the Spirit that there would be a severe famine over all the world; and this took place during the reign of Claudius. 29 The disciples determined that according to their ability, each would send relief to the believers[f] living in Judea; 30 this they did, sending it to the elders by Barnabas and Saul.

12 About that time King Herod laid violent hands upon some who belonged to the church. 2 He had James, the brother of John, killed with the sword. 3 After he saw that it pleased the Jews, he proceeded to arrest Peter also. (This was during the festival of Unleavened Bread.) 4 When he had seized him, he put him in prison and handed him over to four squads of soldiers to guard him, intending to bring him out to the people after the Passover. 5 While Peter was kept in prison, the church prayed fervently to God for him.

6 The very night before Herod was going to bring him out, Peter, bound with two chains, was sleeping between two soldiers, while guards in front of the door were keeping watch over the prison. 7 Suddenly an angel of the Lord appeared and a light shone in the cell. He tapped Peter on the side and woke him, saying, "Get up quickly." And the chains fell off his wrists. 8 The angel said to him, "Fasten your belt and put on your sandals." He did so. Then he said to him, "Wrap your cloak around you and follow me." 9 Peter[g] went out and followed him; he did not realize that what was happening with the angel's help was real; he thought he was seeing a vision. 10 After they had passed the first and the second guard, they came before the iron gate leading into the city. It opened for them of its own accord, and they went outside and walked along a lane, when suddenly the angel left him. 11 Then Peter came to himself and said, "Now I am sure that the Lord has sent his angel and rescued me from the hands of Herod and from all that the Jewish people were expecting."

12 As soon as he realized this, he went to the house of Mary, the mother of John whose other name was Mark, where many had gathered and were praying. 13 When he knocked at the outer gate, a maid named Rhoda came to answer. 14 On recognizing Peter's voice, she was so overjoyed that, instead of opening the gate, she ran in and announced that Peter was standing at the gate. 15 They said to her, "You are out of your mind!" But she insisted that it was so. They said, "It is his angel." 16 Meanwhile Peter continued knocking; and when they opened the gate, they saw him and were amazed. 17 He motioned to them with his hand to be silent, and described for them how the Lord had brought him out of the prison. And he added, "Tell this to James and to the believers."[f] Then he left and went to another place.

18 When morning came, there was no small commotion among the soldiers over what had become of Peter. 19 When Herod had searched for him and could not find him, he examined the guards and ordered them to be put to death. Then he went down from Judea to Caesarea and stayed there.

20 Now Herod[h] was angry with the people of Tyre and Sidon. So they came to him in a body; and after winning over Blastus, the king's chamberlain, they asked for a reconciliation, because their country depended on the king's country for food. 21 On an appointed day Herod put on his royal robes, took his seat on the platform, and delivered a public address to them. 22 The people kept shouting, "The voice of a god, and not of a mortal!" 23 And immediately, because he had not given the glory to God, an angel of the Lord struck him down, and he was eaten by worms and died.

24 But the word of God continued to advance and gain adherents. 25 Then after completing their mission Barnabas and Saul returned to[i] Jerusalem and brought with them John, whose other name was Mark.

13 Now in the church at Antioch there were prophets and teachers: Barnabas, Simeon who was called Niger, Lucius of Cyrene, Manaen a member of the court of Herod the ruler,[j] and Saul. 2 While they were worshiping the Lord and

---

[c]Or *were guests of* [f]Gk *brothers* [g]Gk *He* [h]Gk *he* [i]Other ancient authorities read *from* [j]Gk *tetrarch*

fasting, the Holy Spirit said, "Set apart for me Barnabas and Saul for the work to which I have called them." 3 Then after fasting and praying they laid their hands on them and sent them off.

4 So, being sent out by the Holy Spirit, they went down to Seleucia; and from there they sailed to Cyprus. 5 When they arrived at Salamis, they proclaimed the word of God in the synagogues of the Jews. And they had John also to assist them. 6 When they had gone through the whole island as far as Paphos, they met a certain magician, a Jewish false prophet, named Bar-Jesus. 7 He was with the proconsul, Sergius Paulus, an intelligent man, who summoned Barnabas and Saul and wanted to hear the word of God. 8 But the magician Elymas (for that is the translation of his name) opposed them and tried to turn the proconsul away from the faith. 9 But Saul, also known as Paul, filled with the Holy Spirit, looked intently at him 10 and said, "You son of the devil, you enemy of all righteousness, full of all deceit and villainy, will you not stop making crooked the straight paths of the Lord? 11 And now listen—the hand of the Lord is against you, and you will be blind for a while, unable to see the sun." Immediately mist and darkness came over him, and he went about groping for someone to lead him by the hand. 12 When the proconsul saw what had happened, he believed, for he was astonished at the teaching about the Lord.

13 Then Paul and his companions set sail from Paphos and came to Perga in Pamphylia. John, however, left them and returned to Jerusalem; 14 but they went on from Perga and came to Antioch in Pisidia. And on the sabbath day they went into the synagogue and sat down 15 After the reading of the law and the prophets, the officials of the synagogue sent them a message, saying, "Brothers, if you have any word of exhortation for the people, give it." 16 So Paul stood up and with a gesture began to speak:

"You Israelites,[k] and others who fear God, listen. 17 The God of this people Israel chose our ancestors and made the people great during their stay in the land of Egypt, and with uplifted arm he led them out of it. 18 For about forty years he put up with[l] them in the wilderness. 19 After he had destroyed seven nations in the land of Canaan, he gave them their land as an inheritance 20 for about four hundred fifty years. After that he gave them judges until the time of the prophet Samuel. 21 Then they asked for a king; and God gave them Saul son of Kish, a man of the tribe of Benjamin, who reigned for forty years. 22 When he had removed him, he made David their king. In his testimony about him he said, 'I have found David, son of Jesse, to be a man after my heart, who will carry out all my wishes.'[21] 23 Of this man's posterity God has brought to Israel a Savior, Jesus, as he promised; 24 before his coming John had already proclaimed a baptism of repentance to all the people of Israel. 25 And as John was finishing his work, he said, 'What do you suppose that I am? I am not he. No, but one is coming after me; I am not worthy to untie the thong of the sandals[m] on his feet.'

26 "My brothers, you descendants of Abraham's family, and others who fear God, to us[n] the message of this salvation has been sent. 27 Because the residents of Jerusalem and their leaders did not recognize him or understand the words of the prophets that are read every sabbath, they fulfilled those words by condemning him. 28 Even though they found no cause for a sentence of death, they asked Pilate to have him killed. 29 When they had carried out everything that was written about him, they took him down from the tree and laid him in a tomb. 30 But God raised him from the dead; 31 and for many days he appeared to those who came up with him from Galilee to Jerusalem, and they are now his witnesses to the people. 32 And we bring you the good news that what God promised to our ancestors 33 he has fulfilled for us, their children, by raising Jesus; as also it is written in the second psalm,

'You are my Son;
    today I have begotten you.'[22]
34 As to his raising him from the dead, no more to return to corruption, he has spoken in this way,
'I will give you the holy promises
    made to David.'[23]
35 Therefore he has also said in another psalm,
'You will not let your Holy One
    experience corruption.'[24]

---

[k]Gk *Men, Israelites* [l]Other ancient authorities read *cared for*
[m]Gk *untie the sandals* [n]Other ancient authorities read *you*

[21]Ps 89:20; 1 Sam 13:14 [22]Ps 2:7 [23]Isa 55:3 [24]Ps 16:10

36 For David, after he had served the purpose of God in his own generation, died,[o] was laid beside his ancestors, and experienced corruption; 37 but he whom God raised up experienced no corruption. 38 Let it be known to you therefore, my brothers, that through this man forgiveness of sins is proclaimed to you; 39 by this Jesus[p] everyone who believes is set free from all those sins[q] from which you could not be freed by the law of Moses. 40 Beware, therefore, that what the prophets said does not happen to you:

41   'Look, you scoffers!
          Be amazed and perish,
       for in your days I am doing a
              work,
          a work that you will never
              believe, even if someone
              tells you.'"[25]

42 As Paul and Barnabas[r] were going out, the people urged them to speak about these things again the next sabbath. 43 When the meeting of the synagogue broke up, many Jews and devout converts to Judaism followed Paul and Barnabas, who spoke to them and urged them to continue in the grace of God.

44 The next sabbath almost the whole city gathered to hear the word of the Lord.[s] 45 But when the Jews saw the crowds, they were filled with jealousy; and blaspheming, they contradicted what was spoken by Paul. 46 Then both Paul and Barnabas spoke out boldly, saying, "It was necessary that the word of God should be spoken first to you. Since you reject it and judge yourselves to be unworthy of eternal life, we are now turning to the Gentiles. 47 For so the Lord has commanded us, saying,

       'I have set you to be a light for
          the Gentiles,
       so that you may bring salvation
          to the ends of the earth.'"[26]

48 When the Gentiles heard this, they were glad and praised the word of the Lord; and as many as had been destined for eternal life became believers. 49 Thus the word of the Lord spread throughout the region. 50 But the Jews incited the devout women of high standing and the leading men of the city, and stirred up persecution against Paul and Barnabas, and drove them out of their region. 51 So they shook the dust off their feet in protest against them, and went to Iconium. 52 And the disciples were filled with joy and with the Holy Spirit.

14 The same thing occurred in Iconium, where Paul and Barnabas[r] went into the Jewish synagogue and spoke in such a way that a great number of both Jews and Greeks became believers. 2 But the unbelieving Jews stirred up the Gentiles and poisoned their minds against the brothers. 3 So they remained for a long time, speaking boldly for the Lord, who testified to the word of his grace by granting signs and wonders to be done through them. 4 But the residents of the city were divided; some sided with the Jews, and some with the apostles. 5 And when an attempt was made by both Gentiles and Jews, with their rulers, to mistreat them and to stone them, 6 the apostles[r] learned of it and fled to Lystra and Derbe, cities of Lycaonia, and to the surrounding country; 7 and there they continued proclaiming the good news.

8 In Lystra there was a man sitting who could not use his feet and had never walked, for he had been crippled from birth. 9 He listened to Paul as he was speaking. And Paul, looking at him intently and seeing that he had faith to be healed, 10 said in a loud voice, "Stand upright on your feet." And the man[t] sprang up and began to walk. 11 When the crowds saw what Paul had done, they shouted in the Lycaonian language, "The gods have come down to us in human form!" 12 Barnabas they called Zeus, and Paul they called Hermes, because he was the chief speaker. 13 The priest of Zeus, whose temple was just outside the city,[u] brought oxen and garlands to the gates; he and the crowds wanted to offer sacrifice. 14 When the apostles Barnabas and Paul heard of it, they tore their clothes and rushed out into the crowd, shouting, 15 "Friends,[v] why are you doing this? We are mortals just like you, and we bring you good news, that you should turn from these worthless things to the living God, who made the heaven and the earth and the sea and all that is in them. 16 In past generations he allowed all the nations to

---

[o]Gk *fell asleep* [p]Gk *this* [q]Gk *all* [r]Gk *they* [s]Other ancient authorities read *God* [t]Gk *he* [u]Or *The priest of Zeus-Outside-the-City* [v]Gk *Men*

[25]Hab 1:5 [26]Isa 49:6

follow their own ways; 17 yet he has not left himself without a witness in doing good—giving you rains from heaven and fruitful seasons, and filling you with food and your hearts with joy." 18 Even with these words, they scarcely restrained the crowds from offering sacrifice to them.

19 But Jews came there from Antioch and Iconium and won over the crowds. Then they stoned Paul and dragged him out of the city, supposing that he was dead. 20 But when the disciples surrounded him, he got up and went into the city. The next day he went on with Barnabas to Derbe.

21 After they had proclaimed the good news to that city and had made many disciples, they returned to Lystra, then on to Iconium and Antioch. 22 There they strengthened the souls of the disciples and encouraged them to continue in the faith, saying, "It is through many persecutions that we must enter the kingdom of God." 23 And after they had appointed elders for them in each church, with prayer and fasting they entrusted them to the Lord in whom they had come to believe.

24 Then they passed through Pisidia and came to Pamphylia. 25 When they had spoken the word in Perga, they went down to Attalia. 26 From there they sailed back to Antioch, where they had been commended to the grace of God for the work[w] that they had completed. 27 When they arrived, they called the church together and related all that God had done with them, and how he had opened a door of faith for the Gentiles. 28 And they stayed there with the disciples for some time.

15 Then certain individuals came down from Judea and were teaching the brothers, "Unless you are circumcised according to the custom of Moses, you cannot be saved." 2 And after Paul and Barnabas had no small dissension and debate with them, Paul and Barnabas and some of the others were appointed to go up to Jerusalem to discuss this question with the apostles and the elders. 3 So they were sent on their way by the church, and as they passed through both Phoenicia and Samaria, they reported the conversion of the Gentiles, and brought great joy to all the believers.[x] 4 When they came to Jerusalem, they were welcomed by the church and the apostles and the elders, and they reported all that God had done with them. 5 But some believers who belonged to the sect of the Pharisees stood

up and said, "It is necessary for them to be circumcised and ordered to keep the law of Moses."

6 The apostles and the elders met together to consider this matter. 7 After there had been much debate, Peter stood up and said to them, "My brothers,[y] you know that in the early days God made a choice among you, that I should be the one through whom the Gentiles would hear the message of the good news and become believers. 8 And God, who knows the human heart, testified to them by giving them the Holy Spirit, just as he did to us; 9 and in cleansing their hearts by faith he has made no distinction between them and us. 10 Now therefore why are you putting God to the test by placing on the neck of the disciples a yoke that neither our ancestors nor we have been able to bear? 11 On the contrary, we believe that we will be saved through the grace of the Lord Jesus, just as they will."

12 The whole assembly kept silence, and listened to Barnabas and Paul as they told of all the signs and wonders that God had done through them among the Gentiles. 13 After they finished speaking, James replied, "My brothers,[y] listen to me. 14 Simeon has related how God first looked favorably on the Gentiles, to take from among them a people for his name. 15 This agrees with the words of the prophets, as it is written,

16   'After this I will return,
        and I will rebuild the dwelling of
            David, which has fallen;
        from its ruins I will rebuild it,
            and I will set it up,
17   so that all other peoples may seek
            the Lord—
        even all the Gentiles over whom
            my name has been called.
        Thus says the Lord, who has
            been making these things
18   known from long ago.'[z][27]

19 Therefore I have reached the decision that we should not trouble those Gentiles who are turning to God, 20 but we should write to them to abstain only from things polluted by idols and from forni-

---

[w]Or *committed in the grace of God to the work*   [x]Gk *brothers*
[y]Gk *Men, brothers*   [z]Other ancient authorities read *things.* [18]*Known to God from of old are all his works.'*

---

[27]Amos 9.11–12

cation and from whatever has been strangled[a] and from blood. 21 For in every city, for generations past, Moses has had those who proclaim him, for he has been read aloud every sabbath in the synagogues."

22 Then the apostles and the elders, with the consent of the whole church, decided to choose men from among their members[b] and to send them to Antioch with Paul and Barnabas. They sent Judas called Barsabbas, and Silas, leaders among the brothers, 23 with the following letter: "The brothers, both the apostles and the elders, to the believers[c] of Gentile origin in Antioch and Syria and Cilicia, greetings. 24 Since we have heard that certain persons who have gone out from us, though with no instructions from us, have said things to disturb you and have unsettled your minds,[d] 25 we have decided unanimously to choose representatives[e] and send them to you, along with our beloved Barnabas and Paul, 26 who have risked their lives for the sake of our Lord Jesus Christ. 27 We have therefore sent Judas and Silas, who themselves will tell you the same things by word of mouth. 28 For it has seemed good to the Holy Spirit and to us to impose on you no further burden than these essentials: 29 that you abstain from what has been sacrificed to idols and from blood and from what is strangled[a] and from fornication. If you keep yourselves from these, you will do well. Farewell."

30 So they were sent off and went down to Antioch. When they gathered the congregation together, they delivered the letter. 31 When its members[f] read it, they rejoiced at the exhortation. 32 Judas and Silas, who were themselves prophets, said much to encourage and strengthen the believers.[c] 33 After they had been there for some time, they were sent off in peace by the believers[c] to those who had sent them.[g] 35 But Paul and Barnabas remained in Antioch, and there, with many others, they taught and proclaimed the word of the Lord.

36 After some days Paul said to Barnabas, "Come, let us return and visit the believers[c] in every city where we proclaimed the word of the Lord and see how they are doing." 37 Barnabas wanted to take with them John called Mark. 38 But Paul decided not to take with them one who

had deserted them in Pamphylia and had not accompanied them in the work. 39 The disagreement became so sharp that they parted company; Barnabas took Mark with him and sailed away to Cyprus. 40 But Paul chose Silas and set out, the believers[c] commending him to the grace of the Lord. 41 He went through Syria and Cilicia, strengthening the churches.

16 Paul[h] went on also to Derbe and to Lystra, where there was a disciple named Timothy, the son of a Jewish woman who was a believer; but his father was a Greek. 2 He was well spoken of by the believers[c] in Lystra and Iconium. 3 Paul wanted Timothy to accompany him; and he took him and had him circumcised because of the Jews who were in those places, for they all knew that his father was a Greek. 4 As they went from town to town, they delivered to them for observance the decisions that had been reached by the apostles and elders who were in Jerusalem. 5 So the churches were strengthened in the faith and increased in numbers daily.

6 They went through the region of Phrygia and Galatia, having been forbidden by the Holy Spirit to speak the word in Asia. 7 When they had come opposite Mysia, they attempted to go into Bithynia, but the Spirit of Jesus did not allow them; 8 so, passing by Mysia, they went down to Troas. 9 During the night Paul had a vision: there stood a man of Macedonia pleading with him and saying, "Come over to Macedonia and help us." 10 When he had seen the vision, we immediately tried to cross over to Macedonia, being convinced that God had called us to proclaim the good news to them.

11 We set sail from Troas and took a straight course to Samothrace, the following day to Neapolis, 12 and from there to Philippi, which is a leading city of the district[i] of Macedonia and a Roman colony. We remained in this city for some days. 13 On the sabbath day we went outside the gate by the river, where we supposed there was a place of prayer; and we sat down and spoke to the women who had gathered there. 14 A certain

---

[a]Other ancient authorities lack *and from whatever has been strangled* [b]Gk *from among them* [c]Gk *brothers* [d]Other ancient authorities add *saying, 'You must be circumcised and keep the law,'* [e]Gk *men* [f]Gk *When they* [g]Other ancient authorities add verse 34, *But it seemed good to Silas to remain there* [h]Gk *He* [i]Other authorities read *a city of the first district*

woman named Lydia, a worshiper of God, was listening to us; she was from the city of Thyatira and a dealer in purple cloth. The Lord opened her heart to listen eagerly to what was said by Paul. 15 When she and her household were baptized, she urged us, saying, "If you have judged me to be faithful to the Lord, come and stay at my home." And she prevailed upon us.

16 One day, as we were going to the place of prayer, we met a slave-girl who had a spirit of divination and brought her owners a great deal of money by fortune-telling. 17 While she followed Paul and us, she would cry out, "These men are slaves of the Most High God, who proclaim to you[j] a way of salvation." 18 She kept doing this for many days. But Paul, very much annoyed, turned and said to the spirit, "I order you in the name of Jesus Christ to come out of her." And it came out that very hour.

19 But when her owners saw that their hope of making money was gone, they seized Paul and Silas and dragged them into the marketplace before the authorities. 20 When they had brought them before the magistrates, they said, "These men are disturbing our city; they are Jews 21 and are advocating customs that are not lawful for us as Romans to adopt or observe." 22 The crowd joined in attacking them, and the magistrates had them stripped of their clothing and ordered them to be beaten with rods. 23 After they had given them a severe flogging, they threw them into prison and ordered the jailer to keep them securely. 24 Following these instructions, he put them in the innermost cell and fastened their feet in the stocks.

25 About midnight Paul and Silas were praying and singing hymns to God, and the prisoners were listening to them. 26 Suddenly there was an earthquake, so violent that the foundations of the prison were shaken; and immediately all the doors were opened and everyone's chains were unfastened. 27 When the jailer woke up and saw the prison doors wide open, he drew his sword and was about to kill himself, since he supposed that the prisoners had escaped. 28 But Paul shouted in a loud voice, "Do not harm yourself, for we are all here." 29 The jailer[k] called for lights, and rushing in, he fell down trembling before Paul and Silas. 30 Then he brought them outside and said, "Sirs, what must I do to be saved?" 31 They answered, "Believe on the Lord Jesus, and you will be saved, you and your household." 32 They spoke the word of the Lord[l] to him and to all who were in his house. 33 At the same hour of the night he took them and washed their wounds; then he and his entire family were baptized without delay. 34 He brought them up into the house and set food before them; and he and his entire household rejoiced that he had become a believer in God.

35 When morning came, the magistrates sent the police, saying, "Let those men go." 36 And the jailer reported the message to Paul, saying, "The magistrates sent word to let you go; therefore come out now and go in peace." 37 But Paul replied, "They have beaten us in public, uncondemned, men who are Roman citizens, and have thrown us into prison; and now are they going to discharge us in secret? Certainly not! Let them come and take us out themselves." 38 The police reported these words to the magistrates, and they were afraid when they heard that they were Roman citizens; 39 so they came and apologized to them. And they took them out and asked them to leave the city. 40 After leaving the prison they went to Lydia's home; and when they had seen and encouraged the brothers and sisters[m] there, they departed.

17 After Paul and Silas[n] had passed through Amphipolis and Apollonia, they came to Thessalonica, where there was a synagogue of the Jews. 2 And Paul went in, as was his custom, and on three sabbath days argued with them from the scriptures, 3 explaining and proving that it was necessary for the Messiah[o] to suffer and to rise from the dead, and saying, "This is the Messiah,[o] Jesus whom I am proclaiming to you." 4 Some of them were persuaded and joined Paul and Silas, as did a great many of the devout Greeks and not a few of the leading women. 5 But the Jews became jealous, and with the help of some ruffians in the marketplaces they formed a mob and set the city in an uproar. While they were searching for Paul and Silas to bring them out to the assembly, they attacked Jason's house. 6 When they could not find them, they dragged Jason and some be-

---

[j]Other ancient authorities read *to us* [k]Gk *He* [l]Other ancient authorities read *word of God* [m]Gk *brothers* [n]Gk *they* [o]Or *the Christ*

lievers[p] before the city authorities,[q] shouting, "These people who have been turning the world upside down have come here also, 7 and Jason has entertained them as guests. They are all acting contrary to the decrees of the emperor, saying that there is another king named Jesus." 8 The people and the city officials were disturbed when they heard this, 9 and after they had taken bail from Jason and the others, they let them go.

10 That very night the believers[p] sent Paul and Silas off to Beroea; and when they arrived, they went to the Jewish synagogue. 11 These Jews were more receptive than those in Thessalonica, for they welcomed the message very eagerly and examined the scriptures every day to see whether these things were so. 12 Many of them therefore believed, including not a few Greek women and men of high standing. 13 But when the Jews of Thessalonica learned that the word of God had been proclaimed by Paul in Beroea as well, they came there too, to stir up and incite the crowds. 14 Then the believers[p] immediately sent Paul away to the coast, but Silas and Timothy remained behind. 15 Those who conducted Paul brought him as far as Athens; and after receiving instructions to have Silas and Timothy join him as soon as possible, they left him.

16 While Paul was waiting for them in Athens, he was deeply distressed to see that the city was full of idols. 17 So he argued in the synagogue with the Jews and the devout persons, and also in the marketplace[r] every day with those who happened to be there. 18 Also some Epicurean and Stoic philosophers debated with him. Some said, "What does this babbler want to say?" Others said, "He seems to be a proclaimer of foreign divinities." (This was because he was telling the good news about Jesus and the resurrection.) 19 So they took him and brought him to the Areopagus and asked him, "May we know what this new teaching is that you are presenting? 20 It sounds rather strange to us, so we would like to know what it means." 21 Now all the Athenians and the foreigners living there would spend their time in nothing but telling or hearing something new.

22 Then Paul stood in front of the Areopagus and said, "Athenians, I see how extremely religious you are in every way. 23 For as I went through the city and looked carefully at the objects of your worship, I found among them an altar with the inscription, 'To an unknown god.' What therefore you worship as unknown, this I proclaim to you. 24 The God who made the world and everything in it, he who is Lord of heaven and earth, does not live in shrines made by human hands, 25 nor is he served by human hands, as though he needed anything, since he himself gives to all mortals life and breath and all things. 26 From one ancestor[s] he made all nations to inhabit the whole earth, and he allotted the times of their existence and the boundaries of the places where they would live, 27 so that they would search for God[t] and perhaps grope for him and find him—though indeed he is not far from each one of us. 28 For 'In him we live and move and have our being'; as even some of your own poets have said,

'For we too are his offspring.'

29 Since we are God's offspring, we ought not to think that the deity is like gold, or silver, or stone, an image formed by the art and imagination of mortals. 30 While God has overlooked the times of human ignorance, now he commands all people everywhere to repent, 31 because he has fixed a day on which he will have the world judged in righteousness by a man whom he has appointed, and of this he has given assurance to all by raising him from the dead."

32 When they heard of the resurrection of the dead, some scoffed; but others said, "We will hear you again about this." 33 At that point Paul left them. 34 But some of them joined him and became believers, including Dionysius the Areopagite and a woman named Damaris, and others with them.

18 After this Paul[u] left Athens and went to Corinth. 2 There he found a Jew named Aquila, a native of Pontus, who had recently come from Italy with his wife Priscilla, because Claudius had ordered all Jews to leave Rome. Paul[v] went to see them, 3 and, because he was of the same trade, he stayed with them, and they worked together—by trade they were tentmakers. 4 Every sabbath he would argue in the synagogue and would try to convince Jews and Greeks.

5 When Silas and Timothy arrived from Mace-

---

[p]Gk brothers   [q]Gk politarchs   [r]Or civic center; Gk agora
[s]Gk From one; other ancient authorities read From one blood   [t]Other ancient authorities read the Lord   [u]Gk he   [v]Gk He

donia, Paul was occupied with proclaiming the word,[w] testifying to the Jews that the Messiah[x] was Jesus. 6 When they opposed and reviled him, in protest he shook the dust from his clothes[y] and said to them, "Your blood be on your own heads! I am innocent. From now on I will go to the Gentiles." 7 Then he left the synagogue[z] and went to the house of a man named Titius[a] Justus, a worshiper of God; his house was next door to the synagogue. 8 Crispus, the official of the synagogue, became a believer in the Lord, together with all his household; and many of the Corinthians who heard Paul became believers and were baptized. 9 One night the Lord said to Paul in a vision, "Do not be afraid, but speak and do not be silent; 10 for I am with you, and no one will lay a hand on you to harm you, for there are many in this city who are my people." 11 He stayed there a year and six months, teaching the word of God among them.

12 But when Gallio was proconsul of Achaia, the Jews made a united attack on Paul and brought him before the tribunal. 13 They said, "This man is persuading people to worship God in ways that are contrary to the law." 14 Just as Paul was about to speak, Gallio said to the Jews, "If it were a matter of crime or serious villainy, I would be justified in accepting the complaint of you Jews; 15 but since it is a matter of questions about words and names and your own law, see to it yourselves; I do not wish to be a judge of these matters." 16 And he dismissed them from the tribunal. 17 Then all of them[b] seized Sosthenes, the official of the synagogue, and beat him in front of the tribunal. But Gallio paid no attention to any of these things.

18 After staying there for a considerable time, Paul said farewell to the believers[c] and sailed for Syria, accompanied by Priscilla and Aquila. At Cenchreae he had his hair cut, for he was under a vow. 19 When they reached Ephesus, he left them there, but first he himself went into the synagogue and had a discussion with the Jews. 20 When they asked him to stay longer, he declined; 21 but on taking leave of them, he said, "I[d] will return to you, if God wills." Then he set sail from Ephesus.

22 When he had landed at Caesarea, he went up to Jerusalem[e] and greeted the church, and then went down to Antioch. 23 After spending some time there he departed and went from place to place through the region of Galatia[f] and Phrygia, strengthening all the disciples.

24 Now there came to Ephesus a Jew named Apollos, a native of Alexandria. He was an eloquent man, well-versed in the scriptures. 25 He had been instructed in the Way of the Lord; and he spoke with burning enthusiasm and taught accurately the things concerning Jesus, though he knew only the baptism of John. 26 He began to speak boldly in the synagogue; but when Priscilla and Aquila heard him, they took him aside and explained the Way of God to him more accurately. 27 And when he wished to cross over to Achaia, the believers[c] encouraged him and wrote to the disciples to welcome him. On his arrival he greatly helped those who through grace had become believers, 28 for he powerfully refuted the Jews in public, showing by the scriptures that the Messiah[y] is Jesus.

19 While Apollos was in Corinth, Paul passed through the interior regions and came to Ephesus, where he found some disciples. 2 He said to them, "Did you receive the Holy Spirit when you became believers?" They replied, "No, we have not even heard that there is a Holy Spirit." 3 Then he said, "Into what then were you baptized?" They answered, "Into John's baptism." 4 Paul said, "John baptized with the baptism of repentance, telling the people to believe in the one who was to come after him, that is, in Jesus." 5 On hearing this, they were baptized in the name of the Lord Jesus. 6 When Paul had laid his hands on them, the Holy Spirit came upon them, and they spoke in tongues and prophesied— 7 altogether there were about twelve of them.

8 He entered the synagogue and for three months spoke out boldly, and argued persuasively about the kingdom of God. 9 When some stubbornly refused to believe and spoke evil of the Way before the congregation, he left them, taking the disciples with him, and argued daily in the lecture hall of Tyrannus.[g] 10 This continued for two years, so that all the residents of

---

[w]Gk *with the word*   [x]Or *the Christ*   [y]Gk *reviled him, he shook out his clothes*   [z]Gk *left there*   [a]Other ancient authorities read *Titus*   [b]Other ancient authorities read *all the Greeks*   [c]Gk *brothers*   [d]Other ancient authorities read *I must at all costs keep the approaching festival in Jerusalem, but I*   [e]Gk *went up*   [f]Gk *the Galatian region*   [g]Other ancient authorities read *of a certain Tyrannus, from eleven o'clock in the morning to four in the afternoon*

Asia, both Jews and Greeks, heard the word of the Lord.

11 God did extraordinary miracles through Paul, 12 so that when the handkerchiefs or aprons that had touched his skin were brought to the sick, their diseases left them, and the evil spirits came out of them. 13 Then some itinerant Jewish exorcists tried to use the name of the Lord Jesus over those who had evil spirits, saying, "I adjure you by the Jesus whom Paul proclaims." 14 Seven sons of a Jewish high priest named Sceva were doing this. 15 But the evil spirit said to them in reply, "Jesus I know, and Paul I know; but who are you?" 16 Then the man with the evil spirit leaped on them, mastered them all, and so overpowered them that they fled out of the house naked and wounded. 17 When this became known to all residents of Ephesus, both Jews and Greeks, everyone was awestruck; and the name of the Lord Jesus was praised. 18 Also many of those who became believers confessed and disclosed their practices. 19 A number of those who practiced magic collected their books and burned them publicly; when the value of these books[h] was calculated, it was found to come to fifty thousand silver coins. 20 So the word of the Lord grew mightily and prevailed.

21 Now after these things had been accomplished, Paul resolved in the Spirit to go through Macedonia and Achaia, and then to go on to Jerusalem. He said, "After I have gone there, I must also see Rome." 22 So he sent two of his helpers, Timothy and Erastus, to Macedonia, while he himself stayed for some time longer in Asia.

23 About that time no little disturbance broke out concerning the Way. 24 A man named Demetrius, a silversmith who made silver shrines of Artemis, brought no little business to the artisans. 25 These he gathered together, with the workers of the same trade, and said, "Men, you know that we get our wealth from this business. 26 You also see and hear that not only in Ephesus but in almost the whole of Asia this Paul has persuaded and drawn away a considerable number of people by saying that gods made with hands are not gods. 27 And there is danger not only that this trade of ours may come into disrepute but also that the temple of the great goddess Artemis will be scorned, and she will be deprived of her majesty that brought all Asia and the world to worship her."

28 When they heard this, they were enraged and shouted, "Great is Artemis of the Ephesians!" 29 The city was filled with the confusion; and people[i] rushed together to the theater, dragging with them Gaius and Aristarchus, Macedonians who were Paul's travel companions. 30 Paul wished to go into the crowd, but the disciples would not let him; 31 even some officials of the province of Asia,[j] who were friendly to him, sent him a message urging him not to venture into the theater. 32 Meanwhile, some were shouting one thing, some another; for the assembly was in confusion, and most of them did not know why they had come together. 33 Some of the crowd gave instructions to Alexander, whom the Jews had pushed forward. And Alexander motioned for silence and tried to make a defense before the people. 34 But when they recognized that he was a Jew, for about two hours all of them shouted in unison, "Great is Artemis of the Ephesians!" 35 But when the town clerk had quieted the crowd, he said, "Citizens of Ephesus, who is there that does not know that the city of the Ephesians is the temple keeper of the great Artemis and of the statue that fell from heaven?[k] 36 Since these things cannot be denied, you ought to be quiet and do nothing rash. 37 You have brought these men here who are neither temple robbers nor blasphemers of our[l] goddess. 38 If therefore Demetrius and the artisans with him have a complaint against anyone, the courts are open, and there are proconsuls; let them bring charges there against one another. 39 If there is anything further[m] you want to know, it must be settled in the regular assembly. 40 For we are in danger of being charged with rioting today, since there is no cause that we can give to justify this commotion." 41 When he had said this, he dismissed the assembly.

20 After the uproar had ceased, Paul sent for the disciples; and after encouraging them and saying farewell, he left for Macedonia. 2 When he had gone through those regions and had given the believers[n] much encouragement, he

[h]Gk *them* [i]Gk *they* [j]Gk *some of the Asiarchs* [k]Meaning of Gk uncertain [l]Other ancient authorities read *your* [m]Other ancient authorities read *about other matters* [n]Gk *given them*

came to Greece, 3 where he stayed for three months. He was about to set sail for Syria when a plot was made against him by the Jews, and so he decided to return through Macedonia. 4 He was accompanied by Sopater son of Pyrrhus from Beroea, by Aristarchus and Secundus from Thessalonica, by Gaius from Derbe, and by Timothy, as well as by Tychicus and Trophimus from Asia. 5 They went ahead and were waiting for us in Troas; 6 but we sailed from Philippi after the days of Unleavened Bread, and in five days we joined them in Troas, where we stayed for seven days.

7 On the first day of the week, when we met to break bread, Paul was holding a discussion with them; since he intended to leave the next day, he continued speaking until midnight. 8 There were many lamps in the room upstairs where we were meeting. 9 A young man named Eutychus, who was sitting in the window, began to sink off into a deep sleep while Paul talked still longer. Overcome by sleep, he fell to the ground three floors below and was picked up dead. 10 But Paul went down, and bending over him took him in his arms, and said, "Do not be alarmed, for his life is in him." 11 Then Paul went upstairs, and after he had broken bread and eaten, he continued to converse with them until dawn; then he left. 12 Meanwhile they had taken the boy away alive and were not a little comforted.

13 We went ahead to the ship and set sail for Assos, intending to take Paul on board there; for he had made this arrangement, intending to go by land himself. 14 When he met us in Assos, we took him on board and went to Mitylene. 15 We sailed from there, and on the following day we arrived opposite Chios. The next day we touched at Samos, and[o] the day after that we came to Miletus. 16 For Paul had decided to sail past Ephesus, so that he might not have to spend time in Asia; he was eager to be in Jerusalem, if possible, on the day of Pentecost.

17 From Miletus he sent a message to Ephesus, asking the elders of the church to meet him. 18 When they came to him, he said to them:

"You yourselves know how I lived among you the entire time from the first day that I set foot in Asia, 19 serving the Lord with all humility and with tears, enduring the trials that came to me through the plots of the Jews. 20 I did not shrink from doing anything helpful, proclaiming the message to you and teaching you publicly and from house to house, 21 as I testified to both Jews and Greeks about repentance toward God and faith toward our Lord Jesus. 22 And now, as a captive to the Spirit,[p] I am on my way to Jerusalem, not knowing what will happen to me there, 23 except that the Holy Spirit testifies to me in every city that imprisonment and persecutions are waiting for me. 24 But I do not count my life of any value to myself, if only I may finish my course and the ministry that I received from the Lord Jesus, to testify to the good news of God's grace.

25 "And now I know that none of you, among whom I have gone about proclaiming the kingdom, will ever see my face again. 26 Therefore I declare to you this day that I am not responsible for the blood of any of you, 27 for I did not shrink from declaring to you the whole purpose of God. 28 Keep watch over yourselves and over all the flock, of which the Holy Spirit has made you overseers, to shepherd the church of God[q] that he obtained with the blood of his own Son.[r] 29 I know that after I have gone, savage wolves will come in among you, not sparing the flock. 30 Some even from your own group will come distorting the truth in order to entice the disciples to follow them. 31 Therefore be alert, remembering that for three years I did not cease night or day to warn everyone with tears. 32 And now I commend you to God and to the message of his grace, a message that is able to build you up and to give you the inheritance among all who are sanctified. 33 I coveted no one's silver or gold or clothing. 34 You know for yourselves that I worked with my own hands to support myself and my companions. 35 In all this I have given you an example that by such work we must support the weak, remembering the words of the Lord Jesus, for he himself said, 'It is more blessed to give than to receive.' "

36 When he had finished speaking, he knelt down with them all and prayed. 37 There was much weeping among them all; they embraced Paul and kissed him, 38 grieving especially because of what he had said, that they would not see him again. Then they brought him to the ship.

[o]Other ancient authorities add *after remaining at Trogyllium*
[p]Or *And now, bound in the spirit* [q]Other ancient authorities read *of the Lord* [r]Or *with his own blood*; Gk *with the blood of his Own*

21 When we had parted from them and set sail, we came by a straight course to Cos, and the next day to Rhodes, and from there to Patara.[s] 2 When we found a ship bound for Phoenicia, we went on board and set sail. 3 We came in sight of Cyprus; and leaving it on our left, we sailed to Syria and landed at Tyre, because the ship was to unload its cargo there. 4 We looked up the disciples and stayed there for seven days. Through the Spirit they told Paul not to go on to Jerusalem. 5 When our days there were ended, we left and proceeded on our journey; and all of them, with wives and children, escorted us outside the city. There we knelt down on the beach and prayed 6 and said farewell to one another. Then we went on board the ship, and they returned home.

7 When we had finished[t] the voyage from Tyre, we arrived at Ptolemais; and we greeted the believers[u] and stayed with them for one day. 8 The next day we left and came to Caesarea; and we went into the house of Philip the evangelist, one of the seven, and stayed with him. 9 He had four unmarried daughters[v] who had the gift of prophecy. 10 While we were staying there for several days, a prophet named Agabus came down from Judea. 11 He came to us and took Paul's belt, bound his own feet and hands with it, and said, "Thus says the Holy Spirit, 'This is the way the Jews in Jerusalem will bind the man who owns this belt and will hand him over to the Gentiles.'" 12 When we heard this, we and the people there urged him not to go up to Jerusalem. 13 Then Paul answered, "What are you doing, weeping and breaking my heart? For I am ready not only to be bound but even to die in Jerusalem for the name of the Lord Jesus." 14 Since he would not be persuaded, we remained silent except to say, "The Lord's will be done."

15 After these days we got ready and started to go up to Jerusalem. 16 Some of the disciples from Caesarea also came along and brought us to the house of Mnason of Cyprus, an early disciple, with whom we were to stay.

17 When we arrived in Jerusalem, the brothers welcomed us warmly. 18 The next day Paul went with us to visit James; and all the elders were present. 19 After greeting them, he related one by one the things that God had done among the Gentiles through his ministry. 20 When they heard it, they praised God. Then they said to him, "You see, brother, how many thousands of believers there are among the Jews, and they are all zealous for the law. 21 They have been told about you that you teach all the Jews living among the Gentiles to forsake Moses, and that you tell them not to circumcise their children or observe the customs. 22 What then is to be done? They will certainly hear that you have come. 23 So do what we tell you. We have four men who are under a vow. 24 Join these men, go through the rite of purification with them, and pay for the shaving of their heads. Thus all will know that there is nothing in what they have been told about you, but that you yourself observe and guard the law. 25 But as for the Gentiles who have become believers, we have sent a letter with our judgment that they should abstain from what has been sacrificed to idols and from blood and from what is strangled[w] and from fornication." 26 Then Paul took the men, and the next day, having purified himself, he entered the temple with them, making public the completion of the days of purification when the sacrifice would be made for each of them.

27 When the seven days were almost completed, the Jews from Asia, who had seen him in the temple, stirred up the whole crowd. They seized him, 28 shouting, "Fellow Israelites, help! This is the man who is teaching everyone everywhere against our people, our law, and this place; more than that, he has actually brought Greeks into the temple and has defiled this holy place." 29 For they had previously seen Trophimus the Ephesian with him in the city, and they supposed that Paul had brought him into the temple. 30 Then all the city was aroused, and the people rushed together. They seized Paul and dragged him out of the temple, and immediately the doors were shut. 31 While they were trying to kill him, word came to the tribune of the cohort that all Jerusalem was in an uproar. 32 Immediately he took soldiers and centurions and ran down to them. When they saw the tribune and the soldiers, they stopped beating Paul. 33 Then the tribune came, arrested him, and ordered him to be bound with two chains; he inquired who he was and what he had done. 34 Some

---

[s]Other ancient authorities add *and Myra*   [t]Or *continued*
[u]Gk *brothers*   [v]Gk *four daughters, virgins,*   [w]Other ancient authorities lack *and from what is strangled*

in the crowd shouted one thing, some another; and as he could not learn the facts because of the uproar, he ordered him to be brought into the barracks. 35 When Paul[x] came to the steps, the violence of the mob was so great that he had to be carried by the soldiers. 36 The crowd that followed kept shouting, "Away with him!"

37 Just as Paul was about to be brought into the barracks, he said to the tribune, "May I say something to you?" The tribune[y] replied, "Do you know Greek? 38 Then you are not the Egyptian who recently stirred up a revolt and led the four thousand assassins out into the wilderness?" 39 Paul replied, "I am a Jew, from Tarsus in Cilicia, a citizen of an important city; I beg you, let me speak to the people." 40 When he had given him permission, Paul stood on the steps and motioned to the people for silence; and when there was a great hush, he addressed them in the Hebrew[z] language, saying:

22

"Brothers and fathers, listen to the defense that I now make before you."

2 When they heard him addressing them in Hebrew,[z] they became even more quiet. Then he said:

3 "I am a Jew, born in Tarsus in Cilicia, but brought up in this city at the feet of Gamaliel, educated strictly according to our ancestral law, being zealous for God, just as all of you are today. 4 I persecuted this Way up to the point of death by binding both men and women and putting them in prison, 5 as the high priest and the whole council of elders can testify about me. From them I also received letters to the brothers in Damascus, and I went there in order to bind those who were there and to bring them back to Jerusalem for punishment.

6 "While I was on my way and approaching Damascus, about noon a great light from heaven suddenly shone about me. 7 I fell to the ground and heard a voice saying to me, 'Saul, Saul, why are you persecuting me?' 8 I answered, 'Who are you, Lord?' Then he said to me, 'I am Jesus of Nazareth[a] whom you are persecuting.' 9 Now those who were with me saw the light but did not hear the voice of the one who was speaking to me. 10 I asked, 'What am I to do, Lord?' The Lord said to me, 'Get up and go to Damascus; there you will be told everything that has been assigned to you to do.' 11 Since I could not see because of the bright-

ness of that light, those who were with me took my hand and led me to Damascus.

12 "A certain Ananias, who was a devout man according to the law and well spoken of by all the Jews living there, 13 came to me; and standing beside me, he said, 'Brother Saul, regain your sight!' In that very hour I regained my sight and saw him. 14 Then he said, 'The God of our ancestors has chosen you to know his will, to see the Righteous One and to hear his own voice; 15 for you will be his witness to all the world of what you have seen and heard. 16 And now why do you delay? Get up, be baptized, and have your sins washed away, calling on his name.'

17 "After I had returned to Jerusalem and while I was praying in the temple, I fell into a trance 18 and saw Jesus[b] saying to me, 'Hurry and get out of Jerusalem quickly, because they will not accept your testimony about me.' 19 And I said, 'Lord, they themselves know that in every synagogue I imprisoned and beat those who believed in you. 20 And while the blood of your witness Stephen was shed, I myself was standing by, approving and keeping the coats of those who killed him.' 21 Then he said to me, 'Go, for I will send you far away to the Gentiles.' "

22 Up to this point they listened to him, but then they shouted, "Away with such a fellow from the earth! For he should not be allowed to live." 23 And while they were shouting, throwing off their cloaks, and tossing dust into the air, 24 the tribune directed that he was to be brought into the barracks, and ordered him to be examined by flogging, to find out the reason for this outcry against him. 25 But when they had tied him up with thongs,[c] Paul said to the centurion who was standing by, "Is it legal for you to flog a Roman citizen who is uncondemned?" 26 When the centurion heard that, he went to the tribune and said to him, "What are you about to do? This man is a Roman citizen." 27 The tribune came and asked Paul,[b] "Tell me, are you a Roman citizen?" And he said, "Yes." 28 The tribune answered, "It cost me a large sum of money to get my citizenship." Paul said, "But I was born a citizen." 29 Immediately those who were about to examine him drew back

---

[x]Gk *he* [y]Gk *He* [z]That is, *Aramaic* [a]Gk *the Nazorean* [b]Gk *him*
[c]Or *up for the lashes*

from him; and the tribune also was afraid, for he realized that Paul was a Roman citizen and that he had bound him.

30 Since he wanted to find out what Paul[d] was being accused of by the Jews, the next day he released him and ordered the chief priests and the entire council to meet. He brought Paul down and had him stand before them.

23 While Paul was looking intently at the council he said, "Brothers,[e] up to this day I have lived my life with a clear conscience before God." 2 Then the high priest Ananias ordered those standing near him to strike him on the mouth. 3 At this Paul said to him, "God will strike you, you whitewashed wall! Are you sitting there to judge me according to the law, and yet in violation of the law you order me to be struck?" 4 Those standing nearby said, "Do you dare to insult God's high priest?" 5 And Paul said, "I did not realize, brothers, that he was high priest; for it is written, 'You shall not speak evil of a leader of your people.'"[28]

6 When Paul noticed that some were Sadducees and others were Pharisees, he called out in the council, "Brothers, I am a Pharisee, a son of Pharisees. I am on trial concerning the hope of the resurrection[f] of the dead." 7 When he said this, a dissension began between the Pharisees and the Sadducees, and the assembly was divided. 8 (The Sadducees say that there is no resurrection, or angel, or spirit; but the Pharisees acknowledge all three.) 9 Then a great clamor arose, and certain scribes of the Pharisees' group stood up and contended, "We find nothing wrong with this man. What if a spirit or an angel has spoken to him?" 10 When the dissension became violent, the tribune, fearing that they would tear Paul to pieces, ordered the soldiers to go down, take him by force, and bring him into the barracks.

11 That night the Lord stood near him and said, "Keep up your courage! For just as you have testified for me in Jerusalem, so you must bear witness also in Rome."

12 In the morning the Jews joined in a conspiracy and bound themselves by an oath neither to eat nor drink until they had killed Paul. 13 There were more than forty who joined in this conspiracy. 14 They went to the chief priests and elders and said, "We have strictly bound ourselves by an oath to taste no food until we have killed Paul. 15 Now then, you and the council must notify the tribune to bring him down to you, on the pretext that you want to make a more thorough examination of his case. And we are ready to do away with him before he arrives."

16 Now the son of Paul's sister heard about the ambush; so he went and gained entrance to the barracks and told Paul. 17 Paul called one of the centurions and said, "Take this young man to the tribune, for he has something to report to him." 18 So he took him, brought him to the tribune, and said, "The prisoner Paul called me and asked me to bring this young man to you; he has something to tell you." 19 The tribune took him by the hand, drew him aside privately, and asked, "What is it that you have to report to me?" 20 He answered, "The Jews have agreed to ask you to bring Paul down to the council tomorrow, as though they were going to inquire more thoroughly into his case. 21 But do not be persuaded by them, for more than forty of their men are lying in ambush for him. They have bound themselves by an oath neither to eat nor drink until they kill him. They are ready now and are waiting for your consent." 22 So the tribune dismissed the young man, ordering him, "Tell no one that you have informed me of this."

23 Then he summoned two of the centurions and said, "Get ready to leave by nine o'clock tonight for Caesarea with two hundred soldiers, seventy horsemen, and two hundred spearmen. 24 Also provide mounts for Paul to ride, and take him safely to Felix the governor." 25 He wrote a letter to this effect:

26 "Claudius Lysias to his Excellency the governor Felix, greetings. 27 This man was seized by the Jews and was about to be killed by them, but when I had learned that he was a Roman citizen, I came with the guard and rescued him. 28 Since I wanted to know the charge for which they accused him, I had him brought to their council. 29 I found that he was accused concerning questions of their law, but was charged with nothing deserving death or imprisonment. 30 When I was informed that

---

[d]Gk *he*   [e]Gk *Men, brothers*   [f]Gk *concerning hope and resurrection*

[28]Exod 22:28

there would be a plot against the man, I sent him to you at once, ordering his accusers also to state before you what they have against him.ᵍ"

31 So the soldiers, according to their instructions, took Paul and brought him during the night to Antipatris. 32 The next day they let the horsemen go on with him, while they returned to the barracks. 33 When they came to Caesarea and delivered the letter to the governor, they presented Paul also before him. 34 On reading the letter, he asked what province he belonged to, and when he learned that he was from Cilicia, 35 he said, "I will give you a hearing when your accusers arrive." Then he ordered that he be kept under guard in Herod's headquarters.ʰ

24 Five days later the high priest Ananias came down with some elders and an attorney, a certain Tertullus, and they reported their case against Paul to the governor. 2 When Paulⁱ had been summoned, Tertullus began to accuse him, saying:

"Your Excellency,ʲ because of you we have long enjoyed peace, and reforms have been made for this people because of your foresight. 3 We welcome this in every way and everywhere with utmost gratitude. 4 But, to detain you no further, I beg you to hear us briefly with your customary graciousness. 5 We have, in fact, found this man a pestilent fellow, an agitator among all the Jews throughout the world, and a ringleader of the sect of the Nazarenes.ᵏ 6 He even tried to profane the temple, and so we seized him.ˡ 8 By examining him yourself you will be able to learn from him concerning everything of which we accuse him."

9 The Jews also joined in the charge by asserting that all this was true.

10 When the governor motioned to him to speak, Paul replied:

"I cheerfully make my defense, knowing that for many years you have been a judge over this nation. 11 As you can find out, it is not more than twelve days since I went up to worship in Jerusalem. 12 They did not find me disputing with anyone in the temple or stirring up a crowd either in the synagogues or throughout the city. 13 Neither can they prove to you the charge that they now bring against me. 14 But this I admit to you, that according to the Way, which they call a sect, I worship the God of our ancestors, believing

everything laid down according to the law or written in the prophets. 15 I have a hope in God—a hope that they themselves also accept—that there will be a resurrection of bothᵐ the righteous and the unrighteous. 16 Therefore I do my best always to have a clear conscience toward God and all people. 17 Now after some years I came to bring alms to my nation and to offer sacrifices. 18 While I was doing this, they found me in the temple, completing the rite of purification, without any crowd or disturbance. 19 But there were some Jews from Asia—they ought to be here before you to make an accusation, if they have anything against me. 20 Or let these men here tell what crime they had found when I stood before the council, 21 unless it was this one sentence that I called out while standing before them, 'It is about the resurrection of the dead that I am on trial before you today.'"

22 But Felix, who was rather well informed about the Way, adjourned the hearing with the comment, "When Lysias the tribune comes down, I will decide your case." 23 Then he ordered the centurion to keep him in custody, but to let him have some liberty and not to prevent any of his friends from taking care of his needs.

24 Some days later when Felix came with his wife Drusilla, who was Jewish, he sent for Paul and heard him speak concerning faith in Christ Jesus. 25 And as he discussed justice, self-control, and the coming judgment, Felix became frightened and said, "Go away for the present; when I have an opportunity, I will send for you." 26 At the same time he hoped that money would be given him by Paul, and for that reason he used to send for him very often and converse with him.

27 After two years had passed, Felix was succeeded by Porcius Festus; and since he wanted to grant the Jews a favor, Felix left Paul in prison.

25 Three days after Festus had arrived in the province, he went up from Caesarea to Jerusalem 2 where the chief priests and the leaders of the Jews gave him a report against Paul. They appealed to him 3 and requested, as a favor

---

ᵍOther ancient authorities add *Farewell*   ʰGk *praetorium*   ⁱGk *he*
ʲGk lacks *Your Excellency*   ᵏGk *Nazoreans*   ˡOther ancient
authorities add *and we would have judged him according to our law.*
*⁷But the chief captain Lysias came and with great violence took him
out of our hands, ⁸commanding his accusers to come before you.*
ᵐOther ancient authorities read *of the dead, both of*

to them against Paul,[n] to have him transferred to Jerusalem. They were, in fact, planning an ambush to kill him along the way. 4 Festus replied that Paul was being kept at Caesarea, and that he himself intended to go there shortly. 5 "So," he said, "let those of you who have the authority come down with me, and if there is anything wrong about the man, let them accuse him."

6 After he had stayed among them not more than eight or ten days, he went down to Caesarea; the next day he took his seat on the tribunal and ordered Paul to be brought. 7 When he arrived, the Jews who had gone down from Jerusalem surrounded him, bringing many serious charges against him, which they could not prove. 8 Paul said in his defense, "I have in no way committed an offense against the law of the Jews, or against the temple, or against the emperor." 9 But Festus, wishing to do the Jews a favor, asked Paul, "Do you wish to go up to Jerusalem and be tried there before me on these charges?" 10 Paul said, "I am appealing to the emperor's tribunal; this is where I should be tried. I have done no wrong to the Jews, as you very well know. 11 Now if I am in the wrong and have committed something for which I deserve to die, I am not trying to escape death; but if there is nothing to their charges against me, no one can turn me over to them. I appeal to the emperor." 12 Then Festus, after he had conferred with his council, replied, "You have appealed to the emperor; to the emperor you will go."

13 After several days had passed, King Agrippa and Bernice arrived at Caesarea to welcome Festus. 14 Since they were staying there several days, Festus laid Paul's case before the king, saying, "There is a man here who was left in prison by Felix. 15 When I was in Jerusalem, the chief priests and the elders of the Jews informed me about him and asked for a sentence against him. 16 I told them that it was not the custom of the Romans to hand over anyone before the accused had met the accusers face to face and had been given an opportunity to make a defense against the charge. 17 So when they met here, I lost no time, but on the next day took my seat on the tribunal and ordered the man to be brought. 18 When the accusers stood up, they did not charge him with any of the crimes[o] that I was expecting. 19 Instead they had certain points of disagreement with him

about their own religion and about a certain Jesus, who had died, but whom Paul asserted to be alive. 20 Since I was at a loss how to investigate these questions, I asked whether he wished to go to Jerusalem and be tried there on these charges.[p] 21 But when Paul had appealed to be kept in custody for the decision of his Imperial Majesty, I ordered him to be held until I could send him to the emperor." 22 Agrippa said to Festus, "I would like to hear the man myself." "Tomorrow," he said, "you will hear him."

23 So on the next day Agrippa and Bernice came with great pomp, and they entered the audience hall with the military tribunes and the prominent men of the city. Then Festus gave the order and Paul was brought in. 24 And Festus said, "King Agrippa and all here present with us, you see this man about whom the whole Jewish community petitioned me, both in Jerusalem and here, shouting that he ought not to live any longer. 25 But I found that he had done nothing deserving death; and when he appealed to his Imperial Majesty, I decided to send him. 26 But I have nothing definite to write to our sovereign about him. Therefore I have brought him before all of you, and especially before you, King Agrippa, so that, after we have examined him, I may have something to write— 27 for it seems to me unreasonable to send a prisoner without indicating the charges against him."

26 Agrippa said to Paul, "You have permission to speak for yourself." Then Paul stretched out his hand and began to defend himself:

2 "I consider myself fortunate that it is before you, King Agrippa, I am to make my defense today against all the accusations of the Jews, 3 because you are especially familiar with all the customs and controversies of the Jews; therefore I beg of you to listen to me patiently.

4 "All the Jews know my way of life from my youth, a life spent from the beginning among my own people and in Jerusalem. 5 They have known for a long time, if they are willing to testify, that I have belonged to the strictest sect of our religion and lived as a Pharisee. 6 And now I stand here on

[n]Gk *him* [o]Other ancient authorities read *with anything* [p]Gk *on them*

trial on account of my hope in the promise made by God to our ancestors, 7 a promise that our twelve tribes hope to attain, as they earnestly worship day and night. It is for this hope, your Excellency,q that I am accused by Jews! 8 Why is it thought incredible by any of you that God raises the dead?

9 "Indeed, I myself was convinced that I ought to do many things against the name of Jesus of Nazareth.r 10 And that is what I did in Jerusalem; with authority received from the chief priests, I not only locked up many of the saints in prison, but I also cast my vote against them when they were being condemned to death. 11 By punishing them often in all the synagogues I tried to force them to blaspheme; and since I was so furiously enraged at them, I pursued them even to foreign cities.

12 "With this in mind, I was traveling to Damascus with the authority and commission of the chief priests, 13 when at midday along the road, your Excellency,q I saw a light from heaven, brighter than the sun, shining around me and my companions. 14 When we had all fallen to the ground, I heard a voice saying to me in the Hebrews language, 'Saul, Saul, why are you persecuting me? It hurts you to kick against the goads.' 15 I asked, 'Who are you, Lord?' The Lord answered, 'I am Jesus whom you are persecuting. 16 But get up and stand on your feet; for I have appeared to you for this purpose, to appoint you to serve and testify to the things in which you have seen met and to those in which I will appear to you. 17 I will rescue you from your people and from the Gentiles—to whom I am sending you 18 to open their eyes so that they may turn from darkness to light and from the power of Satan to God, so that they may receive forgiveness of sins and a place among those who are sanctified by faith in me.'

19 "After that, King Agrippa, I was not disobedient to the heavenly vision, 20 but declared first to those in Damascus, then in Jerusalem and throughout the countryside of Judea, and also to the Gentiles, that they should repent and turn to God and do deeds consistent with repentance. 21 For this reason the Jews seized me in the temple and tried to kill me. 22 To this day I have had help from God, and so I stand here, testifying to both small and great, saying nothing but what the prophets and Moses said would take place: 23 that the Messiahu must suffer, and that, by being the first to rise from the dead, he would proclaim light both to our people and to the Gentiles."

24 While he was making this defense, Festus exclaimed, "You are out of your mind, Paul! Too much learning is driving you insane!" 25 But Paul said, "I am not out of my mind, most excellent Festus, but I am speaking the sober truth. 26 Indeed the king knows about these things, and to him I speak freely; for I am certain that none of these things has escaped his notice, for this was not done in a corner. 27 King Agrippa, do you believe the prophets? I know that you believe." 28 Agrippa said to Paul, "Are you so quickly persuading me to become a Christian?"v 29 Paul replied, "Whether quickly or not, I pray to God that not only you but also all who are listening to me today might become such as I am—except for these chains."

30 Then the king got up, and with him the governor and Bernice and those who had been seated with them; 31 and as they were leaving, they said to one another, "This man is doing nothing to deserve death or imprisonment." 32 Agrippa said to Festus, "This man could have been set free if he had not appealed to the emperor."

27 When it was decided that we were to sail for Italy, they transferred Paul and some other prisoners to a centurion of the Augustan Cohort, named Julius. 2 Embarking on a ship of Adramyttium that was about to set sail to the ports along the coast of Asia, we put to sea, accompanied by Aristarchus, a Macedonian from Thessalonica. 3 The next day we put in at Sidon; and Julius treated Paul kindly, and allowed him to go to his friends to be cared for. 4 Putting out to sea from there, we sailed under the lee of Cyprus, because the winds were against us. 5 After we had sailed across the sea that is off Cilicia and Pamphylia, we came to Myra in Lycia. 6 There the centurion found an Alexandrian ship bound for Italy and put us on board. 7 We sailed slowly for a number of days and arrived with difficulty off Cnidus, and as the wind was against us, we sailed under the lee of Crete off Salmone. 8 Sailing past

qGk O king rGk the Nazorean sThat is, Aramaic tOther ancient authorities read the things that you have seen uOr the Christ vOr Quickly you will persuade me to play the Christian

it with difficulty, we came to a place called Fair Havens, near the city of Lasea.

9 Since much time had been lost and sailing was now dangerous, because even the Fast had already gone by, Paul advised them, 10 saying, "Sirs, I can see that the voyage will be with danger and much heavy loss, not only of the cargo and the ship, but also of our lives." 11 But the centurion paid more attention to the pilot and to the owner of the ship than to what Paul said. 12 Since the harbor was not suitable for spending the winter, the majority was in favor of putting to sea from there, on the chance that somehow they could reach Phoenix, where they could spend the winter. It was a harbor of Crete, facing southwest and northwest.

13 When a moderate south wind began to blow, they thought they could achieve their purpose; so they weighed anchor and began to sail past Crete, close to the shore. 14 But soon a violent wind, called the northeaster, rushed down from Crete.ʷ 15 Since the ship was caught and could not be turned head-on into the wind, we gave way to it and were driven. 16 By running under the lee of a small island called Caudaˣ we were scarcely able to get the ship's boat under control. 17 After hoisting it up they took measuresʸ to undergird the ship; then, fearing that they would run on the Syrtis, they lowered the sea anchor and so were driven. 18 We were being pounded by the storm so violently that on the next day they began to throw the cargo overboard, 19 and on the third day with their own hands they threw the ship's tackle overboard. 20 When neither sun nor stars appeared for many days, and no small tempest raged, all hope of our being saved was at last abandoned.

21 Since they had been without food for a long time, Paul then stood up among them and said, "Men, you should have listened to me and not have set sail from Crete and thereby avoided this damage and loss. 22 I urge you now to keep up your courage, for there will be no loss of life among you, but only of the ship. 23 For last night there stood by me an angel of the God to whom I belong and whom I worship, 24 and he said, 'Do not be afraid, Paul; you must stand before the emperor; and indeed, God has granted safety to all those who are sailing with you.' 25 So keep up your courage, men, for I have faith in God that it will be exactly as I have been told. 26 But we will have to run aground on some island."

27 When the fourteenth night had come, as we were drifting across the sea of Adria, about midnight the sailors suspected that they were nearing land. 28 So they took soundings and found twenty fathoms; a little farther on they took soundings again and found fifteen fathoms. 29 Fearing that we might run on the rocks, they let down four anchors from the stern and prayed for day to come. 30 But when the sailors tried to escape from the ship and had lowered the boat into the sea, on the pretext of putting out anchors from the bow, 31 Paul said to the centurion and the soldiers, "Unless these men stay in the ship, you cannot be saved." 32 Then the soldiers cut away the ropes of the boat and set it adrift.

33 Just before daybreak, Paul urged all of them to take some food, saying, "Today is the fourteenth day that you have been in suspense and remaining without food, having eaten nothing. 34 Therefore I urge you to take some food, for it will help you survive; for none of you will lose a hair from your heads." 35 After he had said this, he took bread; and giving thanks to God in the presence of all, he broke it and began to eat. 36 Then all of them were encouraged and took food for themselves. 37 (We were in all two hundred seventy-sixᶻ persons in the ship.) 38 After they had satisfied their hunger, they lightened the ship by throwing the wheat into the sea.

39 In the morning they did not recognize the land, but they noticed a bay with a beach, on which they planned to run the ship ashore, if they could. 40 So they cast off the anchors and left them in the sea. At the same time they loosened the ropes that tied the steering-oars; then hoisting the foresail to the wind, they made for the beach. 41 But striking a reef,ᵃ they ran the ship aground; the bow stuck and remained immovable, but the stern was being broken up by the force of the waves. 42 The soldiers' plan was to kill the prisoners, so that none might swim away and escape; 43 but the centuri-

ʷGk *it*   ˣOther ancient authorities read *Clauda*   ʸGk *helps*   ᶻOther ancient authorities read *seventy-six*; others, *about seventy-six*   ᵃGk *place of two seas*

on, wishing to save Paul, kept them from carrying out their plan. He ordered those who could swim to jump overboard first and make for the land, 44 and the rest to follow, some on planks and others on pieces of the ship. And so it was that all were brought safely to land.

28 After we had reached safety, we then learned that the island was called Malta. 2 The natives showed us unusual kindness. Since it had begun to rain and was cold, they kindled a fire and welcomed all of us around it. 3 Paul had gathered a bundle of brushwood and was putting it on the fire, when a viper, driven out by the heat, fastened itself on his hand. 4 When the natives saw the creature hanging from his hand, they said to one another, "This man must be a murderer; though he has escaped from the sea, justice has not allowed him to live." 5 He, however, shook off the creature into the fire and suffered no harm. 6 They were expecting him to swell up or drop dead, but after they had waited a long time and saw that nothing unusual had happened to him, they changed their minds and began to say that he was a god.

7 Now in the neighborhood of that place were lands belonging to the leading man of the island, named Publius, who received us and entertained us hospitably for three days. 8 It so happened that the father of Publius lay sick in bed with fever and dysentery. Paul visited him and cured him by praying and putting his hands on him. 9 After this happened, the rest of the people on the island who had diseases also came and were cured. 10 They bestowed many honors on us, and when we were about to sail, they put on board all the provisions we needed.

11 Three months later we set sail on a ship that had wintered at the island, an Alexandrian ship with the Twin Brothers as its figurehead. 12 We put in at Syracuse and stayed there for three days; 13 then we weighed anchor and came to Rhegium. After one day there a south wind sprang up, and on the second day we came to Puteoli. 14 There we found believers[b] and were invited to stay with them for seven days. And so we came to Rome. 15 The believers[b] from there, when they heard of us, came as far as the Forum of Appius and Three Taverns to meet us. On seeing them, Paul thanked God and took courage.

16 When we came into Rome, Paul was allowed to live by himself, with the soldier who was guarding him.

17 Three days later he called together the local leaders of the Jews. When they had assembled, he said to them, "Brothers, though I had done nothing against our people or the customs of our ancestors, yet I was arrested in Jerusalem and handed over to the Romans. 18 When they had examined me, the Romans[c] wanted to release me, because there was no reason for the death penalty in my case. 19 But when the Jews objected, I was compelled to appeal to the emperor—even though I had no charge to bring against my nation. 20 For this reason therefore I have asked to see you and speak with you,[d] since it is for the sake of the hope of Israel that I am bound with this chain." 21 They replied, "We have received no letters from Judea about you, and none of the brothers coming here has reported or spoken anything evil about you. 22 But we would like to hear from you what you think, for with regard to this sect we know that everywhere it is spoken against."

23 After they had set a day to meet with him, they came to him at his lodgings in great numbers. From morning until evening he explained the matter to them, testifying to the kingdom of God and trying to convince them about Jesus both from the law of Moses and from the prophets. 24 Some were convinced by what he had said, while others refused to believe. 25 So they disagreed with each other; and as they were leaving, Paul made one further statement: "The Holy Spirit was right in saying to your ancestors through the prophet Isaiah,

26 'Go to this people and say,
You will indeed listen, but never
        understand,
    and you will indeed look, but
        never perceive.
27 For this people's heart has grown
        dull,
    and their ears are hard of hearing,
        and they have shut their eyes;
    so that they might not look
        with their eyes,

---

[b]Gk *brothers* [c]Gk *they* [d]Or *I have asked you to see me and speak with me*

and listen with their ears,
and understand with their heart
and turn—
and I would heal them.'[29]

28 Let it be known to you then that this salvation of God has been sent to the Gentiles; they will listen."[e]

30 He lived there two whole years at his own expense[f] and welcomed all who came to him,

31 proclaiming the kingdom of God and teaching about the Lord Jesus Christ with all boldness and without hindrance.

[e]Other ancient authorities add verse 29, *And when he had said these words, the Jews departed, arguing vigorously among themselves*
[f]Or *in his own hired dwelling*

[29]Isa 6:9–10

The Acts of Paul and Thecla

The *Acts of Paul and Thecla* is a legendary account of the escapades of Thecla, a woman converted to the Christian faith through the preaching of the apostle Paul. Paul himself appears only on the fringes of the story, as a Christian preacher who converts women to a lifestyle of strict asceticism and sexual renunciation, much to the chagrin of their husbands and fiances. When Thecla herself hears Paul's message, she abandons her fiance and joins the apostle on his journeys, liberated from the concerns of marriage and potential domination by a future husband. Thecla's decision to renounce marriage, however, has serious social implications; seeking revenge, her fiance brings her up before the authorities on the charge of being a Christian. In a miraculous series of episodes, however, God intervenes on her behalf, preserving her from death and reuniting her with her beloved apostle, who authorizes her to share fully in his ministry of teaching the word.

It is difficult to know when the *Acts of Paul and Thecla* was written. It appears to have circulated in the second century along with other narratives of the missionary endeavors of Paul that are collectively entitled the *Acts of Paul.* Most scholars identify this collection with a book known to the church father Tertullian, who, around 200 C.E., claimed that it had been forged by a presbyter of Asia Minor who was caught red-handed. According to Tertullian, the author had concocted his account "out of love of Paul."

There is some evidence to suggest, however, that narratives about Thecla were in circulation at a much earlier stage, possibly at the beginning of the second century. Some scholars have maintained, in fact, that the Pastoral Epistles of the New Testament (1 and 2 Timothy and Titus), which warn against women who spread "old wives' tales" (1 Tim 4:7) and who exercise authority over men and teach (see 1 Tim 2:1–11), represent a reaction to views embodied here in the *Acts of Paul and Thecla.*

Whether or not this particular account of Thecla was composed by the beginning of the second century, it appears to incorporate Christian traditions popular then, as women in Christian communities began to recognize the value of an ascetic lifestyle, especially as it could bring liberation from the constraints of male-dominated marriages.

1 As Paul was going to Iconium after his flight from Antioch, his fellow-travelers were Demas and Hermogenes, the coppersmith, who were full of hypocrisy and flattered Paul as if they loved him. Paul, looking only to the goodness of Christ, did them no harm but loved them exceedingly so that he made sweet to them all the words of the Lord and the interpretation of the gospel concerning the birth and resurrection of the Beloved; and he gave them an account, word for word, of the

great deeds of Christ as they were revealed to him.

2 And a certain man, by name Onesiphorus, hearing that Paul was to come to Iconium, went out to meet him with his children Simmias and Zeno and his wife Lectra, in order that he might entertain him. Titus had informed him what Paul looked like, for he had not seen him in the flesh, but only in the spirit.

3 And he went along the royal road to Lystra and kept looking at the passers-by according to the description of Titus. And he saw Paul coming, a man small in size, bald-headed, bandy-legged, of noble mien, with eyebrows meeting, rather hook-nosed, full of grace. Sometimes he seemed like a man, and sometimes he had the face of an angel.

4 And Paul, seeing Onesiphorus, smiled; and Onesiphorus said, "Hail, O servant of the blessed God." And he said, "Grace be with you and your house." And Demas and Hermogenes were jealous and showed greater hypocrisy, so that Demas said, "Are we not of the blessed God that you have not thus saluted us?" And Onesiphorus said, "I do not see in you the fruit of righteousness, but if such you be, come also into my house and refresh yourselves."

5 And after Paul had gone into the house of Onesiphorus there was great joy and bowing of knees and breaking of bread and the word of God about abstinence and the resurrection. Paul said, "Blessed are the pure in heart, for they shall see God;[1] blessed are those who have kept the flesh chaste, for they shall become a temple of God; blessed are the continent, for God shall speak with them; blessed are those who have kept aloof from this world, for they shall be pleasing to God; blessed are those who have wives as not having them, for they shall experience God; blessed are those who have fear of God, for they shall become angels of God.

6 "Blessed are those who respect the word of God, for they shall be comforted; blessed are those who have received the wisdom of Jesus Christ, for they shall be called the sons of the Most High; blessed are those who have kept the baptism, for they shall be refreshed by the Father and the Son; blessed are those who have come to a knowledge of Jesus Christ, for they shall be in the light; blessed are those who through love of God no longer conform to the world, for they shall judge

angels, and shall be blessed at the right hand of the Father; blessed are the merciful, for they shall obtain mercy[2] and shall not see the bitter day of judgment; blessed are the bodies of the virgins, for they shall be well pleasing to God and shall not lose the reward of their chastity. For the word of the Father shall become to them a work of salvation in the day of the Son, and they shall have rest for ever and ever."

7 And while Paul was speaking in the midst of the church in the house of Onesiphorus a certain virgin named Thecla, the daughter of Theoclia, betrothed to a man named Thamyris, was sitting at the window close by and listened day and night to the discourse of virginity, as proclaimed by Paul. And she did not look away from the window, but was led on by faith, rejoicing exceedingly. And when she saw many women and virgins going in to Paul she also had an eager desire to be deemed worthy to stand in Paul's presence and hear the word of Christ. For she had not yet seen Paul in person, but only heard his word.

8 As she did not move from the window her mother sent to Thamyris. And he came gladly as if already receiving her in marriage. And Thamyris said to Theoclia, "Where, then, is my Thecla [that I may see her]?" And Theoclia answered, "I have a strange story to tell you, Thamyris. For three days and three nights Thecla does not rise from the window either to eat or to drink; but looking earnestly as if upon some pleasant sight she is devoted to a foreigner teaching deceitful and artful discourses, so that I wonder how a virgin of her great modesty exposes herself to such extreme discomfort.

9 "Thamyris, this man will overturn the city of the Iconians and your Thecla too; for all the women and the young men go in to him to be taught by him. He says one must fear only one God and live in chastity. Moreover, my daughter, clinging to the window like a spider, lays hold of what is said by him with a strange eagerness and fearful emotion. For the virgin looks eagerly at what is said by him and has been captivated. But go near and speak to her, for she is betrothed to you."

10 And Thamyris greeted her with a kiss, but at the same time being afraid of her overpowering emotion said, "Thecla, my betrothed, why do you

_____

[1]Matt 5:8   [2]Matt 5:7

sit thus? And what sort of feeling holds you distracted? Come back to your Thamyris and be ashamed." Moreover, her mother said the same, "Why do you sit thus looking down, my child, and answering nothing, like a sick woman?" And those who were in the house wept bitterly, Thamyris for the loss of a wife, Theoclia for that of a child, and the maidservants for that of a mistress. And there was a great outpouring of lamentation in the house. And while these things were going on Thecla did not turn away but kept attending to the word of Paul.

11 And Thamyris, jumping up, went into the street, and watched all who went in to Paul and came out. And he saw two men bitterly quarrelling with each other and he said to them, "Men, who are you and tell me who is this man among you, leading astray the souls of young men and deceiving virgins so that they should not marry but remain as they are? I promise you money enough if you tell me about him, for I am the chief man of this city."

12 And Demas and Hermogenes said to him, "Who he is we do not know. But he deprives the husbands of wives and maidens of husbands, saying, 'There is for you no resurrection unless you remain chaste and do not pollute the flesh.'"

13 And Thamyris said to them, "Come into my house and refresh yourselves." And they went to a sumptuous supper and much wine and great wealth and a splendid table. And Thamyris made them drink, for he loved Thecla and wished to take her as wife. And during the supper Thamyris said, "Men, tell me what is his teaching that I also may know it, for I am greatly distressed about Thecla, because she so loves the stranger and I am prevented from marrying."

14 And Demas and Hermogenes said, "Bring him before the Governor Castellius because he persuades the multitude to embrace the new teaching of the Christians, and he will destroy him and you shall have Thecla as your wife. And we shall teach you about the resurrection which he says is to come, that it has already taken place in the children and that we rise again, after having come to the knowledge of the true God."

15 And when Thamyris heard these things he rose up early in the morning and, filled with jealousy and anger, went into the house of Onesiphorus with rulers and officers and a great crowd with batons and said to Paul, "You have deceived the city of the Iconians and especially my betrothed bride so that she will not have me! Let us go to the governor Castellius!" And the whole crowd cried, "Away with the sorcerer for he has misled all our wives!", and the multitude was also incited.

16 And Thamyris standing before the tribunal said with a great shout, "O proconsul, this man—we do not know where he comes from—makes virgins averse to marriage. Let him say before you why he teaches thus." But Demas and Hermogenes said to Thamyris, "Say that he is a Christian and he will die at once." But the governor kept his resolve and called Paul, saying, "Who are you and what do you teach? For they bring no small accusation against you."

17 And Paul, lifting up his voice, said, "If I today must tell any of my teachings then listen, O proconsul. The living God, the God of vengeance, the jealous God, the God who has need of nothing, who seeks the salvation of people, has sent me that I may rescue them from corruption and uncleanness and from all pleasure, and from death, that they may sin no more. On this account God sent his Son whose gospel I preach and teach, that in him people have hope, who alone has had compassion upon a world led astray, that people may be no longer under judgment but may have faith and fear of God and knowledge of honesty and love of truth. If then I teach the things revealed to me by God what harm do I do, O proconsul?" When the governor heard this he ordered Paul to be bound and sent to prison until he had time to hear him more attentively.

18 And Thecla, by night, took off her bracelets and gave them to the gatekeeper; and when the door was opened to her she went into the prison. To the jailer she gave a silver mirror and was thus enabled to go in to Paul and, sitting at his feet, she heard the great deeds of God. And Paul was afraid of nothing, but trusted in God. And her faith also increased and she kissed his bonds.

19 And when Thecla was sought for by her family and Thamyris they were hunting through the streets as if she had been lost. One of the gatekeeper's fellow slaves informed them that she had gone out by night. And they examined the gatekeeper who said to them, "She has gone to the for-

eigner in the prison." And they went and found her, so to say, chained to him by affection. And having gone out from there they incited the people and informed the governor what had happened.

20 And he ordered Paul to be brought before the tribunal, but Thecla was riveted to the place where Paul had sat whilst in prison. And the governor ordered her also to be brought to the tribunal, and she came with an exceedingly great joy. And when Paul had been led forth the crowd vehemently cried out, "He is a sorcerer. Away with him!" But the governor gladly heard Paul speak about the holy works of Christ. And having taken counsel, he summoned Thecla and said, "Why do you not marry Thamyris, according to the law of the Iconians?" But she stood looking earnestly at Paul. And when she gave no answer Theoclia, her mother, cried out saying, "Burn the wicked one; burn her who will not marry in the midst of the theatre, that all the women who have been taught by this man may be afraid."

21 And the governor was greatly moved, and after scourging Paul he cast him out of the city. But Thecla he condemned to be burned. And immediately the governor arose and went away to the theatre. And the whole multitude went out to witness the spectacle. But as a lamb in the wilderness looks around for the shepherd, so Thecla kept searching for Paul. And having looked into the crowd she saw the Lord sitting in the likeness of Paul and said, "As if I were unable to endure, Paul has come to look after me." And she gazed upon him with great earnestness, but he went up into heaven.

22 And the boys and girls brought wood and straw in order that Thecla might be burned. And when she came in naked the governor wept and admired the power that was in her. And the executioners arranged the wood and told her to go up on the pile. And having made the sign of the cross she went up on the pile. And they lighted the fire. And though a great fire was blazing it did not touch her. For God, having compassion upon her, made an underground rumbling, and a cloud full of water and hail overshadowed the theatre from above, and all its contents were poured out so that many were in danger of death. And the fire was put out and Thecla saved.

23 And Paul was fasting with Onesiphorus and his wife and his children in a new tomb on the way which led from Iconium to Daphne. And after many days had been spent in fasting the children said to Paul, "We are hungry." And they had nothing with which to buy bread, for Onesiphorus had left the things of this world and followed Paul with all his house. And Paul, having taken off his cloak, said "Go, my child, sell this and buy some loaves and bring them." And when the child was buying them he saw Thecla their neighbor and was astonished and said, "Thecla, where are you going?" And she said, "I have been saved from the fire and am following Paul." And the child said, "Come, I shall take you to him; for he has been mourning for you and praying and fasting six days already."

24 And when she had come to the tomb Paul was kneeling and praying, "Father of Christ, let not the fire touch Thecla but stand by her, for she is yours"; she, standing behind him, cried out, "O Father who made the heaven and the earth, the Father of your beloved Son Jesus Christ, I praise you that you have saved me from the fire that I may see Paul again." And Paul, rising up, saw her and said, "O God, who knows the heart, Father of our Lord Jesus Christ, I praise you because you have speedily heard my prayer."

25 And there was great love in the tomb as Paul and Onesiphorus and the others all rejoiced. And they had five loaves and vegetables and water, and they rejoiced in the holy works of Christ. And Thecla said to Paul, "I will cut my hair off and I shall follow you wherever you go." But he said, "Times are evil and you are beautiful. I am afraid lest another temptation come upon you worse than the first and that you do not withstand it but become mad after men." And Thecla said, "Only give me the seal in Christ, and no temptation shall touch me." And Paul said, "Thecla, be patient; you shall receive the water."

26 And Paul sent away Onesiphorus and all his family to Iconium and went into Antioch, taking Thecla with him. And as soon as they had arrived a certain Syrian, Alexander by name, an influential citizen of Antioch, seeing Thecla, became enamored of her and tried to bribe Paul with gifts and presents. But Paul said, "I know not the woman of whom you speak, nor is she mine." But he, being of great power, embraced her in the street. But she would not endure it and looked about for Paul. And she cried out bitterly, saying,

"Do not force the stranger; do not force the servant of God. I am one of the chief persons of the Iconians and because I would not marry Thamyris I have been cast out of the city." And taking hold of Alexander, she tore his cloak and pulled off his crown and made him a laughing-stock.

27 And he, although loving her, nevertheless felt ashamed of what had happened and led her before the governor; and as she confessed that she had done these things he condemned her to the wild beasts. The women of the city cried out before the tribunal, "Evil judgment! impious judgment!" and Thecla asked the governor that she might remain pure until she was to fight with the wild beasts. And a rich woman named Queen Tryphaena, whose daughter was dead, took her under her protection and had her for a consolation.

28 And when the beasts were exhibited they bound her to a fierce lioness, and Queen Tryphaena followed her. And the lioness, with Thecla sitting upon her, licked her feet; and all the multitude was astonished. And the charge on her inscription was "Sacrilegious." And the women and children cried out again and again, "O God, outrageous things take place in this city." And after the exhibition Tryphaena received her again. For her dead daughter Falconilla had said to her in a dream, "Mother, receive this stranger, the forsaken Thecla, in my place, that she may pray for me and I may come to the place of the just."

29 And when, after the exhibition, Tryphaena had received her she was grieved because Thecla had to fight on the following day with the wild beasts, but on the other hand she loved her dearly like her daughter Falconilla and said, "Thecla, my second child, come, pray for my child that she may live in eternity, for this I saw in my sleep." And without hesitation she lifted up her voice and said, "My God, Son of the Most High, who are in heaven, grant her wish that her daughter Falconilla may live in eternity." And when Thecla had spoken Tryphaena grieved very much, considering that such beauty was to be thrown to the wild beasts.

30 And when it was dawn Alexander came to her, for it was he who arranged the exhibition of wild beasts, and said, "The governor has taken his seat and the crowd is clamoring for us; get ready, I will take her to fight with the wild beasts." And Tryphaena put him to flight with a loud cry, saying, "A second mourning for my Falconilla has come upon my house, and there is no one to help, neither child for she is dead, nor kinsman for I am a widow. God of Thecla, my child, help Thecla."

31 And the governor sent soldiers to bring Thecla. Tryphaena did not leave her but took her by the hand and led her away saying, "My daughter Falconilla I took away to the tomb, but you, Thecla, I take to fight the wild beasts." And Thecla wept bitterly and sighed to the Lord, "O Lord God, in whom I trust, to whom I have fled for refuge, who did deliver me from the fire, reward Tryphaena who has had compassion on your servant and because she kept me pure."

32 And there arose a tumult: the wild beasts roared, the people and the women sitting together were crying, some saying, "Away with the sacrilegious person!", others saying, "O that the city would be destroyed on account of this iniquity! Kill us all, proconsul; miserable spectacle, evil judgment!"

33 And Thecla, having been taken from the hands of Tryphaena, was stripped and received a girdle and was thrown into the arena. And lions and bears were let loose upon her. And a fierce lioness ran up and lay down at her feet. And the multitude of the women cried aloud. And a bear ran upon her, but the lioness went to meet it and tore the bear to pieces. And again a lion that had been trained to fight against men, which belonged to Alexander, ran upon her. And the lioness, encountering the lion, was killed along with it. And the women cried the more since the lioness, her protector, was dead.

34 Then they sent in many beasts as she was standing and stretching forth her hands and praying. And when she had finished her prayer she turned around and saw a large pit full of water and said, "Now it is time to wash myself." And she threw herself in saying, "In the name of Jesus Christ I baptize myself on my last day." When the women and the multitude saw it they wept and said, "Do not throw yourself into the water!"; even the governor shed tears because the seals were to devour such beauty. She then threw herself into the water in the name of Jesus Christ, but the seals, having seen a flash of lightning, floated dead on the surface. And there was round her a cloud of fire so that neither could the beasts touch her nor could she be seen naked.

35 But the women lamented when other and fiercer animals were let loose; some threw petals, others nard, others cassia, others amomum, so that there was an abundance of perfumes. And all the wild beasts were hypnotized and did not touch her. And Alexander said to the governor, "I have some terrible bulls to which we will bind her." And the governor consented grudgingly, "Do what you will." And they bound her by the feet between the bulls and put red-hot irons under their genitals so that they, being rendered more furious, might kill her. They rushed forward but the burning flame around her consumed the ropes, and she was as if she had not been bound.

36 And Tryphaena fainted standing beside the arena, so that the servants said, "Queen Tryphaena is dead." And the governor put a stop to the games and the whole city was in dismay. And Alexander fell down at the feet of the governor and cried, "Have mercy upon me and upon the city and set the woman free, lest the city also be destroyed. For if Caesar hear of these things he will possibly destroy the city along with us because his kinswoman, Queen Tryphaena, has died at the theatre gate."

37 And the governor summoned Thecla out of the midst of the beasts and said to her, "Who are you? And what is there about you that not one of the wild beasts touched you?" She answered, "I am a servant of the living God and, as to what there is about me, I have believed in the Son of God in whom he is well pleased; that is why not one of the beasts touched me. For he alone is the goal of salvation and the basis of immortal life. For he is a refuge to the tempest-tossed, a solace to the afflicted, a shelter to the despairing; in brief, whoever does not believe in him shall not live but be dead forever."

38 When the governor heard these things he ordered garments to be brought and to be put on her. And she said, "He who clothed me when I was naked among the beasts will in the day of judgment clothe me with salvation." And taking the garments she put them on.

And the governor immediately issued an edict saying, "I release to you the pious Thecla, the servant of God." And the women shouted aloud and with one voice praised God, "One is the God, who saved Thecla", so that the whole city was shaken by their voices.

39 And Tryphaena, having received the good news, went with the multitude to meet Thecla. After embracing her she said, "Now I believe that the dead are raised! Now I believe that my child lives. Come inside and all that is mine I shall assign to you." And Thecla went in with her and rested eight days, instructing her in the word of God, so that many of the maidservants believed. And there was great joy in the house.

40 And Thecla longed for Paul and sought him, looking in every direction. And she was told that he was in Myra. And wearing a mantle that she had altered so as to make a man's cloak, she came with a band of young men and maidens to Myra, where she found Paul speaking the word of God and went to him. And he was astonished at seeing her and her companions, thinking that some new temptation was coming upon her. And perceiving this, she said to him, "I have received baptism, O Paul; for he who worked with you for the gospel has worked with me also for baptism."

41 And Paul, taking her, led her to the house of Hermias and heard everything from her, so that he greatly wondered and those who heard were strengthened and prayed for Tryphaena. And Thecla rose up and said to Paul, "I am going to Iconium." Paul answered, "Go, and teach the word of God." And Tryphaena sent her much clothing and gold so that she could leave many things to Paul for the service of the poor.

42 And coming to Iconium she went into the house of Onesiphorus and fell upon the place where Paul had sat and taught the word of God, and she cried and said, "My God and God of this house where the light shone upon me, Jesus Christ, Son of God, my help in prison, my help before the governors, my help in the fire, my help among the wild beasts, you alone are God and to you be glory for every. Amen."

43 And she found Thamyris dead but her mother alive. And calling her mother she said, "Theoclia, my mother, can you believe that the Lord lives in heaven? For if you desire wealth the Lord will give it to you through me; or if you desire your child, behold, I am standing beside you."

And having thus testified, she went to Seleucia and enlightened many by the word of God; then she rested in a glorious sleep.

The Martyrdom of Polycarp

Although the Martyrdom of Polycarp does not fall within the strict chronological limits of this collection, there are good reasons for including it here among the earliest Christian writings. The main character, Polycarp, bishop of Smyrna (in Asia Minor, modern Turkey), figured prominently among the proto-orthodox Christians in the early years of the second century. Even within this collection itself there is a letter addressed *to* him by Ignatius of Antioch and another letter written *by* him to the Christians of Philippi. Moreover, this account of his death is the first surviving Christian martyrology from outside the New Testament (cf. the death of Stephen in Acts 7). Such narratives of Christians tried and executed by the state became standard fare in the Christian literature of the second and third centuries. For anyone interested in the persecution of the Christians at the hands of the Romans—persecution that goes all the way back to the earliest years of the movement—this narrative will be of real interest.

The account is embodied in a letter sent from a member of Polycarp's own congregation to the church of Philomelium in the province of Phrygia in Asia Minor. It is clear that the account, even though contemporary with the events it describes, cannot be taken as an objective, factual description, for it involves a good deal of artistry, as the author portrays Polycarp's death as "conformable to the gospel" (1:1)—that is, comparable to the martyrdom of Jesus himself as described in the early Christian traditions. A number of literary flourishes convey the point: The account indicates that Polycarp knew in advance how he was to die (5:2); he was betrayed by his own companions (6:2); the police chief in charge of his arrest was named Herod (6:2); Polycarp refused to escape, but instead prayed that "God's will be done" (7:1); he entered the city mounted on a donkey (8:1); he was tried before the Roman proconsul, who wanted to release him but was pressured by the crowds, especially the Jews among them, to have him executed (chaps. 9–13).

In addition to these literary touches, there are certain legendary accretions to the martyrdom itself, such as the inability of the flames to touch Polycarp's body, the smell of precious spices that exuded from the pyre, the dousing of the conflagration by the martyr's blood, and, at his death, the emergence of a dove (his [holy?] spirit) from Polycarp's side.

Legendary additions aside, the legal grounds for Polycarp's execution are relatively clear: He refused to pay homage to the divine spirit of the Roman emperor and was opposed to the state gods (chaps. 9–12). The author of the account is fully sympathetic with this stance; for him, Polycarp, and other Christian martyrs like him, were willing to exchange any torments they might experience in this life for the ecstasies they would enjoy in the hereafter: "they despised the torments of the world, in one hour purchasing for themselves eternal life. And the fire of their inhuman torturers was cold to them, because they kept their eyes on the goal of escaping the fire that is eternal and never extinguished" (2:3).

Scholars debate when the martyrdom took place; most think that it was sometime in the mid 150s C.E.

The church of God that temporarily resides in Smyrna to the church of God that temporarily resides in Philomelium, and to all congregations of temporary residents everywhere, who belong to the holy and universal[a] church. May the mercy, peace, and love of God the Father and of our Lord Jesus Christ be multiplied.

1 We are writing you, brothers, about those who were martyred, along with the blessed Polycarp, who put an end to the persecution by, as it were, setting a seal on it through his death as a martyr. For nearly everything leading up to his death occurred so that the Lord might show us from above[b] a martyrdom in conformity with the gospel. 2 For Polycarp waited to be betrayed, as also did the Lord, that we in turn might imitate him, thinking not only of ourselves, but also of our neighbors.[1] For anyone with true and certain love wants not only himself but also all the brothers to be saved.

2 Blessed and noble, therefore, are all the martyrdoms that have occurred according to the will of God. For we must be reverent and attribute the ultimate authority to God. 2 For who would not be astounded by their nobility, endurance, and love of the Master? For they endured even when their skin was ripped to shreds by whips, revealing the very anatomy of their flesh, down to the inner veins and arteries, while bystanders felt pity and wailed. But they displayed such nobility that none of them either grumbled or moaned, clearly showing us all that in that hour, while under torture, the martyrs of Christ had journeyed far away from the flesh, or rather, that the Lord was standing by, speaking to them. 3 And clinging to the gracious gift of Christ, they despised the torments of the world, in one hour purchasing for themselves eternal life. And the fire of their inhuman torturers was cold to them, because they kept their eyes on the goal of escaping the fire that is eternal and never extinguished. And with the eyes of their

hearts they looked above to the good things preserved for those who endure, which no ear has heard nor eye seen, which have never entered into the human heart,[2] but which the Lord revealed to them, who were no long humans but already angels.

4 In a similar way, those who were condemned to the wild beasts endured horrible torments, stretched out on sharp shells and punished with various other kinds of tortures, that, if possible, he[c] might force them to make a denial through continuous torment.

3 For the devil devised many torments against them. But thanks be to God: He had no power over any of them. For the most noble Germanicus strengthened their cowardice through his endurance, and he fought the wild beasts impressively. For when the proconsul wanted to persuade him, saying "Take pity on your age," he forcefully dragged the wild beast onto himself, wanting to leave their unjust and lawless life without delay. 2 Because of this, the entire multitude, astounded by the great nobility of the godly and reverent race of the Christians, cried out, "Away with the atheists! Find Polycarp!"

4 But there was a person named Quintus, a Phrygian who had recently come from Phrygia, who was overcome with cowardice once he saw the wild beasts. This is the one who compelled both himself and several others to turn themselves in. But the insistent pleas of the proconsul convinced him to take the oath and offer a sacrifice. Because of this, brothers, we do not praise those who hand themselves over, since this is not what the gospel teaches.

5 Now when the most marvelous Polycarp first heard, he was not disturbed, but wanted

---

[a]Or *catholic*   [b]Or *again*   [c]That is, *the devil*; see 3.1

[1]Phil 2:4   [2]1 Cor 2:9

to remain in the city. But most of the others were urging him to leave. And so he left for a small country house not far from the city and stayed there with a few others, night and day doing nothing but pray for everyone and for the churches throughout the world, as was his custom. 2 Three days before he was arrested, while praying, he had a vision and saw his pillow being consumed by fire. Then he turned to those with him and said, "I must be burned alive."

6 While they continued searching for him, he moved to a different country house—just as those who were seeking him arrived at the other. Since they could not find him, they arrested two young slaves, one of whom made a confession under torture. 2 For it was impossible for him to keep in hiding, since the ones who betrayed him were members of his household. And the chief of police, who was called by the same name—for his name was Herod—was eager to lead him into the stadium, that he might fulfill his special destiny as a partner with Christ, while those who betrayed him might suffer the punishment of Judas himself.

7 And so, taking the young slave, on the Day of Preparation[d] around the dinner hour, the mounted police and horsemen went out with their usual weapons, as if running down a thief.[e3] And when the hour was late, they converged and found Polycarp lying down in a small room upstairs. He could have fled elsewhere even from there, but he chose not to do so, saying, "God's will be done."[4] 2 And so, when he heard them come in, he came downstairs and talked with them; and those who were there were astonished at how old and composed he was, and they wondered why there was so much haste to arrest an old man like him. Straight away he ordered them to be given everything they wanted to eat and drink, then and there. And he asked them for an hour to pray without being disturbed. 3 When they gave their permission, he stood and prayed, being so filled with God's grace that for two hours he could not be silent. Those who heard him were amazed, and many of them regretted coming out for such a godly old man.

8 Then he finished his prayer, having remembered everyone he had ever met, both small and great, reputable and disreputable, as well as the entire universal[f] church throughout the world;

and when it came time for him to leave, they seated him on a donkey and led him into the city. It was a great sabbath.[5] 2 The chief of police Herod, along with his father Nicetas, met him and transferred him to their carriage. Sitting on either side, they were trying to persuade him, saying, "Why is it so wrong to save yourself by saying 'Caesar is Lord,' making a sacrifice, and so on?" He did not answer them at first; but when they persisted, he said, "I am not about to do what you advise." 3 Having failed to persuade him, they began speaking horrible words and hastily shoved him out, so that when he came down out of the carriage he scraped his shin. He did not turn around, but quickly walked on in haste as if he had not been hurt. And he was led into the stadium, where there was such an uproar that no one could be heard.

9 But as he entered the stadium a voice came to Polycarp from heaven: "Be strong, Polycarp, and be a man."[g6] No one saw who had spoken, but those among our people who were there heard the voice. Finally, when he was brought forward, there was a great uproar among those who heard that Polycarp had been arrested. 2 When he was brought forward the proconsul asked if he was Polycarp. When he said he was, the proconsul began trying to persuade him to make a denial, saying, "Have respect for your age," along with other related things they customarily say: "Swear by the Fortune of Caesar, repent, and say 'Away with the atheists.'" But Polycarp looked with a stern face at the entire crowd of lawless Gentiles in the stadium; and gesturing to them with his hand, he sighed, looked up to heaven, and said, "Away with the atheists." 3 The proconsul became more insistent and said, "Take the oath and I will release you. Revile Christ." But Polycarp responded, "For eighty-six years I have served him, and he has done me no wrong. How can I blaspheme my king who has saved me?"

10 When the proconsul persisted and said, "Swear by the Fortune of Caesar," Polycarp answered, "If you are so foolish as to think that I will swear by the Fortune of Caesar, as you say, and if you pretend not to know who I am, lis-

---

[d]That is, *Friday*   [e]Or *armed rebel*   [f]Or *catholic*   [g]Or *be courageous*

[3]Matt 26:55   [4]Acts 21:14; cf. Luke 22:42; Matt 6:10   [5]Cf. John 19:31   [6]Josh 1:6

ten closely: I am a Christian. But if you wish to learn an account of Christianity, appoint a day and listen." 2 The proconsul replied, "Persuade the people." Polycarp said, "I think you deserve an account, for we are taught to render all due honor to rulers and authorities appointed by God,[7] in so far as it does us no harm. But as to those, I do not consider them worthy to hear a reasoned defense."

11 The proconsul said, "I have wild beasts, and I will cast you to them if you do not repent." He replied, "Call them! For it is impossible for us to repent from better to worse; it is good, though, to change from what is wicked to what is right." 2 Again the proconsul said to him, "If you despise the wild beasts, I will have you consumed by fire, if you do not repent." Polycarp replied, "You threaten with a fire that burns for an hour and after a short while is extinguished; for you do not know about the fire of the coming judgment and eternal torment, reserved for the ungodly. But why are you waiting? Bring on what you wish."

12 While he was saying these and many other things, he was filled with courage and joy, and his face was full of grace, so that not only did he not collapse to the ground from being unnerved at what he heard, but on the contrary, the proconsul was amazed and sent his herald into the center of the stadium to proclaim three times, "Polycarp has confessed himself to be a Christian." 2 When the herald said this, the entire multitude of both Gentiles and Jews who lived in Smyrna cried out with uncontrolled rage and a great voice, "This is the teacher of impiety, the father of the Christians, the destroyer of our own gods, the one who teaches many not to sacrifice or worship the gods." Saying these things, they began calling out to Philip, the Asiarch, asking him to release a lion on Polycarp. But he said that he could not do so, since he had already concluded the animal hunts. 3 Then they decided to call out in unison for him to burn Polycarp alive. For the vision that had been revealed about the pillow had to be fulfilled; for he had seen it burning while he prayed. And when he turned he said prophetically to the faithful who were with him, "I must be burned alive."

13 These things then happened with incredible speed, quicker than can be described.

The crowds immediately gathered wood and kindling from the workplaces and the baths, with the Jews proving especially eager to assist, as is their custom. 2 When the pyre was prepared, Polycarp laid aside all his garments and loosened his belt. He was also trying to undo his sandals, even though he was not accustomed to do so, since each of the faithful was always eager to do it, to see who could touch his skin most quickly. For he was adorned with every good thing[h] because of his exemplary way of life, even before he bore his testimony unto death. 3 Immediately the instruments prepared for the pyre were placed around him. When they were about to nail him, he said, "Leave me as I am; for the one who enables me to endure the fire will also enable me to remain in the pyre without moving, even without the security of your nails."

14 So they did not nail him, but they tied him. And when he placed his hands behind his back and was tied, he was like an exceptional ram taken from a great flock for a sacrifice, prepared as a whole burnt offering that is acceptable to God. Looking up into heaven he said, "Lord God Almighty, Father of your beloved and blessed child Jesus Christ, through whom we have received knowledge of you, the God of angels, of powers, and of all creation, and of every race of the upright who live before you, 2 I bless you for making me worthy of this day and hour, that I may receive a share among the number of the martyrs in the cup of your Christ, unto the resurrection of eternal life in both soul and body in the immortality of the Holy Spirit. Among them may I be received before you today as a sacrifice that is rich and acceptable, just as you prepared and revealed in advance and now fulfilled—the true God who does not lie. 3 For this reason and for all things I praise you, I bless you, I glorify you through the eternal and heavenly high priest Jesus Christ, your beloved child, through whom be glory to you, with him and the Holy Spirit, both now and for the ages to come. Amen."

15 When he sent up the "Amen" and finished the prayer, the men in charge of the

---

[h]Or *was treated with all respect*

---

[7]Rom 13:1; 1 Pet 2:13

fire touched it off. And as a great flame blazoned forth we beheld a marvel—we to whom it was granted to see, who have also been preserved to report the events to the others. 2 For the fire, taking on the appearance of a vaulted room, like a boat's sail filled with the wind, formed a wall around the martyr's body. And he was in the center, not like burning flesh but like baking bread or like gold and silver being refined in a furnace. And we perceived a particularly sweet aroma, like wafting incense or some other precious perfume.

16 Finally, when the lawless ones saw that his body could not be consumed by the fire, they ordered an executioner to go up and stab him with a dagger. When he did so, a dove came forth, along with such a quantity of blood that it extinguished the fire, striking the entire crowd with amazement that there could be so much difference between the unbelievers and the elect. 2 One of the latter was this most astounding Polycarp, who in our time was an apostolic and prophetic teacher and bishop of the universal[i] church in Smyrna. For every word that came forth from his mouth was fulfilled and will be fulfilled.

17 But the jealous and envious Evil One, the enemy of the race of the upright, having seen the greatness of Polycarp's death as a martyr and the irreproachable way of life that he had from the beginning—and that he had received the crown of immortality and was awarded with the incontestible prize—made certain that his poor body was not taken away by us, even though many were desiring to do so and to have a share in[j] his holy flesh. 2 So he incited Nicetas, the father of Herod and brother of Alce, to petition the magistrate not to hand over his body, "Lest," he said, "they desert the one who was crucified and begin to worship this one." The Jews instigated and strongly urged these things, and kept watch when we were about to take him from the fire. For they did not realize that we are never able to abandon Christ, who suffered for the salvation of the entire world of those who are being saved the one who was blameless for sinners; nor are we able to worship any other. 3 For we worship this one who is the Son of God, but we love the martyrs as disciples and imitators of the Lord. And they are worthy, because of their unsurpassable affection for their own king and teacher. May we also become partners and fellow disciples with them!

18 When the centurion saw the contentiousness caused by the Jews, he placed Polycarp's body in the center and burned it, as is their custom. 2 And so, afterwards, we removed his bones, which were more valuable than expensive gems and more precious than gold, and put them in a suitable place. 3 There, whenever we can gather together in joy and happiness, the Lord will allow us to commemorate the birthday of his martyrdom, both in memory of those who have already engaged in the struggle and as a training and preparation for those who are about to do so.

19 Such are the matters pertaining to the blessed Polycarp, who along with those from Philadelphia was the twelfth martyr in Smyrna; but he alone is remembered by all, discussed even by the outsiders[k] in every place. For he was not only an exceptional teacher but also a superb martyr. Everyone longs to imitate his martyrdom, since it occurred in conformity with the gospel of Christ. 2 Through endurance he overcame the unjust ruler and thus received the crown of immortality. And now he rejoices together with the apostles and all those who are upright, and he glorifies God the Father and blesses our Lord Jesus Christ, the savior of our souls, pilot of our bodies, and shepherd of the universal[l] church throughout the world.

20 You had asked for a lengthier explanation of what took place, but for the present we have mentioned only the principal points through our brother Marcion. When you have learned these things, send our letter to the brothers who are farther afield, that they may also glorify the Lord who selects his chosen ones from among his own slaves. 2 And now to the one who is able to lead us all by his grace and gift into his eternal kingdom, through his child, the unique one, Jesus Christ, be the glory, honor, power, and greatness forever. Greet all the saints. Those who are with us greet you, as does Evaristus, the one who is writing the letter, with his entire household.

21 But the blessed Polycarp bore his witness unto death on the second day of the new

---

[i]Or *catholic*   [j]Or *to commune with*; or *to have fellowship with*
[k]Literally, *Gentiles or nations*   [l]Or *catholic*

month of Xanthikos, February 23,[m] on a great sabbath, at 2:00 in the afternoon.[n] But he was arrested by Herod while Philip of Tralles was high priest, Statius Quadratus was proconsul, and Jesus Christ was ruling as king forever.[o] To him be the glory, honor, greatness, and eternal throne, from one generation to the next. Amen.

22 We bid you farewell, brothers, you who conduct yourselves in the word of Jesus Christ according to the gospel; with him be glory to God, both Father and Holy Spirit[p] for the salvation of his holy chosen ones, just as the blessed Polycarp bore witness unto death. May we be found to have followed in his footsteps in the kingdom of Jesus Christ! 2 Gaius transcribed these things from the papers of Irenaeus, a disciple of Polycarp; he also lived in the same city as Irenaeus. And I, Socrates, have written these things in Corinth from the copies made by Gaius. May grace be with everyone. 3 And I, Pionius, then sought out these things and produced a copy from the one mentioned above, in accordance with a revelation of the blessed Polycarp, who showed it to me, as I will explain in what follows. And I gathered these papers together when they were nearly worn out by age, so that the Lord Jesus Christ may gather me together with his chosen ones into his heavenly kingdom. To him be the glory with the Father and the Holy Spirit forever and ever. Amen.

Another Epilogue, from the Moscow Manuscript

Gaius transcribed these things from the writings of Irenaeus; he also lived in the same city with Irenaeus, a disciple of the holy Polycarp.

2 For this Irenaeus was in Rome when the bishop Polycarp was martyred, and he taught many people. And many of his writings—which are excellent and supremely true—are in circulation; in them he remembers Polycarp, because he studied under him. He powerfully refuted every heresy and passed on the ecclesiastical and universal[q] rule of faith, as he received it from the holy one. 3 He also says that Marcion, from whom come those who are called Marcionites, once met the holy Polycarp and said, "You need to recognize us, Polycarp." But he then replied to Marcion, "I do recognize you—I recognize the firstborn of Satan!" 4 This also is found in the writings of Irenaeus, that on the day and hour that Polycarp was martyred in Smyrna, Irenaeus, who was in the city of the Romans, heard a voice like a trumpet saying, "Polycarp has been martyred." 5 And so, as was indicated before, Gaius made a transcription from the writings of Irenaeus, as Isocrates did, in Corinth, from the copies of Gaius. And then I, Pionius, wrote a copy from those of Isocrates, in accordance with a revelation of the holy Polycarp, after seeking out these writings and gathering them together when they were nearly worn out by age, so that the Lord Jesus Christ may gather me together with his chosen ones into his heavenly kingdom. To him be the glory, with the Father and the Son and the Holy Spirit, forever and ever. Amen.

[m]Literally, *seven days before the Calends of March*   [n]Literally, *the eighth hour*   [o]Or *over the aeons*   [p]Or *God, and the Father, and the Holy Spirit*   [q]Or *catholic*

EARLY CHRISTIAN LETTERS ATTRIBUTED TO PAUL

The Letter to the Romans

The Letter to the Romans is unique among the Pauline epistles. Whereas each of Paul's other letters was written to address doctrinal or practical problems that had arisen in churches that Paul himself had founded, Romans is directed to a community he had never seen. This is not to say that the letter lacks a concrete occasion. On the contrary, Paul's own circumstances appear to have prompted his writing.

Near the end of the letter Paul indicates that he plans to make a missionary journey to Spain and to spend time with the Christians in Rome en route; in particular, he hopes that the Roman Christians will speed him along his journey (15:23–24). Before seeing them, however, he plans to deliver money that he has collected from his churches for the poor saints in Jerusalem (15:25–28). The delivery of this collection from Gentile to Jewish believers was important for Paul because it symbolized the unity of Jew and Gentile in Christ. Indeed, the message of this unity lies at the very heart of Paul's gospel. Paul devotes the bulk of Romans to expounding this message. It appears that Paul's principal reason for the exposition is to win the support of the Roman community, either moral or financial, for his westward mission. It is possible that he is impelled to do so, in part, because the Romans have been misinformed about his message, or at least that he thinks they have been.

Because of this unusual occasion, the letter to the Romans preserves the clearest and most carefully reasoned expression of Paul's gospel. In it he explains how both Jew and Gentile are in need of God's salvation, how the Jewish Law is unable to provide that salvation, and how God has instead provided it through the death and resurrection of Christ (chaps. 1–3). Those who believe in Christ are restored to a right relationship with God (or "justified"; chaps 3–4); being restored to this right relationship brings a release from the dreaded cosmic powers that have been unleashed against this world, including the powers of sin, the flesh, and death (chaps. 5–8).

Paul insists that God's act of justification of Jew and Gentile apart from works prescribed by the Law does not mean that God has gone back on his promises to the Jews to be his chosen people (chaps. 9–11). On the contrary, God's word cannot be revoked; indeed, the Jewish Scriptures themselves demonstrate that God justifies all people, Jew and Gentile, on the basis of faith rather than law (3:31; 4:1–25). Moreover, even though many Jews have rejected the message of God's salvation, in the end, in fulfillment of God's promises, all of Israel too will be saved (11:25–26).

Finally, Paul is adamant that, contrary to what some persons have maintained, his law-free gospel does not lead to lawless behavior. Instead, those who have been restored to a right standing with God will live upright and responsible lives in the Spirit, manifesting love for their neighbors and thereby fulfilling the injunctions of the Law (chaps. 12–15).

1 Paul, a servant[a] of Jesus Christ, called to be an apostle, set apart for the gospel of God, 2 which he promised beforehand through his prophets in the holy scriptures, 3 the gospel concerning his Son, who was descended from David according to the flesh 4 and was declared to be Son of God with power according to the spirit[b] of holiness by resurrection from the dead, Jesus Christ our Lord, 5 through whom we have received grace and apostleship to bring about the obedience of faith among all the Gentiles for the sake of his name, 6 including yourselves who are called to belong to Jesus Christ,

7 To all God's beloved in Rome, who are called to be saints:

Grace to you and peace from God our Father and the Lord Jesus Christ.

8 First, I thank my God through Jesus Christ for all of you, because your faith is proclaimed throughout the world. 9 For God, whom I serve with my spirit by announcing the gospel[c] of his Son, is my witness that without ceasing I remember you always in my prayers, 10 asking that by God's will I may somehow at last succeed in coming to you. 11 For I am longing to see you so that I may share with you some spiritual gift to strengthen you— 12 or rather so that we may be mutually encouraged by each other's faith, both yours and mine. 13 I want you to know, brothers and sisters,[d] that I have often intended to come to you (but thus far have been prevented), in order that I may reap some harvest among you as I have among the rest of the Gentiles. 14 I am a debtor both to Greeks and to barbarians, both to the wise and to the foolish 15 —hence my eagerness to proclaim the gospel to you also who are in Rome.

 Universal Solution

16 For I am not ashamed of the gospel; it is the power of God for salvation to everyone who has faith, to the Jew first and also to the Greek. 17 For in it the righteousness of God is revealed through faith for faith; as it is written, "The one who is righteous will live by faith."[e][1]

18 For the wrath of God is revealed from heaven against all ungodliness and wickedness of those who by their wickedness suppress the truth. 19 For what can be known about God is plain to them, because God has shown it to them. 20 Ever since the creation of the world his eternal power and divine nature, invisible though they are, have been understood and seen through the things he has made. So they are without excuse; 21 for though they knew God, they did not honor him as God or give thanks to him, but they became futile in their thinking, and their senseless minds were darkened. 22 Claiming to be wise, they became fools; 23 and they exchanged the glory of the immortal God for images resembling a mortal human being or birds or four-footed animals or reptiles.

24 Therefore God gave them up in the lusts of their hearts to impurity, to the degrading of their bodies among themselves, 25 because they exchanged the truth about God for a lie and worshiped and served the creature rather than the Creator, who is blessed forever! Amen.

26 For this reason God gave them up to degrading passions. Their women exchanged natural intercourse for unnatural, 27 and in the same way also the men, giving up natural intercourse with women, were consumed with passion for one another. Men committed shameless acts with men and received in their own persons the due penalty for their error.

28 And since they did not see fit to acknowledge God, God gave them up to a debased mind and to things that should not be done. 29 They were filled with every kind of wickedness, evil, covetousness, malice. Full of envy, murder, strife, deceit, craftiness, they are gossips, 30 slanderers, God-haters,[f] insolent, haughty, boastful, inventors of evil, rebellious toward parents, 31 foolish, faithless, heartless, ruthless. 32 They know God's decree, that those who practice such things deserve to die—yet they not only do them but even applaud others who practice them.

2 Therefore you have no excuse, whoever you are, when you judge others; for in passing judgment on another you condemn yourself, because you, the judge, are doing the very same things. 2 You say,[g] "We know that God's judgment on those who do such things is in accordance with truth." 3 Do you imagine, whoever you are, that when you judge those who do such things and

---

[a]Gk *slave* [b]Or *Spirit* [c]Gk *my spirit in the gospel* [d]Gk *brothers*
[e]Or *The one who is righteous through faith will live* [f]Or *God-hated*
[g]Gk lacks *You say*

---

[1]Hab 2:4

yet do them yourself, you will escape the judgment of God? 4 Or do you despise the riches of his kindness and forbearance and patience? Do you not realize that God's kindness is meant to lead you to repentance? 5 But by your hard and impenitent heart you are storing up wrath for yourself on the day of wrath, when God's righteous judgment will be revealed. 6 For he will repay according to each one's deeds: 7 to those who by patiently doing good seek for glory and honor and immortality, he will give eternal life; 8 while for those who are self-seeking and who obey not the truth but wickedness, there will be wrath and fury. 9 There will be anguish and distress for everyone who does evil, the Jew first and also the Greek, 10 but glory and honor and peace for everyone who does good, the Jew first and also the Greek. 11 For God shows no partiality.

12 All who have sinned apart from the law will also perish apart from the law, and all who have sinned under the law will be judged by the law. 13 For it is not the hearers of the law who are righteous in God's sight, but the doers of the law who will be justified. 14 When Gentiles, who do not possess the law, do instinctively what the law requires, these, though not having the law, are a law to themselves. 15 They show that what the law requires is written on their hearts, to which their own conscience also bears witness; and their conflicting thoughts will accuse or perhaps excuse them 16 on the day when, according to my gospel, God, through Jesus Christ, will judge the secret thoughts of all.

17 But if you call yourself a Jew and rely on the law and boast of your relation to God 18 and know his will and determine what is best because you are instructed in the law, 19 and if you are sure that you are a guide to the blind, a light to those who are in darkness, 20 a corrector of the foolish, a teacher of children, having in the law the embodiment of knowledge and truth, 21 you, then, that teach others, will you not teach yourself? While you preach against stealing, do you steal? 22 You that forbid adultery, do you commit adultery? You that abhor idols, do you rob temples? 23 You that boast in the law, do you dishonor God by breaking the law? 24 For, as it is written, "The name of God is blasphemed among the Gentiles because of you."[2]

25 Circumcision indeed is of value if you obey the law; but if you break the law, your circumcision has become uncircumcision. 26 So, if those who are uncircumcised keep the requirements of the law, will not their uncircumcision be regarded as circumcision? 27 Then those who are physically uncircumcised but keep the law will condemn you that have the written code and circumcision but break the law. 28 For a person is not a Jew who is one outwardly, nor is true circumcision something external and physical. 29 Rather, a person is a Jew who is one inwardly, and real circumcision is a matter of the heart—it is spiritual and not literal. Such a person receives praise not from others but from God.

3 Then what advantage has the Jew? Or what is the value of circumcision? 2 Much, in every way. For in the first place the Jews[h] were entrusted with the oracles of God. 3 What if some were unfaithful? Will their faithlessness nullify the faithfulness of God? 4 By no means! Although everyone is a liar, let God be proved true, as it is written,

> "So that you may be justified in
>   your words,
>   and prevail in your judging."[i3]

5 But if our injustice serves to confirm the justice of God, what should we say? That God is unjust to inflict wrath on us? (I speak in a human way.) 6 By no means! For then how could God judge the world? 7 But if through my falsehood God's truthfulness abounds to his glory, why am I still being condemned as a sinner? 8 And why not say (as some people slander us by saying that we say), "Let us do evil so that good may come"? Their condemnation is deserved!

9 What then? Are we any better off?[j] No, not at all; for we have already charged that all, both Jews and Greeks, are under the power of sin, 10 as it is written:

> "There is no one who is righteous,
>   not even one;[4]
> 11   there is no one who has
>   understanding,
>   there is no one who seeks
>   God.

[h]Gk *they*   [i]Gk *when you are being judged*   [j]Or *at any disadvantage?*

---

[2]Isa 52:5; Ezek 36:20   [3]Ps 51:4   [4]Eccl 7:20

12   All have turned aside, together
         they have become
         worthless;
      there is no one who shows
         kindness,
         there is not even one."[5]
13   "Their throats are opened graves;
         they use their tongues to
         deceive."[6]
      "The venom of vipers is under
         their lips."[7]
14   "Their mouths are full of
         cursing and bitterness."[8]
15   "Their feet are swift to shed
         blood;
16   ruin and misery are in their
         paths,
17   and the way of peace they have
         not known."[9]
18   "There is no fear of God before
         their eyes."[10]

19 Now we know that whatever the law says, it speaks to those who are under the law, so that every mouth may be silenced, and the whole world may be held accountable to God. 20 For "no human being will be justified in his sight" by deeds prescribed by the law, for through the law comes the knowledge of sin.

21 But now, apart from law, the righteousness of God has been disclosed, and is attested by the law and the prophets, 22 the righteousness of God through faith in Jesus Christ[k] for all who believe. For there is no distinction, 23 since all have sinned and fall short of the glory of God; 24 they are now justified by his grace as a gift, through the redemption that is in Christ Jesus, 25 whom God put forward as a sacrifice of atonement[l] by his blood, effective through faith. He did this to show his righteousness, because in his divine forbearance he had passed over the sins previously committed; 26 it was to prove at the present time that he himself is righteous and that he justifies the one who has faith in Jesus.[m]

27 Then what becomes of boasting? It is excluded. By what law? By that of works? No, but by the law of faith. 28 For we hold that a person is justified by faith apart from works prescribed by the law. 29 Or is God the God of Jews only? Is he not the God of Gentiles also? Yes, of Gentiles also, 30 since God is one; and he will justify the circumcised on the ground of faith and the uncircumcised through that same faith. 31 Do we then overthrow the law by this faith? By no means! On the contrary, we uphold the law.

4 What then are we to say was gained by[n] Abraham, our ancestor according to the flesh? 2 For if Abraham was justified by works, he has something to boast about, but not before God. 3 For what does the scripture say? "Abraham believed God, and it was reckoned to him as righteousness."[11] 4 Now to one who works, wages are not reckoned as a gift but as something due. 5 But to one who without works trusts him who justifies the ungodly, such faith is reckoned as righteousness. 6 So also David speaks of the blessedness of those to whom God reckons righteousness apart from works:

7   "Blessed are those whose iniquities
         are forgiven,
      and whose sins are covered;
8   blessed is the one against whom
         the Lord will not reckon
         sin."[12]

9 Is this blessedness, then, pronounced only on the circumcised, or also on the uncircumcised? We say, "Faith was reckoned to Abraham as righteousness."[13] 10 How then was it reckoned to him? Was it before or after he had been circumcised? It was not after, but before he was circumcised. 11 He received the sign of circumcision as a seal of the righteousness that he had by faith while he was still uncircumcised. The purpose was to make him the ancestor of all who believe without being circumcised and who thus have righteousness reckoned to them, 12 and likewise the ancestor of the circumcised who are not only circumcised but who also follow the example of the faith that our ancestor Abraham had before he was circumcised.

13 For the promise that he would inherit the world did not come to Abraham or to his descen-

[k]Or *through the faith of Jesus Christ* [l]Or *a place of atonement* [m]Or *who has the faith of Jesus* [n]Other ancient authorities read *say about*

[5]Ps 14:1–3; 53:1–3 [6]Ps 5:9 [7]Ps 140:3 [8]Ps 10:7 [9]Isa 59:7–8 [10]Ps 36:1 [11]Gen 15:6 [12]Ps 32:1–2 [13]Gen 15:6

dants through the law but through the righteousness of faith. 14 If it is the adherents of the law who are to be the heirs, faith is null and the promise is void. 15 For the law brings wrath; but where there is no law, neither is there violation.

16 For this reason it depends on faith, in order that the promise may rest on grace and be guaranteed to all his descendants, not only to the adherents of the law but also to those who share the faith of Abraham (for he is the father of all of us, 17 as it is written, "I have made you the father of many nations"[14])—in the presence of the God in whom he believed, who gives life to the dead and calls into existence the things that do not exist. 18 Hoping against hope, he believed that he would become "the father of many nations,"[15] according to what was said, "So numerous shall your descendants be."[16] 19 He did not weaken in faith when he considered his own body, which was already[o] as good as dead (for he was about a hundred years old), or when he considered the barrenness of Sarah's womb. 20 No distrust made him waver concerning the promise of God, but he grew strong in his faith as he gave glory to God, 21 being fully convinced that God was able to do what he had promised. 22 Therefore his faith[p] "was reckoned to him as righteousness."[17] 23 Now the words, "it was reckoned to him," were written not for his sake alone, 24 but for ours also. It will be reckoned to us who believe in him who raised Jesus our Lord from the dead, 25 who was handed over to death for our trespasses and was raised for our justification.

5 Therefore, since we are justified by faith, we[q] have peace with God through our Lord Jesus Christ, 2 through whom we have obtained access[r] to this grace in which we stand; and we[s] boast in our hope of sharing the glory of God. 3 And not only that, but we[s] also boast in our sufferings, knowing that suffering produces endurance, 4 and endurance produces character, and character produces hope, 5 and hope does not disappoint us, because God's love has been poured into our hearts through the Holy Spirit that has been given to us.

6 For while we were still weak, at the right time Christ died for the ungodly. 7 Indeed, rarely will anyone die for a righteous person—though perhaps for a good person someone might actually dare to die. 8 But God proves his love for us in that while we still were sinners Christ died for us. 9 Much more surely then, now that we have been justified by his blood, will we be saved through him from the wrath of God.[t] 10 For if while we were enemies, we were reconciled to God through the death of his Son, much more surely, having been reconciled, will we be saved by his life. 11 But more than that, we even boast in God through our Lord Jesus Christ, through whom we have now received reconciliation.

12 Therefore, just as sin came into the world through one man, and death came through sin, and so death spread to all because all have sinned— 13 sin was indeed in the world before the law, but sin is not reckoned when there is no law. 14 Yet death exercised dominion from Adam to Moses, even over those whose sins were not like the transgression of Adam, who is a type of the one who was to come.

15 But the free gift is not like the trespass. For if the many died through the one man's trespass, much more surely have the grace of God and the free gift in the grace of the one man, Jesus Christ, abounded for the many. 16 And the free gift is not like the effect of the one man's sin. For the judgment following one trespass brought condemnation, but the free gift following many trespasses brings justification. 17 If, because of the one man's trespass, death exercised dominion through that one, much more surely will those who receive the abundance of grace and the free gift of righteousness exercise dominion in life through the one man, Jesus Christ.

18 Therefore just as one man's trespass led to condemnation for all, so one man's act of righteousness leads to justification and life for all. 19 For just as by the one man's disobedience the many were made sinners, so by the one man's obedience the many will be made righteous. 20 But law came in, with the result that the trespass multiplied; but where sin increased, grace abounded all the more, 21 so that, just as sin exercised do-

°Other ancient authorities lack *already* PGk *Therefore it* qOther ancient authorities read *let us* rOther ancient authorities add *by faith* sOr *let us* tGk *the wrath*

14Gen 17:5 15Gen 17:5 16Gen 15:5 17Gen 15:6

minion in death, so grace might also exercise dominion through justification[u] leading to eternal life through Jesus Christ our Lord.

6 What then are we to say? Should we continue in sin in order that grace may abound? 2 By no means! How can we who died to sin go on living in it? 3 Do you not know that all of us who have been baptized into Christ Jesus were baptized into his death? 4 Therefore we have been buried with him by baptism into death, so that, just as Christ was raised from the dead by the glory of the Father, so we too might walk in newness of life.

5 For if we have been united with him in a death like his, we will certainly be united with him in a resurrection like his. 6 We know that our old self was crucified with him so that the body of sin might be destroyed, and we might no longer be enslaved to sin. 7 For whoever has died is freed from sin. 8 But if we have died with Christ, we believe that we will also live with him. 9 We know that Christ, being raised from the dead, will never die again; death no longer has dominion over him. 10 The death he died, he died to sin, once for all; but the life he lives, he lives to God. 11 So you also must consider yourselves dead to sin and alive to God in Christ Jesus.

12 Therefore, do not let sin exercise dominion in your mortal bodies, to make you obey their passions. 13 No longer present your members to sin as instruments[v] of wickedness, but present yourselves to God as those who have been brought from death to life, and present your members to God as instruments[v] of righteousness. 14 For sin will have no dominion over you, since you are not under law but under grace.

15 What then? Should we sin because we are not under law but under grace? By no means! 16 Do you not know that if you present yourselves to anyone as obedient slaves, you are slaves of the one whom you obey, either of sin, which leads to death, or of obedience, which leads to righteousness? 17 But thanks be to God that you, having once been slaves of sin, have become obedient from the heart to the form of teaching to which you were entrusted, 18 and that you, having been set free from sin, have become slaves of righteousness. 19 I am speaking in human terms because of your natural limitations.[w] For just as you once pre-

sented your members as slaves to impurity and to greater and greater iniquity, so now present your members as slaves to righteousness for sanctification.

20 When you were slaves of sin, you were free in regard to righteousness. 21 So what advantage did you then get from the things of which you now are ashamed? The end of those things is death. 22 But now that you have been freed from sin and enslaved to God, the advantage you get is sanctification. The end is eternal life. 23 For the wages of sin is death, but the free gift of God is eternal life in Christ Jesus our Lord.

7 Do you not know, brothers and sisters[x]—for I am speaking to those who know the law—that the law is binding on a person only during that person's lifetime? 2 Thus a married woman is bound by the law to her husband as long as he lives; but if her husband dies, she is discharged from the law concerning the husband. 3 Accordingly, she will be called an adulteress if she lives with another man while her husband is alive. But if her husband dies, she is free from that law, and if she marries another man, she is not an adulteress.

4 In the same way, my friends,[x] you have died to the law through the body of Christ, so that you may belong to another, to him who has been raised from the dead in order that we may bear fruit for God. 5 While we were living in the flesh, our sinful passions, aroused by the law, were at work in our members to bear fruit for death. 6 But now we are discharged from the law, dead to that which held us captive, so that we are slaves not under the old written code but in the new life of the Spirit.

7 What then should we say? That the law is sin? By no means! Yet, if it had not been for the law, I would not have known sin. I would not have known what it is to covet if the law had not said, "You shall not covet."[18] 8 But sin, seizing an opportunity in the commandment, produced in me all kinds of covetousness. Apart from the law sin lies dead. 9 I was once alive apart from the law, but when the commandment came, sin revived 10 and I died, and the very commandment that promised

---

[u]Or righteousness [v]Or weapons [w]Gk the weakness of your flesh
[x]Gk brothers

---

[18]Exod 20:17; Deut 5:21

life proved to be death to me. 11 For sin, seizing an opportunity in the commandment, deceived me and through it killed me. 12 So the law is holy, and the commandment is holy and just and good.

13 Did what is good, then, bring death to me? By no means! It was sin, working death in me through what is good, in order that sin might be shown to be sin, and through the commandment might become sinful beyond measure.

14 For we know that the law is spiritual; but I am of the flesh, sold into slavery under sin.[y] 15 I do not understand my own actions. For I do not do what I want, but I do the very thing I hate. 16 Now if I do what I do not want, I agree that the law is good. 17 But in fact it is no longer I that do it, but sin that dwells within me. 18 For I know that nothing good dwells within me, that is, in my flesh. I can will what is right, but I cannot do it. 19 For I do not do the good I want, but the evil I do not want is what I do. 20 Now if I do what I do not want, it is no longer I that do it, but sin that dwells within me.

21 So I find it to be a law that when I want to do what is good, evil lies close at hand. 22 For I delight in the law of God in my inmost self, 23 but I see in my members another law at war with the law of my mind, making me captive to the law of sin that dwells in my members. 24 Wretched man that I am! Who will rescue me from this body of death? 25 Thanks be to God through Jesus Christ our Lord!

So then, with my mind I am a slave to the law of God, but with my flesh I am a slave to the law of sin.

8 There is therefore now no condemnation for those who are in Christ Jesus. 2 For the law of the Spirit[z] of life in Christ Jesus has set you[a] free from the law of sin and of death. 3 For God has done what the law, weakened by the flesh, could not do: by sending his own Son in the likeness of sinful flesh, and to deal with sin,[b] he condemned sin in the flesh, 4 so that the just requirement of the law might be fulfilled in us, who walk not according to the flesh but according to the Spirit.[z] 5 For those who live according to the flesh set their minds on the things of the flesh, but those who live according to the Spirit[z] set their minds on the things of the Spirit.[z] 6 To set the mind on the flesh is death, but to set the mind on the Spirit[z] is life and peace. 7 For this reason the mind that is set on the flesh is hostile to God; it does not submit to God's law—indeed it cannot, 8 and those who are in the flesh cannot please God.

9 But you are not in the flesh; you are in the Spirit,[z] since the Spirit of God dwells in you. Anyone who does not have the Spirit of Christ does not belong to him. 10 But if Christ is in you, though the body is dead because of sin, the Spirit[z] is life because of righteousness. 11 If the Spirit of him who raised Jesus from the dead dwells in you, he who raised Christ[c] from the dead will give life to your mortal bodies also through[d] his Spirit that dwells in you.

12 So then, brothers and sisters,[e] we are debtors, not to the flesh, to live according to the flesh— 13 for if you live according to the flesh, you will die; but if by the Spirit you put to death the deeds of the body, you will live. 14 For all who are led by the Spirit of God are children of God. 15 For you did not receive a spirit of slavery to fall back into fear, but you have received a spirit of adoption. When we cry, "Abba![f] Father!" 16 it is that very Spirit bearing witness[g] with our spirit that we are children of God, 17 and if children, then heirs, heirs of God and joint heirs with Christ—if, in fact, we suffer with him so that we may also be glorified with him.

18 I consider that the sufferings of this present time are not worth comparing with the glory about to be revealed to us. 19 For the creation waits with eager longing for the revealing of the children of God; 20 for the creation was subjected to futility, not of its own will but by the will of the one who subjected it, in hope 21 that the creation itself will be set free from its bondage to decay and will obtain the freedom of the glory of the children of God. 22 We know that the whole creation has been groaning in labor pains until now; 23 and not only the creation, but we ourselves, who have the first fruits of the Spirit, groan inwardly while we wait for adoption, the redemption of our bodies.

Thinks world has changed

[y]Gk *sold under sin* [z]Or *spirit* [a]Here the Greek word *you* is singular number; other ancient authorities read *me* or *us* [b]Or *and as a sin offering* [c]Other ancient authorities read *the Christ* or *Christ Jesus* or *Jesus Christ* [d]Other ancient authorities read *on account of* [e]Gk *brothers* [f]Aramaic for *Father* [g]Or [15]*a spirit of adoption, by which we cry, "Abba! Father!"* [16]*The Spirit itself bears witness*

24 For in[h] hope we were saved. Now hope that is seen is not hope. For who hopes[i] for what is seen? 25 But if we hope for what we do not see, we wait for it with patience.

26 Likewise the Spirit helps us in our weakness; for we do not know how to pray as we ought, but that very Spirit intercedes[j] with sighs too deep for words. 27 And God,[k] who searches the heart, knows what is the mind of the Spirit, because the Spirit[l] intercedes for the saints according to the will of God.[m]

28 We know that all things work together for good[n] for those who love God, who are called according to his purpose. 29 For those whom he foreknew he also predestined to be conformed to the image of his Son, in order that he might be the firstborn within a large family.[o] 30 And those whom he predestined he also called; and those whom he called he also justified; and those whom he justified he also glorified.

31 What then are we to say about these things? If God is for us, who is against us? 32 He who did not withhold his own Son, but gave him up for all of us, will he not with him also give us everything else? 33 Who will bring any charge against God's elect? It is God who justifies. 34 Who is to condemn? It is Christ Jesus, who died, yes, who was raised, who is at the right hand of God, who indeed intercedes for us.[p] 35 Who will separate us from the love of Christ? Will hardship, or distress, or persecution, or famine, or nakedness, or peril, or sword? 36 As it is written,

> "For your sake we are being killed
>   all day long;
> we are accounted as sheep to be
>   slaughtered."[19]

37 No, in all these things we are more than conquerors through him who loved us. 38 For I am convinced that neither death, nor life, nor angels, nor rulers, nor things present, nor things to come, nor powers, 39 nor height, nor depth, nor anything else in all creation, will be able to separate us from the love of God in Christ Jesus our Lord.

9 I am speaking the truth in Christ—I am not lying; my conscience confirms it by the Holy Spirit— 2 I have great sorrow and unceasing anguish in my heart. 3 For I could wish that I myself were accursed and cut off from Christ for the sake of my own people,[q] my kindred according to the flesh. 4 They are Israelites, and to them belong the adoption, the glory, the covenants, the giving of the law, the worship, and the promises; 5 to them belong the patriarchs, and from them, according to the flesh, comes the Messiah,[r] who is over all, God blessed forever.[s] Amen.

6 It is not as though the word of God had failed. For not all Israelites truly belong to Israel, 7 and not all of Abraham's children are his true descendants; but "It is through Isaac that descendants shall be named for you."[20] 8 This means that it is not the children of the flesh who are the children of God, but the children of the promise are counted as descendants. 9 For this is what the promise said, "About this time I will return and Sarah shall have a son."[21] 10 Nor is that all; something similar happened to Rebecca when she had conceived children by one husband, our ancestor Isaac. 11 Even before they had been born or had done anything good or bad (so that God's purpose of election might continue, 12 not by works but by his call) she was told, "The elder shall serve the younger."[22] 13 As it is written,

> "I have loved Jacob,
>   but I have hated Esau."[23]

14 What then are we to say? Is there injustice on God's part? By no means! 15 For he says to Moses,

> "I will have mercy on whom I
>   have mercy,
> and I will have compassion on
>   whom I have compassion."[24]

16 So it depends not on human will or exertion, but on God who shows mercy. 17 For the scripture says to Pharaoh, "I have raised you up for the very purpose of showing my power in you, so that my name may be proclaimed in all the earth."[25] 18 So then he has mercy on whomever he chooses, and he hardens the heart of whomever he chooses.

[h]Or by [i]Other ancient authorities read *awaits* [j]Other ancient authorities add *for us* [k]Gk *the one* [l]Gk *he* or *it* [m]Gk *according to God* [n]Other ancient authorities read *God makes all things work together for good*, or *in all things God works for good* [o]Gk *among many brothers* [p]Or *Is it Christ Jesus . . . for us?* [q]Gk *my brothers* [r]Or *the Christ* [s]Or *Messiah, who is God over all, blessed forever*; or *Messiah. May he who is God over all be blessed forever*

[19]Ps 44:22 [20]Gen 21:12 [21]Gen 18:10, 14 [22]Gen 25:23 [23]Mal 1:2–3 [24]Exod 33:19 [25]Exod 9:16

19 You will say to me then, "Why then does he still find fault? For who can resist his will?" 20 But who indeed are you, a human being, to argue with God? Will what is molded say to the one who molds it, "Why have you made me like this?" 21 Has the potter no right over the clay, to make out of the same lump one object for special use and another for ordinary use? 22 What if God, desiring to show his wrath and to make known his power, has endured with much patience the objects of wrath that are made for destruction; 23 and what if he has done so in order to make known the riches of his glory for the objects of mercy, which he has prepared beforehand for glory— 24 including us whom he has called, not from the Jews only but also from the Gentiles? 25 As indeed he says in Hosea,

> "Those who were not my people I
>   will call 'my people'
> and her who was not beloved I
>   will call 'beloved.'"[26]

26   "And in the very place where it
>   was said to them, 'You are
>   not my people,'
>   there they shall be called
>   children of the living God."[27]

27 And Isaiah cries out concerning Israel, "Though the number of the children of Israel were like the sand of the sea, only a remnant of them will be saved; 28 for the Lord will execute his sentence on the earth quickly and decisively."[t28] 29 And as Isaiah predicted,

> "If the Lord of hosts had not left
>   survivors[u] to us,
> we would have fared like
>   Sodom
> and been made like Gomorrah."[29]

30 What then are we to say? Gentiles, who did not strive for righteousness, have attained it, that is, righteousness through faith; 31 but Israel, who did strive for the righteousness that is based on the law, did not succeed in fulfilling that law. 32 Why not? Because they did not strive for it on the basis of faith, but as if it were based on works. They have stumbled over the stumbling stone, 33 as it is written,

> "See, I am laying in Zion a stone
>   that will make people
>   stumble, a rock that will

make them fall,
> and whoever believes in him[v]
>   will not be put to shame."[30]

10

Brothers and sisters,[w] my heart's desire and prayer to God for them is that they may be saved. 2 I can testify that they have a zeal for God, but it is not enlightened. 3 For, being ignorant of the righteousness that comes from God, and seeking to establish their own, they have not submitted to God's righteousness. 4 For Christ is the end of the law so that there may be righteousness for everyone who believes.

5 Moses writes concerning the righteousness that comes from the law, that "the person who does these things will live by them."[31] 6 But the righteousness that comes from faith says, "Do not say in your heart, 'Who will ascend into heaven?'" (that is, to bring Christ down) 7 "or 'Who will descend into the abyss?'" (that is, to bring Christ up from the dead). 8 But what does it say?

> "The word is near you,
>   on your lips and in your heart"[32]

(that is, the word of faith that we proclaim); 9 because[x] if you confess with your lips that Jesus is Lord and believe in your heart that God raised him from the dead, you will be saved. [*accept and trust*] 10 For one believes with the heart and so is justified, and one confesses with the mouth and so is saved. 11 The scripture says, "No one who believes in him will be put to shame."[33] 12 For there is no distinction between Jew and Greek; the same Lord is Lord of all and is generous to all who call on him. 13 For, "Everyone who calls on the name of the Lord shall be saved."[34]

14 But how are they to call on one in whom they have not believed? And how are they to believe in one of whom they have never heard? And how are they to hear without someone to proclaim him? 15 And how are they to proclaim him unless they are sent? As it is written, "How beautiful are the feet of those who bring good news!"[35] 16 But not all have obeyed the good news;[y] for Isaiah says,

---

[t]Other ancient authorities read *for he will finish his work and cut it short in righteousness, because the Lord will make the sentence shortened on the earth* [u]Or *descendants*; Gk *seed* [v]Or *trusts in it* [w]Gk *Brothers* [x]Or *namely, that* [y]Or *gospel*

[26]Hos 2:23 [27]Hos 1:10 [28]Isa 10:22–23 [29]Isa 1:9 [30]Isa 28:16; 8:14 [31]Lev 18:5 [32]Deut 30:12–14 [33]Isa 28:16 [34]Joel 2:32 [35]Isa 52:7

"Lord, who has believed our message?"[36] 17 So faith comes from what is heard, and what is heard comes through the word of Christ.[z]

18 But I ask, have they not heard? Indeed they have; for

> "Their voice has gone out to all
> the earth,
> and their words to the ends of
> the world."[37]

19 Again I ask, did Israel not understand? First Moses says,

> "I will make you jealous of those
> who are not a nation;
> with a foolish nation I will
> make you angry."[38]

20 Then Isaiah is so bold as to say,

> "I have been found by those who
> did not seek me;
> I have shown myself to those
> who did not ask for me."[39]

21 But of Israel he says, "All day long I have held out my hands to a disobedient and contrary people."[40]

11 I ask, then, has God rejected his people? By no means! I myself am an Israelite, a descendant of Abraham, a member of the tribe of Benjamin. 2 God has not rejected his people whom he foreknew. Do you not know what the scripture says of Elijah, how he pleads with God against Israel? 3 "Lord, they have killed your prophets, they have demolished your altars; I alone am left, and they are seeking my life."[41] 4 But what is the divine reply to him? "I have kept for myself seven thousand who have not bowed the knee to Baal."[42] 5 So too at the present time there is a remnant, chosen by grace. 6 But if it is by grace, it is no longer on the basis of works, otherwise grace would no longer be grace.[a]

7 What then? Israel failed to obtain what it was seeking. The elect obtained it, but the rest were hardened, 8 as it is written,

> "God gave them a sluggish spirit,
> eyes that would not see
> and ears that would not hear,
> down to this very day."[43]

9 And David says,

> "Let their table become a snare
> and a trap,

> a stumbling block and a
> retribution for them;
> 10   let their eyes be darkened so that
> they cannot see,
> and keep their backs forever
> bent."[44]

11 So I ask, have they stumbled so as to fall? By no means! But through their stumbling[b] salvation has come to the Gentiles, so as to make Israel[c] jealous. 12 Now if their stumbling[b] means riches for the world, and if their defeat means riches for Gentiles, how much more will their full inclusion mean!

13 Now I am speaking to you Gentiles. Inasmuch then as I am an apostle to the Gentiles, I glorify my ministry 14 in order to make my own people[d] jealous, and thus save some of them. 15 For if their rejection is the reconciliation of the world, what will their acceptance be but life from the dead! 16 If the part of the dough offered as first fruits is holy, then the whole batch is holy; and if the root is holy, then the branches also are holy.

17 But if some of the branches were broken off, and you, a wild olive shoot, were grafted in their place to share the rich root[e] of the olive tree, 18 do not boast over the branches. If you do boast, remember that it is not you that support the root, but the root that supports you. 19 You will say, "Branches were broken off so that I might be grafted in." 20 That is true. They were broken off because of their unbelief, but you stand only through faith. So do not become proud, but stand in awe. 21 For if God did not spare the natural branches, perhaps he will not spare you.[f] 22 Note then the kindness and the severity of God: severity toward those who have fallen, but God's kindness toward you, provided you continue in his kindness; otherwise you also will be cut off. 23 And even those of Israel,[g] if they do not persist

---

[z]Or *about Christ*; other ancient authorities read *of God*   [a]Other ancient authorities add *But if it is by works, it is no longer on the basis of grace, otherwise work would no longer be work*   [b]Gk *transgression*   [c]Gk *them*   [d]Gk *my flesh*   [e]Other ancient authorities read *the richness*   [f]Other ancient authorities read *neither will he spare you*   [g]Gk lacks *of Israel*

---

[36]Isa 53:1   [37]Ps 19:4   [38]Deut 32:21   [39]Isa 65:1   [40]Isa 65:2   [41]1 Kgs 19:10, 14   [42]1 Kgs 19:18   [43]Deut 29:4; Isa 29:10   [44]Ps 69:22–23

in unbelief, will be grafted in, for God has the power to graft them in again. 24 For if you have been cut from what is by nature a wild olive tree and grafted, contrary to nature, into a cultivated olive tree, how much more will these natural branches be grafted back into their own olive tree.

25 So that you may not claim to be wiser than you are, brothers and sisters,[h] I want you to understand this mystery: a hardening has come upon part of Israel, until the full number of the Gentiles has come in. 26 And so all Israel will be saved; as it is written,

"Out of Zion will come the
    Deliverer;
he will banish ungodliness from
    Jacob."
27   "And this is my covenant with
        them,
    when I take away their sins."[45]

28 As regards the gospel they are enemies of God[i] for your sake; but as regards election they are beloved, for the sake of their ancestors; 29 for the gifts and the calling of God are irrevocable. 30 Just as you were once disobedient to God but have now received mercy because of their disobedience, 31 so they have now been disobedient in order that, by the mercy shown to you, they too may now[j] receive mercy. 32 For God has imprisoned all in disobedience so that he may be merciful to all.

33 O the depth of the riches and wisdom and knowledge of God! How unsearchable are his judgments and how inscrutable his ways!
34   "For who has known the mind of
        the Lord?
    Or who has been his
        counselor?"[46]
35   "Or who has given a gift to him,
        to receive a gift in return?"[47]
36 For from him and through him and to him are all things. To him be the glory forever. Amen.

12 I appeal to you therefore, brothers and sisters,[h] by the mercies of God, to present your bodies as a living sacrifice, holy and acceptable to God, which is your spiritual[k] worship. 2 Do not be conformed to this world, but be transformed by the renewing of your minds, so that you

may discern what is the will of God—what is good and acceptable and perfect.[m]

3 For by the grace given to me I say to everyone among you not to think of yourself more highly than you ought to think, but to think with sober judgment, each according to the measure of faith that God has assigned. 4 For as in one body we have many members, and not all the members have the same function, 5 so we, who are many, are one body in Christ, and individually we are members one of another. 6 We have gifts that differ according to the grace given to us: prophecy, in proportion to faith; 7 ministry, in ministering; the teacher, in teaching; 8 the exhorter, in exhortation; the giver, in generosity; the leader, in diligence; the compassionate, in cheerfulness.

9 Let love be genuine; hate what is evil, hold fast to what is good; 10 love one another with mutual affection; outdo one another in showing honor. 11 Do not lag in zeal, be ardent in spirit, serve the Lord.[n] 12 Rejoice in hope, be patient in suffering, persevere in prayer. 13 Contribute to the needs of the saints; extend hospitality to strangers.

14 Bless those who persecute you; bless and do not curse them. 15 Rejoice with those who rejoice, weep with those who weep. 16 Live in harmony with one another; do not be haughty, but associate with the lowly;[o] do not claim to be wiser than you are. 17 Do not repay anyone evil for evil, but take thought for what is noble in the sight of all. 18 If it is possible, so far as it depends on you, live peaceably with all. 19 Beloved, never avenge yourselves, but leave room for the wrath of God;[p] for it is written, "Vengeance is mine, I will repay, says the Lord."[48] 20 No, "if your enemies are hungry, feed them; if they are thirsty, give them something to drink; for by doing this you will heap burning coals on their heads."[49] 21 Do not be overcome by evil, but overcome evil with good.

13 Let every person be subject to the governing authorities; for there is no authority except from God, and those authorities that ex-

[h]Gk brothers [i]Gk lacks of God [j]Other ancient authorities lack now [k]Or reasonable [l]Gk age [m]Or what is the good and acceptable and perfect will of God [n]Other ancient authorities read serve the opportune time [o]Or give yourselves to humble tasks [p]Gk the wrath

[45]Isa 59:20–21; 27:9 [46]Isa 40:13 [47]Job 41:3, 11 [48]Deut 32:35 [49]Prov 25:21–22

ist have been instituted by God. 2 Therefore whoever resists authority resists what God has appointed, and those who resist will incur judgment. 3 For rulers are not a terror to good conduct, but to bad. Do you wish to have no fear of the authority? Then do what is good, and you will receive its approval; 4 for it is God's servant for your good. But if you do what is wrong, you should be afraid, for the authority[q] does not bear the sword in vain! It is the servant of God to execute wrath on the wrongdoer. 5 Therefore one must be subject, not only because of wrath but also because of conscience. 6 For the same reason you also pay taxes, for the authorities are God's servants, busy with this very thing. 7 Pay to all what is due them—taxes to whom taxes are due, revenue to whom revenue is due, respect to whom respect is due, honor to whom honor is due.

8 Owe no one anything, except to love one another; for the one who loves another has fulfilled the law. 9 The commandments, "You shall not commit adultery; You shall not murder; You shall not steal; You shall not covet";[50] and any other commandment, are summed up in this word, "Love your neighbor as yourself."[51] 10 Love does no wrong to a neighbor; therefore, love is the fulfilling of the law.

11 Besides this, you know what time it is, how it is now the moment for you to wake from sleep. For salvation is nearer to us now than when we became believers; 12 the night is far gone, the day is near. Let us then lay aside the works of darkness and put on the armor of light; 13 let us live honorably as in the day, not in reveling and drunkenness, not in debauchery and licentiousness, not in quarreling and jealousy. 14 Instead, put on the Lord Jesus Christ, and make no provision for the flesh, to gratify its desires.

14 Welcome those who are weak in faith,[r] but not for the purpose of quarreling over opinions. 2 Some believe in eating anything, while the weak eat only vegetables. 3 Those who eat must not despise those who abstain, and those who abstain must not pass judgment on those who eat; for God has welcomed them. 4 Who are you to pass judgment on servants of another? It is before their own lord that they stand or fall. And they will be upheld, for the Lord[s] is able to make them stand.

5 Some judge one day to be better than another, while others judge all days to be alike. Let all be fully convinced in their own minds. 6 Those who observe the day, observe it in honor of the Lord. Also those who eat, eat in honor of the Lord, since they give thanks to God; while those who abstain, abstain in honor of the Lord and give thanks to God.

7 We do not live to ourselves, and we do not die to ourselves. 8 If we live, we live to the Lord, and if we die, we die to the Lord; so then, whether we live or whether we die, we are the Lord's. 9 For to this end Christ died and lived again, so that he might be Lord of both the dead and the living.

10 Why do you pass judgment on your brother or sister?[t] Or you, why do you despise your brother or sister?[t] For we will all stand before the judgment seat of God.[u] 11 For it is written,

"As I live, says the Lord, every
    knee shall bow to me,
and every tongue shall give
    praise to[v] God."[52]

12 So then, each of us will be accountable to God.[w]

13 Let us therefore no longer pass judgment on one another, but resolve instead never to put a stumbling block or hindrance in the way of another.[x] 14 I know and am persuaded in the Lord Jesus that nothing is unclean in itself; but it is unclean for anyone who thinks it unclean. 15 If your brother or sister[t] is being injured by what you eat, you are no longer walking in love. Do not let what you eat cause the ruin of one for whom Christ died. 16 So do not let your good be spoken of as evil. 17 For the kingdom of God is not food and drink but righteousness and peace and joy in the Holy Spirit. 18 The one who thus serves Christ is acceptable to God and has human approval. 19 Let us then pursue what makes for peace and for mutual upbuilding. 20 Do not, for the sake of food, destroy the work of God. Everything is indeed clean, but it is wrong for you to make others fall by what you eat; 21 it is good not to eat meat or drink wine or do anything that makes your

---

[q]Gk *it*   [r]Or *conviction*   [s]Other ancient authorities read *for God*
[t]Gk *brother*   [u]Other ancient authorities read *of Christ*   [v]Or *confess*
[w]Other ancient authorities lack *to God*   [x]Gk *of a brother*

[50]Exod 20:13–15, 17; Deut 5:17–19, 21   [51]Lev 19:18   [52]Isa 45:23

brother or sister[y] stumble.[z] 22 The faith that you have, have as your own conviction before God. Blessed are those who have no reason to condemn themselves because of what they approve. 23 But those who have doubts are condemned if they eat, because they do not act from faith;[a] for whatever does not proceed from faith[a] is sin.[b]

15 We who are strong ought to put up with the failings of the weak, and not to please ourselves. 2 Each of us must please our neighbor for the good purpose of building up the neighbor. 3 For Christ did not please himself; but, as it is written, "The insults of those who insult you have fallen on me."[53] 4 For whatever was written in former days was written for our instruction, so that by steadfastness and by the encouragement of the scriptures we might have hope. 5 May the God of steadfastness and encouragement grant you to live in harmony with one another, in accordance with Christ Jesus, 6 so that together you may with one voice glorify the God and Father of our Lord Jesus Christ.

7 Welcome one another, therefore, just as Christ has welcomed you, for the glory of God. 8 For I tell you that Christ has become a servant of the circumcised on behalf of the truth of God in order that he might confirm the promises given to the patriarchs, 9 and in order that the Gentiles might glorify God for his mercy. As it is written,

"Therefore I will confess[c] you
among the Gentiles,
and sing praises to your name";[54]

10 and again he says,

"Rejoice, O Gentiles, with his
people";[55]

11 and again,

"Praise the Lord, all you Gentiles,
and let all the peoples praise
him";[56]

12 and again Isaiah says,

"The root of Jesse shall come,
the one who rises to rule the
Gentiles;[57]
in him the Gentiles shall hope."

13 May the God of hope fill you with all joy and peace in believing, so that you may abound in hope by the power of the Holy Spirit.

14 I myself feel confident about you, my brothers and sisters,[d] that you yourselves are full of goodness, filled with all knowledge, and able to instruct one another. 15 Nevertheless on some points I have written to you rather boldly by way of reminder, because of the grace given me by God 16 to be a minister of Christ Jesus to the Gentiles in the priestly service of the gospel of God, so that the offering of the Gentiles may be acceptable, sanctified by the Holy Spirit. 17 In Christ Jesus, then, I have reason to boast of my work for God. 18 For I will not venture to speak of anything except what Christ has accomplished[e] through me to win obedience from the Gentiles, by word and deed, 19 by the power of signs and wonders, by the power of the Spirit of God,[f] so that from Jerusalem and as far around as Illyricum I have fully proclaimed the good news[g] of Christ. 20 Thus I make it my ambition to proclaim the good news,[e] not where Christ has already been named, so that I do not build on someone else's foundation, 21 but as it is written,

"Those who have never been told
of him shall see,
and those who have never heard
of him shall understand."[58]

22 This is the reason that I have so often been hindered from coming to you. 23 But now, with no further place for me in these regions, I desire, as I have for many years, to come to you 24 when I go to Spain. For I do hope to see you on my journey and to be sent on by you, once I have enjoyed your company for a little while. 25 At present, however, I am going to Jerusalem in a ministry to the saints; 26 for Macedonia and Achaia have been pleased to share their resources with the poor among the saints at Jerusalem. 27 They were pleased to do this, and indeed they owe it to them; for if the Gentiles have come to share in their spiritual blessings, they ought also to be of service to them in material things. 28 So, when I have completed this, and have delivered to them what has

---

[y]Gk brother [z]Other ancient authorities add or be upset or be weakened [a]Or conviction [b]Other authorities, some ancient, add here 16.25-27 [c]Or thank [d]Gk brothers [e]Gk speak of those things that Christ has not accomplished [f]Other ancient authorities read of the Spirit or of the Holy Spirit [g]Or gospel

[53]Ps 69:9 [54]Ps 18:49; 2 Sam 22:50 [55]Deut 32:43 [56]Ps 117:1 [57]Isa 11:10 [58]Isa 52:15

been collected,[h] I will set out by way of you to Spain; 29 and I know that when I come to you, I will come in the fullness of the blessing[i] of Christ.

30 I appeal to you, brothers and sisters,[j] by our Lord Jesus Christ and by the love of the Spirit, to join me in earnest prayer to God on my behalf, 31 that I may be rescued from the unbelievers in Judea, and that my ministry[k] to Jerusalem may be acceptable to the saints, 32 so that by God's will I may come to you with joy and be refreshed in your company. 33 The God of peace be with all of you.[l] Amen.

16 I commend to you our sister Phoebe, a deacon[m] of the church at Cenchreae, 2 so that you may welcome her in the Lord as is fitting for the saints, and help her in whatever she may require from you, for she has been a benefactor of many and of myself as well.

3 Greet Prisca and Aquila, who work with me in Christ Jesus, 4 and who risked their necks for my life, to whom not only I give thanks, but also all the churches of the Gentiles. 5 Greet also the church in their house. Greet my beloved Epaenetus, who was the first convert[n] in Asia for Christ. 6 Greet Mary, who has worked very hard among you. 7 Greet Andronicus and Junia,[o] my relatives[p] who were in prison with me; they are prominent among the apostles, and they were in Christ before I was. 8 Greet Ampliatus, my beloved in the Lord. 9 Greet Urbanus, our co-worker in Christ, and my beloved Stachys. 10 Greet Apelles, who is approved in Christ. Greet those who belong to the family of Aristobulus. 11 Greet my relative[q] Herodion. Greet those in the Lord who belong to the family of Narcissus. 12 Greet those workers in the Lord, Tryphaena and Tryphosa. Greet the beloved Persis, who has worked hard in the Lord. 13 Greet Rufus, chosen in the Lord; and greet his mother—a mother to me also. 14 Greet Asyncritus, Phlegon, Hermes, Patrobas, Hermas, and the brothers and sisters[j] who are with them. 15 Greet Philologus, Julia, Nereus

and his sister, and Olympas, and all the saints who are with them. 16 Greet one another with a holy kiss. All the churches of Christ greet you.

17 I urge you, brothers and sisters,[j] to keep an eye on those who cause dissensions and offenses, in opposition to the teaching that you have learned; avoid them. 18 For such people do not serve our Lord Christ, but their own appetites,[r] and by smooth talk and flattery they deceive the hearts of the simple-minded. 19 For while your obedience is known to all, so that I rejoice over you, I want you to be wise in what is good and guileless in what is evil. 20 The God of peace will shortly crush Satan under your feet. The grace of our Lord Jesus Christ be with you.[r]

21 Timothy, my co-worker, greets you; so do Lucius and Jason and Sosipater, my relatives.[p]

22 I Tertius, the writer of this letter, greet you in the Lord.[t]

23 Gaius, who is host to me and to the whole church, greets you. Erastus, the city treasurer, and our brother Quartus, greet you.[u]

25 Now to God[v] who is able to strengthen you according to my gospel and the proclamation of Jesus Christ, according to the revelation of the mystery that was kept secret for long ages 26 but is now disclosed, and through the prophetic writings is made known to all the Gentiles, according to the command of the eternal God, to bring about the obedience of faith— 27 to the only wise God, through Jesus Christ, to whom[w] be the glory forever! Amen.[x]

---

[h]Gk *have sealed to them this fruit*   [i]Other ancient authorities add *of the gospel*   [j]Gk *brothers*   [k]Other ancient authorities read *my bringing of a gift*   [l]One ancient authority adds 16.25-27 here   [m]Or *minister*   [n]Gk *first fruits*   [o]Or *Junias*; other ancient authorities read *Julia*   [p]Or *compatriots*   [q]Or *compatriot*   [r]Gk *their own belly*   [s]Other ancient authorities lack this sentence   [t]Or *I Tertius, writing this letter in the Lord, greet you*   [u]Other ancient authorities add verse 24, *The grace of our Lord Jesus Christ be with all of you. Amen.*   [v]Gk *the one*   [w]Other ancient authorities lack *to whom*. The verse then reads, *to the only wise God be the glory through Jesus Christ forever. Amen.*   [x]Other ancient authorities lack 16.25-27 or include it after 14.23 or 15.33; others put verse 24 after verse 27

The First Letter to the Corinthians

Paul himself established the church in Corinth, the capital of the Roman province of Achaia (in modern-day Greece), along with his two companions Timothy and Silvanus. The three of them spent considerable time in the city (a year and a half, according to Acts 18:11), preaching the gospel and teaching their converts.

After leaving Corinth, Paul journeyed across the Aegean to the city of Ephesus. While there, he heard word concerning his Corinthian converts from several persons called "Chloe's people" (possibly slaves of a prominent Corinthian woman named Chloe, who were conducting business in Ephesus; 1:11); moreover, he received a letter from members of the congregation who had pressing ethical concerns (cf. 7:1). From Paul's perspective, the news he learned from these sources was not good. He wrote the letter of 1 Corinthians to deal with the problems.

The church had grown fragmented, as different leaders asserted themselves, each claiming special spiritual powers, each acquiring a following (chaps. 1–4). The resultant disunity of the community manifested itself in numerous ways: some members were taking others to court (over what, we are not told; chap. 6); during the communal meals, some were gorging themselves and getting drunk, others had to come late and got nothing to eat (chap. 11); the worship services were chaotic, as different members tried to manifest their spiritual abilities, especially the ability to speak in "tongues" (i.e., unknown languages given by God), more loudly and forcefully than the others (chaps. 12–14). And there were other ethical problems; some men were visiting prostitutes and bragging about it in church (chap. 6); one man was sleeping with his stepmother (chap. 5).

Paul addresses these issues one by one in the letter. But near the end he gets to the heart of the matter. The sundry problems had arisen because the Corinthians did not understand the full meaning of the gospel. Having put their faith in Christ, many Corinthians believed that the salvation they had received was already complete, that they were already living an exalted spiritual life with Christ, ruling with him, not subject to the powers of sin and death that were in the world. Their physical and social lives were therefore of no ultimate consequence to them. Paul, however, thought otherwise. Those who believe in Christ do indeed have a right standing with God, but evil is still present in the world and will continue to be so until the end of the age, when Christ returns to destroy all that is opposed to God and to raise all believers out of their mortal, sinful bodies into bodies that are imperishable and perfect (chap. 15).

Until that time, according to Paul, believers do not yet reign in the heavenly places with Christ; instead, they still partake of this weak and sinful existence. The Corinthians were to realize that they lived in an age of sin and death, and they were to refrain from participating in it. They were to manifest love for one another and to maintain an upright demeanor for those who were outside the church. Above all, they were to await the return of Christ from heaven, when he would dispose of this evil world and bring his followers into his glorious kingdom.

From the New Revised Standard Version Bible, © 1989.

1 Paul, called to be an apostle of Christ Jesus by the will of God, and our brother Sosthenes,

2 To the church of God that is in Corinth, to those who are sanctified in Christ Jesus, called to be saints, together with all those who in every place call on the name of our Lord Jesus Christ, both their Lord[a] and ours:

3 Grace to you and peace from God our Father and the Lord Jesus Christ.

4 I give thanks to my[b] God always for you because of the grace of God that has been given you in Christ Jesus, 5 for in every way you have been enriched in him, in speech and knowledge of every kind— 6 just as the testimony of[c] Christ has been strengthened among you— 7 so that you are not lacking in any spiritual gift as you wait for the revealing of our Lord Jesus Christ. 8 He will also strengthen you to the end, so that you may be blameless on the day of our Lord Jesus Christ. 9 God is faithful; by him you were called into the fellowship of his Son, Jesus Christ our Lord.

10 Now I appeal to you, brothers and sisters,[d] by the name of our Lord Jesus Christ, that all of you be in agreement and that there be no divisions among you, but that you be united in the same mind and the same purpose. 11 For it has been reported to me by Chloe's people that there are quarrels among you, my brothers and sisters.[e] 12 What I mean is that each of you says, "I belong to Paul," or "I belong to Apollos," or "I belong to Cephas," or "I belong to Christ." 13 Has Christ been divided? Was Paul crucified for you? Or were you baptized in the name of Paul? 14 I thank God[f] that I baptized none of you except Crispus and Gaius, 15 so that no one can say that you were baptized in my name. 16 (I did baptize also the household of Stephanas; beyond that, I do not know whether I baptized anyone else.) 17 For Christ did not send me to baptize but to proclaim the gospel, and not with eloquent wisdom, so that the cross of Christ might not be emptied of its power.

18 For the message about the cross is foolishness to those who are perishing, but to us who are being saved it is the power of God. 19 For it is written,

"I will destroy the wisdom of the
wise,

and the discernment of the
discerning I will thwart."[1]

20 Where is the one who is wise? Where is the scribe? Where is the debater of this age? Has not God made foolish the wisdom of the world? 21 For since, in the wisdom of God, the world did not know God through wisdom, God decided, through the foolishness of our proclamation, to save those who believe. 22 For Jews demand signs and Greeks desire wisdom, 23 but we proclaim Christ crucified, a stumbling block to Jews and foolishness to Gentiles, 24 but to those who are the called, both Jews and Greeks, Christ the power of God and the wisdom of God. 25 For God's foolishness is wiser than human wisdom, and God's weakness is stronger than human strength.

26 Consider your own call, brothers and sisters:[d] not many of you were wise by human standards,[g] not many were powerful, not many were of noble birth. 27 But God chose what is foolish in the world to shame the wise; God chose what is weak in the world to shame the strong; 28 God chose what is low and despised in the world, things that are not, to reduce to nothing things that are, 29 so that no one[h] might boast in the presence of God. 30 He is the source of your life in Christ Jesus, who became for us wisdom from God, and righteousness and sanctification and redemption, 31 in order that, as it is written, "Let the one who boasts, boast in[i] the Lord."[2]

2 When I came to you, brothers and sisters,[d] I did not come proclaiming the mystery[j] of God to you in lofty words or wisdom. 2 For I decided to know nothing among you except Jesus Christ, and him crucified. 3 And I came to you in weakness and in fear and in much trembling. 4 My speech and my proclamation were not with plausible words of wisdom,[k] but with a demonstration of the Spirit and of power, 5 so that your faith might rest not on human wisdom but on the power of God.

6 Yet among the mature we do speak wisdom,

[a]Gk theirs [b]Other ancient authorities lack my [c]Or to
[d]Gk brothers [e]Gk my brothers [f]Other ancient authorities read I am thankful [g]Gk according to the flesh [h]Gk no flesh [i]Or of [j]Other ancient authorities read testimony [k]Other ancient authorities read the persuasiveness of wisdom

[1]Isa 29:14 [2]Jer 9:24

though it is not a wisdom of this age or of the rulers of this age, who are doomed to perish. 7 But we speak God's wisdom, secret and hidden, which God decreed before the ages for our glory. 8 None of the rulers of this age understood this; for if they had, they would not have crucified the Lord of glory. 9 But, as it is written,

> "What no eye has seen, nor ear
> heard,
> nor the human heart conceived,
> what God has prepared for those
> who love him"—[3]

10 these things God has revealed to us through the Spirit; for the Spirit searches everything, even the depths of God. 11 For what human being knows what is truly human except the human spirit that is within? So also no one comprehends what is truly God's except the Spirit of God. 12 Now we have received not the spirit of the world, but the Spirit that is from God, so that we may understand the gifts bestowed on us by God. 13 And we speak of these things in words not taught by human wisdom but taught by the Spirit, interpreting spiritual things to those who are spiritual.[1]

14 Those who are unspiritual[m] do not receive the gifts of God's Spirit, for they are foolishness to them, and they are unable to understand them because they are spiritually discerned. 15 Those who are spiritual discern all things, and they are themselves subject to no one else's scrutiny.

16   "For who has known the mind of
     the Lord
     so as to instruct him?"[4]

But we have the mind of Christ.

3 And so, brothers and sisters,[n] I could not speak to you as spiritual people, but rather as people of the flesh, as infants in Christ. 2 I fed you with milk, not solid food, for you were not ready for solid food. Even now you are still not ready, 3 for you are still of the flesh. For as long as there is jealousy and quarreling among you, are you not of the flesh, and behaving according to human inclinations? 4 For when one says, "I belong to Paul," and another, "I belong to Apollos," are you not merely human?

5 What then is Apollos? What is Paul? Servants through whom you came to believe, as the Lord assigned to each. 6 I planted, Apollos watered, but God gave the growth. 7 So neither the one

who plants nor the one who waters is anything, but only God who gives the growth. 8 The one who plants and the one who waters have a common purpose, and each will receive wages according to the labor of each. 9 For we are God's servants, working together; you are God's field, God's building.

10 According to the grace of God given to me, like a skilled master builder I laid a foundation, and someone else is building on it. Each builder must choose with care how to build on it. 11 For no one can lay any foundation other than the one that has been laid; that foundation is Jesus Christ. 12 Now if anyone builds on the foundation with gold, silver, precious stones, wood, hay, straw— 13 the work of each builder will become visible, for the Day will disclose it, because it will be revealed with fire, and the fire will test what sort of work each has done. 14 If what has been built on the foundation survives, the builder will receive a reward. 15 If the work is burned up, the builder will suffer loss; the builder will be saved, but only as through fire.

16 Do you not know that you are God's temple and that God's Spirit dwells in you?[o] 17 If anyone destroys God's temple, God will destroy that person. For God's temple is holy, and you are that temple.

18 Do not deceive yourselves. If you think that you are wise in this age, you should become fools so that you may become wise. 19 For the wisdom of this world is foolishness with God. For it is written,

> "He catches the wise in their
> craftiness,"[5]

20 and again,

> "The Lord knows the thoughts of
> the wise,
> that they are futile."[6]

21 So let no one boast about human leaders. For all things are yours, 22 whether Paul or Apollos or Cephas or the world or life or death or the present or the future—all belong to you, 23 and you belong to Christ, and Christ belongs to God.

---

[1] Or *interpreting spiritual things in spiritual language*, or *comparing spiritual things with spiritual*   [m] Or *natural*   [n] Gk *brothers*
[o] In verses 16 and 17 the Greek word for *you* is plural

---

[3] Isa 64:4 52:15   [4] Isa 40:13   [5] Job 5:13   [6] Ps 94:11

4 Think of us in this way, as servants of Christ and stewards of God's mysteries. 2 Moreover, it is required of stewards that they be found trustworthy. 3 But with me it is a very small thing that I should be judged by you or by any human court. I do not even judge myself. 4 I am not aware of anything against myself, but I am not thereby acquitted. It is the Lord who judges me. 5 Therefore do not pronounce judgment before the time, before the Lord comes, who will bring to light the things now hidden in darkness and will disclose the purposes of the heart. Then each one will receive commendation from God.

factions 6 I have applied all this to Apollos and myself for your benefit, brothers and sisters,[p] so that you may learn through us the meaning of the saying, "Nothing beyond what is written," so that none of you will be puffed up in favor of one against another. 7 For who sees anything different in you?[q] What do you have that you did not receive? And if you received it, why do you boast as if it were not a gift?

8 Already you have all you want! Already you have become rich! Quite apart from us you have become kings! Indeed, I wish that you had become kings, so that we might be kings with you! 9 For I think that God has exhibited us apostles as last of all, as though sentenced to death, because we have become a spectacle to the world, to angels and to mortals. 10 We are fools for the sake of Christ, but you are wise in Christ. We are weak, but you are strong. You are held in honor, but we in disrepute. 11 To the present hour we are hungry and thirsty, we are poorly clothed and beaten and homeless, 12 and we grow weary from the work of our own hands. When reviled, we bless; when persecuted, we endure; 13 when slandered, we speak kindly. We have become like the rubbish of the world, the dregs of all things, to this very day.

14 I am not writing this to make you ashamed, but to admonish you as my beloved children. 15 For though you might have ten thousand guardians in Christ, you do not have many fathers. Indeed, in Christ Jesus I became your father through the gospel. 16 I appeal to you, then, be imitators of me. 17 For this reason I sent[r] you Timothy, who is my beloved and faithful child in the Lord, to remind you of my ways in Christ Jesus, as I teach them everywhere in every church. 18 But some of you, thinking that I am not coming

to you, have become arrogant. 19 But I will come to you soon, if the Lord wills, and I will find out not the talk of these arrogant people but their power. 20 For the kingdom of God depends not on talk but on power. 21 What would you prefer? Am I to come to you with a stick, or with love in a spirit of gentleness?

5 It is actually reported that there is sexual immorality among you, and of a kind that is not found even among pagans; for a man is living with his father's wife. 2 And you are arrogant! Should you not rather have mourned, so that he who has done this would have been removed from among you?

3 For though absent in body, I am present in spirit; and as if present I have already pronounced judgment 4 in the name of the Lord Jesus on the man who has done such a thing.[s] When you are assembled, and my spirit is present with the power of our Lord Jesus, 5 you are to hand this man over to Satan for the destruction of the flesh, so that his spirit may be saved in the day of the Lord.[t]

6 Your boasting is not a good thing. Do you not know that a little yeast leavens the whole batch of dough? 7 Clean out the old yeast so that you may be a new batch, as you really are unleavened. For our paschal lamb, Christ, has been sacrificed. 8 Therefore, let us celebrate the festival, not with the old yeast, the yeast of malice and evil, but with the unleavened bread of sincerity and truth.

9 I wrote to you in my letter not to associate with sexually immoral persons— 10 not at all meaning the immoral of this world, or the greedy and robbers, or idolaters, since you would then need to go out of the world. 11 But now I am writing to you not to associate with anyone who bears the name of brother or sister[u] who is sexually immoral or greedy, or is an idolater, reviler, drunkard, or robber. Do not even eat with such a one. 12 For what have I to do with judging those outside? Is it not those who are inside that you are to judge? 13 God will judge those outside. "Drive out the wicked person from among you."[7]

[p]Gk *brothers* [q]Or *Who makes you different from another?* [r]Or *am sending* [s]Or *on the man who has done such a thing in the name of the Lord Jesus* [t]Other ancient authorities add *Jesus* [u]Gk *brother*

[7]Deut 17:7

Using ancient medical terms?

6

When any of you has a grievance against another, do you dare to take it to court before the unrighteous, instead of taking it before the saints? 2 Do you not know that the saints will judge the world? And if the world is to be judged by you, are you incompetent to try trivial cases? 3 Do you not know that we are to judge angels—*No* to say nothing of ordinary matters? 4 If you have *worldly* ordinary cases, then, do you appoint as judges those who have no standing in the church? 5 I say this to your shame. Can it be that there is no one among you wise enough to decide between one believer[v] and another, 6 but a believer[v] goes to court against a believer[v]—and before unbelievers at that?

7 In fact, to have lawsuits at all with one another is already a defeat for you. Why not rather be wronged? Why not rather be defrauded? 8 But you yourselves wrong and defraud—and believers[w] at that.

9 Do you not know that wrongdoers will not inherit the kingdom of God? Do not be deceived! Fornicators, idolaters, adulterers, male prostitutes, sodomites, 10 thieves, the greedy, drunkards, revilers, robbers—none of these will inherit the kingdom of God. 11 And this is what some of you used to be. But you were washed, you were sanctified, you were justified in the name of the Lord Jesus Christ and in the Spirit of our God.

12 "All things are lawful for me," but not all things are beneficial. "All things are lawful for me," but I will not be dominated by anything. 13 "Food is meant for the stomach and the stomach for food,"[x] and God will destroy both one and the other. The body is meant not for fornication but for the Lord, and the Lord for the body. 14 And God raised the Lord and will also raise us by his power. 15 Do you not know that your bodies are members of Christ? Should I therefore take the members of Christ and make them members of a prostitute? Never! 16 Do you not know that whoever is united to a prostitute becomes one body with her? For it is said, "The two shall be one flesh."[8] 17 But anyone united to the Lord becomes one spirit with him. 18 Shun fornication! Every sin that a person commits is outside the body; but the fornicator sins against the body itself. 19 Or do you not know that your body is a temple[y] of the Holy Spirit within you, which you

Antinomianism

have from God, and that you are not your own? 20 For you were bought with a price; therefore glorify God in your body.

(7: Don't change your state / what you are doing)

7

Now concerning the matters about which you wrote: "It is well for a man not to touch a woman." 2 But because of cases of sexual immorality, each man should have his own wife and each woman her own husband. 3 The husband should give to his wife her conjugal rights, and likewise the wife to her husband. 4 For the wife does not have authority over her own body, but the husband does; likewise the husband does not have authority over his own body, but the wife does. 5 Do not deprive one another except perhaps by agreement for a set time, to devote yourselves to prayer, and then come together again, so that Satan may not tempt you because of your lack of self-control. 6 This I say by way of concession, not of command. 7 I wish that all were as I myself am. But each has a particular gift from God, one having one kind and another a different kind.

8 To the unmarried and the widows I say that it is well for them to remain unmarried as I am. 9 But if they are not practicing self-control, they should marry. For it is better to marry than to be aflame with passion.

10 To the married I give this command—not I but the Lord—that the wife should not separate from her husband 11 (but if she does separate, let her remain unmarried or else be reconciled to her husband), and that the husband should not divorce his wife.

12 To the rest I say—I and not the Lord—that if any believer[z] has a wife who is an unbeliever, and she consents to live with him, he should not divorce her. 13 And if any woman has a husband who is an unbeliever, and he consents to live with her, she should not divorce him. 14 For the unbelieving husband is made holy through his wife, and the unbelieving wife is made holy through her husband. Otherwise, your children would be unclean, but as it is, they are holy. 15 But if the unbelieving partner separates, let it be so; in such a case the brother or sister is not bound. It is to peace

Prostitutes

---

[v]Gk *brother* [w]Gk *brothers* [x]The quotation may extend to the word *other* [y]Or *sanctuary* [z]Gk *brother*

---

[8]Gen 2:24

that God has called you.[a] 16 Wife, for all you know, you might save your husband. Husband, for all you know, you might save your wife.

17 However that may be, let each of you lead the life that the Lord has assigned, to which God called you. This is my rule in all the churches. 18 Was anyone at the time of his call already circumcised? Let him not seek to remove the marks of circumcision. Was anyone at the time of his call uncircumcised? Let him not seek circumcision. 19 Circumcision is nothing, and uncircumcision is nothing; but obeying the commandments of God is everything. 20 Let each of you remain in the condition in which you were called.

21 Were you a slave when called? Do not be concerned about it. Even if you can gain your freedom, make use of your present condition now more than ever.[b] 22 For whoever was called in the Lord as a slave is a freed person belonging to the Lord, just as whoever was free when called is a slave of Christ. 23 You were bought with a price; do not become slaves of human masters. 24 In whatever condition you were called, brothers and sisters,[c] there remain with God.

25 Now concerning virgins, I have no command of the Lord, but I give my opinion as one who by the Lord's mercy is trustworthy. 26 I think that, in view of the impending[d] crisis, it is well for you to remain as you are. 27 Are you bound to a wife? Do not seek to be free. Are you free from a wife? Do not seek a wife. 28 But if you marry, you do not sin, and if a virgin marries, she does not sin. Yet those who marry will experience distress in this life,[e] and I would spare you that. 29 I mean, brothers and sisters,[c] the appointed time has grown short; from now on, let even those who have wives be as though they had none, 30 and those who mourn as though they were not mourning, and those who rejoice as though they were not rejoicing, and those who buy as though they had no possessions, 31 and those who deal with the world as though they had no dealings with it. For the present form of this world is passing away.

32 I want you to be free from anxieties. The unmarried man is anxious about the affairs of the Lord, how to please the Lord; 33 but the married man is anxious about the affairs of the world, how to please his wife, 34 and his interests are divided. And the unmarried woman and the virgin are anxious about the affairs of the Lord, so that they may be holy in body and spirit; but the married woman is anxious about the affairs of the world, how to please her husband. 35 I say this for your own benefit, not to put any restraint upon you, but to promote good order and unhindered devotion to the Lord.

36 If anyone thinks that he is not behaving properly toward his fiancée,[f] if his passions are strong, and so it has to be, let him marry as he wishes; it is no sin. Let them marry. 37 But if someone stands firm in his resolve, being under no necessity but having his own desire under control, and has determined in his own mind to keep her as his fiancée,[f] he will do well. 38 So then, he who marries his fiancée[f] does well; and he who refrains from marriage will do better.

39 A wife is bound as long as her husband lives. But if the husband dies,[g] she is free to marry anyone she wishes, only in the Lord. 40 But in my judgment she is more blessed if she remains as she is. And I think that I too have the Spirit of God.

8 Now concerning food sacrificed to idols: we know that "all of us possess knowledge." Knowledge puffs up, but love builds up. 2 Anyone who claims to know something does not yet have the necessary knowledge; 3 but anyone who loves God is known by him.

4 Hence, as to the eating of food offered to idols, we know that "no idol in the world really exists," and that "there is no God but one." 5 Indeed, even though there may be so-called gods in heaven or on earth—as in fact there are many gods and many lords— 6 yet for us there is one God, the Father, from whom are all things and for whom we exist, and one Lord, Jesus Christ, through whom are all things and through whom we exist.

7 It is not everyone, however, who has this knowledge. Since some have become so accustomed to idols until now, they still think of the food they eat as food offered to an idol; and their conscience, being weak, is defiled. 8 "Food will not bring us close to God."[h] We are no worse off if we do not eat, and no better off if we do. 9 But

---

[a]Other ancient authorities read *us*   [b]Or *avail yourself of the opportunity*   [c]Gk *brothers*   [d]Or *present*   [e]Gk *in the flesh*   [f]Gk *virgin*   [g]Gk *falls asleep*   [h]The quotation may extend to the end of the verse

take care that this liberty of yours does not somehow become a stumbling block to the weak. 10 For if others see you, who possess knowledge, eating in the temple of an idol, might they not, since their conscience is weak, be encouraged to the point of eating food sacrificed to idols? 11 So by your knowledge those weak believers for whom Christ died are destroyed.[i] 12 But when you thus sin against members of your family,[j] and wound their conscience when it is weak, you sin against Christ. 13 Therefore, if food is a cause of their falling,[k] I will never eat meat, so that I may not cause one of them[l] to fall.

You should Pay me, but I'm not looking for

9 Am I not free? Am I not an apostle? Have I not seen Jesus our Lord? Are you not my *for* work in the Lord? 2 If I am not an apostle to others, at least I am to you; for you are the seal of my apostleship in the Lord.

Just as I

3 This is my defense to those who would examine me. 4 Do we not have the right to our food and *did* drink? 5 Do we not have the right to be accompanied by a believing wife,[m] as do the other apostles and the brothers of the Lord and Cephas? 6 Or is it only Barnabas and I who have no right to refrain *should* from working for a living? 7 Who at any time pays the expenses for doing military service? Who plants a vineyard and does not eat any of its fruit? Or who tends a flock and does not get any of its milk?

8 Do I say this on human authority? Does not the law also say the same? 9 For it is written in the law of Moses, "You shall not muzzle an ox while it is treading out the grain."[9] Is it for oxen that God is concerned? 10 Or does he not speak entirely for our sake? It was indeed written for our sake, for whoever plows should plow in hope and whoever threshes should thresh in hope of a share in the crop. 11 If we have sown spiritual good among you, is it too much if we reap your material benefits? 12 If others share this rightful claim on you, do not we still more?

Nevertheless, we have not made use of this right, but we endure anything rather than put an obstacle in the way of the gospel of Christ. 13 Do you not know that those who are employed in the temple service get their food from the temple, and those who serve at the altar share in what is sacrificed on the altar? 14 In the same way, the Lord

commanded that those who proclaim the gospel should get their living by the gospel.

15 But I have made no use of any of these rights, nor am I writing this so that they may be applied in my case. Indeed, I would rather die than that— no one will deprive me of my ground for boasting! 16 If I proclaim the gospel, this gives me no ground for boasting, for an obligation is laid on me, and woe to me if I do not proclaim the gospel! 17 For if I do this of my own will, I have a reward; but if not of my own will, I am entrusted with a commission. 18 What then is my reward? Just this: that in my proclamation I may make the gospel free of charge, so as not to make full use of my rights in the gospel.

19 For though I am free with respect to all, I have made myself a slave to all, so that I might win more of them. 20 To the Jews I became as a Jew, in order to win Jews. To those under the law I became as one under the law (though I myself am not under the law) so that I might win those under the law. 21 To those outside the law I became as one outside the law (though I am not free from God's law but am under Christ's law) so that I might win those outside the law. 22 To the weak I became weak, so that I might win the weak. I have become all things to all people, that I might by all means save some. 23 I do it all for the sake of the gospel, so that I may share in its blessings.

24 Do you not know that in a race the runners all compete, but only one receives the prize? Run in such a way that you may win it. 25 Athletes exercise self-control in all things; they do it to receive a perishable wreath, but we an imperishable one. 26 So I do not run aimlessly, nor do I box as though beating the air; 27 but I punish my body and enslave it, so that after proclaiming to others I myself should not be disqualified.

10 I do not want you to be unaware, brothers and sisters,[n] that our ancestors were all under the cloud, and all passed through the sea, 2 and all were baptized into Moses in the cloud and in the sea, 3 and all ate the same spiritual food,

[i]Gk *the weak brother . . . is destroyed*   [j]Gk *against the brothers*   [k]Gk *my brother's falling*   [l]Gk *cause my brother*   [m]Gk *a sister as wife*   [n]Gk *brothers*

[9]Deut 25:4

1-5 : Jewish groups

4 and all drank the same spiritual drink. For they drank from the spiritual rock that followed them, and the rock was Christ. 5 Nevertheless, God was not pleased with most of them, and they were struck down in the wilderness.

6 Now these things occurred as examples for us, so that we might not desire evil as they did. 7 Do not become idolaters as some of them did; as it is written, "The people sat down to eat and drink, and they rose up to play."[10] 8 We must not indulge in sexual immorality as some of them did, and twenty-three thousand fell in a single day. 9 We must not put Christ[o] to the test, as some of them did, and were destroyed by serpents. 10 And do not complain as some of them did, and were destroyed by the destroyer. 11 These things happened to them to serve as an example, and they were written down to instruct us, on whom the ends of the ages have come. 12 So if you think you are standing, watch out that you do not fall. 13 No testing has overtaken you that is not common to everyone. God is faithful, and he will not let you be tested beyond your strength, but with the testing he will also provide the way out so that you may be able to endure it.

14 Therefore, my dear friends,[p] flee from the worship of idols. 15 I speak as to sensible people; judge for yourselves what I say. 16 The cup of blessing that we bless, is it not a sharing in the blood of Christ? The bread that we break, is it not a sharing in the body of Christ? 17 Because there is one bread, we who are many are one body, for we all partake of the one bread. 18 Consider the people of Israel;[q] are not those who eat the sacrifices partners in the altar? 19 What do I imply then? That food sacrificed to idols is anything, or that an idol is anything? 20 No, I imply that what pagans sacrifice, they sacrifice to demons and not to God. I do not want you to be partners with demons. 21 You cannot drink the cup of the Lord and the cup of demons. You cannot partake of the table of the Lord and the table of demons. 22 Or are we provoking the Lord to jealousy? Are we stronger than he?

23 "All things are lawful," but not all things are beneficial. "All things are lawful," but not all things build up. 24 Do not seek your own advantage, but that of the other. 25 Eat whatever is sold in the meat market without raising any question on

the ground of conscience, 26 for "the earth and its fullness are the Lord's."[11] 27 If an unbeliever invites you to a meal and you are disposed to go, eat whatever is set before you without raising any question on the ground of conscience. 28 But if someone says to you, "This has been offered in sacrifice," then do not eat it, out of consideration for the one who informed you, and for the sake of conscience— 29 I mean the other's conscience, not your own. For why should my liberty be subject to the judgment of someone else's conscience? 30 If I partake with thankfulness, why should I be denounced because of that for which I give thanks?

31 So, whether you eat or drink, or whatever you do, do everything for the glory of God. 32 Give no offense to Jews or to Greeks or to the church of God, 33 just as I try to please everyone in everything I do, not seeking my own advantage, but that of many, so that they may be saved.

11
Be imitators of me, as I am of Christ.

2 I commend you because you remember me in everything and maintain the traditions just as I handed them on to you. 3 But I want you to understand that Christ is the head of every man, and the husband[r] is the head of his wife,[s] and God is the head of Christ. 4 Any man who prays or prophesies with something on his head disgraces his head, 5 but any woman who prays or prophesies with her head unveiled disgraces her head—it is one and the same thing as having her head shaved. 6 For if a woman will not veil herself, then she should cut off her hair; but if it is disgraceful for a woman to have her hair cut off or to be shaved, she should wear a veil. 7 For a man ought not to have his head veiled, since he is the image and reflection[t] of God; but woman is the reflection[t] of man. 8 Indeed, man was not made from woman, but woman from man. 9 Neither was man created for the sake of woman, but woman for the sake of man. 10 For this reason a woman ought to have a symbol of[u] authority on

---

[o]Other ancient authorities read *the Lord*   [p]Gk *my beloved*   [q]Gk *Israel according to the flesh*   [r]The same Greek word means *man* or *husband*   [s]Or *head of the woman*   [t]Or *glory*   [u]Gk lacks *a symbol of*

---

[10]Exod 32:6   [11]Ps 24:1

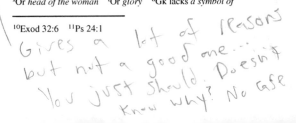

her head,[v] because of the angels. 11 Nevertheless, in the Lord woman is not independent of man or man independent of woman. 12 For just as woman came from man, so man comes through woman; but all things come from God. 13 Judge for yourselves: is it proper for a woman to pray to God with her head unveiled? 14 Does not nature itself teach you that if a man wears long hair, it is degrading to him, 15 but if a woman has long hair, it is her glory? For her hair is given to her for a covering. 16 But if anyone is disposed to be contentious—we have no such custom, nor do the churches of God.

17 Now in the following instructions I do not commend you, because when you come together it is not for the better but for the worse. 18 For, to begin with, when you come together as a church, I hear that there are divisions among you; and to some extent I believe it. 19 Indeed, there have to be factions among you, for only so will it become clear who among you are genuine. 20 When you come together, it is not really to eat the Lord's supper. 21 For when the time comes to eat, each of you goes ahead with your own supper, and one goes hungry and another becomes drunk. 22 What! Do you not have homes to eat and drink in? Or do you show contempt for the church of God and humiliate those who have nothing? What should I say to you? Should I commend you? In this matter I do not commend you!

23 For I received from the Lord what I also handed on to you, that the Lord Jesus on the night when he was betrayed took a loaf of bread, 24 and when he had given thanks, he broke it and said, "This is my body that is for[w] you. Do this in remembrance of me." 25 In the same way he took the cup also, after supper, saying, "This cup is the new covenant in my blood. Do this, as often as you drink it, in remembrance of me." 26 For as often as you eat this bread and drink the cup, you proclaim the Lord's death until he comes.

27 Whoever, therefore, eats the bread or drinks the cup of the Lord in an unworthy manner will be answerable for the body and blood of the Lord. 28 Examine yourselves, and only then eat of the bread and drink of the cup. 29 For all who eat and drink[x] without discerning the body,[y] eat and drink judgment against themselves. 30 For this reason many of you are weak and ill, and some have died.[z] 31 But if we judged ourselves, we would not be judged. 32 But when we are judged by the Lord, we are disciplined[a] so that we may not be condemned along with the world.

33 So then, my brothers and sisters,[b] when you come together to eat, wait for one another. 34 If you are hungry, eat at home, so that when you come together, it will not be for your condemnation. About the other things I will give instructions when I come.

12 Now concerning spiritual gifts,[c] brothers and sisters,[b] I do not want you to be uninformed. 2 You know that when you were pagans, you were enticed and led astray to idols that could not speak. 3 Therefore I want you to understand that no one speaking by the Spirit of God ever says "Let Jesus be cursed!" and no one can say "Jesus is Lord" except by the Holy Spirit.

gentile

4 Now there are varieties of gifts, but the same Spirit; 5 and there are varieties of services, but the same Lord; 6 and there are varieties of activities, but it is the same God who activates all of them in everyone. 7 To each is given the manifestation of the Spirit for the common good. 8 To one is given through the Spirit the utterance of wisdom, and to another the utterance of knowledge according to the same Spirit, 9 to another faith by the same Spirit, to another gifts of healing by the one Spirit, 10 to another the working of miracles, to another prophecy, to another the discernment of spirits, to another various kinds of tongues, to another the interpretation of tongues. 11 All these are activated by one and the same Spirit, who allots to each one individually just as the Spirit chooses.

12 For just as the body is one and has many members, and all the members of the body, though many, are one body, so it is with Christ. 13 For in the one Spirit we were all baptized into one body—Jews or Greeks, slaves or free—and we were all made to drink of one Spirit.

14 Indeed, the body does not consist of one member but of many. 15 If the foot would say, "Because I am not a hand, I do not belong to the

[v]Or *have freedom of choice regarding her head*   [w]Other ancient authorities read *is broken for*   [x]Other ancient authorities add *in an unworthy manner*,   [y]Other ancient authorities read *the Lord's body*   [z]Gk *fallen asleep*   [a]Or *When we are judged, we are being disciplined by the Lord*   [b]Gk *brothers*   [c]Or *spiritual persons*

body," that would not make it any less a part of the body. 16 And if the ear would say, "Because I am not an eye, I do not belong to the body," that would not make it any less a part of the body. 17 If the whole body were an eye, where would the hearing be? If the whole body were hearing, where would the sense of smell be? 18 But as it is, God arranged the members in the body, each one of them, as he chose. 19 If all were a single member, where would the body be? 20 As it is, there are many members, yet one body. 21 The eye cannot say to the hand, "I have no need of you," nor again the head to the feet, "I have no need of you." 22 On the contrary, the members of the body that seem to be weaker are indispensable, 23 and those members of the body that we think less honorable we clothe with greater honor, and our less respectable members are treated with greater respect; 24 whereas our more respectable members do not need this. But God has so arranged the body, giving the greater honor to the inferior member, 25 that there may be no dissension within the body, but the members may have the same care for one another. 26 If one member suffers, all suffer together with it; if one member is honored, all rejoice together with it.

27 Now you are the body of Christ and individually members of it. 28 And God has appointed in the church first apostles, second prophets, third teachers; then deeds of power, then gifts of healing, forms of assistance, forms of leadership, various kinds of tongues. 29 Are all apostles? Are all prophets? Are all teachers? Do all work miracles? 30 Do all possess gifts of healing? Do all speak in tongues? Do all interpret? 31 But strive for the greater gifts. And I will show you a still more excellent way.

13 If I speak in the tongues of mortals and of angels, but do not have love, I am a noisy gong or a clanging cymbal. 2 And if I have prophetic powers, and understand all mysteries and all knowledge, and if I have all faith, so as to remove mountains, but do not have love, I am nothing. 3 If I give away all my possessions, and if I hand over my body so that I may boast,[d] but do not have love, I gain nothing.

4 Love is patient; love is kind; love is not envious or boastful or arrogant 5 or rude. It does not insist on its own way; it is not irritable or resent-

ful; 6 it does not rejoice in wrongdoing, but rejoices in the truth. 7 It bears all things, believes all things, hopes all things, endures all things.

8 Love never ends. But as for prophecies, they will come to an end; as for tongues, they will cease; as for knowledge, it will come to an end. 9 For we know only in part, and we prophesy only in part; 10 but when the complete comes, the partial will come to an end. 11 When I was a child, I spoke like a child, I thought like a child, I reasoned like a child; when I became an adult, I put an end to childish ways. 12 For now we see in a mirror, dimly,[e] but then we will see face to face. Now I know only in part; then I will know fully, even as I have been fully known. 13 And now faith, hope, and love abide, these three; and the greatest of these is love.

14 Pursue love and strive for the spiritual gifts, and especially that you may prophesy. 2 For those who speak in a tongue do not speak to other people but to God; for nobody understands them, since they are speaking mysteries in the Spirit. 3 On the other hand, those who prophesy speak to other people for their upbuilding and encouragement and consolation. 4 Those who speak in a tongue build up themselves, but those who prophesy build up the church. 5 Now I would like all of you to speak in tongues, but even more to prophesy. One who prophesies is greater than one who speaks in tongues, unless someone interprets, so that the church may be built up.

6 Now, brothers and sisters,[f] if I come to you speaking in tongues, how will I benefit you unless I speak to you in some revelation or knowledge or prophecy or teaching? 7 It is the same way with lifeless instruments that produce sound, such as the flute or the harp. If they do not give distinct notes, how will anyone know what is being played? 8 And if the bugle gives an indistinct sound, who will get ready for battle? 9 So with yourselves; if in a tongue you utter speech that is not intelligible, how will anyone know what is being said? For you will be speaking into the air. 10 There are doubtless many different kinds of sounds in the world, and nothing is without sound. 11 If then I do not know the meaning of a sound, I

---

[d]Other ancient authorities read *body to be burned*   [e]Gk *in a riddle*   [f]Gk *brothers*

will be a foreigner to the speaker and the speaker a foreigner to me. 12 So with yourselves; since you are eager for spiritual gifts, strive to excel in them for building up the church.

13 Therefore, one who speaks in a tongue should pray for the power to interpret. 14 For if I pray in a tongue, my spirit prays but my mind is unproductive. 15 What should I do then? I will pray with the spirit, but I will pray with the mind also; I will sing praise with the spirit, but I will sing praise with the mind also. 16 Otherwise, if you say a blessing with the spirit, how can anyone in the position of an outsider say the "Amen" to your thanksgiving, since the outsider does not know what you are saying? 17 For you may give thanks well enough, but the other person is not built up. 18 I thank God that I speak in tongues more than all of you; 19 nevertheless, in church I would rather speak five words with my mind, in order to instruct others also, than ten thousand words in a tongue.

20 Brothers and sisters,[g] do not be children in your thinking; rather, be infants in evil, but in thinking be adults. 21 In the law it is written,

"By people of strange tongues
    and by the lips of foreigners
I will speak to this people;
    yet even then they will not
        listen to me,"[12]

says the Lord. 22 Tongues, then, are a sign not for believers but for unbelievers, while prophecy is not for unbelievers but for believers. 23 If, therefore, the whole church comes together and all speak in tongues, and outsiders or unbelievers enter, will they not say that you are out of your mind? 24 But if all prophesy, an unbeliever or outsider who enters is reproved by all and called to account by all. 25 After the secrets of the unbeliever's heart are disclosed, that person will bow down before God and worship him, declaring, "God is really among you."

26 What should be done then, my friends?[g] When you come together, each one has a hymn, a lesson, a revelation, a tongue, or an interpretation. Let all things be done for building up. 27 If anyone speaks in a tongue, let there be only two or at most three, and each in turn; and let one interpret. 28 But if there is no one to interpret, let them be silent in church and speak to themselves and to

God. 29 Let two or three prophets speak, and let the others weigh what is said. 30 If a revelation is made to someone else sitting nearby, let the first person be silent. 31 For you can all prophesy one by one, so that all may learn and all be encouraged. 32 And the spirits of prophets are subject to the prophets, 33 for God is a God not of disorder but of peace.

(As in all the churches of the saints, 34 women should be silent in the churches. For they are not permitted to speak, but should be subordinate, as the law also says. 35 If there is anything they desire to know, let them ask their husbands at home. For it is shameful for a woman to speak in church.[h] 36 Or did the word of God originate with you? Or are you the only ones it has reached?)

37 Anyone who claims to be a prophet, or to have spiritual powers, must acknowledge that what I am writing to you is a command of the Lord. 38 Anyone who does not recognize this is not to be recognized. 39 So, my friends,[i] be eager to prophesy, and do not forbid speaking in tongues; 40 but all things should be done decently and in order.

15 Now I would remind you, brothers and sisters,[g] of the good news[j] that I proclaimed to you, which you in turn received, in which also you stand, 2 through which also you are being saved, if you hold firmly to the message that I proclaimed to you—unless you have come to believe in vain.

3 For I handed on to you as of first importance what I in turn had received: that Christ died for our sins in accordance with the scriptures, 4 and that he was buried, and that he was raised on the third day in accordance with the scriptures, 5 and that he appeared to Cephas, then to the twelve. 6 Then he appeared to more than five hundred brothers and sisters[g] at one time, most of whom are still alive, though some have died.[k] 7 Then he appeared to James, then to all the apostles. 8 Last of all, as to one untimely born, he appeared also to me. 9 For I am the least of the apostles, unfit to be called an apostle, because I persecuted the church

---

[g]Gk *brothers*   [h]Other ancient authorities put verses 34-35 after verse 40   [i]Gk *my brothers*   [j]Or *gospel*   [k]Gk *fallen asleep*

---

[12]Isa 28:11–12

of God. 10 But by the grace of God I am what I am, and his grace toward me has not been in vain. On the contrary, I worked harder than any of them—though it was not I, but the grace of God that is with me. 11 Whether then it was I or they, so we proclaim and so you have come to believe. 12 Now if Christ is proclaimed as raised from the dead, how can some of you say there is no resurrection of the dead? 13 If there is no resurrection of the dead, then Christ has not been raised; 14 and if Christ has not been raised, then our proclamation has been in vain and your faith has been in vain. 15 We are even found to be misrepresenting God, because we testified of God that he raised Christ—whom he did not raise if it is true that the dead are not raised. 16 For if the dead are not raised, then Christ has not been raised. 17 If Christ has not been raised, your faith is futile and you are still in your sins. 18 Then those also who have died[l] in Christ have perished. 19 If for this life only we have hoped in Christ, we are of all people most to be pitied.

20 But in fact Christ has been raised from the dead, the first fruits of those who have died.[l] 21 For since death came through a human being, the resurrection of the dead has also come through a human being; 22 for as all die in Adam, so all will be made alive in Christ. 23 But each in his own order: Christ the first fruits, then at his coming those who belong to Christ. 24 Then comes the end,[m] when he hands over the kingdom to God the Father, after he has destroyed every ruler and every authority and power. 25 For he must reign until he has put all his enemies under his feet. 26 The last enemy to be destroyed is death. 27 For "God[n] has put all things in subjection under his feet."[13] But when it says, "All things are put in subjection," it is plain that this does not include the one who put all things in subjection under him. 28 When all things are subjected to him, then the Son himself will also be subjected to the one who put all things in subjection under him, so that God may be all in all.

29 Otherwise, what will those people do who receive baptism on behalf of the dead? If the dead are not raised at all, why are people baptized on their behalf?

30 And why are we putting ourselves in danger every hour? 31 I die every day! That is as certain, brothers and sisters,[o] as my boasting of you—a boast that I make in Christ Jesus our Lord. 32 If with merely human hopes I fought with wild animals at Ephesus, what would I have gained by it? If the dead are not raised,

"Let us eat and drink,
for tomorrow we die."[14]

33 Do not be deceived:

"Bad company ruins good
morals."

34 Come to a sober and right mind, and sin no more; for some people have no knowledge of God. I say this to your shame.

35 But someone will ask, "How are the dead raised? With what kind of body do they come?" 36 Fool! What you sow does not come to life unless it dies. 37 And as for what you sow, you do not sow the body that is to be, but a bare seed, perhaps of wheat or of some other grain. 38 But God gives it a body as he has chosen, and to each kind of seed its own body. 39 Not all flesh is alike, but there is one flesh for human beings, another for animals, another for birds, and another for fish. 40 There are both heavenly bodies and earthly bodies, but the glory of the heavenly is one thing, and that of the earthly is another. 41 There is one glory of the sun, and another glory of the moon, and another glory of the stars; indeed, star differs from star in glory.

42 So it is with the resurrection of the dead. What is sown is perishable, what is raised is imperishable. 43 It is sown in dishonor, it is raised in glory. It is sown in weakness, it is raised in power. 44 It is sown a physical body, it is raised a spiritual body. If there is a physical body, there is also a spiritual body. 45 Thus it is written, "The first man, Adam, became a living being";[15] the last Adam became a life-giving spirit. 46 But it is not the spiritual that is first, but the physical, and then the spiritual. 47 The first man was from the earth, a man of dust; the second man is[p] from heaven. 48 As was the man of dust, so are those who are of the dust; and as is the man of heaven, so are those

[l]Gk *fallen asleep*   [m]Or *Then come the rest*   [n]Gk *he*   [o]Gk *brothers*
[p]Other ancient authorities add *the Lord*

[13]Ps 8:6   [14]Isa 22:13   [15]Gen 2:7

who are of heaven. 49 Just as we have borne the image of the man of dust, we will[q] also bear the image of the man of heaven.

50 What I am saying, brothers and sisters,[r] is this: flesh and blood cannot inherit the kingdom of God, nor does the perishable inherit the imperishable. 51 Listen, I will tell you a mystery! We will not all die,[s] but we will all be changed, 52 in a moment, in the twinkling of an eye, at the last trumpet. For the trumpet will sound, and the dead will be raised imperishable, and we will be changed. 53 For this perishable body must put on imperishability, and this mortal body must put on immortality. 54 When this perishable body puts on imperishability, and this mortal body puts on immortality, then the saying that is written will be fulfilled:

> "Death has been swallowed up in
>   victory."[16]

55   "Where, O death, is your
>   victory?
>   Where, O death, is your
>   sting?"[17]

56 The sting of death is sin, and the power of sin is the law. 57 But thanks be to God, who gives us the victory through our Lord Jesus Christ.

58 Therefore, my beloved,[t] be steadfast, immovable, always excelling in the work of the Lord, because you know that in the Lord your labor is not in vain.

16 Now concerning the collection for the saints: you should follow the directions I gave to the churches of Galatia. 2 On the first day of every week, each of you is to put aside and save whatever extra you earn, so that collections need not be taken when I come. 3 And when I arrive, I will send any whom you approve with letters to take your gift to Jerusalem. 4 If it seems advisable that I should go also, they will accompany me.

5 I will visit you after passing through Macedonia—for I intend to pass through Macedonia—6 and perhaps I will stay with you or even spend the winter, so that you may send me on my way, wherever I go. 7 I do not want to see you now just in passing, for I hope to spend some time with you, if the Lord permits. 8 But I will stay in Ephesus until Pentecost, 9 for a wide door for effective work has opened to me, and there are many adversaries.

10 If Timothy comes, see that he has nothing to fear among you, for he is doing the work of the Lord just as I am; 11 therefore let no one despise him. Send him on his way in peace, so that he may come to me; for I am expecting him with the brothers.

12 Now concerning our brother Apollos, I strongly urged him to visit you with the other brothers, but he was not at all willing[u] to come now. He will come when he has the opportunity.

13 Keep alert, stand firm in your faith, be courageous, be strong. 14 Let all that you do be done in love.

15 Now, brothers and sisters,[r] you know that members of the household of Stephanas were the first converts in Achaia, and they have devoted themselves to the service of the saints; 16 I urge you to put yourselves at the service of such people, and of everyone who works and toils with them. 17 I rejoice at the coming of Stephanas and Fortunatus and Achaicus, because they have made up for your absence; 18 for they refreshed my spirit as well as yours. So give recognition to such persons.

19 The churches of Asia send greetings. Aquila and Prisca, together with the church in their house, greet you warmly in the Lord. 20 All the brothers and sisters[r] send greetings. Greet one another with a holy kiss.

21 I, Paul, write this greeting with my own hand. 22 Let anyone be accursed who has no love for the Lord. Our Lord, come![v] 23 The grace of the Lord Jesus be with you. 24 My love be with all of you in Christ Jesus.[w]

---

[q]Other ancient authorities read *let us*   [r]Gk *brothers*   [s]Gk *fall asleep*
[t]Gk *beloved brothers*   [u]Or *it was not at all God's will for him*
[v]Gk *Marana tha*. These Aramaic words can also be read *Maran atha*, meaning *Our Lord has come*   [w]Other ancient authorities add *Amen*

---

[16]Isa 25:8   [17]Hos 13:14

The Second Letter to the Corinthians

To speak of Paul's "second" letter to the Corinthians may be something of a misnomer, for in the opinion of many scholars, 2 Corinthians represents at least two different Pauline letters (or possibly four or five), which were later cut and pasted together for broader circulation, possibly by someone in the Corinthian community. The principal reason for this scholarly opinion is the drastic shift from the joyful and caring tone of chapters 1–9 to the harsh and condemnatory language of chapters 10–13. If this theory is right, then the final four chapters were taken from a letter that was written earlier than the one embodied in chapters 1–9. Neither letter, on this score, is preserved intact.

Establishing a plausible historical backdrop for each of the letter fragments can facilitate our understanding of their message. In 1 Corinthians 16:5–7 Paul had promised to pay the Corinthians another visit. He evidently fulfilled this promise prior to the writing of 2 Corinthians 1–9, because there he indicates that he does not wish to make "another" painful visit to them (2:1–4). This suggests that the second time he came things did not go well (he was there for the first time when he established the congregation, a visit that was by no means painful). It appears that while he was there, another group of apostles, whom he disparagingly calls the "super-apostles" (11:5), had arrived, claiming for themselves special supernatural gifts and powers that Paul himself could not match. Paul evidently left town in a huff.

He then fired off a letter attacking the super-apostles and all they stood for. In this letter, embodied in part in chapters 10–13, he reasserted some of the main points he had made in 1 Corinthians, but more forcefully and in response to the situation at hand. Contrary to the claims of the super-apostles, Christian existence in the present age is not one of glory and exaltation but of pain and suffering (12:9–10). The true apostle in particular experiences the pain of this world (11:20–31). Anyone who claims to live an exalted existence, therefore, is not a true apostle. Paul threatens now to come a third time in judgment (13:1–4).

He sent this letter through his companion Titus, and it evidently brought remarkable success. The Corinthians had a change of heart, returned to his fold (7:5–12), and punished a person who had publicly humiliated Paul on his second visit (2:5–11). Paul then wrote a friendly and grateful letter in response; most of this letter is now found in chapters 1–9. In it he reaffirms his conviction that, while this is an age dominated by the forces of evil, God's grace is sufficient for those who suffer (1:3–11). He urges his converts to look forward to the time when salvation will be complete, in which present affliction will be rewarded with "an eternal weight of glory beyond all measure" (4:17). This is the final word we hear from Paul concerning his Corinthian congregation; it is impossible for us to know whether the breach was completely mended or whether similar problems arose again later in their relationship with one another.

From the New Revised Standard Version Bible, © 1989.

1 Paul, an apostle of Christ Jesus by the will of God, and Timothy our brother,

To the church of God that is in Corinth, including all the saints throughout Achaia:

2 Grace to you and peace from God our Father and the Lord Jesus Christ.

3 Blessed be the God and Father of our Lord Jesus Christ, the Father of mercies and the God of all consolation, 4 who consoles us in all our affliction, so that we may be able to console those who are in any affliction with the consolation with which we ourselves are consoled by God. 5 For just as the sufferings of Christ are abundant for us, so also our consolation is abundant through Christ. 6 If we are being afflicted, it is for your consolation and salvation; if we are being consoled, it is for your consolation, which you experience when you patiently endure the same sufferings that we are also suffering. 7 Our hope for you is unshaken; for we know that as you share in our sufferings, so also you share in our consolation.

8 We do not want you to be unaware, brothers and sisters,[a] of the affliction we experienced in Asia; for we were so utterly, unbearably crushed that we despaired of life itself. 9 Indeed, we felt that we had received the sentence of death so that we would rely not on ourselves but on God who raises the dead. 10 He who rescued us from so deadly a peril will continue to rescue us; on him we have set our hope that he will rescue us again, 11 as you also join in helping us by your prayers, so that many will give thanks on our[b] behalf for the blessing granted us through the prayers of many.

12 Indeed, this is our boast, the testimony of our conscience: we have behaved in the world with frankness[c] and godly sincerity, not by earthly wisdom but by the grace of God—and all the more toward you. 13 For we write you nothing other than what you can read and also understand; I hope you will understand until the end— 14 as you have already understood us in part—that on the day of the Lord Jesus we are your boast even as you are our boast.

15 Since I was sure of this, I wanted to come to you first, so that you might have a double favor;[d] 16 I wanted to visit you on my way to Macedonia, and to come back to you from Macedonia and have

you send me on to Judea. 17 Was I vacillating when I wanted to do this? Do I make my plans according to ordinary human standards,[e] ready to say "Yes, yes" and "No, no" at the same time? 18 As surely as God is faithful, our word to you has not been "Yes and No." 19 For the Son of God, Jesus Christ, whom we proclaimed among you, Silvanus and Timothy and I, was not "Yes and No"; but in him it is always "Yes." 20 For in him every one of God's promises is a "Yes." For this reason it is through him that we say the "Amen," to the glory of God. 21 But it is God who establishes us with you in Christ and has anointed us, 22 by putting his seal on us and giving us his Spirit in our hearts as a first installment.

23 But I call on God as witness against me: it was to spare you that I did not come again to Corinth. 24 I do not mean to imply that we lord it over your faith; rather, we are workers with you for your joy, because you stand firm in the faith.

2 So I made up my mind not to make you another painful visit. 2 For if I cause you pain, who is there to make me glad but the one whom I have pained? 3 And I wrote as I did, so that when I came, I might not suffer pain from those who should have made me rejoice; for I am confident about all of you, that my joy would be the joy of all of you. 4 For I wrote you out of much distress and anguish of heart and with many tears, not to cause you pain, but to let you know the abundant love that I have for you.

5 But if anyone has caused pain, he has caused it not to me, but to some extent—not to exaggerate it—to all of you. 6 This punishment by the majority is enough for such a person; 7 so now instead you should forgive and console him, so that he may not be overwhelmed by excessive sorrow. 8 So I urge you to reaffirm your love for him. 9 I wrote for this reason: to test you and to know whether you are obedient in everything. 10 Anyone whom you forgive, I also forgive. What I have forgiven, if I have forgiven anything, has been for your sake in the presence of Christ. 11 And we do this so that we may not be outwitted by Satan; for we are not ignorant of his designs.

12 When I came to Troas to proclaim the good

---

[a]Gk brothers [b]Other ancient authorities read your [c]Other ancient authorities read holiness [d]Other ancient authorities read pleasure [e]Gk according to the flesh

news of Christ, a door was opened for me in the Lord; 13 but my mind could not rest because I did not find my brother Titus there. So I said farewell to them and went on to Macedonia.

14 But thanks be to God, who in Christ always leads us in triumphal procession, and through us spreads in every place the fragrance that comes from knowing him. 15 For we are the aroma of Christ to God among those who are being saved and among those who are perishing; 16 to the one a fragrance from death to death, to the other a fragrance from life to life. Who is sufficient for these things? 17 For we are not peddlers of God's word like so many;[f] but in Christ we speak as persons of sincerity, as persons sent from God and standing in his presence.

3 Are we beginning to commend ourselves again? Surely we do not need, as some do, letters of recommendation to you or from you, do we? 2 You yourselves are our letter, written on our[g] hearts, to be known and read by all; 3 and you show that you are a letter of Christ, prepared by us, written not with ink but with the Spirit of the living God, not on tablets of stone but on tablets of human hearts.

4 Such is the confidence that we have through Christ toward God. 5 Not that we are competent of ourselves to claim anything as coming from us; our competence is from God, 6 who has made us competent to be ministers of a new covenant, not of letter but of spirit; for the letter kills, but the Spirit gives life.

7 Now if the ministry of death, chiseled in letters on stone tablets,[h] came in glory so that the people of Israel could not gaze at Moses' face because of the glory of his face, a glory now set aside, 8 how much more will the ministry of the Spirit come in glory? 9 For if there was glory in the ministry of condemnation, much more does the ministry of justification abound in glory! 10 Indeed, what once had glory has lost its glory because of the greater glory; 11 for if what was set aside came through glory, much more has the permanent come in glory!

12 Since, then, we have such a hope, we act with great boldness, 13 not like Moses, who put a veil over his face to keep the people of Israel from gazing at the end of the glory that[i] was being set aside. 14 But their minds were hardened. Indeed, to this

very day, when they hear the reading of the old covenant, that same veil is still there, since only in Christ is it set aside. 15 Indeed, to this very day whenever Moses is read, a veil lies over their minds; 16 but when one turns to the Lord, the veil is removed. 17 Now the Lord is the Spirit, and where the Spirit of the Lord is, there is freedom. 18 And all of us, with unveiled faces, seeing the glory of the Lord as though reflected in a mirror, are being transformed into the same image from one degree of glory to another; for this comes from the Lord, the Spirit.

4 Therefore, since it is by God's mercy that we are engaged in this ministry, we do not lose heart. 2 We have renounced the shameful things that one hides; we refuse to practice cunning or to falsify God's word; but by the open statement of the truth we commend ourselves to the conscience of everyone in the sight of God. 3 And even if our gospel is veiled, it is veiled to those who are perishing. 4 In their case the god of this world has blinded the minds of the unbelievers, to keep them from seeing the light of the gospel of the glory of Christ, who is the image of God. 5 For we do not proclaim ourselves; we proclaim Jesus Christ as Lord and ourselves as your slaves for Jesus' sake. 6 For it is the God who said, "Let light shine out of darkness," who has shone in our hearts to give the light of the knowledge of the glory of God in the face of Jesus Christ.

7 But we have this treasure in clay jars, so that it may be made clear that this extraordinary power belongs to God and does not come from us. 8 We are afflicted in every way, but not crushed; perplexed, but not driven to despair; 9 persecuted, but not forsaken; struck down, but not destroyed; 10 always carrying in the body the death of Jesus, so that the life of Jesus may also be made visible in our bodies. 11 For while we live, we are always being given up to death for Jesus' sake, so that the life of Jesus may be made visible in our mortal flesh. 12 So death is at work in us, but life in you.

13 But just as we have the same spirit of faith that is in accordance with scripture—"I believed, and so I spoke"[1]—we also believe, and so we

---

[f]Other ancient authorities read *like the others*   [g]Other ancient authorities read *your*   [h]Gk *on stones*   [i]Gk *of what*

[1]Ps 116:10

speak, 14 because we know that the one who raised the Lord Jesus will raise us also with Jesus, and will bring us with you into his presence. 15 Yes, everything is for your sake, so that grace, as it extends to more and more people, may increase thanksgiving, to the glory of God.

16 So we do not lose heart. Even though our outer nature is wasting away, our inner nature is being renewed day by day. 17 For this slight momentary affliction is preparing us for an eternal weight of glory beyond all measure, 18 because we look not at what can be seen but at what cannot be seen; for what can be seen is temporary, but what cannot be seen is eternal.

5 For we know that if the earthly tent we live in is destroyed, we have a building from God, a house not made with hands, eternal in the heavens. 2 For in this tent we groan, longing to be clothed with our heavenly dwelling— 3 if indeed, when we have taken it off[j] we will not be found naked. 4 For while we are still in this tent, we groan under our burden, because we wish not to be unclothed but to be further clothed, so that what is mortal may be swallowed up by life. 5 He who has prepared us for this very thing is God, who has given us the Spirit as a guarantee.

6 So we are always confident; even though we know that while we are at home in the body we are away from the Lord— 7 for we walk by faith, not by sight. 8 Yes, we do have confidence, and we would rather be away from the body and at home with the Lord. 9 So whether we are at home or away, we make it our aim to please him. 10 For all of us must appear before the judgment seat of Christ, so that each may receive recompense for what has been done in the body, whether good or evil.

11 Therefore, knowing the fear of the Lord, we try to persuade others; but we ourselves are well known to God, and I hope that we are also well known to your consciences. 12 We are not commending ourselves to you again, but giving you an opportunity to boast about us, so that you may be able to answer those who boast in outward appearance and not in the heart. 13 For if we are beside ourselves, it is for God; if we are in our right mind, it is for you. 14 For the love of Christ urges us on, because we are convinced that one has died for all; therefore all have died. 15 And he died for

all, so that those who live might live no longer for themselves, but for him who died and was raised for them.

16 From now on, therefore, we regard no one from a human point of view;[k] even though we once knew Christ from a human point of view,[k] we know him no longer in that way. 17 So if anyone is in Christ, there is a new creation: everything old has passed away; see, everything has become new! 18 All this is from God, who reconciled us to himself through Christ, and has given us the ministry of reconciliation; 19 that is, in Christ God was reconciling the world to himself,[l] not counting their trespasses against them, and entrusting the message of reconciliation to us. 20 So we are ambassadors for Christ, since God is making his appeal through us; we entreat you on behalf of Christ, be reconciled to God. 21 For our sake he made him to be sin who knew no sin, so that in him we might become the righteousness of God.

6 As we work together with him,[m] we urge you also not to accept the grace of God in vain. 2 For he says,

"At an acceptable time I have
  listened to you,
and on a day of salvation I have
  helped you."[2]

See, now is the acceptable time; see, now is the day of salvation! 3 We are putting no obstacle in anyone's way, so that no fault may be found with our ministry, 4 but as servants of God we have commended ourselves in every way: through great endurance, in afflictions, hardships, calamities, 5 beatings, imprisonments, riots, labors, sleepless nights, hunger; 6 by purity, knowledge, patience, kindness, holiness of spirit, genuine love, 7 truthful speech, and the power of God; with the weapons of righteousness for the right hand and for the left; 8 in honor and dishonor, in ill repute and good repute. We are treated as impostors, and yet are true; 9 as unknown, and yet are well known; as dying, and see—we are alive; as punished, and yet not killed; 10 as sorrowful, yet al-

---

[j]Other ancient authorities read *put it on*   [k]Gk *according to the flesh*
[l]Or *God was in Christ reconciling the world to himself*   [m]Gk *As we work together*

[2]Isa 49:8

ways rejoicing; as poor, yet making many rich; as having nothing, and yet possessing everything.

11 We have spoken frankly to you Corinthians; our heart is wide open to you. 12 There is no restriction in our affections, but only in yours. 13 In return—I speak as to children—open wide your hearts also.

14 Do not be mismatched with unbelievers. For what partnership is there between righteousness and lawlessness? Or what fellowship is there between light and darkness? 15 What agreement does Christ have with Beliar? Or what does a believer share with an unbeliever? 16 What agreement has the temple of God with idols? For we[n] are the temple of the living God; as God said,

> "I will live in them and walk
>   among them,
>   and I will be their God,
>   and they shall be my people.[3]

17   Therefore come out from them,
>   and be separate from them, says
>   the Lord,
>   and touch nothing unclean;
>   then I will welcome you,[4]

18   and I will be your father,
>   and you shall be my sons and
>   daughters,
>   says the Lord Almighty."[5]

7 Since we have these promises, beloved, let us cleanse ourselves from every defilement of body and of spirit, making holiness perfect in the fear of God.

2 Make room in your hearts[o] for us; we have wronged no one, we have corrupted no one, we have taken advantage of no one. 3 I do not say this to condemn you, for I said before that you are in our hearts, to die together and to live together. 4 I often boast about you; I have great pride in you; I am filled with consolation; I am overjoyed in all our affliction.

5 For even when we came into Macedonia, our bodies had no rest, but we were afflicted in every way—disputes without and fears within. 6 But God, who consoles the downcast, consoled us by the arrival of Titus, 7 and not only by his coming, but also by the consolation with which he was consoled about you, as he told us of your longing, your

mourning, your zeal for me, so that I rejoiced still more. 8 For even if I made you sorry with my letter, I do not regret it (though I did regret it, for I see that I grieved you with that letter, though only briefly). 9 Now I rejoice, not because you were grieved, but because your grief led to repentance; for you felt a godly grief, so that you were not harmed in any way by us. 10 For godly grief produces a repentance that leads to salvation and brings no regret, but worldly grief produces death. 11 For see what earnestness this godly grief has produced in you, what eagerness to clear yourselves, what indignation, what alarm, what longing, what zeal, what punishment! At every point you have proved yourselves guiltless in the matter. 12 So although I wrote to you, it was not on account of the one who did the wrong, nor on account of the one who was wronged, but in order that your zeal for us might be made known to you before God. 13 In this we find comfort.

In addition to our own consolation, we rejoiced still more at the joy of Titus, because his mind has been set at rest by all of you. 14 For if I have been somewhat boastful about you to him, I was not disgraced; but just as everything we said to you was true, so our boasting to Titus has proved true as well. 15 And his heart goes out all the more to you, as he remembers the obedience of all of you, and how you welcomed him with fear and trembling. 16 I rejoice, because I have complete confidence in you.

8 We want you to know, brothers and sisters,[p] about the grace of God that has been granted to the churches of Macedonia; 2 for during a severe ordeal of affliction, their abundant joy and their extreme poverty have overflowed in a wealth of generosity on their part. 3 For, as I can testify, they voluntarily gave according to their means, and even beyond their means, 4 begging us earnestly for the privilege[q] of sharing in this ministry to the saints— 5 and this, not merely as we expected; they gave themselves first to the Lord and, by the will of God, to us, 6 so that we might

---

[n]Other ancient authorities read *you*   [o]Gk lacks *in your hearts*
[p]Gk *brothers*   [q]Gk *grace*

[3]Lev 26:11–12; Jer 32:38; Ezek 37:27   [4]Isa 52:11; Ezek 20:34, 41
[5]2 Sam 7:8, 14; Isa 43:6; Jer 31:9

urge Titus that, as he had already made a beginning, so he should also complete this generous undertaking[r] among you. 7 Now as you excel in everything—in faith, in speech, in knowledge, in utmost eagerness, and in our love for you[s]—so we want you to excel also in this generous undertaking.[r]

8 I do not say this as a command, but I am testing the genuineness of your love against the earnestness of others. 9 For you know the generous act[t] of our Lord Jesus Christ, that though he was rich, yet for your sakes he became poor, so that by his poverty you might become rich. 10 And in this matter I am giving my advice: it is appropriate for you who began last year not only to do something but even to desire to do something— 11 now finish doing it, so that your eagerness may be matched by completing it according to your means. 12 For if the eagerness is there, the gift is acceptable according to what one has— not according to what one does not have. 13 I do not mean that there should be relief for others and pressure on you, but it is a question of a fair balance between 14 your present abundance and their need, so that their abundance may be for your need, in order that there may be a fair balance. 15 As it is written,

> "The one who had much did not
>   have too much,
> and the one who had little did
>   not have too little."[6]

16 But thanks be to God who put in the heart of Titus the same eagerness for you that I myself have. 17 For he not only accepted our appeal, but since he is more eager than ever, he is going to you of his own accord. 18 With him we are sending the brother who is famous among all the churches for his proclaiming the good news;[u] 19 and not only that, but he has also been appointed by the churches to travel with us while we are administering this generous undertaking[r] for the glory of the Lord himself[v] and to show our goodwill. 20 We intend that no one should blame us about this generous gift that we are administering, 21 for we intend to do what is right not only in the Lord's sight but also in the sight of others. 22 And with them we are sending our brother whom we have often tested and found eager in many matters, but who is now more eager than ever because of

his great confidence in you. 23 As for Titus, he is my partner and co-worker in your service; as for our brothers, they are messengers[w] of the churches, the glory of Christ. 24 Therefore openly before the churches, show them the proof of your love and of our reason for boasting about you.

9 Now it is not necessary for me to write you about the ministry to the saints, 2 for I know your eagerness, which is the subject of my boasting about you to the people of Macedonia, saying that Achaia has been ready since last year; and your zeal has stirred up most of them. 3 But I am sending the brothers in order that our boasting about you may not prove to have been empty in this case, so that you may be ready, as I said you would be; 4 otherwise, if some Macedonians come with me and find that you are not ready, we would be humiliated—to say nothing of you—in this undertaking.[x] 5 So I thought it necessary to urge the brothers to go on ahead to you, and arrange in advance for this bountiful gift that you have promised, so that it may be ready as a voluntary gift and not as an extortion.

6 The point is this: the one who sows sparingly will also reap sparingly, and the one who sows bountifully will also reap bountifully. 7 Each of you must give as you have made up your mind, not reluctantly or under compulsion, for God loves a cheerful giver. 8 And God is able to provide you with every blessing in abundance, so that by always having enough of everything, you may share abundantly in every good work. 9 As it is written,

> "He scatters abroad, he gives to
>   the poor;
> his righteousness[y] endures
>   forever."[7]

10 He who supplies seed to the sower and bread for food will supply and multiply your seed for sowing and increase the harvest of your righteousness.[y] 11 You will be enriched in every way for your great generosity, which will produce thanksgiving to God through us; 12 for the rendering of

[r]Gk this grace   [s]Other ancient authorities read your love for us
[t]Gk the grace   [u]Or the gospel   [v]Other ancient authorities lack
himself   [w]Gk apostles   [x]Other ancient authorities add of boasting
[y]Or benevolence

[6]Exod 16:18   [7]Ps 112:9

this ministry not only supplies the needs of the saints but also overflows with many thanksgivings to God. 13 Through the testing of this ministry you glorify God by your obedience to the confession of the gospel of Christ and by the generosity of your sharing with them and with all others, 14 while they long for you and pray for you because of the surpassing grace of God that he has given you. 15 Thanks be to God for his indescribable gift!

10 I myself, Paul, appeal to you by the meekness and gentleness of Christ—I who am humble when face to face with you, but bold toward you when I am away!— 2 I ask that when I am present I need not show boldness by daring to oppose those who think we are acting according to human standards.[z] 3 Indeed, we live as human beings,[a] but we do not wage war according to human standards;[z] 4 for the weapons of our warfare are not merely human,[b] but they have divine power to destroy strongholds. We destroy arguments 5 and every proud obstacle raised up against the knowledge of God, and we take every thought captive to obey Christ. 6 We are ready to punish every disobedience when your obedience is complete.

7 Look at what is before your eyes. If you are confident that you belong to Christ, remind yourself of this, that just as you belong to Christ, so also do we. 8 Now, even if I boast a little too much of our authority, which the Lord gave for building you up and not for tearing you down, I will not be ashamed of it. 9 I do not want to seem as though I am trying to frighten you with my letters. 10 For they say, "His letters are weighty and strong, but his bodily presence is weak, and his speech contemptible." 11 Let such people understand that what we say by letter when absent, we will also do when present.

12 We do not dare to classify or compare ourselves with some of those who commend themselves. But when they measure themselves by one another, and compare themselves with one another, they do not show good sense. 13 We, however, will not boast beyond limits, but will keep within the field that God has assigned to us, to reach out even as far as you. 14 For we were not overstepping our limits when we reached you; we were the first to come all the way to you with the good news[c] of Christ. 15 We do not boast beyond limits, that is, in the labors of others; but our hope is that, as your faith increases, our sphere of action among you may be greatly enlarged, 16 so that we may proclaim the good news[c] in lands beyond you, without boasting of work already done in someone else's sphere of action. 17 "Let the one who boasts, boast in the Lord."[8] 18 For it is not those who commend themselves that are approved, but those whom the Lord commends.

11 I wish you would bear with me in a little foolishness. Do bear with me! 2 I feel a divine jealousy for you, for I promised you in marriage to one husband, to present you as a chaste virgin to Christ. 3 But I am afraid that as the serpent deceived Eve by its cunning, your thoughts will be led astray from a sincere and pure[d] devotion to Christ. 4 For if someone comes and proclaims another Jesus than the one we proclaimed, or if you receive a different spirit from the one you received, or a different gospel from the one you accepted, you submit to it readily enough. 5 I think that I am not in the least inferior to these super-apostles. 6 I may be untrained in speech, but not in knowledge; certainly in every way and in all things we have made this evident to you.

7 Did I commit a sin by humbling myself so that you might be exalted, because I proclaimed God's good news[c] to you free of charge? 8 I robbed other churches by accepting support from them in order to serve you. 9 And when I was with you and was in need, I did not burden anyone, for my needs were supplied by the friends[f] who came from Macedonia. So I refrained and will continue to refrain from burdening you in any way. 10 As the truth of Christ is in me, this boast of mine will not be silenced in the regions of Achaia. 11 And why? Because I do not love you? God knows I do!

12 And what I do I will also continue to do, in order to deny an opportunity to those who want an opportunity to be recognized as our equals in what they boast about. 13 For such boasters are false apostles, deceitful workers, disguising themselves

---

[z]Gk *according to the flesh*   [a]Gk *in the flesh*   [b]Gk *fleshly*   [c]Or *the gospel*   [d]Other ancient authorities lack *and pure*   [e]Gk *the gospel of God*   [f]Gk *brothers*

---

[8]Jer 9:24

as apostles of Christ. 14 And no wonder! Even Satan disguises himself as an angel of light. 15 So it is not strange if his ministers also disguise themselves as ministers of righteousness. Their end will match their deeds.

16 I repeat, let no one think that I am a fool; but if you do, then accept me as a fool, so that I too may boast a little. 17 What I am saying in regard to this boastful confidence, I am saying not with the Lord's authority, but as a fool; 18 since many boast according to human standards,[g] I will also boast. 19 For you gladly put up with fools, being wise yourselves! 20 For you put up with it when someone makes slaves of you, or preys upon you, or takes advantage of you, or puts on airs, or gives you a slap in the face. 21 To my shame, I must say, we were too weak for that!

But whatever anyone dares to boast of—I am speaking as a fool—I also dare to boast of that. 22 Are they Hebrews? So am I. Are they Israelites? So am I. Are they descendants of Abraham? So am I. 23 Are they ministers of Christ? I am talking like a madman—I am a better one: with far greater labors, far more imprisonments, with countless floggings, and often near death. 24 Five times I have received from the Jews the forty lashes minus one. 25 Three times I was beaten with rods. Once I received a stoning. Three times I was shipwrecked; for a night and a day I was adrift at sea; 26 on frequent journeys, in danger from rivers, danger from bandits, danger from my own people, danger from Gentiles, danger in the city, danger in the wilderness, danger at sea, danger from false brothers and sisters;[h] 27 in toil and hardship, through many a sleepless night, hungry and thirsty, often without food, cold and naked. 28 And, besides other things, I am under daily pressure because of my anxiety for all the churches. 29 Who is weak, and I am not weak? Who is made to stumble, and I am not indignant?

30 If I must boast, I will boast of the things that show my weakness. 31 The God and Father of the Lord Jesus (blessed be he forever!) knows that I do not lie. 32 In Damascus, the governor[i] under King Aretas guarded the city of Damascus in order to[j] seize me, 33 but I was let down in a basket through a window in the wall,[k] and escaped from his hands.

12 It is necessary to boast; nothing is to be gained by it, but I will go on to visions and revelations of the Lord. 2 I know a person in Christ who fourteen years ago was caught up to the third heaven—whether in the body or out of the body I do not know; God knows. 3 And I know that such a person—whether in the body or out of the body I do not know; God knows— 4 was caught up into Paradise and heard things that are not to be told, that no mortal is permitted to repeat. 5 On behalf of such a one I will boast, but on my own behalf I will not boast, except of my weaknesses. 6 But if I wish to boast, I will not be a fool, for I will be speaking the truth. But I refrain from it, so that no one may think better of me than what is seen in me or heard from me, 7 even considering the exceptional character of the revelations. Therefore, to keep[l] me from being too elated, a thorn was given me in the flesh, a messenger of Satan to torment me, to keep me from being too elated.[m] 8 Three times I appealed to the Lord about this, that it would leave me, 9 but he said to me, "My grace is sufficient for you, for power[n] is made perfect in weakness." So, I will boast all the more gladly of my weaknesses, so that the power of Christ may dwell in me. 10 Therefore I am content with weaknesses, insults, hardships, persecutions, and calamities for the sake of Christ; for whenever I am weak, then I am strong.

11 I have been a fool! You forced me to it. Indeed you should have been the ones commending me, for I am not at all inferior to these super-apostles, even though I am nothing. 12 The signs of a true apostle were performed among you with utmost patience, signs and wonders and mighty works. 13 How have you been worse off than the other churches, except that I myself did not burden you? Forgive me this wrong!

14 Here I am, ready to come to you this third time. And I will not be a burden, because I do not want what is yours but you; for children ought not to lay up for their parents, but parents for their children. 15 I will most gladly spend and be spent for you. If I love you more, am I to be loved less?

[g]Gk *according to the flesh*   [h]Gk *brothers*   [i]Gk *ethnarch*   [j]Other ancient authorities read *and wanted to*   [k]Gk *through the wall*   [l]Other ancient authorities read *To keep*   [m]Other ancient authorities lack *to keep me from being too elated*   [n]Other ancient authorities read *my power*

16 Let it be assumed that I did not burden you. Nevertheless (you say) since I was crafty, I took you in by deceit. 17 Did I take advantage of you through any of those whom I sent to you? 18 I urged Titus to go, and sent the brother with him. Titus did not take advantage of you, did he? Did we not conduct ourselves with the same spirit? Did we not take the same steps?

19 Have you been thinking all along that we have been defending ourselves before you? We are speaking in Christ before God. Everything we do, beloved, is for the sake of building you up. 20 For I fear that when I come, I may find you not as I wish, and that you may find me not as you wish; I fear that there may perhaps be quarreling, jealousy, anger, selfishness, slander, gossip, conceit, and disorder. 21 I fear that when I come again, my God may humble me before you, and that I may have to mourn over many who previously sinned and have not repented of the impurity, sexual immorality, and licentiousness that they have practiced.

13 This is the third time I am coming to you. "Any charge must be sustained by the evidence of two or three witnesses."[9] 2 I warned those who sinned previously and all the others, and I warn them now while absent, as I did when present on my second visit, that if I come again, I will not be lenient— 3 since you desire proof that Christ is speaking in me. He is not weak in dealing with you, but is powerful in you. 4 For he was crucified in weakness, but lives by the power of God. For we are weak in him,[o] but in dealing with you we will live with him by the power of God.

5 Examine yourselves to see whether you are living in the faith. Test yourselves. Do you not realize that Jesus Christ is in you?—unless, indeed, you fail to meet the test! 6 I hope you will find out that we have not failed. 7 But we pray to God that you may not do anything wrong—not that we may appear to have met the test, but that you may do what is right, though we may seem to have failed. 8 For we cannot do anything against the truth, but only for the truth. 9 For we rejoice when we are weak and you are strong. This is what we pray for, that you may become perfect. 10 So I write these things while I am away from you, so that when I come, I may not have to be severe in using the authority that the Lord has given me for building up and not for tearing down.

11 Finally, brothers and sisters,[p] farewell.[q] Put things in order, listen to my appeal,[r] agree with one another, live in peace; and the God of love and peace will be with you. 12 Greet one another with a holy kiss. All the saints greet you.

13 The grace of the Lord Jesus Christ, the love of God, and the communion of[s] the Holy Spirit be with all of you.

[o]Other ancient authorities read *with him*   [p]Gk *brothers*   [q]Or *rejoice*   [r]Or *encourage one another*   [s]Or *and the sharing in*

[9]Deut 19:15

The Letter to the Galatians

Paul wrote the letter of Galatians to churches in the Roman province of Galatia in central Asia Minor (modern-day Turkey). The letter does not indicate where in the province, exactly, these churches were located, whether among the southern cities evangelized by Paul in Acts (Acts 14) or in the more northern climes, where people were historically more apt to call themselves "Galatians" (3:1). In any event, the occasion for the letter is relatively clear. After Paul had established churches among Gentiles in this region (4:12–20), other Christian missionaries arrived proclaiming a message different from his. According to them, Gentiles who had placed their faith in Christ should also follow the prescriptions of the Jewish Law. Specifically, the males of the congregation were to be circumcised.

We do not know how these missionaries argued their case; they may simply have claimed that since Jesus was the Jewish messiah sent from the Jewish God to the Jewish people in fulfillment of the promises given to the Jewish patriarchs in the Jewish Scriptures, anyone who believes in Christ must obviously accept the Jewish Law. Paul, however, had maintained that people were made right with God through Christ alone, apart from doing the works of the Law. For him, this was not an honest disagreement among well-meaning Christian brothers and sisters. His opponents' views were a frontal attack on the core of his gospel message and on his own authorization to preach it.

Paul's anger is clear at the outset; this is his only letter that does not begin by thanking God for the congregation but, instead, with a rebuke to those who have abandoned Paul's message for "another gospel." Far from having earned God's blessing, such persons stand under God's curse (1:6–9).

Paul devotes the first portion of the letter (most of the first two chapters) to showing that his gospel was "not of human origin," but instead was given to him directly "through a revelation of Jesus Christ" (1:11–12). Contrary to the claims of his opponents, Paul did not modify the original Christian message preached by the apostles before him, because he did not receive his message from them. He got it directly from God (1:13–2:14). Paul then argues at length, in the heart of the letter (2:15–5:12), that a person is made right with God (justified) not by doing works of the Law, but by faith in Christ. Those who insist on doing works of the Law for justification have totally misunderstood and misrepresented the gospel. For if justification could come through the Law, then Christ "died for nothing" (2:21).

This is not to say, however, that those who have been justified apart from the Law can lead lawless lives. Paul concludes the letter by showing that those who now belong to God's people through Christ have received God's Spirit and so are empowered to do God's will, loving their neighbors as themselves, and so fulfilling the Law (5:13–26).

From the New Revised Standard Version Bible, © 1989.

1 Paul an apostle—sent neither by human commission nor from human authorities, but through Jesus Christ and God the Father, who raised him from the dead— 2 and all the members of God's family[a] who are with me,

To the churches of Galatia:

3 Grace to you and peace from God our Father and the Lord Jesus Christ, 4 who gave himself for our sins to set us free from the present evil age, according to the will of our God and Father, 5 to whom be the glory forever and ever. Amen.

6 I am astonished that you are so quickly deserting the one who called you in the grace of Christ and are turning to a different gospel— 7 not that there is another gospel, but there are some who are confusing you and want to pervert the gospel of Christ. 8 But even if we or an angel[b] from heaven should proclaim to you a gospel contrary to what we proclaimed to you, let that one be accursed! 9 As we have said before, so now I repeat, if anyone proclaims to you a gospel contrary to what you received, let that one be accursed!

10 Am I now seeking human approval, or God's approval? Or am I trying to please people? If I were still pleasing people, I would not be a servant[c] of Christ.

11 For I want you to know, brothers and sisters,[d] that the gospel that was proclaimed by me is not of human origin; 12 for I did not receive it from a human source, nor was I taught it, but I received it through a revelation of Jesus Christ.

13 You have heard, no doubt, of my earlier life in Judaism. I was violently persecuting the church of God and was trying to destroy it. 14 I advanced in Judaism beyond many among my people of the same age, for I was far more zealous for the traditions of my ancestors. 15 But when God, who had set me apart before I was born and called me through his grace, was pleased 16 to reveal his Son to me,[e] so that I might proclaim him among the Gentiles, I did not confer with any human being, 17 nor did I go up to Jerusalem to those who were already apostles before me, but I went away at once into Arabia, and afterwards I returned to Damascus.

18 Then after three years I did go up to Jerusalem to visit Cephas and stayed with him fifteen days; 19 but I did not see any other apostle except James the Lord's brother. 20 In wh; writing to you, before God, I do not lie! 2 I went into the regions of Syria and Cilicia, I was still unknown by sight to the churc Judea that are in Christ; 23 they only heard "The one who formerly was persecuting us proclaiming the faith he once tried to de 24 And they glorified God because of me.

2 Then after fourteen years I went up a Jerusalem with Barnabas, taking Titu: with me. 2 I went up in response to a reve Then I laid before them (though only in a meeting with the acknowledged leader gospel that I proclaim among the Gentiles der to make sure that I was not running, or I run, in vain. 3 But even Titus, who was w: was not compelled to be circumcised, tho was a Greek. 4 But because of false believe cretly brought in, who slipped in to spy on tl dom we have in Christ Jesus, so that they enslave us— 5 we did not submit to them e a moment, so that the truth of the gospel mi ways remain with you. 6 And from thos were supposed to be acknowledged leaders they actually were makes no difference to m shows no partiality)—those leaders contι nothing to me. 7 On the contrary, when thι that I had been entrusted with the gospel uncircumcised, just as Peter had been en with the gospel for the circumcised 8 (for I worked through Peter making him an apc the circumcised also worked through me ir ing me to the Gentiles), 9 and when Jam Cephas and John, who were acknowledged recognized the grace that had been given they gave to Barnabas and me the right hand lowship, agreeing that we should go to th tiles and they to the circumcised. 10 They only one thing, that we remember the poor, was actually what I was[g] eager to do.

11 But when Cephas came to Antioch, I oι him to his face, because he stood self-condε 12 for until certain people came from Jan used to eat with the Gentiles. But after they he drew back and kept himself separate for the circumcision faction. 13 And the othe

---

[a] Gk *all the brothers*   [b] Or *a messenger*   [c] Gk *slave*   [d] Gk *br*
[e] Gk *in me*   [f] Gk *false brothers*   [g] Or *had been*

joined him in this hypocrisy, so that even Barnabas was led astray by their hypocrisy. 14 But when I saw that they were not acting consistently with the truth of the gospel, I said to Cephas before them all, "If you, though a Jew, live like a Gentile and not like a Jew, how can you compel the Gentiles to live like Jews?"[h]

15 We ourselves are Jews by birth and not Gentile sinners; 16 yet we know that a person is justified[i] not by the works of the law but through faith in Jesus Christ.[j] And we have come to believe in Christ Jesus, so that we might be justified by faith in Christ,[k] and not by doing the works of the law, because no one will be justified by the works of the law. 17 But if, in our effort to be justified in Christ, we ourselves have been found to be sinners, is Christ then a servant of sin? Certainly not! 18 But if I build up again the very things that I once tore down, then I demonstrate that I am a transgressor. 19 For through the law I died to the law, so that I might live to God. I have been crucified with Christ; 20 and it is no longer I who live, but it is Christ who lives in me. And the life I now live in the flesh I live by faith in the Son of God,[l] who loved me and gave himself for me. 21 I do not nullify the grace of God; for if justification[m] comes through the law, then Christ died for nothing.

3 You foolish Galatians! Who has bewitched you? It was before your eyes that Jesus Christ was publicly exhibited as crucified! 2 The only thing I want to learn from you is this: Did you receive the Spirit by doing the works of the law or by believing what you heard? 3 Are you so foolish? Having started with the Spirit, are you now ending with the flesh? 4 Did you experience so much for nothing?—if it really was for nothing. 5 Well then, does God[n] supply you with the Spirit and work miracles among you by your doing the works of the law, or by your believing what you heard?

6 Just as Abraham "believed God, and it was reckoned to him as righteousness,"[1] 7 so, you see, those who believe are the descendants of Abraham. 8 And the scripture, foreseeing that God would justify the Gentiles by faith, declared the gospel beforehand to Abraham, saying, "All the Gentiles shall be blessed in you."[2] 9 For this reason, those who believe are blessed with Abraham who believed.

10 For all who rely on the works of the under a curse; for it is written, "Cursed i one who does not observe and obey all th written in the book of the law."[3] 11 Now dent that no one is justified before God by for "The one who is righteous will live by 12 But the law does not rest on faith; on trary, "Whoever does the works of the law[p] by them."[5] 13 Christ redeemed us from the the law by becoming a curse for us—for i ten, "Cursed is everyone who hangs on a 14 in order that in Christ Jesus the blessing ham might come to the Gentiles, so that v receive the promise of the Spirit through

15 Brothers and sisters,[q] I give an exam daily life: once a person's will[r] has been no one adds to it or annuls it. 16 Now the es were made to Abraham and to his offs does not say, "And to offsprings,"[t] as of m it says, "And to your offspring,"[s7] that is person, who is Christ. 17 My point is this: which came four hundred thirty years la nct annul a covenant previously ratified so as to nullify the promise. 18 For if th tance comes from the law, it no longer con the promise; but God granted it to A through the promise.

19 Why then the law? It was added be transgressions, until the offspring[s] would whom the promise had been made; and it dained through angels by a mediator. 20 mediator involves more than one party; is one.

21 Is the law then opposed to the proi God? Certainly not! For if a law had bee that could make alive, then righteousnes indeed come through the law. 22 But the s has imprisoned all things under the powe so that what was promised through faith Christ[u] might be given to those who belie

[h]Some interpreters hold that the quotation extends into the paragraph [i]Or reckoned as righteous; and so elsewhere faith of Jesus Christ [k]Or the faith of Christ [l]Or by the fc Son of God [m]Or righteousness [n]Gk he [o]Or The one w righteous through faith will live [p]Gk does them [q]Gk Bn [r]Or covenant (as in verse 17) [s]Gk seed [t]Gk seeds [u]Or faith of Jesus Christ

[1]Gen 15:6 [2]Gen 12:3 [3]Deut 27:26; 28:58 [4]Hab 2:4
[6]Deut 21 23 [7]Gen 12:7; 13:15; 17:7; 24:7

faithed

Genesis

15 before 17 - shows importance in faith
(faith)   (circumcision)

23 Now before faith came, we were imprisoned and guarded under the law until faith would be revealed. 24 Therefore the law was our disciplinarian until Christ came, so that we might be justified by faith. 25 But now that faith has come, we are no longer subject to a disciplinarian, 26 for in Christ Jesus you are all children of God through faith. 27 As many of you as were baptized into Christ have clothed yourselves with Christ. 28 There is no longer Jew or Greek, there is no longer slave or free, there is no longer male and female; for all of you are one in Christ Jesus. 29 And if you belong to Christ, then you are Abraham's offspring,ᵛ heirs according to the promise.

4 My point is this: heirs, as long as they are minors, are no better than slaves, though they are the owners of all the property; 2 but they remain under guardians and trustees until the date set by the father. 3 So with us; while we were minors, we were enslaved to the elemental spiritsʷ of the world. 4 But when the fullness of time had come, God sent his Son, born of a woman, born under the law, 5 in order to redeem those who were under the law, so that we might receive adoption as children. 6 And because you are children, God has sent the Spirit of his Son into ourˣhearts, crying, "Abba!ʸ Father!" 7 So you are no longer a slave but a child, and if a child then also an heir, through God.ᶻ

8 Formerly, when you did not know God, you were enslaved to beings that by nature are not gods. 9 Now, however, that you have come to know God, or rather to be known by God, how can you turn back again to the weak and beggarly elemental spirits?ᵃ How can you want to be enslaved to them again? 10 You are observing special days, and months, and seasons, and years. 11 I am afraid that my work for you may have been wasted.

12 Friends,ᵇ I beg you, become as I am, for I also have become as you are. You have done me no wrong. 13 You know that it was because of a physical infirmity that I first announced the gospel to you; 14 though my condition put you to the test, you did not scorn or despise me, but welcomed me as an angel of God, as Christ Jesus. 15 What has become of the goodwill you felt? For I testify that, had it been possible, you would have torn out your eyes and given them to me. 16 Have I now become

your enemy by telling you the truth? 1 make much of you, but for no good purpos want to exclude you, so that you may make of them. 18 It is good to be made much o good purpose at all times, and not only whe present with you. 19 My little children, for I am again in the pain of childbirth until C formed in you, 20 I wish I were present wi now and could change my tone, for I am per about you.

21 Tell me, you who desire to be subject law, will you not listen to the law? 22 Fo written that Abraham had two sons, one by woman and the other by a free woman. 2 the child of the slave, was born according flesh; the other, the child of the free woma born through the promise. 24 Now this is a gory: these women are two covenants woman, in fact, is Hagar, from Mount Sinai ing children for slavery. 25 Now Hagar is Sinai in Arabiaᶜ and corresponds to the ↓ Jerusalem, for she is in slavery with her ch 26 But the other woman corresponds Jerusalem above; she is free, and she is our er. 27 For it is written,

"Rejoice, you childless one, you
    who bear no children,
burst into song and shout, you
    who endure no birth pangs;
for the children of the desolate
    woman are more numerous
than the children of the one
    who is married."⁸

28 Now you,ᵈ my friends,ᵉ are children promise, like Isaac. 29 But just as at that ti child who was born according to the flesh cuted the child who was born according Spirit, so it is now also. 30 But what do scripture say? "Drive out the slave and her for the child of the slave will not share the tance with the child of the free woman."⁹ then, friends,ᵉ we are children, not of the sla of the free woman.

ᵛGk *seed*   ʷOr *the rudiments*   ˣOther ancient authorities rea ʸAramaic for *Father*   ᶻOther ancient authorities read *an heir through Christ*   ᵃOr *beggarly rudiments*   ᵇGk *Brothers*   ᶜO ancient authorities read *For Sinai is a mountain in Arabia*   ᵈ ancient authorities read *we*   ᵉGk *brothers*

8Isa 54:1   9Gen 21:10

5 For freedom Christ has set us free. Stand firm, therefore, and do not submit again to a yoke of slavery.

2 Listen! I, Paul, am telling you that if you let yourselves be circumcised, Christ will be of no benefit to you. 3 Once again I testify to every man who lets himself be circumcised that he is obliged to obey the entire law. 4 You who want to be justified by the law have cut yourselves off from Christ; you have fallen away from grace. 5 For through the Spirit, by faith, we eagerly wait for the hope of righteousness. 6 For in Christ Jesus neither circumcision nor uncircumcision counts for anything; the only thing that counts is faith working[f] through love.

7 You were running well; who prevented you from obeying the truth? 8 Such persuasion does not come from the one who calls you. 9 A little yeast leavens the whole batch of dough. 10 I am confident about you in the Lord that you will not think otherwise. But whoever it is that is confusing you will pay the penalty. 11 But my friends,[g] why am I still being persecuted if I am still preaching circumcision? In that case the offense of the cross has been removed. 12 I wish those who unsettle you would castrate themselves!

13 For you were called to freedom, brothers and sisters;[g] only do not use your freedom as an opportunity for self-indulgence,[h] but through love become slaves to one another. 14 For the whole law is summed up in a single commandment, "You shall love your neighbor as yourself."[10] 15 If, however, you bite and devour one another, take care that you are not consumed by one another.

16 Live by the Spirit, I say, and do not gratify the desires of the flesh. 17 For what the flesh desires is opposed to the Spirit, and what the Spirit desires is opposed to the flesh; for these are opposed to each other, to prevent you from doing what you want. 18 But if you are led by the Spirit, you are not subject to the law. 19 Now the works of the flesh are obvious: fornication, impurity, licentiousness, 20 idolatry, sorcery, enmities, strife, jealousy, anger, quarrels, dissensions, factions, 21 envy,[i] drunkenness, carousing, and things like these. I am warning you, as I warned you before: those who do such things will not inherit the kingdom of God.

22 By contrast, the fruit of the Spirit is love, joy, peace, patience, kindness, generosity, fait[h] 23 gentleness, and self-control. There is against such things. 24 And those who b Christ Jesus have crucified the flesh with sions and desires. 25 If we live by the Spi also be guided by the Spirit. 26 Let us not conceited, competing against one anothe ing one another.

6 My friends,[j] if anyone is detected in gression, you who have received t[h] should restore such a one in a spirit of ge[n] Take care that you yourselves are not 1 2 Bear one another's burdens, and in this will fulfill[k] the law of Christ. 3 For if th[e] are nothing think they are something, they themselves. 4 All must test their own wo that work, rather than their neighbor's wo become a cause for pride. 5 For all mu their own loads.

6 Those who are taught the word must all good things with their teacher.

7 Do not be deceived; God is not moc you reap whatever you sow. 8 If you sow own flesh, you will reap corruption from t but if you sow to the Spirit, you will rea[p] life from the Spirit. 9 So let us not grow doing what is right, for we will reap at harv if we do not give up. 10 So then, when have an opportunity, let us work for the go and especially for those of the family of f[a]

11 See what large letters I make when I ing in my own hand! 12 It is those who make a good showing in the flesh that try pel you to be circumcised—only that they be persecuted for the cross of Christ. 13 I circumcised do not themselves obey the they want you to be circumcised so that t[h] boast about your flesh. 14 May I never anything except the cross of our Lord Jesu by which[l] the world has been crucified to I to the world. 15 For[m] neither circumci uncircumcision is anything; but a new cr[o]

[f]Or made effective [g]Gk brothers [h]Gk the flesh [i]Other authorities add murder [j]Gk Brothers [k]Other ancient aut read in this way fulfill [l]Or through whom [m]Other ancien[t] authorities add in Christ Jesus

---

[10]Lev 19:18

everything! 16 As for those who will follow this rule—peace be upon them, and mercy, and upon the Israel of God.

17 From now on, let no one make trouble for me; for I carry the marks of Jesus branded on my body.

18 May the grace of our Lord Jesus Ch with your spirit, brothers and sisters.[n] Ame

[n]Gk brothers

The Letter to the Ephesians

Ephesians is unique among the letters that go under Paul's name in that it appears to have originally been a circular letter. In the earliest and best manuscripts, the words "in Ephesus" are lacking from 1:1, so that rather than being addressed to the saints of Ephesus, it was addressed to saints everywhere (including, no doubt, Ephesus, where a copyist then supplied the words "in Ephesus" in order to personalize the letter). Indeed, the problems that are addressed in this letter are not specific to a particular locale; they are problems that had emerged in numerous Christian communities, possibly throughout Asia Minor, at the time of its writing.

The overriding purpose of the letter is to remind its Gentile readers that, whereas they had formerly been alienated from both God and his people, the Jews, they have now been reconciled through the work of Christ (2:1–22). Jesus' death tore down the barrier that had previously separated Jew and Gentile—that is the Jewish Law—so that both groups were now equal and able to live in harmony with one another (2:11–18). Moreover, through Christ's death all people, Jew and Gentile, have become united with God (2:18–22) and raised up to enjoy a glorified existence in the heavenly places (2:1–10). This was the "mystery" that God had concealed from earlier generations but had now revealed through Paul to the world (3:1–13).

While still living in the world, believers are to manifest the unity that they have in Christ in their various relationships: among themselves in the church (4:1–16), with respect to the rest of society (4:17–5:20), and in the social roles in which they find themselves (5:21–6:9). The letter closes with exhortation to continue the fight against the Satanic forces trying to disrupt the life of the congregation (6:10–20).

Even though Ephesians has a number of similarities with some of the undisputedly Pauline letters (e.g., Romans), the majority of critical scholars today are persuaded that Paul himself did not write this letter. Even more than Colossians (see that introduction), the vocabulary and especially the style of writing are strikingly different from Paul's; the exalted view of the believers as already reigning with Christ is even more pronounced here than in Colossians (contrast 2:5–6 with Rom 6:1–6 and 1 Corinthians 15); and several Pauline ideas have taken on new shades of meaning (e.g., Paul's opposition to "works" of the Jewish Law as a means of salvation has here become an opposition to reliance on "good deeds"; 2:1–10). It appears, then, that an author living near the end of the first century has developed some of Paul's views in directions not taken by the apostle himself. Possibly using some of the letters circulating under Paul's name (especially Colossians, with which Ephesians has a good deal in common), the author writes a circular letter to reaffirm what he saw to be the core of Paul's message, that Christ brought a unification of Jew and Gentile with one another and of both with God, and that those who are in Christ should manifest this unity in their lives together.

1 Paul, an apostle of Christ Jesus by the will of God,

To the saints who are in Ephesus and are faithful[a] in Christ Jesus:

2 Grace to you and peace from God our Father and the Lord Jesus Christ.

3 Blessed be the God and Father of our Lord Jesus Christ, who has blessed us in Christ with every spiritual blessing in the heavenly places, 4 just as he chose us in Christ[b] before the foundation of the world to be holy and blameless before him in love. 5 He destined us for adoption as his children through Jesus Christ, according to the good pleasure of his will, 6 to the praise of his glorious grace that he freely bestowed on us in the Beloved. 7 In him we have redemption through his blood, the forgiveness of our trespasses, according to the riches of his grace 8 that he lavished on us. With all wisdom and insight 9 he has made known to us the mystery of his will, according to his good pleasure that he set forth in Christ, 10 as a plan for the fullness of time, to gather up all things in him, things in heaven and things on earth. 11 In Christ we have also obtained an inheritance,[c] having been destined according to the purpose of him who accomplishes all things according to his counsel and will, 12 so that we, who were the first to set our hope on Christ, might live for the praise of his glory. 13 In him you also, when you had heard the word of truth, the gospel of your salvation, and had believed in him, were marked with the seal of the promised Holy Spirit; 14 this[d] is the pledge of our inheritance toward redemption as God's own people, to the praise of his glory.

15 I have heard of your faith in the Lord Jesus and your love[e] toward all the saints, and for this reason 16 I do not cease to give thanks for you as I remember you in my prayers. 17 I pray that the God of our Lord Jesus Christ, the Father of glory, may give you a spirit of wisdom and revelation as you come to know him, 18 so that, with the eyes of your heart enlightened, you may know what is the hope to which he has called you, what are the riches of his glorious inheritance among the saints, 19 and what is the immeasurable greatness of his power for us who believe, according to the working of his great power. 20 God[f] put this power to work in Christ when he raised him from the dead

and seated him at his right hand in the heavenly places, 21 far above all rule and authority and power and dominion, and above every name that is named, not only in this age but also in the age to come. 22 And he has put all things under his feet and has made him the head over all things for the church, 23 which is his body, the fullness of him who fills all in all.

2 You were dead through the trespasses and sins 2 in which you once lived, following the course of this world, following the ruler of the power of the air, the spirit that is now at work among those who are disobedient. 3 All of us once lived among them in the passions of our flesh, following the desires of flesh and senses, and we were by nature children of wrath, like everyone else. 4 But God, who is rich in mercy, out of the great love with which he loved us 5 even when we were dead through our trespasses, made us alive together with Christ[g]—by grace you have been saved— 6 and raised us up with him and seated us with him in the heavenly places in Christ Jesus, 7 so that in the ages to come he might show the immeasurable riches of his grace in kindness toward us in Christ Jesus. 8 For by grace you have been saved through faith, and this is not your own doing; it is the gift of God— 9 not the result of works, so that no one may boast. 10 For we are what he has made us, created in Christ Jesus for good works, which God prepared beforehand to be our way of life.

11 So then, remember that at one time you Gentiles by birth,[h] called "the uncircumcision" by those who are called "the circumcision"—a physical circumcision made in the flesh by human hands— 12 remember that you were at that time without Christ, being aliens from the commonwealth of Israel, and strangers to the covenants of promise, having no hope and without God in the world. 13 But now in Christ Jesus you who once were far off have been brought near by the blood of Christ. 14 For he is our peace; in his flesh he has made both groups into one and has broken down the dividing wall, that is, the hostility between us. 15 He has abolished the law with its

---

[a]Other ancient authorities lack *in Ephesus*, reading *saints who are also faithful* [b]Gk *in him* [c]Or *been made a heritage* [d]Other ancient authorities read *who* [e]Other ancient authorities lack *and your love* [f]Gk *He* [g]Other ancient authorities read *in Christ* [h]Gk *in the flesh*

commandments and ordinances, that he might create in himself one new humanity in place of the two, thus making peace, 16 and might reconcile both groups to God in one body[i] through the cross, thus putting to death that hostility through it.[j] 17 So he came and proclaimed peace to you who were far off and peace to those who were near; 18 for through him both of us have access in one Spirit to the Father. 19 So then you are no longer strangers and aliens, but you are citizens with the saints and also members of the household of God, 20 built upon the foundation of the apostles and prophets, with Christ Jesus himself as the cornerstone.[k] 21 In him the whole structure is joined together and grows into a holy temple in the Lord; 22 in whom you also are built together spiritually[l] into a dwelling place for God.

3 This is the reason that I Paul am a prisoner for[m] Christ Jesus for the sake of you Gentiles— 2 for surely you have already heard of the commission of God's grace that was given me for you, 3 and how the mystery was made known to me by revelation, as I wrote above in a few words, 4 a reading of which will enable you to perceive my understanding of the mystery of Christ. 5 In former generations this mystery[n] was not made known to humankind, as it has now been revealed to his holy apostles and prophets by the Spirit: 6 that is, the Gentiles have become fellow heirs, members of the same body, and sharers in the promise in Christ Jesus through the gospel.

7 Of this gospel I have become a servant according to the gift of God's grace that was given me by the working of his power. 8 Although I am the very least of all the saints, this grace was given to me to bring to the Gentiles the news of the boundless riches of Christ, 9 and to make everyone see[o] what is the plan of the mystery hidden for ages in[p] God who created all things; 10 so that through the church the wisdom of God in its rich variety might now be made known to the rulers and authorities in the heavenly places. 11 This was in accordance with the eternal purpose that he has carried out in Christ Jesus our Lord, 12 in whom we have access to God in boldness and confidence through faith in him.[q] 13 I pray therefore that you[r] may not lose heart over my sufferings for you; they are your glory.

14 For this reason I bow my knees before the Father,[s] 15 from whom every family[t] in heaven and on earth takes its name. 16 I pray that, according to the riches of his glory, he may grant that you may be strengthened in your inner being with power through his Spirit, 17 and that Christ may dwell in your hearts through faith, as you are being rooted and grounded in love. 18 I pray that you may have the power to comprehend, with all the saints, what is the breadth and length and height and depth, 19 and to know the love of Christ that surpasses knowledge, so that you may be filled with all the fullness of God.

20 Now to him who by the power at work within us is able to accomplish abundantly far more than all we can ask or imagine, 21 to him be glory in the church and in Christ Jesus to all generations, forever and ever. Amen.

4 I therefore, the prisoner in the Lord, beg you to lead a life worthy of the calling to which you have been called, 2 with all humility and gentleness, with patience, bearing with one another in love, 3 making every effort to maintain the unity of the Spirit in the bond of peace. 4 There is one body and one Spirit, just as you were called to the one hope of your calling, 5 one Lord, one faith, one baptism, 6 one God and Father of all, who is above all and through all and in all.

7 But each of us was given grace according to the measure of Christ's gift. 8 Therefore it is said,
   "When he ascended on high he
       made captivity itself a
           captive;
       he gave gifts to his people."[1]
9 (When it says, "He ascended," what does it mean but that he had also descended[u] into the lower parts of the earth? 10 He who descended is the same one who ascended far above all the heavens, so that he might fill all things.) 11 The gifts he gave were that some would be apostles, some prophets, some evangelists, some pastors and teachers, 12 to equip the saints for the work of ministry, for building up the body of Christ,

---

[i]Or reconcile both of us in one body for God [j]Or in him, or in himself [k]Or keystone [l]Gk in the Spirit [m]Or of [n]Gk it [o]Other ancient authorities read to bring to light [p]Or by [q]Or the faith of him [r]Or I [s]Other ancient authorities add of our Lord Jesus Christ [t]Gk fatherhood [u]Other ancient authorities add first

---

[1]Ps 68:18

13 until all of us come to the unity of the faith and of the knowledge of the Son of God, to maturity, to the measure of the full stature of Christ. 14 We must no longer be children, tossed to and fro and blown about by every wind of doctrine, by people's trickery, by their craftiness in deceitful scheming. 15 But speaking the truth in love, we must grow up in every way into him who is the head, into Christ, 16 from whom the whole body, joined and knit together by every ligament with which it is equipped, as each part is working properly, promotes the body's growth in building itself up in love.

17 Now this I affirm and insist on in the Lord: you must no longer live as the Gentiles live, in the futility of their minds. 18 They are darkened in their understanding, alienated from the life of God because of their ignorance and hardness of heart. 19 They have lost all sensitivity and have abandoned themselves to licentiousness, greedy to practice every kind of impurity. 20 That is not the way you learned Christ! 21 For surely you have heard about him and were taught in him, as truth is in Jesus. 22 You were taught to put away your former way of life, your old self, corrupt and deluded by its lusts, 23 and to be renewed in the spirit of your minds, 24 and to clothe yourselves with the new self, created according to the likeness of God in true righteousness and holiness.

25 So then, putting away falsehood, let all of us speak the truth to our neighbors, for we are members of one another. 26 Be angry but do not sin; do not let the sun go down on your anger, 27 and do not make room for the devil. 28 Thieves must give up stealing; rather let them labor and work honestly with their own hands, so as to have something to share with the needy. 29 Let no evil talk come out of your mouths, but only what is useful for building up,[v] as there is need, so that your words may give grace to those who hear. 30 And do not grieve the Holy Spirit of God, with which you were marked with a seal for the day of redemption. 31 Put away from you all bitterness and wrath and anger and wrangling and slander, together with all malice, 32 and be kind to one another, tenderhearted, forgiving one another, as God in Christ has forgiven you.[w]

5 Therefore be imitators of God, as beloved children, 2 and live in love, as Christ loved us[x] and gave himself up for us, a fragrant offering and sacrifice to God.

3 But fornication and impurity of any kind, or greed, must not even be mentioned among you, as is proper among saints. 4 Entirely out of place is obscene, silly, and vulgar talk; but instead, let there be thanksgiving. 5 Be sure of this, that no fornicator or impure person, or one who is greedy (that is, an idolater), has any inheritance in the kingdom of Christ and of God.

6 Let no one deceive you with empty words, for because of these things the wrath of God comes on those who are disobedient. 7 Therefore do not be associated with them. 8 For once you were darkness, but now in the Lord you are light. Live as children of light— 9 for the fruit of the light is found in all that is good and right and true. 10 Try to find out what is pleasing to the Lord. 11 Take no part in the unfruitful works of darkness, but instead expose them. 12 For it is shameful even to mention what such people do secretly; 13 but everything exposed by the light becomes visible, 14 for everything that becomes visible is light. Therefore it says,

> "Sleeper, awake!
> Rise from the dead,
> and Christ will shine on you."

15 Be careful then how you live, not as unwise people but as wise, 16 making the most of the time, because the days are evil. 17 So do not be foolish, but understand what the will of the Lord is. 18 Do not get drunk with wine, for that is debauchery; but be filled with the Spirit, 19 as you sing psalms and hymns and spiritual songs among yourselves, singing and making melody to the Lord in your hearts, 20 giving thanks to God the Father at all times and for everything in the name of our Lord Jesus Christ.

21 Be subject to one another out of reverence for Christ.

22 Wives, be subject to your husbands as you are to the Lord. 23 For the husband is the head of the wife just as Christ is the head of the church, the body of which he is the Savior. 24 Just as the church is subject to Christ, so also wives ought to be, in everything, to their husbands.

---

[v]Other ancient authorities read *building up faith*   [w]Other ancient authorities read *us*   [x]Other ancient authorities read *you*

25 Husbands, love your wives, just as Christ loved the church and gave himself up for her, 26 in order to make her holy by cleansing her with the washing of water by the word, 27 so as to present the church to himself in splendor, without a spot or wrinkle or anything of the kind—yes, so that she may be holy and without blemish. 28 In the same way, husbands should love their wives as they do their own bodies. He who loves his wife loves himself. 29 For no one ever hates his own body, but he nourishes and tenderly cares for it, just as Christ does for the church, 30 because we are members of his body.[y] 31 "For this reason a man will leave his father and mother and be joined to his wife, and the two will become one flesh."[2] 32 This is a great mystery, and I am applying it to Christ and the church. 33 Each of you, however, should love his wife as himself, and a wife should respect her husband.

6 Children, obey your parents in the Lord,[z] for this is right. 2 "Honor your father and mother"—this is the first commandment with a promise: 3 "so that it may be well with you and you may live long on the earth."[3]

4 And, fathers, do not provoke your children to anger, but bring them up in the discipline and instruction of the Lord.

5 Slaves, obey your earthly masters with fear and trembling, in singleness of heart, as you obey Christ; 6 not only while being watched, and in order to please them, but as slaves of Christ, doing the will of God from the heart. 7 Render service with enthusiasm, as to the Lord and not to men and women, 8 knowing that whatever good we do, we will receive the same again from the Lord, whether we are slaves or free.

9 And, masters, do the same to them. Stop threatening them, for you know that both of you have the same Master in heaven, and with him there is no partiality.

10 Finally, be strong in the Lord and in the strength of his power. 11 Put on the whole armor of God, so that you may be able to stand against the wiles of the devil. 12 For our[a] struggle is not against enemies of blood and flesh, but against the rulers, against the authorities, against the cosmic powers of this present darkness, against the spiritual forces of evil in the heavenly places. 13 Therefore take up the whole armor of God, so that you may be able to withstand on that evil day, and having done everything, to stand firm. 14 Stand therefore, and fasten the belt of truth around your waist, and put on the breastplate of righteousness. 15 As shoes for your feet put on whatever will make you ready to proclaim the gospel of peace. 16 With all of these,[b] take the shield of faith, with which you will be able to quench all the flaming arrows of the evil one. 17 Take the helmet of salvation, and the sword of the Spirit, which is the word of God.

18 Pray in the Spirit at all times in every prayer and supplication. To that end keep alert and always persevere in supplication for all the saints. 19 Pray also for me, so that when I speak, a message may be given to me to make known with boldness the mystery of the gospel,[c] 20 for which I am an ambassador in chains. Pray that I may declare it boldly, as I must speak.

21 So that you also may know how I am and what I am doing, Tychicus will tell you everything. He is a dear brother and a faithful minister in the Lord. 22 I am sending him to you for this very purpose, to let you know how we are, and to encourage your hearts.

23 Peace be to the whole community,[d] and love with faith, from God the Father and the Lord Jesus Christ. 24 Grace be with all who have an undying love for our Lord Jesus Christ.[e]

---

[y]Other ancient authorities add *of his flesh and of his bones* [z]Other ancient authorities lack *in the Lord* [a]Other ancient authorities read *your* [b]Or *in all circumstances* [c]Other ancient authorities lack *of the gospel* [d]Gk *to the brothers* [e]Other ancient authorities add *Amen*

[2]Gen 2:24 [3]Exod 20:12; Deut 5:16

The Letter to the Philippians

Scholars debate whether Paul's letter to the Philippians represents a solitary letter or a collection of two or more letters, later spliced together for broader distribution (cf. 2 Corinthians). In any event, it is clear that prior to the writing of the letter(s) a considerable amount of correspondence had been going on between Paul and the church that he founded in Philippi, in the province of Macedonia.

At the time of his writing, Paul was in prison awaiting trial and anticipating his own death (1:7, 12–26). We do not know where he was, exactly, whether in Rome, Ephesus, or somewhere else. His Philippian converts had learned of his situation and sent one of their members, a man named Epaphroditus, with a monetary gift to assist him in his time of suffering (4:10–20). After arriving, however, Epaphroditus himself fell gravely ill, nearly to the point of death. The Philippians heard of the situation and grew deeply concerned. When Epaphroditus's health returned he himself became distraught over the anxiety he had caused.

All of these issues, and several others, are addressed in the short and joyful letter (or letters) that Paul wrote from the midst of his own sufferings to those who had made a tangible expression of their love and concern for him. In part, the letter serves as a thank-you note for the gift Paul had received (4:10–20); in part it provides reassurance to the Philippians concerning the recovery of Epaphroditus (2:25–30); and in part it expresses Paul's joy in the midst of suffering and his urgent request that others follow him in rejoicing that God's work goes forward despite the harsh realities of life in this evil world (1:3–30).

Perhaps most important, Paul uses the occasion of the letter to urge the Philippians not only to rejoice in what God was doing, but also to model themselves after what he had already done through his servants. They are to give themselves to one another, following the examples provided by Epaphroditus and ultimately by Christ himself, who for the sake of others humbled himself by "taking the form of a slave," being "born in human likeness," and ultimately becoming "obedient to the point of death" (2:6–8). It was because of Christ's self-condescension that God then exalted him (2:9–11), and the Philippians should follow his lead. There should be no strife or contention in the congregation; they should treat one another as more important than themselves (2:1–4); and they should stay true to the teachings they have received, avoiding teachers in their midst who might possibly lead them astray (3:2–11).

From the New Revised Standard Version Bible, © 1989.

238

1 Paul and Timothy, servants[a] of Christ Jesus,
To all the saints in Christ Jesus who are in
Philippi, with the bishops[b] and deacons:[c]

2 Grace to you and peace from God our Father
and the Lord Jesus Christ.

3 I thank my God every time I remember you,
4 constantly praying with joy in every one of my
prayers for all of you, 5 because of your sharing
in the gospel from the first day until now. 6 I am
confident of this, that the one who began a good
work among you will bring it to completion by the
day of Jesus Christ. 7 It is right for me to think this
way about all of you, because you hold me in your
heart,[d] for all of you share in God's grace[e] with me,
both in my imprisonment and in the defense and
confirmation of the gospel. 8 For God is my witness, how I long for all of you with the compassion of Christ Jesus. 9 And this is my prayer, that
your love may overflow more and more with
knowledge and full insight 10 to help you to determine what is best, so that in the day of Christ you
may be pure and blameless, 11 having produced
the harvest of righteousness that comes through
Jesus Christ for the glory and praise of God.

12 I want you to know, beloved,[f] that what has
happened to me has actually helped to spread the
gospel, 13 so that it has become known throughout
the whole imperial guard[g] and to everyone else that
my imprisonment is for Christ; 14 and most of the
brothers and sisters,[f] having been made confident
in the Lord by my imprisonment, dare to speak the
word[h] with greater boldness and without fear.

15 Some proclaim Christ from envy and rivalry,
but others from goodwill. 16 These proclaim
Christ out of love, knowing that I have been put
here for the defense of the gospel; 17 the others
proclaim Christ out of selfish ambition, not sin-
cerely but intending to increase my suffering in
my imprisonment. 18 What does it matter? Just
this, that Christ is proclaimed in every way,
whether out of false motives or true; and in that I
rejoice.

Yes, and I will continue to rejoice, 19 for I
know that through your prayers and the help of the
Spirit of Jesus Christ this will turn out for my de-
liverance. 20 It is my eager expectation and hope
that I will not be put to shame in any way, but that
by my speaking with all boldness, Christ will be-
exalted now as always in my body, whether by life
or by death. 21 For to me, living is Christ and dying is gain. 22 If I am to live in the flesh, that
means fruitful labor for me; and I do not know
which I prefer. 23 I am hard pressed between the
two: my desire is to depart and be with Christ, for
that is far better; 24 but to remain in the flesh is
more necessary for you. 25 Since I am convinced
of this, I know that I will remain and continue with
all of you for your progress and joy in faith, 26 so
that I may share abundantly in your boasting in
Christ Jesus when I come to you again.

27 Only, live your life in a manner worthy of the
gospel of Christ, so that, whether I come and see
you or am absent and hear about you, I will know
that you are standing firm in one spirit, striving
side by side with one mind for the faith of the
gospel, 28 and are in no way intimidated by your
opponents. For them this is evidence of their destruction, but of your salvation. And this is God's
doing. 29 For he has graciously granted you the
privilege not only of believing in Christ, but of
suffering for him as well— 30 since you are having the same struggle that you saw I had and now
hear that I still have.

2 If then there is any encouragement in Christ,
any consolation from love, any sharing in
the Spirit, any compassion and sympathy, 2 make
my joy complete: be of the same mind, having the
same love, being in full accord and of one mind.
3 Do nothing from selfish ambition or conceit, but
in humility regard others as better than yourselves.
4 Let each of you look not to your own interests,
but to the interests of others. 5 Let the same mind
be in you that was[i] in Christ Jesus,

6   who, though he was in the form
        of God,
      did not regard equality with
        God
      as something to be exploited,
7   but emptied himself,
      taking the form of a slave,
      being born in human
        likeness.

Johannie (handwritten margin note)

---

[a]Gk slaves [b]Or overseers [c]Or overseers and helpers [d]Or because
I hold you in my heart [e]Gk in grace [f]Gk brothers [g]Gk whole
praetorium [h]Other ancient authorities read word of God [i]Or that
you have

And being found in human
form,

8   he humbled himself
and became obedient to the
point of death—
even death on a cross.

9   Therefore God also highly exalted
him
and gave him the name
that is above every name,

10   so that at the name of Jesus
every knee should bend,
in heaven and on earth and
under the earth,

11   and every tongue should confess
that Jesus Christ is Lord,
to the glory of God the Father.

Johannine [handwritten annotation]

Luke [handwritten annotation]

12 Therefore, my beloved, just as you have always obeyed me, not only in my presence, but much more now in my absence, work out your own salvation with fear and trembling; 13 for it is God who is at work in you, enabling you both to will and to work for his good pleasure.

14 Do all things without murmuring and arguing, 15 so that you may be blameless and innocent, children of God without blemish in the midst of a crooked and perverse generation, in which you shine like stars in the world. 16 It is by your holding fast to the word of life that I can boast on the day of Christ that I did not run in vain or labor in vain. 17 But even if I am being poured out as a libation over the sacrifice and the offering of your faith, I am glad and rejoice with all of you— 18 and in the same way you also must be glad and rejoice with me.

19 I hope in the Lord Jesus to send Timothy to you soon, so that I may be cheered by news of you. 20 I have no one like him who will be genuinely concerned for your welfare. 21 All of them are seeking their own interests, not those of Jesus Christ. 22 But Timothy's[j] worth you know, how like a son with a father he has served with me in the work of the gospel. 23 I hope therefore to send him as soon as I see how things go with me; 24 and I trust in the Lord that I will also come soon.

25 Still, I think it necessary to send to you Epaphroditus—my brother and co-worker and fel-

low soldier, your messenger[k] and minister to my need; 26 for he has been longing for[l] all of you, and has been distressed because you heard that he was ill. 27 He was indeed so ill that he nearly died. But God had mercy on him, and not only on him but on me also, so that I would not have one sorrow after another. 28 I am the more eager to send him, therefore, in order that you may rejoice at seeing him again, and that I may be less anxious. 29 Welcome him then in the Lord with all joy, and honor such people, 30 because he came close to death for the work of Christ,[m] risking his life to make up for those services that you could not give me.

3 Finally, my brothers and sisters,[n] rejoice[o] in the Lord.

To write the same things to you is not troublesome to me, and for you it is a safeguard.

2 Beware of the dogs, beware of the evil workers, beware of those who mutilate the flesh![p] 3 For it is we who are the circumcision, who worship in the Spirit of God[q] and boast in Christ Jesus and have no confidence in the flesh— 4 even though I, too, have reason for confidence in the flesh.

If anyone else has reason to be confident in the flesh, I have more: 5 circumcised on the eighth day, a member of the people of Israel, of the tribe of Benjamin, a Hebrew born of Hebrews; as to the law, a Pharisee; 6 as to zeal, a persecutor of the church; as to righteousness under the law, blameless.

7 Yet whatever gains I had, these I have come to regard as loss because of Christ. 8 More than that, I regard everything as loss because of the surpassing value of knowing Christ Jesus my Lord. For his sake I have suffered the loss of all things, and I regard them as rubbish, in order that I may gain Christ 9 and be found in him, not having a righteousness of my own that comes from the law, but one that comes through faith in Christ,[r] the righteousness from God based on faith. 10 I want to know Christ[s] and the power of his resurrection and the sharing of his sufferings by becoming like him

[j]Gk *his*   [k]Gk *apostle*   [l]Other ancient authorities read *longing to see*   [m]Other ancient authorities read *of the Lord*   [n]Gk *my brothers*   [o]Or *farewell*   [p]Gk *the mutilation*   [q]Other ancient authorities read *worship God in spirit*   [r]Or *through the faith of Christ*   [s]Gk *him*

in his death, 11 if somehow I may attain the resurrection from the dead.

12 Not that I have already obtained this or have already reached the goal;[t] but I press on to make it my own, because Christ Jesus has made me his own. 13 Beloved,[u] I do not consider that I have made it my own;[v] but this one thing I do: forgetting what lies behind and straining forward to what lies ahead, 14 I press on toward the goal for the prize of the heavenly[w] call of God in Christ Jesus. 15 Let those of us then who are mature be of the same mind; and if you think differently about anything, this too God will reveal to you. 16 Only let us hold fast to what we have attained.

17 Brothers and sisters,[a] join in imitating me, and observe those who live according to the example you have in us. 18 For many live as enemies of the cross of Christ; I have often told you of them, and now I tell you even with tears. 19 Their end is destruction; their god is the belly; and their glory is in their shame; their minds are set on earthly things. 20 But our citizenship[x] is in heaven, and it is from there that we are expecting a Savior, the Lord Jesus Christ. 21 He will transform the body of our humiliation[y] that it may be conformed to the body of his glory,[z] by the power that also enables him to make all things subject to himself.

4 Therefore, my brothers and sisters,[a] whom I love and long for, my joy and crown, stand firm in the Lord in this way, my beloved.

2 I urge Euodia and I urge Syntyche to be of the same mind in the Lord. 3 Yes, and I ask you also, my loyal companion,[b] help these women, for they have struggled beside me in the work of the gospel, together with Clement and the rest of my co-workers, whose names are in the book of life.

4 Rejoice[c] in the Lord always; again I will say, Rejoice.[c] 5 Let your gentleness be known to everyone. The Lord is near. 6 Do not worry about anything, but in everything by prayer and supplication with thanksgiving let your requests be made known to God. 7 And the peace of God, which surpasses all understanding, will guard your hearts and your minds in Christ Jesus.

8 Finally, beloved,[d] whatever is true, whatever is honorable, whatever is just, whatever is pure, whatever is pleasing, whatever is commendable, if there is any excellence and if there is anything worthy of praise, think about[e] these things. 9 Keep on doing the things that you have learned and received and heard and seen in me, and the God of peace will be with you.

10 I rejoice[f] in the Lord greatly that now at last you have revived your concern for me; indeed, you were concerned for me, but had no opportunity to show it.[g] 11 Not that I am referring to being in need; for I have learned to be content with whatever I have. 12 I know what it is to have little, and I know what it is to have plenty. In any and all circumstances I have learned the secret of being well-fed and of going hungry, of having plenty and of being in need. 13 I can do all things through him who strengthens me. 14 In any case, it was kind of you to share my distress.

15 You Philippians indeed know that in the early days of the gospel, when I left Macedonia, no church shared with me in the matter of giving and receiving, except you alone. 16 For even when I was in Thessalonica, you sent me help for my needs more than once. 17 Not that I seek the gift, but I seek the profit that accumulates to your account. 18 I have been paid in full and have more than enough; I am fully satisfied, now that I have received from Epaphroditus the gifts you sent, a fragrant offering, a sacrifice acceptable and pleasing to God. 19 And my God will fully satisfy every need of yours according to his riches in glory in Christ Jesus. 20 To our God and Father be glory forever and ever. Amen.

21 Greet every saint in Christ Jesus. The friends[d] who are with me greet you. 22 All the saints greet you, especially those of the emperor's household.

23 The grace of the Lord Jesus Christ be with your spirit.[h]

---

[t] Or *have already been made perfect* [u] Gk *Brothers* [v] Other ancient authorities read *my own yet* [w] Gk *upward* [x] Or *commonwealth* [y] Or *our humble bodies* [z] Or *his glorious body* [a] Gk *my brothers* [b] Or *loyal Syzygus* [c] Or *Farewell* [d] Gk *brothers* [e] Gk *take account of* [f] Gk *I rejoiced* [g] Gk lacks *to show it* [h] Other ancient authorities add *Amen*

The Letter to the Colossians

The letter to the Colossians is directed against a group of "false teachers" who had infiltrated the Christian community (2:4). The author does not indicate the precise nature of the teaching, which he labels a "philosophy and empty deceit" (2:8). It appears to have involved some kind of Jewish mysticism, in which aspects of the Jewish Law were to be rigorously followed (2:11–17), an ascetic lifestyle was to be maintained (2:18), and angelic beings were to be worshipped (2:19). These mystical practices were evidently intended to unite believers with the divine.

In response, the author insists that Christ himself is "the image of the invisible God," and that "the fullness of God" dwells in him (1:15, 19). There is no need, therefore, to worship other beings; indeed, Christ himself created these beings and is lord over them (1:16). It is Christ who bestows all blessings on believers (1:21–22; 2:13–15), including the true "spiritual circumcision" (2:9–10). Through his death he destroyed everything that brings alienation from God, including the "legal demands" (2:14) so cherished by the author's opponents.

According to this author, believers in Christ have already been raised with him and are dwelling with him in the heavenly places (3:1); they do not therefore need "visions" of the divine realm. Nor do they need purity regulations that bring only the appearance of piety; in Christ, believers have the full experience of the divine itself (2:20–23). This does not mean, however, that they are free to neglect social and moral obligations in this world. Until Christ himself returns they must continue to avoid vice (3:5–11), embrace virtue (3:12–17), and live appropriately according to their social roles (3:18–4:1).

Scholars continue to debate whether Paul himself wrote this letter. On the one hand, the prescript, the basic layout of the letter, and the closing all sound like Paul, and a number of Pauline themes are sounded throughout. On the other hand, the writing style (as seen in the Greek) is quite different from Paul's, especially in the use of long complex sentences. Even more important, the central claim of the letter, that believers have already been raised with Christ and are presently enjoying the full blessings of heaven (e.g., 3:1), seems to stand at direct odds with what Paul himself says elsewhere. For Paul, believers have already "died" with Christ, but they have *not* yet been raised with him; nor will they be until he returns (cf. Rom 6:1–6, where he is emphatic about just this point). In fact, 1 Corinthians appears to oppose precisely the perspective advanced here, that believers are already residing in the heavenly places and ruling with Christ.

For these reasons many scholars believe this letter to be pseudonymous, written perhaps a generation after Paul by a member of one of his churches who chose to address a new problem that had arisen in his community by appealing to the authority of the apostle in support of his views.

1 Paul, an apostle of Christ Jesus by the will of God, and Timothy our brother,

2 To the saints and faithful brothers and sisters[a] in Christ in Colossae:

Grace to you and peace from God our Father.

3 In our prayers for you we always thank God, the Father of our Lord Jesus Christ, 4 for we have heard of your faith in Christ Jesus and of the love that you have for all the saints, 5 because of the hope laid up for you in heaven. You have heard of this hope before in the word of the truth, the gospel 6 that has come to you. Just as it is bearing fruit and growing in the whole world, so it has been bearing fruit among yourselves from the day you heard it and truly comprehended the grace of God. 7 This you learned from Epaphras, our beloved fellow servant.[b] He is a faithful minister of Christ on your[c] behalf, 8 and he has made known to us your love in the Spirit.

9 For this reason, since the day we heard it, we have not ceased praying for you and asking that you may be filled with the knowledge of God's[d] will in all spiritual wisdom and understanding, 10 so that you may lead lives worthy of the Lord, fully pleasing to him, as you bear fruit in every good work and as you grow in the knowledge of God. 11 May you be made strong with all the strength that comes from his glorious power, and may you be prepared to endure everything with patience, while joyfully 12 giving thanks to the Father, who has enabled[e] you[f] to share in the inheritance of the saints in the light. 13 He has rescued us from the power of darkness and transferred us into the kingdom of his beloved Son, 14 in whom we have redemption, the forgiveness of sins.[g]

15 He is the image of the invisible God, the firstborn of all creation; 16 for in[h] him all things in heaven and on earth were created, things visible and invisible, whether thrones or dominions or rulers or powers—all things have been created through him and for him. 17 He himself is before all things, and in[h] him all things hold together. 18 He is the head of the body, the church; he is the beginning, the firstborn from the dead, so that he might come to have first place in everything. 19 For in him all the fullness of God was pleased to dwell, 20 and through him God was pleased to reconcile to himself all things, whether on earth or in heaven, by making peace through the blood of his cross.

21 And you who were once estranged and hostile in mind, doing evil deeds, 22 he has now reconciled[i] in his fleshly body[j] through death, so as to present you holy and blameless and irreproachable before him— 23 provided that you continue securely established and steadfast in the faith, without shifting from the hope promised by the gospel that you heard, which has been proclaimed to every creature under heaven. I, Paul, became a servant of this gospel.

24 I am now rejoicing in my sufferings for your sake, and in my flesh I am completing what is lacking in Christ's afflictions for the sake of his body, that is, the church. 25 I became its servant according to God's commission that was given to me for you, to make the word of God fully known, 26 the mystery that has been hidden throughout the ages and generations but has now been revealed to his saints. 27 To them God chose to make known how great among the Gentiles are the riches of the glory of this mystery, which is Christ in you, the hope of glory. 28 It is he whom we proclaim, warning everyone and teaching everyone in all wisdom, so that we may present everyone mature in Christ. 29 For this I toil and struggle with all the energy that he powerfully inspires within me.

2 For I want you to know how much I am struggling for you, and for those in Laodicea, and for all who have not seen me face to face. 2 I want their hearts to be encouraged and united in love, so that they may have all the riches of assured understanding and have the knowledge of God's mystery, that is, Christ himself,[k] 3 in whom are hidden all the treasures of wisdom and knowledge. 4 I am saying this so that no one may deceive you with plausible arguments. 5 For though I am absent in body, yet I am with you in spirit, and I rejoice to see your morale and the firmness of your faith in Christ.

6 As you therefore have received Christ Jesus

---

[a] Gk brothers [b] Gk slave [c] Other ancient authorities read our [d] Gk his [e] Other ancient authorities read called [f] Other ancient authorities read us [g] Other ancient authorities add through his blood [h] Or by [i] Other ancient authorities read you have now been reconciled [j] Gk in the body of his flesh [k] Other ancient authorities read of the mystery of God, both of the Father and of Christ

the Lord, continue to live your lives[l] in him, 7 rooted and built up in him and established in the faith, just as you were taught, abounding in thanksgiving.

8 See to it that no one takes you captive through philosophy and empty deceit, according to human tradition, according to the elemental spirits of the universe,[m] and not according to Christ. 9 For in him the whole fullness of deity dwells bodily, 10 and you have come to fullness in him, who is the head of every ruler and authority. 11 In him also you were circumcised with a spiritual circumcision,[n] by putting off the body of the flesh in the circumcision of Christ; 12 when you were buried with him in baptism, you were also raised with him through faith in the power of God, who raised him from the dead. 13 And when you were dead in trespasses and the uncircumcision of your flesh, God[o] made you[p] alive together with him, when he forgave us all our trespasses, 14 erasing the record that stood against us with its legal demands. He set this aside, nailing it to the cross. 15 He disarmed[q] the rulers and authorities and made a public example of them, triumphing over them in it.

16 Therefore do not let anyone condemn you in matters of food and drink or of observing festivals, new moons, or sabbaths. 17 These are only a shadow of what is to come, but the substance belongs to Christ. 18 Do not let anyone disqualify you, insisting on self-abasement and worship of angels, dwelling[r] on visions,[s] puffed up without cause by a human way of thinking,[t] 19 and not holding fast to the head, from whom the whole body, nourished and held together by its ligaments and sinews, grows with a growth that is from God.

20 If with Christ you died to the elemental spirits of the universe,[m] why do you live as if you still belonged to the world? Why do you submit to regulations, 21 "Do not handle, Do not taste, Do not touch"? 22 All these regulations refer to things that perish with use; they are simply human commands and teachings. 23 These have indeed an appearance of wisdom in promoting self-imposed piety, humility, and severe treatment of the body, but they are of no value in checking self-indulgence.[u]

Already been raised w/ Christ

3 So if you have been raised with Christ, seek the things that are above, where Christ is, seated at the right hand of God. 2 Set your minds on things that are above, not on things that are on earth, 3 for you have died, and your life is hidden with Christ in God. 4 When Christ who is your[v] life is revealed, then you also will be revealed with him in glory.

5 Put to death, therefore, whatever in you is earthly: fornication, impurity, passion, evil desire, and greed (which is idolatry). 6 On account of these the wrath of God is coming on those who are disobedient.[w] 7 These are the ways you also once followed, when you were living that life.[x] 8 But now you must get rid of all such things—anger, wrath, malice, slander, and abusive[y] language from your mouth. 9 Do not lie to one another, seeing that you have stripped off the old self with its practices 10 and have clothed yourselves with the new self, which is being renewed in knowledge according to the image of its creator. 11 In that renewal[z] there is no longer Greek and Jew, circumcised and uncircumcised, barbarian, Scythian, slave and free; but Christ is all and in all!

12 As God's chosen ones, holy and beloved, clothe yourselves with compassion, kindness, humility, meekness, and patience. 13 Bear with one another and, if anyone has a complaint against another, forgive each other; just as the Lord[a] has forgiven you, so you also must forgive. 14 Above all, clothe yourselves with love, which binds everything together in perfect harmony. 15 And let the peace of Christ rule in your hearts, to which indeed you were called in the one body. And be thankful. 16 Let the word of Christ[b] dwell in you richly; teach and admonish one another in all wisdom; and with gratitude in your hearts sing psalms, hymns, and spiritual songs to God.[c] 17 And whatever you do, in word or deed, do everything in the name of the Lord Jesus, giving thanks to God the Father through him.

---

[l]Gk *to walk*   [m]Or *the rudiments of the world*   [n]Gk *a circumcision made without hands*   [o]Gk *he*   [p]Other ancient authorities read *made us*; others, *made*   [q]Or *divested himself of*   [r]Other ancient authorities read *not dwelling*   [s]Meaning of Gk uncertain   [t]Gk *by the mind of his flesh*   [u]Or *are of no value, serving only to indulge the flesh*   [v]Other authorities read *our*   [w]Other ancient authorities lack *on those who are disobedient* (Gk *the children of disobedience*)   [x]Or *living among such people*   [y]Or *filthy*   [z]Gk *its creator,*   [11]where   [a]Other ancient authorities read *just as Christ*   [b]Other ancient authorities read *of God,* or *of the Lord*   [c]Other ancient authorities read *to the Lord*

18 Wives, be subject to your husbands, as is fitting in the Lord. 19 Husbands, love your wives and never treat them harshly.

20 Children, obey your parents in everything, for this is your acceptable duty in the Lord. 21 Fathers, do not provoke your children, or they may lose heart. 22 Slaves, obey your earthly masters[d] in everything, not only while being watched and in order to please them, but wholeheartedly, fearing the Lord.[d] 23 Whatever your task, put yourselves into it, as done for the Lord and not for your masters,[e] 24 since you know that from the Lord you will receive the inheritance as your reward; you serve[f] the Lord Christ. 25 For the wrongdoer will be paid back for whatever wrong has been done, and there is no partiality.

4 Masters, treat your slaves justly and fairly, for you know that you also have a Master in heaven.

2 Devote yourselves to prayer, keeping alert in it with thanksgiving. 3 At the same time pray for us as well that God will open to us a door for the word, that we may declare the mystery of Christ, for which I am in prison, 4 so that I may reveal it clearly, as I should.

5 Conduct yourselves wisely toward outsiders, making the most of the time.[g] 6 Let your speech always be gracious, seasoned with salt, so that you may know how you ought to answer everyone.

7 Tychicus will tell you all the news about me; he is a beloved brother, a faithful minister, and a fellow servant[h] in the Lord. 8 I have sent him to you for this very purpose, so that you may know how we are[i] and that he may encourage your hearts; 9 he is coming with Onesimus, the faithful and beloved brother, who is one of you. They will tell you about everything here.

10 Aristarchus my fellow prisoner greets you, as does Mark the cousin of Barnabas, concerning whom you have received instructions—if he comes to you, welcome him. 11 And Jesus who is called Justus greets you. These are the only ones of the circumcision among my co-workers for the kingdom of God, and they have been a comfort to me. 12 Epaphras, who is one of you, a servant[h] of Christ Jesus, greets you. He is always wrestling in his prayers on your behalf, so that you may stand mature and fully assured in everything that God wills. 13 For I testify for him that he has worked hard for you and for those in Laodicea and in Hierapolis. 14 Luke, the beloved physician, and Demas greet you. 15 Give my greetings to the brothers and sisters[j] in Laodicea, and to Nym-pha and the church in her house. 16 And when this letter has been read among you, have it read also in the church of the Laodiceans; and see that you read also the letter from Laodicea. 17 And say to Archippus, "See that you complete the task that you have received in the Lord."

18 I, Paul, write this greeting with my own hand. Remember my chains. Grace be with you.[k]

---

[d]In Greek the same word is used for *master* and *Lord*   [e]Gk *not for men*   [f]Or *you are slaves of, or be slaves of*   [g]Or *opportunity*   [h]Gk *slave*   [i]Other authorities read *that I may know how you are*   [j]Gk *brothers*   [k]Other ancient authorities add *Amen*

Gentiles
1:9

—Small grp (8/15 people)

The First Letter to the Thessalonians

live in Greek city

very friendly letter, gentle
—building them up
—uses "brothers" a lot
—form into family

First Thessalonians was the first book of the New Testament to be written (ca. 50 C.E.). This makes it the oldest surviving piece of literature from early Christianity. It is addressed by Paul and his two companions, Timothy and Silvanus, to the church that they jointed founded in Thessalonica, capital of the province of Macedonia. It is a particularly personal and joyful letter, full of fond recollections of the relationship these three missionaries shared with their converts when they first were with them.

The community was comprised of Gentiles who had been converted from their polytheistic worship of idols "to serve a living and true God, and to wait for his Son from heaven whom he raised from the dead" (1:9–10). Possibly because Paul had not spent much time among the Thessalonian Christians before moving on, questions had arisen in his absence. Having sent Timothy back to check up on the congregation and having learned of the problems that had emerged, Paul, along with his two fellow-missionaries, now writes this letter in response (3:1–6).

The principal problem appears to have involved Paul's message of the imminent return of Christ in judgment. Paul had persuaded his converts that Jesus, who was now exalted to heaven, was soon to appear again to remove those who believe in him from this sinful world and to allow them to enter into the glorious kingdom that he would bring. But Christ had not yet returned, and in the meantime some of the members of the Thessalonian congregation had died. This caused some consternation among those left behind (4:13). Have those who died missed out on their heavenly reward? Will they not enjoy the blessings of the kingdom when Christ returns?

Paul writes not only to reestablish friendly contact with his Thessalonian converts and to encourage them in their faith, but also to console them in the face of their loss and to affirm that in fact the dead in Christ have not lost out on the glories to be brought at his return. For when Jesus appears from heaven, "the dead in Christ will rise first"; and then "we who are alive, who are left will be caught up in the clouds together with them, to meet the Lord in the air" (4:16–17). The Thessalonians can continue to be assured that this cataclysmic event will come soon. And they should be alert and ready, lest they be caught unawares; for it will come unexpectedly, "like a thief in the night" (5:1–11).

In the meantime, the Thessalonians are to keep the faith, even in the midst of opposition by their non-Christian opponents (4:13–16). They are to live moral and upright lives, avoiding sexual impurity among themselves (4:1–8). And they are to project an acceptable and attractive image to those outside the church by the way they live and relate to one another (4:9–12).

—Remind them

—keeps thanking (3 times)

Deeds of Power
1:4

1

Paul, Silvanus, and Timothy,

To the church of the Thessalonians in God the Father and the Lord Jesus Christ: *Re character of thessalonians*

Grace to you and peace. *prayer*

2 We always give thanks to God for all of you and mention you in our prayers, constantly 3 remembering before our God and Father your work *describe* of faith and labor of love and steadfastness of hope *prayer* in our Lord Jesus Christ. 4 For we know, brothers *hstreaty* and sisters[a] beloved by God, that he has chosen you, 5 because our message of the gospel came to you not in word only, but also in power and in the Holy Spirit and with full conviction; just as you know what kind of persons we proved to be among you for your sake. 6 And you became imitators of us and of the Lord, for in spite of persecution you received the word with joy inspired by the Holy Spirit, 7 so that you became an example to all the believers in Macedonia and in Achaia. 8 For the word of the Lord has sounded forth from you not only in Macedonia and Achaia, but in every place your faith in God has become known, so that we have no need to speak about it. 9 For the people of those regions[b] report about us what kind of welcome we had among you, and how you turned to God from idols, to serve a living and true God, 10 and to wait for his Son from heaven, whom he raised from the dead—Jesus, who rescues us from the wrath that is coming. *eschatology*

2

You yourselves know, brothers and sisters,[a] that our coming to you was not in vain, 2 but though we had already suffered and been shamefully mistreated at Philippi, as you know, we had courage in our God to declare to you the gospel of God in spite of great opposition. 3 For our appeal *some one* does not spring from deceit or impure motives or *accuse* trickery, 4 but just as we have been approved by *of* God to be entrusted with the message of the *deceit* gospel, even so we speak, not to please mortals, but to please God who tests our hearts. 5 As you know and as God is our witness, we never came with words of flattery or with a pretext for greed; 6 nor did we seek praise from mortals, whether from you or from others, 7 though we might have made demands as apostles of Christ. But we were gentle[c] among you, like a nurse tenderly caring for her own children. 8 So deeply do we care for you that we are determined to share with you not only

the gospel of God but also our own selves, because you have become very dear to us.

9 You remember our labor and toil, brothers and sisters;[a] we worked night and day, so that we might not burden any of you while we proclaimed to you the gospel of God. 10 You are witnesses, and God also, how pure, upright, and blameless our conduct was toward you believers. 11 As you know, we dealt with each one of you like a father with his children, 12 urging and encouraging you and pleading that you lead a life worthy of God, who calls you into his own kingdom and glory. *Motives were pure -I did not rip you off*

13 We also constantly give thanks to God for this, that when you received the word of God that you heard from us, you accepted it not as a human word but as what it really is, God's word, which is also at work in you believers. 14 For you, brothers and sisters,[a] became imitators of the churches of God in Christ Jesus that are in Judea, for you suffered the same things from your own compatriots as they did from the Jews, 15 who killed both the Lord Jesus and the prophets,[d] and drove us out; they displease God and oppose everyone 16 by hindering us from speaking to the Gentiles so that they may be saved. Thus they have constantly been filling up the measure of their sins; but God's wrath has overtaken them at last.[e]

17 As for us, brothers and sisters,[a] when, for a short time, we were made orphans by being separated from you—in person, not in heart—we longed with great eagerness to see you face to face. 18 For we wanted to come to you—certainly I, Paul, wanted to again and again—but Satan blocked our way. 19 For what is our hope or joy or crown of boasting before our Lord Jesus at his coming? Is it not you? 20 Yes, you are our glory and joy!

3

Therefore when we could bear it no longer, we decided to be left alone in Athens; 2 and we sent Timothy, our brother and co-worker for God in proclaiming[f] the gospel of Christ, to strengthen and encourage you for the sake of your faith, 3 so that no one would be shaken by these persecutions. Indeed, you yourselves know that this is what we are destined for. 4 In fact, when we were with you, we told you beforehand that we

---

[a] Gk *brothers*   [b] Gk *For they*   [c] Other ancient authorities read *infants*
[d] Other ancient authorities read *their own prophets*   [e] Or *completely* or *forever*   [f] Gk lacks *proclaiming*

hired by family to nurse children (not her own)

were to suffer persecution; so it turned out, as you know. 5 For this reason, when I could bear it no longer, I sent to find out about your faith; I was afraid that somehow the tempter had tempted you and that our labor had been in vain.

6 But Timothy has just now come to us from you, and has brought us the good news of your faith and love. He has told us also that you always remember us kindly and long to see us—just as we long to see you. 7 For this reason, brothers and sisters,[g] during all our distress and persecution we have been encouraged about you through your faith. 8 For we now live, if you continue to stand firm in the Lord. 9 How can we thank God enough for you in return for all the joy that we feel before our God because of you? 10 Night and day we pray most earnestly that we may see you face to face and restore whatever is lacking in your faith.

11 Now may our God and Father himself and our Lord Jesus direct our way to you. 12 And may the Lord make you increase and abound in love for one another and for all, just as we abound in love for you. 13 And may he so strengthen your hearts in holiness that you may be blameless before our God and Father at the coming of our Lord Jesus with all his saints.

Possible Benediction

looks like end of letter. possible seam?

4 Finally, brothers and sisters,[g] we ask and urge you in the Lord Jesus that, as you learned from us how you ought to live and to please God (as, in fact, you are doing), you should do so more and more. 2 For you know what instructions we gave you through the Lord Jesus. 3 For this is the will of God, your sanctification: that you abstain from fornication; 4 that each one of you know how to control your own body[h] in holiness and honor, 5 not with lustful passion, like the Gentiles who do not know God; 6 that no one wrong or exploit a brother or sister[i] in this matter, because the Lord is an avenger in all these things, just as we have already told you beforehand and solemnly warned you. 7 For God did not call us to impurity but in holiness. 8 Therefore whoever rejects this rejects not human authority but God, who also gives his Holy Spirit to you.

Spirit + church ethical life is meshed with life w/ God/Spirit

9 Now concerning love of the brothers and sisters,[g] you do not need to have anyone write to you, for you yourselves have been taught by God to love one another; 10 and indeed you do love all the brothers and sisters[g] throughout Macedonia. But we urge you, beloved,[g] to do so more and more, 11 to aspire to live quietly, to mind your own affairs, and to work with your hands, as we directed you, 12 so that you may behave properly toward outsiders and be dependent on no one.

13 But we do not want you to be uninformed, brothers and sisters,[g] about those who have died,[j] so that you may not grieve as others do who have no hope. 14 For since we believe that Jesus died and rose again, even so, through Jesus, God will bring with him those who have died.[j] 15 For this we declare to you by the word of the Lord, that we who are alive, who are left until the coming of the Lord, will by no means precede those who have died.[j] 16 For the Lord himself, with a cry of command, with the archangel's call and with the sound of God's trumpet, will descend from heaven, and the dead in Christ will rise first. 17 Then we who are alive, who are left, will be caught up in the clouds together with them to meet the Lord in the air; and so we will be with the Lord forever. 18 Therefore encourage one another with these words.

5 Now concerning the times and the seasons, brothers and sisters,[g] you do not need to have anything written to you. 2 For you yourselves know very well that the day of the Lord will come like a thief in the night. 3 When they say, "There is peace and security," then sudden destruction will come upon them, as labor pains come upon a pregnant woman, and there will be no escape! 4 But you, beloved,[g] are not in darkness, for that day to surprise you like a thief; 5 for you are all children of light and children of the day; we are not of the night or of darkness. 6 So then let us not fall asleep as others do, but let us keep awake and be sober; 7 for those who sleep sleep at night, and those who are drunk get drunk at night. 8 But since we belong to the day, let us be sober, and put on the breastplate of faith and love, and for a helmet the hope of salvation. 9 For God has destined us not for wrath but for obtaining salvation through our Lord Jesus Christ,

[g]Gk *brothers*   [h]Or *how to take a wife for himself*   [i]Gk *brother*
[j]Gk *fallen asleep*

doesn't mean community is a bunch of drunks, could just be general advice

10 who died for us, so that whether we are awake or asleep we may live with him. 11 Therefore encourage one another and build up each other, as indeed you are doing.

12 But we appeal to you, brothers and sisters,[k] to respect those who labor among you, and have charge of you in the Lord and admonish you; 13 esteem them very highly in love because of their work. Be at peace among yourselves. 14 And we urge you, beloved,[k] to admonish the idlers, encourage the fainthearted, help the weak, be patient with all of them. 15 See that none of you repays evil for evil, but always seek to do good to one another and to all. 16 Rejoice always, 17 pray without ceasing, 18 give thanks in all circumstances; for this is the will of God in Christ Jesus for you. 19 Do not quench the Spirit. 20 Do not despise the words of prophets,[l] 21 but test everything; hold fast to what is good; 22 abstain from every form of evil.

23 May the God of peace himself sanctify you entirely; and may your spirit and soul and body be kept sound[m] and blameless at the coming of our Lord Jesus Christ. 24 The one who calls you is faithful, and he will do this.

25 Beloved,[n] pray for us.

26 Greet all the brothers and sisters[o] with a holy kiss. 27 I solemnly command you by the Lord that this letter be read to all of them.[p]

28 The grace of our Lord Jesus Christ be with you.[q]

[k]Gk brothers [l]Gk despise prophecies [m]Or complete
[n]Gk Brothers [o]Gk brothers [p]Gk to all the brothers [q]Other ancient authorities add Amen

The Second Letter to the Thessalonians

One of the Deutero-Pauline epistles, 2 Thessalonians is a letter assigned by many scholars, not to Paul himself, but to a member of one of his churches—a "second" Paul—some years after the apostle's death (see also the introductions to Ephesians and Colossians). Whoever actually wrote the letter, its occasion and purpose are relatively clear. The people to whom it is addressed are experiencing persecution for their faith (1:4–6); moreover, their suffering has led some of their number to believe that the end of the age is absolutely imminent (2:1–2). Some of them have taken this belief to an extreme, having quit their jobs in anticipation of Christ's immediate return. Problems within the community have erupted as a result; those who continue to earn a living are having to support those who do not (3:6–15).

The letter was written in part to comfort those who were being persecuted for their faith. Their enemies would be punished with "eternal destruction" at Christ's return, whereas they themselves would enter into their glorious reward (1:7–12). This cataclysmic event, however, was not to take place in the immediate future. Notwithstanding prophecies made in the church and a letter allegedly from the apostle, the end had not yet arrived (2:1–3). According to this author, an entire sequence of events was to transpire before Christ would return: an anti-Christ figure was to arise who would establish himself in the Jerusalem temple and declare himself to be God (2:3–5). Only then would Christ come for a final confrontation with the forces of evil (2:6–12). The Thessalonians, therefore, were not to think that the end was absolutely imminent. They were to return to work and patiently wait for the end that was destined, eventually, to come (3:6–12).

Parts of this letter bear a close resemblance to writings that are undisputably from Paul, including the prescript (2 Thess 1:1; cf. 1 Thess 2:1) and certain echoes of 1 Thessalonians (3:7–9; cf. 1 Thess 2:9). The difficulty with ascribing it to Paul himself, however, is the apocalyptic scenario that lies at its core. For if in fact a series of earthly events was to transpire before the end could come (such as the public appearance of the anti-Christ), how could Paul have earlier warned the Thessalonians to be prepared at all times for the imminent return of Christ, which would happen "suddenly," "like a thief in the night" (1 Thess 5:1–10)? In the view of most scholars, either Paul seriously changed his mind about a major component of his teaching, or the second letter to the Thessalonians came from a different hand, possibly a member of one of Paul's churches living a generation later, when some Christians *continued* to believe that the end was to come in the immediate future and had begun to act upon this conviction.

1 Paul, Silvanus, and Timothy,
To the church of the Thessalonians in God our Father and the Lord Jesus Christ:

2 Grace to you and peace from God our[a] Father and the Lord Jesus Christ.

3 We must always give thanks to God for you, brothers and sisters,[b] as is right, because your faith is growing abundantly, and the love of everyone of you for one another is increasing. 4 Therefore we ourselves boast of you among the churches of God for your steadfastness and faith during all your persecutions and the afflictions that you are enduring.

5 This is evidence of the righteous judgment of God, and is intended to make you worthy of the kingdom of God, for which you are also suffering. 6 For it is indeed just of God to repay with affliction those who afflict you, 7 and to give relief to the afflicted as well as to us, when the Lord Jesus is revealed from heaven with his mighty angels 8 in flaming fire, inflicting vengeance on those who do not know God and on those who do not obey the gospel of our Lord Jesus. 9 These will suffer the punishment of eternal destruction, separated from the presence of the Lord and from the glory of his might, 10 when he comes to be glorified by his saints and to be marveled at on that day among all who have believed, because our testimony to you was believed. 11 To this end we always pray for you, asking that our God will make you worthy of his call and will fulfil by his power every good resolve and work of faith, 12 so that the name of our Lord Jesus may be glorified in you, and you in him, according to the grace of our God and the Lord Jesus Christ.

2 As to the coming of our Lord Jesus Christ and our being gathered together to him, we beg you, brothers and sisters,[b] 2 not to be quickly shaken in mind or alarmed, either by spirit or by word or by letter, as though from us, to the effect that the day of the Lord is already here. 3 Let no one deceive you in any way; for that day will not come unless the rebellion comes first and the lawless one[c] is revealed, the one destined for destruction.[d] 4 He opposes and exalts himself above every so-called god or object of worship, so that he takes his seat in the temple of God, declaring himself to be God. 5 Do you not remember that I told you these things when I was still with you? 6 And you know what is now restraining him, so

that he may be revealed when his time comes. 7 For the mystery of lawlessness is already at work, but only until the one who now restrains it is removed. 8 And then the lawless one will be revealed, whom the Lord Jesus[e] will destroy[f] with the breath of his mouth, annihilating him by the manifestation of his coming. 9 The coming of the lawless one is apparent in the working of Satan, who uses all power, signs, lying wonders, 10 and every kind of wicked deception for those who are perishing, because they refused to love the truth and so be saved. 11 For this reason God sends them a powerful delusion, leading them to believe what is false, 12 so that all who have not believed the truth but took pleasure in unrighteousness will be condemned.

13 But we must always give thanks to God for you, brothers and sisters[b] beloved by the Lord, because God chose you as the first fruits[g] for salvation through sanctification by the Spirit and through belief in the truth. 14 For this purpose he called you through our proclamation of the good news,[h] so that you may obtain the glory of our Lord Jesus Christ. 15 So then, brothers and sisters,[b] stand firm and hold fast to the traditions that you were taught by us, either by word of mouth or by our letter.

16 Now may our Lord Jesus Christ himself and God our Father, who loved us and through grace gave us eternal comfort and good hope, 17 comfort your hearts and strengthen them in every good work and word.

3 Finally, brothers and sisters,[b] pray for us, so that the word of the Lord may spread rapidly and be glorified everywhere, just as it is among you, 2 and that we may be rescued from wicked and evil people; for not all have faith. 3 But the Lord is faithful; he will strengthen you and guard you from the evil one.[i] 4 And we have confidence in the Lord concerning you, that you are doing and will go on doing the things that we command. 5 May the Lord direct your hearts to the love of God and to the steadfastness of Christ.

---

[a]Other ancient authorities read *the* [b]Gk *brothers* [c]Gk *the man of lawlessness*; other ancient authorities read *the man of sin* [d]Gk *the son of destruction* [e]Other ancient authorities lack *Jesus* [f]Other ancient authorities read *consume* [g]Other ancient authorities read *from the beginning* [h]Or *through our gospel* [i]Or *from evil*

6 Now we command you, beloved,[j] in the name of our Lord Jesus Christ, to keep away from believers who are[k] living in idleness and not according to the tradition that they[l] received from us. 7 For you yourselves know how you ought to imitate us; we were not idle when we were with you, 8 and we did not eat anyone's bread without paying for it; but with toil and labor we worked night and day, so that we might not burden any of you. 9 This was not because we do not have that right, but in order to give you an example to imitate. 10 For even when we were with you, we gave you this command: Anyone unwilling to work should not eat. 11 For we hear that some of you are living in idleness, mere busybodies, not doing any work. 12 Now such persons we command and exhort in the Lord Jesus Christ to do their work qui-

etly and to earn their own living. 13 Brothers and sisters,[m] do not be weary in doing what is right.

14 Take note of those who do not obey what we say in this letter; have nothing to do with them, so that they may be ashamed. 15 Do not regard them as enemies, but warn them as believers.[n]

16 Now may the Lord of peace himself give you peace at all times in all ways. The Lord be with all of you.

17 I, Paul, write this greeting with my own hand. This is the mark in every letter of mine; it is the way I write. 18 The grace of our Lord Jesus Christ be with all of you.[o]

[j]Gk brothers [k]Ck from every brother who is [l]Other ancient authorities read you [m]Gk Brothers [n]Gk a brother [o]Other ancient authorities add Amen

The First Letter to Timothy

1 and 2 Timothy and Titus are commonly designated the Pastoral Epistles. Each of these letters purports to be written by the apostle Paul to a person he has chosen to lead one of his churches; the letters contain pastoral advice concerning how these appointed representatives ("pastors") should tend their Christian flocks. Although each epistle presupposes a slightly different situation, the overarching issues are the same: (a) false teachers creating problems for the congregations, and (b) the internal organization of the Christian communities.

Because the vocabulary, theological ideas, and presupposed historical contexts of these letters differ so markedly from those of the undisputedly Pauline letters, the majority of scholars today maintain that the Pastoral Epistles did not actually come from Paul's hand, but from a later author of one of his churches, who wrote in the apostle's name to authorize his own opposition to "false" teachers and to sanction his vision of how the church should be organized. Both the rigorous church structure promoted here and the gnostic character of the author's opponents point to a time of composition several decades after Paul's death, possibly near the end of the first century or the beginning of the second.

In order to advance his views, this pseudonymous and otherwise unknown author embedded a plausible historical context within each of his letters. The letter of 1 Timothy presupposes that Paul has left Timothy behind in the city of Ephesus in order to bring the false teachers within the Christian congregation under control (1:3–11), to establish order in the church (2:1–15), and to appoint moral and upright leaders to administer the community's affairs (3:1–13). Most of the letter consists of instructions concerning Christian living and social interaction, with respect, for example, to Christians' treatment of the elderly, widows, and their own leaders, and Christians' disposition toward needless asceticism, material wealth, and heretics who corrupt the truth.

Since these heretics are said to have been enthralled with "myths and endless genealogies" (1:4), to have used the Jewish Scriptures to support their views (1:6), to have demanded strict ascetic practices (4:3), and to have promoted the "contradictions of what is falsely called knowledge" (*gnosis*) (6:20), they may have represented an early form of Jewish-Christian Gnosticism. It may be that some of the prominent women in the congregation were particularly attracted to this perspective; this would explain the author's insistence that women be silenced and brought under control (see 2:11–15 and 5:4–16). In any event, the author of this letter urges his readers to spurn these gnostic teachers and to organize the leadership of the church in such a way as to present a unified front against them.

From the New Revised Standard Version Bible, © 1989.

1 Paul, an apostle of Christ Jesus by the command of God our Savior and of Christ Jesus our hope,

2 To Timothy, my loyal child in the faith:

Grace, mercy, and peace from God the Father and Christ Jesus our Lord.

3 I urge you, as I did when I was on my way to Macedonia, to remain in Ephesus so that you may instruct certain people not to teach any different doctrine, 4 and not to occupy themselves with myths and endless genealogies that promote speculations rather than the divine training[a] that is known by faith. 5 But the aim of such instruction is love that comes from a pure heart, a good conscience, and sincere faith. 6 Some people have deviated from these and turned to meaningless talk, 7 desiring to be teachers of the law, without understanding either what they are saying or the things about which they make assertions.

8 Now we know that the law is good, if one uses it legitimately. 9 This means understanding that the law is laid down not for the innocent but for the lawless and disobedient, for the godless and sinful, for the unholy and profane, for those who kill their father or mother, for murderers, 10 fornicators, sodomites, slave traders, liars, perjurers, and whatever else is contrary to the sound teaching 11 that conforms to the glorious gospel of the blessed God, which he entrusted to me.

12 I am grateful to Christ Jesus our Lord, who has strengthened me, because he judged me faithful and appointed me to his service, 13 even though I was formerly a blasphemer, a persecutor, and a man of violence. But I received mercy because I had acted ignorantly in unbelief, 14 and the grace of our Lord overflowed for me with the faith and love that are in Christ Jesus. 15 The saying is sure and worthy of full acceptance, that Christ Jesus came into the world to save sinners—of whom I am the foremost. 16 But for that very reason I received mercy, so that in me, as the foremost, Jesus Christ might display the utmost patience, making me an example to those who would come to believe in him for eternal life. 17 To the King of the ages, immortal, invisible, the only God, be honor and glory forever and ever.[b] Amen.

18 I am giving you these instructions, Timothy, my child, in accordance with the prophecies made earlier about you, so that by following them you may fight the good fight, 19 having faith and a good conscience. By rejecting conscience, certain persons have suffered shipwreck in the faith; 20 among them are Hymenaeus and Alexander, whom I have turned over to Satan, so that they may learn not to blaspheme.

2 First of all, then, I urge that supplications, prayers, intercessions, and thanksgivings be made for everyone, 2 for kings and all who are in high positions, so that we may lead a quiet and peaceable life in all godliness and dignity. 3 This is right and is acceptable in the sight of God our Savior, 4 who desires everyone to be saved and to come to the knowledge of the truth. 5 For

there is one God;
there is also one mediator
between God and
humankind,
Christ Jesus, himself human,
6   who gave himself a ransom for
all

—this was attested at the right time. 7 For this I was appointed a herald and an apostle (I am telling the truth,[c] I am not lying), a teacher of the Gentiles in faith and truth.

8 I desire, then, that in every place the men should pray, lifting up holy hands without anger or argument; 9 also that the women should dress themselves modestly and decently in suitable clothing, not with their hair braided, or with gold, pearls, or expensive clothes, 10 but with good works, as is proper for women who profess reverence for God. 11 Let a woman[d] learn in silence with full submission. 12 I permit no woman[d] to teach or to have authority over a man;[e] she is to keep silent. 13 For Adam was formed first, then Eve; 14 and Adam was not deceived, but the woman was deceived and became a transgressor. 15 Yet she will be saved through childbearing, provided they continue in faith and love and holiness, with modesty.

3 The saying is sure:[f] whoever aspires to the office of bishop[g] desires a noble task.

[a]Or *plan* [b]Gk *to the ages of the ages* [c]Other ancient authorities add *in Christ* [d]Or *wife* [e]Or *her husband* [f]Some interpreters place these words at the end of the previous paragraph. Other ancient authorities read *The saying is commonly accepted* [g]Or *overseer*

2 Now a bishop[h] must be above reproach, married only once,[i] temperate, sensible, respectable, hospitable, an apt teacher, 3 not a drunkard, not violent but gentle, not quarrelsome, and not a lover of money. 4 He must manage his own household well, keeping his children submissive and respectful in every way— 5 for if someone does not know how to manage his own household, how can he take care of God's church? 6 He must not be a recent convert, or he may be puffed up with conceit and fall into the condemnation of the devil. 7 Moreover, he must be well thought of by outsiders, so that he may not fall into disgrace and the snare of the devil.

8 Deacons likewise must be serious, not double-tongued, not indulging in much wine, not greedy for money; 9 they must hold fast to the mystery of the faith with a clear conscience. 10 And let them first be tested; then, if they prove themselves blameless, let them serve as deacons. 11 Women[j] likewise must be serious, not slanderers, but temperate, faithful in all things. 12 Let deacons be married only once,[k] and let them manage their children and their households well; 13 for those who serve well as deacons gain a good standing for themselves and great boldness in the faith that is in Christ Jesus.

14 I hope to come to you soon, but I am writing these instructions to you so that, 15 if I am delayed, you may know how one ought to behave in the household of God, which is the church of the living God, the pillar and bulwark of the truth. 16 Without any doubt, the mystery of our religion is great:

He[l] was revealed in flesh,
vindicated[m] in spirit,[n]
seen by angels,
proclaimed among Gentiles,
believed in throughout the
world,
taken up in glory.

4 Now the Spirit expressly says that in later[o] times some will renounce the faith by paying attention to deceitful spirits and teachings of demons, 2 through the hypocrisy of liars whose consciences are seared with a hot iron. 3 They forbid marriage and demand abstinence from foods, which God created to be received with thanksgiving by those who believe and know the truth. 4 For everything created by God is good, and nothing is to be rejected, provided it is received with thanksgiving; 5 for it is sanctified by God's word and by prayer.

6 If you put these instructions before the brothers and sisters,[p] you will be a good servant[q] of Christ Jesus, nourished on the words of the faith and of the sound teaching that you have followed. 7 Have nothing to do with profane myths and old wives' tales. Train yourself in godliness, 8 for, while physical training is of some value, godliness is valuable in every way, holding promise for both the present life and the life to come. 9 The saying is sure and worthy of full acceptance. 10 For to this end we toil and struggle,[r] because we have our hope set on the living God, who is the Savior of all people, especially of those who believe.

11 These are the things you must insist on and teach. 12 Let no one despise your youth, but set the believers an example in speech and conduct, in love, in faith, in purity. 13 Until I arrive, give attention to the public reading of scripture,[s] to exhorting, to teaching. 14 Do not neglect the gift that is in you, which was given to you through prophecy with the laying on of hands by the council of elders.[t] 15 Put these things into practice, devote yourself to them, so that all may see your progress. 16 Pay close attention to yourself and to your teaching; continue in these things, for in doing this you will save both yourself and your hearers.

5 Do not speak harshly to an older man,[u] but speak to him as to a father, to younger men as brothers, 2 to older women as mothers, to younger women as sisters—with absolute purity.

3 Honor widows who are really widows. 4 If a widow has children or grandchildren, they should first learn their religious duty to their own family and make some repayment to their parents; for this is pleasing in God's sight. 5 The real widow, left alone, has set her hope on God and continues in

[h]Or an overseer [i]Gk the husband of one wife [j]Or Their wives, or Women deacons [k]Gk be husbands of one wife [l]Gk Who; other ancient authorities read God; others, Which [m]Or justified [n]Or by the Spirit [o]Or the last [p]Gk brothers [q]Or deacon [r]Other ancient authorities read suffer reproach [s]Gk to the reading [t]Gk by the presbytery [u]Or an elder, or a presbyter

supplications and prayers night and day; 6 but the widow[v] who lives for pleasure is dead even while she lives. 7 Give these commands as well, so that they may be above reproach. 8 And whoever does not provide for relatives, and especially for family members, has denied the faith and is worse than an unbeliever.

9 Let a widow be put on the list if she is not less than sixty years old and has been married only once;[w] 10 she must be well attested for her good works, as one who has brought up children, shown hospitality, washed the saints' feet, helped the afflicted, and devoted herself to doing good in every way. 11 But refuse to put younger widows on the list; for when their sensual desires alienate them from Christ, they want to marry, 12 and so they incur condemnation for having violated their first pledge. 13 Besides that, they learn to be idle, gadding about from house to house; and they are not merely idle, but also gossips and busybodies, saying what they should not say. 14 So I would have younger widows marry, bear children, and manage their households, so as to give the adversary no occasion to revile us. 15 For some have already turned away to follow Satan. 16 If any believing woman[x] has relatives who are really widows, let her assist them; let the church not be burdened, so that it can assist those who are real widows.

17 Let the elders who rule well be considered worthy of double honor,[y] especially those who labor in preaching and teaching; 18 for the scripture says, "You shall not muzzle an ox while it is treading out the grain,"[1] and, "The laborer deserves to be paid."[2] 19 Never accept any accusation against an elder except on the evidence of two or three witnesses. 20 As for those who persist in sin, rebuke them in the presence of all, so that the rest also may stand in fear. 21 In the presence of God and of Christ Jesus and of the elect angels, I warn you to keep these instructions without prejudice, doing nothing on the basis of partiality. 22 Do not ordain[z] anyone hastily, and do not participate in the sins of others; keep yourself pure.

23 No longer drink only water, but take a little wine for the sake of your stomach and your frequent ailments.

24 The sins of some people are conspicuous and precede them to judgment, while the sins of others follow them there. 25 So also good works are conspicuous; and even when they are not, they cannot remain hidden.

6 Let all who are under the yoke of slavery regard their masters as worthy of all honor, so that the name of God and the teaching may not be blasphemed. 2 Those who have believing masters must not be disrespectful to them on the ground that they are members of the church;[a] rather they must serve them all the more, since those who benefit by their service are believers and beloved.[b]

Teach and urge these duties. 3 Whoever teaches otherwise and does not agree with the sound words of our Lord Jesus Christ and the teaching that is in accordance with godliness, 4 is conceited, understanding nothing, and has a morbid craving for controversy and for disputes about words. From these come envy, dissension, slander, base suspicions, 5 and wrangling among those who are depraved in mind and bereft of the truth, imagining that godliness is a means of gain.[c] 6 Of course, there is great gain in godliness combined with contentment; 7 for we brought nothing into the world, so that[d] we can take nothing out of it; 8 but if we have food and clothing, we will be content with these. 9 But those who want to be rich fall into temptation and are trapped by many senseless and harmful desires that plunge people into ruin and destruction. 10 For the love of money is a root of all kinds of evil, and in their eagerness to be rich some have wandered away from the faith and pierced themselves with many pains.

11 But as for you, man of God, shun all this; pursue righteousness, godliness, faith, love, endurance, gentleness. 12 Fight the good fight of the faith; take hold of the eternal life, to which you were called and for which you made[e] the good confession in the presence of many witnesses. 13 In the presence of God, who gives life to all things, and of Christ Jesus, who in his testimony

---

[v]Gk *she*   [w]Gk *the wife of one husband*   [x]Other ancient authorities read *believing man or woman*; others, *believing man*
[y]Or *compensation*   [z]Gk *Do not lay hands on*   [a]Gk *are brothers*
[b]Or *since they are believers and beloved, who devote themselves to good deeds*   [c]Other ancient authorities add *Withdraw yourself from such people*   [d]Other ancient authorities read *world—it is certain that*
[e]Gk *confessed*

---

[1]Deut 25:4   [2]Matt 10:10; Luke 10:7

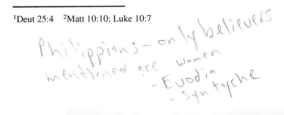

before Pontius Pilate made the good confession, I charge you 14 to keep the commandment without spot or blame until the manifestation of our Lord Jesus Christ, 15 which he will bring about at the right time—he who is the blessed and only Sovereign, the King of kings and Lord of lords. 16 It is he alone who has immortality and dwells in unapproachable light, whom no one has ever seen or can see; to him be honor and eternal dominion. Amen.

17 As for those who in the present age are rich, command them not to be haughty, or to set their hopes on the uncertainty of riches, but rather on God who richly provides us with everything for our enjoyment. 18 They are to do good, to be rich in good works, generous, and ready to share, 19 thus storing up for themselves the treasure of a good foundation for the future, so that they may take hold of the life that really is life.

20 Timothy, guard what has been entrusted to you. Avoid the profane chatter and contradictions of what is falsely called knowledge; 21 by professing it some have missed the mark as regards the faith.

Grace be with you.[f]

The Second Letter to Timothy

Even though 2 Timothy differs from the other Pastoral Epistles in content and tone, it appears to have been written by the same pseudonymous author (see the introduction to 1 Timothy). The vocabulary and writing style are similar to those of 1 Timothy (cf. 1 Tim 1:2 and 2 Tim 1:2), and the concerns for the administration of the church and the weeding out of false teachers are still to the fore.

Unlike the other Pastoral Epistles, in this letter "Paul" is in prison in Rome (1:8, 16–17), expecting soon to be put to death after a second judicial proceeding (4:6–8, 17; the first one evidently did not go well). He writes Timothy not only to encourage him in his pastoral duties and to urge him, yet again, to contend with the false teachers in his church (2:14–19), but also to ask him to come to Rome as soon as possible with some of the apostle's personal belongings (4:13, 21).

Timothy appears to be portrayed here as a third-generation Christian who was preceded in his faith by his mother Eunice and grandmother Lois (1:5). He is said to have been trained in the Scriptures from his childhood (3:15); as an adult, he became a companion of "Paul" and collaborated with him in his mission to Asia Minor (3:10–11). He was ordained to the ministry through a ceremony of laying on of hands (1:6; 4:1–5). As one of Paul's few trusted companions (see 1:16–17; 4:10–18), he was put in charge of the major church of Ephesus and especially commissioned with overcoming those who were leading the saints astray with their idle talk and corrupt lives (2:16–18, 23–26; 3:1–9; 4:3–5).

Because this letter has a far more personal tone to it than the other Pastoral Epistles, some scholars have maintained that it has been interspersed with fragments of Paul's genuine correspondence. Recently, though, scholars have come to think that its personal character relates more closely to its unique genre; unlike 1 Timothy and Titus, 2 Timothy represents the "last will and testament" of the apostle Paul, a kind of letter that we know about from other pseudonymous writings, especially Jewish, of the period. Here the apostle bids his farewell to a person dear to him, extending his final blessings, warnings, and exhortations, and urging his reader(s) to endure suffering with the same fortitude and faithfulness that he himself has displayed.

1 Paul, an apostle of Christ Jesus by the will of God, for the sake of the promise of life that is in Christ Jesus,

2 To Timothy, my beloved child:

Grace, mercy, and peace from God the Father and Christ Jesus our Lord.

3 I am grateful to God—whom I worship with a clear conscience, as my ancestors did—when I remember you constantly in my prayers night and day. 4 Recalling your tears, I long to see you so that I may be filled with joy. 5 I am reminded of your sincere faith, a faith that lived first in your

grandmother Lois and your mother Eunice and now, I am sure, lives in you. 6 For this reason I remind you to rekindle the gift of God that is within you through the laying on of my hands; 7 for God did not give us a spirit of cowardice, but rather a spirit of power and of love and of self-discipline.

8 Do not be ashamed, then, of the testimony about our Lord or of me his prisoner, but join with me in suffering for the gospel, relying on the power of God, 9 who saved us and called us with a holy calling, not according to our works but according to his own purpose and grace. This grace was given to us in Christ Jesus before the ages began, 10 but it has now been revealed through the appearing of our Savior Christ Jesus, who abolished death and brought life and immortality to light through the gospel. 11 For this gospel I was appointed a herald and an apostle and a teacher,[a] 12 and for this reason I suffer as I do. But I am not ashamed, for I know the one in whom I have put my trust, and I am sure that he is able to guard until that day what I have entrusted to him.[b] 13 Hold to the standard of sound teaching that you have heard from me, in the faith and love that are in Christ Jesus. 14 Guard the good treasure entrusted to you, with the help of the Holy Spirit living in us.

15 You are aware that all who are in Asia have turned away from me, including Phygelus and Hermogenes. 16 May the Lord grant mercy to the household of Onesiphorus, because he often refreshed me and was not ashamed of my chain; 17 when he arrived in Rome, he eagerly[c] searched for me and found me 18 —may the Lord grant that he will find mercy from the Lord on that day! And you know very well how much service he rendered in Ephesus.

2 You then, my child, be strong in the grace that is in Christ Jesus; 2 and what you have heard from me through many witnesses entrust to faithful people who will be able to teach others as well. 3 Share in suffering like a good soldier of Christ Jesus. 4 No one serving in the army gets entangled in everyday affairs; the soldier's aim is to please the enlisting officer. 5 And in the case of an athlete, no one is crowned without competing according to the rules. 6 It is the farmer who does the work who ought to have the first share of the crops. 7 Think over what I say, for the Lord will give you understanding in all things.

8 Remember Jesus Christ, raised from the dead, a descendant of David—that is my gospel, 9 for which I suffer hardship, even to the point of being chained like a criminal. But the word of God is not chained. 10 Therefore I endure everything for the sake of the elect, so that they may also obtain the salvation that is in Christ Jesus, with eternal glory. 11 The saying is sure:

If we have died with him, we will
     also live with him;
12   if we endure, we will also reign
          with him;
     if we deny him, he will also deny
          us;
13   if we are faithless, he remains
          faithful—
     for he cannot deny himself.

14 Remind them of this, and warn them before God[d] that they are to avoid wrangling over words, which does no good but only ruins those who are listening. 15 Do your best to present yourself to God as one approved by him, a worker who has no need to be ashamed, rightly explaining the word of truth. 16 Avoid profane chatter, for it will lead people into more and more impiety, 17 and their talk will spread like gangrene. Among them are Hymenaeus and Philetus, 18 who have swerved from the truth by claiming that the resurrection has already taken place. They are upsetting the faith of some. 19 But God's firm foundation stands, bearing this inscription: "The Lord knows those who are his,"[1] and, "Let everyone who calls on the name of the Lord turn away from wickedness."[2]

20 In a large house there are utensils not only of gold and silver but also of wood and clay, some for special use, some for ordinary. 21 All who cleanse themselves of the things I have mentioned[e] will become special utensils, dedicated and useful to the owner of the house, ready for every good work. 22 Shun youthful passions and pursue righteousness, faith, love, and peace, along with those who

---

[a]Other ancient authorities add *of the Gentiles* [b]Or *what has been entrusted to me* [c]Or *promptly* [d]Other ancient authorities read *the Lord* [e]Gk *of these things*

---

[1]Num 16:5 [2]Num 16:26; Job 36:10; Isa 26:13

call on the Lord from a pure heart. 23 Have nothing to do with stupid and senseless controversies; you know that they breed quarrels. 24 And the Lord's servant[f] must not be quarrelsome but kindly to everyone, an apt teacher, patient, 25 correcting opponents with gentleness. God may perhaps grant that they will repent and come to know the truth, 26 and that they may escape from the snare of the devil, having been held captive by him to do his will.[g]

3 You must understand this, that in the last days distressing times will come. 2 For people will be lovers of themselves, lovers of money, boasters, arrogant, abusive, disobedient to their parents, ungrateful, unholy, 3 inhuman, implacable, slanderers, profligates, brutes, haters of good, 4 treacherous, reckless, swollen with conceit, lovers of pleasure rather than lovers of God, 5 holding to the outward form of godliness but denying its power. Avoid them! 6 For among them are those who make their way into households and captivate silly women, overwhelmed by their sins and swayed by all kinds of desires, 7 who are always being instructed and can never arrive at a knowledge of the truth. 8 As Jannes and Jambres opposed Moses, so these people, of corrupt mind and counterfeit faith, also oppose the truth. 9 But they will not make much progress, because, as in the case of those two men,[h] their folly will become plain to everyone.

10 Now you have observed my teaching, my conduct, my aim in life, my faith, my patience, my love, my steadfastness, 11 my persecutions, and my suffering the things that happened to me in Antioch, Iconium, and Lystra. What persecutions I endured! Yet the Lord rescued me from all of them. 12 Indeed, all who want to live a godly life in Christ Jesus will be persecuted. 13 But wicked people and impostors will go from bad to worse, deceiving others and being deceived. 14 But as for you, continue in what you have learned and firmly believed, knowing from whom you learned it, 15 and how from childhood you have known the sacred writings that are able to instruct you for salvation through faith in Christ Jesus. 16 All scripture is inspired by God and is[i] useful for teaching, for reproof, for correction, and for training in righteousness, 17 so that everyone who belongs to God may be proficient, equipped for every good work.

4 In the presence of God and of Christ Jesus, who is to judge the living and the dead, and in view of his appearing and his kingdom, I solemnly urge you: 2 proclaim the message; be persistent whether the time is favorable or unfavorable; convince, rebuke, and encourage, with the utmost patience in teaching. 3 For the time is coming when people will not put up with sound doctrine, but having itching ears, they will accumulate for themselves teachers to suit their own desires, 4 and will turn away from listening to the truth and wander away to myths. 5 As for you, always be sober, endure suffering, do the work of an evangelist, carry out your ministry fully.

6 As for me, I am already being poured out as a libation, and the time of my departure has come. 7 I have fought the good fight, I have finished the race, I have kept the faith. 8 From now on there is reserved for me the crown of righteousness, which the Lord, the righteous judge, will give me on that day, and not only to me but also to all who have longed for his appearing.

9 Do your best to come to me soon, 10 for Demas, in love with this present world, has deserted me and gone to Thessalonica; Crescens has gone to Galatia,[j] Titus to Dalmatia. 11 Only Luke is with me. Get Mark and bring him with you, for he is useful in my ministry. 12 I have sent Tychicus to Ephesus. 13 When you come, bring the cloak that I left with Carpus at Troas, also the books, and above all the parchments. 14 Alexander the coppersmith did me great harm; the Lord will pay him back for his deeds. 15 You also must beware of him, for he strongly opposed our message.

16 At my first defense no one came to my support, but all deserted me. May it not be counted against them! 17 But the Lord stood by me and gave me strength, so that through me the message might be fully proclaimed and all the Gentiles might hear it. So I was rescued from the lion's mouth. 18 The Lord will rescue me from every

[f]Gk *slave*   [g]Or *by him, to do his* (that is, God's) *will*   [h]Gk lacks *two men*   [i]Or *Every scripture inspired by God is also*   [j]Other ancient authorities read *Gaul*

evil attack and save me for his heavenly kingdom. To him be the glory forever and ever. Amen.

19 Greet Prisca and Aquila, and the household of Onesiphorus. 20 Erastus remained in Corinth; Trophimus I left ill in Miletus. 21 Do your best to come before winter. Eubulus sends greetings to you, as do Pudens and Linus and Claudia and all the brothers and sisters.[k]

22 The Lord be with your spirit. Grace be with you.[l]

[k]Gk *all the brothers*   [l]The Greek word for *you* here is plural. Other ancient authorities add *Amen*

The Letter to Titus

There can be little doubt that the Letter to Titus was produced by the same pseudonymous author who wrote the two other Pastoral Epistles (see the introduction to 1 Timothy). In many ways Titus seems like a condensed version of 1 Timothy: its overarching concern with church organization, its lists of qualifications for church leaders, and the nature of its moral instructions are very much the same.

The situation presupposed in this letter is that "Paul" has left his entrusted colleague Titus behind on the island of Crete to appoint Christian elders in the churches there (1:4–9). He is now writing to urge Titus to correct the erroneous ideas promoted by false teachers; as in 1 Timothy, these teachings involve complicated "mythologies" that confuse the faithful (1:10–16), "genealogies," and "quarrels about the law" (3:9). Here again, then, the opponents may have represented an early form of Jewish-Christian Gnosticism. Titus is not to argue with such people, but to warn them twice to change their views and afterwards simply to ignore them (3:9–11). It appears that, as with 1 Timothy, the tight church organization promoted by the letter is designed to provide a unified front against those who advance such dangerous opinions.

A good portion of the epistle provides advice to various social groups within the Christian congregation, "older men" (2:2), "older women" (2:3), "younger women" (2:4–5), "younger men" (2:6–8), and "slaves" (2:9–10). Near the conclusion of the letter, the advice becomes more general in nature, involving basic admonitions to Christians to engage in the kind of moral behavior that is appropriate for those who have been saved (3:1–7).

1 Paul, a servant[a] of God and an apostle of Jesus Christ, for the sake of the faith of God's elect and the knowledge of the truth that is in accordance with godliness, 2 in the hope of eternal life that God, who never lies, promised before the ages began— 3 in due time he revealed his word through the proclamation with which I have been entrusted by the command of God our Savior,

4 To Titus, my loyal child in the faith we share:

Grace[b] and peace from God the Father and Christ Jesus our Savior.

5 I left you behind in Crete for this reason, so that you should put in order what remained to be done, and should appoint elders in every town, as I directed you: 6 someone who is blameless, married only once,[c] whose children are believers, not accused of debauchery and not rebellious. 7 For a bishop,[d] as God's steward, must be blameless; he must not be arrogant or quick-tempered or addicted to wine or violent or greedy for gain; 8 but he must be hospitable, a lover of goodness, prudent, upright, devout, and self-controlled. 9 He must have a firm grasp of the word that is trustworthy in accordance with the teaching, so that he may be able both to preach with sound doctrine and to refute those who contradict it.

10 There are also many rebellious people, idle talkers and deceivers, especially those of the circumcision; 11 they must be silenced, since they are upsetting whole families by teaching for sor-

---

[a]Gk slave [b]Other ancient authorities read Grace, mercy,
[c]Gk husband of one wife [d]Or an overseer

did gain what it is not right to teach. 12 It was one of them, their very own prophet, who said,

"Cretans are always liars, vicious
brutes, lazy gluttons."

13 That testimony is true. For this reason rebuke them sharply, so that they may become sound in the faith, 14 not paying attention to Jewish myths or to commandments of those who reject the truth. 15 To the pure all things are pure, but to the corrupt and unbelieving nothing is pure. Their very minds and consciences are corrupted. 16 They profess to know God, but they deny him by their actions. They are detestable, disobedient, unfit for any good work.

2 But as for you, teach what is consistent with sound doctrine. 2 Tell the older men to be temperate, serious, prudent, and sound in faith, in love, and in endurance.

3 Likewise, tell the older women to be reverent in behavior, not to be slanderers or slaves to drink; they are to teach what is good, 4 so that they may encourage the young women to love their husbands, to love their children, 5 to be self-controlled, chaste, good managers of the household, kind, being submissive to their husbands, so that the word of God may not be discredited.

6 Likewise, urge the younger men to be self-controlled. 7 Show yourself in all respects a model of good works, and in your teaching show integrity, gravity, 8 and sound speech that cannot be censured; then any opponent will be put to shame, having nothing evil to say of us.

9 Tell slaves to be submissive to their masters and to give satisfaction in every respect; they are not to talk back, 10 not to pilfer, but to show complete and perfect fidelity, so that in everything they may be an ornament to the doctrine of God our Savior.

11 For the grace of God has appeared, bringing salvation to all,[e] 12 training us to renounce impiety and worldly passions, and in the present age to live lives that are self-controlled, upright, and godly, 13 while we wait for the blessed hope and the manifestation of the glory of our great God and Savior,[f] Jesus Christ. 14 He it is who gave himself for us that he might redeem us from all iniquity and purify for himself a people of his own who are zealous for good deeds.

15 Declare these things; exhort and reprove with all authority.[g] Let no one look down on you.

3 Remind them to be subject to rulers and authorities, to be obedient, to be ready for every good work, 2 to speak evil of no one, to avoid quarreling, to be gentle, and to show every courtesy to everyone. 3 For we ourselves were once foolish, disobedient, led astray, slaves to various passions and pleasures, passing our days in malice and envy, despicable, hating one another. 4 But when the goodness and loving kindness of God our Savior appeared, 5 he saved us, not because of any works of righteousness that we had done, but according to his mercy, through the water[h] of rebirth and renewal by the Holy Spirit. 6 This Spirit he poured out on us richly through Jesus Christ our Savior, 7 so that, having been justified by his grace, we might become heirs according to the hope of eternal life. 8 The saying is sure.

I desire that you insist on these things, so that those who have come to believe in God may be careful to devote themselves to good works; these things are excellent and profitable to everyone. 9 But avoid stupid controversies, genealogies, dissensions, and quarrels about the law, for they are unprofitable and worthless. 10 After a first and second admonition, have nothing more to do with anyone who causes divisions, 11 since you know that such a person is perverted and sinful, being self-condemned.

12 When I send Artemas to you, or Tychicus, do your best to come to me at Nicopolis, for I have decided to spend the winter there. 13 Make every effort to send Zenas the lawyer and Apollos on their way, and see that they lack nothing. 14 And let people learn to devote themselves to good works in order to meet urgent needs, so that they may not be unproductive.

15 All who are with me send greetings to you. Greet those who love us in the faith.

Grace be with all of you.[i]

---

[e]Or has appeared to all, bringing salvation   [f]Or of the great God and our Savior   [g]Gk commandment   [h]Gk washing   [i]Other ancient authorities add Amen

The Letter to Philemon

No more than a page in length, Philemon is the only undisputed Pauline letter written to an individual. Rather than addressing practical and doctrinal problems that had arisen in the church, the letter concerns a single man, the runaway slave Onesimus, and his fate at the hands of his master, a Christian named Philemon.

At the time of his writing, Paul is in prison (v. 1), although it is impossible to determine whether he is in Ephesus, Rome, or elsewhere. While in prison, he has seen and converted Onesimus, who has become his servant (v. 10). He is now sending him back to his legal owner, Philemon, whom Paul knows well, evidently as another of his converts (v. 19).

Tradition says that Philemon lived in the small town of Colossae in Asia Minor. Paul wants him to receive Onesimus back without punishing him or charging him for the financial loss that he incurred (he may have run off with some of his master's property; v. 18). He appeals to Philemon's personal indebtedness to him, and informs him that he himself will make up any loss he has suffered, possibly in anticipation that this will not be necessary (v. 19). Onesimus, Paul informs Philemon, has proved "useful" to him and can still be "useful" to Philemon (v. 11). Here Paul is playing on words. The name Onesimus means "useful" in Greek.

Scholars have sometimes had difficulty explaining how Onesimus and Paul happened to meet. Given the enormity of the empire, it seems unlikely that Paul and the slave of a former convert would end up in the same jail cell by chance. The problem has been resolved by recent studies of ancient slavery, which have shown that it was an accepted practice for mistreated or runaway slaves to appeal to a respected friend of their master for help in pleading their cause. Evidently, Onesimus took advantage of this practice. When he met Paul, however, he heard the same gospel that had converted his master and, like him, came then to believe in Christ.

Onesimus's conversion made it easier for him to return home without penalty, for Paul could now encourage Philemon to receive him "no longer as a slave but more than a slave, a beloved brother" (v. 16). It may be that Paul hopes for even something more, that Philemon will set Onesimus free or, possibly, give him over to the apostle for his own ongoing work (vv. 20–21).

1 Paul, a prisoner of Christ Jesus, and Timothy our brother,[a]

To Philemon our dear friend and co-worker, 2 to Apphia our sister,[b] to Archippus our fellow soldier, and to the church in your house:

3 Grace to you and peace from God our Father and the Lord Jesus Christ.

4 When I remember you[c] in my prayers, I always thank my God 5 because I hear of your love for all the saints and your faith toward the Lord Jesus. 6 I pray that the sharing of your faith may become effective when you perceive all the good that we[d] may do for Christ. 7 I have indeed received much joy and encouragement from your love, because the hearts of the saints have been refreshed through you, my brother.

8 For this reason, though I am bold enough in Christ to command you to do your duty, 9 yet I would rather appeal to you on the basis of love—and I, Paul, do this as an old man, and now also as a prisoner of Christ Jesus.[e] 10 I am appealing to you for my child, Onesimus, whose father I have become during my imprisonment. 11 Formerly he was useless to you, but now he is indeed useful[f] both to you and to me. 12 I am sending him, that is, my own heart, back to you. 13 I wanted to keep him with me, so that he might be of service to me in your place during my imprisonment for the gospel; 14 but I preferred to do nothing without your consent, in order that your good deed might be voluntary and not something forced. 15 Perhaps this is the reason he was separated from you for a while, so that you might have him back forever, 16 no longer as a slave but more than a slave, a beloved brother—especially to me but how much more to you, both in the flesh and in the Lord.

17 So if you consider me your partner, welcome him as you would welcome me. 18 If he has wronged you in any way, or owes you anything, charge that to my account. 19 I, Paul, am writing this with my own hand: I will repay it. I say nothing about your owing me even your own self. 20 Yes, brother, let me have this benefit from you in the Lord! Refresh my heart in Christ. 21 Confident of your obedience, I am writing to you, knowing that you will do even more than I say.

22 One thing more—prepare a guest room for me, for I am hoping through your prayers to be restored to you.

23 Epaphras, my fellow prisoner in Christ Jesus, sends greetings to you,[g] 24 and so do Mark, Aristarchus, Demas, and Luke, my fellow workers.

25 The grace of the Lord Jesus Christ be with your spirit.[h]

---

[a]Gk the brother   [b]Gk the sister   [c]From verse 4 through verse 21, you is singular   [d]Other ancient authorities read you (plural)   [e]Or as an ambassador of Christ Jesus, and now also his prisoner   [f]The name Onesimus means useful or (compare verse 20) beneficial   [g]Here you is singular   [h]Other ancient authorities add Amen

The Third Letter to the Corinthians

As its name suggests, *3 Corinthians* is a letter pseudonymously penned in Paul's name, ostensibly to the Christian community that he founded in Corinth. Near the end of the second century, the letter came to be included in the narrative of Paul's missionary travels known as the *Acts of Paul*. The letter itself, however, may have been in circulation at an earlier date. It addresses theological issues known already to have been debated during the first half of the second century, and many of its views are reminiscent of those advanced by the Pastoral Epistles at the end of the first century and by Ignatius of Antioch at the beginning of the second. The letter may have been composed, then, sometime in the early part of the second century.

Within the *Acts of Paul, 3 Corinthians* represents Paul's response to a letter sent to him by the Corinthian congregation, in which they express their concern over the views of two false teachers in their midst, Simon and Cleobius. These heretics have led members of the church astray into a form of gnostic teaching that maintains that the true God did not create the world or inspire the Jewish prophets, that there is to be no future fleshly resurrection, and that Jesus himself was not a fleshly human being, born of a human mother.

In opposition to these teachings, *3 Corinthians* emphasizes the fleshly nature both of Jesus and of the salvation that he brings; the flesh is not destined for annihilation but for redemption. Thus Jesus really was "born to Mary," after the Holy Spirit came into her from heaven (v. 5; cf. vv. 12–14); Jesus came into this world "to redeem all flesh through his own flesh" (v. 6; cf. vv. 14–15); and there is to be a resurrection of all flesh from the dead (vv. 6, 24, 17, 33).

All these things had been taught, according to the author, through the Jewish prophets (vv. 9–10), the earliest apostles (v. 4), and Paul himself. Those who accept this teaching will "receive a reward" by being raised bodily from the dead for eternal life (v. 36); but those who turn away from it are destined for the destruction of fire (vv. 37–38).

1 Paul, the prisoner of Jesus Christ, to the brethren at Corinth—greeting! 2 Being in many afflictions, I marvel not that the teachings of the evil one had such rapid success. 3 For my Lord Jesus Christ will quickly come, since he is rejected by those who falsify his teaching. 4 For I delivered to you first of all what I received from the apostles before me who were always with Jesus Christ, 5 that our Lord Jesus Christ was born of Mary of the seed of David, the Father having sent the spir-

it from heaven into her 6 that he might come into this world and save all flesh by his own flesh and that he might raise us in the flesh from the dead as he has presented himself to us as our example. 7 And since man is created by his Father, 8 for this reason was he sought by him when he was lost, to become alive by adoption. 9 For the almighty God, maker of heaven and earth, sent the prophets first to the Jews to deliver them from their sins, 10 for he wished to save the house of Israel; therefore he took from the spirit of Christ and poured it out upon the prophets who proclaimed the true worship of God for a long period of time. 11 For the wicked prince who wished to be God himself laid his hands on them and killed them and bound all flesh of man to his pleasure. 12 But the almighty God, being just, and not wishing to repudiate his creation had mercy 13 and sent his Spirit into Mary the Galilean, 15 that the evil one might be conquered by the same flesh by which he held sway, and be convinced that he is not God. 16 For by his own body Jesus Christ saved all flesh, 17 presenting in his own body a temple of righteousness 18 through which we are saved. 19 They who follow them are not children of righteousness but of wrath, who despise the wisdom of God and in their disbelief assert that heaven and earth and all that is in them are not a work of God. 20 They have the accursed belief of the serpent. 21 Turn away from them and keep aloof from their teaching. 24 And those who say that there is no resurrection of the flesh shall have no resurrection, 25 for they do not believe him who had thus risen. 26 For they do not know, O Corinthians, about the sowing of wheat or some other grain that it is cast naked into the ground and having perished rises up again by the will of God in a body and clothed. 27 And he not only raises the body which is sown, but blesses it manifold. 28 And if one will not take the parable of the seeds 29 let him look at Jonah, the son of Amathios who, being unwilling to preach to the Ninevites, was swallowed up by the whale. 30 And after three days and three nights God heard the prayer of Jonah out of deepest hell, and nothing was corrupted, not even a hair nor an eyelid. 31 How much more will he raise you up, who have believed in Christ Jesus, as he himself was raised up. 32 When a corpse was thrown on the bones of the prophet Elisha by one of the children of Israel the corpse rose from death; how much more shall you rise up on that day with a whole body, after you have been thrown upon the body and bones and Spirit of the Lord. 34 If, however, you receive anything else let no one trouble me, 35 for I have these bonds on me that I may win Christ, and I bear his marks that I may attain to the resurrection of the dead. 36 And whoever accepts this rule which we have received by the blessed prophets and the holy gospel, shall receive a reward, 37 but for whomsoever deviates from this rule fire shall be for him and for those who preceded him therein 38 since they are Godless people, a generation of vipers. 39 Resist them in the power of the Lord. 40 Peace be with you.

GENERAL EPISTLES
AND OTHER EARLY
CHRISTIAN WRITINGS

The Letter to the Hebrews

The book traditionally called "Paul's Letter to the Hebrews" is probably misnamed. It was not written by Paul, it is not a letter, and it was evidently not addressed to Jews.

The book was eventually accepted as canonical only when enough fourth-century Christian leaders became convinced that Paul had written it; the book itself, however, makes no such claim. Already in antiquity there were scholars who knew that Paul did not write it. The writing style and vocabulary differ from his, some of its important terms (e.g., "faith," 11:1) mean something other than in Paul's letters, and its major concerns are issues Paul never discusses, let alone emphasizes (e.g., Jesus' superiority to the Jewish priests and the Jewish sacrificial system).

Although the book has an epistolary conclusion, it does not begin as a letter. There is, for example, no prescript that names its author or addressees. Instead the book appears to be a sermon addressed by a Christian preacher to his congregation (13:22). The congregation may have been comprised largely of Gentile converts to Christianity: in the course of his exhortation, when the preacher recalls the instructions they had received upon first coming into the fold, he mentions faith in God, the resurrection of the dead, and eternal judgment (6:1–2). It seems unlikely that converts from Judaism would have needed instruction about such matters.

The sermon is principally concerned with the superiority of Christ to the Jewish religion. According to this author, the Jewish Law is partial and imperfect, unable to bring people into a right standing before God. The inadequacy of Judaism, he maintains, is recognized by the Jewish Scriptures themselves, which state that God had planned all along to provide a "new covenant" to do what the "old" one could not (8:7–13). This old covenant was foreshadowed in the legislation given by Moses (8:5, 10:1), but has been fulfilled only in the work of Christ. Christ, in fact, is superior to the religion of Judaism: he surpasses the Jewish prophets (1:1–3), the Jewish lawgiver Moses (3:1–6), the Jewish priests (chaps. 4–7), and the Jewish sacrifices (chap. 10).

The point of this exposition is a practical one. Some members of the preacher's community had forsaken the Christian church for the synagogue, or at least were being tempted to do so, perhaps in an effort to avoid persecution (see 10:32–34). The author wants to stop them. For him, Christians would be foolish to turn to the "imperfect" religion of Judaism after they have already experienced the full reality of Christ. Indeed, to do so would be to call the wrath of God down upon themselves (6:1–6; 10:26–29).

We do not know when this book was written. Given the fact that the references to Judaism are drawn exclusively from the Jewish Scriptures rather than from cultic practices of the first century, many scholars prefer a date after the Jerusalem Temple was destroyed (70 C.E.), possibly sometime nearer the end of the first century.

From the New Revised Standard Version Bible, © 1989.

1 Long ago God spoke to our ancestors in many and various ways by the prophets, 2 but in these last days he has spoken to us by a Son,[a] whom he appointed heir of all things, through whom he also created the worlds. 3 He is the reflection of God's glory and the exact imprint of God's very being, and he sustains[b] all things by his powerful word. When he had made purification for sins, he sat down at the right hand of the Majesty on high, 4 having become as much superior to angels as the name he has inherited is more excellent than theirs.

5 For to which of the angels did God ever say,
"You are my Son;
        today I have begotten you"?[1]
Or again,
    "I will be his Father,
        and he will be my Son"?[2]
6 And again, when he brings the firstborn into the world, he says,
    "Let all God's angels worship
        him."[3]
7 Of the angels he says,
    "He makes his angels winds,
        and his servants flames of fire."[4]
8 But of the Son he says,
    "Your throne, O God, is[c] forever
        and ever,
    and the righteous scepter is the
        scepter of your[d] kingdom.[5]
9   You have loved righteousness and
        hated wickedness;
    therefore God, your God, has
        anointed you
    with the oil of gladness beyond
        your companions."[5]
10 And,
    "In the beginning, Lord, you
        founded the earth,
    and the heavens are the work of
        your hands;
11 they will perish, but you remain;
        they will all wear out like
            clothing;
12 like a cloak you will roll them up,
        and like clothing[e] they will be
            changed.
    But you are the same,
        and your years will never end."[6]

13 But to which of the angels has he ever said,
    "Sit at my right hand
        until I make your enemies a
            footstool for your feet"?[7]
14 Are not all angels[f] spirits in the divine service, sent to serve for the sake of those who are to inherit salvation?

2 Therefore we must pay greater attention to what we have heard, so that we do not drift away from it. 2 For if the message declared through angels was valid, and every transgression or disobedience received a just penalty, 3 how can we escape if we neglect so great a salvation? It was declared at first through the Lord, and it was attested to us by those who heard him, 4 while God added his testimony by signs and wonders and various miracles, and by gifts of the Holy Spirit, distributed according to his will.

5 Now God[g] did not subject the coming world, about which we are speaking, to angels. 6 But someone has testified somewhere,
    "What are human beings that you
        are mindful of them,[h]
    or mortals, that you care for
        them?[i]
7   You have made them for a little
        while lower[j] than the
            angels;
    you have crowned them with
        glory and honor,[k]
8   subjecting all things under their
        feet."[8]
Now in subjecting all things to them, God[g] left nothing outside their control. As it is, we do not yet see everything in subjection to them, 9 but we do see Jesus, who for a little while was made lower[l] than the angels, now crowned with glory and honor because of the suffering of death, so that by the grace of God[m] he might taste death for everyone. 10 It was fitting that God,[g] for whom and

[a]Or the Son [b]Or bears along [c]Or God is your throne [d]Other ancient authorities read his [e]Other ancient authorities lack like clothing [f]Gk all of them [g]Gk he [h]Gk What is man that you are mindful of him? [i]Gk or the son of man that you care for him? In the Hebrew of Psalm 8.4-6 both man and son of man refer to all humankind [j]Or them only a little lower [k]Other ancient authorities add and set them over the works of your hands [l]Or who was made a little lower [m]Other ancient authorities read apart from God

[1]Ps 2:7 [2]2 Sam 7:14; 1 Chron 17:13 [3]Deut 32:43 [4]Ps 104:4 [5]Ps 45:6–7 [6]Ps 102:25–27 [7]Ps 110:1 [8]Ps 8:4–6

through whom all things exist, in bringing many children to glory, should make the pioneer of their salvation perfect through sufferings. 11 For the one who sanctifies and those who are sanctified all have one Father.[n] For this reason Jesus[o] is not ashamed to call them brothers and sisters,[p] 12 saying,

"I will proclaim your name to my
brothers and sisters,[p]
in the midst of the congregation
I will praise you."[9]

13 And again,

"I will put my trust in him."

And again,

"Here am I and the children
whom God has given me."[10]

14 Since, therefore, the children share flesh and blood, he himself likewise shared the same things, so that through death he might destroy the one who has the power of death, that is, the devil, 15 and free those who all their lives were held in slavery by the fear of death. 16 For it is clear that he did not come to help angels, but the descendants of Abraham. 17 Therefore he had to become like his brothers and sisters[p] in every respect, so that he might be a merciful and faithful high priest in the service of God, to make a sacrifice of atonement for the sins of the people. 18 Because he himself was tested by what he suffered, he is able to help those who are being tested.

3 Therefore, brothers and sisters,[p] holy partners in a heavenly calling, consider that Jesus, the apostle and high priest of our confession, 2 was faithful to the one who appointed him, just as Moses also "was faithful in all[q] God's[r] house."[11] 3 Yet Jesus[s] is worthy of more glory than Moses, just as the builder of a house has more honor than the house itself. 4 (For every house is built by someone, but the builder of all things is God.) 5 Now Moses was faithful in all God's[r] house as a servant, to testify to the things that would be spoken later. 6 Christ, however, was faithful over God's[r] house as a son, and we are his house if we hold firm[t] the confidence and the pride that belong to hope.

7 Therefore, as the Holy Spirit says,

"Today, if you hear his voice,

8   do not harden your hearts as in

the rebellion,
as on the day of testing in the
wilderness,

9   where your ancestors put me to
the test,
though they had seen my works

10   for forty years.
Therefore I was angry with that
generation,
and I said, 'They always go astray
in their hearts,
and they have not known my
ways.'

11   As in my anger I swore,
'They will not enter my rest.'"[12]

12 Take care, brothers and sisters,[p] that none of you may have an evil, unbelieving heart that turns away from the living God. 13 But exhort one another every day, as long as it is called "today," so that none of you may be hardened by the deceitfulness of sin. 14 For we have become partners of Christ, if only we hold our first confidence firm to the end. 15 As it is said,

"Today if you hear his voice,
do not harden your hearts as in
the rebellion."[13]

16 Now who were they who heard and yet were rebellious? Was it not all those who left Egypt under the leadership of Moses? 17 But with whom was he angry forty years? Was it not those who sinned, whose bodies fell in the wilderness? 18 And to whom did he swear that they would not enter his rest, if not to those who were disobedient? 19 So we see that they were unable to enter because of unbelief.

4 Therefore, while the promise of entering his rest is still open, let us take care that none of you should seem to have failed to reach it. 2 For indeed the good news came to us just as to them; but the message they heard did not benefit them, because they were not united by faith with those who listened.[u] 3 For we who have believed enter that rest, just as God[v] has said,

---

[n]Gk are all of one   [o]Gk he   [p]Gk brothers   [q]Other ancient authorities lack all   [r]Gk his   [s]Gk this one   [t]Other ancient authorities add to the end   [u]Other ancient authorities read it did not meet with faith in those who listened   [v]Gk he

---

[9]Ps 22:22   [10]Isa 8:17–18   [11]Num 12:7   [12]Ps 95:7–11   [13]Ps 95:7–8

"As in my anger I swore,
   'They shall not enter my rest,'"[14]
though his works were finished at the foundation
of the world. 4 For in one place it speaks about the
seventh day as follows, "And God rested on the
seventh day from all his works."[15] 5 And again in
this place it says, "They shall not enter my rest."[16]
6 Since therefore it remains open for some to enter it, and those who formerly received the good
news failed to enter because of disobedience,
7 again he sets a certain day—"today"—saying
through David much later, in the words already
quoted,

"Today, if you hear his voice,
   do not harden your hearts."[17]

8 For if Joshua had given them rest, God[w] would
not speak later about another day. 9 So then, a
sabbath rest still remains for the people of God;
10 for those who enter God's rest also cease from
their labors as God did from his. 11 Let us therefore make every effort to enter that rest, so that no
one may fall through such disobedience as theirs.

12 Indeed, the word of God is living and active,
sharper than any two-edged sword, piercing until
it divides soul from spirit, joints from marrow; it
is able to judge the thoughts and intentions of the
heart. 13 And before him no creature is hidden,
but all are naked and laid bare to the eyes of the
one to whom we must render an account.

14 Since, then, we have a great high priest who
has passed through the heavens, Jesus, the Son of
God, let us hold fast to our confession. 15 For we
do not have a high priest who is unable to sympathize with our weaknesses, but we have one who
in every respect has been tested[x] as we are, yet
without sin. 16 Let us therefore approach the
throne of grace with boldness, so that we may receive mercy and find grace to help in time of need.

5 Every high priest chosen from among mortals is put in charge of things pertaining to
God on their behalf, to offer gifts and sacrifices for
sins. 2 He is able to deal gently with the ignorant
and wayward, since he himself is subject to weakness; 3 and because of this he must offer sacrifice
for his own sins as well as for those of the people.
4 And one does not presume to take this honor, but
takes it only when called by God, just as Aaron
was.

5 So also Christ did not glorify himself in becoming a high priest, but was appointed by the one
who said to him,

"You are my Son,
   today I have begotten you";[18]
6 as he says also in another place,
   "You are a priest forever,
      according to the order of
        Melchizedek."[19]

7 In the days of his flesh, Jesus[w] offered up
prayers and supplications, with loud cries and
tears, to the one who was able to save him from
death, and he was heard because of his reverent
submission. 8 Although he was a Son, he learned
obedience through what he suffered; 9 and having
been made perfect, he became the source of eternal salvation for all who obey him, 10 having
been designated by God a high priest according to
the order of Melchizedek.

11 About this[y] we have much to say that is hard
to explain, since you have become dull in understanding. 12 For though by this time you ought to
be teachers, you need someone to teach you again
the basic elements of the oracles of God. You need
milk, not solid food; 13 for everyone who lives on
milk, being still an infant, is unskilled in the word
of righteousness. 14 But solid food is for the mature, for those whose faculties have been trained
by practice to distinguish good from evil.

6 Therefore let us go on toward perfection,[z]
leaving behind the basic teaching about
Christ, and not laying again the foundation: repentance from dead works and faith toward God,
2 instruction about baptisms, laying on of hands,
resurrection of the dead, and eternal judgment.
3 And we will do[a] this, if God permits. 4 For it is
impossible to restore again to repentance those
who have once been enlightened, and have tasted
the heavenly gift, and have shared in the Holy
Spirit, 5 and have tasted the goodness of the word
of God and the powers of the age to come, 6 and
then have fallen away, since on their own they are
crucifying again the Son of God and are holding
him up to contempt. 7 Ground that drinks up the

---

[w]Gk *he* [x]Or *tempted* [y]Or *him* [z]Or *toward maturity* [a]Other
ancient authorities read *let us do*

---

[14]Ps 95:11 [15]Gen 2:2 [16]Ps 95:11 [17]Ps 95:7–8 [18]Ps 2:7 [19]Ps
110:4

rain falling on it repeatedly, and that produces a crop useful to those for whom it is cultivated, receives a blessing from God. 8 But if it produces thorns and thistles, it is worthless and on the verge of being cursed; its end is to be burned over.

9 Even though we speak in this way, beloved, we are confident of better things in your case, things that belong to salvation. 10 For God is not unjust; he will not overlook your work and the love that you showed for his sake[b] in serving the saints, as you still do. 11 And we want each one of you to show the same diligence so as to realize the full assurance of hope to the very end, 12 so that you may not become sluggish, but imitators of those who through faith and patience inherit the promises.

13 When God made a promise to Abraham, because he had no one greater by whom to swear, he swore by himself, 14 saying, "I will surely bless you and multiply you."[20] 15 And thus Abraham,[c] having patiently endured, obtained the promise. 16 Human beings, of course, swear by someone greater than themselves, and an oath given as confirmation puts an end to all dispute. 17 In the same way, when God desired to show even more clearly to the heirs of the promise the unchangeable character of his purpose, he guaranteed it by an oath, 18 so that through two unchangeable things, in which it is impossible that God would prove false, we who have taken refuge might be strongly encouraged to seize the hope set before us. 19 We have this hope, a sure and steadfast anchor of the soul, a hope that enters the inner shrine behind the curtain, 20 where Jesus, a forerunner on our behalf, has entered, having become a high priest forever according to the order of Melchizedek.

7 This "King Melchizedek of Salem, priest of the Most High God, met Abraham as he was returning from defeating the kings and blessed him"; 2 and to him Abraham apportioned "one-tenth of everything." His name, in the first place, means "king of righteousness"; next he is also king of Salem, that is, "king of peace."[21] 3 Without father, without mother, without genealogy, having neither beginning of days nor end of life, but resembling the Son of God, he remains a priest forever.

4 See how great he is! Even[d] Abraham the patriarch gave him a tenth of the spoils. 5 And those descendants of Levi who receive the priestly office have a commandment in the law to collect tithes[e] from the people, that is, from their kindred,[f] though these also are descended from Abraham. 6 But this man, who does not belong to their ancestry, collected tithes[e] from Abraham and blessed him who had received the promises. 7 It is beyond dispute that the inferior is blessed by the superior. 8 In the one case, tithes are received by those who are mortal; in the other, by one of whom it is testified that he lives. 9 One might even say that Levi himself, who receives tithes, paid tithes through Abraham, 10 for he was still in the loins of his ancestor when Melchizedek met him.

11 Now if perfection had been attainable through the levitical priesthood—for the people received the law under this priesthood—what further need would there have been to speak of another priest arising according to the order of Melchizedek, rather than one according to the order of Aaron? 12 For when there is a change in the priesthood, there is necessarily a change in the law as well. 13 Now the one of whom these things are spoken belonged to another tribe, from which no one has ever served at the altar. 14 For it is evident that our Lord was descended from Judah, and in connection with that tribe Moses said nothing about priests.

15 It is even more obvious when another priest arises, resembling Melchizedek, 16 one who has become a priest, not through a legal requirement concerning physical descent, but through the power of an indestructible life. 17 For it is attested of him,

> "You are a priest forever,
>   according to the order of
>   Melchizedek."[22]

18 There is, on the one hand, the abrogation of an earlier commandment because it was weak and ineffectual 19 (for the law made nothing perfect); there is, on the other hand, the introduction of a better hope, through which we approach God.

20 This was confirmed with an oath; for others who became priests took their office without an

---

[b]Gk *for his name*   [c]Gk *he*   [d]Other ancient authorities lack *Even*
[e]Or *a tenth*   [f]Gk *brothers*

---

[20]Gen 22:16–17   [21]Gen 14:17–20   [22]Ps 110:4

oath, 21 but this one became a priest with an oath, because of the one who said to him,

> "The Lord has sworn
>   and will not change his mind,
>   'You are a priest forever'"—[23]

22 accordingly Jesus has also become the guarantee of a better covenant.

23 Furthermore, the former priests were many in number, because they were prevented by death from continuing in office; 24 but he holds his priesthood permanently, because he continues forever. 25 Consequently he is able for all time to save[g] those who approach God through him, since he always lives to make intercession for them.

26 For it was fitting that we should have such a high priest, holy, blameless, undefiled, separated from sinners, and exalted above the heavens. 27 Unlike the other[h] high priests, he has no need to offer sacrifices day after day, first for his own sins, and then for those of the people; this he did once for all when he offered himself. 28 For the law appoints as high priests those who are subject to weakness, but the word of the oath, which came later than the law, appoints a Son who has been made perfect forever.

8 Now the main point in what we are saying is this: we have such a high priest, one who is seated at the right hand of the throne of the Majesty in the heavens, 2 a minister in the sanctuary and the true tent[i] that the Lord, and not any mortal, has set up. 3 For every high priest is appointed to offer gifts and sacrifices; hence it is necessary for this priest also to have something to offer. 4 Now if he were on earth, he would not be a priest at all, since there are priests who offer gifts according to the law. 5 They offer worship in a sanctuary that is a sketch and shadow of the heavenly one; for Moses, when he was about to erect the tent,[i] was warned, "See that you make everything according to the pattern that was shown you on the mountain."[24] 6 But Jesus[j] has now obtained a more excellent ministry, and to that degree he is the mediator of a better covenant, which has been enacted through better promises. 7 For if that first covenant had been faultless, there would have been no need to look for a second one.

8 God[k] finds fault with them when he says:

> "The days are surely coming, says
>   the Lord,
>   when I will establish a new
>   covenant with the house of
>   Israel
>   and with the house of Judah;
>
> 9   not like the covenant that I made
>   with their ancestors,
>   on the day when I took them
>   by the hand to lead them
>   out of the land of Egypt;
>   for they did not continue in my
>   covenant,
>   and so I had no concern for
>   them, says the Lord.
>
> 10   This is the covenant that I will
>   make with the house of
>   srael
>   after those days, says the Lord:
>   I will put my laws in their minds,
>   and write them on their hearts,
>   and I will be their God,
>   and they shall be my people.
>
> 11   And they shall not teach one
>   another
>   or say to each other, 'Know the
>   Lord,'
>   for they shall all know me,
>   from the least of them to the
>   greatest.
>
> 12   For I will be merciful toward their
>   iniquities,
>   and I will remember their sins
>   no more."[25]

13 In speaking of "a new covenant," he has made the first one obsolete. And what is obsolete and growing old will soon disappear.

9 Now even the first covenant had regulations for worship and an earthly sanctuary. 2 For a tent[i] was constructed, the first one, in which were the lampstand, the table, and the bread of the Presence;[l] this is called the Holy Place. 3 Behind the second curtain was a tent[i] called the Holy of

---

[g]Or *able to save completely* [h]Gk lacks *other* [i]Or *tabernacle*
[j]Gk *he* [k]Gk *He* [l]Gk *the presentation of the loaves*

---

[23]Ps 110:4 [24]Exod 25:40 [25]Jer 31:31–34

Holies. 4 In it stood the golden altar of incense and the ark of the covenant overlaid on all sides with gold, in which there were a golden urn holding the manna, and Aaron's rod that budded, and the tablets of the covenant; 5 above it were the cherubim of glory overshadowing the mercy seat.[m] Of these things we cannot speak now in detail.

6 Such preparations having been made, the priests go continually into the first tent[n] to carry out their ritual duties; 7 but only the high priest goes into the second, and he but once a year, and not without taking the blood that he offers for himself and for the sins committed unintentionally by the people. 8 By this the Holy Spirit indicates that the way into the sanctuary has not yet been disclosed as long as the first tent[n] is still standing. 9 This is a symbol[o] of the present time, during which gifts and sacrifices are offered that cannot perfect the conscience of the worshiper, 10 but deal only with food and drink and various baptisms, regulations for the body imposed until the time comes to set things right.

11 But when Christ came as a high priest of the good things that have come,[p] then through the greater and perfect[q] tent[n] (not made with hands, that is, not of this creation), 12 he entered once for all into the Holy Place, not with the blood of goats and calves, but with his own blood, thus obtaining eternal redemption. 13 For if the blood of goats and bulls, with the sprinkling of the ashes of a heifer, sanctifies those who have been defiled so that their flesh is purified, 14 how much more will the blood of Christ, who through the eternal Spirit[r] offered himself without blemish to God, purify our[s] conscience from dead works to worship the living God!

15 For this reason he is the mediator of a new covenant, so that those who are called may receive the promised eternal inheritance, because a death has occurred that redeems them from the transgressions under the first covenant.[t] 16 Where a will[t] is involved, the death of the one who made it must be established. 17 For a will[t] takes effect only at death, since it is not in force as long as the one who made it is alive. 18 Hence not even the first covenant was inaugurated without blood. 19 For when every commandment had been told to

all the people by Moses in accordance with the law he took the blood of calves and goats,[u] with water and scarlet wool and hyssop, and sprinkled both the scroll itself and all the people, 20 saying, "This is the blood of the covenant that God has ordained for you."[26] 21 And in the same way he sprinkled with the blood both the tent[n] and all the vessels used in worship. 22 Indeed, under the law almost everything is purified with blood, and without the shedding of blood there is no forgiveness of sins.

23 Thus it was necessary for the sketches of the heavenly things to be purified with these rites, but the heavenly things themselves need better sacrifices than these. 24 For Christ did not enter a sanctuary made by human hands, a mere copy of the true one, but he entered into heaven itself, now to appear in the presence of God on our behalf. 25 Nor was it to offer himself again and again, as the high priest enters the Holy Place year after year with blood that is not his own; 26 for then he would have had to suffer again and again since the foundation of the world. But as it is, he has appeared once for all at the end of the age to remove sin by the sacrifice of himself. 27 And just as it is appointed for mortals to die once, and after that the judgment, 28 so Christ, having been offered once to bear the sins of many, will appear a second time, not to deal with sin, but to save those who are eagerly waiting for him.

10 Since the law has only a shadow of the good things to come and not the true form of these realities, it[v] can never, by the same sacrifices that are continually offered year after year, make perfect those who approach. 2 Otherwise, would they not have ceased being offered, since the worshipers, cleansed once for all, would no longer have any consciousness of sin? 3 But in these sacrifices there is a reminder of sin year after year. 4 For it is impossible for the blood of bulls and goats to take away sins. 5 Conse-

---

[m] Or *the place of atonement*   [n] Or *tabernacle*   [o] Gk *parable*   [p] Other ancient authorities read *good things to come*   [q] Gk *more perfect*   [r] Other ancient authorities read *Holy Spirit*   [s] Other ancient authorities read *your*   [t] The Greek word used here means both *covenant* and *will*   [u] Other ancient authorities lack *and goats*   [v] Other ancient authorities read *they*

---

[26] Exod 24:8

quently, when Christ[w] came into the world, he said,

> "Sacrifices and offerings you have
>   not desired,
>   but a body you have prepared
>   for me;
> 6   in burnt offerings and sin
>   offerings
>   you have taken no pleasure.
> 7   Then I said, 'See, God, I have
>   come to do your will,
>   O God'
>   (in the scroll of the book[x] it is
>   written of me)."[27]

8 When he said above, "You have neither desired nor taken pleasure in sacrifices and offerings and burnt offerings and sin offerings"[28] (these are offered according to the law), 9 then he added, "See, I have come to do your will."[29] He abolishes the first in order to establish the second. 10 And it is by God's will[y] that we have been sanctified through the offering of the body of Jesus Christ once for all.

11 And every priest stands day after day at his service, offering again and again the same sacrifices that can never take away sins. 12 But when Christ[z] had offered for all time a single sacrifice for sins, "he sat down at the right hand of God," 13 and since then has been waiting "until his enemies would be made a footstool for his feet."[30] 14 For by a single offering he has perfected for all time those who are sanctified. 15 And the Holy Spirit also testifies to us, for after saying,

> 16   "This is the covenant that I will
>   make with them
>   after those days, says the Lord:
>   I will put my laws in their hearts,
>   and I will write them on their
>   minds,"[31]

17 he also adds,

> "I will remember[a] their sins and
>   their lawless deeds no
>   more."[32]

18 Where there is forgiveness of these, there is no longer any offering for sin.

19 Therefore, my friends,[b] since we have confidence to enter the sanctuary by the blood of Jesus, 20 by the new and living way that he opened for us through the curtain (that is, through his flesh),

21 and since we have a great priest over the house of God, 22 let us approach with a true heart in full assurance of faith, with our hearts sprinkled clean from an evil conscience and our bodies washed with pure water. 23 Let us hold fast to the confession of our hope without wavering, for he who has promised is faithful. 24 And let us consider how to provoke one another to love and good deeds, 25 not neglecting to meet together, as is the habit of some, but encouraging one another, and all the more as you see the Day approaching.

26 For if we willfully persist in sin after having received the knowledge of the truth, there no longer remains a sacrifice for sins, 27 but a fearful prospect of judgment, and a fury of fire that will consume the adversaries. 28 Anyone who has violated the law of Moses dies without mercy "on the testimony of two or three witnesses."[33] 29 How much worse punishment do you think will be deserved by those who have spurned the Son of God, profaned the blood of the covenant by which they were sanctified, and outraged the Spirit of grace? 30 For we know the one who said, "Vengeance is mine, I will repay."[34] And again, "The Lord will judge his people."[35] 31 It is a fearful thing to fall into the hands of the living God.

32 But recall those earlier days when, after you had been enlightened, you endured a hard struggle with sufferings, 33 sometimes being publicly exposed to abuse and persecution, and sometimes being partners with those so treated. 34 For you had compassion for those who were in prison, and you cheerfully accepted the plundering of your possessions, knowing that you yourselves possessed something better and more lasting. 35 Do not, therefore, abandon that confidence of yours; it brings a great reward. 36 For you need endurance, so that when you have done the will of God, you may receive what was promised. 37 For yet

> "in a very little while,
>   the one who is coming will
>   come and will not delay;
> 38   but my righteous one will live by
>   faith.

---

[w]Gk he   [x]Meaning of Gk uncertain   [y]Gk by that will   [z]Gk this one   [a]Gk on their minds and I will remember   [b]Gk Therefore, brothers

[27]Ps 40:6–8   [28]Ps 40:6   [29]Ps 40:7   [30]Ps 110:1   [31]Jer 31:33   [32]Jer 31:34   [33]Deut 19:15   [34]Deut 32:35   [35]Deut 32:36; Ps 135:14

My soul takes no pleasure in
anyone who shrinks back."[36]
39 But we are not among those who shrink back
and so are lost, but among those who have faith
and so are saved.

11 Now faith is the assurance of things
hoped for, the conviction of things not
seen. 2 Indeed, by faith[c] our ancestors received
approval. 3 By faith we understand that the
worlds were prepared by the word of God, so that
what is seen was made from things that are not
visible.[d]

4 By faith Abel offered to God a more acceptable[e] sacrifice than Cain's. Through this he received approval as righteous, God himself giving
approval to his gifts; he died, but through his faith[f]
he still speaks. 5 By faith Enoch was taken so that
he did not experience death; and "he was not
found, because God had taken him."[37] For it was
attested before he was taken away that "he had
pleased God."[38] 6 And without faith it is impossible to please God, for whoever would approach
him must believe that he exists and that he rewards
those who seek him. 7 By faith Noah, warned by
God about events as yet unseen, respected the
warning and built an ark to save his household; by
this he condemned the world and became an heir
to the righteousness that is in accordance with
faith.

8 By faith Abraham obeyed when he was called
to set out for a place that he was to receive as an
inheritance; and he set out, not knowing where he
was going. 9 By faith he stayed for a time in the
land he had been promised, as in a foreign land,
living in tents, as did Isaac and Jacob, who were
heirs with him of the same promise. 10 For he
looked forward to the city that has foundations,
whose architect and builder is God. 11 By faith he
received power of procreation, even though he
was too old—and Sarah herself was barren—because he considered him faithful who had promised.[g] 12 Therefore from one person, and this one
as good as dead, descendants were born, "as many
as the stars of heaven and as the innumerable
grains of sand by the seashore."[39]

13 All of these died in faith without having received the promises, but from a distance they saw
and greeted them. They confessed that they were
strangers and foreigners on the earth, 14 for people who speak in this way make it clear that they
are seeking a homeland. 15 If they had been
thinking of the land that they had left behind, they
would have had opportunity to return. 16 But as it
is, they desire a better country, that is, a heavenly
one. Therefore God is not ashamed to be called
their God; indeed, he has prepared a city for them.

17 By faith Abraham, when put to the test, offered up Isaac. He who had received the promises
was ready to offer up his only son, 18 of whom he
had been told, "It is through Isaac that descendants
shall be named for you."[40] 19 He considered the
fact that God is able even to raise someone from
the dead—and figuratively speaking, he did receive him back. 20 By faith Isaac invoked blessings for the future on Jacob and Esau. 21 By faith
Jacob, when dying, blessed each of the sons of
Joseph, "bowing in worship over the top of his
staff."[41] 22 By faith Joseph, at the end of his life,
made mention of the exodus of the Israelites and
gave instructions about his burial.[h]

23 By faith Moses was hidden by his parents for
three months after his birth, because they saw that
the child was beautiful; and they were not afraid
of the king's edict.[i] 24 By faith Moses, when he
was grown up, refused to be called a son of
Pharaoh's daughter, 25 choosing rather to share
ill-treatment with the people of God than to enjoy
the fleeting pleasures of sin. 26 He considered
abuse suffered for the Christ[j] to be greater wealth
than the treasures of Egypt, for he was looking
ahead to the reward. 27 By faith he left Egypt, un-
afraid of the king's anger; for he persevered as
though[k] he saw him who is invisible. 28 By faith
he kept the Passover and the sprinkling of blood,
so that the destroyer of the firstborn would not
touch the firstborn of Israel.[l]

29 By faith the people passed through the Red
Sea as if it were dry land, but when the Egyptians
attempted to do so they were drowned. 30 By faith

[c]Gk by this [d]Or was not made out of visible things [e]Gk greater
[f]Gk through it [g]Or By faith Sarah herself, though barren, received
power to conceive, even when she was too old, because she
considered him faithful who had promised. [h]Gk his bones [i]Other
ancient authorities add By faith Moses, when he was grown up, killed
the Egyptian, because he observed the humiliation of his people (Gk
brothers) [j]Or the Messiah [k]Or because [l]Gk would not touch them

[35]Hab 2:3–4 [37]Gen 5:24; Sir 44:16 [38]Gen 5:22 [39]Gen 22:17
[40]Gen 21:12 [41]Gen 47:31

the walls of Jericho fell after they had been encircled for seven days. 31 By faith Rahab the prostitute did not perish with those who were disobedient,[m] because she had received the spies in peace.

32 And what more should I say? For time would fail me to tell of Gideon, Barak, Samson, Jephthah, of David and Samuel and the prophets— 33 who through faith conquered kingdoms, administered justice, obtained promises, shut the mouths of lions, 34 quenched raging fire, escaped the edge of the sword, won strength out of weakness, became mighty in war, put foreign armies to flight. 35 Women received their dead by resurrection. Others were tortured, refusing to accept release, in order to obtain a better resurrection. 36 Others suffered mocking and flogging, and even chains and imprisonment. 37 They were stoned to death, they were sawn in two,[n] they were killed by the sword; they went about in skins of sheep and goats, destitute, persecuted, tormented— 38 of whom the world was not worthy. They wandered in deserts and mountains, and in caves and holes in the ground.

39 Yet all these, though they were commended for their faith, did not receive what was promised, 40 since God had provided something better so that they would not, apart from us, be made perfect.

12 Therefore, since we are surrounded by so great a cloud of witnesses, let us also lay aside every weight and the sin that clings so closely,[o] and let us run with perseverance the race that is set before us, 2 looking to Jesus the pioneer and perfecter of our faith, who for the sake of[p] the joy that was set before him endured the cross, disregarding its shame, and has taken his seat at the right hand of the throne of God.

3 Consider him who endured such hostility against himself from sinners,[q] so that you may not grow weary or lose heart. 4 In your struggle against sin you have not yet resisted to the point of shedding your blood. 5 And you have forgotten the exhortation that addresses you as children—

"My child, do not regard lightly
        the discipline of the Lord,
    or lose heart when you are
            punished by him;
6   for the Lord disciplines those
            whom he loves,

and chastises every child whom
            he accepts."[42]
7 Endure trials for the sake of discipline. God is treating you as children; for what child is there whom a parent does not discipline? 8 If you do not have that discipline in which all children share, then you are illegitimate and not his children. 9 Moreover, we had human parents to discipline us, and we respected them. Should we not be even more willing to be subject to the Father of spirits and live? 10 For they disciplined us for a short time as seemed best to them, but he disciplines us for our good, in order that we may share his holiness. 11 Now, discipline always seems painful rather than pleasant at the time, but later it yields the peaceful fruit of righteousness to those who have been trained by it.

12 Therefore lift your drooping hands and strengthen your weak knees, 13 and make straight paths for your feet, so that what is lame may not be put out of joint, but rather be healed.

14 Pursue peace with everyone, and the holiness without which no one will see the Lord. 15 See to it that no one fails to obtain the grace of God; that no root of bitterness springs up and causes trouble, and through it many become defiled. 16 See to it that no one becomes like Esau, an immoral and godless person, who sold his birthright for a single meal. 17 You know that later, when he wanted to inherit the blessing, he was rejected, for he found no chance to repent,[r] even though he sought the blessing[s] with tears.

18 You have not come to something[t] that can be touched, a blazing fire, and darkness, and gloom, and a tempest, 19 and the sound of a trumpet, and a voice whose words made the hearers beg that not another word be spoken to them. 20 (For they could not endure the order that was given, "If even an animal touches the mountain, it shall be stoned to death."[43] 21 Indeed, so terrifying was the sight that Moses said, "I tremble with fear."[44]) 22 But you have come to Mount Zion and to the city of the living God, the heavenly Jerusalem, and to in-

---

[m]Or *unbelieving* [n]Other ancient authorities add *they were tempted* [o]Other ancient authorities read *sin that easily distracts* [p]Or *who instead of* [q]Other ancient authorities read *such hostility from sinners against themselves* [r]Or *no chance to change his father's mind* [s]Gk *it* [t]Other ancient authorities read *a mountain*

[42]Prov 3:11–12   [43]Exod 19:12–13   [44]Deut 9:19

numerable angels in festal gathering, 23 and to the assembly[u] of the firstborn who are enrolled in heaven, and to God the judge of all, and to the spirits of the righteous made perfect, 24 and to Jesus, the mediator of a new covenant, and to the sprinkled blood that speaks a better word than the blood of Abel.

25 See that you do not refuse the one who is speaking; for if they did not escape when they refused the one who warned them on earth, how much less will we escape if we reject the one who warns from heaven! 26 At that time his voice shook the earth; but now he has promised, "Yet once more I will shake not only the earth but also the heaven."[45] 27 This phrase, "Yet once more," indicates the removal of what is shaken—that is, created things—so that what cannot be shaken may remain. 28 Therefore, since we are receiving a kingdom that cannot be shaken, let us give thanks, by which we offer to God an acceptable worship with reverence and awe; 29 for indeed our God is a consuming fire.

13 Let mutual love continue. 2 Do not neglect to show hospitality to strangers, for by doing that some have entertained angels without knowing it. 3 Remember those who are in prison, as though you were in prison with them; those who are being tortured, as though you yourselves were being tortured.[v] 4 Let marriage be held in honor by all, and let the marriage bed be kept undefiled; for God will judge fornicators and adulterers. 5 Keep your lives free from the love of money, and be content with what you have; for he has said, "I will never leave you or forsake you."[46] 6 So we can say with confidence,

"The Lord is my helper;
I will not be afraid.
What can anyone do to me?"[47]

7 Remember your leaders, those who spoke the word of God to you; consider the outcome of their way of life, and imitate their faith. 8 Jesus Christ is the same yesterday and today and forever. 9 Do not be carried away by all kinds of strange teachings; for it is well for the heart to be strengthened by grace, not by regulations about food,[w] which

have not benefited those who observe them. 10 We have an altar from which those who officiate in the tent[x] have no right to eat. 11 For the bodies of those animals whose blood is brought into the sanctuary by the high priest as a sacrifice for sin are burned outside the camp. 12 Therefore Jesus also suffered outside the city gate in order to sanctify the people by his own blood. 13 Let us then go to him outside the camp and bear the abuse he endured. 14 For here we have no lasting city, but we are looking for the city that is to come. 15 Through him, then, let us continually offer a sacrifice of praise to God, that is, the fruit of lips that confess his name. 16 Do not neglect to do good and to share what you have, for such sacrifices are pleasing to God.

17 Obey your leaders and submit to them, for they are keeping watch over your souls and will give an account. Let them do this with joy and not with sighing—for that would be harmful to you.

18 Pray for us; we are sure that we have a clear conscience, desiring to act honorably in all things. 19 I urge you all the more to do this, so that I may be restored to you very soon.

20 Now may the God of peace, who brought back from the dead our Lord Jesus, the great shepherd of the sheep, by the blood of the eternal covenant, 21 make you complete in everything good so that you may do his will, working among us[y] that which is pleasing in his sight, through Jesus Christ, to whom be the glory forever and ever. Amen.

22 I appeal to you, brothers and sisters,[z] bear with my word of exhortation, for I have written to you briefly. 23 I want you to know that our brother Timothy has been set free; and if he comes in time, he will be with me when I see you. 24 Greet all your leaders and all the saints. Those from Italy send you greetings 25 Grace be with all of you.[a]

---

[*]Or *angels, and to the festal gathering* [23]*and assembly* [v]Gk *were in the body* [w]Gk *not by foods* [x]Or *tabernacle* [y]Other ancient authorities read *you* [z]Gk *brothers* [a]Other ancient authorities add *Amen*

---

[45]Hag 2:6 [46]Deut 31:6, 8; Josh 1:5 [47]Ps 118:6

The Letter of James

The Letter of James consists of a series of ethical admonitions to those who "believe in our glorious Lord Jesus Christ" (2:1). The author, who calls himself "James, a servant of God" (1:1), has been traditionally identified as James the brother of Jesus (see Gal 1:19). It is not clear, however, that the author intends this identification. For one thing, "James" was a common name in the first century; even within the New Testament several other persons have it (see, e.g., Matt 4:21; 10:3; 27:56). Moreover, nowhere in the letter does the author claim to be a member of Jesus' family or to have any firsthand knowledge of his teachings.

Scholars occasionally have been struck by the unique character of this book, especially by how little of it seems distinctively Christian: the figure of Jesus himself appears only on the periphery (he is named only in 1:1 and 2:1), nearly all of the moral injunctions are paralleled in non-Christian Jewish writings, and the examples of ethical behavior are consistently drawn, not from the lives of Jesus and his apostles, but from stories of the Jewish Scriptures (Abraham, 2:21; Rahab, 2:25; Job, 5:11; Elijah, 5:17). Even the communities of believers who are addressed are portrayed in Jewish guise: they are "the twelve tribes in the Dispersion" (1:1), and their assembly place is literally called a "synagogue" (2:2).

Both the author and his audience, however, are clearly Christian (1:1; 2:1). Moreover, as a number of scholars have observed, many of the ethical injunctions here are similar to Jesus' own teachings as preserved in the Gospels (cf. 2:8 with Matt 19:23–24; 5:1–6 with Matt 19:23–24; and 5:12 with Matt 5:33–37). It appears, then, that the author has culled a number of important ethical admonitions from a variety of sources, such as Jewish books of wisdom (comparable to the book of Proverbs) and traditions of Jesus' own teaching. In doing so he has been particularly keen to admonish his readers to control their speech (1:26; 3:1–12), to beware of the dangers of wealth (1:9–11; 4:13–17; 5:1–6), and to be patient in the midst of suffering (1:2–8, 12–16; 5:7–11).

Above all else, James is concerned to show that no one can be made right with God by faith alone, without doing good deeds (1:22–27; 2:14–26). Since the Reformation, some interpreters have thought that James is directly opposing Paul's teaching that a person is "justified by faith, not by works of the law" (Rom 3:28). It may be more accurate to say, however, that James is opposed to an extreme interpretation of Paul, which states that people can live any way they want, so long as they have "faith." For James, faith must be manifest in one's life, for "faith without works is dead" (2:26).

From the New Revised Standard Version Bible, © 1989.

1 James, a servant[a] of God and of the Lord Jesus Christ,

To the twelve tribes in the Dispersion:
Greetings.

2 My brothers and sisters,[b] whenever you face trials of any kind, consider it nothing but joy, 3 because you know that the testing of your faith produces endurance; 4 and let endurance have its full effect, so that you may be mature and complete, lacking in nothing.

5 If any of you is lacking in wisdom, ask God, who gives to all generously and ungrudgingly, and it will be given you. 6 But ask in faith, never doubting, for the one who doubts is like a wave of the sea, driven and tossed by the wind; 7, 8 for the doubter, being double-minded and unstable in every way, must not expect to receive anything from the Lord.

9 Let the believer[c] who is lowly boast in being raised up, 10 and the rich in being brought low, because the rich will disappear like a flower in the field. 11 For the sun rises with its scorching heat and withers the field; its flower falls, and its beauty perishes. It is the same way with the rich; in the midst of a busy life, they will wither away.

12 Blessed is anyone who endures temptation. Such a one has stood the test and will receive the crown of life that the Lord[d] has promised to those who love him. 13 No one, when tempted, should say, "I am being tempted by God"; for God cannot be tempted by evil and he himself tempts no one. 14 But one is tempted by one's own desire, being lured and enticed by it; 15 then, when that desire has conceived, it gives birth to sin, and that sin, when it is fully grown, gives birth to death. 16 Do not be deceived, my beloved.[e]

17 Every generous act of giving, with every perfect gift, is from above, coming down from the Father of lights, with whom there is no variation or shadow due to change.[f] 18 In fulfillment of his own purpose he gave us birth by the word of truth, so that we would become a kind of first fruits of his creatures.

19 You must understand this, my beloved:[e] let everyone be quick to listen, slow to speak, slow to anger; 20 for your anger does not produce God's righteousness. 21 Therefore rid yourselves of all sordidness and rank growth of wickedness, and welcome with meekness the implanted word that has the power to save your souls.

22 But be doers of the word, and not merely hearers who deceive themselves. 23 For if any are hearers of the word and not doers, they are like those who look at themselves[g] in a mirror; 24 for they look at themselves and, on going away, immediately forget what they were like. 25 But those who look into the perfect law, the law of liberty, and persevere, being not hearers who forget but doers who act—they will be blessed in their doing.

26 If any think they are religious, and do not bridle their tongues but deceive their hearts, their religion is worthless. 27 Religion that is pure and undefiled before God, the Father, is this: to care for orphans and widows in their distress, and to keep oneself unstained by the world.

2 My brothers and sisters,[h] do you with your acts of favoritism really believe in our glorious Lord Jesus Christ?[i] 2 For if a person with gold rings and in fine clothes comes into your assembly, and if a poor person in dirty clothes also comes in, 3 and if you take notice of the one wearing the fine clothes and say, "Have a seat here, please," while to the one who is poor you say, "Stand there," or, "Sit at my feet,"[j] 4 have you not made distinctions among yourselves, and become judges with evil thoughts? 5 Listen, my beloved brothers and sisters.[b] Has not God chosen the poor in the world to be rich in faith and to be heirs of the kingdom that he has promised to those who love him? 6 But you have dishonored the poor. Is it not the rich who oppress you? Is it not they who drag you into court? 7 Is it not they who blaspheme the excellent name that was invoked over you?

8 You do well if you really fulfill the royal law according to the scripture, "You shall love your neighbor as yourself."[1] 9 But if you show partiality, you commit sin and are convicted by the law

---

[a]Gk slave [b]Gk brothers [c]Gk brother [d]Gk he; other ancient authorities read God [e]Gk my beloved brothers [f]Other ancient authorities read variation due to a shadow of turning [g]Gk at the face of his birth [h]Gk My brothers [i]Or hold the faith of our glorious Lord Jesus Christ without acts of favoritism [j]Gk Sit under my footstool

---

[1]Lev 19:18

as transgressors. 10 For whoever keeps the whole law but fails in one point has become accountable for all of it. 11 For the one who said, "You shall not commit adultery,"[2] also said, "You shall not murder."[3] Now if you do not commit adultery but if you murder, you have become a transgressor of the law. 12 So speak and so act as those who are to be judged by the law of liberty. 13 For judgment will be without mercy to anyone who has shown no mercy; mercy triumphs over judgment.

14 What good is it, my brothers and sisters,[k] if you say you have faith but do not have works? Can faith save you? 15 If a brother or sister is naked and lacks daily food, 16 and one of you says to them, "Go in peace; keep warm and eat your fill," and yet you do not supply their bodily needs, what is the good of that? 17 So faith by itself, if it has no works, is dead.

18 But someone will say, "You have faith and I have works." Show me your faith apart from your works, and I by my works will show you my faith. 19 You believe that God is one; you do well. Even the demons believe—and shudder. 20 Do you want to be shown, you senseless person, that faith apart from works is barren? 21 Was not our ancestor Abraham justified by works when he offered his son Isaac on the altar? 22 You see that faith was active along with his works, and faith was brought to completion by the works. 23 Thus the scripture was fulfilled that says, "Abraham believed God, and it was reckoned to him as righteousness,"[4] and he was called the friend of God. 24 You see that a person is justified by works and not by faith alone. 25 Likewise, was not Rahab the prostitute also justified by works when she welcomed the messengers and sent them out by another road? 26 For just as the body without the spirit is dead, so faith without works is also dead.

3 Not many of you should become teachers, my brothers and sisters,[k] for you know that we who teach will be judged with greater strictness. 2 For all of us make many mistakes. Anyone who makes no mistakes in speaking is perfect, able to keep the whole body in check with a bridle. 3 If we put bits into the mouths of horses to make them obey us, we guide their whole bodies. 4 Or look at ships: though they are so large that it takes strong winds to drive them, yet they are

guided by a very small rudder wherever the will of the pilot directs. 5 So also the tongue is a small member, yet it boasts of great exploits.

How great a forest is set ablaze by a small fire! 6 And the tongue is a fire. The tongue is placed among our members as a world of iniquity; it stains the whole body, sets on fire the cycle of nature,[l] and is itself set on fire by hell.[m] 7 For every species of beast and bird, of reptile and sea creature, can be tamed and has been tamed by the human species, 8 but no one can tame the tongue—a restless evil, full of deadly poison. 9 With it we bless the Lord and Father, and with it we curse those who are made in the likeness of God. 10 From the same mouth come blessing and cursing. My brothers and sisters,[n] this ought not to be so. 11 Does a spring pour forth from the same opening both fresh and brackish water? 12 Can a fig tree, my brothers and sisters,[o] yield olives, or a grapevine figs? No more can salt water yield fresh.

13 Who is wise and understanding among you? Show by your good life that your works are done with gentleness born of wisdom. 14 But if you have bitter envy and selfish ambition in your hearts, do not be boastful and false to the truth. 15 Such wisdom does not come down from above, but is earthly, unspiritual, devilish. 16 For where there is envy and selfish ambition, there will also be disorder and wickedness of every kind. 17 But the wisdom from above is first pure, then peaceable, gentle, willing to yield, full of mercy and good fruits, without a trace of partiality or hypocrisy. 18 And a harvest of righteousness is sown in peace for[p] those who make peace.

4 Those conflicts and disputes among you, where do they come from? Do they not come from your cravings that are at war within you? 2 You want something and do not have it; so you commit murder. And you covet[q] something and cannot obtain it; so you engage in disputes and conflicts. You do not have, because you do not ask. 3 You ask and do not receive, because you ask wrongly, in order to spend what you get on your pleasures. 4 Adulterers! Do you not know that friendship with the world is enmity with God?

[k]Gk *brothers*   [l]Or *wheel of birth*   [m]Gk *Gehenna*   [n]Gk *My brothers*
[o]Gk *my brothers*   [p]Or *by*   [q]Or *you murder and you covet*

---

[2]Exod 20:14; Deut 5:18   [3]Exod 20:13; Deut 5:17   [4]Gen 15:6

Therefore whoever wishes to be a friend of the world becomes an enemy of God. 5 Or do you suppose that it is for nothing that the scripture says, "God^r yearns jealously for the spirit that he has made to dwell in us"? 6 But he gives all the more grace; therefore it says,

"God opposes the proud,
  but gives grace to the humble."⁵

7 Submit yourselves therefore to God. Resist the devil, and he will flee from you. 8 Draw near to God, and he will draw near to you. Cleanse your hands, you sinners, and purify your hearts, you double-minded. 9 Lament and mourn and weep. Let your laughter be turned into mourning and your joy into dejection. 10 Humble yourselves before the Lord, and he will exalt you.

11 Do not speak evil against one another, brothers and sisters.^s Whoever speaks evil against another or judges another, speaks evil against the law and judges the law; but if you judge the law, you are not a doer of the law but a judge. 12 There is one lawgiver and judge who is able to save and to destroy. So who, then, are you to judge your neighbor?

13 Come now, you who say, "Today or tomorrow we will go to such and such a town and spend a year there, doing business and making money." 14 Yet you do not even know what tomorrow will bring. What is your life? For you are a mist that appears for a little while and then vanishes. 15 Instead you ought to say, "If the Lord wishes, we will live and do this or that." 16 As it is, you boast in your arrogance; all such boasting is evil. 17 Anyone, then, who knows the right thing to do and fails to do it, commits sin.

5 Come now, you rich people, weep and wail for the miseries that are coming to you. 2 Your riches have rotted, and your clothes are moth-eaten. 3 Your gold and silver have rusted, and their rust will be evidence against you, and it will eat your flesh like fire. You have laid up treasure^t for the last days. 4 Listen! The wages of the laborers who mowed your fields, which you kept back by fraud, cry out, and the cries of the harvesters have reached the ears of the Lord of hosts. 5 You have lived on the earth in luxury and in plea-

sure; you have fattened your hearts in a day of slaughter. 6 You have condemned and murdered the righteous one, who does not resist you.

7 Be patient, therefore, beloved,^s until the coming of the Lord. The farmer waits for the precious crop from the earth, being patient with it until it receives the early and the late rains. 8 You also must be patient. Strengthen your hearts, for the coming of the Lord is near.^u 9 Beloved,^v do not grumble against one another, so that you may not be judged. See, the Judge is standing at the doors! 10 As an example of suffering and patience, beloved,^s take the prophets who spoke in the name of the Lord. 11 Indeed we call blessed those who showed endurance. You have heard of the endurance of Job, and you have seen the purpose of the Lord, how the Lord is compassionate and merciful.

12 Above all, my beloved,^s do not swear, either by heaven or by earth or by any other oath, but let your "Yes" be yes and your "No" be no, so that you may not fall under condemnation.

13 Are any among you suffering? They should pray. Are any cheerful? They should sing songs of praise. 14 Are any among you sick? They should call for the elders of the church and have them pray over them, anointing them with oil in the name of the Lord. 15 The prayer of faith will save the sick, and the Lord will raise them up; and anyone who has committed sins will be forgiven. 16 Therefore confess your sins to one another, and pray for one another, so that you may be healed. The prayer of the righteous is powerful and effective. 17 Elijah was a human being like us, and he prayed fervently that it might not rain, and for three years and six months it did not rain on the earth. 18 Then he prayed again, and the heaven gave rain and the earth yielded its harvest.

19 My brothers and sisters,^w if anyone among you wanders from the truth and is brought back by another, 20 you should know that whoever brings back a sinner from wandering will save the sinner's^x soul from death and will cover a multitude of sins.

---

^rGk *He*   ^sGk *brothers*   ^tOr *will eat your flesh, since you have stored up fire*   ^uOr *is at hand*   ^vGk *Brothers*   ^wGk *My brothers*   ^xGk *his*

---

⁵Prov 3:34

The Letter of 1 Peter

The Letter of 1 Peter is addressed to Christian "exiles" scattered throughout several provinces of Asia Minor: "Pontus, Galatia, Cappadocia, Asia, and Bithynia" (1:1). Scholars have debated whether the recipients were literally "exiles" and "aliens" (2:1)—that is, people who were socially marginalized as foreigners in their places of residence—or whether these terms are figurative designations for Christians whose real allegiance is heaven and who are, therefore, simply "in exile" here on earth for a short while (cf. 1:13, 17). In either case, the immediate social context of the letter is clear. The people addressed are experiencing persecution and it has grown serious (2:12; 3:14; 4:12). The word for suffering occurs more frequently in this short letter than in any other book of the New Testament.

The antagonism toward the Christians has evidently come from the grass roots; they are being opposed by former colleagues and friends who do not understand or appreciate their new allegiances to the church (4:4). Some Christians may have been placed on trial before civil authorities simply for being Christian (3:15).

The author of the letter is concerned that his readers not abandon the Christian faith because of their suffering. And so he repeatedly reminds them that they are special before God as the chosen people set apart from the rest of the world (1:4, 17, 19, 23; 2:4–9). He is even more emphatic that Christians should suffer for doing what is right, in imitation of Christ, rather than for what is wrong (3:15–17). They are, therefore, to continue to lead moral, upright lives and to be good family members and model citizens, showing that they have done nothing to deserve their punishment and putting to shame those who wrongly harm them (3:16; 4:16–16).

The letter claims to have been written by Simon Peter, Jesus' disciple, evidently from Rome (assuming that "Babylon" in 5:13 is a codeword for the capital of the empire; see Rev 17:5; 18:2). Scholars, however, have long questioned this claim. Virtually the only things known about Peter are that he was a Jewish fisherman from Galilee, a peasant known to be illiterate, whose native language was probably Aramaic (Mark 1:6; Acts 4:13). This letter, on the other hand, was written by a highly literate Greek-speaking Christian familiar with the Greek Old Testament and Greek rhetorical strategies.

Some scholars have resolved this dilemma by suggesting that Silvanus, mentioned in 5:12, was the actual author of the letter (or that, as Peter's scribe, Silvanus put the letter into more rhetorically effective language). Others have noted the large number of other early Christian writings pseudonymously produced in Peter's name, including three apocalypses, several Acts, and other letters. 1 Peter may itself belong to this group of Petrine pseudepigrapha, a letter written in the apostle's name to deal with problems that had arisen some decades after his death.

1 Peter, an apostle of Jesus Christ,
To the exiles of the Dispersion in Pontus, Galatia, Cappadocia, Asia, and Bithynia, 2 who have been chosen and destined by God the Father and sanctified by the Spirit to be obedient to Jesus Christ and to be sprinkled with his blood:

May grace and peace be yours in abundance.

3 Blessed be the God and Father of our Lord Jesus Christ! By his great mercy he has given us a new birth into a living hope through the resurrection of Jesus Christ from the dead, 4 and into an inheritance that is imperishable, undefiled, and unfading, kept in heaven for you, 5 who are being protected by the power of God through faith for a salvation ready to be revealed in the last time. 6 In this you rejoice,[a] even if now for a little while you have had to suffer various trials, 7 so that the genuineness of your faith—being more precious than gold that, though perishable, is tested by fire—may be found to result in praise and glory and honor when Jesus Christ is revealed. 8 Although you have not seen[b] him, you love him; and even though you do not see him now, you believe in him and rejoice with an indescribable and glorious joy, 9 for you are receiving the outcome of your faith, the salvation of your souls.

10 Concerning this salvation, the prophets who prophesied of the grace that was to be yours made careful search and inquiry, 11 inquiring about the person or time that the Spirit of Christ within them indicated when it testified in advance to the sufferings destined for Christ and the subsequent glory. 12 It was revealed to them that they were serving not themselves but you, in regard to the things that have now been announced to you through those who brought you good news by the Holy Spirit sent from heaven—things into which angels long to look!

13 Therefore prepare your minds for action;[c] discipline yourselves; set all your hope on the grace that Jesus Christ will bring you when he is revealed. 14 Like obedient children, do not be conformed to the desires that you formerly had in ignorance. 15 Instead, as he who called you is holy, be holy yourselves in all your conduct; 16 for it is written, "You shall be holy, for I am holy."[1]

17 If you invoke as Father the one who judges all people impartially according to their deeds, live in reverent fear during the time of your exile.

18 You know that you were ransomed from the futile ways inherited from your ancestors, not with perishable things like silver or gold, 19 but with the precious blood of Christ, like that of a lamb without defect or blemish. 20 He was destined before the foundation of the world, but was revealed at the end of the ages for your sake. 21 Through him you have come to trust in God, who raised him from the dead and gave him glory, so that your faith and hope are set on God.

22 Now that you have purified your souls by your obedience to the truth[d] so that you have genuine mutual love, love one another deeply[e] from the heart.[f] 23 You have been born anew, not of perishable but of imperishable seed, through the living and enduring word of God.[g] 24 For

"All flesh is like grass
    and all its glory like the flower
        of grass.
The grass withers,
    and the flower falls,
25   but the word of the Lord endures
        forever."[2]

That word is the good news that was announced to you.

2 Rid yourselves, therefore, of all malice, and all guile, insincerity, envy, and all slander. 2 Like newborn infants, long for the pure, spiritual milk, so that by it you may grow into salvation— 3 if indeed you have tasted that the Lord is good.

4 Come to him, a living stone, though rejected by mortals yet chosen and precious in God's sight, and 5 like living stones, let yourselves be built[h] into a spiritual house, to be a holy priesthood, to offer spiritual sacrifices acceptable to God through Jesus Christ. 6 For it stands in scripture:

"See, I am laying in Zion a stone,
    a cornerstone chosen and
        precious;
and whoever believes in him[i] will
    not be put to shame."[3]

_____

[a] Or Rejoice in this   [b] Other ancient authorities read known   [c] Gk gird up the loins of your mind   [d] Other ancient authorities add through the Spirit   [e] Or constantly   [f] Other ancient authorities read a pure heart   [g] Or through the word of the living and enduring God   [h] Or you yourselves are being built   [i] Or it

_____

[1] Lev 11:45; 19:2   [2] Isa 40:6–8   [3] Isa 28:16

Jesus is coming -Apocalyptic

7 To you then who believe, he is precious; but for those who do not believe,

> "The stone that the builders
>   rejected
>   has become the very head of the
>   corner,"[4]

8 and

> "A stone that makes them
>   stumble,
>   and a rock that makes them
>   fall."[5]

They stumble because they disobey the word, as they were destined to do.

9 But you are a chosen race, a royal priesthood, a holy nation, God's own people,[j] in order that you may proclaim the mighty acts of him who called you out of darkness into his marvelous light.

10   Once you were not a people,
>   but now you are God's people;
>   once you had not received mercy,
>   but now you have received
>   mercy.

11 Beloved, I urge you as aliens and exiles to abstain from the desires of the flesh that wage war against the soul. 12 Conduct yourselves honorably among the Gentiles, so that, though they malign you as evildoers, they may see your honorable deeds and glorify God when he comes to judge.[k]

13 For the Lord's sake accept the authority of every human institution,[l] whether of the emperor as supreme, 14 or of governors, as sent by him to punish those who do wrong and to praise those who do right. 15 For it is God's will that by doing right you should silence the ignorance of the foolish. 16 As servants[m] of God, live as free people, yet do not use your freedom as a pretext for evil. 17 Honor everyone. Love the family of believers.[n] Fear God. Honor the emperor.

18 Slaves, accept the authority of your masters with all deference, not only those who are kind and gentle but also those who are harsh. 19 For it is a credit to you if, being aware of God, you endure pain while suffering unjustly. 20 If you endure when you are beaten for doing wrong, what credit is that? But if you endure when you do right and suffer for it, you have God's approval. 21 For to this you have been called, because Christ also suffered for you, leaving you an example, so that you should follow in his steps.

22   "He committed no sin,
>   and no deceit was found in his
>   mouth."[6]

23 When he was abused, he did not return abuse; when he suffered, he did not threaten; but he entrusted himself to the one who judges justly. 24 He himself bore our sins in his body on the cross,[o] so that, free from sins, we might live for righteousness; by his wounds[p] you have been healed. 25 For you were going astray like sheep, but now you have returned to the shepherd and guardian of your souls.

3 Wives, in the same way, accept the authority of your husbands, so that, even if some of them do not obey the word, they may be won over without a word by their wives' conduct, 2 when they see the purity and reverence of your lives. 3 Do not adorn yourselves outwardly by braiding your hair, and by wearing gold ornaments or fine clothing; 4 rather, let your adornment be the inner self with the lasting beauty of a gentle and quiet spirit, which is very precious in God's sight. 5 It was in this way long ago that the holy women who hoped in God used to adorn themselves by accepting the authority of their husbands. 6 Thus Sarah obeyed Abraham and called him lord. You have become her daughters as long as you do what is good and never let fears alarm you.

7 Husbands, in the same way, show consideration for your wives in your life together, paying honor to the woman as the weaker sex,[q] since they too are also heirs of the gracious gift of life—so that nothing may hinder your prayers.

8 Finally, all of you, have unity of spirit, sympathy, love for one another, a tender heart, and a humble mind. 9 Do not repay evil for evil or abuse for abuse; but, on the contrary, repay with a blessing. It is for this that you were called—that you might inherit a blessing. 10 For

> "Those who desire life
>   and desire to see good days,
>   let them keep their tongues from
>   evil

[j]Gk *a people for his possession*   [k]Gk *God on the day of visitation*
[l]Or *every institution ordained for human beings*   [m]Gk *slaves*
[n]Gk *Love the brotherhood*   [o]Or *carried up our sins in his body to the tree*   [p]Gk *bruise*   [q]Gk *vessel*

[4]Ps 118:22   [5]Isa 8:14   [6]Isa 53:9

and their lips from speaking
    deceit;
11   let them turn away from evil and
       do good;
    let them seek peace and pursue
       it.
12   For the eyes of the Lord are on
       the righteous,
    and his ears are open to their
       prayer.
    But the face of the Lord is against
       those who do evil."[7]

13 Now who will harm you if you are eager to do what is good? 14 But even if you do suffer for doing what is right, you are blessed. Do not fear what they fear,[r] and do not be intimidated, 15 but in your hearts sanctify Christ as Lord. Always be ready to make your defense to anyone who demands from you an accounting for the hope that is in you; 16 yet do it with gentleness and reverence.[s] Keep your conscience clear, so that, when you are maligned, those who abuse you for your good conduct in Christ may be put to shame. 17 For it is better to suffer for doing good, if suffering should be God's will, than to suffer for doing evil. 18 For Christ also suffered[t] for sins once for all, the righteous for the unrighteous, in order to bring you[u] to God. He was put to death in the flesh, but made alive in the spirit, 19 in which also he went and made a proclamation to the spirits in prison, 20 who in former times did not obey, when God waited patiently in the days of Noah, during the building of the ark, in which a few, that is, eight persons, were saved through water. 21 And baptism, which this prefigured, now saves you—not as a removal of dirt from the body, but as an appeal to God for[v] a good conscience, through the resurrection of Jesus Christ, 22 who has gone into heaven and is at the right hand of God, with angels, authorities, and powers made subject to him.

4 Since therefore Christ suffered in the flesh,[w] arm yourselves also with the same intention (for whoever has suffered in the flesh has finished with sin), 2 so as to live for the rest of your earthly life[x] no longer by human desires but by the will of God. 3 You have already spent enough time in doing what the Gentiles like to do, living in licentiousness, passions, drunkenness, revels, carous-

ing, and lawless idolatry. 4 They are surprised that you no longer join them in the same excesses of dissipation, and so they blaspheme.[y] 5 But they will have to give an accounting to him who stands ready to judge the living and the dead. 6 For this is the reason the gospel was proclaimed even to the dead, so that, though they had been judged in the flesh as everyone is judged, they might live in the spirit as God does.

7 The end of all things is near;[z] therefore be serious and discipline yourselves for the sake of your prayers. 8 Above all, maintain constant love for one another, for love covers a multitude of sins. 9 Be hospitable to one another without complaining. 10 Like good stewards of the manifold grace of God, serve one another with whatever gift each of you has received. 11 Whoever speaks must do so as one speaking the very words of God; whoever serves must do so with the strength that God supplies, so that God may be glorified in all things through Jesus Christ. To him belong the glory and the power forever and ever. Amen.

12 Beloved, do not be surprised at the fiery ordeal that is taking place among you to test you, as though something strange were happening to you. 13 But rejoice insofar as you are sharing Christ's sufferings, so that you may also be glad and shout for joy when his glory is revealed. 14 If you are reviled for the name of Christ, you are blessed, because the spirit of glory,[a] which is the Spirit of God, is resting on you.[b] 15 But let none of you suffer as a murderer, a thief, a criminal, or even as a mischief maker. 16 Yet if any of you suffers as a Christian, do not consider it a disgrace, but glorify God because you bear this name. 17 For the time has come for judgment to begin with the household of God; if it begins with us, what will be the end for those who do not obey the gospel of God? 18 And

    "If it is hard for the righteous to
       be saved,

[r]Gk *their fear* [s]Or *respect* [t]Other ancient authorities read *died*
[u]Other ancient authorities read *us* [v]Or *a pledge to God from*
[w]Other ancient authorities add *for us*; others, *for you* [x]Gk *rest of the time in the flesh* [y]Or *they malign you* [z]Or *is at hand* [a]Other ancient authorities add *and of power* [b]Other ancient authorities add *On their part he is blasphemed, but on your part he is glorified*

[7]Ps 34:12–16

what will become of the
ungodly and the sinners?"[8]
19 Therefore, let those suffering in accordance with God's will entrust themselves to a faithful Creator, while continuing to do good.

5 Now as an elder myself and a witness of the sufferings of Christ, as well as one who shares in the glory to be revealed, I exhort the elders among you 2 to tend the flock of God that is in your charge, exercising the oversight,[c] not under compulsion but willingly, as God would have you do it[d]—not for sordid gain but eagerly. 3 Do not lord it over those in your charge, but be examples to the flock. 4 And when the chief shepherd appears, you will win the crown of glory that never fades away. 5 In the same way, you who are younger must accept the authority of the elders.[e] And all of you must clothe yourselves with humility in your dealings with one another, for

"God opposes the proud,
    but gives grace to the humble."[9]

6 Humble yourselves therefore under the mighty hand of God, so that he may exalt you in due time. 7 Cast all your anxiety on him, because he cares for you. 8 Discipline yourselves, keep alert.[f] Like a roaring lion your adversary the devil prowls around, looking for someone to devour. 9 Resist him, steadfast in your faith, for you know that your brothers and sisters[g] in all the world are undergoing the same kinds of suffering. 10 And after you have suffered for a little while, the God of all grace, who has called you to his eternal glory in Christ, will himself restore, support, strengthen, and establish you. 11 To him be the power forever and ever. Amen.

12 Through Silvanus, whom I consider a faithful brother, I have written this short letter to encourage you and to testify that this is the true grace of God. Stand fast in it. 13 Your sister church[h] in Babylon, chosen together with you, sends you greetings; and so does my son Mark. 14 Greet one another with a kiss of love.

Peace to all of you who are in Christ.[i]

---

[c]Other ancient authorities lack *exercising the oversight* [d]Other ancient authorities lack *as God would have you do it* [e]Or *of those who are older* [f]Or *be vigilant* [g]Gk *your brotherhood* [h]Gk *She who is* [i]Other ancient authorities add *Amen*

[8]Prov 11:31 [9]Prov 3:34

The Letter of 2 Peter

The author of 2 Peter claims to be the apostle "Simeon Peter," who beheld Jesus' glory and heard the voice from heaven on the Mount of Transfiguration (1:1, 17–18). On the basis of internal evidence in the letter itself, however, the majority of critical scholars have concluded that it is pseudonymous, written some decades after Peter's death by an author intent on providing apostolic support for his own views. For one thing, the book was written at a time when the imminent end of the world, so widely anticipated among the earliest Christians, had become a source of ridicule against them (3:3–10). Moreover, as is sometimes pointed out, it was written by a relatively sophisticated Greek-speaking Christian, rather than an Aramaic-speaking Jewish peasant. It is striking that no church writer evidences any knowledge of this book at all until the beginning of the third century; this would be peculiar if it were known to be an actual letter by Jesus' apostle.

The author claims to be Peter precisely in order to show that, unlike his opponents, he has no need of "cleverly devised myths" to understand Jesus (1:16); he knows about him firsthand. His opponents appear to be early Christian Gnostics who propound idiosyncratic interpretations of Scripture (1:20) and who appeal to the writings of Paul for support (3:16). The author never explains what, exactly, these views were, but instead launches an attack on the immoral lives of those who advance them (chap. 2). They are said to be "insatiable for sin," they speak "bombastic nonsense," and they are full of "licentious desires" (2:14, 18). Much of this vituperative attack appears to have been borrowed from the book of Jude.

In particular, the author opposes those who scoff at Christians for thinking, against all appearances, that the end of the world is imminent (3:3–4). For him, the end is indeed soon to come, and those who mock have erred in measuring time in human terms. For with God "one day is like a thousand years and a thousand years are like one day" (3:8). The end, the author maintains, has been delayed for good reason: to allow people a chance to repent. This they must do without delay, for when the "day of God" comes, "the heavens will be set ablaze and dissolved, and the elements will melt with fire," but those who are prepared will be rewarded with "new heavens and a new earth, where righteousness is at home" (3:12–13).

1 Simeon[a] Peter, a servant[b] and apostle of Jesus Christ,

To those who have received a faith as precious as ours through the righteousness of our God and Savior Jesus Christ:[c]

2 May grace and peace be yours in abundance in the knowledge of God and of Jesus our Lord.

3 His divine power has given us everything needed for life and godliness, through the knowledge of him who called us by[d] his own glory and goodness. 4 Thus he has given us, through these things, his precious and very great promises, so that through them you may escape from the cor-

[a]Other ancient authorities read *Simon* [b]Gk *slave* [c]Or *of our God and the Savior Jesus Christ* [d]Other ancient authorities read *through*

ruption that is in the world because of lust, and may become participants of the divine nature. 5 For this very reason, you must make every effort to support your faith with goodness, and goodness with knowledge, 6 and knowledge with self-control, and self-control with endurance, and endurance with godliness, 7 and godliness with mutual[c] affection, and mutual[c] affection with love. 8 For if these things are yours and are increasing among you, they keep you from being ineffective and unfruitful in the knowledge of our Lord Jesus Christ. 9 For anyone who lacks these things is nearsighted and blind, and is forgetful of the cleansing of past sins. 10 Therefore, brothers and sisters,[f] be all the more eager to confirm your call and election, for if you do this, you will never stumble. 11 For in this way, entry into the eternal kingdom of our Lord and Savior Jesus Christ will be richly provided for you.

12 Therefore I intend to keep on reminding you of these things, though you know them already and are established in the truth that has come to you. 13 I think it right, as long as I am in this body,[g] to refresh your memory, 14 since I know that my death[h] will come soon, as indeed our Lord Jesus Christ has made clear to me. 15 And I will make every effort so that after my departure you may be able at any time to recall these things.

16 For we did not follow cleverly devised myths when we made known to you the power and coming of our Lord Jesus Christ, but we had been eyewitnesses of his majesty. 17 For he received honor and glory from God the Father when that voice was conveyed to him by the Majestic Glory, saying, "This is my Son, my Beloved,[i] with whom I am well pleased."[1] 18 We ourselves heard this voice come from heaven, while we were with him on the holy mountain.

19 So we have the prophetic message more fully confirmed. You will do well to be attentive to this as to a lamp shining in a dark place, until the day dawns and the morning star rises in your hearts. 20 First of all you must understand this, that no prophecy of scripture is a matter of one's own interpretation, 21 because no prophecy ever came by human will, but men and women moved by the Holy Spirit spoke from God.[j]

2 But false prophets also arose among the people, just as there will be false teachers among you, who will secretly bring in destructive opinions. They will even deny the Master who bought them—bringing swift destruction on themselves. 2 Even so, many will follow their licentious ways, and because of these teachers[k] the way of truth will be maligned. 3 And in their greed they will exploit you with deceptive words. Their condemnation, pronounced against them long ago, has not been idle, and their destruction is not asleep.

4 For if God did not spare the angels when they sinned, but cast them into hell[l] and committed them to chains[m] of deepest darkness to be kept until the judgment; 5 and if he did not spare the ancient world, even though he saved Noah, a herald of righteousness, with seven others, when he brought a flood on a world of the ungodly; 6 and if by turning the cities of Sodom and Gomorrah to ashes he condemned them to extinction[n] and made them an example of what is coming to the ungodly;[o] 7 and if he rescued Lot, a righteous man greatly distressed by the licentiousness of the lawless 8 (for that righteous man, living among them day after day, was tormented in his righteous soul by their lawless deeds that he saw and heard), 9 then the Lord knows how to rescue the godly from trial, and to keep the unrighteous under punishment until the day of judgment 10 —especially those who indulge their flesh in depraved lust, and who despise authority.

Bold and willful, they are not afraid to slander the glorious ones,[p] 11 whereas angels, though greater in might and power, do not bring against them a slanderous judgment from the Lord.[q] 12 These people, however, are like irrational animals, mere creatures of instinct, born to be caught and killed. They slander what they do not understand, and when those creatures are destroyed,[r] they also will be destroyed, 13 suffering[s] the penalty for doing wrong. They count it a pleasure to revel in the daytime. They are blots and blem-

---

[c]Gk brotherly [f]Gk brothers [g]Gk tent [h]Gk the putting off of my tent [i]Other ancient authorities read my beloved Son [j]Other ancient authorities read but moved by the Holy Spirit saints of God spoke [k]Gk because of them [l]Gk Tartaros [m]Other ancient authorities read pits [n]Other ancient authorities lack to extinction [o]Other ancient authorities read an example to those who were to be ungodly [p]Or angels; Gk glories [q]Other ancient authorities read before the Lord; others lack the phrase [r]Gk in their destruction [s]Other ancient authorities read receiving

---

[1]Matt 17:5; Mk 9:7

ishes, reveling in their dissipation[t] while they feast with you. 14 They have eyes full of adultery, insatiable for sin. They entice unsteady souls. They have hearts trained in greed. Accursed children! 15 They have left the straight road and have gone astray, following the road of Balaam son of Bosor,[u] who loved the wages of doing wrong, 16 but was rebuked for his own transgression; a speechless donkey spoke with a human voice and restrained the prophet's madness.

17 These are waterless springs and mists driven by a storm; for them the deepest darkness has been reserved. 18 For they speak bombastic nonsense, and with licentious desires of the flesh they entice people who have just[v] escaped from those who live in error. 19 They promise them freedom, but they themselves are slaves of corruption; for people are slaves to whatever masters them. 20 For if, after they have escaped the defilements of the world through the knowledge of our Lord and Savior Jesus Christ, they are again entangled in them and overpowered, the last state has become worse for them than the first. 21 For it would have been better for them never to have known the way of righteousness than, after knowing it, to turn back from the holy commandment that was passed on to them. 22 It has happened to them according to the true proverb,

> "The dog turns back to its own
> vomit,"[2]

and,

> "The sow is washed only to
> wallow in the mud."

3 This is now, beloved, the second letter I am writing to you; in them I am trying to arouse your sincere intention by reminding you 2 that you should remember the words spoken in the past by the holy prophets, and the commandment of the Lord and Savior spoken through your apostles. 3 First of all you must understand this, that in the last days scoffers will come, scoffing and indulging their own lusts 4 and saying, "Where is the promise of his coming? For ever since our ancestors died,[w] all things continue as they were from the beginning of creation!" 5 They deliberately ignore this fact, that by the word of God heavens existed long ago and an earth was formed out of water and by means of water, 6 through

which the world of that time was deluged with water and perished. 7 But by the same word the present heavens and earth have been reserved for fire, being kept until the day of judgment and destruction of the godless.

8 But do not ignore this one fact, beloved, that with the Lord one day is like a thousand years, and a thousand years are like one day. 9 The Lord is not slow about his promise, as some think of slowness, but is patient with you,[x] not wanting any to perish, but all to come to repentance. 10 But the day of the Lord will come like a thief, and then the heavens will pass away with a loud noise, and the elements will be dissolved with fire, and the earth and everything that is done on it will be disclosed.[y]

11 Since all these things are to be dissolved in this way, what sort of persons ought you to be in leading lives of holiness and godliness, 12 waiting for and hastening[z] the coming of the day of God, because of which the heavens will be set ablaze and dissolved, and the elements will melt with fire? 13 But, in accordance with his promise, we wait for new heavens and a new earth, where righteousness is at home.

14 Therefore, beloved, while you are waiting for these things, strive to be found by him at peace, without spot or blemish; 15 and regard the patience of our Lord as salvation. So also our beloved brother Paul wrote to you according to the wisdom given him, 16 speaking of this as he does in all his letters. There are some things in them hard to understand, which the ignorant and unstable twist to their own destruction, as they do the other scriptures. 17 You therefore, beloved, since you are forewarned, beware that you are not carried away with the error of the lawless and lose your own stability. 18 But grow in the grace and knowledge of our Lord and Savior Jesus Christ. To him be the glory both now and to the day of eternity. Amen.[a]

---

[t] Other ancient authorities read *love-feasts* [u] Other ancient authorities read *Beor* [v] Other ancient authorities read *actually* [w] Gk *our fathers fell asleep* [x] Other ancient authorities read *on your account* [y] Other ancient authorities read *will be burned up* [z] Or *earnestly desiring* [a] Other ancient authorities lack *Amen*

---

[2] Prov 26:11

The Letter of 1 John

Although traditionally called an "epistle," the book of 1 John lacks the standard conventions of ancient letters: the author does not introduce himself, name his addressees, or offer an opening greeting or prayer on their behalf; nor does he conclude with well-wishings, final prayers, or even a farewell. The book appears to be a persuasive essay written by a Christian leader to a Christian community; it was possibly accompanied by a cover letter that has since been lost.

The occasion for the essay is relatively clear. The author refers to a group of persons who had formerly belonged to the community but have since left: "They went out from us, but they did not belong to us; for if they had belonged to us, they would have remained with us" (2:19). In other places he calls these persons "liars" and "antichrists" (i.e., those who are opposed to Christ; 2:4, 18, 22). Some evidence in the letter suggests that these persons were Christians who believed so strongly in the divinity of Jesus that they had come to deny his humanity. That is to say, they did not think that, as a divine being, Jesus fully participated in human existence; he did not have have a real flesh-and-blood body. Not finding acceptance in the community, these people withdrew, possibly in order to start a new community of their own.

The author counteracts his opponents' views by stressing that Christ actually did "come in the flesh" (4:2), that the "Word of Life" could be "heard . . . seen with our eyes . . . and touched with our hands" (1:1–2), and that it was his real blood that brought forgiveness of sins (1:7; 2:2; 4:10). Moreover, he maintains that the real fleshly existence of Christ has moral implications for the believer. He charges that his opponents, more concerned with the spirit than the flesh, are lax in keeping God's commandments and in loving their brothers and sisters (2:4, 9–11); they practice sin while claiming to be spiritual beings who have no contact with it (1:6–10). In contrast, the author stresses that his readers are to manifest real, active love among one another as the children of God (e.g., 3:18; 4:7).

We do not know who actually wrote this book, as the writer kept his identity anonymous. Readers have long noted the similarity in vocabulary and theology to the Fourth Gospel, and so have traditionally ascribed the book to the same author. Since, however, the issues raised here differ markedly from those addressed by the Gospel—the conflict with the Jewish synagogue, for example, is entirely lacking—most scholars today prefer to see the book as stemming from a later author living in the same community, one who possibly knew the gospel traditions and understood himself (as opposed to those who withdrew from the community) to stand in continuity with them.

1 We declare to you what was from the beginning, what we have heard, what we have seen with our eyes, what we have looked at and touched with our hands, concerning the word of life— 2 this life was revealed, and we have seen it and testify to it, and declare to you the eternal life that was with the Father and was revealed to us— 3 we declare to you what we have seen and heard

From the New Revised Standard Version Bible, © 1989.

so that you also may have fellowship with us; and truly our fellowship is with the Father and with his Son Jesus Christ. 4 We are writing these things so that our[a] joy may be complete.

5 This is the message we have heard from him and proclaim to you, that God is light and in him there is no darkness at all. 6 If we say that we have fellowship with him while we are walking in darkness, we lie and do not do what is true; 7 but if we walk in the light as he himself is in the light, we have fellowship with one another, and the blood of Jesus his Son cleanses us from all sin. 8 If we say that we have no sin, we deceive ourselves, and the truth is not in us. 9 If we confess our sins, he who is faithful and just will forgive us our sins and cleanse us from all unrighteousness. 10 If we say that we have not sinned, we make him a liar, and his word is not in us.

2 My little children, I am writing these things to you so that you may not sin. But if anyone does sin, we have an advocate with the Father, Jesus Christ the righteous; 2 and he is the atoning sacrifice for our sins, and not for ours only but also for the sins of the whole world.

3 Now by this we may be sure that we know him, if we obey his commandments. 4 Whoever says, "I have come to know him," but does not obey his commandments, is a liar, and in such a person the truth does not exist; 5 but whoever obeys his word, truly in this person the love of God has reached perfection. By this we may be sure that we are in him: 6 whoever says, "I abide in him," ought to walk just as he walked.

7 Beloved, I am writing you no new commandment, but an old commandment that you have had from the beginning; the old commandment is the word that you have heard. 8 Yet I am writing you a new commandment that is true in him and in you, because[b] the darkness is passing away and the true light is already shining. 9 Whoever says, "I am in the light," while hating a brother or sister,[c] is still in the darkness. 10 Whoever loves a brother or sister[d] lives in the light, and in such a person[e] there is no cause for stumbling. 11 But whoever hates another believer[f] is in the darkness, walks in the darkness, and does not know the way to go, because the darkness has brought on blindness.

12   I am writing to you, little
            children,
                because your sins are forgiven
                on account of his name.
13   I am writing to you, fathers,
            because you know him who is
                from the beginning.
       I am writing to you, young
            people,
            because you have conquered the
                evil one.
14   I write to you, children,
            because you know the Father.
       I write to you, fathers,
            because you know him who is
                from the beginning.
       I write to you, young people,
            because you are strong
            and the word of God abides in
                you,
            and you have overcome the
                evil one.

15 Do not love the world or the things in the world. The love of the Father is not in those who love the world; 16 for all that is in the world—the desire of the flesh, the desire of the eyes, the pride in riches—comes not from the Father but from the world. 17 And the world and its desire[g] are passing away, but those who do the will of God live forever.

18 Children, it is the last hour! As you have heard that antichrist is coming, so now many antichrists have come. From this we know that it is the last hour. 19 They went out from us, but they did not belong to us; for if they had belonged to us, they would have remained with us. But by going out they made it plain that none of them belongs to us. 20 But you have been anointed by the Holy One, and all of you have knowledge.[h] 21 I write to you, not because you do not know the truth, but because you know it, and you know that no lie comes from the truth. 22 Who is the liar but the one who denies that Jesus is the Christ?[i] This is the antichrist, the one who denies the Father and the Son. 23 No one who denies the Son has the Father; everyone who confesses the Son has the Father also. 24 Let what you heard from the begin-

---

[a]Other ancient authorities read *your* [b]Or *that* [c]Gk *hating a brother* [d]Gk *loves a brother* [e]Or *in it* [f]Gk *hates a brother* [g]Or *the desire for it* [h]Other ancient authorities read *you know all things* [i]Or *the Messiah*

ning abide in you. If what you heard from the beginning abides in you, then you will abide in the Son and in the Father. 25 And this is what he has promised us,[j] eternal life.

26 I write these things to you concerning those who would deceive you. 27 As for you, the anointing that you received from him abides in you, and so you do not need anyone to teach you. But as his anointing teaches you about all things, and is true and is not a lie, and just as it has taught you, abide in him.[k]

28 And now, little children, abide in him, so that when he is revealed we may have confidence and not be put to shame before him at his coming.

29 If you know that he is righteous, you may be sure that everyone who does right has been born of him.

3 See what love the Father has given us, that we should be called children of God; and that is what we are. The reason the world does not know us is that it did not know him. 2 Beloved, we are God's children now; what we will be has not yet been revealed. What we do know is this: when he[k] is revealed, we will be like him, for we will see him as he is. 3 And all who have this hope in him purify themselves, just as he is pure.

4 Everyone who commits sin is guilty of lawlessness; sin is lawlessness. 5 You know that he was revealed to take away sins, and in him there is no sin. 6 No one who abides in him sins; no one who sins has either seen him or known him. 7 Little children, let no one deceive you. Everyone who does what is right is righteous, just as he is righteous. 8 Everyone who commits sin is a child of the devil; for the devil has been sinning from the beginning. The Son of God was revealed for this purpose, to destroy the works of the devil. 9 Those who have been born of God do not sin, because God's seed abides in them;[l] they cannot sin, because they have been born of God. 10 The children of God and the children of the devil are revealed in this way: all who do not do what is right are not from God, nor are those who do not love their brothers and sisters.[m]

11 For this is the message you have heard from the beginning, that we should love one another. 12 We must not be like Cain who was from the evil one and murdered his brother. And why did he murder him? Because his own deeds were evil and his brother's righteous. 13 Do not be astonished, brothers and sisters,[n] that the world hates you. 14 We know that we have passed from death to life because we love one another. Whoever does not love abides in death. 15 All who hate a brother or sister[m] are murderers, and you know that murderers do not have eternal life abiding in them. 16 We know love by this, that he laid down his life for us—and we ought to lay down our lives for one another. 17 How does God's love abide in anyone who has the world's goods and sees a brother or sister[o] in need and yet refuses help?

18 Little children, let us love, not in word or speech, but in truth and action. 19 And by this we will know that we are from the truth and will reassure our hearts before him 20 whenever our hearts condemn us; for God is greater than our hearts, and he knows everything. 21 Beloved, if our hearts do not condemn us, we have boldness before God; 22 and we receive from him whatever we ask, because we obey his commandments and do what pleases him.

23 And this is his commandment, that we should believe in the name of his Son Jesus Christ and love one another, just as he has commanded us. 24 All who obey his commandments abide in him, and he abides in them. And by this we know that he abides in us, by the Spirit that he has given us.

4 Beloved, do not believe every spirit, but test the spirits to see whether they are from God; for many false prophets have gone out into the world. 2 By this you know the Spirit of God: every spirit that confesses that Jesus Christ has come in the flesh is from God, 3 and every spirit that does not confess Jesus[p] is not from God. And this is the spirit of the antichrist, of which you have heard that it is coming; and now it is already in the world. 4 Little children, you are from God, and have conquered them; for the one who is in you is greater than the one who is in the world. 5 They are from the world; therefore what they say is from the world, and the world listens to them. 6 We are from God. Whoever knows God listens to us, and whoever is not from God does not listen to us.

[j]Other ancient authorities read *you* [k]Or *it* [l]Or *because the children of God abide in him* [m]Gk *his brother* [n]Gk *brothers* [o]Gk *brother* [p]Other ancient authorities read *does away with Jesus* (Gk *dissolves Jesus*)

From this we know the spirit of truth and the spirit of error.

7 Beloved, let us love one another, because love
is from God; everyone who loves is born of God
and knows God. 8 Whoever does not love does
not know God, for God is love. 9 God's love was
revealed among us in this way: God sent his only
Son into the world so that we might live through
him. 10 In this is love, not that we loved God but
that he loved us and sent his Son to be the atoning
sacrifice for our sins. 11 Beloved, since God
loved us so much, we also ought to love one another. 12 No one has ever seen God; if we love
one another, God lives in us, and his love is perfected in us.

13 By this we know that we abide in him and he
in us, because he has given us of his Spirit. 14 And
we have seen and do testify that the Father has sent
his Son as the Savior of the world. 15 God abides
in those who confess that Jesus is the Son of God,
and they abide in God. 16 So we have known and
believe the love that God has for us.

God is love, and those who abide in love abide
in God, and God abides in them. 17 Love has been
perfected among us in this: that we may have boldness on the day of judgment, because as he is, so
are we in this world. 18 There is no fear in love,
but perfect love casts out fear; for fear has to
do with punishment, and whoever fears has not
reached perfection in love. 19 We love[q] because
he first loved us. 20 Those who say, "I love God,"
and hate their brothers or sisters,[r] are liars; for
those who do not love a brother or sister[s] whom
they have seen, cannot love God whom they have
not seen. 21 The commandment we have from
him is this: those who love God must love their
brothers and sisters[r] also.

5 Everyone who believes that Jesus is the
Christ[t] has been born of God, and everyone
who loves the parent loves the child. 2 By this we
know that we love the children of God, when we
love God and obey his commandments. 3 For the
love of God is this, that we obey his commandments. And his commandments are not burden-
some, 4 for whatever is born of God conquers the
world. And this is the victory that conquers the
world, our faith. 5 Who is it that conquers the
world but the one who believes that Jesus is
the Son of God?

6 This is the one who came by water and blood,
Jesus Christ, not with the water only but with the
water and the blood. And the Spirit is the one that
testifies, for the Spirit is the truth. 7 There are
three that testify:[u] 8 the Spirit and the water and
the blood, and these three agree. 9 If we receive
human testimony, the testimony of God is greater;
for this is the testimony of God that he has testified to his Son. 10 Those who believe in the Son
of God have the testimony in their hearts. Those
who do not believe in God[v] have made him a liar
by not believing in the testimony that God has giv-
en concerning his Son. 11 And this is the testimony: God gave us eternal life, and this life is in his
Son. 12 Whoever has the Son has life; whoever
does not have the Son of God does not have life.

13 I write these things to you who believe in the
name of the Son of God, so that you may know that
you have eternal life.

14 And this is the boldness we have in him, that
if we ask anything according to his will, he hears
us. 15 And if we know that he hears us in whatever we ask, we know that we have obtained the
requests made of him. 16 If you see your brother
or sister[w] committing what is not a mortal sin, you
will ask, and God[x] will give life to such a one—to
those whose sin is not mortal. There is sin that is
mortal; I do not say that you should pray about
that. 17 All wrongdoing is sin, but there is sin that
is not mortal.

18 We know that those who are born of God do
not sin, but the one who was born of God protects
them, and the evil one does not touch them. 19 We
know that we are God's children, and that the
whole world lies under the power of the evil one.
20 And we know that the Son of God has come and
has given us understanding so that we may know
him who is true;[y] and we are in him who is true, in
his Son Jesus Christ. He is the true God and eternal life.

21 Little children, keep yourselves from idols.[z]

[q]Other ancient authorities add *him*; others add *God* [r]Gk *brothers* [s]Gk *brother* [t]Or *the Messiah* [u]A few other authorities read (with variations) [7]*There are three that testify in heaven, the Father, the Word, and the Holy Spirit, and these three are one.* [8]*And there are three that testify on earth:* [v]Other ancient authorities read *in the Son* [w]Gk *your brother* [x]Gk *he* [y]Other ancient authorities read *know the true God* [z]Other ancient authorities add *Amen*

The Letter of 2 John

Unlike 1 John (see that introduction), the book of 2 John is an actual epistle, sent by someone who calls himself "the elder" to an unnamed person called "the elect lady" (v. 1). Because in the course of his letter the author stops speaking to this "lady" and begins addressing a group of people ("you," plural, in v. 6), many scholars assume that the term *elect lady* refers to a Christian community that understands itself to be the chosen of God.

The issues and concerns of this letter are closely aligned with those of 1 John, as are the vocabulary and writing style, leading most scholars to conclude that they were written by the same author, probably to the same community. Here too there is a concern over "deceivers" and "antichrists" who deny that "Jesus has come in the flesh" (v. 7); here too there is an emphasis on the need for those within the community to love one another by keeping God's commandments (vv. 5–6).

The author strongly opposes those who do not share his views in such matters, insisting that the community show no hospitality to anyone who takes a contrary position (vv. 9–11). He concludes by indicating his eagerness to join the congregation soon and by sending greetings from its "elect sister," that is, presumably, his own Christian community (v. 13). Like 1 John, the book was probably produced after the Fourth Gospel, sometime near the end of the first century.

1 The elder to the elect lady and her children, whom I love in the truth, and not only I but also all who know the truth, 2 because of the truth that abides in us and will be with us forever:

3 Grace, mercy, and peace will be with us from God the Father and from[a] Jesus Christ, the Father's Son, in truth and love.

4 I was overjoyed to find some of your children walking in the truth, just as we have been commanded by the Father. 5 But now, dear lady, I ask you, not as though I were writing you a new commandment, but one we have had from the beginning, let us love one another. 6 And this is love, that we walk according to his commandments; this is the commandment just as you have heard it from the beginning—you must walk in it.

7 Many deceivers have gone out into the world, those who do not confess that Jesus Christ has come in the flesh; any such person is the deceiver and the antichrist! 8 Be on your guard, so that you do not lose what we[b] have worked for, but may receive a full reward. 9 Everyone who does not abide in the teaching of Christ, but goes beyond it, does not have God; whoever abides in the teaching has both the Father and the Son. 10 Do not receive into the house or welcome anyone who comes to you and does not bring this teaching; 11 for to welcome is to participate in the evil deeds of such a person.

12 Although I have much to write to you, I would rather not use paper and ink; instead I hope to come to you and talk with you face to face, so that our joy may be complete.

13 The children of your elect sister send you their greetings.[c]

[a]Other ancient authorities add *the Lord* [b]Other ancient authorities read *you* [c]Other ancient authorities add *Amen*

The Letter of 3 John

Like 2 John, the book of 3 John is a real letter; it was evidently written by the same author. Rather than addressing the entire Christian community, however, here the author addresses an individual within it, a man named Gaius. It appears that Gaius had shown some hospitality to a group of traveling Christians (missionaries?), possibly sent by the author himself, and the author is writing to express his gratitude (vv. 5–8).

At the same time, the letter reveals a serious bit of tension in Gaius's Christian community, for another leader named Diotrephes has refused to receive these visitors and has defamed the author of the letter himself (vv. 9–10). It remains unclear whether Gaius and Diotrephes were heads of different house churches within the same community or were, instead, leading spokespersons within the same church.

In any event, the author commends to Gaius another of his envoys, Demetrius, possibly as the one bearing the letter (v. 12). As in 2 John, he concludes by expressing his desire to visit soon and by sending greetings from members of his own church (vv. 13–15).

1 The elder to the beloved Gaius, whom I love in truth.

2 Beloved, I pray that all may go well with you and that you may be in good health, just as it is well with your soul. 3 I was overjoyed when some of the friends[a] arrived and testified to your faithfulness to the truth, namely how you walk in the truth. 4 I have no greater joy than this, to hear that my children are walking in the truth.

5 Beloved, you do faithfully whatever you do for the friends,[a] even though they are strangers to you; 6 they have testified to your love before the church. You will do well to send them on in a manner worthy of God; 7 for they began their journey for the sake of Christ,[b] accepting no support from non-believers.[c] 8 Therefore we ought to support such people, so that we may become co-workers with the truth.

9 I have written something to the church; but Diotrephes, who likes to put himself first, does not acknowledge our authority. 10 So if I come, I will call attention to what he is doing in spreading false charges against us. And not content with those charges, he refuses to welcome the friends,[a] and even prevents those who want to do so and expels them from the church.

11 Beloved, do not imitate what is evil but imitate what is good. Whoever does good is from God; whoever does evil has not seen God. 12 Everyone has testified favorably about Demetrius, and so has the truth itself. We also testify for him,[d] and you know that our testimony is true.

13 I have much to write to you, but I would rather not write with pen and ink; 14 instead I hope to see you soon, and we will talk together face to face.

15 Peace to you. The friends send you their greetings. Greet the friends there, each by name.

[a]Gk brothers [b]Gk for the sake of the name [c]Gk the Gentiles
[d]Gk lacks for him

From the New Revised Standard Version Bible, © 1989.

The Letter of Jude

The brief Letter of Jude is principally concerned with false teachers who have infiltrated the Christian community and led many of its members astray (v. 4). The author does not indicate what, exactly, these "intruders" taught, but he considers their teachings extremely dangerous: he maintains that they actually "deny our Master and Lord Jesus Christ" (v. 4). In particular he is concerned with the moral views these teachers embody. He claims that they behave like "irrational animals" (v. 10), engage in ungodly activities (v. 15), and indulge in their own lusts (v. 16). He likens them to the children of Israel who reveled in their wanton acts of adultery and idolatry after escaping Egypt, and to the inhabitants of Sodom and Gomorrah who "indulged in sexual immorality and pursued unnatural lust" (vv. 5–7).

Much of the epistle is filled with invective and name-calling against these opponents (see vv. 12–13). The author warns them to take heed and repent, or, like the inhabitants of Sodom and Gomorrah, they would be made "an example by undergoing a punishment of eternal fire" (v. 7).

The letter claims to be written by "Jude . . . the brother of James" (v. 1). Since Jesus was known to have two brothers named Jude and James (Mark 6:3), the latter of whom became the leader of the Jerusalem church (e.g., Gal 1:19; 2:9), the author appears to be claiming to be Jesus' own brother. Many scholars, however, suspect that the letter is pseudonymous. We know from historical sources that Jude's family was comprised of uneducated peasants, whereas this book is written by someone well-trained in Greek and conversant with a wide range of apocryphal Jewish literature (he quotes, for example from a lost apocryphal account in v. 9 and the book of 1 Enoch in v. 14). The book may have been written near the end of the first century, when Christian communities were coming under the influence of a wide array of teachers and leaders, many of whom stood at odds with one another and engaged in vitriolic attacks on one another's moral character.

1 Jude,[a] a servant[b] of Jesus Christ and brother of James,

To those who are called, who are beloved[c] in[d] God the Father and kept safe for[d] Jesus Christ:

2 May mercy, peace, and love be yours in abundance.

3 Beloved, while eagerly preparing to write to you about the salvation we share, I find it necessary to write and appeal to you to contend for the faith that was once for all entrusted to the saints. 4 For certain intruders have stolen in among you, people who long ago were designated for this condemnation as ungodly, who pervert the grace of our God into licentiousness and deny our only Master and Lord, Jesus Christ.[e]

[a]Gk Judas [b]Gk slave [c]Other ancient authorities read sanctified [d]Or by [e]Or the only Master and our Lord Jesus Christ

5 Now I desire to remind you, though you are fully informed, that the Lord, who once for all saved[f] a people out of the land of Egypt, afterward destroyed those who did not believe. 6 And the angels who did not keep their own position, but left their proper dwelling, he has kept in eternal chains in deepest darkness for the judgment of the great day. 7 Likewise, Sodom and Gomorrah and the surrounding cities, which, in the same manner as they, indulged in sexual immorality and pursued unnatural lust,[g] serve as an example by undergoing a punishment of eternal fire.

8 Yet in the same way these dreamers also defile the flesh, reject authority, and slander the glorious ones.[h] 9 But when the archangel Michael contended with the devil and disputed about the body of Moses, he did not dare to bring a condemnation of slander[i] against him, but said, "The Lord rebuke you!" 10 But these people slander whatever they do not understand, and they are destroyed by those things that, like irrational animals, they know by instinct. 11 Woe to them! For they go the way of Cain, and abandon themselves to Balaam's error for the sake of gain, and perish in Korah's rebellion. 12 These are blemishes[j] on your love-feasts, while they feast with you without fear, feeding themselves.[k] They are waterless clouds carried along by the winds; autumn trees without fruit, twice dead, uprooted; 13 wild waves of the sea, casting up the foam of their own shame; wandering stars, for whom the deepest darkness has been reserved forever.

14 It was also about these that Enoch, in the seventh generation from Adam, prophesied, saying, "See, the Lord is coming[l] with ten thousands of his holy ones, 15 to execute judgment on all, and to convict everyone of all the deeds of ungodliness that they have committed in such an ungodly way, and of all the harsh things that ungodly sinners have spoken against him."[1] 16 These are grumblers and malcontents; they indulge their own lusts; they are bombastic in speech, flattering people to their own advantage.

17 But you, beloved, must remember the predictions of the apostles of our Lord Jesus Christ; 18 for they said to you, "In the last time there will be scoffers, indulging their own ungodly lusts." 19 It is these worldly people, devoid of the Spirit, who are causing divisions. 20 But you, beloved, build yourselves up on your most holy faith; pray in the Holy Spirit; 21 keep yourselves in the love of God; look forward to the mercy of our Lord Jesus Christ that leads to[m] eternal life. 22 And have mercy on some who are wavering; 23 save others by snatching them out of the fire; and have mercy on still others with fear, hating even the tunic defiled by their bodies.[n]

24 Now to him who is able to keep you from falling, and to make you stand without blemish in the presence of his glory with rejoicing, 25 to the only God our Savior, through Jesus Christ our Lord, be glory, majesty, power, and authority, before all time and now and forever. Amen.

---

[f]Other ancient authorities read *though you were once for all fully informed, that Jesus* (or *Joshua*) *who saved* [g]Gk *went after other flesh* [h]Or *angels*; Gk *glories* [i]Or *condemnation for blasphemy* [j]Or *reefs* [k]Or *without fear. They are shepherds who care only for themselves* [l]Gk *came* [m]Gk *Christ to* [n]Gk *by the flesh*. The Greek text of verses 22-23 is uncertain at several points

---

[1]1 Enoc 1:9

The Letter of 1 Clement

The letter of 1 Clement was sent from "the church of God . . . in Rome" to "the church of God . . . in Corinth" (1:1). Although traditionally ascribed to Clement, thought to have been the third bishop of Rome, the letter itself never names its actual author or mentions Clement. The purpose of the writing, in any event, is perfectly clear. There has been a division in the church in Corinth, a "vile and profane faction that is alien and foreign to God's chosen people" (1:1), in which the elders of the church have been forcibly deposed from their office and others have taken their place (3:2–4). For the Roman Christians, this is an altogether unacceptable arrangement: "it is shameful . . . exceedingly shameful and unworthy of your conduct in Christ, that the most secure and ancient church of the Corinthians is reported to have created a faction against its presbyters, at the instigation of one or two persons" (47:6). This letter urges the congregation to do something about the situation: they are to remove the new leaders and reinstate the old.

At the core of the letter's argument against the Corinthian usurpers lies one of the earliest expressions of the notion of "apostolic succession," which came to play such a significant role in theological controversies of the second century. According to this view, the original leaders of the Christian churches had been appointed by the apostles, who were themselves chosen by Christ, who was sent from God. Anyone who deposes these leaders, therefore, is in direct rebellion against God himself (chaps. 42–44).

Much of the argument revolves around the history of the people of God as known from the Jewish Scriptures. According to 1 Clement, from the time of Cain and Abel onwards, envy and strife have always been promoted by sinners opposed to the righteous. The new leaders of the Corinthian congregation stand within this nefarious line: they have swindled their way into power out of jealousy and rivalry. But for this author, God opposes those who exalt themselves over the ones he himself has chosen. This is shown not only from writings of the Jewish prophets, but also from the teachings of Jesus and the writings of the apostles (e.g., chaps. 12 and 46).

The letter provides several hints as to the time of its composition. It indicates that there were still church leaders throughout the Christian world who had been hand-picked by the apostles (chap. 44), and yet the Corinthian church is called "ancient" (chap. 47). Moreover, Peter and Paul are said here to have been martyred in Rome in "our own generation" (chap. 5; they are generally thought to have been executed under Nero, ca. 64 C.E.), and hostilities against the Christians have recently been renewed. These various hints suggest that the book was written near the end of the first century, possibly around 95 C.E., during the reign of Domitian.

"The Letter of Clement" from *The Apostolic Fathers,* translated by Bart D. Ehrman. Loeb Classical Library; © 2003. Reprinted by permission of Harvard University Press.

The church of God that temporarily resides in Rome, to the church of God that temporarily resides in Corinth, to those who have been called and made holy by the will of God through our Lord Jesus Christ. May grace and peace be increased among you, from the all-powerful God, through Jesus Christ.

1 Because of the sudden and repeated misfortunes and setbacks we have experienced, we realize that we have been slow to turn our attention to the matters causing disputes among you, loved ones, involving that vile and profane faction that is alien and foreign to God's chosen people—a faction stoked by a few reckless and headstrong persons to such a pitch of madness that your venerable and renowned reputation, worthy of everyone's love, has been greatly slandered. 2 For who has ever visited you and not approved your highly virtuous and stable faith? And not been astonished by your temperate and gentle piety in Christ? And not proclaimed the magnificent character of your hospitality? And not uttered a blessing for your perfect and unwavering knowledge? 3 For you used to act impartially in all that you did, and you walked according to the ordinances of God, submitting yourselves to your leaders and rendering all due honor to those who were older[a] among you. You instructed your young people to think moderate and respectful thoughts. You directed women to accomplish all things with a blameless, respectful, and pure conscience, dutifully loving their husbands. And you taught them to run their households respectfully, living under the rule of submission, practicing discretion in every way.

2 And all of you used to be humble in mind, not arrogant in the least, being submissive rather than forcing submission, giving more gladly than receiving,[1] being satisfied with the provisions supplied by Christ. You heeded his words, carefully storing them up in your inner selves. And his sufferings were present before your eyes.

2 For this reason a deep and rich peace was given to all, along with an insatiable desire for doing good; and a full outpouring of the Holy Spirit came upon everyone. 3 And being filled with his holy will, you used to stretch out your hands to the all-powerful God, zealous for the good, with pious confidence, begging him to be gracious if you inadvertently committed any sin. 4 Day and night you struggled on behalf of the entire brotherhood, that the total number of his chosen ones might be saved, with mortal fear and self-awareness.[b] 5 You were sincere and innocent and bore no grudges against one another. 6 Every faction and schism was loathsome to you. You used to grieve over the unlawful acts of your neighbors and considered their shortcomings your own. 7 You had no regrets when doing good; you were prepared for every good deed.[2] 8 You were adorned with a highly virtuous and honorable way of life, and you accomplished all things in reverential awe of him. The commandments and righteous demands of the Lord were inscribed upon the tablets of your heart.[3]

3 All glory and enlargement was given to you, and that which was written was fulfilled: "My loved one ate and drank and became large and grew fat and kicked out with his heels."[4] 2 From this came jealousy and envy, strife and faction, persecution and disorderliness, war and captivity. 3 And so the dishonorable rose up against the honorable, the disreputable against the reputable, the senseless against the sensible, the young against the old.[c][5] 4 For this reason, righteousness and peace are far removed,[6] since each has abandoned the reverential awe of God and become dim-sighted in faith, failing to proceed in the ordinances of his commandments and not living according to what is appropriate in Christ. Instead, each one walks according to the desires of his evil heart, which have aroused unrighteous and impious jealousy—through which also death entered the world.[7]

4 For so it is written, "It came about that after some days, Cain brought an offering to God from the fruits of the earth; and for his part, Abel brought from the firstborn of the sheep and their fat. 2 And God looked favorably upon Abel and his gifts but paid no regard to Cain and his offerings. 3 And Cain was extremely upset and became downcast. 4 And God said to Cain, 'Why have you become so upset and

---

[a]Or *presbyters*   [b]Or *conscientiously*; meaning obscure   [c]Or *the presbyters*

---

[1]Acts 20:35   [2]Titus 3:1   [3]Prov 7:3   [4]Deut 32:15   [5]Isa 3:5   [6]Isa 59:14   [7]Wis 2:24

downcast? If you brought the proper sacrifice but did not exercise proper discernment, have you not sinned?[d] 5 Be calm. He will return to you and you will rule over him.'[e] 6 And Cain said to his brother Abel, 'Let us go into the field.' And it came about that when they were in the field, Cain rose up against his brother Abel and murdered him."[8]

7 You see, brothers, jealousy and envy brought about the murder of a brother. 8 Because of jealousy our father Jacob fled from the presence of Esau, his brother.[9] 9 Jealousy caused Joseph to be persecuted to the point of death and to enter into slavery.[10] 10 Jealousy forced Moses to flee from the presence of Pharoah, king of Egypt, when he heard from his fellow countryman, "Who made you an arbitrator or judge over us? Do you want to kill me, as you killed the Egyptian yesterday?"[11] 11 Because of jealousy Aaron and Miriam had to stay outside the camp.[12] 12 Jealousy brought Dathan and Abiram down into Hades while still alive because they created a faction against the servant of God, Moses.[13] 13 Because of jealousy not only did David incur envy from foreigners, but he was even persecuted by Saul, the king of Israel.[14]

5 But to stop giving ancient examples, let us come to those who became athletic contenders in quite recent times. We should consider the noble examples of our own generation. 2 Because of jealousy and envy the greatest and most upright pillars were persecuted, and they struggled in the contest even to death. 3 We should set before our eyes the good apostles. 4 There is Peter, who because of unjust jealousy bore up under hardships not just once or twice, but many times; and having thus borne his witness he went to the place of glory that he deserved. 5 Because of jealousy and strife Paul pointed the way to the prize for endurance. 6 Seven times he bore chains; he was sent into exile and stoned; he served as a herald in both the East and the West; and he received the noble reputation for his faith. 7 He taught righteousness to the whole world, and came to the limits of the West, bearing his witness before the rulers. And so he was set free from this world and transported up to the holy place, having become the greatest example of endurance.

6 To these men who have conducted themselves in such a holy way there has been added a great multitude of the elect, who have set a superb example among us by the numerous torments and tortures they suffered because of jealousy. 2 Women were persecuted as Danaids and Dircae[f] and suffered terrifying and profane torments because of jealousy. But they confidently completed the race of faith, and though weak in body, they received a noble reward. 3 Jealousy estranged wives from their husbands and nullified what was spoken by our father Adam, "This now is bone from my bones and flesh from my flesh."[15] 4 Jealousy and strife overturned great cities and uprooted great nations.

7 We are writing these things, loved ones, not only to admonish you but also to remind ourselves. For we are in the same arena and the same contest is set before us. 2 For this reason we should leave behind empty and frivolous thoughts and come to the famous and venerable rule of our tradition. 3 We should realize what is good and pleasing and acceptable before the one who made us. 4 We should gaze intently on the blood of Christ and realize how precious it is to his Father; for when it was poured out for our salvation, it brought the gracious gift of repentance to the entire world. 5 Let us review all the generations and learn that from one generation to the

[d]Or *If you brought the proper sacrifice but did not divide it up properly, have you not sinned?*; Or, *If you have rightly brought an offering but have not brought the right portion, have you not sinned?*; Or, *If you have brought, as was right, an offering but have not correctly discerned which one to bring, have you not sinned?* Meaning obscure, both in the Hebrew of Genesis and in this Greek translation
[e]Or, *It will turn to you and you will rule over it*; meaning obscure
[f]The author's meaning is unclear. Some scholars have suggested that he is referring to Christian women martyred under Nero, who was known for his creatively brutal excesses (see Suetonius, *Nero* 11, 12). If so, women executed as Dircae may have been dragged to death in the arena, bound to the horns of a bull, like Dirce of Greek myth. The reference to the Danaids is more puzzling. Some scholars have seen it as an allusion to the legend that the daughters of Danaus were taken by men against their will—that is, the Christian women were publicly raped before being put to death. Others have thought that it refers to the punishment of Danaus's daughters in the afterlife, where they were compelled perpetually to fill leaking vessels—that is, the Christian women were subject to pointless and seemingly endless torments prior to their deaths. In either event, the text is so difficult that several emendations have been suggested to eliminate the reference to "Danaids and Dircae" altogether, the most popular of which is: "persecuted as women, maidens, and slave-girls".

[8]Gen 4:3–8   [9]Gen 27:41ff   [10]Genesis 37   [11]Exod 2:14
[12]Numbers 12   [13]Num 16:13   [14]1 Samuel 18ff   [15]Gen 2:23

next the Master has provided an opportunity for repentance to those wanting to return to him. 6 Noah proclaimed repentance, and those who heeded were saved from danger.[16] 7 Jonah proclaimed an impending disaster to the Ninevites; and those who repented of their sins appeased God through their fervent pleas and received salvation, even though they had been estranged from God.[17]

8 Those who administered the gracious gift of God spoke through the Holy Spirit about repentance. 2 And the Master of all things himself spoke about repentance with an oath: "For as I live, says the Lord, I do not want the sinner to die but to repent."[18] And to this he added a good pronouncement: 3 "Repent from your lawlessness, house of Israel. Say to the children of my people, 'If your sins extend from the earth to the sky and are redder than scarlet and blacker than sackcloth, but you return to me with your whole heart and say, "Father," I will listen to you as to a holy people.'"[19] 4 And in another place he speaks as follows: "Wash and become clean; remove from yourselves the evils that are before my eyes; put an end to your evil deeds; learn to do good; pursue justice, rescue those who are treated unjustly, render a decision for the orphan and do what is right for the widow. And come, let us reason together, says the Lord. Even if your sins are like crimson, I will make them white as snow; and if they are like scarlet, I will make them white as wool. If you are willing and obey me, you will eat the good things of the earth; but if you are not willing and do not obey me, a sword will devour you. For the mouth of the Lord has spoken these things."[20] 5 Because he wanted all his loved ones to have a share in repentance, he set it in place by his all-powerful will.

9 For this reason we should obey his magnificent and glorious will and, as petitioners of his mercy and kindness, fall down before him and turn to his compassionate ways, leaving behind our pointless toil and strife and the jealousy that leads to death. 2 We should gaze intently on those who have perfectly served his magnificent glory. 3 We should consider Enoch, who was transported to another place because he was found to be righteous in his obedience; and his death was never found.[21] 4 Noah, who was found to be faithful through his service, proclaimed a new beginning to the world; and through him the Master saved the living creatures that entered the ark in harmony.[22]

10 Abraham, who was called "The Friend,"[23] was found to be faithful when he became obedient to God's words. 2 In obedience he left his land, his family, and his father's house, so that by abandoning a paltry land, an insignificant family, and a small house he might inherit the promises of God. For God said to him, 3 "Depart from your land, your family, and your father's house to the land I will show you. And I will form you into a great nation and I will bless you and make your name great; and you will be blessed. And I will bless those who bless you and curse those who curse you, and all the tribes of the earth will be blessed in you."[24] 4 And again when Abraham separated from Lot, God said to him, "Lift up your eyes and look out from where you are now to the north, south, east, and west; for I will give all the land that you see to you and your offspring forever. 5 And I will make your offspring like the sand of the earth. If anyone is able to count the sand of the earth, your offspring will also be counted."[25] 6 Again it says, "God led Abraham out and said to him, 'Look up into the sky and count the stars, if you are able to number them. So will your offspring be.' And Abraham trusted God, and it was accounted to him as righteousness."[26] 7 Because of his faith and hospitality, a son was given to him in his old age; and in obedience he offered him up as a sacrifice to God on one of the mountains that he showed him.[27]

11 Because of his hospitality and piety, Lot was saved out of Sodom when all the surrounding countryside was judged by fire and brimstone.[28] The Master thus made it clear that he does not abandon those who hope in him, but hands over to punishment and torment those who turn away. 2 Lot's wife was made a sign of this: for when she left with him but then changed her

---

[16]Gen 7 [17]Jon 3 [18]Cf. Ezek 33:11 [19]Possibly drawn from Ezek 33 [20]Isa 1:16–20 [21]Gen 5:24; Heb 11:5 [22]Gen 6:8; Heb 11:7 [23]Cf. Isa 41:8; Jas 2:23 [24]Gen 12:1–3 [25]Gen 13:14–16 [26]Gen 15:5–6; Rom 4:3 [27]Gen 18:21; Gen 22; Heb 11:17 [28]The following account is drawn from Gen 19

mind and fell out of harmony, she was turned into a pillar of salt until this day—so that everyone may know that those who are of two minds and who doubt the power of God enter into judgment and become a visible sign for all generations.

12 Because of her faith and hospitality Rahab the prostitute was saved from danger.[29] 2 For when reconnaissance scouts had been sent into Jericho by Joshua, the son of Nun, the king of the land discovered that they had come to scout out their country and sent men to arrest them, so that once detained they could be executed. 3 And so, the hospitable Rahab brought them inside and hid them in the upper room under a pile of thatching straw.[g] 4 When the king's men arrived and said, "Those who are scouting out our land came into your house; bring them out, for so the king has ordered," she replied, "The men you are seeking did come in to see me, but they left right away and are going on down the road." And she pointed them in the wrong direction. 5 And she said to the men, "I know full well that the Lord God is handing this land over to you, for fear and trembling has seized its inhabitants because of you. When you take the land, save me and my father's household." 6 They said to her, "It will be just as you have spoken to us. So, when you know that we are approaching, gather all your family under your roof and they will be saved. For whoever is found outside the house will perish." 7 And they proceeded to give her a sign,[h] that she should hang a piece of scarlet from her house—making it clear that it is through the blood of the Lord that redemption will come to all who believe and hope in God. 8 You see, loved ones, not only was faith found in the woman, but prophecy as well.

13 And so we should be humble-minded, brothers, laying aside all arrogance, conceit, foolishness, and forms of anger; and we should act in accordance with what is written. For the Holy Spirit says, "The one who is wise should not boast about his wisdom, nor the one who is strong about his strength, nor the one who is wealthy about his wealth; instead, the one who boasts should boast about the Lord, seeking after him and doing what is just and right."[30] We should

especially remember the words the Lord Jesus spoke when teaching about gentleness and patience. 2 For he said, "Show mercy, that you may be shown mercy; forgive, that it may be forgiven you. As you do, so it will be done to you; as you give, so it will be given to you; as you judge, so you will be judged; as you show kindness, so will kindness be shown to you; the amount you dispense will be the amount you receive."[31] 3 Let us strengthen one another in this commandment and these demands, so that we may forge ahead, obedient to his words (which are well-suited for holiness) and humble-minded. For the holy word says, 4 "Upon whom will I look, but upon the one who is meek and mild and who trembles at my sayings?"[32]

14 And so it is right and holy for us to obey God, brothers, rather than follow those who instigate a foul jealousy with arrogance and disorderliness. 2 For we will subject ourselves not to some ordinary harm, but to real danger, if we rashly hand ourselves over to the desires of those who rush headlong into strife and faction and so estrange us from what is good for us. 3 We should treat one another kindly, according to the compassion and sweet character of the one who made us. 4 For it is written, "Those who are kind will inhabit the land, and the innocent will be left upon it; but those who break the law will be destroyed from it."[33] 5 And again it says, "I saw one who was impious greatly exalted and raised high as the cedars of Lebanon. Then I passed by and look! He was no more. And I searched for his place, but did not find it. Protect what is innocent and focus on what is upright, because the one who lives in peace will have a posterity."[34]

15 Therefore we should cling to those who keep the peace with piety, not those who wish for peace out of hypocrisy. 2 For it says somewhere, "This people honors me with their lips, but their heart is far removed from me."[35] 3 And again, "They blessed with their mouth but

[g]Or *fine linen*; or *flax* [h]Or *in addition they told her to give a sign*

[29]The following account is drawn from Josh 2. Cf. Heb 11:31; Jas 2:25 [30]Jer 9:23–24; 1 Cor 1:31; 2 Cor 10:17 [31]Matt 5:7; 6:14–15; 7:1–2, 12; Luke 6:31, 36–38 [32]Isa 66:2 [33]Prov 2:21–22; Ps 37:9, 38 [34]Ps 37:35–37 [35]Isa 29:13; Mark 7:6; Matt 15:8

cursed in their heart."[36] 4 And again it says, "They loved him with their mouth and with their tongue they lied against him; but their heart was not right with him, nor did they prove faithful to his covenant."[37] 5 "For this reason let the deceitful lips that speak a lawless word against the righteous one be silenced."[38] And again, "May the Lord destroy all deceitful lips, the boastful tongue, and those who say, 'We will exalt our tongue; our lips are under our control. Who is lord over us?' 6 Now, says the Lord, I will rise up because of the humility of the poor and the groaning of the needy. I will establish him in salvation 7 and deal boldly with him."[39]

16

For Christ belongs to those who are humble-minded, not to those who vaunt themselves over his flock. 2 The scepter of God's majesty, the Lord Jesus Christ, did not come with an ostentatious show of arrogance or haughtiness—even though he could have done so—but with a humble mind, just as the Holy Spirit spoke concerning him. For he says, 3 "Lord, who believed our report? And to whom was the arm of the Lord revealed? We made our announcement before him: He was like a child, like a root in a dry land. He had no striking form or glorious presence. We saw him, and he had no striking form or beauty; but his form was dishonorable, inferior to the form of others. He experienced trauma and toil; he knew what it meant to bear weakness. For his face was turned aside; he was dishonored and given no regard. 4 This one bears our sins and for our sake experiences pain. And we regarded him as having borne toil, trauma, and oppression. 5 But he was wounded because of our sins and weakened because of our lawless acts. The punishment that brought us peace came upon him. By his bruising we were healed. 6 We have all wandered astray like sheep; each has wandered on his own path. 7 The Lord handed him over for our sins, but he did not open his mouth because of his mistreatment. He was led like a sheep going to slaughter; and like a lamb, silent before the one who shears it, so he did not open his mouth. Justice was denied him in his humiliation. 8 Who will describe his generation? For his life is removed from the earth. 9 Because of the lawless acts of my people, he has entered the realm of death. 10 And I will exchange those who are evil for his burial and

those who are wealthy for his death; for he broke no law, nor was any deceit found in his mouth. And the Lord wants to cleanse him of his wound. 11 If you give an offering for sin, your soul will see offspring who live long. 12 And the Lord wants to remove the burden from his soul, to reveal a light to him and to mold him with understanding, to give justice to the one who is just, who serves many people well. And he himself will bear their sins. 13 For this reason he will inherit many and will divide the spoils of the strong; for his soul was handed over to death and he was counted among the lawless. 14 He bore the sins of many and was handed over because of their sins."[40] 15 And again he himself says, "I am a worm, not a human, reproached by others and despised by the people. 16 Everyone who sees me has mocked me; they spoke with their lips and shook their heads, 'He hoped in the Lord; let the Lord rescue him. Let him save him, since he desires him.'"[41]

17 You see, beloved men, the example that he has given us. For if the Lord was humble-minded in this way, what shall we ourselves do, who through him have assumed the yoke of his gracious favor?

17

We should become imitators also of those who went about in the skins of goats and sheep,[42] proclaiming the coming of Christ. We mean Elijah and Elisha, and also Ezekiel, the prophets; and in addition to these, those who had a good reputation. 2 Abraham was given a great reputation and was called "Friend of God." While he gazed intently upon the glory of God with a humble mind, he said, "I am just dust and ashes."[43] 3 Also concerning Job it is written: "But Job was upright and blameless, truthful, one who revered God and was far removed from all evil."[44] 4 But he accused himself, saying, ""No one is clean from filth, even if his life lasts for a single day."[45] 5 Moses was called faithful in his entire house,[46] and through his service God judged Egypt through their plagues and torments; but even though he was greatly exalted, he did not boast aloud. Instead, when the revelation was given to him from the bush, he said, "Who am I that you send me?

---

[36]Ps 62:4   [37]Ps 78:36–37   [38]Ps 31:18   [39]Ps 12:4–6   [40]Isa 53:1–12
[41]Ps 22:6–8   [42]Heb 11:37   [43]Gen 18:27   [44]Job 1:1   [45]Job 14:4–5
[46]Num 12:7; Heb 3:2

For I am feeble in speech and slow in tongue."[47] 6 And again he said, "I am just steam from a pot."[48]

18 And what shall we say about David, who had such a good reputation? God said concerning him,[i] "I have found a man after my own heart, David the son of Jesse. I have anointed him with a mercy that will last forever."[49] 2 But he himself said to God, "Have mercy on me, O God, according to your great mercy, and according to the abundance of your compassion wipe away my unlawful behavior. 3 Even more, wash my lawlessness away from me and cleanse me from my sin; for I know my lawlessness and my sin is always before my eyes. 4 Against you alone have I sinned and done what is evil before your eyes, so that you are shown to be right in your words and victorious when you are brought to court. 5 For indeed, in lawless acts was I conceived and in sinful deeds did my mother come to bear me. 6 For indeed, you loved truth. You have unveiled to me the veiled and hidden matters of your wisdom. 7 You will sprinkle me with hyssop, and I will be cleansed. You will wash me, and I will be whiter than snow. 8 You will allow me to hear rejoicing and gladness; bones that have been humbled will rejoice. 9 Turn your face from my sins and wipe away all my lawless deeds. 10 Create a clean heart within me, O God, and restore a right spirit in my inner being. 11 Do not cast me out from your presence, and do not remove your holy spirit from me. 12 Restore to me the joy of your salvation and strengthen me with your ruling spirit. 13 I will teach your ways to those who are lawless and those who are unholy will turn back to you. 14 Deliver me from acts of bloodshed, O God, the God of my salvation. 15 My tongue will rejoice in your righteousness. Lord, you will open my mouth and my lips will sound forth your praise. 16 For if you had desired a sacrifice, I would have given it. You will not be pleased with whole burnt offerings. 17 A crushed spirit is a sacrifice to God; and God will not despise a crushed and humbled heart."[50]

19 The humility and obedient lowliness of so many people with such strong reputation have improved not only us, but also the generations that came before us—indeed all those who received the sayings of God in reverential

awe and truth. 2 And so, since we have shared in such numerous, great, and glorious deeds, we should forge ahead to the goal of peace that has been delivered to us from the beginning.[51] And we should gaze intently on the Father and Creator of the entire world and cling to his magnificent and superior gifts of peace and acts of kindness. 3 We should observe him with understanding and look upon his patient will with the eyes of our soul. We should realize how he feels no anger toward his entire creation.

20 The heavens, which move about under his management, are peacefully subject to him. 2 Day and night complete the racecourse laid out by him, without impeding one another in the least. 3 Sun and moon and the chorus of stars roll along the tracks that have been appointed to them, in harmony, never crossing their lines, in accordance with the arrangement he has made. 4 By his will and in the proper seasons, the fertile earth brings forth its rich abundance of nourishment for humans, beasts, and all living things that dwell on it, without dissenting or altering any of the decrees he has set forth. 5 Both the inscrutable regions of the abysses and the indescribable realms of the depths are constrained by the same commands. 6 The basin of the boundless sea, established by his workmanship to hold the waters collected, does not cross its restraining barriers, but acts just as he ordered. 7 For he said, "You shall come this far, and your waves shall crash down within you."[52] 8 The ocean, boundless to humans, and the worlds beyond it are governed by the same decrees of the Master. 9 The seasons—spring, summer, fall, and winter—succeed one another in peace. 10 The forces[j] of the winds complete their service in their own proper season, without faltering. And the eternal fountains, created for enjoyment and health, provide their life-giving breasts to humans without ceasing. The most insignificant living creatures associate with one another[k] in harmony and peace. 11 The great Creator and Master of all appointed all these things to be in peace and harmony, bringing great benefits to all things, but most especially to us, who flee to his compassion

---

[i]Or *to him*   [j]Or *stations*   [k]Or *have sexual intercourse*

[47]Exod 3:11; 4:10   [48]Source unknown   [49]1 Sam 13:14; Acts 13:22
[50]Ps 51:1–17   [51]Cf. Heb 12:1–2   [52]Job 38:11

through our Lord Jesus Christ. 12 To him be the glory and the majesty forever and ever. Amen.

21 Loved ones, you should take care that his many acts of kindness do not lead to judgment against all of us. For this will happen if we fail to conduct ourselves worthily of him and to do the things that are good and pleasing before him, in harmony. 2 For somewhere it says, "The Spirit of the Lord is a lamp that searches out the recesses deep within us."[53] 3 We should realize how near he is, and that none of our thoughts or the disputes we have had is hidden from him. 4 And so it is right for us not to desert from his will. 5 It is better for us to offend foolish, senseless, and presumptuous people who boast in the arrogance of their own talk than to offend God. 6 We should revere the Lord Jesus Christ, whose blood was given for us; we should respect our leaders; we should honor the elderly;[l] we should discipline our youth in the reverential fear of God; we should set our wives along the straight path that leads to the good. 7 Let them display a character of purity, worthy of love; let them exhibit the innocent will of their meekness; let them manifest the gentleness of their tongues through how they speak; let them show their love not with partiality, but equally to all those who stand in reverential awe of God in a holy way. 8 Let our children partake of the discipline that is in Christ. Let them learn the strength of humility before God and the power of pure love before God. Let them learn how the reverential awe of him is beautiful and great, and how it saves all those who conduct themselves in it[m] in a holy way, with a clear understanding. 9 For he is the one who explores our understandings and desires. His breath is in us, and when he wishes, he will remove it.

22 The faith that is in Christ guarantees all these things. For he himself calls to us through the Holy Spirit: "Come, children, and hear me; I will teach you the reverential awe of the Lord. 2 Who is the person who wants to live and yearns to see good days? 3 Stop your tongue from speaking evil and your lips from spouting deceit. 4 Move away from evil and do what is good. 5 Seek after peace and pursue it. 6 The eyes of the Lord are upon the upright, and his ears attend to their prayer. But the face of the Lord is against those who do evil and destroys any recollection of them from the face of the earth. 7 The one who is upright has called out, and the Lord has heard him and delivered him from all his afflictions."[54] 8 "Many are the plagues of the sinner, but mercy will surround those who hope in the Lord."[55]

23 The beneficent Father, compassionate in every way, has pity on those who stand in awe of him; gently and kindly does he bestow his gracious gifts on those who approach him with a pure resolve. 2 And so, we should not be of two minds, nor should we entertain wild notions about his superior and glorious gifts. 3 May this Scripture be far removed from us that says "How miserable are those who are of two minds, who doubt in their soul, who say, 'We have heard these things from the time of our parents, and look! We have grown old, and none of these things has happened to us.' 4 You fools! Compare yourselves to a tree. Take a vine: First it sheds its leaves, then a bud appears, then a leaf, then a flower, and after these an unripe grape, and then an entire bunch fully grown."[56] You see that the fruit of the tree becomes ripe in just a short time. 5 In truth, his plan will come to completion quickly and suddenly, as even the Scripture testifies, when it says, "He will come quickly and not delay. And suddenly the Lord will come to his temple—he who is holy, the one you await."[57]

24 We should consider, loved ones, how the Master continuously shows us the future resurrection that is about to occur, of which he made the Lord Jesus Christ the first fruit by raising him from the dead.[58] 2 We should look, loved ones, at the resurrection that happens time after time. 3 Day and night reveal to us a resurrection: The night sleeps and the day arises; the day departs and the night arrives. 4 We should consider the crops: How, and in what way, does the sowing occur? 5 The sower goes out and casts each of the seeds onto the soil.[59] Because they are dry and barren, they decay when they fall onto the soil. But then the magnificent forethought of the Master raises them up out of their decay, and from the one seed grow more, and so bring forth the crop.

---

[l]Or the presbyters   [m]Or in him

---

[53]Prov 20:27   [54]Ps 34:11–17, 19   [55]Ps 32:10   [56]Source unknown. Cf. 2 Clem 11:2–3   [57]Cf. Isa 13:22 (LXX); Mal 3:1   [58]1 Cor 15:20   [59]Mark 4:3; cf. 1 Cor 15:36ff

25 Let us consider the incredible sign that occurs in the eastern climes, that is, in the regions near Arabia. 2 For there is a bird called the Phoenix. This unique creature lives five hundred years. And when at last it approaches its dissolution through death, it makes a tomb for itself out of frankincense, myrrh, and other spices. Then, when the time has been fulfilled, it enters into the tomb and dies. 3 But when its flesh rots, a worm is born. And nourished by the secretions of the dead creature, it sprouts wings. Then when it becomes strong, it takes the tomb containing the bones of its predecessor and bears these from Arabia to Egypt, to the city called Heliopolis. 4 In the daytime, while all are watching, it flies onto the altar of the sun and deposits these things, and so hastens back. 5 Then the priests examine the records of the times and discover that it has come after five hundred years have elapsed.

26 Do we then think that it is so great and marvelous that the Creator of all things will raise everyone who has served him in a holy way with the confidence of good faith, when he shows us the magnificence of his promise even through a bird? 2 For it says somewhere, "You will raise me up and I will praise you,"[60] and, "I lay down and slept, and I arose, because you are with me."[61] 3 And again, Job says, "You will raise this flesh of mine, which has endured all these things."[62]

27 Let our souls, therefore, be bound by this hope to the one who is faithful in his promises and upright in his judgments. 2 The one who commanded us not to lie, how much more will he not lie? For nothing is impossible for God, except lying. 3 Let his faithfulness[n] be rekindled within us and let us realize that all things are near to him. 4 By the word of his majesty he has established all things, and by his word he is able to destroy them. 5 "Who will say to him, 'What are you doing?' Or who will oppose his mighty power?"[63] He will do all things when he wishes and as he wishes, and nothing decreed by him will pass away. 6 Everything is before him, and nothing escapes his will. 7 "For the heavens declare the glory of God and the firmament proclaims the work of his hands. One day utters a word to another, and one night proclaims knowledge to the next. And

there are no words or speeches whose voices are not heard."[64]

28 Since everything is seen and heard, we should stand in awe of him, leaving behind depraved desires for evil works, that by his mercy we may be protected from the judgments that are to come. 2 For where can any of us flee from the power of his hand? And what world will welcome any of those who desert him? For the Scripture somewhere says, 3 "Where will I go and where will I hide from your presence? If I ascend to heaven, you are there. If I journey to the ends of the earth, your right hand is there. If I make my bed in the netherworld, your spirit is there."[65] 4 Where then can a person go, or where escape the one who encompasses all things?

29 And so we should approach him with devout souls, raising pure and undefiled hands to him and loving our gentle and kind-hearted Father, who made us his own chosen portion. 2 For so it is written: "When the Most High divided the nations and scattered the descendants of Adam, he established the boundaries of the nations according to the number of the angels of God. His people, Jacob, became the portion for the Lord; Israel became the allotment of his inheritance."[66] 3 And in another place it says, "See, the Lord takes for himself a nation from among the nations, just as a person takes the first fruit of his crops from the threshing floor. From that nation will come forth that which is most holy."[o67]

30 Since then we are a holy portion, we should do everything that pertains to holiness, fleeing slander and vile and impure sexual embraces, drunken revelries, rebellions and loathsome passions, foul adultery and loathsome haughtiness. 2 "For God," it says, "opposes the haughty but gives grace to the humble."[68] 3 We should, therefore, cling to those who have been bestowed with God's gracious gift; we should be clothed with harmony, being humble in mind, showing self-restraint, distancing ourselves from all gossip and slander, acquiring an upright character

[n]Or *faith in him*   [o]Or *"the Holy of the Holies"*

[60]Ps 28:7   [61]Ps 3:5   [62]Job 19:26   [63]Wis 12:12   [64]Ps 19:1–3   [65]Ps 139:7–8   [66]Deut 32:8–9   [67]Cf. Deut 4:34; 14:2; Num 18:27   [68]Prov 3:34; Jas 4:6; 1 Pet 5:5

through deeds, not just words. 4 For it says, "The one who speaks many things must also listen in return. Or does someone who is eloquent think he is right? 5 Blessed is one born of a woman but who lives a short life. Do not be profuse in your words."[69] 6 Let our praise be with God and not from ourselves. For God hates those who praise themselves. 7 Let the testimony of our good behavior be given by others, just as it was given to our ancestors who were upright. 8 Audacity, insolence, and effrontery belong to those who are cursed by God; gentleness, humility, and meekness to those blessed by God.

31 And so we should cling to his blessing and discern the paths that lead to it. We should unravel in our minds what has taken place from the beginning. 2 Why was our father Abraham blessed? Was it not because he did what was righteous and true through faith?[70] 3 Isaac gladly allowed himself to be brought forward as a sacrifice, confident in the knowledge of what was about to happen.[71] 4 Jacob departed with humility from his land on account of his brother and went to Laban to serve as a slave; and the twelve scepters of Israel were given to him.[72]

32 Whoever will honestly consider each of these matters will recognize the greatness of the gifts given by God.[p]

2 For from Jacob[q] came the priests and all the Levites who minister at the altar of God. From him came the Lord Jesus according to the flesh. From him came the kings, rulers, and leaders in the line of Judah. And his other scepters enjoyed no small glory either, since God had promised, "Your offspring will be like the stars of heaven."[73] 3 All of these, therefore, were glorified and exalted not through themselves or their deeds or the upright actions they did, but through his own will. 4 So too we who have been called through his will in Christ Jesus are made upright not through ourselves—through our own wisdom or understanding or piety or the deeds we have done with a devout heart—but through faith, through which the all-powerful God has made all these people upright, from the beginning of the ages. To him be the glory forever and ever. Amen.

33 What then shall we do, brothers? Shall we grow idle and not do what is good?

Shall we abandon our acts of love? May the Master never let this happen to us! Instead, we should hasten with fervor and zeal to complete every good work. 2 For the Creator and Master of all things rejoices in his works. 3 For he established the heavens by his all-superior power, and by his incomprehensible understanding he set them in order. And he separated the earth from the water that surrounded it, and established it upon the firm foundation of his own will. By his own decree he commanded the living creatures that roam about on it to come into being. Having prepared in advance the sea and all the living beings in it, he then enclosed them by his own power. 4 And with his holy and perfect hands he formed the one who was preeminent and superior in intelligence to all, the human, stamped with his own image. 5 For as God says, "Let us make a human according to our own image and likeness. And God made the human; male and female he made them."[74] 6 When he had finished all these things, he praised and blessed them, and said "Increase and become numerous."[75] 7 We should realize that all those who are upright have been adorned with good works, and even the Lord himself, when he adorned himself with good works, rejoiced. 8 With such a model before us, we should come to do his will without delay; with all our strength we should engage in righteous work.

34 The good worker receives bread for his toil with forthright confidence; the one who is lazy and slovenly does not look his employer in the eye. 2 And so we must be eager to do what is good. For all things come from him. 3 For he tells us in advance, "Behold the Lord! And the wage he offers is before him, to bestow on each according to his work."[76] 4 Thus he urges us who believe in him with our entire heart not to be idle or slovenly in every good work. 5 Our boast and forthright confidence should be in him. We should be submissive to his will. We should consider how the entire multitude of his angels stands beside him, administering his will. 6 For the Scripture

[p]Gk by him   [q]Gk him

[69]Job 11:2–3   [70]Gen 15:6   [71]Genesis 22   [72]Genesis 28ff   [73]Cf. Gen 15:5; 22:17; 26:4   [74]Gen 1:26–27   [75]Gen 1:28   [76]Cf. Rev 22:12; Isa 40:10

says, "Myriads upon myriads stood before him, and thousands upon thousands were ministering to him; and they cried out, 'Holy, holy, holy, Lord Sabaoth, all of creation is full of his glory.'"[77] 7 So too we should gather together in harmony, conscientiously, as we fervently cry out to him with one voice, that we may have a share in his great and glorious promises. 8 For he says, "No eye has seen nor ear heard, nor has it entered into the human heart, what the Lord has prepared for those who await him."[78]

35 Loved ones, how blessed and marvelous are the gifts of God: 2 life in immortality, splendor in righteousness, truth in boldness, faith in confidence, self-restraint in holiness; and all these things are subject to our understanding. 3 What therefore has been prepared for those who wait? The Maker and Father of the ages, the All Holy One, he himself knows both their magnitude and their beauty. 4 We should therefore strive to be counted among those who wait, so that we may receive the gifts he has promised. 5 But how will this be, loved ones? When our understanding is faithfully fixed on God, when we seek after what is pleasing and acceptable to him, when we accomplish what accords with his perfect will and follow in the path of truth, casting from ourselves all injustice and lawlessness, greed, strife, malice and deceit, gossip and slander, hatred of God, haughtiness and arrogance, vanity and inhospitality. 6 For those who do these things are hateful to God—and not only those who do them, but also those who approve of them. 7 For the Scripture says, "God says to the sinner, 'Why do you declare my righteous deeds and receive my covenant in your mouth? 8 For you despised discipline and tossed my words aside. When you saw a robber, you ran along with him; and you joined forces with adulterers. Your mouth multiplied evil and your tongue wove threads of deceit. You sat and spoke slanders against your brother and caused the son of your mother to stumble. 9 You did these things and I was silent. You have supposed, oh lawless one, that I will be like you. 10 I will convict you and set you up against your own face. 11 So, understand these things, you who forget about God—lest like a lion he seize you, and there be no one to deliver you. 12 A sacrifice of praise will glorify me; there is the path I will show him as the salvation of God.'"[79]

36 This is the path, loved ones, in which we have found our salvation—Jesus Christ, the high priest of our offerings, the benefactor[r] who helps us in our weaknesses.[80] 2 Through this one we gaze into the heights of the heavens; through this one we see the reflection of his perfect and superior countenance; through this one the eyes of our hearts have been opened; through this one our foolish and darkened understanding springs up into the light; through this one the Master has wished us to taste the knowledge of immortality. He is the radiance of his magnificence, as superior to the angels as he has inherited a more excellent name.[81] 3 For so it is written: "The one who makes his angels spirits and his ministers a tongue of fire."[82] 4 But the Master says this about his Son: "You are my Son; today I have given you birth. Ask from me, and I will give you the nations as your inheritance, and the ends of the earth as your possession."[83] 5 And again he says to him, "Sit at my right hand, until I make your enemies a footstool for your feet."[84] 6 Who then are the enemies? Those who are evil and oppose his will.

37 And so, brothers, with all eagerness let us do battle as soldiers under his blameless commands. 2 Consider those who soldier under our own leaders, how they accomplish what is demanded of them with such order, habit, and submission. 3 For not all are commanders-in-chief or commanders over a thousand troops, or a hundred, or fifty, and so on. But each one, according to his own rank, accomplishes what is ordered by the king and the leaders. 4 Those who are great cannot survive without the lowly nor the lowly without the great. There is a certain commixture in all things, and this proves to be useful for them. 5 Take our own body. The head is nothing without the feet, just as the feet are nothing without the head. And our body's most insignificant parts are necessary and useful for the whole. But all parts work together in subjection to a single order, to keep the whole body healthy.[s85]

38 And so, let our whole body be healthy[t] in Christ Jesus, and let each person be sub-

---

[r]Or *patron*   [s]Or *safe*   [t]Or *be saved*

[77]Dan 7:10; Isa 6:3   [78]1 Cor 2:9   [79]Ps 50:16–23   [80]Cf. Heb 3:1; 2:18   [81]Cf. Heb. 1:3, 4   [82]Heb 1:7; Ps 104:4   [83]Ps 2:7–8; Heb 1:5   [84]Ps 110:1; Heb 1:13   [85]1 Cor 12:21

ject to his neighbor, in accordance with the gracious gift he has received. 2 Let the one who is strong take care of the weak; and let the weak show due respect to the strong. Let the wealthy provide what is needed to the poor, and let the poor offer thanks to God, since he has given him someone to supply his need. Let the one who is wise show forth wisdom not through words but through good deeds. Let the one who is humble not testify to himself but permit another to testify on his behalf. Let the one who is pure in the flesh not act arrogantly, knowing that another has provided him with his self-restraint. 3 Let us carefully consider, brothers, the material from which we have been made, and who and what sort of people we were when we entered into the world; and let us consider from what kind of tomb and darkness we were led into the world by the one who fashioned and made us, after he prepared his kindly acts in advance, even before we were born. 4 Since we have all these things from him, we ought to thank him in every way. To him be the glory forever and ever. Amen.

39 Those who are ignorant, unlearned, foolish, and uneducated mock and ridicule us, wishing to vaunt themselves in their own thoughts. 2 But what can a mortal accomplish? Or what power belongs to the one born of earth? 3 For it is written, "There was no form before my eyes, but I heard a puff of air and the sound of a voice. 4 What then? Can a mortal be pure before the Lord? Or can a man be blameless in what he does, when he does not trust his own servants and detects something crooked in his own messengers?[u] 5 Not even heaven is pure before him. But see! We who inhabit clay houses are ourselves made from the same clay. He smashed them like a moth, and from dawn to dusk they are no more. They perished, unable to come to their own assistance. 6 He breathed upon them and they died for want of wisdom. 7 But call out; see if anyone listens or if you observe any of the holy angels. For wrath[v] destroys the ignorant and zeal[w] kills the one who has been deceived. 8 I have seen the ignorant casting forth their roots, but their sustenance was immediately consumed. 9 May their children be far removed from safety; may they be derided before the doors of their inferiors, with no one there to deliver them. For the food prepared for them will be devoured by the upright, and they will not be delivered from those who are evil."[86]

40 Since these matters have been clarified for us in advance and we have gazed into the depths of divine knowledge, we should do everything the Master has commanded us to perform in an orderly way and at appointed times. 2 He commanded that the sacrificial offerings and liturgical rites be performed not in a random or haphazard way, but according to set times and hours. 3 In his superior plan he set forth both where and through whom he wished them to be performed, so that everything done in a holy way and according to his good pleasure might be acceptable to his will. 4 Thus, those who make their sacrificial offerings at the arranged times are acceptable and blessed. And since they follow the ordinances of the Master, they commit no sin. 5 For special liturgical rites have been assigned to the high priest, and a special place has been designated for the regular priests, and special ministries are established for the Levites. The lay person is assigned to matters enjoined on the laity.

41 Brothers, let each of us be pleasing to God by keeping to our special assignments with a good conscience, not violating the established rule of his ministry, acting in reverence. 2 The sacrifices made daily, or for vows, or for sin and transgression are not offered everywhere, brothers, but in Jerusalem alone; and even there a sacrifice is not made in just any place, but before the sanctuary on the altar, after the sacrificial animal has been inspected for blemishes by both the high priest and the ministers mentioned earlier. 3 Thus, those who do anything contrary to his plan bear the penalty of death. 4 You see, brothers, the more knowledge we have been deemed worthy to receive, the more we are subject to danger.

42 The apostles were given the gospel for us by the Lord Jesus Christ, and Jesus Christ was sent forth from God. 2 Thus Christ came from God and the apostles from Christ. Both things happened, then, in an orderly way according to the will of God. 3 When, therefore, the

---

[u]Meaning obscure   [v]Or *his wrath*   [w]Or *his zeal*

---

[86]Job 4:16–18; 15:15; 4:19–5:5

apostles received his commands and were fully convinced through the resurrection of our Lord Jesus Christ and persuaded by the word of God, they went forth proclaiming the good news that the Kingdom of God was about to come, brimming with confidence through the Holy Spirit. 4 And as they preached throughout the countryside and in the cities, they appointed the first fruits of their ministries as bishops and deacons of those who were about to believe, testing them by the Spirit. 5 And this was no recent development. For indeed, bishops and deacons had been mentioned in writings long before. For thus the Scripture says in one place, "I will appoint their bishops in righteousness and their deacons in faith."[87]

43 And why should it be so amazing if those who were in Christ and entrusted by God with such a work appointed the leaders mentioned earlier? For even the most fortunate Moses, a faithful servant in all the house,[88] recorded in the sacred books all the directives that had been given him. And he was followed by all the other prophets, who together testified to the laws he laid down. 2 For when jealousy fell upon the tribes and created internal factions over the priesthood—concerning which of them should be adorned with that glorious name—Moses commanded the twelve tribal leaders to bring him rods, each one inscribed with the tribe's name.[89] Taking these he bound them together, sealed them with the rings of the tribal leaders, and set them in the Tent of Testimony on the table of God. 3 He shut the Tent and sealed the keys just as he had done with the rods. 4 He said to them, "Brothers, the tribe whose rod will blossom has been chosen by God to serve as his priests and ministers." 5 When early morning came he called together all Israel, some six hundred thousand men, and showed the tribal leaders the seals. He opened the Tent of Testimony and brought out the rods. And the rod of Aaron was found not only to have blossomed, but even to be bearing fruit. 6 What do you think, loved ones? That Moses did not know in advance this would happen? Of course he knew. But he did this so that there might be no disorderliness in Israel, that the name of the one who is true and unique might be glorified. To him be the glory forever and ever. Amen.

44 So too our apostles knew through our Lord Jesus Christ that strife would arise over the office of the bishop. 2 For this reason, since they understood perfectly well in advance what would happen, they appointed those we have already mentioned; and afterwards they added a codicil[x] to the effect that if these should die, other approved men should succeed them in their ministry. 3 Thus we do not think it right to remove from the ministry those who were appointed by them or, afterwards, by other reputable men, with the entire church giving its approval. For they have ministered over the flock of Christ blamelessly and with humility, gently and unselfishly, receiving a good witness by all, many times over. 4 Indeed we commit no little sin if we remove from the bishop's office those who offer the gifts in a blameless and holy way. 5 How fortunate are the presbyters who passed on before, who enjoyed a fruitful and perfect departure from this life. For they have no fear that someone will remove them from the place established for them. 6 But we see that you have deposed some from the ministry held blamelessly in honor among them, even though they had been conducting themselves well.

45 You should strive hard, brothers, and be zealous[y] in matters that pertain to salvation! 2 You have gazed into the holy and true Scriptures that were given through the Holy Spirit. 3 You realize that there is nothing unjust or counterfeit written in them. There you will not find the upright cast out by men who were holy. 4 The upright were persecuted, but by the lawless. They were imprisoned, but by the unholy. They were stoned by those who transgressed the law and killed by those who embraced vile and unjust envy. 5 And they bore up gloriously while suffering these things. 6 For what shall we say, brothers? Was Daniel cast into the lions' den by those who feared God?[90] 7 Or were Ananias, Azarias, and Misael shut up in the fiery furnace by those who participated in the magnificent and glorious worship of the Most High?[91] This could

---

[x]The text appears here to be corrupt   [y]Or *You are contentious, brothers, and envious*

[87]Isa 60:17 (LXX)   [88]Num 12:7; Heb 3:5   [89]The following account is drawn from Num 17   [90]Dan 6:16   [91]Dan 3:19ff

never be! Who then did these things? Those who were hateful and full of every evil were roused to such a pitch of anger that they tortured those who served God with holy and blameless resolve. But they did not know that the Most High is the champion and protector of those who minister to his all-virtuous name with a pure conscience. To him be the glory forever and ever. Amen. 8 But those who endured in confidence inherited glory and honor; and they were exalted and inscribed by God in their own memorial forever and ever. Amen.

46 And so, we too must cling to these examples, brothers. 2 For it is written, "Cling to those who are holy; for those who cling to them will themselves be made holy."[92] 3 And again in another place it says, "With an innocent man, you too will be innocent and with one who is chosen, you will be chosen. But with one who is corrupt, you will cause corruption."[93] 4 Therefore we should cling to those who are innocent and upright, for these are God's chosen. 5 Why are there conflicts, fits of anger, dissensions, factions, and war among you? 6 Do we not have one God, and one Christ, and one gracious Spirit that has been poured out upon us, and one calling in Christ?[94] 7 Why do we mangle and mutilate the members of Christ and create factions in our own body? Why do we come to such a pitch of madness as to forget that we are members of one another? Remember the words of our Lord Jesus, 8 for he said, "Woe to that person! It would have been good for him not to be born, rather than cause one of my chosen to stumble. Better for him to have a millstone cast about his neck and be drowned in the sea than to have corrupted one of my chosen."[95] 9 Your schism has corrupted many and cast many into despondency, many into doubt, and all of us into grief. And your faction persists even now!

47 Take up the epistle of that blessed apostle, Paul. 2 What did he write to you at first, at the beginning of his proclamation of the gospel? 3 To be sure, he sent you a letter in the Spirit[z] concerning himself and Cephas and Apollos, since you were even then engaged in partisanship.[96] 4 But that partisanship involved you in a relatively minor sin, for you were partisan toward reputable apostles and a man approved by them.

5 But now consider who has corrupted you and diminished the respect you had because of your esteemed love of others. 6 It is shameful, loved ones, exceedingly shameful and unworthy of your conduct in Christ, that the most secure and ancient church of the Corinthians is reported to have created a faction against its presbyters, at the instigation of one or two persons. 7 And this report has reached not only us but even those who stand opposed to us, so that blasphemies have been uttered against the Lord's name because of your foolishness; and you are exposing yourselves to danger.

48 And so let us dispose of this problem quickly and fall down before the Master and weep, begging him to be merciful and to be reconciled to us, and to restore us to our respected and holy conduct, seen in our love of others. 2 For this is a gate of righteousness that opens up onto life, just as it is written, "Open up for me gates of righteousness; when I enter through them I will give praises to the Lord. 3 This is the gate of the Lord, and the upright will enter through it."[97] 4 Although many gates open, this is the one that leads to righteousness—the one that is in Christ. All those who enter it are most fortunate; they make their path straight in holiness and righteousness, accomplishing all things without disorder.

5 Let a person be faithful, let him be able to speak forth knowledge, let him be wise in his discernment of words, let him be pure in deeds. 6 For the more he appears to be great, the more he should be humble, striving for the good of all, not just of himself.

49 The one who experiences love in Christ should do what Christ commanded. 2 Who can explain the bond of God's love? 3 Who is able to recount the greatness of its beauty? 4 The height to which love leads is beyond description. 5 Love binds us to God; love hides a multitude of sins;[98] love bears all things and endures all things. There is nothing vulgar in love, nothing haughty. Love has no schism, love creates

---

[z]Or with spiritual concerns

---

[92]Source unknown   [93]Ps 18:25–26   [94]Eph 4:4–6   [95]Matt 26:24; Luke 17:2   [96]1 Cor 1:12   [97]Ps 118:19–20   [98]1 Pet 4:8

no faction, love does all things in harmony. Everyone chosen by God has been perfected in love; apart from love nothing is pleasing to God.[99] 6 The Master has received us in love. Because of the love he had for us, our Lord Jesus Christ gave his blood for us, by God's will—his flesh for our flesh, his soul for our souls.

50 You see, loved ones, how great and amazing love is; there can be no exposition of its perfection. 2 Who is adequate to be found in it, except those whom God has made worthy? And so we should implore and plead for his mercy, that we may be found in his love, removed from any human partisanship, blameless. 3 All the generations from Adam till today have passed away, but those perfected in love through the gracious gift of God have a place among the godly. And they will be revealed when the kingdom of Christ appears. 4 For it is written, "Come into the inner rooms for just a short while, until my anger and wrath pass by; and I will remember a good day and raise you up from your tombs."[100] 5 We are blessed, loved ones, when we keep God's commandments in the harmony of love, that our sins may be forgiven us through love. 6 For it is written, "Blessed are those whose lawless acts are forgiven and whose sins have been covered over. Blessed is the man whose sin the Lord does not take into account and in whose mouth is found no deceit."[101] 7 This blessing comes to those who have been chosen by God through our Lord Jesus Christ. To him be the glory forever and ever. Amen.

51 And so we should ask to be forgiven for all the errors we have committed and the deeds we have performed through any of the machinations of the Enemy. In addition, those who became the leaders of the faction and dissension should consider the common ground of hope. 2 For those who conduct themselves with reverential awe and love prefer to undergo torture themselves than to have their neighbors do so. They would rather have condemnation fall on themselves than on the unity that has been nobly and justly delivered over to us. 3 For it is more noble for a person to confess his transgressions than to harden his heart. Indeed, the hearts of those who rebelled against the servant of God, Moses, were hardened, and their judgment was publicly seen.

4 For they descended into Hades alive, and Death will be their shepherd.[102] 5 Pharoah and his army and all the leaders of Egypt, both the chariots and those who rode in them, were plunged into the Red Sea and perished for no other reason than this: their foolish hearts were hardened after the signs and wonders occurred in Egypt through Moses, the servant of God.[103]

52 The Master is in need of nothing, brothers, and craves nothing from anyone, but to be praised. 2 For the chosen one, David, says, "I will praise the Lord and it will please him more than a young calf bearing horns and hooves. Let those who are poor see this and rejoice."[104] 3 And again he says, "Give to God a sacrifice of your praise and render to the Most High your prayers. And call upon me in the day of your affliction, and I will rescue you; and you will give glory to me."[105] 4 "For a crushed spirit is a sacrifice to God."[106]

53 For you know the sacred Scriptures, loved ones—and know them quite well—and you have gazed into the sayings of God. And so we write these things simply as a reminder. 2 For after Moses went up onto the mountain and spent forty days and nights in fasting and humility,[107] God said to him, "Moses, Moses, go down from here at once: Your people, whom you brought out of the land of Egypt, have broken the Law. They have departed quickly from the path you commanded them to take and have cast metal idols for themselves." 3 And the Lord said to him, "I have spoken with you once and again: I have seen this people and know they are stiff-necked. Let me destroy them and I will blot their name out from beneath the sky; and I will make you into a great and spectacular nation, much greater than this one." 4 And Moses said, "May it never be, Lord! Forgive the sin of this people—or blot me also out from the book of the living."

5 O great love! O incomparable perfection! The servant speaks boldly to the Lord, and asks for the multitude to be forgiven—or pleads for himself to be blotted out with them.

---

[99]Cf. 1 Cor 13:4–7　[100]Isa 26:20; Ezek 37:12　[101]Ps 32:1–2; Rom 4:7–9　[102]Num 16:33; Ps 49:14　[103]Exod 14:23　[104]Ps 69:30–32 [105]Ps 50:14–15　[106]Ps 51:17　[107]The following account is drawn from Exod 32:7–10, 31–32 and Deut 9:12–14

54 Who, therefore, among you is noble? Or compassionate? Or filled with love? 2 Let that one say, "If I am the cause of faction, strife, and schisms, I will depart; I will go wherever you wish and do what is commanded by the congregation. Only allow the flock of Christ to be at peace with the presbyters who have been appointed." 3 The one who does this will have made himself eminent in Christ and will be welcomed everywhere. "For the earth, and all that is in it, belongs to the Lord."[108] 4 Those who have performed their civic duty to God, without regrets, have done these things and will continue to do them.

55 But we should bring in examples from the Gentiles as well. Many kings and rulers, after receiving instruction from an oracle, have handed themselves over to death during the time of plague, in order to deliver their fellow citizens by shedding their own blood. Many left their own cities to avoid creating more factions. 2 Among ourselves, we know many who put themselves in prison in order to ransom others; many placed themselves in slavery and fed others with the purchase price they received. 3 Many women were empowered by the gracious gift of God to perform numerous "manly" deeds. 4 The blessed Judith, when her city lay under siege, asked the elders for permission to go out to the foreigners' camp.[109] 5 And so she handed herself over to danger, going out because she loved her homeland and the people under siege. And the Lord handed Holofernes over to the hand of a female. 6 No less did Esther, a woman perfect in faith, put herself in danger to rescue the twelve tribes of Israel who were about to perish.[110] For through her fasting and humility she petitioned the all-seeing Master, the God of eternity, who saw the humbleness of her soul and rescued the people for whom she put herself in danger.

56 And so we should pray for those caught up in any unlawful act, that gentleness and humility may be given them, so that they may yield themselves not to us but to the will of God. For so the compassionate remembrance of them by God and the saints will be fruitful and perfect.[a] 2 We should welcome discipline, loved ones; no one should be irritated by it. It is good and supremely useful to rebuke one another, for this binds us to the will of God. 3 For thus says the holy word: "The Lord disciplined me harshly but did not hand me over to death. 4 For the Lord disciplines the one he loves and whips every son he receives."[111] 5 "For the one who is upright will discipline me in his mercy," it says, "and he will set me straight. But may the oil of sinners not anoint my head."[112] 6 And again it says, "How fortunate is the one whom the Lord sets straight. Do not spurn the rebuke of the All-powerful. For he causes pain and again brings relief. 7 He strikes and his hands provide healing. 8 Six times he will rescue you from anguish and the seventh time evil will not touch you. 9 During time of famine he will rescue you from death, and in time of war he will free you from the hand that wields the sword. 10 He will hide you from the scourge of the tongue and you will not be afraid when evils draw near. 11 You will mock those who are unjust and lawless; you will not fear the wild beasts. 12 For wild beasts will be at peace with you. 13 Then you will know that your household will be at peace, and the tent you inhabit will never fail. 14 And you will know that your descendants will be numerous, your children like all the plants of the field. 15 And you will enter the grave like ripened grain harvested at the proper time, or like a heap of sheaves on the threshing floor, gathered together at the right hour."[113]

16 You see, loved ones, what a great protection there is for those who are disciplined by the Master. For since he is a good father, he disciplines us, that through his holy discipline we may receive mercy.

57 Thus you who laid the foundation of the faction should be subject to the presbyters and accept the discipline that leads to repentance, falling prostrate in your heart. 2 Learn to be submissive; lay aside the arrogant and haughty insolence of your tongue. For it is better for you to be considered insignificant but reputable in the flock of Christ than to appear prominent while sundered from his hope. 3 For thus says his all-virtuous Wisdom: "Look, I will utter a

---

[a]Meaning obscure

[108]Ps 24:1   [109]The account is drawn from Jth 8ff   [110]The account is drawn from Esther 7; 4:16   [111]Prov 3:12; cf. Heb 12:6   [112]Ps 141:5   [113]Job 5:17–26

saying to you with my breath and teach you my word. 4 For I was calling and you did not listen, and I was sending forth my words and you paid no attention. But you repudiated my advice and disobeyed when I reproached you. For this reason I too will mock when you are annihilated and rejoice when destruction comes upon you and turmoil suddenly appears among you, when catastrophe arrives like a tempest, or when adversity and distress come upon you. 5 For then when you call on me, I will not listen to you. Those who are evil will seek me out but not find me. For they hated wisdom and chose not to accept the reverential awe of the Lord. Nor did they wish to accept my advice, but they mocked when I rebuked them. 6 For this reason they will consume the fruits of their own path and be filled with their own impious deeds. 7 For since they treated the young with injustice, they will be murdered, and an inquiry will destroy those who are impious. But the one who hears me will dwell in hope with all confidence; he will be at rest, fearing no evil."[114]

58 For this reason we should be obedient to his most holy and glorious name, fleeing the dangers foretold by Wisdom, which threaten the disobedient. In this way we will dwell with confidence in the most holy name of his magnificence. 2 Take our advice and you will have no regrets. For as God, the Lord Jesus Christ, and the Holy Spirit all live—as do[b] the faith and hope of those who are chosen —the one who does the righteous demands and commandments given by God with humility and fervent gentleness, and without regret, will be included and held in esteem among the number of those who will be saved through Jesus Christ. Through whom be glory to him forever and ever. Amen.

59 But if some disobey the words he has spoken through us, they should realize that they entangle themselves in transgression and no little danger. 2 But we ourselves will be innocent of this sin, and we will ask with a fervent prayer and petition that the Creator of all safeguard the number of those counted among his elect throughout the entire world, through his beloved child Jesus Christ, through whom he called us out of darkness into light, from ignorance into the knowledge of his glorious name. 3 Grant us, O Lord, that we may hope in your name, the ultimate source of all creation. Open the eyes of our heart, that we may recognize you as the one alone who is the highest among the highest, the holy one who rests among the holy, the one who humbles the insolence of the proud, who destroys the reasonings of the nations, who exalts the humble to the heights and humiliates the exalted, the one who enriches and impoverishes, who kills and brings to life, the sole benefactor of spirits and the God of all flesh, the one who peers into the places of the abyss, who observes the works of humans and helps those in danger, the savior of those who have abandoned hope, the creator and overseer of every spirit, the one who multiplies the nations upon the earth and who from them all has chosen those who love you through Jesus Christ, your beloved child, through whom you have disciplined, sanctified, and honored us. 4 We ask you, O Master, to be our helper and defender. Save those of us who are in affliction, show mercy to those who are humble, raise those who have fallen, show yourself to those who are in need, heal those who are sick, set straight those among your people who are going astray. Feed the hungry, ransom our prisoners, raise up the weak, encourage the despondent. Let all the nations know you, that you alone are God, that Jesus Christ is your child, and that we are your people and the sheep of your pasture.

60 For you have made plain the eternal structure of the world through the works you have accomplished. You, O Lord, created the world in which we live; you are faithful from one generation to the next, upright in your judgments, spectacular in your strength and magnificence; you are wise when you create and understanding when you establish what exists; you are good in what is seen and kind to those who trust you. You who are merciful and compassionate, forgive us for our lawless acts, unjust deeds, transgressions, and faults. 2 Take into account none of the sins committed by your male slaves and female servants, but cleanse us with your truth. Set our steps straight that we may go forward with devout hearts, to do what is good and pleasing to you and to those who rule us.

---

[b]Or *who are*

[114]Prov 1:23–33

3 Yes, Master, make your face shine on us in peace, for our own good, that we may be protected by your powerful hand and rescued from our every sin by your exalted arm. And rescue us from those who hate us without cause. 4 Give harmony and peace both to us and to all those who inhabit the earth, just as you gave it to our ancestors when they called upon you in a holy way, in faith and truth; and allow us to be obedient to your all-powerful and all-virtuous name, and to those who rule and lead us here on earth.

61 You have given them, O Master, the authority to rule through your magnificent and indescribable power, that we may both recognize the glory and honor you have given them and subject ourselves to them, resisting nothing that conforms to your will. Give to them, O Lord, health, peace, harmony, and stability, so that without faltering they may administer the rule that you have given to them. 2 For you, O Master, Heavenly King forever, give humans glory, honor, and authority over the creatures of the earth. O Lord, make their plan conform with what is good and acceptable before you, that when they administer with piety the authority you have given them, in peace and meekness, they may attain your mercy. 3 You who alone can to do these things for us, and do what is more abundantly good, we praise you through the high priest and benefactor of our souls, Jesus Christ, through whom the glory and majesty be yours both now and for all generations and forever. Amen.

62 Brothers, we have written you enough about what is fitting for our worship and what is most profitable for the virtuous life, for those who want to conduct themselves in a pious and upright way. 2 For we have touched on every aspect of faith, repentance, genuine love, self-restraint, moderation, and endurance, reminding you that you must be pleasing, in a holy way, both to the all-powerful God—by acting in righteousness, truth, and patience, living in harmony, holding no grudges, living in love and peace with fervent gentleness, just as our ancestors, whom we mentioned before, were pleasing to God by being humble-minded toward the Father, who is both God and Creator—and to all people. 3 And we were all the more happy to bring these things to mind, since we knew full well that we were writing to faithful and highly respectable men, who have gazed into the sayings of God's teaching.[c]

63 Now that we have considered such great and so many examples, it is right for us to bow our necks in submission and assume a position of obedience. In this way, by putting a halt to the futile faction, we will truly reach the goal set before us, with no blame attached. 2 For you will make us joyful and happy if you become obedient to what we have written through the Holy Spirit and excise the wanton anger expressed through your jealousy, in accordance with the request we have made in this letter for your peace and harmony.

3 We have sent faithful and temperate men who have lived blamelessly among us from youth to old age; these also will serve as witnesses between you and us. 4 We have done this that you may know that our every concern has been—and is—for you to establish the peace quickly.

64 And finally, may the God who observes all things—the Master of spirits and Lord of all flesh, who chose both the Lord Jesus Christ and us through him to be his special people—may he grant to every soul that is called by his magnificent and holy name faith, reverential awe, peace, endurance and patience, self-restraint, purity, and moderation, that they may be found pleasing to his name through our high priest and benefactor, Jesus Christ. Through whom to him be glory and greatness, power and honor, both now and forevermore. Amen.

65 But send back to us quickly our envoys Claudius Ephebus and Valerius Bito, along with Fortunatus, in peace and with joy, that they may inform us without delay about the peace and harmony that we have prayed and desired for you. Then we will rejoice more quickly in your stability.

2 The grace of our Lord Jesus Christ be with you and with all those everywhere who are called by God through him. Through whom be to him all glory, honor, power, greatness, and the eternal throne, forever and ever. Amen.

---

[c]Or *the sayings of God that bring discipline*

The Didache

Discovered in 1873 in a monastary library in Constantinople, the *Didache* (literally, *The Teaching*) *of the Twelve Apostles* has made a significant impact on the way in which scholars understand the social life and ritual practices of the early church. It is, in fact, the first "church manual" to have survived from early Christianity.

The book was probably written around 100 C.E., since it appears to be familiar with earlier Christian traditions such as those embodied in Matthew's Gospel in the latter half of the first century, yet does not evidence the rigid form of church hierarchy that had developed later in the second century (even though it speaks of bishops and deacons).

The first part of the book describes the "Two Paths of Life and Death" (see the introduction to the *Letter of Barnabas*). The Path of Life (chaps. 1–4) is paved with upright behavior: the author's readers are to love one another, avoid evil desires, jealousy, and anger, give alms to the poor, obey God's commandments, and generally lead morally respectable lives. Many of these instructions reflect the teachings of Jesus from Matthew's Sermon on the Mount (e.g., praying for one's enemies, turning the other cheek, and going the extra mile). As might be expected, the Path of Death (chap. 5) involves the opposite sorts of behavior: "murders, adulteries, passions, sexual immoralities, robberies," and sundry other transgressive activities.

The bulk of the rest of the book gives instructions for the ritual practices and social interactions of the Christian community (chaps. 7–15), including directions for how to perform baptisms (preferably in cold, running water), when to fast (every Wednesday and Friday), what to pray (the Lord's Prayer, three times a day), and how to celebrate the Eucharist (first giving thanks for the cup, then the bread). Near the end of these instructions the author addresses the problem of wandering "apostles," "teachers," and "prophets" of dubious moral character; evidently, some scoundrels had become itinerant Christian preachers simply for financial gain. The communities are to test the sincerity of these wandering ministers and to limit the length of their stay at the community's expense; moreover, the communities are to appoint leaders of their own to direct their affairs.

The book concludes with a kind of apocalyptic discourse, an exhortation to be prepared for the imminent end of the world, to be brought by "the Lord coming on the clouds of the sky" (16:7).

The Didache, from *The Apostolic Fathers,* translated by Bart D. Ehrman. Loeb Classical Library; © 2003. Reprinted by permission of Harvard University Press.

The teaching of the Lord through the twelve apostles to the Gentiles.[a]

1 There are two paths, one of life and one of death, and the difference between the two paths is great.

2 This then is the path of life. First, love the God who made you, and second, your neighbor as yourself.[1] And whatever you do not want to happen to you, do not do to another.[2]

3 This is the teaching relating to these matters: Bless those who curse you, pray for your enemies, and fast for those who persecute you. For why is it so great to love those who love you? Do the Gentiles[a] not do this as well? But you should love those who hate you[3]—then you will have no enemy. 4 Abstain from fleshly passions.[4] If anyone slaps your right cheek, turn the other to him as well,[5] and you will be perfect.[6] If anyone compels you to go one mile, go with him two. If anyone takes your cloak, give him your shirt as well. If anyone seizes what is yours, do not ask for it back,[7] for you will not be able to get it. 5 Give to everyone who asks, and do not ask for anything back.[8] For the Father wants everyone to be given something from the gracious gifts he himself provides.[c] How fortunate is the one who gives according to the commandment, for he is without fault. Woe to the one who receives. For if anyone receives because he is in need, he is without fault. But the one who receives without a need will have to testify why he received what he did, and for what purpose. And he will be thrown in prison and interrogated about what he did; and he will not get out until he pays back every last cent.[9] 6 For it has also been said concerning this, "Let your gift to charity sweat in your hands until you know to whom to give it."[10]

2 And now the second commandment of the teaching. 2 Do not murder, do not commit adultery,[11] do not engage in pederasty, do not engage in sexual immorality. Do not steal, do not practice magic, do not use enchanted potions, do not abort a fetus or kill a child that is born. 3 Do not desire what belongs to your neighbor, do not commit perjury, do not give false testimony, do not speak insults, do not bear grudges. 4 Do not be of two minds or speak from both sides of your mouth, for speaking from both sides of your mouth is a deadly trap. 5 Your word must not be empty or false. 6 Do not be greedy, rapacious, hypocritical, spiteful, or haughty. Do not entertain a wicked plot against your neighbor. 7 Do not hate anyone—but reprove some, pray for others, and love still others more than yourself.

3 My child, flee from all evil and everything like it. 2 Do not be prone to anger, for anger leads to murder; nor be zealous, contentious, or irascible. For from all these are born acts of murder.

3 My child, do not be filled with passion, for passion leads to sexual immorality; nor be foulmouthed or lecherous. For from all these are born acts of adultery.

4 My child, do not practice divination,[d] since this leads to idolatry; nor use incantations or astrology or rites of purification, nor even wish to see or hear these things. For from all these is born idolatry.

5 My child, do not be a liar, since lying leads to robbery; nor be fond of money or vain. For from all these are born acts of robbery.

6 My child, do not be a complainer, since this leads to blasphemy; nor be insolent or evil-minded. For from all these are born blasphemies. 7 But be meek, since the meek will inherit the earth.[12] 8 Be patient, merciful, innocent, gentle, and good, trembling at the words you have heard. 9 Do not exalt yourself or become impertinent. You should not join forces with the high and mighty, but you should associate with the upright and humble. 10 Welcome whatever happens to you as good, knowing that nothing occurs apart from God.

4 My child, night and day remember the one who speaks the word of God to you; honor him as the Lord. For where his lordship is discussed, there the Lord himself is. 2 Every day seek out the company of the saints, that you may find comfort in their words. 3 Do not create a schism, but bring peace to those who are at odds.

[a]Or *nations* [b]Or *nations* [c]Meaning obscure [d]That is, through observing the flight of birds

[1]Matt 22:37–39; Mark 12:30–31; Luke 10:27; Deut 6:5; Lev 19:18 [2]Cf. Matt 7:12; Luke 6:31 [3]Cf. Matt 5:44, 46–47; Luke 6:28, 32–33, 35 [4]1 Pet 2:11 [5]Matt 5:39 [6]Matt 5:48 [7]Matt 4:41, 40; Luke 6:29–30 [8]Luke 6:30 [9]Cf. Matt 5:26; Luke 12:59 [10]Source unknown [11]The following passage elaborates Exod 20:13–17; cf. Matt 19:18; 5:33 [12]Matt 5:5; Ps 37:11

Give a fair judgment; do not show favoritism when you reproach others for their unlawful acts. 4 Do not be of two minds, whether this should happen or not.

5 Do not be one who reaches out your hands to receive but draws them back from giving. 6 If you acquire something with your hands, give it as a ransom for your sins. 7 Do not doubt whether to give, nor grumble while giving. For you should recognize the good paymaster of the reward. 8 Do not shun a person in need, but share all things with your brother and do not say that anything is your own.[13] For if you are partners in what is immortal, how much more in what is mortal?

9 Do not remove your hand from[e] your son or daughter, but from their youth teach them the reverential fear of God. 10 Do not give orders to your male slave or female servant (who hope in the same God) out of bitterness, lest they stop fearing the God who is over you both. For he does not come to call those of high status, but those whom the Spirit has prepared. 11 And you who are slaves must be subject to your masters as to a replica[f] of God, with respect and reverential fear.

12 Hate all hypocrisy and everything that is not pleasing to the Lord. 13 Do not abandon the commandments of the Lord, but guard what you have received, neither adding to them nor taking away.[14] 14 Confess your unlawful acts in church, and do not come to your prayer with an evil conscience. This is the path of life.

5 And the path of death is this. First of all it is evil and filled with a curse: murders, adulteries, passions, sexual immoralities, robberies, idolatries, feats of magic, sorceries, rapacious acts, false testimonies, hypocrisies, split affection, deceit, arrogance, malice, insolence, greed, obscenity, jealousy, impertinence, pride, haughtiness, irreverence.

2 It is filled with persecutors of the good, haters of the truth, lovers of the lie, who do not know the reward of righteousness, nor cling to the good nor to a fair judgment, who are alert not to do good but to do evil; from whom meekness and patience are far removed. For they love what is vain and pursue a reward, showing no mercy to the poor nor toiling for the oppressed nor knowing the one who made them; murderers of children and corruptors of what God has fashioned, who turn their backs on the needy, oppress the afflicted, and support the wealthy. They are lawless judges of the impoverished, altogether sinful. Be delivered, children, from all such people.

6 Take care that no one lead you astray from the path of this teaching, since that one teaches you apart from God.

2 For if you can bear the entire yoke of the Lord, you will be perfect; but if you cannot, do as much as you can.

3 And concerning food, bear what you can. But especially abstain from food sacrificed to idols; for this is a ministry to dead gods.

7 But with respect to baptism, baptize as follows. Having said all these things in advance, baptize in the name of the Father and of the Son and of the Holy Spirit,[15] in running water. 2 But if you do not have running water, baptize in some other water. And if you cannot baptize in cold water, use warm. 3 But if you have neither, pour water on the head three times in the name of Father and Son and Holy Spirit. 4 But both the one baptizing and the one being baptized should fast before the baptism, along with some others if they can. But command the one being baptized to fast one or two days in advance.

8 And do not keep your fasts with the hypocrites.[16] For they fast on Monday and Thursday; but you should fast on Wednesday and Friday.

2 Nor should you pray like the hypocrites,[17] but as the Lord commanded in his gospel, you should pray as follows: "Our Father in heaven, may your name be kept holy; may your kingdom come, may your will be done on earth as in heaven. Give us today our daily bread.[g] And forgive us our debt, as we forgive our debtors. And do not bring us into temptation but deliver us from the Evil One.[h] For the power and the glory are yours forever."[18]

3 Pray like this three times a day.

9 And with respect to the thanksgiving meal,[i] you shall give thanks as follows. 2 First, with respect to the cup: "We give you thanks, our

Eucharist

---

[e]Or *Do not refrain from disciplining*; or *Do not shirk your responsibility towards* [f]Or *type* [g]Or *the bread that we need*; or *our bread for tomorrow* [h]Or *from evil* [i]Literally, *eucharist*

[13]Acts 4:32 [14]Deut 4:2; 12:32 [15]Matt 28:19 [16]Cf. Matt 6:16 [17]Cf. Matt 6:5 [18]Matt 6:9–13

Father, for the holy vine of David, your child, which you made known to us through Jesus your child. To you be the glory forever."

3 And with respect to the fragment of bread: "We give you thanks, our Father, for the life and knowledge that you made known to us through Jesus your child. To you be the glory forever. 4 As this fragment of bread was scattered upon the mountains and was gathered to become one, so may your church be gathered together from the ends of the earth into your kingdom. For the glory and the power are yours through Jesus Christ forever."

5 But let no one eat or drink from your thanksgiving meal[j] unless they have been baptized in the name of the Lord. For also the Lord has said about this, "Do not give what is holy to the dogs."[19]

10 And when you have had enough to eat, you should give thanks as follows: 2 "We give you thanks, holy Father, for your holy name which you have made reside in our hearts, and for the knowledge, faith, and immortality that you made known to us through Jesus your child. To you be the glory forever. 3 You, O Master Almighty, created all things for the sake of your name, and gave both food and drink to humans for their refreshment, that they might give you thanks. And you graciously provided us with spiritual food and drink, and eternal life through your child. 4 Above all we thank you because you are powerful. To you be the glory forever. 5 Remember your church, O Lord; save it from all evil, and perfect it in your love. And gather it from the four winds into your kingdom, which you prepared for it. For yours is the power and the glory forever. 6 May grace come and this world pass away. Hosanna to the God of David. If anyone is holy, let him come; if anyone is not, let him repent. Maranatha![20] Amen."

7 But permit the prophets to give thanks[k] as often as they wish.[l]

11 And so, welcome anyone who comes and teaches you everything mentioned above. 2 But if the teacher should himself turn away and teach something different, undermining these things, do not listen to him. But if his teaching brings righteousness and the knowledge of the Lord, then welcome him as the Lord.

3 But act towards the apostles and prophets as the gospel decrees. 4 Let every apostle who comes to you be welcomed as the Lord. 5 But he should not remain more than[m] a day. If he must, he may stay one more. But if he stays three days, he is a false prophet. 6 When an apostle leaves he should take nothing except bread, until he arrives at his night's lodging. If he asks for money, he is a false prophet.

7 Do not test or condemn a prophet speaking in the Spirit. For every sin will be forgiven, but not this sin.[21] 8 Not everyone who speaks in the Spirit is a prophet, but only one who conducts himself like the Lord. Thus the false prophet and the prophet will both be known by their conduct. 9 No prophet who orders a meal[n] in the Spirit eats of it; if he does, he is a false prophet. 10 Every prophet who teaches the truth but does not do what he himself teaches is a false prophet. 11 You are not to condemn any prophet who has been approved and is true, and who acts on behalf of the earthly[o] mystery of the church, even if he does not teach others to do what he himself does, since he has his judgment with God. For even the ancient prophets behaved in this way. 12 Do not listen to anyone who says in the Spirit, "Give me money" (or something else). But if he tells you to give to others who are in need, let no one judge him.

12 Everyone who comes in the name of the Lord should be welcomed. Then, when you exercise your critical judgment, you will know him; for you understand what is true and what is false.[p] 2 If the one who comes is simply passing through, help him as much as you can. He should not stay with you more than two or three days, if need be. 3 If he wants to remain with you, and is a tradesman, let him work and eat. 4 If he does not have a trade, use your foresight to determine how he as a Christian may live among you without being idle.[q] 5 If he does not want to be-

[j]Literally, *eucharist* [k]Or *hold the eucharist* [l]Two important witnesses add a verse (with variations): "But concerning the matter of the ointment, give thanks as follows, saying, 'We give you thanks, O Father, for the ointment you have made known to us through Jesus your child. To you be the glory forever, Amen.'" [m]"more than" is not found in the Greek, but the context and 12:2 justify the emendation [n]Literally, *appoints a table.* This may refer to a meal for the needy [o]Or *cosmic;* meaning obscure [p]Literally *both the right side and the left* [q]Or *through your understanding you should know in advance that no idle Christian is to live among you*

[19]Matt 7:6   [20]Cf. 1 Cor 16:22   [21]Cf. Matt 12:31

have like this, he is a Christmonger. Avoid such people.

13 Every true prophet who wants to settle down with you deserves his food. 2 So too a true teacher, like the worker, deserves his food.[22] 3 Therefore you shall take every first portion[r] of the produce from the wine vat and the threshing floor, and the first portion of both cattle and sheep, and give it to the prophets. For they are your high priests. 4 If you do not have a prophet, then give it to the poor. 5 If you make bread, take the first portion and give it according to the commandment. 6 So too if you open a jar of wine or oil, take the first portion of it and give it to the prophets. 7 And take the first portion of your money, clothing, and everything you own, as it seems good to you, and give it according to the commandment.

14 On the Lord's own day,[s] when you gather together, break bread and give thanks[t] after you have confessed your unlawful deeds, that your sacrifice may be pure. 2 Let no one quarreling with his neighbor join you until they are reconciled, that your sacrifice may not be defiled.[23] 3 For this is the sacrifice mentioned by the Lord: "In every place and time, bring me a pure sacrifice. For I am a great King, says the Lord, and my name is considered marvelous among the Gentiles."[u24]

15 And so, elect for yourselves bishops and deacons who are worthy of the Lord, gentle men who are not fond of money, who are true and approved. For these also conduct the ministry of the prophets and teachers among you. 2 And so, do not disregard them. For these are the ones who have found honor among you, along with the prophets and teachers.

3 Do not reprimand one another in anger, but in peace, as you have learned from the gospel. Let no one speak with a person who has committed a sin

against his neighbor, nor let him hear anything from you, until he repents. 4 But say your prayers, give to charity, and engage in all your activities as you have learned in the gospel of our Lord.

16 Be watchful for your life. Do not let your lamps be extinguished or your robes[v] be loosed; but be prepared. For you do not know the hour when our Lord is coming.[25] 2 Gather together frequently, seeking what is appropriate for your souls. For the entire time of your faith will be of no use to you if you are not found perfect at the final moment. 3 For in the final days the false prophets and corruptors of the faith will be multiplied. The sheep will be turned into wolves, and love into hatred. 4 For when lawlessness increases they will hate, persecute, and betray one another.[26] Then the world-deceiver will be manifest as a son of God. He will perform signs and wonders,[27] and the earth will be delivered over into his hands. He will perform lawless deeds, unlike anything done from eternity. 5 Then all human creation will come to the fire of testing, and many will fall away and perish, but those who endure in their faith will be saved[28] by the curse itself.[w] 6 Then the signs of truth will be manifest[29]: first a sign of a rip[x] in the sky, then a sign of the sound of a trumpet,[30] and third a resurrection of the dead. 7 But not of all the dead. For as it has been said, "The Lord will come and all of his holy ones with him.[31] 8 Then the world will see the Lord coming on the clouds of the sky. . . ."[y32]

---

[r]Literally, *first fruit*; so too in verses 3b, 5–7   [s]Literally, *On the Lord's day of the Lord*   [t]Or *celebrate the eucharist*   [u]Or *nations*   [v]Literally, *loins*   [w]Meaning obscure   [x]Or *of a stretching*   [y]The conclusion is evidently lost

---

[22]Matt 10:10   [23]Cf. Matt 5:23–24   [24]Mal 1:11, 14   [25]Cf. Matt 24:42; Luke 12:40; cf. Mark 13:35,37   [26]Cf. Matt 24:10–12   [27]Cf. Mark 13:22   [28]Cf. Matt 24:10, 13   [29]Cf. Matt 24:30   [30]Cf. Matt 24:31; 1 Cor 15:52; 1 Thess 4:16   [31]Zech. 14:5; 1 Thess 3:13   [32]Cf. Matt 24:30

The Letter of Ignatius to the Ephesians

Ignatius is one of the first Christians known to have been executed on order of the Roman authorities. Arrested in Antioch of Syria, where he served as bishop of the church, Ignatius was sent in chains to face the wild beasts in the Roman amphitheater (Ign Eph 1:2; 21:2). While traveling by land through Asia Minor, he was met at various stopping points by representatives of local Christian communities who had heard of his plight. Ignatius in turn penned letters to several of these churches. Altogether, seven letters survive from his hand. They appear to date from around 110 C.E.

The letter to the church in Ephesus was written from the city of Smyrna (21:1). The Ephesian Christians had sent a five-person delegation to meet with Ignatius, headed by the bishop of the church, Onesimus, and one of its deacons, Burrhus (1:3–2:1). Having learned about their congregation, Ignatius writes to express his gratitude and to encourage them in their faith.

Several themes recur throughout this short letter. Most noticably, Ignatius is concerned that the Ephesian Christians live in harmony with one another and, especially, with their bishop. They are "to run together in harmony with the mind of the bishop" (4:1) and to "be eager not to oppose the bishop [so as to] be subject to God" (5:3). Indeed, the Ephesians are told to regard Onesimus, their bishop, "as the Lord himself" (6:1).

Much of the letter provides basic instruction on Christian living; the Ephesians are encouraged, for example, to live in love toward one another (14:1), to avoid sin (14:2), not to be overly garrulous (15:1), and to practice what they preach (15:1). In particular, Ignatius had learned that outsiders have come into the congregation proclaiming "evil teaching" (9:1). He does not indicate the precise nature of the problem, but he does warn the Ephesians to give these interlopers no heed and to remain true to their basic beliefs about Christ. His own summary of these beliefs is strikingly paradoxical: "There is one physician, both fleshly and spiritual, born and unborn, God come in the flesh, true life in death, from both Mary and God, first subject to suffering then beyond suffering, Jesus Christ our Lord" (7:1).

Ignatius appears to be familiar with a number of traditions about Jesus from the Gospels, and he interprets them in somewhat unusual ways: The star of Bethlehem astonished all the other stars of heaven, which gathered about it in adoration (19:2–3); Jesus' baptism in water purified the waters used in (Christian) baptism (18:2); and his being anointed with oil allowed him to "breathe immortality into the church" (17:1). It is debated among scholars whether Ignatius had actually read any of our written Gospels (e.g., Matthew) or had instead simply heard some of the oral traditions about Jesus' life.

"The Letter of Ignatius to the Ephesians," from *The Apostolic Fathers,* translated by Bart D. Ehrman. Loeb Classical Library; © 2003. Reprinted by permission of Harvard University Press.

Ignatius, who is also called God-bearer, to the church that is blessed with greatness by the fullness of God the Father, a church foreordained from eternity past to obtain a constant glory which is enduring and unchanging, a church that has been unified and chosen in true suffering by the will of the Father and of Jesus Christ, our God; to the church in Ephesus of Asia, which is worthy of all good fortune. Warmest greetings in Jesus Christ and in blameless joy!

1 Now that I have received in God your greatly loved name, which you have obtained because of your upright nature, according to the faith and love that is in Christ Jesus our Savior—for you are imitators of God and have rekindled, through the blood of God, the work we share as members of the same family, and brought it to perfect completion. 2 For you were eager to see me, since you heard that I was being brought in chains from Syria because of the name and hope we share, and that I was hoping, through your prayer, to be allowed to fight the beasts in Rome, that by doing so I might be able to be a disciple. 3 Since, then, I have received your entire congregation in the name of God through Onesimus, who abides in a love that defies description and serves as your bishop in the flesh—and I ask by Jesus Christ that you love him, and that all of you be like him. For blessed is the one who has graciously granted you, who are worthy, to obtain such a bishop.

2 But as to my fellow slave Burrhus, your godly deacon who is blessed in all things, I ask that he stay here for the honor of both you and the bishop. And Crocus as well—who is worthy of God and of you, whom I received as an embodiment of your love—has revived me in every way. So may the Father of Jesus Christ refresh him, along with Onesimus, Burrhus, Euplus, and Fronto, those through whom I lovingly saw all of you. 2 I hope to enjoy you at all times, if indeed I am worthy. For it is fitting for you in every way to give glory to Jesus Christ, the one who glorified you, so that you may be holy in all respects, being made complete through a single subjection, being subject to the bishop and the presbytery.

3 I am not giving you orders as if I were someone. For even though I have been bound in the name, I have not yet been perfected in Jesus Christ. For now I have merely begun to be a disci-

ple and am speaking to you as my fellow learners. For I have needed you to prepare me for the struggle[a] in faith, admonishment, endurance, and patience. 2 But since love does not allow me to be silent concerning you, I decided to encourage you, that you may run together in harmony with the mind of God. For also Jesus Christ, who cannot be distinguished from our life, is the Father's mind, just as also the bishops who have been appointed throughout the world share the mind of Jesus Christ.

4 For this reason it is fitting for you to run together in harmony with the mind of the bishop, which is exactly what you are doing. For your presbytery, which is both worthy of the name and worthy of God, is attuned to the bishop as strings to the lyre. Therefore Jesus Christ is sung in your harmony and symphonic love. 2 And each of you should join the chorus, that by being symphonic in your harmony, taking up God's pitch in unison, you may sing in one voice through Jesus Christ to the Father, that he may both hear and recognize you through the things you do well, since you are members of his Son. Therefore it is useful for you to be in flawless unison, that you may partake of God at all times as well.

5 For since I was able to establish such an intimacy with your bishop so quickly (an intimacy that was not human but spiritual), how much more do I consider you fortunate, you who are mingled together with him as the church is mingled with Jesus Christ and Jesus Christ with the Father, so that all things may be symphonic in unison. 2 Let no one be deceived. Anyone who is not inside the sanctuary lacks the bread of God. For if the prayer of one or two persons has such power, how much more will that of the bishop and the entire church? 3 Therefore the one who does not join the entire congregation is already haughty and passes judgment on himself. For it is written, "God opposes the haughty."[1] And so we should be eager not to oppose the bishop, that we may be subject to God.

6 The more one notices that the bishop is silent, the more he should stand in awe of him. For we must receive everyone that the mas-

---

[a]Literally, *to be anointed by you*

[1]Prov 3:34; cf. Jas 4:6; 1 Pet 5:5

ter of the house sends to take care of his affairs as if he were the sender himself. And so we are clearly obliged to look upon the bishop as the Lord himself. 2 Thus Onesimus himself praises you highly for being so well ordered in God, because all of you live according to the truth and no heresy resides among you. On the contrary, you no longer listen to anyone, except one who speaks truthfully about Jesus Christ.

7 For some are accustomed to bear the name in wicked deceit, while acting in ways that are unworthy of God. You must shun them as wild animals. For they are raving dogs who bite when no one is looking. You must guard against them, for they are hard to tame.[b] 2 For there is one physician, both fleshly and spiritual, born and unborn, God come in the flesh, true life in death, from both Mary and God, first subject to suffering and then beyond suffering, Jesus Christ our Lord.

8 And so let no one deceive you, just as you are not deceived, since you belong entirely to God. For when no strife that is able to torment you is rooted within you, then you are living as God wants. I am your lowly scapegoat;[c] I give myself as a sacrificial offering[d] for you Ephesians, a church of eternal renown. 2 Those who belong to the flesh cannot do spiritual things, nor can those who belong to the spirit do fleshly things;[2] so too, faith cannot do what is faithless nor can faithlessness do what is faithful. But even what you do according to the flesh is spiritual, for you do all things in Jesus Christ.

9 I have learned that some people have passed through on their way from there with an evil teaching. But you did not permit them to sow any seeds among you, plugging your ears so as not to receive anything sown by them. You are stones of the Father's temple, prepared for the building of God the Father. For you are being carried up to the heights by the crane of Jesus Christ, which is the cross, using as a cable the Holy Spirit; and your faith is your hoist, and love is the path that carries you up to God.

2 And so you are all traveling companions bearing God, bearing the temple, bearing Christ, and bearing the holy things, adorned in every way with the commandments of Jesus Christ. I exult in you, since I have been deemed worthy through the things that I write to speak with you and to rejoice together with you; for you love nothing in human life but God alone.

10 Constantly pray for others; for there is still hope that they may repent so as to attain to God. And so, allow them to learn from you, at least by your deeds.[e] 2 In response to their anger, show meekness; to their boasting, be humble; to their blasphemies, offer up prayers; to their wandering in error, be firmly rooted in faith; to their savage behavior, act civilized. Do not be eager to imitate their example. 3 We should be found their brothers through gentleness. And we should be eager to imitate the Lord. Who was mistreated more than he? Or defrauded? Or rejected? Do this, so that no weed planted by the Devil may be found in you and you may abide in Jesus Christ both in the flesh and in the spirit, with all holiness and self-control.

11 These are the end times. And so we should feel shame and stand in fear of God's patience, that it not turn into our judgment. For we should either fear the wrath that is coming or love the gracious gift that is already here—one or the other, so long as we acquire true life by being found in Christ Jesus. 2 Apart from him nothing should seem right to you. In him I am bearing my chains, which are spiritual pearls; in them I hope to rise again, through your prayer. May I always have a share of it! Then I will be found to share the lot of the Ephesian Christians, who have always agreed with the apostles by the power of Jesus Christ.

12 I know who I am and to whom I am writing. I am condemned, you have been shown mercy; I am in danger, you are secure. 2 You are a passageway for those slain for God; you are fellow initiates with Paul, the holy one who received a testimony and proved worthy of all fortune. When I attain to God, may I be found in his footsteps, this one who mentions you in every epistle in Christ Jesus.

13 Be eager, therefore, to come together more frequently to give thanks and glory[f] to God. For when you frequently gather as a con-

---

[b]Or *difficult to cure*   [c]Or *your humble servant*; literally, *your offscouring*   [d]Or *I dedicate myself*   [e]Meaning obscure   [f]Or *to celebrate the eucharist and give glory*

[2]Rom 8:5, 8

gregation, the powers of Satan are destroyed, and his destructive force is vanquished by the harmony of your faith. 2 Nothing is better than peace, by which every battle is abolished, whether waged by those in heaven or by those on earth.

14 None of these things escapes your notice if you completely adhere to the faith and love that are in Jesus Christ. This is the beginning and end of life: faith is the beginning, love is the end. And the two together in unity are God; all other things that lead to nobility of character follow. 2 No one who professes faith sins, nor does anyone hate after acquiring love. The tree is known by its fruit;[3] so those who profess to belong to Christ will be seen by what they do. For the deed is not a matter of profession in the present but of being found in the power of faith at the end.[g]

15 It is better to be silent and to exist than to speak and not exist. It is good to teach, if the one who speaks also acts. For there was one teacher who spoke and it happened.[4] And the things he has done while remaining silent are worthy of the Father. 2 The one who truly possesses the word of Jesus is able to hear his silence as well. He will, as a result, be perfect, acting through what he says and being understood through what he does not say.[h]

3 Nothing escapes the notice of the Lord, but even what we have kept hidden is near to him. And so, we should do everything knowing that he is dwelling within us, that we may be his temples and he our God in us,[5] as in fact he is. And he will be made visible before our eyes. For these reasons, let us love him in an upright way.

16 Do not be deceived, my brothers; those who corrupt their households will not inherit the kingdom of God.[6] 2 If then those who do such things according to the flesh die, how much more the one who corrupts the faith of God through an evil teaching, the faith for which Jesus Christ was crucified? Such a person is filthy and will depart into the unquenchable fire; so too the one who listens to him.

17 For this reason the Lord received perfumed ointment on his head,[7] that he might breathe immortality into the church. Do not be anointed with the stench of the teaching of the ruler of this age, lest he take you captive from the life set before you. 2 Why do we all not become wise by receiving the knowledge of God, which is Jesus Christ? Why do we foolishly perish, remaining ignorant of the gracious gift the Lord has truly sent?

18 My spirit is a sacrificial offering bound to the cross,[i] which is a scandal to those who do not believe but salvation and eternal life to us. Where is the one who is wise? Where is the debater?[8] Where is the boast of those called intelligent? 2 For our God, Jesus Christ, was conceived by Mary according to the plan of God; he was from the seed of David, but also from the Holy Spirit. He was born and baptized, that he might cleanse the water by his suffering.

19 The virginity of Mary and her giving birth escaped the notice of the ruler of this age; so too did the death of the Lord—three mysteries of a cry which were accomplished in the silence of God. 2 How then did he become manifest to the aeons?[j] A star in the sky shone brighter than all the stars. Its light was indescribable and its novelty created astonishment. All the other stars, along with the sun and the moon, formed a chorus to that star, and its light surpassed all the others. And there was a disturbance over whence it had come, this novel thing, so different from the others. 3 Hence all magic was vanquished and every bondage of evil came to nought. Ignorance was destroyed and the ancient realm was brought to ruin, when God became manifest in a human way, for the newness of eternal life. And that which had been prepared by God received its beginning. From that time on, all things were put in commotion because the dissolution of death was taking place.

20 If Jesus Christ finds me worthy through your prayer and it be his will, in the second small book that I am about to write you I will show you plainly what I have begun to discuss about the divine plan that leads to the new person Jesus Christ, involving his faithfulness and love, his suffering and resurrection. 2 I will especially do so if the Lord shows me that all of you to a per-

---

[g]Meaning obscure   [h]Or *being recognized through keeping silent*
[i]Literally, *scapegoat of the cross*; or *offscouring of the cross*
[j]Or *ages*; or *world*

[3]Matt 12:33   [4]Ps 33:9   [5]Cf. 1 Cor 3:16   [6]Cf. 1 Cor 6:9   [7]Matt 26:7; Mark 14:3   [8]1 Cor 1:20, 23

son are gathering together one by one[k] in God's grace, in one faith and in Jesus Christ—who is from the race of David according to the flesh, and is both son of man and son of God—so that you may obey the bishop and the presbytery (which is undistracted in mind), breaking one bread, which is a medicine that brings immortality, an antidote that allows us not to die but to live at all times in Jesus Christ.

21 I am giving my life for you, and for those you sent to Smyrna for the honor of God.

I am writing you from there, giving thanks to the Lord and loving Polycarp as also I love you. Remember me as Jesus Christ remembers you. 2 Pray on behalf of the church in Syria; I am being taken from there to Rome in chains—even though I am the least of those who believe there—since I have been deemed worthy to be found honorable to God. Farewell in God the Father and in Jesus Christ, our mutual hope.

[k]Meaning obscure

The Letter of Ignatius to the Magnesians

Ignatius's letter to the Magnesians is similar in many ways to his letter to the Ephesians (see the Introduction to that selection). It too was written from Smyrna (15:1), a stopping point along Ignatius's journey to martyrdom in Rome. It too is a response to the support shown Ignatius by the church: The Magnesians had sent a four-person delegation to meet with him, headed by their bishop, Damas.

Here too Ignatius stresses the need for the members of the church to live in harmony with one another and with their bishop. In particular, he is concerned that the Magnesian Christians not look down upon their bishop for his youthfulness (3:1). They are to "render him all due respect according to the power of God the Father" (3:1), they are to "be submissive" to him (13:2), they are to allow him to preside "in the place of God" (6:1). Under the bishop are the "elders" or "presbyters," whom Ignatius insists are to be respected as the apostles themselves (6:1).

The Magnesian delegation had evidently informed Ignatius of "false teaching" in their midst, and he writes the congregation to be wary of it. In this instance, unlike the letter to the Ephesians, we learn something about the nature of the problem. There were some members of the congregation who were urging Christians to adopt Jewish customs (8:1; 9:1; 10:3). For Ignatius, this idea is "outlandish" (10:3); for Christianity, he claims, is not based on Judaism, but Judaism on Christianity (10:3). Indeed, for Ignatius, "if we have lived according to Judaism until now, we admit that we have not received God's gracious gift" (8:1). For even the prophets of the Jewish Scriptures were persecuted for proclaiming that the one true God has "manifested himself through Jesus Christ his Son" (8:2). This letter thus shows that already by the early second century Christians had begun to claim that the Hebrew Bible was a Christian, not a Jewish, book.

Ignatius, who is also called God-bearer, to the one that has been blessed by the gracious gift of God the Father in Christ Jesus our Savior, in whom I greet the church that is in Magnesia on the Meander and extend warmest greetings in God the Father and in Jesus Christ.

1 Knowing the great orderliness of your godly love, I have joyfully decided to speak with you in the faith of Jesus Christ. 2 For since I have been made worthy of a most godly name, by the bonds that I bear I sing the praises of the churches, praying that they may experience the unity of the flesh and spirit of Jesus Christ—our constant life—and of faith and love, to which nothing is preferred, and (more important still) of Jesus and the Father. If we endure in him all the abusive treatment of the ruler of this age and escape, we will attain to God.

2 Since, then, I have been found worthy to see you through Damas, your bishop who is worthy of God, through your worthy presbyters Bassus and Apollonius, and through my fellow slave, the deacon Zotion—whom I hope to enjoy, for he is subject to the bishop as to the grace of God, and to the presbytery as to the law of Jesus Christ.

3 But it is not right for you to take advantage of your bishop because of his age. You should render him all due respect according to the power of God the Father, just as I have learned that even your holy presbyters have not exploited his seemingly youthful appearance;[a] but they have deferred to him as one who is wise in God—and not to him, but to the Father of Jesus Christ, the bishop of all. 2 And so it is fitting for us to be obedient apart from all hypocrisy, for the honor of the one who has desired us. For it is not that a person deceives this bishop who is seen, but he deals falsely with the one who is invisible. In such a case, an account must be rendered not to human flesh, but to God, who knows the things that are hidden.

4 And so it is fitting not only to be called Christians, but also to be Christians, just as there are some who call a person the bishop but do everything without him. Such persons do not seem to me to be acting in good conscience, because they do not hold valid meetings in accordance with the commandment.

5 Since, then, these matters have an end, and the two things are set together, death and life, and each person is about to depart to his own place— 2 for just as there are two kinds of coin, one from God and the other from the world, and each of them has its own stamp set upon it: the unbelievers the stamp of this world and the believers the stamp of God the Father, in love, through Jesus Christ. If we do not choose to die voluntarily in his suffering, his life is not in us.

6 Since, then, I have observed, by the eyes of faith, your entire congregation through those I have already mentioned, and loved it, I urge you to hasten to do all things in the harmony of God, with the bishop presiding in the place of God and the presbyters in the place of the council of the apostles, and the deacons, who are especially dear to me, entrusted with the ministry of Jesus Christ,

who was with the Father before the ages and has been manifest at the end.

2 You should assume the character of God and all respect one another. No one should consider his neighbor in a fleshly way, but you should love one another in Jesus Christ at all times. Let there be nothing among you that can divide you, but be unified with the bishop and with those who preside according to the model and teaching of incorruptibility.

7 And so, just as the Lord did nothing apart from the Father—being united with him—neither on his own nor through the apostles, so too you should do nothing apart from the bishop and the presbyters. Do not try to maintain that it is reasonable for you to do something among yourselves in private;[b] instead, for the common purpose, let there be one prayer, one petition, one mind, one hope in love and in blameless joy, which is Jesus Christ. Nothing is superior to him.

2 You should all run together, as into one temple of God, as upon one altar, upon one Jesus Christ, who came forth from one Father and was with the one[c] and returned to the one.[1]

8 Do not be deceived by false opinions[d] or old fables that are of no use. For if we have lived according to Judaism until now, we admit that we have not received God's gracious gift. 2 For the most divine prophets lived according to Jesus Christ. For this reason also they were persecuted. But they were inspired by his gracious gift, so that the disobedient became fully convinced that there is one God, who manifested himself through Jesus Christ his Son, who is his Word that came forth from silence, who was pleasing in every way to the one who sent him.

9 And so those who lived according to the old ways came to a new hope, no longer keeping the sabbath but living according to the Lord's day, on which also our life arose through him and his death—which some deny. Through this mystery we came to believe, and for this reason we endure, that we may be found to be disciples of Jesus Christ, our only teacher. 2 How then are we able to live apart from him? Even the prophets who

[a]Or *rank*; or *position*   [b]Meaning obscure   [c]Or *and was one with him*
[d]Literally, *heterodoxies*

[1]Cf. John 16:28

were his disciples in the spirit awaited him as their teacher. And for this reason, the one they righteously expected raised them from the dead when he arrived.

10 We should not fail to perceive his kindness. For if he were to imitate our actions, we would no longer exist. For this reason, since we are his disciples, let us learn to live according to Christianity. For whoever is called by a name other than this does not belong to God. 2 So lay aside the bad yeast, which has grown old and sour, and turn to the new yeast, which is Jesus Christ. Be salted in him, that no one among you become rotten; for you will be shown for what you are by your smell. 3 It is outlandish to proclaim Jesus Christ and practice Judaism. For Christianity did not believe in Judaism, but Judaism in Christianity—in which every tongue that believes in God has been gathered together.[2]

11 I am not writing these things, my beloved, because I have learned that some of you are behaving like this. But as one who is less important than you I want to protect you from being snagged by the fish hooks of worthless ideas. You should be fully convinced of the birth and suffering and resurrection that occurred in the time of the governor Pontius Pilate. These things were truly and certainly done by Jesus Christ, our hope. From this hope may none of you turn away.

12 May I enjoy you in every way, if I should be worthy. For even though I am in chains, I am not worth one of you who is free. I know you are not haughty; for you have Jesus Christ in you. On the contrary, when I praise you, I know you are respectful. As it is written, "the one who is upright is his own accuser."[3]

13 Be eager therefore to stand securely in the decrees of the Lord and the apostles, that you may prosper in everything you do in flesh and spirit, in faith and love, in the Son and the Father and in the Spirit, in the beginning and end, along with your most worthy bishop and your presbytery, which is a spiritual crown worthily woven, and your godly deacons. 2 Be submissive to the bishop and to one another—as Jesus Christ was to the Father according to the flesh, and as the apostles were to Christ and to the Father and to the Spirit—so that there may be unity, both fleshly and spiritually.

14 Because I know that you are filled with God, I have exhorted you briefly. Remember me in your prayers, that I may attain to God; and remember the church in Syria, from which I am not worthy to be called. For I am in need of your unified prayer and love in God, that the church in Syria may be deemed worthy to be refreshed with dew through your church.

15 The Ephesians greet you from Smyrna; I am writing you from there. They are here for the glory of God, as you are as well. They have refreshed me in every way, along with Polycarp, the bishop of the Smyrnaeans. And the other churches also greet you in the honor of Jesus Christ. In the harmony of God, farewell to you who have obtained a spirit[e] that is not divided,[f] which is Jesus Christ.

---

[e]Or *Spirit*   [f]Or *is unwavering*

---

[2]Cf. Isa 66:18   [3]Prov 18:17

The Letter of Ignatius to the Trallians

Like his letters to the Ephesians and the Magnesians, Ignatius's letter to the Trallians was sent from Smyrna (12:1) in response to the support he had received. The church in Tralles had sent its bishop, Polybius, to meet with Ignatius on his road to martyrdom (1:1). Having learned about the congregation, Ignatius writes to urge them to stay united and to stand against heresy.

Thus Ignatius urges the Trallians "not [to] angage in any activity apart from the bishop" (2:2) who is the "image the Father" (3:1) and to "be subject also to the presbytery as to the apostles of Jesus Christ," (2:2). He suggests that "the one who does anything apart from the bishop, the presbytery, and the deacons is not pure in conscience" (7:2).

He is also concerned with false teaching in the congregation; but rather than opposing Judaism, as he does in the letter to the Magnesians, here Ignatius warns against those who claim that Jesus "only appeared to suffer" (10:1). These Christians—whom Ignatius labels "atheists" and "unbelievers" (10:1)—evidently maintained that since Jesus was God, he could not have been a real flesh-and-blood human being, capable of being born, suffering, and dying. In response, Ignatius insists that Jesus "was truly born, both ate and drank, was truly persecuted at the time of Pontius Pilate, was truly crucified and died . . . [and] was also truly raised from the dead" (9:1–2).

Ignatius concludes his letter by urging the Trallians to flee false teachings (11:1–2), to continue in their harmony with one another (12:1), to pray for his own situation (12:3) and for the church in Syria that he left behind (13:1), and to be submissive to their bishop and presbytery (13:2).

Ignatius, who is also called God-bearer, to the holy church in Tralles of Asia, beloved of God, the Father of Jesus Christ, chosen and worthy of God, a church made at peace in flesh and spirit by the suffering of Jesus Christ, who is our hope for[a] a resurrection that leads to him, a church which I also greet in fullness in the apostolic manner and to which I extend warmest greetings.

1 I have learned that your way of thinking is blameless and unwavering in endurance, not by force of habit but by your very nature, just as Polybius, your bishop showed me. He arrived in Smyrna by the will of God and Jesus Christ, and so rejoiced together with me, who am in chains in Christ Jesus, so that I saw your entire congregation in him. 2 I was exultant when I received your act of godly kindness through him, for I found that you were imitators of God, as I had known.

2 For when you are subject to the bishop as to Jesus Christ, you appear to me to live not in a human way but according to Jesus Christ, who died for us that you may escape dying by believ-

[a] Or *through*

"The Letter of Ignatius to the Trallians," from *The Apostolic Fathers,* translated by Bart D. Ehrman. Loeb Classical Library: © 2003. Reprinted by permission of Harvard University Press.

ing in his death. 2 And so—as is already the case—you must not engage in any activity apart from the bishop, but be subject also to the presbytery as to the apostles of Jesus Christ, our hope. If we live in him, we will be found in him. 3 And those who are deacons of the mysteries of Jesus Christ must also be pleasing in every way to all people. For they are not deacons dealing with food and drink; they are servants of the church of God. And so they must guard themselves against accusations as against fire.

3 So too let everyone respect the deacons like Jesus Christ, and also the bishop, who is the image of the Father; and let them respect the presbyters like the council of God and the band of the apostles. Apart from these a gathering cannot be called a church. 2 I am convinced that you agree about this. For I have received the embodiment of your love and have it with me in the person of your bishop, whose very deportment is a great lesson and whose meekness is power–who is respected, I believe, even by the godless.

3 I am sparing you out of love, though I could write more sharply about this matter. But I have not thought that I, a condemned man, should give you orders like an apostle.[b]

4 I am thinking many things in God, but I take measure of myself so as not to be destroyed by my boasting. For now I must fear all the more and pay no attention to those who make me self-important. For those who speak to me flog me. 2 For indeed I love to suffer; but I do not know if I am worthy. For envy is not obvious to many, but it is escalating its war against me. And so I need humility, by which the ruler of this age is destroyed.

5 Am I not able to write to you about heavenly things? But I am afraid that I may harm you who are still infants.[1] Grant me this concession—otherwise you may choke, not being able to swallow enough. 2 For not even I am a disciple already, simply because I am in bondage and am able to understand the heavenly realms and the angelic regions and hierarchies of the cosmic rulers, both visible and invisible.[2] For many things are still lacking to us, that we may not be lacking God.

6 Therefore I am urging you—not I, but the love of Jesus Christ: Make use only of Christian food and abstain from a foreign plant, which

is heresy. 2 Even though such persons seem to be trustworthy, they mingle Jesus Christ with themselves, as if giving a deadly drug mixed with honeyed wine, which the unsuspecting gladly takes with evil pleasure, but then dies.

7 Guard against such people. You will be able to do this when you are not haughty and are inseparable from God—that is, Jesus Christ—and from the bishop and from the injunctions of the apostles. 2 The one who is inside the sanctuary is pure, but the one outside the sanctuary is not pure. This means that the one who does anything apart from the bishop, the presbytery, and the deacons is not pure in conscience.

8 It is not that I know of any such problem among you, but I am protecting you, my loved ones, anticipating the snares of the devil. You should therefore take up gentleness and create yourselves anew in faith, which is the flesh of the Lord, and in love, which is the blood of Jesus Christ. 2 Let none of you hold a grudge against your neighbor. Give no occasion to the outsiders[c] lest on account of a few foolish persons the entire congregation in God be slandered. "For woe to that one through whom my name is slandered in vain by some."[3]

9 And so, be deaf when someone speaks to you apart from Jesus Christ, who was from the race of David and from Mary, who was truly born, both ate and drank, was truly persecuted at the time of Pontius Pilate, was truly crucified and died, while those in heaven and on earth and under the earth looked on. 2 He was also truly raised from the dead, his Father having raised him. In the same way his Father will also raise us in Christ Jesus, we who believe in him, apart from whom we do not have true life.

10 But if, as some who are atheists—that is, unbelievers—say, that he only appeared to suffer (it is they who are the appearance), why am I in bondage, and why also do I pray to fight the wild beasts? I am then dying in vain and am, even more, lying about the Lord.

11 Flee therefore the evil offshoots that produce deadly fruit; anyone who tastes it

[b]The text of this verse is corrupt; the translation attempts to convey the sense [c]Literally, *Gentiles*; or *nations*

[1]Cf. 1 Cor. 3:1–2   [2]Cf. Col 1:16   [3]Cf. Isa 52:5

dies at once. For these are not the Father's planting. 2 If they were, they would appear as branches of the cross and their fruit would be imperishable. Through the cross, by his suffering, he calls you who are the parts of his body. Thus the head cannot be born without the other parts, because God promises unity, which he himself is.

12 I greet you from Smyrna, along with the churches of God that are present with me and that have refreshed me in every way, in both flesh and spirit. 2 My chains exhort you; I bear them on account of Jesus Christ, asking that I may attain to God. Remain in your harmony and in prayer with one another. For it is fitting for each one of you, and especially the presbyters, to refresh the bishop for the honor of the Father and of Jesus Christ and of the apostles.

3 I ask you to hear me in love, that I may not be a witness against you by having written. And pray also for me, since I stand in need of your love by God's mercy, that I may be found worthy of the lot I am bound to obtain, lest I be discovered to have failed the test.[4]

13 The love of the Smyrnaeans and of the Ephesians greets you. Remember the church in Syria in your prayers; I am not worthy to be called from there, since I am the least of them. 2 Farewell in Jesus Christ. Be subject to the bishop as to the commandment, and to the presbytery as well. And let each of you love one another with an undivided heart. 3 My own spirit is sacrificed for you, not only now but also when I attain to God. For I am still in danger; but the Father is faithful in Jesus Christ to fulfill my request and yours. In him may you be found blameless.

---

[4]Cf. 1 Cor 9:27

The Letter of Ignatius to the Romans

Ignatius's letter to the Romans is unique among the seven writings that survive from his hand. It is not addressed to a church that had sent delegates to support him en route to his martyrdom, nor to a church with which he had stayed. It is sent instead to the Christians of Rome, his destination. The letter has one overarching purpose: to persuade these Christians not to interfere with Ignatius's approaching martyrdom. Ignatius is bound for the amphitheater, where he will be thrown to the wild beasts; he pleads with the Roman Christians not to hinder the proceedings.

In Ignatius's own words: "I am willingly dying for God, unless you hinder me. I urge you, do not become an untimely kindness to me. Allow me to be bread for the wild beasts; through them I am able to attain to God. I am the wheat of God and am ground by the teeth of the wild beasts, that I may be found to be the pure bread of Christ" (4:1–2). Some of Ignatius's rhetoric has struck modern readers as almost pathological: "May I have the full pleasure of the wild beasts prepared for me . . . I will coax them to devour me quickly . . . And even if they do not wish to do so willingly, I will force them to it . . . Fire and cross and packs of wild beasts, cuttings and being torn apart, the scattering of bones, the mangling of limbs, the grinding of the whole body, the evil torments of the devil—let them come upon me, only that I may attain to Jesus Christ (5:2–3).

In any event, the reason for Ignatius's passionate longing for death is reasonably clear. Ignatius claims to have no desire to live in this world (7:3); he wants to leave it so that he can "attain to God" (4:1). Moreover, just as Christ suffered a violent death, so must he, if he wants "truly [to] be a disciple of Jesus Christ" (4:2). Only then will he "be an imitator of the suffering of my God" (6:3). In particular, Ignatius appears concerned that his nerves may fail him when he actually arrives in Rome,. And so he beseeches the Christian community there in advance to not to intervene on his behalf (1:2), "even if I urge you otherwise when I arrive" (7:2).

As with the letters to the Ephesians, Magnesians, and Trallians, this letter was written from Smyrna; unlike them, it is dated, August 24 (10:3). We are not told the year, but most scholars put it around 110 C.E.

Ignatius, who is also called God-bearer, to the church that has obtained mercy by the greatness of the Father Most High and Jesus Christ his only Son; the church that is loved and enlightened by the will of the one who has willed everything that is, according to the faith and love of Jesus Christ, our God; the church that is presiding in the land of the Romans, worthy of God, worthy of honor, worthy of blessing, worthy of praise, worthy of success, worthy of holiness, and preeminent in love, a church that keeps the law of Christ and bears the name of the Father; this is the church that I greet in the name of Jesus Christ, the Son of the Father. And I extend warmest greetings blame-

"The Letter of Ignatius to the Romans," from *The Apostolic Fathers,* translated by Bart D. Ehrman. Loeb Classical Library; © 2003. Reprinted by permission of Harvard University Press.

lessly in Jesus Christ, our God, to those who are united in both flesh and spirit in his every commandment, filled with the gracious gift of God without wavering, and filtered from every unsuitable taint.

1 Since by my prayer to God I have managed to see your faces, which are worthy of God—as indeed I have asked to receive even more, for I hope to greet you while in chains in Christ Jesus, if indeed it be the will of the one who has made me worthy to endure until the end. 2 For the beginning is auspicious, if I can indeed obtain the gracious gift I need in order to receive my lot without any impediment. For I am afraid of your love, that it may do me harm. For it is easy for you to do what you want, but it is difficult for me to attain to God, if you do not spare me.

2 For I do not want you to please people but to please God,[1] as indeed you are doing. For I will have no other such opportunity to attain to God, nor can you be enlisted for a better work—if, that is, you keep silent. For if you keep silent about me, I will be a word of God; but if you desire my flesh, I will once again be a mere noise. 2 But grant me nothing more than to be poured out as a libation to God while there is still an altar at hand, that by becoming a chorus in love, you may sing forth to the Father in Jesus Christ, saying that God has deemed the bishop of Syria worthy to be found at the setting of the sun, after sending him from where it rises. For it is good for me to set from the world to God, that I may rise up to him.

3 At no time have you been envious of anyone; instead you have taught others. But my wish is that the instructions you enjoin on others be firm, when you make them disciples.[a] 2 For me, ask only that I have power both inside and out, that I not only speak but also have the desire, that I not only be called a Christian but also be found one. For if I be found a Christian, I can also be called one and then be faithful—when I am no longer visible in the world. 3 Nothing that is visible is good. For our God Jesus Christ, since he is in the Father, is all the more visible.[b] The work is not a matter of persuasion, but Christianity is a matter of greatness, when it is hated by the world.[c]

4 I am writing all the churches and giving instruction to all, that I am willingly dying for God, unless you hinder me. I urge you, do not be-

come an untimely kindness to me. Allow me to be bread for the wild beasts; through them I am able to attain to God. I am the wheat of God and am ground by the teeth of the wild beasts, that I may be found to be the pure bread of Christ. 2 Rather, coax the wild beasts, that they may become a tomb for me and leave no part of my body behind, that I may burden no one once I have died. Then I will truly be a disciple of Jesus Christ, when the world does not see even my body. Petition Christ on my behalf, that I may be found a sacrifice through these instruments of God. 3 I am not enjoining you as Peter and Paul did. They were apostles, I am condemned; they were free, until now I have been a slave. But if I suffer, I will become a freed person who belongs to Jesus Christ, and I will rise up, free, in him. In the meantime I am learning to desire nothing while in chains.

5 From Syria to Rome I have been fighting the wild beasts, through land and sea, night and day, bound to ten leopards, which is a company of soldiers, who become worse when treated well. But I am becoming more of a disciple by their mistreatment. Still, it is not because of this that I have been made upright.[2] 2 May I have the full pleasure of the wild beasts prepared for me; I pray they will be found ready for me. Indeed, I will coax them to devour me quickly—not as happens with some, whom they are afraid to touch. And even if they do not wish to do so willingly, I will force them to it. 3 Grant this to me; I know what benefits me. Now I am beginning to be a disciple. May nothing visible or invisible show any envy toward me, that I may attain to Jesus Christ. Fire and cross and packs of wild beasts, cuttings and being torn apart, the scattering of bones, the mangling of limbs, the grinding of the whole body, the evil torments of the devil—let them come upon me, only that I may attain to Jesus Christ.

6 Neither the ends of the world nor the kingdoms of this age will benefit me in the least. It is better for me to die in Jesus Christ than to rule the ends of the earth. That is the one I seek, who died on our behalf; that is the one I desire, who arose for us. But pains of birth have come upon

[a]Meaning obscure [b]Meaning obscure [c]Meaning obscure

[1]Cf. 2 Thess 2:4 [2]1 Cor 4:4

me. 2 Grant this to me, brothers: Do not keep me from living; do not wish me to die; do not hand over to the world the one who wants to belong to God or deceive him by what is material. Allow me to receive the pure light; when I have arrived there, I will be a human. 3 Allow me to be an imitator of the suffering of my God. If anyone has him within himself, let him both understand what I want and sympathize with me, realizing the things that constrain me.

7 The ruler of this age wishes to snatch me away and corrupt my mind, which is directed toward God. And so let none of you who are present assist him; rather be on my side—that is, on God's. Do not speak about Jesus Christ but long for the world. 2 Let no envy dwell among you. Even if I urge you otherwise when I arrive, do not be persuaded; instead be persuaded by what I am writing you now. For I write to you while living, desiring to die. My passion has been crucified[3] and there is no burning love within me for material things; instead there is living water,[4] which also is speaking in me, saying to me from within: "Come to the Father." 3 I have no pleasure in the food that perishes nor in the pleasures of this life. I desire the bread of God, which is the flesh of Jesus Christ, from the seed of David; and for drink I desire his blood, which is imperishable love.

8 I no longer desire to live like a human; and I will succeed, if you also desire it. Desire it, that you may also be desired. 2 Through just a few words I ask you: trust me! Jesus Christ will show you that I speak the truth. He is the mouth that does not lie, by whom the Father spoke the truth. 3 Pray for me, that I may attain to God. I have not written you according to the flesh but according to the mind of God. If I suffer, you have desired it; if I am rejected, you have hated me.

9 In your prayer remember the church of Syria, which has God as its shepherd in my place. Jesus Christ alone will oversee it,[d] along with your love. 2 But I am ashamed to be called one of them; for I am not at all worthy, as the least of them and a miscarriage.[5] But I have found mercy to be someone, if I attain to God.

3 My spirit greets you, as does the love of the churches that received me in the name of Jesus Christ, and not just as one passing by. For even those that did not lie on my actual route went ahead of me from city to city.

10 I am writing this to you from Smyrna, through the Ephesians, who are worthy to be blessed. Along with many others, Crocus is with me, a name that is dear to me. 2 I believe you know about those who have preceded me from Syria to Rome for the glory of God. Tell them I am near. For they are all worthy of God and of you. It is fitting for you to refresh them in every way. 3 I am writing this to you on August 24.[e] Farewell until the end, in the endurance of Jesus Christ.

[d]Or: *be its bishop*   [e]Literally, *on the ninth day before the calends of September*

---

[3]Cf. Gal 6:14   [4]Cf. John 4:10, 14   [5]1 Cor 15:8–9

The Letter of Ignatius to the Philadelphians

After Ignatius left Smyrna, he passed through the Asia Minor city of Philadelphia, spending time with the church there before journeying on to Troas, still en route to his martyrdom in Rome (Ign Phil 6:3–7:1). It was from Troas that he wrote a letter back to the Philadelphians through his traveling companion, Burrhus, a Christian from Ephesus (11:2).

Most of the themes sounded in Ignatius's earlier letters are present here as well. He speaks highly of the bishop of Philadelphia (whom he does not name), being particularly impressed with his quiet strength (1:1) and upright life (1:2). He writes to the church that it needs to be united behind the bishop. It appears that while among them, Ignatius had seen divisions; at the time, he claims, he tried to resolve the problems, "acting on my own accord as a person set on unity" (8:1). The divisions, he believed, had a simple solution: "I cried out while among you, speaking in a great voice, the voice of God, 'Pay attention to the bishop and the presbytery and the deacons'" (7:1). He urged the community to "do nothing apart from the bishop; keep your flesh as the temple of God; love unity; flee divisions" (7:2).

The divisions were evidently rooted in different theological and practical perspectives advanced by some members of the congregation. Among the Philadelphians were Gentile believers who had come to think that Christians needed to follow the practices of Judaism. This was a position toward which Ignatius showed little sympathy: "if anyone should interpret Judaism to you, do not hear him. For it is better to hear Christianity from a man who is circumcised than Judaism from one who is uncircumcised" (6:1). While his opponents claimed not to accept anything as true that was not supported in their "ancient records," the Hebrew Bible, Ignatius claimed that "Jesus Christ is the ancient records" (8:2). For him, the Old Testament patriarchs and prophets were looking forward to Christ and themselves had salvation only through Christ (9:1–2).

The letter concludes with an expression of gratitude that his own church, in Antioch of Syria, had begun to enjoy peace, as the divisions earlier evidenced there had been resolved. Ignatius hopes that the Philadelphian church can send an ambassador to convey its congratulations (10:1).

Ignatius, who is also called God-bearer, to the church of God the Father and of the Lord Jesus Christ that is in Philadelphia of Asia, that has received mercy and been founded in the harmony that comes from God, that rejoices without wavering in the suffering of our Lord and that is fully convinced by all mercy in his resurrection; this is the church that I greet by the blood of Jesus Christ, which is an eternal and enduring joy, especially if they are at one with the bishop and with the presbyters with him, and with the deacons who have been appointed in accordance with the mind of Jesus Christ—those who have been securely set in place by his Holy Spirit according to his own will.

1 I have learned that your bishop did not obtain his ministry to the community[a] from himself, nor through humans, nor according to pure vanity, but by the love of God the Father and the Lord Jesus Christ. I have been amazed at his gentleness; by being silent he can do more than those who speak idle thoughts. 2 For he is attuned to the commandments like a lyre to the strings. For this reason my soul blesses his mind fixed in God—knowing it to be virtuous and perfect— along with his solid and anger-free character, manifest in all gentleness, which comes from the living God.

2 Therefore, children of the light of truth, flee division and evil teachings. Where the shepherd is, there you should follow as sheep. 2 For many seemingly trustworthy wolves use wicked pleasure to capture those who run in God's race; but they will have no place in your unity.

3 Abstain from evil plants which Jesus Christ does not cultivate, since they are not a planting of the Father. Not that I found a division among you, but a filter. 2 For all who belong to God and Jesus Christ are with the bishop, and all those who come into the unity of the church through repentance will belong to God, so that they may live according to Jesus Christ. 3 Do not be deceived my brothers; no one who follows someone creating a schism will inherit the kingdom of God;[1] anyone who thinks otherwise does not agree with the Passion.

4 And so be eager to celebrate just one eucharist. For there is one flesh of our Lord Jesus Christ and one cup that brings the unity of his blood, and one altar, as there is one bishop together with the presbytery and the deacons, my fellow slaves. Thus, whatever you do, do according to God.

5 My brothers, I am completely overflowing with love for you and out of extreme joy am I watching over you—not I, but Jesus Christ. Even though I bear my chains in him, I am even more afraid, since I am still not perfected. But your prayer to God will perfect me, so that I may attain to God by the lot that I have been mercifully assigned, when I flee to the gospel as to the flesh of Jesus and to the apostles as to the presbytery of the church. 2 And we should also love the prophets, because their proclamation anticipated the gospel and they hoped in him and awaited him. And they were saved by believing in him, because they stood in the unity of Jesus Christ, saints who were worthy of love and admiration, who were testified to by Jesus Christ and counted as belonging to the gospel of our mutual hope.

6 But if anyone should interpret Judaism to you, do not hear him. For it is better to hear Christianity from a man who is circumcised than Judaism from one who is uncircumcised. But if neither one speaks about Jesus Christ, they both appear to me as monuments and tombs of the dead, on which are written merely human names. 2 And so flee the evil designs and snares of the ruler of this age, lest being oppressed by his way of thinking you be weakened in love. But all of you should stand in agreement with an undivided heart. 3 I thank my God that I have a good conscience among you and that no one can boast against me, whether in secret or in public, that I burdened anyone in either a trifling matter or great. But I pray that none of those who heard me speak may encounter my word as a witness against himself.

7 For even if some people have wanted to deceive me according to the flesh, the Spirit is not deceived, since it comes from God. For it knows whence it comes and where it is going, and it exposes the things that are hidden.[2] I cried out while among you, speaking in a great voice, the

---

[a]Or *for the common good*

[1]Cf. 1 Cor 6:9–10   [2]Cf. John 3:8; 1 Cor. 2:10

voice of God, "Pay attention to the bishop and the presbytery and the deacons." 2 But some suspected that I said these things because I knew in advance that there was a division among you. But the one in whom I am bound is my witness that I knew it from no human source; but the Spirit was preaching, saying, "Do nothing apart from the bishop; keep your flesh as the Temple of God; love unity; flee divisions; be imitators of Jesus Christ as he is of his Father."

8 I was therefore acting on my own accord as a person set on unity. But where there is division and anger, God does not dwell. Thus the Lord forgives all who repent, if they return[b] to the unity of God and the council of the bishop. I believe in the gracious gift that comes from Jesus Christ, who will loose every bond from you.

2 But I urge you to do nothing in a contentious way, but in accordance with what you have learned in Christ. For I heard some saying, "If I do not find it in the ancient records, I do not believe in the gospel." And when I said to them, "It is written," they replied to me, "That is just the question." But for me, Jesus Christ is the ancient records; the sacred ancient records are his cross and death, and his resurrection, and the faith that comes through him—by which things I long to be made righteous by your prayer.

9 The priests are good, but the high priest who has been entrusted with the holy of holies is better; he alone is entrusted with the hidden things that belong to God. He is the door of the Father,[3] through which Abraham and Isaac and Jacob and the prophets and the apostles and the church enter. All these things are bound together in the unity of God. 2 But there is something distinct about the gospel—that is, the coming of the Savior, our Lord Jesus Christ, his suffering and resurrection. For the beloved prophets made their proclamation looking ahead to him; but the gospel is the com-

pletion of immortality.[c] All things together are good, if you believe while showing forth love.

10 Since it has been reported to me that the church of God in Antioch of Syria is at peace—in accordance with your prayer and the compassion that you have in Christ Jesus—it is fitting for you as the church of God to elect a deacon to go as an ambassador of God there, that you may rejoice together with those who have achieved a common purpose and so give glory to the name. 2 Most fortunate in Jesus Christ is the one who will be considered worthy of this ministry, and you too will be glorified. And for you who wish to do this, on behalf of the name of God, it is not an impossible task, since the churches that are nearer have even sent bishops, while others have sent presbyters and deacons.

11 But concerning Philo, the deacon from Cilicia, a man who has received a good testimony and who now serves me in the word of God along with Rheus Agathopous, one of the elect who is following me from Syria, who has bid farewell to life—these also bear testimony to you. And I thank God for you that you welcomed them as also the Lord welcomed you. But may those who dishonored them be redeemed by the gracious gift that comes from Jesus Christ. 2 The love of the brothers in Troas greets you; it is from there that I am writing you through Burrhus, who has been sent together with me from the Ephesians and Smyrneans as a pledge of honor. The Lord Jesus Christ will honor them; in him they hope, in flesh, soul, spirit, faith, love, and harmony. Farewell in Christ Jesus, our mutual hope.

---

[b]Literally, *repent*   [c]Or *incorrupt completion*; or *completion that leads to incorruption*; meaning obscure

---

[3]Cf. John 10:7, 9

The Letter of Ignatius to the Smyrneans

Ignatius had evidently gotten to know the church at Smyrna rather well during his stay there. After leaving town, he traveled to Troas, where he wrote a letter (12:1), greeting a number of the Smyrnean Christians (13:1–2) and urging them to avoid heresy and to remain united behind their bishop.

Ignatius is particularly concerned over those who claimed that Jesus' passion was only a sham—that is, that Jesus was not an actual flesh-and-blood human being who really suffered (2:1). Ignatius denies that such persons are "believers" (2:1) and warns his readers not even to meet and talk with them (4:1). In opposition to their views, Ignatius insists that Jesus was "truly born" (1:1) and was "truly nailed for us in the flesh" (1:2), he "truly suffered" and "truly raised himself" (2:1). Even after his resurrection he was "in the flesh" (3:1), as evidenced by the fact that his disciples touched him and saw him eat and drink (3:2–3).

Ignatius is deeply troubled by this Christological issue, in part because it relates to his own situation. He himself is on the road to martyrdom; if Christ did not actually suffer in the flesh, there would be little reason for Ignatius himself to do so: "If these things were accomplished by our Lord only in appearance, I also am in chains only in appearance. But why then have I handed myself over to death, to fire, to the sword, to wild beasts?" (4:2).

The community can best withstand these pernicious teachers, in Ignatius's view, by uniting behind their bishop, the representative of God among the congregation. Whoever "honors the bishop is honored by God," whereas anyone "who does anything behind the bishop's back serves the devil" (9:1). No one, therefore, should be allowed to conduct baptisms or eucharistic meals without the bishop present (8:1).

Near the end of the letter Ignatius enjoins the church to send a delegate to his own church in Antioch, with a letter to "exult with them in the tranquility that has come to them from God" (11:3); he concludes by sending final greetings to members of the congregation he had come to know during his time among them (13:1–2).

Ignatius, who is also called God-bearer, to the church of God the Father and the beloved Jesus Christ which is in Smyrna of Asia, which has been shown mercy in every gracious gift, filled with faith and love, and lacking no gracious gift, a church that is most worthy of God and bears what is holy. Warmest greetings in a blameless spirit and the word of God.

1 I give glory to Jesus Christ, the God who has made you so wise. For I know that you have been made complete in a faith that cannot be moved—as if you were nailed to the cross of the Lord Jesus Christ in both flesh and spirit—and that you have been established in love by the blood of Christ. For you are fully convinced about our Lord, that he was truly from the family of David according to the flesh, Son of God according to the will and power of God, truly born from a virgin, and baptized by John that all righteousness might be fulfilled by him.[1] 2 In the time of Pontius Pilate and the tetrarch Herod, he was truly nailed for us in the flesh—we ourselves come from the fruit of his divinely blessed suffering—so that through his resurrection he might eternally[a] lift up the standard for his holy and faithful ones, whether among Jews or Gentiles, in the one body of his church.

2 For he suffered all these things for our sake, that we might be saved; and he truly suffered, just as he also truly raised himself—not as some unbelievers say, that he suffered only in appearance. They are the ones who are only an appearance; and it will happen to them just as they think, since they are without bodies, like the daimons.

3 For I know and believe that he was in the flesh even after the resurrection. 2 And when he came to those who were with Peter, he said to them, "Reach out, handle me and see that I am not a bodiless daimon."[2] And immediately they touched him and believed, having been intermingled with his flesh and spirit. For this reason they also despised death, for they were found to be beyond death. 3 And after his resurrection he ate and drank with them as a fleshly being, even though he was spiritually united with the Father.

4 I am advising you about these things, beloved, even though I know that you already agree. But I am guarding you ahead of time from the wild beasts in human form. Not only should you refrain from welcoming such people, if possible you should not even meet with them. Instead pray for them that they might somehow repent, though even this is difficult. But Jesus Christ, our true life, has authority over this. 2 For if these things were accomplished by our Lord only in appearance, I also am in chains only in appearance. But why then have I handed myself over to death, to fire, to the sword, to wild beasts? But to be near the sword is to be near God, to be in the presence

of the wild beasts is to be in the presence of God—so long as it is in the name of Jesus Christ. I am enduring all things in order to suffer along with him, while he, the one who became the perfect human, empowers me.

5 Some deny him out of ignorance, or rather, they are denied by him: These are public advocates of death, not truth. They have been convinced neither by the words of the prophets nor the Law of Moses, nor, until now, by the gospel, nor by the suffering each of us has experienced. 2 For they think the same things about us. For how does anyone benefit me if he praises me but blasphemes my Lord, not confessing that he bore flesh? The one who refuses to say this denies him completely, as one who bears a corpse. 3 But I see no point in recording their disbelieving names. I do not even want to recall them, until they repent concerning the Passion, which is our resurrection.

6 Let no one be deceived. Judgment is prepared even for the heavenly beings, for the glory of the angels, and for the rulers both visible and invisible, if they do not believe in the blood of Christ. Let the one who can receive this receive it.[3] Let no one become haughty because of his position. For faith and love are everything; nothing is preferable to them.

2 But take note of those who spout false opinions[b] about the gracious gift of Jesus Christ that has come to us, and see how they are opposed to the mind of God. They have no interest in love, in the widow, the orphan, the oppressed, the one who is in chains or the one set free, the one who is hungry or the one who thirsts.

7 They abstain from the eucharist and prayer, since they do not confess that the eucharist is the flesh of our savior Jesus Christ, which suffered on behalf of our sins and which the Father raised in his kindness. And so, those who dispute the gift of God perish while still arguing the point. It would be better for them to engage in acts of love, that they might also rise up. 2 And so it is fitting to avoid such people and not even to speak about them, either privately or in public, but in-

---

[a]Or *for the cosmic rulers*; literally *unto the aeons*   [b]Literally, *heterodoxies*

[1]Cf. Matt 3:15   [2]Cf. Luke 24:39   [3]Matt 19:12

stead to pay attention to the prophets, and especially to the gospel, in which the passion is clearly shown to us and the resurrection is perfected. But flee divisions as the beginning of evils.

8 All of you should follow the bishop as Jesus Christ follows the Father; and follow the presbytery as you would the apostles. Respect the deacons as the commandment of God. Let no one do anything involving the church without the bishop. Let that eucharist be considered valid that occurs under the bishop or the one to whom he entrusts it. 2 Let the congregation be wherever the bishop is; just as wherever Jesus Christ is, there also is the universal[c] church. It is not permitted either to baptize or to hold a love feast without the bishop. But whatever he approves is acceptable to God, so that everything you do should be secure and valid.

9 Finally, it is reasonable for us to return to sobriety, while we still have time to repent to God. It is good to know both God and the bishop. The one who honors the bishop is honored by God; the one who does anything behind the bishop's back serves the devil.

2 Let all things abound to you in grace, for you are worthy. You have refreshed me in every way and Jesus Christ has refreshed you. You have loved me when absent as well as when present. God is your recompense; if you endure all things for his sake, you will attain to him.

10 You did well to receive Philo and Rheus Agathopous as deacons of the Christ of God;[d] they have followed me in the word of God. And they give thanks to the Lord for you, because you refreshed them in every way. Nothing will be lost to you. 2 My spirit is given in exchange for yours, as are my chains, which you did not treat with haughtiness or shame. Neither will the perfect hope, Jesus Christ, be ashamed of you.

11 Your prayer has gone out to the church in Antioch of Syria. I greet everyone, having come from there bound in chains that are most acceptable to God; but I am not worthy to be from there, since I am the least of them. Still, I have been deemed worthy according to God's will—not by my own conscience but by the gracious gift of

God. I ask that it may be given to me perfectly, that I may attain to God by your prayer. 2 So then, that your work may be made perfect both on earth and in heaven, it is fitting for the honor of God that your church elect an ambassador of God to go to Syria and rejoice together with them. For they have found peace and have recovered their own greatness, and their own corporate body has been restored to them. 3 And so it seems to me a matter worthy of God that you send one of your own with a letter, that he may exult with them in the tranquility that has come to them from God, because they have already reached a harbor by your prayer. As those who are perfect, you should also think perfect things.[4] For God is ready to supply what is needed for you who wish to do good.

12 The love of the brothers who are in Troas greets you; from there I am writing to you through Burrhus, whom you sent along with me, together with your brothers the Ephesians. He has refreshed me in every way. Would that everyone imitated him, as he is the embodiment of the ministry of God. But the gracious gift of God will reward him in every way. 2 I greet the bishop who is worthy of God, the godly presbytery, the deacons who are my fellow slaves, and all individually and together in the name of Jesus Christ, in his flesh and blood, in his passion and resurrection, which pertains to both flesh and spirit, in unity with God and with you. May grace, mercy, peace, and endurance be yours at all times.

13 I greet the households of my brothers, along with their wives and children, and the virgins who are called widows. I wish you farewell in the power of the Father. Philo, who is with me, greets you. 2 I greet the household of Tavia, whom I pray will be firm in faith and in a love that is both fleshly and spiritual. I greet Alce, a name dear to me, and the incomparable Daphnus and Eutecnus, and all by name. Farewell in the gracious gift of God.

[c]Or *catholic*   [d]Or *of Christ, who is God*

[4]Cf. Phil 3:15

The Letter of Ignatius to Polycarp

All of Ignatius's other surviving letters are addressed to Christian communities; the letter to Polycarp is the only one sent to an individual. Polycarp was the bishop of Smyrna, one of the churches that Ignatius had visited en route to Rome and to which he addressed one of his other letters. The letter to Polycarp consists principally of advice to the bishop concerning how to shepherd his flock; it is particularly noteworthy for its rich imagery, as Ignatius repeatedly likens the labor of the bishop to the discipline of an athlete and to the work of a sailor. He urges his friend to be diligent, to bring unruly members of his congregation under subjection, to overcome false teachers, and to promote the social well-being of his community (1:2–5:2).

It is interesting to note that after the first five chapters, the letter suddenly shifts to address the community at large; it was evidently meant to be read, therefore, to the entire church. Members of the community are urged to heed the bishop, to be united with one another, and to continue the good fight of the faith (6:1–2). The letter includes another request for the church to send a delegate to Ignatius's home church in Antioch, which had just overcome its own internal struggles.

In his conclusion, Ignatius indicates that he is to sail immediately for Neapolis (8:1). He asks Polycarp to write the churches on his route to inform them of his coming. His final greetings are the last words we have from his hand.

Ignatius, who is also called God-bearer, to Polycarp, bishop of the church of the Smyrnaeans—rather, the one who has God the Father and the Lord Jesus Christ as his bishop. Warmest greetings.

1 I welcome your godly way of thinking, which is fixed firmly as upon an unmoveable rock; and I exult all the more, having been found worthy of your blameless face. I hope to enjoy it in God! 2 But I urge you by the gracious gift with which you are clothed, to forge ahead in your race and urge all to be saved. Vindicate your position[a] with all fleshly and spiritual diligence. Consider unity, for nothing is better. Bear with all people, just as the Lord bears with you. Tolerate everyone in love, just as you are already doing.[1] 3 Be assiduous in constant prayers; ask for greater understanding than you have. Be alert, as one who has

[a] Or office

[1] Cf. Eph 4:2

obtained a spirit that never slumbers. Speak to each one according to God's own character. Bear the illnesses of all as a perfect athlete. Where there is more toil, there is great gain.

2 It is nothing special[b] for you to love good disciples; instead, gently bring those who are more pestiferous into subjection. Not every wound is cured with the same plaster. Soothe paroxysms of fever with cold compresses. 2 Be wise as a serpent in all things and always pure as the dove.[2] You are fleshly and spiritual for this reason, that you may deal gently with what is visible before you. But ask that what is unseen be made visible to you, that you may lack nothing and abound in every gracious gift.

3 The season seeks for you—as sailors at the helm seek for winds and the one driven by storm a harbor—so that you may attain to God. Be sober as an athlete of God. The prize is immortality and eternal life, about which you have already been convinced. I am given in exchange for you in every way, as are the bonds I bear, which you have loved.

3 Do not allow those who appear trustworthy yet who deliver contrary teachings to daze you. Stand firm as an anvil that is struck. It is the mark of a great athlete to bear up under blows and still claim the victory. But especially, for God's sake, we must endure everything, that he may endure us. 2 Be more eager than you are. Take note of the seasons. Await the one who is beyond the season, the one who is timeless, the one who is invisible, who became visible for us, the one who cannot be handled, the one who is beyond suffering, who suffered for us, enduring in every way on our account.

4 Do not allow the widows to be neglected. After the Lord, it is you who must be mindful of them. Let nothing be done apart from your consent, and do nothing apart from God. You are already acting in this way. Be imperturbable. 2 Let there be more frequent gatherings; seek out everyone by name. 3 Do not be arrogant toward male and female slaves, but neither let them become haughty; rather, let them serve even more as slaves for the glory of God, that they may receive a greater freedom from God. And they should not long to be set free through the common fund, lest they be found slaves of passion.

5 Flee the evil arts; indeed, deliver a sermon about them. Instruct my sisters to love the Lord and to be satisfied with their husbands in flesh and spirit. So too enjoin my brothers in the name of Jesus Christ to love their wives as the Lord loves the church.[3] 2 If anyone is able to honor the flesh of the Lord by maintaining a state of purity, let him do so without boasting. If he boasts, he has been destroyed, and if it becomes known to anyone beyond the bishop, he is ruined. But it is right for men and women who marry to make their union with the consent of the bishop, that their marriage may be for the Lord and not for passion. Let all things be done for the honor of God.

6 All of you should pay attention to the bishop, that God may pay attention to you. I am giving my life in exchange for those who are subject to the bishop, the presbyters, and the deacons. And I hope to have my lot together with them in God. Labor together with one another, compete together, run together, suffer together, lie down together, and be raised together as the household slaves, attendants, and servants of God. 2 Be pleasing to the one in whose army you serve,[4] from whom also you receive your wages. Let none of you be found a deserter. Let your baptism remain as your weaponry, your faith as a helmet, your love as a spear, your endurance as a full set of armor.[5] Let your works be a down payment on your wages, that you may receive the back pay you deserve. Be patient therefore with one another in gentleness, as God is with you. May I enjoy you at all times.

7 Since the church in Antioch of Syria is now at peace because of your prayer, as has been shown to me, I too, having been removed from all earthly cares by God, have become more eager to be found your disciple in the resurrection, if indeed I attain to God through suffering. 2 It is fitting, O Polycarp, most blessed by God, for you to call a council that is pleasing to God and to elect someone whom you hold most dear and resolved, who can be called the runner of God. Deem this one worthy to go to Syria and glorify your resolute love for the glory of God. 3 A Christian has no au-

---

[b]Or *requires no special gift*

[2]Matt 10:16   [3]Eph 5:25, 29   [4]Cf. 2 Tim 2:4   [5]Cf. Eph 6:11–17

thority over himself, but is diligent for God. When you bring it to completion, this work belongs to both God and you. For by grace I believe that you are prepared to do the good deeds that are appropriate to God. Because I know the zeal you have for the truth, I have urged you through just these few words.

8 Because I have not been able to write to all the churches—since, as the divine will enjoins, I am unexpectedly to set sail from Troas to Neapolis—you are to write to the churches that lie before me,[c] as one who has the mind of God, that they may do the same thing as well. Some can send messengers by foot; but others can send letters through those whom you send yourself, so that all of you may be glorified by an eternal work, since you yourself are worthy.

2 I greet all by name, and the wife of Epitropus, along with the entire household of her and her children. I greet Attalus, my beloved. I greet the one who is about to be deemed worthy to go to Syria. God's grace will be with him constantly, and with Polycarp who sends him. 3 I bid you constant farewell in our God, Jesus Christ. May you remain in him, in the unity and care that comes from God. I greet Alce, a name dear to me. Farewell in the Lord.

---

[c] Or *on this side*, possibly referring to the churches that lie between Smyrna and Antioch or between Troas and Rome

The Letter of Polycarp
to the Philippians

Sometime after Ignatius visited and wrote to Polycarp, the bishop of Smyrna in Asia Minor, Polycarp himself addressed a letter to the Christian community of Philippi. Scholars have debated the date of this letter: in one passage, Polycarp intimates that Ignatius had just left town, putting its date around 110 C.E. (13:1, where Polycarp indicates that he plans to visit the church in Antioch at Ignatius's request). Another passage implies that Ignatius had already experienced martyrdom (9:1). This has sometimes been taken to suggest that the letter was penned many years later, possibly as late as 135 C.E. Other scholars, however, have maintained that our present book represents two different letters written at different times, later cut and pasted together to form one larger letter for circulation.

Whether representing one writing or two, the occasion of the bulk of the letter as we have it is relatively clear. Polycarp is writing the Philippian church because they have asked his advice on a problem that had arisen in their community: a man named Valens, a leader of the church, along with his wife, had been caught embezzling church funds, and the community was not certain how to handle the situation (chap. 11). Polycarp uses the opportunity to denounce those who crave worldly goods and to issue other moral exhortations to his readers; in terms of the specific situation, he advises the Philippians to allow the offending couple to repent and return to the church's good graces.

Polycarp does not recommend a similarly kind treatment to the false teachers that he has learned were plaguing the Philippian church with their denials of the future resurrection of believers and of the fleshly existence of Christ (7:1). Polycarp denounces these teachings and urges the congregation to give such persons no heed.

Much of the rest of the letter consists of general ethical exhortations for the Philippians to love one another, pray for one another, give alms insofar as possible, and live moral, upright lives. Many of these exhortations are drawn from other Christian writings, including the Synoptic Gospels and the letters of Paul. Indeed, in places the letter reads almost like a pastiche of earlier Christian traditions known to the author and, presumably, to many of his Philippian readers.

Polycarp and the presbyters who are with him to the church of God that temporarily resides in Philippi. May mercy and peace be multiplied to you from God Almighty and Jesus Christ our savior.

1 I greatly rejoice together with you in our Lord Jesus Christ. For you have received the replicas of true love and have, as was incumbent upon you, sent ahead those who were confined in chains fitting for the saints, crowns for those who have truly been chosen by God and our Lord. 2 And I rejoice that the secure root of your faith, proclaimed from ancient times, even now continues to abide and bear fruit in our Lord Jesus Christ. He persevered to the point of death on behalf of our sins; and God raised him up after loosing the labor pains of Hades.[1] 3 Even without seeing him, you believe in him with an inexpressible and glorious joy[2] that many long to experience. For you know that you have been saved by a gracious gift—not from works[3] but by the will of God through Jesus Christ.

2 Therefore, bind up your loose robes[a] and serve as God's slaves in reverential fear and truth, abandoning futile reasoning and the error that deceives many, and believing in the one who raised our Lord Jesus Christ from the dead and gave him glory[4] and a throne at his right hand. Everything in heaven and on earth is subject to him;[5] everything that breathes will serve him; he is coming as a judge of the living and the dead;[6] and God will hold those who disobey him accountable for his blood. 2 But the one who raised him from the dead will raise us as well[7] if we do his will, walking in his commandments and loving the things he loved, abstaining from every kind of injustice, greed, love of money, slander, and false witness, not paying back evil for evil, or abuse for abuse,[8] or blow for blow, or curse for curse, 3 but remembering what the Lord said when he taught: "Do not judge lest you be judged; forgive and it will be forgiven you; show mercy that you may be shown mercy; the amount you dispense will be the amount you receive in return."[9] And, "blessed are the poor and those persecuted for the sake of righteousness, because the kingdom of God belongs to them."[10]

3 I am writing these things about righteousness, brothers, not on my own initiative but at your request. 2 For neither I nor anyone like me is able to replicate the wisdom of the blessed and glorious Paul. When he was with you he accurately and reliably taught the word of truth to those who were there at the time. And when he was absent he wrote you letters. If you carefully peer into them, you will be able to be built up in the faith that was given you. 3 This faith is the mother of us all,[11] with hope following close after, and the love of God, Christ, and neighbor leading the way. For anyone centered in these has fulfilled the commandment of righteousness. For the one who has love is far removed from all sin.

4 The love of money is the beginning of all difficulties.[12] And so, since we know that we brought nothing into the world and can take nothing out of it,[13] we should arm ourselves with the weapons of righteousness and teach one another, first of all, to walk in the commandment of the Lord.

2 Then we should teach our wives to walk in the faith given them and in love and purity; to be affectionate towards their own husbands in all truth [14] to love everyone equally, with all self-restraint; and to discipline their children in the reverential fear of God.[15] 3 We should teach the widows to be self-controlled with respect to faith in the Lord, to pray without ceasing for everyone, and to be distant from all libel, slander, false witness, love of money, and all evil, knowing that they are God's altar and that each offering is inspected for a blemish[16] and that nothing escapes his notice, whether thoughts, ideas,[17] or any of the things hidden in the heart.[18]

5 Since we know that God is not mocked,[19] we should walk in a manner worthy of his commandment and glory.

2 So too the deacons should be blameless[20] before his righteousness as ministers of God and of Christ, not of humans. They should not be slanderous or insincere, but free from the love of money, self-restrained in every way, compassionate,

---

[a]Literally *gird up your loins*

[1]Acts 2:24 [2]1 Pet 1:8 [3]Eph 2:5, 8–9 [4]1 Pet 1:21 [5]Cf. 1 Cor 15:28; Phil 2:10; 3:21 [6]Acts 10:42 [7]Cf. 2 Cor 4:14 [8]1 Pet 3:9 [9]Matt 7:1–2; Luke 6:36–38; cf. 1 Clem 13:2 [10]Luke 6:20; Matt 5:10 [11]Gal 4:26 [12]Cf. 1 Tim 6:10 [13]Cf. 1 Tim 6:7 [14]Cf. 1 Clem 1:3 [15]Cf. 1 Clem 21:6–8 [16]Cf. 1 Clem 41:2 [17]Cf. 1 Clem 21:3 [18]1 Cor 14:25 [19]Gal 6:7 [20]Cf. 1 Tim 3:8–13

attentive, and proceeding according to the truth of the Lord, who became a minister for everyone. If we are pleasing to him in the present age we will receive also the age that is coming, just as he promised that he would raise us from the dead and that, if we conducted ourselves worthily of him, we would also rule together with him[21]—so long as we believe.

3 So too let the young men be blameless in all things, concerned above all else for their purity, keeping themselves in check with respect to all evil. For it is good to be cut off from the passions of the world, since every passion wages war against the spirit,[22] and neither the sexually immoral, nor the effeminate, nor male prostitutes will inherit the kingdom of God;[23] nor will those who engage in aberrant behavior. Therefore we must abstain from all these things, and be subject to the presbyters and deacons as to God and Christ. And the virgins must walk in a blameless and pure conscience.

6 The presbyters also should be compassionate, merciful to all, turning back those who have gone astray, caring for all who are sick, not neglecting the widow, the orphan, or the poor, but always taking thought for what is good before both God and others,[24] abstaining from all anger, prejudice, and unfair judgment, avoiding all love of money, not quick to believe a rumor against anyone, not severe in judgment, knowing that we are all in debt because of sin. 2 And so if we ask the Lord to forgive us, we ourselves also ought to forgive; for we are before the eyes of the Lord and of God, and everyone must appear before the judgment seat of Christ, each rendering an account of himself.[25] 3 And so we should serve as his slaves, with reverential fear and all respect, just as he commanded, as did the apostles who proclaimed the gospel to us and the prophets who preached, in advance, the coming of our Lord. We should be zealous for what is good, avoiding stumbling blocks, false brothers, and those who carry the name of the Lord in hypocrisy, leading the empty-minded astray.

7 For anyone who does not confess that Jesus Christ has come in the flesh is an <u>an</u>-<u>tichrist</u>;[26] and whoever does not confess the witness of the cross is from the devil;[27] and whoever distorts the words of the Lord for his own pas-

sions, saying that there is neither resurrection nor judgment—this one is the firstborn of Satan. 2 And so, let us leave behind the idle speculation of the multitudes and false teachings and turn to the word that was delivered to us from the beginning, being alert in prayer and persistent in fasting. Through our entreaties let us ask the God who sees all things not to bring us into temptation,[28] just as the Lord said, "For the spirit is willing but the flesh is weak."[29]

8 Thus we should persevere, unremitting in our hope and in the down payment of our righteousness, which is Christ Jesus, who bore our sins in his own body on the tree, who did not commit sin nor was deceit found in his mouth;[30] but he endured all things on our account, that we might live in him. 2 Therefore we should be imitators of his endurance, and if we suffer for his name, we should give him the glory. For he set this example for us through what he did,[31] and we have believed it.

9 Therefore I urge all of you to obey the word of righteousness and to practice all endurance, which you also observed with your own eyes not only in the most fortunate Ignatius, Zosimus, and Rufus, but also in others who lived among you, and in Paul himself and the other apostles. 2 You should be convinced that none of them acted[b] in vain,[32] but in faith and righteousness, and that they are in the place they deserved, with the Lord, with whom they also suffered. For they did not love the present age;[33] they loved the one who died for us and who was raised by God for our sakes.

10 And so, you should stand firm in these things and follow the example of the Lord, secure and unmoveable in your faith, loving the brotherhood, caring for one another, united in the truth, waiting on one another in the gentleness of the Lord, looking down on no one. 2 When you are able to do good, do not put it off,[34] since giving to charity frees a person from death.[35] Let all of you be subject to one another, keeping your in-

[b]Literally, *ran*

[21]2 Tim 2:12 [22]1 Pet 2:11 [23]1 Cor 6:9 [24]Prov 3:4; cf. 2 Cor 8:21 [25]Cf. Rom 14:10, 12; 2 Cor 5:10 [26]Cf. 1 John 4:2–3 [27]Cf. 1 John 3:8 [28]Matt 6:13 [29]Matt 26:41 [30]1 Pet 2:24, 22 [31]Cf. 1 Pet 2:21 [32]Phil 2:16 [33]Cf. 2 Tim 4:10 [34]Cf. Prov 3:28 [35]Tob 4:10

teractions with the outsiders[c] above reproach, that by your good works you may receive praise and the Lord not be blasphemed because of you. 3 For woe to the one through whom the name of the Lord is blasphemed.[36] Teach all, therefore, to conduct themselves in a sober way, as you yourselves are doing.

11 I am extremely sad for Valens, once a presbyter among you, that he should so misunderstand the office that was given him. Thus I urge you to abstain from love of money and to be pure and truthful. Abstain from every kind of evil.[37] 2 For if someone cannot control himself in such things, how can he preach self-control to another?[38] Anyone who cannot avoid the love of money will be defiled by idolatry, and will be judged as if among the outsiders[d] who know nothing about the judgment of the Lord. Or do we not realize that "the saints will judge the world?"[39] For so Paul teaches. 3 But I have neither perceived nor heard that you have any such thing in your midst, among whom the most fortunate Paul labored and who are found in the beginning of his epistle. For he exulted in you among all his churches, which alone knew God at that time; for we had not yet come to know him. 4 And so, my brothers, I am very sad for that man and his wife; may the Lord give them true repentance. And you yourselves should act in a sober way in this matter. Rather than judge such people as enemies, call them back as frail and wayward members, so as to heal your entire body. For when you do this, you build yourselves up.

12 I am confident that you are well trained in the sacred Scriptures and that nothing is hidden from you; but to me this has not been granted. Only, as it is written in these Scriptures, "Be angry and do not sin, and do not let the sun go down on your anger."[40] How fortunate is the one who remembers this; and I believe this to be the case among you. 2 So may the God and Father of our Lord Jesus Christ, and the eternal priest himself, the Son of God, Jesus Christ, build you up in faith and truth and in all gentleness, without anger, and in patience, forbearance, tolerance, and purity; and may he grant to you the lot and portion to be among his saints—and to us as well with you, and to everyone under heaven who is about to believe in our Lord and God, Jesus Christ, and in his Father, who raised him from the dead. 3 Pray for all the saints.[41] Pray also for kings and magistrates and rulers, as well as for those who persecute and hate you[42] and for the enemies of the cross, that your fruit may be manifest to all and you may be made perfect in him.

13 Both you and Ignatius have written to me that if anyone is going to Syria he should take along your letter. I will do so if I have the opportunity—either I or someone I send as a representative on your behalf and mine. 2 We have forwarded to you the letters of Ignatius that he sent to us, along with all the others we had with us, just as you directed us to do. These accompany this letter; you will be able to profit greatly from them, for they deal with faith and endurance and all edification that is suitable in our Lord. And let us know what you have learned more definitely about Ignatius himself and those who are with him.

14 I am writing these things to you through Crescens, whom I commended to you recently[e] and now commend again. For he has conducted himself blamelessly among us; and I believe that he will do the same among you. And his sister will be commended to you when she comes to you. Farewell in the Lord Jesus Christ in grace, with all who are yours. Amen.

---

[c]Literally, *Gentiles*; or *nations* [d]Literally, *Gentiles*; or *nations* [e]Or *when I was with you*; Latin obscure

---

[36]Cf. Isa 52:5 [37]Cf. 1 Thess 5:22 [38]Cf. 1 Tim 3:5 [39]1 Cor 6:2 [40]Eph 4:26; Ps 4:5 [41]Cf. Eph 6:18 [42]Cf. Matt 5:44; Luke 6:27

The Letter of Barnabas

The book of Barnabas has traditionally been called an epistle, even though its opening contains only a greeting, with neither its author nor its recipients named. The second- and third-century Christians who refer to the book attribute it to Barnabas, the companion of the apostle Paul. But this may have involved little more than guesswork on the part of Christians who were eager to have the book read and accepted as "apostolic." It was considered part of the New Testament Scriptures in some Christian communities down to the fourth century.

The book in fact appears to have been written long after Barnabas himself had died: it mentions, for example, the destruction of the Temple (70 C.E.) and refers to the possibility of its soon being rebuilt (16:3–4). This possibility was very much alive in the early decades of the second century, but evaporated when the Emperor Hadrian (132–134 C.E.) had a Roman shrine constructed over the Temple's ruins. Most scholars have concluded, on these grounds, that the book was written sometime during the first half of the second century, possibly around 130 C.E.

The book is concerned with the relationship of Judaism and Christianity. Its basic thrust is that Judaism is, and always has been, a false religion. According to this author, Jews violated God's covenant from the very beginning (4:6–8); they have, as a result, never been God's people or understood their own Scriptures. For this author, the Jewish Scriptures can be understood only in light of Christ; indeed, for him, the Old Testament is a Christian, not a Jewish, book.

As a corollary, Jews who claim that their religion was given by God have been misled by an evil angel who persuaded them to take the laws of Moses literally (9:5). In fact, claims the author, the laws of sabbath observance, kosher food, and circumcision were meant not as literal descriptions of how the Jewish people were to live, but as figurative pointers to Christ and the religion that he was to establish (chaps. 9–10, 15). A good deal of this book, therefore, tries to show how Christ and the Christian religion were foreshadowed in the Old Testament Scriptures.

The book ends on a different note, by describing the Christian doctrine of the "Two Paths": there is the morally upright path of "light" and the morally perverse path of "darkness" (chaps. 18–20; see the introduction to the *Didache*). All people must choose between these two paths, following the righteous practices of the one or the moral improprieties of the other.

"The Letter of Barnabas," from *The Apostolic Fathers,* translated by Bart D. Ehrman. Loeb Classical Library; © 2003. Reprinted by permission of Harvard University Press.

1 Greetings, sons and daughters, in the name of the Lord who loved us, in peace.

2 So great and abundant are the righteous acts of God toward you that I am exceedingly overjoyed, beyond measure, by your blessed and glorious spirits. For you have received such a measure of his grace planted within you, the spiritual gift! 3 And so I share your joy all the more within myself,[a] hoping to be saved; for truly I see that, in your midst, the Spirit has been poured out upon you from the abundance of the Lord's fountain— so amazed have I been by the sight of your face, which I have so desired.

4 And so, since I have been persuaded about this and realize that I who have spoken to you know many things (since the Lord has traveled along with me in the path of righteousness), I have also felt fully compelled to love you more than my own soul. For a great faith and love dwell within you in the hope of his life. 5 I have thus come to realize that I will be rewarded for serving spirits like yours, if I care for you enough to hand over a portion of what I have received. I have hastened, then, to send you a brief letter, that you may have perfect knowledge to accompany your faith.

6 There are three firm teachings of the Lord of life: hope, which is the beginning and end of our faith; righteousness, which is the beginning and end of judgment; and love, which is a testament to our joy and gladness in upright deeds.

7 For through the prophets the Master has made known to us what has happened and what now is; and he has given us the first fruits of the taste of what is yet to be. And as we see that each and every thing has happened just as he indicated, we should make a more abundant and exalted offering in awe of him. 8 But I will show a few matters to you, not as a teacher but as one of your own; these will gladden your hearts in the present circumstances.

2 Since, then, the days are evil and the one who is at work holds sway, we should commit ourselves to seeking after the righteous acts of the Lord. 2 Reverential awe and endurance assist our faith, and patience and self-restraint do battle on our side. 3 And so while these things remain in a holy state before the Lord, wisdom, understanding, perception, and knowledge rejoice together with them.

4 For through all the prophets he has shown us

that he has no need of sacrifices, whole burnt offerings, or regular offerings. For he says in one place,

5 "What is the multitude of your sacrifices to me? says the Lord. I am sated with whole burnt offerings, and have no desire for the fat of lambs, the blood of bulls and goats—not even if you should come to appear before me. For who sought these things from your hands? Trample my court no longer. If you bring fine flour, it is futile; incense is loathsome to me. I cannot stand your new moons and sabbaths."[1] 6 And so he nullified these things that the new law of our Lord Jesus Christ, which is without the yoke of compulsion, should provide an offering not made by humans.

7 And again he says to them, "Did I command your fathers who came out from the land of Egypt to offer whole burnt offerings and sacrifices to me?"[2] 8 "No, this is what I commanded them: Let none of you bear a grudge against your neighbor in your heart, and do not love a false oath."[3] 9 And so, since we are not ignorant, we should perceive the good intention of our Father. For he is speaking to us, wanting us to seek how to make an offering to him without being deceived like them.

10 And so he says to us, "A sacrifice to the Lord is a crushed heart; a sweet fragrance to the Lord is a heart that glorifies the one who made it."[4] And so, brothers, we ought to learn clearly about our salvation, to keep the Evil One from hurling us away from our life after bringing error in through the back door.

3 And so he speaks to them again concerning these things: "Why do you fast for me, says the Lord, so that your voice is heard crying out today? This is not the fast I have chosen, says the Lord—not a person humbling his soul. 2 Not even if you bend your neck into a circle and put on sackcloth and make for yourself a bed of ashes— not even so should you call this a proper fast."[5] 3 But he says to us, "See, this is the fast I have chosen, says the Lord. Loosen every bond of injustice; unravel the stranglehold of coercive agreements; send forth in forgiveness those who are downtrod-

---

[a]Or I congratulate myself all the more

[1]Isa 1:11–13 [2]Jer 7:22 [3]Zech 8:17 [4]Ps 51:17 [5]Isa 58:3–5

den; tear up every unfair contract. Break your bread for the hungry, and provide clothing for anyone you see naked. Bring the homeless under your roof. And if you see anyone who has been humbled, do not despise him—neither you nor anyone from your children's household. 4 Then your light will burst forth at dawn, your garments will quickly rise up,[b] your righteousness will go forth before you, and the glory of God will clothe you. 5 Then you will cry out and God will hear you. While you are still speaking he will say, 'See! Here I am!'—if, that is, you remove from yourself bondage, the threatening gesture, and the word of complaint, and from your heart you give your bread to the poor and show mercy to the person who has been humbled."[6] 6 The one who is patient anticipated, brothers, that the people he prepared in his beloved would believe, in a state of innocence. And so he revealed all things to us in advance, that we not be dashed against[c] their law as newcomers.[d]

4 And so by carefully investigating what is here and now, we must seek for the things that can save us. We should flee, entirely, all the works of lawlessness; otherwise, they may overwhelm us. And we should hate the error of the present age, that we may be loved in the age to come. 2 We should not allow our souls to relax, thinking they can consort with sinners and the wicked; otherwise we may become like them.

3 The final stumbling block is at hand, about which it has been written, just as Enoch says. For this reason the Master shortened the seasons and the days, that his beloved may hurry and arrive at his inheritance. 4 For also the prophet says, "Ten kingdoms will rule the earth and a small king will rise up afterwards; he will humble three of the kings at one time."[e7] 5 So too Daniel speaks about the same thing: "I saw the fourth beast, wicked and strong, and worse than all the beasts of the sea, and I saw how ten horns rose up from him, and from them a small horn as an offshoot; and I saw how he humbled three of the great horns at one time."[f8] 6 And so you should understand. And yet again, I am asking you this as one who is from among you and who loves each and every one of you more than my own soul: Watch yourselves now and do not become like some people by piling up your sins, saying that the covenant is both theirs and ours. 7 For it is ours. But they permanently lost it, in this way, when Moses had just received it. For the Scripture says, "Moses was on the mountain fasting for forty days and forty nights, and he received the covenant from the Lord, stone tablets written with the finger of the Lord's own hand."[9] 8 But when they turned back to idols they lost it. For the Lord says this: "Moses, Moses, go down quickly, because your people, whom you led from the land of Egypt, has broken the law."[10] Moses understood and cast the two tablets from his hands. And their covenant was smashed—that the covenant of his beloved, Jesus, might be sealed in our hearts, in the hope brought by faith in him.

9 Since I want to write many things, not as a teacher, but as is fitting for one who is eager to abandon none of the things we have, I hasten to write, as your lowly scapegoat.[g] Therefore, we should pay close attention here in the final days. For the entire time of our faith will be of no use to us if we do not stand in resistance, as is fitting for the children of God, both against this present lawless age and against the stumbling blocks that are yet to come, 10 that the Black One not sneak in among us. We should flee from all that is futile and completely hate the works of the evil path. Do not sink into yourselves and live alone, as if you were already made upright; instead, gathering together for the same purpose, seek out what is profitable for the common good. 11 For the Scripture says, "Woe to those who have understanding in themselves and are knowledgeable before their own eyes."[11] We should be spiritual; we should be a perfect temple to God. As much as we can, we should concern ourselves with the reverential awe of God and struggle to guard his commandments, that we may be glad in his righteous acts.[h] 12 The Lord will judge the world, playing no favorites. Each will receive according to what he has done. If he is good, his righteousness will precede him; if evil, the reward for his wickedness will be before him. 13 As those who are called we must

[b]Meaning obscure [c]Or *shipwrecked on* [d]Or *proselytes* [e]Or *under one of them*; or *with a single blow*; meaning obscure [f]Or *under one of them*; or *with a single blow*; meaning obscure [g]Or *your humble servant*; literally, *offscouring* [h]Or *righteous demands*

[6]Isa 58:6–10 [7]Dan 7:24 [8]Dan 7:7–8 [9]Exod 31:18; 34:28 [10]Exod 32:7 [11]Isa 5:21

never lie down and lose consciousness of our sins, allowing the evil ruler to receive the authority against us and force us out of the Lord's kingdom. 14 And still, my brothers, consider: When you observe that Israel was abandoned even after such signs and wonders had occurred in it, we too should pay close attention, lest, as it is written, "many of us were found called, but few chosen."[12]

5 This is why the Lord allowed his flesh to be given over[i] to corruption, that we might be made holy through the forgiveness of sins, which comes in the sprinkling of his blood. 2 For some of the things written about him concern Israel; others concern us. And so it says, "He was wounded because of our lawless acts and weakened because of our sins. By his bruising we were healed. He was led like a sheep going to slaughter; and like a lamb, silent before the one who shears it."[13]

3 Therefore we ought to give thanks to the Lord even more abundantly, because he revealed to us the things that have taken place and made us wise in the things that are now; and we are not ignorant of the things that are yet to happen. 4 And the Scripture says, "Not unjustly are the nets spread out for the birds."[14] It says this because the person who knows the path of righteousness but keeps himself in the path of darkness deserves to perish.

5 Consider this, my brothers: If the Lord allowed himself to suffer for our sake, even though he was the Lord of the entire world, the one to whom God said at the foundation of the world, "Let us make a human according to our image and likeness,"[15] how then did he allow himself to suffer by the hand of humans? Learn this! 6 Because the prophets received his gracious gift, they prophesied looking ahead to him. He allowed himself to suffer in order to destroy death and to show that there is a resurrection of the dead. For he had to be manifest in the flesh. 7 And he allowed himself to suffer in order to redeem the promise given to the fathers and to show, while he was on earth preparing a new people for himself, that he is to execute judgment after raising the dead.

8 Moreover, while teaching Israel and doing such wonders and signs, he preached to them and loved them deeply. 9 And when he selected his own apostles who were about to preach his gospel, they were altogether lawless beyond all sin. This was to show that he did not come to call the up-

right but sinners. Then he revealed that he was the Son of God. 10 For if he had not come in the flesh, how would people have been able to look upon him and survive? For they cannot even look intently at the sun, gazing directly into its rays, even though it is the work of his hands and will eventually cease to exist. 11 Therefore, the Son of God came in the flesh for this reason, that he might total up all the sins of those who persecuted his prophets to death. 12 And so this is why he allowed himself to suffer. For God speaks of the blow they delivered against his flesh: "When they smite their own shepherd, then the sheep of the flock will perish."[16] 13 But he wished to suffer in this way, for he had to suffer on a tree. For the one who prophesied about him said, "Spare my life from the sword," and "Nail my flesh, because an assembly[j] of evildoers has risen up against me."[17] 14 Again he says, "See! I have set my back to whips and my cheeks to blows; and I have set my face as a hard rock."[18]

6 And so, when he issued the commandment, what did he say? "Who is the one who takes me to court? Let him oppose me! Or who acquits himself before me? Let him approach the servant of the Lord! 2 Woe to you, for you will all grow old like a garment and a moth will devour you."[19] And again, since he was set in place as a strong stone used for crushing, the prophet says, "See, I will cast into Zion's foundation a precious stone that is chosen, a cornerstone, one to be valued." 3 Then what does he say? "The one who believes in him will live forever."[20] Is our hope then built on a stone? May it never be! But he says this because the Lord has set his flesh up in strength. For he says, "He set me up as a hard rock."[21] 4 And again the prophet says, "A stone that the builders rejected has become the very cornerstone." And again he says, "This is the great and marvelous day the Lord has made."[22]

5 I am writing to you in very simple terms, that you may understand. I am a lowly scapegoat[k] for your love.

---

[i]Literally, *endured to deliver his flesh over*   [j]Or *synagogue*   [k]Or *a humble servant*; literally, *an offscouring*

---

[12]Matt 22:14   [13]Isa 53:5, 7   [14]Prov 1:17   [15]Gen 1:26   [16]Cf. Zech 13:7; Matt 26:31   [17]Ps 22:20, 16   [18]Isa 50:6–7   [19]Isa 50:8–9 [20]Isa 28:16   [21]Isa 50:7   [22]Ps 118:22, 24; cf. 1 Pet 2:7

6 And so what again does the prophet say? "An assembly[1] of evildoers surrounded me, they swarmed about me like bees around a honeycomb,"[23] and, "They cast lots for my clothing."[24] 7 And so, because he was about to be revealed and suffer in the flesh, his suffering was revealed in advance. For the prophet says about Israel, "Woe to their souls, because they hatched an evil plot against themselves, saying, 'Let us bind the upright one, because he is trouble for us.'"[25] 8 What does the other prophet, Moses, say to them? "See, this is what the Lord God says, 'Enter into the good land, which the Lord swore to give to Abraham, Isaac, and Jacob; and receive it as an inheritance, a land flowing with milk and honey.'"[26] 9 Learn what knowledge says. "Hope," it says, "in Jesus, who is about to be revealed to you in the flesh." For a human is earth that suffers. For Adam was formed out of the face of the earth. 10 Why then does he say, "Into the good land, a land flowing with milk and honey"? Blessed is our Lord, brothers, who placed the wisdom and knowledge of his secrets within us. For the prophet is speaking a parable of the Lord. Who will understand it, except one who is wise and learned, who loves his Lord?

11 Since, then, he renewed us through the forgiveness of our sins, he made us into a different type of person, that we might have the soul of children, as if he were indeed forming us all over again. 12 For the Scripture speaks about us when he says to his Son, "Let us make humans according to our image and likeness, and let them rule over the wild beasts of the land and the birds of the sky and the fish of the sea."[27] Once the Lord saw our beautiful form, he said "Increase and multiply and fill the earth."[28] He said these things to the Son.

13 Again I will show you how he speaks to us. He made yet a second human form in the final days. And the Lord says, "See! I am making the final things like the first."[29] This is why the prophet proclaimed, "Enter into a land flowing with milk and honey, and rule over it."[30] 14 See, then, that we have been formed anew, just as he again says in another prophet, "See, says the Lord, I will remove from these people their hearts of stone" (that is to say, from those whom the Spirit of the Lord foresaw) "and cast into them hearts of flesh."[31] For

he was about to be revealed in the flesh and to dwell among us. 15 For the dwelling place of our heart, my brothers, is a temple holy to the Lord. 16 For again the Lord says, "And how will I appear before the Lord my God and be glorified?"[32] He answers: "I will praise you in the assembly[m] of my brothers, and sing your praise in the midst of the assembly[n] of saints."[33] And so we are the ones he has brought into the good land.

17 Why then does he speak of milk and honey? Because the child is first nourished by honey and then milk. So also, when we are nourished by faith in the promise and then by the word, we will live as masters over the earth. 18 For he already said above, "Let them increase and multiply and rule over the fish."[34] Who can now rule over wild beasts and fish and birds of the sky? For we ought to realize that ruling is a matter of authority, so that the one who issues commands is the master. 19 Since this is not happening now, he has told us when it will happen: when we have ourselves been perfected so as to become heirs of the Lord's covenant.

7 And so you should understand, children of gladness, that the good Lord has revealed everything to us in advance, that we may know whom to praise when we give thanks for everything.

2 And so, if the Son of God suffered, that by being beaten he might give us life (even though he is the Lord and is about to judge the living and the dead), we should believe that the Son of God could not suffer unless it was for our sakes.

3 But also when he was crucified he was given vinegar and gall to drink. Listen how the priests in the Temple made a revelation about this. For the Lord gave the written commandment that "Whoever does not keep the fast must surely die,"[35] because he himself was about to offer the vessel of the Spirit as a sacrifice for our own sins, that the type might also be fulfilled that was set forth in Isaac, when he was offered on the altar. 4 What then does he say in the prophet? "Let them eat some of the goat offered for all sins on the day of

---

[1]Or *synagogue*   [m]Or *church*   [n]Or *church*

[23]Ps 22:16; 118:12   [24]Ps 22:18   [25]Isa 3:9–10   [26]Exod 33:1, 3   [27]Gen 1:26   [28]Gen 1:28   [29]Source unknown   [30]Exod 33:3   [31]Ezek 11:19   [32]Ps 42:4   [33]Ps 22:22, 25   [34]Gen 1:28   [35]Lev 23:29

fasting." Now pay careful attention: "And let all the priests alone eat the intestines, unwashed, with vinegar."[36] 5 Why is this? Since you are about to give me gall mixed with vinegar to drink—when I am about to offer my flesh on behalf of the sins of my new people—you alone are to eat, while the people fast and mourn in sackcloth and ashes. He says this to show that he had to suffer at their hands. 6 Pay attention to what he commands: "Take two fine goats who are alike and offer them as a sacrifice; and let the priest take one of them as a whole burnt offering for sins."[37] 7 But what will they do with the other? "The other," he says, "is cursed."[38] Pay attention to how the type of Jesus is revealed.

8 "And all of you shall spit on it and pierce it and wrap a piece of scarlet wool around its head, and so let it be cast into the wilderness."[39] When this happens, the one who takes the goat leads it into the wilderness and removes the wool, and places it on a blackberry bush,[o] whose buds we are accustomed to eat when we find it in the countryside. (Thus the fruit of the blackberry bush[p] alone is sweet.) 9 And so, what does this mean? Pay attention: "The one they take to the altar, but the other is cursed," and the one that is cursed is crowned. For then they will see him in that day wearing a long scarlet robe around his flesh, and they will say, "Is this not the one we once crucified, despising, piercing, and spitting on him? Truly this is the one who was saying at the time that he was himself the Son of God." 10 For how is he like that one? This is why "the goats are alike, fine, and equal," that when they see him coming at that time, they may be amazed at how much he is like the goat. See then the type of Jesus who was about to suffer.

11 But why do they place the wool in the midst of the thorns? This is a type of Jesus established for[q] the church, because whoever wishes to remove the scarlet wool must suffer greatly, since the thorn is a fearful thing, and a person can retrieve the wool only by experiencing pain. And so he says: Those who wish to see me and touch my kingdom must take hold of me through pain and suffering.

8 And what do you suppose is the type found in his command to Israel, that men who are full of sin should offer up a heifer, and after

slaughtering it burn it, and that children should then take the ashes and cast them into vessels, and then tie scarlet wool around a piece of wood (see again the type of the cross and the scarlet wool!), along with the hyssop, and that the children should thus sprinkle the people one by one, that they might be purified from their sins? 2 Understand how he speaks to you simply. The calf is Jesus; the sinful men who make the offering are those who offered him up for slaughter. Then they are no longer men and the glory of sinners is no more.[r] 3 The children who sprinkle are those who proclaimed to us the forgiveness of sins and the purification of our hearts. To them he has given the authority to preach the gospel. There are twelve of them as a witness to the tribes, for there were twelve tribes in Israel. 4 But why are there three children who sprinkle? As a witness to Abraham, Isaac, and Jacob, because these were great before God.

5 And why is the wool placed on a piece of wood? Because the kingdom of Jesus is on the tree, and because those who hope in him will live forever. 6 But why are the wool and hyssop together? Because in his kingdom there will be evil and foul days, in which we will be saved. And because the one who is sick in the flesh is healed by the foul juice of the hyssop.

7 And thus the things that have happened in this way are clear to us, but they are obscure to them, because they have not heard the voice of the Lord.

9 For he speaks again about the ears, indicating how he has circumcised our hearts. The Lord says in the prophet, "They obeyed me because of what they heard with their ears."[40] Again he says, "Those who are far off will clearly hear; they will know what I have done."[41] And, "Circumcise your hearts,"[42] says the Lord.

2 Again he says, "Hear O Israel, for thus says the Lord your God."[43] And again the Spirit of the Lord prophesies, "Who is the one who wants to live forever? Let him clearly hear the voice of my servant."[44] 3 Again he says, "Hear, O heaven, and

---

[o]Greek obscure   [p]Greek obscure   [q]Or *placed in*   [r]Greek obscure

[36]Source unknown. Cf. Leviticus 16   [37]Lev 16:7, 9   [38]Cf. Lev 16:8
[39]Cf. Lev 16:10, 20–22   [40]Ps 18:44   [41]Cf. Isa 33:13   [42]Isa 33:13;
Jer 4:4   [43]Cf. Jer 7:2–3; Ps 34:12–13   [44]Cf. Ps 34:12–13; Isa 50:10;
Exod. 15:26

give ear, O earth, for the Lord has said these things as a witness."[45] And again he says, "Hear the word of the Lord, you rulers of this people."[46] And again he says, "Hear, O children, the voice of one crying in the wilderness."[47] Thus he circumcised our hearing, that once we heard the word we might believe. 4 But even the circumcision in which they trusted has been nullified. For he has said that circumcision is not a matter of the flesh. But they violated his law, because an evil angel instructed them. 5 He says to them, "Thus says the Lord your God" (here is where I find a commandment), "Do not sow among the thorns; be circumcised to your Lord."[48] And what does he say? "Circumcise your hardened hearts and do not harden your necks."[49] Or consider again, "See, says the Lord, all the nations are uncircumcised in their foreskins, but this people is uncircumcised in their hearts."[50]

6 But you will say, "Yet surely the people have been circumcised as a seal."[s] But every Syrian and Arab and all the priests of the idols are circumcised as well. So then, do those belong to their covenant? Even the people of Egypt are circumcised! 7 Thus learn about the whole matter fully, children of love. For Abraham, the first to perform circumcision, was looking ahead in the Spirit to Jesus when he circumcised. For he received the firm teachings of the three letters. 8 For it says, "Abraham circumcised eighteen and three hundred men from his household."[51] What knowledge, then, was given to him? Notice that first he mentions the eighteen and then, after a pause, the three hundred. The number eighteen (in Greek) consists of an Iota (J), ten, and an Eta (E), eight. There you have Jesus.[t] And because the cross was about to have grace in the letter Tau (T), he next gives the three hundred, Tau. And so he shows the name Jesus by the first two letters, and the cross by the other.

9 For the one who has placed the implanted gift of his covenant in us knew these things. No one has learned a more reliable lesson from me. But I know that you are worthy.

10

And when Moses said, "Do not eat the pig, or the eagle, or the hawk, or the crow, or any fish without scales,"[52] he received three firm teachings in his understanding. 2 Moreover, he said to them in the book of Deuteronomy, "I will establish a covenant with this people in my

righteous demands."[53] So, then, the commandment of God is not a matter of avoiding food; but Moses spoke in the Spirit.

3 This is why he spoke about the pig: "Do not cling," he says, "to such people, who are like pigs." That is to say, when they live in luxury, they forget the Lord, but when they are in need, they remember the Lord. This is just like the pig: When it is eating, it does not know its master, but when hungry, it cries out—until it gets its food, and then is silent again.

4 "And do not eat the eagle, the hawk, the kite, or the crow."[54] "You must not," he says, "cling to such people or be like them, people who do not know how to procure food for themselves through toil and sweat, but by their lawless behavior seize food that belongs to others. And they are always on the watch, strolling about with ostensible innocence, but looking to see what they can plunder because of their greed." For these are the only birds that do not procure their own food, but sit by idly, waiting to see how they might devour the flesh procured by others, being pestilent in their evil.

5 "And do not," he says, "eat the lamprey eel, the octopus, or the cuttlefish."[55] "You must not," he says, "be like such people, who are completely impious and condemned already to death." For these fish alone are cursed and hover in the depths, not swimming like the others but dwelling in the mud beneath the depths.

6 But also "do not eat the hare."[56] For what reason? "You must not," he says, "be one who corrupts children or be like such people." For the rabbit adds an orifice every year; it has as many holes as years it has lived.

7 "Nor shall you eat the hyena."[57] "You must not," he says, "be an adulterer or a pervert nor be like such people." For what reason? Because this animal changes its nature every year, at one time it is male, the next time female.

8 And he has fully hated the weasel. "You must

---

[s]I.e., of the covenant   [t]I.e., the number eighteen in Greek is JE, taken here as an abbreviation for the name "Jesus"

---

[45]Cf. Isa 1:2   [46]Cf. Isa 1:10; 28:14   [47]Cf. Isa 40:3   [48]Jer 4:3–4   [49]Cf. Deut 10:16   [50]Jer 9:26   [51]Cf. Gen 14:14; 17:23   [52]Cf. Lev 11:7–15; Deut 14:8–14   [53]Cf. Deut 4:10, 13   [54]Cf. Lev 11:13–16   [55]Source unknown   [56]Cf. Lev 11:6   [57]Source unknown

not," he says, "be like those who are reputed to perform a lawless deed in their mouth because of their uncleanness, nor cling to unclean women who perform the lawless deed in their mouth." For this animal conceives with its mouth.

9 And so, Moses received the three firm teachings about food and spoke in the Spirit. But they received his words according to the desires of their own flesh, as if he were actually speaking about food.

10 And David received the knowledge of the same three firm teachings and spoke in a similar way: "How fortunate is the man who does not proceed in the counsel of the impious" (like the fish who proceed in darkness in the depths) "and does not stand in the path of sinners" (like those who appear to fear God but sin like the pig) "and does not sit in the seat of the pestilent"[58] (like the birds who sit waiting for something to seize). Here you have a perfect lesson about food. 11 Again Moses said, "Eat every animal with a split hoof and that chews the cud."[59] What does he mean? He means that the one who receives food knows who has provided it and appears to be glad, having relied on him. He spoke well, looking to the commandment. What does he mean then? Cling to those who fear the Lord, to those who meditate on the special meaning of the teaching they have received in their heart, to those who discuss and keep the upright demands of the Lord, to those who know that meditation is a work that produces gladness, and to those who carefully chew over the word of the Lord. But why does he mention the split hoof? Because the one who is upright both walks in this world and waits for the holy age. Do you see how well Moses has given the Law? 12 But how could they know or understand these things? We, however, speak as those who know the commandments in an upright way, as the Lord wished. For this reason he circumcised our hearing and our hearts, that we might understand these things.

11 But we should look closely to see if the Lord was concerned to reveal anything in advance about the water and the cross. On the one hand, it is written about the water that Israel will not at all accept the baptism that brings forgiveness of sins, but will create something in its place for themselves.[u] 2 For the prophet says, "Be as-

tounded, O heaven, and shudder even more at this, O earth. For this people has done two wicked things: They have deserted me, the fountain of life, and dug for themselves a pit of death. 3 Is my holy mountain, Sinai, a rock that has been abandoned? For you will be like young birds who flutter about after being taken from their nest."[60] 4 Again the prophet says, "I will go before you to flatten mountains, crush gates of bronze, and smash bars of iron, and I will give you treasures that are dark, hidden, and unseen, that they may know that I am the Lord God."[61] 5 And, "You will dwell in a high cave, built of solid rock, and its water will not fail. You will see a king with glory, and your soul will meditate on the reverential fear of the Lord."[62] 6 Again in another prophet he says, "The one who does these things will be like a tree planted beside springs of water; it will produce its fruit in its season, and its leaf will not fall, and everything it does will prosper. 7 Not so with the impious, not so; but they will be like chaff driven by the wind from the face of the earth. For this reason the impious will not rise up in judgment nor sinners in the counsel of the upright; for the Lord knows the path of the upright, but the path of the impious will perish."[63] 8 Notice how he describes the water and the cross in the same place. He means this: How fortunate are those who went down into the water hoping in the cross, for he indicates the reward will come "in its season." "At that time," he says, "I will pay it." Now when he says, "the leaves will not fall," he means that every word your mouth utters in faith and love will lead many to convert and hope.

9 And again another prophet says, "The land of Jacob was praised more than every other land." This means that he glorifies the vessel of his Spirit. 10 What does he say then? "And a river was flowing from the right side, and beautiful trees were rising up from it. Whoever eats from them will live forever."[64] 11 This means that we descend into the water full of sins and filth, but come up out of it bearing the fruit of reverential fear in our heart and having the hope in Jesus in our spir-

---

[u]Literally, will build for themselves; Greek obscure

[58]Ps 1:1 [59]Cf. Lev 11:3; Deut 14:6 [60]Jer 2:12–13; cf. Isa 16:1–2 [61]Cf. Isa 45:2–3 [62]Cf. Isa 33:16–18 [63]Ps 1:3–6 [64]Cf. Ezek 47:1–12

its.[v] And "whoever eats from these will live forever" means this: Whoever, he says, hears and believes what has been said will live forever.

12 In a similar way he makes another declaration about the cross in another prophet, who says, "'When will these things be fulfilled?' says the Lord. 'When a tree falls and rises up, and when blood flows from a tree.'"[65] Again you have a message about the cross and the one who was about to be crucified.

2 And he again tells Moses, when Israel was attacked by a foreign people, to remind those under assault that they were being handed over to death because of their sins. The Spirit speaks to the heart of Moses that he should make a type of the cross and of the one who was about to suffer, that they might realize, he says, that if they refused to hope in him, they would be attacked forever. And so Moses stacked weapons one on the other in the midst of the battle, and standing high above all the people he began stretching out his hands; and so Israel again gained the victory. But then, when he lowered his hands, they began to be killed.[66] 3 Why was that? So that they may know that they cannot be saved unless they hope in him.

4 And again in another prophet he says, "All day long I have stretched out my hands to a disobedient people that opposes my upright path."[67]

5 Again Moses made a type of Jesus, showing that he had to suffer and that he will again make alive this one whom they will think they have destroyed. This type came in a sign given when Israel was falling. For the Lord made every serpent bite them and they were dying (since the act of transgression came by Eve through the serpent). This was to convince them that they will be handed over to the affliction of death because of their transgression.

6 Moreover, even though Moses himself issued this command—"You will have no molten or carved image as your god"[68]—he himself made one, that he might show forth a type of Jesus. And so Moses made a bronze serpent and displayed it prominently, and he called the people through a proclamation. 7 And when they came together they begged Moses to offer up a prayer on their behalf, that they might be healed. But Moses said to them, "When any of you is bitten, come to the serpent that is displayed on the tree and hope, in faith, that even though dead, it can restore a person to life; and you will then immediately be saved."[w] And they did this.[69] Again you have the glory of Jesus in these things, for everything is in him and for him. 8 Again, why does Moses say to Jesus the son of Naue,[x] when he gave this name to him who was a prophet, that all the people should listen to him alone? Because the Father reveals everything about his Son Jesus. 9 And so, after Moses gave Jesus the son of Naue[y] this name, he sent him as a reconnaissance scout over the land and said, "Take a small book in your hands and record what the Lord says, that in the last days the Son of God will chop down the entire house of Amalek at its roots."[70] 10 Again you see Jesus, not as son of man but as Son of God, manifest here in the flesh as a type. And so, since they are about to say that the Christ is the son of David, David himself speaks a prophecy in reverential awe, understanding the error of the sinners: "The Lord said to my Lord, 'Sit at my right side until I make your enemies a footstool for your feet.'"[71] 11 And again Isaiah says the following: "The Lord said to Christ my Lord, 'I have grasped his right hand that the nations will obey him, and I will shatter the power of kings.'"[72] See how David calls him Lord; he does not call him son.

13 Now let us see whether it is this people or the first one that receives the inheritance, and whether the covenant is for us or them.

2 Hear what the Scripture says concerning the people: "Isaac prayed for Rebecca his wife, because she was infertile. And then she conceived." Then, "Rebecca went to inquire of the Lord, and the Lord said to her, 'There are two nations in your womb and two peoples in your belly, and one people will dominate the other and the greater will serve the lesser.'"[73] 3 You ought to perceive who Isaac represents and who Rebecca, and whom he means when he shows that this people is greater than that one.

4 In another prophecy Jacob speaks more plain-

---

[v]Or *in the Spirit*   [w]Or *healed*   [x]Or *Joshua the son of Nun*; "Jesus" is the Greek equivalent of the Hebrew name Joshua   [y]Or *Joshua the son of Nun*; "Jesus" is the Greek equivalent of the Hebrew name Joshua

---

[65]4 Ezra 4:33; 5:5   [66]Cf. Exod 17:8–13   [67]Cf. Isa 65:2   [68]Cf. Lev 26:1; Deut 27:15   [69]Cf. Num 21:4–8   [70]Cf. Exod 17:14   [71]Ps 110:1   [72]Cf. Isa 45:1   [73]Cf. Gen 25:21–23

ly to Joseph his son, when he says, "See, the Lord has not kept me from your presence. Bring your sons to me that I may bless them."[74] 5 He brought Ephraim and Manasseh, wanting him to bless Manasseh since he was the elder. So Joseph brought him to the right hand of his father Jacob. But Jacob saw in the Spirit a type of the people who was to come later. And what does it say? "Jacob crossed his hands and placed his right hand on the head of Ephraim, the second and younger, and blessed him. And Joseph said to Jacob, 'Switch your right hand onto Manasseh's head, because he is my firstborn son.' Jacob said to Joseph, 'I know, my child, I know. But the greater will serve the lesser, and it is this one who will be blessed.'"[75] 6 You see about whom he has decreed, that this people will be first, and the heir of the covenant.

7 And if this is also brought to mind through Abraham, we maintain that our knowledge is now perfect. What then does he say to Abraham, when he alone believed and was appointed for righteousness? "See, Abraham, I have made you a father of the nations who believe in God while uncircumcised."[76]

14 Yes indeed. But we should see if he has given the covenant that he swore to the fathers he would give the people. Let us pursue the question. He has given it, but they were not worthy to receive it because of their sins. 2 For the prophet says, "Moses was fasting on Mount Sinai for forty days and forty nights, that he might receive the covenant of the Lord for the people. And Moses received from the Lord the two tablets written with the finger of the Lord's hand in the Spirit."[77] When Moses received them he brought them down to give to the people. 3 And the Lord said to Moses, "Moses, Moses, go down at once, because your people, whom you brought out of the land of Egypt, has broken the Law." Moses understood that they had again made molten images for themselves, and he hurled the tablets from his hands. And the tablets of the Lord's covenant were smashed.[78] 4 So Moses received the covenant, but they were not worthy. Now learn how we have received it. Moses received it as a servant, but the Lord himself gave it to us, as a people of the inheritance, by enduring suffering for us. 5 He was made manifest so that those people might be completely filled with sins, and that we might receive

the covenant through the Lord Jesus, who inherited it. He was prepared for this end, that when he became manifest he might make a covenant with us by his word, after redeeming our hearts from darkness, hearts that were already paid out to death and given over to the lawlessness of deceit. 6 For it is written how the Father commanded him to prepare for himself a holy people after he redeemed us from darkness. 7 And so the prophet says, "I the Lord your God called you in righteousness; and I will grasp your hand and strengthen you. I have given you as a covenant of the people, as a light to the nations, to open the eyes of the blind, to bring out of their bondage those in shackles and out of prison those who sit in darkness."[79] And so we know the place from which we have been redeemed. 8 Again the prophet says, "See, I have set you as a light to the nations that you may bring salvation to the end of the earth; so says the Lord God who redeems you."[80] 9 Again the prophet says, "The Spirit of the Lord is upon me, because he anointed me to preach the good news of grace to the humble; he sent me to heal those whose hearts are crushed, to proclaim a release to the captives and renewed sight to the blind, to call out the acceptable year of the Lord and the day of recompense, to comfort all those who mourn."[81]

15 Something is also written about the sabbath in the ten commandments, which God spoke to Moses face-to-face on Mount Sinai: "Make the sabbath of the Lord holy, with pure hands and a pure heart."[82] 2 In another place it says, "If my children keep the sabbath, I will bestow my mercy on them."[83] 3 This refers to the sabbath at the beginning of creation: "God made the works of his hands in six days, and he finished on the seventh day; and he rested on it and made it holy."[84] 4 Pay attention, children, to what it means that "he finished in six days." This means that in six thousand years the Lord will complete all things. For with him a day represents a thousand years. He himself testifies that I am right, when he says, "See, a day of the Lord will be like a thousand years."[85] And so, children, all things

---

[74]Gen 48:11, 9   [75]Cf. Gen 48:14, 19   [75]Cf. Gen 15:6; 17:4   [77]Cf. Exod. 24:18; 31:18   [78]Cf. Exod 32:7–19   [79]Isa 42:6–7   [80]Cf. Isa 49:6–7   [81]Isa 61:1–2   [82]Cf. Exod 20:8; Deut 5:12   [83]Cf. Jer 17:24–25   [84]Gen 2:2–3   [85]Cf. Ps 90:4; 2 Pet 3:8

will be completed in six days—that is to say, in six thousand years.

5 "And he rested on the seventh day." This means that when his Son comes he will put an end to the age of the lawless one, judge the impious, and alter the sun, moon, and stars; then he will indeed rest on the seventh day.

6 Moreover, it says, "Make it holy with pure hands and a pure heart." We are very much mistaken if we think that at the present time anyone, by having a pure heart, can make holy the day that the Lord has made holy. 7 And so you see that at that time, when we are given a good rest, we will make it holy—being able to do so because we ourselves have been made upright and have received the promise, when lawlessness is no more and all things have been made new by the Lord. Then we will be able to make the day holy, after we ourselves have been made holy.

8 Moreover he says to them, "I cannot stand your new moons and sabbaths."[86] You see what he means: It is not the sabbaths of the present time that are acceptable to me, but the one I have made, in which I will give rest to all things and make a beginning of an eighth day, which is the beginning of another world. 9 Therefore also we celebrate the eighth day with gladness, for on it Jesus arose from the dead, and appeared, and ascended into heaven.

16 I will also speak to you about the Temple, since those wretches were misguided in hoping in the building rather than in their God who made them, as if the Temple were actually the house of God. 2 For they consecrated him in the Temple almost like the Gentiles do. But consider what the Lord says in order to invalidate it: "Who has measured the sky with the span of his hand or the earth with his outstretched fingers? Is it not I, says the Lord? The sky is my throne and the earth is the footstool for my feet. What sort of house will you build me, or where is the place I can rest?"[87] You knew that their hope was in vain! 3 Moreover he says again, "See, those who have destroyed this temple will themselves build it."[88] 4 This is happening. For because of their war, it was destroyed by their enemies. And now the servants of the enemies will themselves rebuild it.

5 Again it was revealed how the city, the temple, and the people of Israel were about to be hand-

ed over. For the Scripture says, "It will be in the last days that the Lord will hand over to destruction the sheep of the pasture along with their enclosure and tower."[89] And it has happened just as the Lord said. 6 But let us inquire if a temple of God still exists. It does exist, where he says that he is making and completing it. For it is written, "It will come about that when the seventh day is finished, a temple of God will be gloriously built in the name of the Lord."[90] 7 And so I conclude that a temple exists. But learn how it will be built in the name of the Lord. Before we believed in God, the dwelling place of our heart was corrupt and feeble, since it really was a temple built by hand; for it was full of idolatry and was a house of demons, because we did everything that was opposed to God. 8 "But it will be built in the name of the Lord." Now pay attention, so that the temple of the Lord may be gloriously built. And learn how: We have become new, created again from the beginning, because we have received the forgiveness of sins and have hoped in the name. Therefore God truly resides within our place of dwelling—within us. 9 How so? His word of faith, his call to us through his promise, the wisdom of his upright demands, the commandments of the teaching, he himself prophesying in us and dwelling in us who had served death, opening up to us the door of the temple, which is the mouth, and giving repentance to us—thus he brings us into his imperishable temple. 10 For the one who longs to be saved looks not merely to a person but to the one who dwells and speaks in him. For he is amazed at him since he has never heard him speak these words from his mouth nor even ever desired to hear them. This is a spiritual temple built for the Lord.

17 Insofar as I have been able to set forth these matters to you simply, I hope to have fulfilled my desire not to have omitted anything that pertains to salvation. 2 For if I should write to you about things present or things to come, you would not understand, because they are set forth in parables. And so these things will suffice.

18 But let us turn to another area of knowledge and teaching. There are two paths of

---

[86]Isa 1:13   [87]Cf. Isa 40:12; 66:1   [88]Cf. Isa 49:17   [89]Cf. 1 Enoch 89:56   [90]Cf. Dan 9:24; 1 Enoch 91:13

teaching and authority, the path of light and the path of darkness. And the difference between the two paths is great. For over the one are appointed light-bearing angels of God, but over the other angels of Satan. 2 And the one is Lord from eternity past to eternity to come; but the other is the ruler over the present age of lawlessness.

19 This then is the path of light. Anyone who wants to travel to the place that has been appointed should be diligent in his works. Such is the knowledge given to us, that we may walk in it. 2 Love the one who made you; stand in reverential awe of the one who formed you; glorify the one who ransomed you from death. Be simple in heart and rich in spirit. Do not mingle with those who walk along the path of death; hate everything that is not pleasing to God; hate all hypocrisy; do not abandon the commandments of the Lord. 3 Do not exalt yourself but be humble in every way. Do not heap glory on yourself. Do not entertain a wicked plot against your neighbor; do not make your soul impertinent. 4 Do not engage in sexual immorality, do not commit adultery, do not engage in pederasty. The word of God must not go out from you to any who are impure.ᶻ Do not show favoritism when you reproach someone for an unlawful act. Be meek and gentle; tremble at the words you have heard. Do not hold a grudge against your brother. 5 Do not be of two minds whether this should happen or not. Do not take the Lord's name for a futile purpose. Love your neighbor more than yourself. Do not abort a fetus or kill a child that is already born. Do not remove your hand fromᵃ your son or daughter, but from their youth teach them the reverential fear of God. 6 Do not desire your neighbor's belongings; do not be greedy. Do not join forces with the high and mighty but associate with the humble and upright. Welcome whatever happens to you as good, knowing that nothing occurs apart from God. 7 Do not be of two minds or speak from both sides of your mouth, for speaking from both sides of your mouth is a deadly trap. Be subject to your masters as to a replicaᵇ of God, with respect and reverential fear. Do not give orders to your male slave or female servant out of bitterness (since they hope in the same God) lest they stop fearing the God who is over you both. For he did not come to call those of high status but those

whom the Spirit had prepared. 8 Share all things with your neighbor and do not say that anything is your own. For if you are partners in what is imperishable, how much more in what is perishable? Do not be garrulous, for the mouth is a deadly trap. In so far as you are able, be pure within. 9 Do not be one who reaches out your hands to receive but draws them back from giving. Love like the apple of your eye everyone who speaks the word of the Lord to you. 10 Think about the day of judgment night and day, and seek out the company of the saints every day, either laboring through the word and going out to comfort another, being concerned to save a life through the word, or working with your hands as a ransom for your sins. 11 Do not doubt whether to give, nor grumble while giving. But recognize who is the good paymaster of the reward. Guard the injunctions you have received, neither adding to them nor taking away. Completely hate what is evil. Give a fair judgment. 12 Do not create a schism, but make peace by bringing together those who are at odds. Confess your sins. Do not come to prayer with an evil conscience. This is the path of light.

20 But the path of the Black One is crooked and filled with a curse. For it is the path of eternal death which comes with punishment; on it are those things that destroy people's souls: idolatry, impertinence, glorification of power, hypocrisy, duplicity, adultery, murder, robbery, arrogance, transgression, deceit, malice, insolence, sorcery, magic, greed, irreverence toward God. 2 It is filled with persecutors of the good, haters of the truth, lovers of the lie; those who do not know the reward of righteousness, nor cling to the good nor to a fair judgment, who do not look out for the widow and the orphan, who are alert not to the reverential fear of God but to evil, from whom meekness and patience are far removed and remote. For they love what is vain and pursue a reward, showing no mercy to the poor nor toiling for the oppressed; they are prone to slander, not knowing the one who made them; murderers of children and corruptors of what God has fashioned; they turn their backs on the needy, oppress the afflicted, and

---

ᶻGreek obscure   ᵃOr *refrain from disciplining*; or *do not shirk your responsibility toward*   ᵇOr *type*

support the wealthy. They are lawless judges of the impoverished, altogether sinful.

21 And so it is good for one who has learned all the upright demands of the Lord that have been written to walk in them. For the one who does these things will be glorified in the kingdom of God. The one who chooses those other things will be destroyed, along with his works. This is why there is a resurrection; this is why a recompense.

2 I ask those of you who are in high positions, if you are willing to receive advice from my good counsel: Keep some people among yourselves for whom you can do good, and do not fail. 3 The day is near when all things will perish, along with the Wicked One. The Lord is near, as is his reward.[91]

4 Again and again I ask you, be your own good lawgivers, remain faithful advisors to yourselves, remove all hypocrisy from yourselves. 5 And may God, the one who rules the entire world, give you wisdom, understanding, perception, knowledge of his righteous demands, and patience.

6 Become those who are taught by God, enquiring into what the Lord seeks from you. And do it, that you may be found in the day of judgment. 7 And if there is any recollection of what is good, remember me by practicing these things, that my desire and vigilance may lead to a good result. I ask this of you, begging for a favor.

8 While the good vessel is still with you, do not fail in any of these things, but enquire fervently after them and fulfill every commandment. For they are worth doing. 9 Therefore I have been all the more eager to write what I could, to make you glad. Be well,[c] children of love and peace. May the Lord of glory and of every gracious gift be with your spirit.

[c]Or *Be saved*

---

[91]Cf. Isa 40:10; Rev 22:12

The Preaching of Peter

A popular document in the early church, the *Preaching of Peter* was widely assumed by early church fathers to have been composed by the apostle Peter himself. Most scholars today, however, think that it was written sometime during the first part of the second century.

The book no longer survives intact but is known only through the quotations of later authors, especially Clement of Alexandria, who lived at the end of the second century and the beginning of the third. On the basis of these fragmentary remains it is impossible to judge the original length or contents of the document. Some of its major emphases, however, are reasonably clear: according to its author, Christianity is superior both to the cults of pagans, who naively worship idols and living creatures, and to the religion of the Jews, who in their ignorance worship angels and celestial bodies rather than the true God. In particular, the book emphasizes that Christ fulfilled the predictions of the Jewish Scriptures and brought salvation to all people. Everyone who learns the truth of Christ is to repent for the forgiveness of their sins.

It is possible, given its themes, that the book was one of the first "apologies" for early Christianity, that is, a reasoned defense of the views of Christians against the attacks of their cultured despisers, both pagans and Jews.

1. Clement of Alexandria *Strom.* 1.29.182

And in the Preaching of Peter you may find the Lord called "Law and Word."

2. Clement of Alexandria, *Strom.* 6.5.39–41

But that the most notable of the Greeks do not know God by direct knowledge but indirectly, Peter says in his Preaching, "Know then that there is one God who made the beginning of all things and has power over their end," and "The invisible who sees all things, uncontainable, who contains all, who needs nothing, of whom all things stand in need and for whose sake they exist, incomprehensible, perpetual, incorruptible, uncreated, who made all things by the word of his power . . . that is, the Son." Then he goes on, "This God you must worship, not after the manner of the Greeks . . . showing that we and the notable Greeks worship the same God, though not according to perfect knowledge for they had not learned the tradition of the Son." "Do not," he says, "worship"—he does not say "the God whom the Greeks worship," but "not in the manner of the Greeks": he would change the method of worship of God, not proclaim another God. What, then, is meant by "not in the manner of the Greeks"? Peter himself will explain, for he continues, "Carried away by ignorance and not knowing God as we do, according to the perfect knowledge, but shaping those things over which he gave them power for their use, wood and stones, brass and iron, gold and silver, forgetting their material and proper use, they set up things subservient to their existence and worship them; and what things God has given them for food, the fowls of the air and the creatures that swim in the sea and creep on the earth, wild beasts and four-footed cattle of the field, weasels too and mice, cats and dogs and apes; even their own foodstuffs do they sacrifice to animals that can be consumed and, offering dead things to the dead as if they were gods, they show ingratitude to God since by these practices they deny that he exists. . ." He continues again in this fashion, "Neither worship him as the Jews do for they, who suppose that they alone know God, do not know him, serving angels and archangels, the month and the moon: and if no moon be seen, they do not celebrate what is called the first sabbath, nor keep the new moon, nor the days of unleavened bread, nor the feast of tabernacles, nor the great day (of atonement)."

Then he adds the finale of what is required: "So then learn in a holy and righteous manner that which we deliver to you, observe, worshipping God through Christ in a new way. For we have found in the Scriptures, how the Lord said, 'Behold, I make with you a new covenant, not as the covenant with your fathers in mount Horeb.'[1] He has made a new one with us: for the ways of the Greeks and Jews are old, but we are Christians who worship him in a new way as a third generation."

3. Clement of Alexandria *Strom.* 6.5.43

Therefore Peter says that the Lord said to the apostles, "If then any of Israel will repent and believe in God through my name, his sins shall be forgiven him: and after twelve years go out into the world, lest any say, 'We did not hear'."

4. Clement of Alexandria *Strom.* 6.6.48

For example, in the Preaching of Peter the Lord says, "I chose you twelve, judging you to be disciples worthy of me, whom the Lord willed, and thinking you faithful apostles I sent you into the world to preach the gospel to people throughout the world, that they should know that there is one God; to declare by faith in me [the Christ] what shall be, so that those who have heard and believed may be saved, and that those who have not believed may hear and bear witness, not having any defence so as to say, 'We did not hear.' . . ."

And to all reasonable souls it has been said above: Whatever things any of you did in ignorance, not knowing God clearly, all his sins shall be forgiven him, if he comes to God and repents.

5. Clement of Alexandria *Strom.* 6.15.128

Peter in the Preaching, speaking of the apostles, says, "But, having opened the books of the prophets which we had, we found, sometimes expressed by parables, sometimes by riddles, and sometimes directly and in so many words the name Jesus Christ, both his coming and his death and the cross and all the other torments which the Jews inflicted on him, and his resurrection and assumption into the heavens before Jerusalem was founded, all these things that had been written, what he must suffer and what shall be after him. When, therefore, we gained knowledge of these things, we believed in God through that which had been written of him."

And a little after he adds that the prophecies came by divine providence, in these terms, "For we know that God commanded them, and without the Scripture we say nothing."

6. John of Damascus, *Parall.* A 12

(Of Peter): Wretched that I am, I remembered not that God sees the mind and observes the voice of the soul. Allying myself with sin, I said to myself, "God is merciful, and will bear with me; and be-

---

[1]Jer 31:31–32

cause I was not immediately smitten, I ceased not, but rather despised pardon, and exhausted the long-suffering of God."

(From the Teaching of Peter): Rich is the man who has mercy on many, and, imitating God, gives what he has. For God has given all things to all his creation. Understand then, you rich, that you ought to minister, for you have received more than you yourselves need. Learn that others lack the things you have in superfluity. Be ashamed to keep things that belong to others. Imitate the fairness of God, and no one will be poor.

7. Origen, *de Principiis* i, prol. 8

But if any would produce to us from that book which is called The Doctrine of Peter, the passage where the Saviour is represented as saying to the disciples, "I am not a bodiless demon," . . .

8. Gregory of Nazianaus, *epp.* 16 and 20

"A soul in trouble is near to God," as Peter says somewhere—a marvellous utterance.

The Fragments of Papias

According to the church father Irenaeus, Papias was a companion of Polycarp. The fourth-century church historian Eusebius claims that Papias had been the bishop of Hieropolis in Asia Minor. Otherwise we know very little about the man.

Sometime between 110 and 140 C.E. Papias wrote a five-volume work entitled *Expositions of the Sayings of the Lord*. The work no longer survives intact, but several fragments from it are quoted and discussed by such church fathers as Irenaeus and Eusebius. Papias claims to have acquired his information about Jesus from followers of the disciples; in particular, he names Aristion and "the presbyter John." Eusebius points out that the latter could not have been John the son of Zebedee, whom Papias mentions elsewhere.

Among the most interesting features of the surviving fragments of Papias are the following:

(1)   He is forthright in stating his preference for *oral* traditions about Jesus (the "living and abiding voice") over written accounts about him (i.e., the Gospels; it is uncertain if he knew of any besides Matthew and Mark).

(2)   He asserts that Mark recorded stories about Jesus as they were told by Peter, but acknowledges that Peter often changed the stories as occasion demanded, that he did not tell them sequentially, and that Mark did not record them "in order." (Many scholars believe that Papias is referring to our canonical Mark, but that is not at all certain; in any event, it should be recalled that he is writing nearly six decades after Mark had been placed in circulation.)

(3)   He maintains that Matthew collected Jesus' sayings in Hebrew, and that these sayings were translated (into Greek?) in different ways by different people. (Again, it is not clear that Papias has in mind the New Testament Gospel of Matthew, since this book, unlike the collection of sayings that Papias mentions, was originally composed in Greek rather than Hebrew.)

Eusebius discusses several other features of Papias's writings without quoting them directly. Papias had evidently related the story of a dead person raised to life in his own congregation, an account of a Christian man who drank deadly poison to no ill effect, and an episode similar to the story of the woman taken in adultery that later found its way into manuscripts of the Gospel of John (7:53–8:12).

In particular, Papias emphasized a materialistic understanding of the end time, asserting that there was to be a literal thousand-year millenium on earth after the resurrection of the dead. This teaching did not ingratiate Papias with later church writers. Eusebius, for instance, calls him "a man of exceedingly small intelligence" (*Ecclesiastical History* 3.39.13). Perhaps as a result of such views, Papias's writings were not copied and preserved for posterity.

1. Irenaeus of Lyons, *Against Heresies*, 5.33.3–4

Thus the blessing that is foretold belongs without question to the times of the kingdom, when the righteous will rise from the dead and rule, and the creation that is renewed and set free will bring forth from the dew of heaven and the fertility of the soil[1] an abundance of food of all kinds. Thus the elders who saw John, the disciple of the Lord, remembered hearing him say how the Lord used to teach about those times, saying:

2 "The days are coming when vines will come forth, each with ten thousand boughs; and on a single bough will be ten thousand branches. And indeed, on a single branch will be ten thousand shoots and on every shoot ten thousand clusters; and in every cluster will be ten thousand grapes, and every grape, when pressed, will yield twenty-five measures of wine. 3 And when any of the saints grabs hold of a cluster, another will cry out, 'I am better, take me; bless the Lord through me.' So too a grain of wheat will produce ten thousand heads and every head will have ten thousand grains and every grain will yield ten pounds of pure, exceptionally fine flour. So too the remaining fruits and seeds and vegetation will produce in similar proportions. And all the animals who eat this food drawn from the earth will come to be at peace and harmony with one another, yielding in complete submission to humans."

4 Papias as well, an ancient man—the one who heard John and was a companion of Polycarp—gives a written account of these things in the fourth of his books. For he wrote five books. And in addition he says 5 "These things can be believed by those who believe. And the betrayer Judas," he said, "did not believe, but asked, 'How then can the Lord bring forth such produce?'" The Lord then replied, "Those who come into those times will see."

2. Eusebius, *Ecclesiastical History*, 2.15

But such a light of piety shone on the minds of those who heard Peter that they were not nearly satisfied with a single hearing or with an unwritten account of the divine proclamation. And so with all kinds of entreaties they begged Mark (whose Gospel is now in circulation), a follower of Peter, that he might leave behind a written record of the teaching that had been given to them orally. And they did not rest until they had prevailed upon him. To this extent they were the impetus for the writing called the Gospel according to Mark. And they say that when the apostle came to know what had happened, after the Spirit revealed it to him, he delighted in their eagerness and authorized the writing to be read in the churches. Clement passes along this story in the sixth book of the *Outlines,* and the one who is called Papias, the bishop of Hierapolis, corroborates his account, pointing out in addition that Peter makes mention of Mark in his first epistle, which also they maintain was composed in Rome itself . . .

3. Eusebius, *Ecclesiastical History*, 3.39

There are five books written by Papias in circulation, entitled *An Exposition of the Sayings of the Lord.* Irenaeus remembers these as the only ones Papias wrote, as he somewhere says, "And Papias as well, an ancient man—the one who heard John and was a companion of Polycarp—gives a written account of these things in the fourth of his books. For he wrote five books."[a] 2 Thus Irenaeus. But Papias himself, in the preface of his work, makes it clear that he himself neither heard nor saw in person any of the holy apostles. Instead, he declares that he received the matters of faith from those known to them. As he says:

[a]Cf. Irenaeus, *Against Heresies*, 5.33.4

---

[1]Cf. Gen 27:28

3 "I also will not hesitate to draw up for you, along with these expositions, an orderly account of all the things I carefully learned and have carefully recalled from the elders; for I have certified their truth. For unlike most people, I took no pleasure in hearing those who had a lot to say, but only those who taught the truth, and not those who recalled commandments from strangers, but only those who recalled the commandments which have been given faithfully by the Lord and which proceed from the truth itself. 4 But whenever someone arrived who had been a companion of one of the elders, I would carefully inquire after their words, what Andrew or Peter had said, or what Philip or what Thomas had said, or James or John or Matthew or any of the other disciples of the Lord, and what things Aristion and the elder John, disciples of the Lord, were saying. For I did not suppose that what came out of books would benefit me as much as that which came from a living and abiding voice."

. . . 7 This Papias, whom we have just been discussing, acknowledges that he received the words of the apostles from those who had been their followers, and he indicates that he himself had listened to Aristion and the elder John. And so he often recalls them by name, and in his books he sets forth the traditions that they passed along. These remarks should also be of some use to us. 8 But it would be worthwhile to supplement these remarks of Papias with some of his other words, through which he recounts certain miracles and other matters, which would have come to him from the tradition. 9 We have already seen that the apostle Philip resided in Hieropolis with his daughters;[b] but now I should point out that Papias, who was their contemporary, recalls an amazing story that he learned from Philip's daughters. For he indicates that a person was raised from the dead in his own time. Moreover, he tells another miracle about Justus (also called Barsabbas), who drank deadly poison but suffered no ill effects because he was sustained by the grace of the Lord. . . . 11 And he sets forth other matters that came to him from the unwritten tradition, including some bizarre parables of the Savior, his teachings, and several other more legendary accounts. 12 Among these things he says that after the resurrection of the dead there will be a thousand-year period, dur-

ing which the Kingdom of Christ will exist tangibly, here on this very earth. . . . 14 And in his own book he passes along other accounts of the sayings of the Lord from Aristion, whom we have already mentioned, as well as traditions from the elder John. We have referred knowledgeable readers to these and now feel constrained to add to these reports already quoted from him a tradition that he gives about Mark, who wrote the Gospel. These are his words: 15 "And this is what the elder used to say,

'When Mark was the interpreter[c] of Peter, he wrote down accurately everything that he recalled of the Lord's words and deeds—but not in order. For he neither heard the Lord nor accompanied him; but later, as I indicated, he accompanied Peter, who used to adapt his teachings for the needs at hand, not arranging, as it were, an orderly composition of the Lord's sayings. And so Mark did nothing wrong by writing some of the matters as he remembered them. For he was intent on just one purpose: to leave out nothing that he heard or to include any falsehood among them.'"

This then is what Papias says about Mark. 16 And this is what he says about Matthew:

"And so Matthew composed the sayings in the Hebrew tongue, and each one interpreted[d] them to the best of his ability."

17 And Papias made use of the testimonies found in the first epistle of John, and from the epistle of Peter as well. And he set forth another account about a woman who was falsely accused of many sins before the Lord,[2] which is also found in the Gospel according to the Hebrews . . .

4. Apollinaris of Laodicea (Drawn from a Number of Sources)

Judas did not die by hanging, but he survived after being taken down, before he had choked to death. The Acts of the Apostles signifies this as well: "Falling headfirst he burst forth in the middle, and his intestines spilled out."[3] And Pa-

[b]See *Ecclesiastical History* 3.31   [c]Or *translator*   [d]Or *translated*

[2]Cf. John 7:53–8:11   [3]Cf. Acts 1:18

pias, the disciple of John, relates this very clearly in the fourth book of his *Exposition of the Sayings of the Lord*:

2 "But Judas went about in this world as a great model of impiety. He became so bloated in the flesh that he could not pass through a place that was easily wide enough for a wagon—not even his swollen head could fit. They say that his eyelids swelled to such an extent that he could not see the light at all; and a doctor could not see his eyes even with an optical device, so deeply sunken they were in the surrounding flesh. And his genitals became more disgusting and larger than anyone's; simply by relieving himself, to his wanton shame, he emitted pus and worms that flowed through his entire body. 3 And they say that after he suffered numerous torments and punishments, he died on his own land, and that land has been, until now, desolate and uninhabited because of the stench. Indeed, even to this day no one can pass by the place without holding their nose. This was how great an outpouring he made from his flesh on the ground."

5. Jerome, *Lives of Illustrious Men,* 18

Papias, the hearer of John and bishop of Hierapolis in Asia, wrote only five volumes, which he called *An Exposition of the Sayings of the Lord.* When he claims in the Preface that he did not follow various opinions, but had the apostles as his authorities, he says:

"I used to make careful inquiry into what Andrew and Peter said, and what Philip said, and Thomas, and James, and John, and Matthew, and any of the other disciples of the Lord; and what Aristion and the elder John, the Lord's disciples, would say. For books that can be read are less useful to me than a living voice that resounds through authorities still alive in our own day."

. . . He is said to have propagated the Jewish tradition of the millennium, adopted by Irenaeus, Apollinarius, and others, who say that the Lord will rule in the flesh, with his saints, after the resurrection.

6. Maximus the Confessor, Scolia on Dionysius the Areopagite, *On the Heavenly Hierarchy,* chap. 2

They used to call those who were trained in divine innocence "children," as Papias shows in the first book of *The Expositions of the Lord's Sayings.*

7. Maximus the Confessor, *On the Heavenly Hierarchy,* chap. 7

When he said these things, I think he[e] was alluding to Papias who was then a bishop of Hierapolis in Asia, flourishing during the time of the Evangelist John. For this Papias, in his fourth book of *The Expositions of the Lord's Sayings,* spoke about the pleasures of food in the resurrection. . . . And Irenaeus of Lyons says the same thing in the fifth book of his work, *Against Heresies,* citing this one we have named, Papias, as a witness to the things he said.

8. Andreas of Caesarea, *Preface to the Apocalypse*

Nonetheless, we think it superfluous to speak at length about the inspiration of the book,[f] since such blessed writers as Gregory (I mean the theologian) and Cyril, not to mention such ancient writers as Papias, Irenaeus, Methodius, and Hippolytus have borne witness to its trustworthiness.

9. Andreas of Caesarea, *On the Apocalypse,* chap. 34

And the following is exactly what Papias says: "He appointed some of them (he clearly means the holy angels of old) to rule over the administration of the earth, and he ordered them to rule it well." And later he says, "But it turned out that their assignment came to nothing."

10. Anastasius of Sinai, *Contemplations on the Hexamaron*

They take their lead from the renowned Papias of Hierapolis, the close companion of the one who

---

[e] I.e., Dionysius the Areopagite   [f] I.e., the Apocalypse of John

leaned on Jesus' breast, and Clement, and Pantaenus the priest of the Alexandrian church, and the most wise Ammonius—ancient exegetes who lived before the councils, who understood the entire six days of creation to refer to Christ and the church.

11. Anastasius of Sinai, *Contemplations on the Hexamaron,* book 7

And so, the very ancient exegetes of the church, I mean the philosopher Philo, who lived in the time of the apostles, and the great Papias of Hierapolis, who was a close companion of the Evangelist John . . . and those who were their associates, understood the stories about Paradise in a spiritual way, as referring to the church of Christ.

12. Philip of Side, *Ecclesiastical History*

Papias, bishop of Hierapolis, hearer of the theologian John and friend of Polycarp, wrote five books about the sayings of the Lord. In these, in a list that he made of the apostles, after Peter and John, Philip and Thomas and Matthew, he indicated that Aristion and another John, whom he also called an elder, were disciples of the Lord . . . Papias was also mistaken about the future millennium; Irenaeus got his ideas from him. 2 In his second book Papias says that John the theologian and his brother James were killed by Jews. And this Papias we have been discussing related a story that he evidently received from the daughters of Philip, that when Barsabbas, also called Justus, was put to the test by unbelievers, he drank snake poison but was preserved unharmed by the name of Christ. And he tells other amazing stories—especially one about Manaim's mother, who was raised from the dead. And he relates that those who were raised from the dead by Christ lived until the time of Hadrian.

13. George the Sinner, *Chronicle*

And after Domitian, Nerva reigned for one year. He recalled John from his island and allowed him to live in Ephesus. He alone of the twelve disciples remained alive at that time; and after he composed his Gospel he was found worthy to become a martyr. 2 For Papias, bishop of Hierapolis, an eyewitness of John, asserts in the second book of the Lord's sayings that John was killed by Jews. And so he, along with his brother, clearly fulfilled the prediction of Christ about them and the confession and consent that they gave to it. For the Lord said to them, "Are you able to drink the cup that I drink?" And when they eagerly nodded their assent and agreed to do so, he said, "You will drink my cup, and you will be baptized with the baptism that I experience."[4] And it makes sense that this happened, because God cannot lie. 3 So too the polymath Origen sets forth clearly in his commentary on Matthew[g] that John was martyred, indicating that he learned this from the successors to the apostles.

14. Photius, *Bibliotheca*

[Stephen Gorbarus] did not [go along with] Papias the bishop and martyr of Hierapolis or with Irenaeus, the holy bishop of Lyons, when they said that the kingdom of heaven involved the enjoyment of foods palpable to the senses.

15. Catena of the Greek Fathers on Saint John

For when the last of these, John, called "Son of Thunder,"[5] had become a very old man (as Irenaeus, Eusebius, and other reliable historians who followed in their train have handed down to us), fearful heresies had sprouted up; and he dictated the Gospel to his own disciple, the respectable Papias of Hierapolis, so as to complete the work of those before him who had proclaimed the word to the nations throughout the world.

16. Codex Vaticanus Alexandrinus, 14

Here begins an overview[h] of the Gospel according to John.

The Gospel of John was published and given to the churches by John while he was still living, just as Papias, also called the Hierapolite, a close disciple of John, mentions in the more accessible part of his five books—that is to say, near the end. In fact, he carefully transcribed the Gospel while John dictated it to him.

[g]Origen, *Commentary on Matthew,* 16.6   [h]Or *the subject matter*

[4]Cf. Mark 10:38–39   [5]Mark 3:18

EARLY CHRISTIAN
APOCALYPSES

The Revelation to John

No book of the Christian Bible has so mystified and intrigued readers over the centuries as the Revelation (or Apocalypse) to John. Nor has any other been subject to such wild and divergent interpretations, as readers have tried to demonstrate that its visions of the end time relate directly to events transpiring in their own day.

The book records a series of visions given by God to his prophet John on the island of Patmos (1:9). The author does not claim to be Jesus' disciple, John the son of Zebedee, although tradition has so identified him. In any event, modern scholars have recognized on linguistic grounds that, whoever wrote this book (John was a common name), it was not the author of the Fourth Gospel.

The first vision is of Christ himself, who appears to the author as "one like the Son of Man" (chap. 1; cf. Dan 7:13) and dictates letters to the seven churches of Asia Minor to comfort and/or admonish them in their Christian lives (chaps. 2–3). The rest of the book narrates a series of heavenly visions concerning the future course of events on earth; the events are catastrophic and take place in three series of sevens: the breaking of seven seals of a scroll that records earth's destiny (chaps. 5–6); the blowing of seven trumpets (chaps. 8–9), which also leads to the appearance of the anti-Christ and his prophet (chaps. 12–13); and the pouring out of seven bowls of God's wrath (chaps. 15–16).

The earthly disasters reach their climax with the destruction of the Great Whore of Babylon, representing Rome, the city "built on seven hills" (17:9, 18), followed by a cosmic battle in which Christ destroys the forces of evil aligned against him (chaps. 17–19). In the end, God sends his kingdom to earth, in which his saints will live a blessed existence forever (chaps. 20–22).

Whereas this description of future events may seem bizarre and unique to modern readers, it is a kind of book that would have been familiar to Jewish and Christian readers in the ancient world. Most of the other ancient "apocalypses" are pseudonymous, written in the names of famous persons from the past like Abraham, Enoch, or Adam. These books record highly symbolic visions given to the prophet by God and interpreted through an angelic mediator; the visions typically reveal the future course of worldly events or indicate the real but hidden meaning of earthly realities. In every instance, the visions are meant to provide hope for their readers: despite appearances to the contrary, God is ultimately in control of the world and its destiny, and those who remain faithful to him will be rewarded in the end. For the Book of Revelation, the enemy of believers is the city of Rome and its emperors (chaps. 17–19); the author's visions show that God will soon intervene on behalf of his persecuted saints, overthrow the evil empire aligned against them, and bestow eternal rewards on those who remain faithful.

While it is difficult to assign a date to the Book of Revelation, most scholars think that some of its visions date to the reign of Nero (ca. 64 C.E.), but that the book as a whole was not completed until near the end of the first century, possibly around 95 C.E. during the reign of Domitian.

From the New Revised Standard Version Bible, © 1989.

Not by John (John referred to in 3rd person)   *Slave*

1

The revelation of Jesus Christ, which God gave him to show his servants what must soon take place; he made[b] it known by sending his angel to his servant John, 2 who testified to the word of God and to the testimony of Jesus Christ, even to all that he saw.

Beatitude (7 in Rev)

3 Blessed is the one who reads aloud the words of the prophecy, and blessed are those who hear and who keep what is written in it; for the time is near.

Starts as a Letter (Similar to Paul)

4 John to the seven churches that are in Asia: Grace to you and peace from him who is and who was and who is to come, and from the seven spirits who are before his throne, 5 and from Jesus Christ, the faithful witness, the firstborn of the dead, and the ruler of the kings of the earth.

Could be out the text

To him who loves us and freed[d] us from our sins by his blood, 6 and made[b] us to be a kingdom, priests serving[e] his God and Father, to him be glory and dominion forever and ever. Amen.

Dan 7:13

7 Look! He is coming with the
   clouds;
every eye will see him,
   even those who pierced him;
and on his account all the tribes
   of the earth will wail.

So it is to be. Amen.

1st time God spoke in Rev

8 "I am the Alpha and the Omega," says the Lord God, who is and who was and who is to come, the Almighty.

9 I, John, your brother who share with you in Jesus the persecution and the kingdom and the patient endurance, was on the island called Patmos because of the word of God and the testimony of Jesus.[f] 10 I was in the spirit[g] on the Lord's day, and I heard behind me a loud voice like a trumpet 11 saying, "Write in a book what you see and send it to the seven churches, to Ephesus, to Smyrna, to Pergamum, to Thyatira, to Sardis, to Philadelphia, and to Laodicea."

12 Then I turned to see whose voice it was that spoke to me, and on turning I saw seven golden lampstands, 13 and in the midst of the lampstands I saw one like the Son of Man, clothed with a long robe and with a golden sash across his chest. 14 His head and his hair were white as white wool, white as snow; his eyes were like a flame of fire, 15 his feet were like burnished bronze, refined as

Dan 7 + Dan 10

in a furnace, and his voice was like the sound of many waters. 16 In his right hand he held seven stars, and from his mouth came a sharp, two-edged sword, and his face was like the sun shining with full force.

17 When I saw him, I fell at his feet as though dead. But he placed his right hand on me, saying, "Do not be afraid; I am the first and the last, 18 and the living one. I was dead, and see, I am alive forever and ever; and I have the keys of Death and of Hades. 19 Now write what you have seen, what is, and what is to take place after this. 20 As for the mystery of the seven stars that you saw in my right hand, and the seven golden lampstands: the seven stars are the angels of the seven churches, and the seven lampstands are the seven churches.

2

"To the angel of the church in Ephesus write: These are the words of him who holds the seven stars in his right hand, who walks among the seven golden lampstands:

2 "I know your works, your toil and your patient endurance. I know that you cannot tolerate evildoers; you have tested those who claim to be apostles but are not, and have found them to be false. 3 I also know that you are enduring patiently and bearing up for the sake of my name, and that you have not grown weary. 4 But I have this against you, that you have abandoned the love you had at first. 5 Remember then from what you have fallen; repent, and do the works you did at first. If not, I will come to you and remove your lampstand from its place, unless you repent. 6 Yet this is to your credit: you hate the works of the Nicolaitans, which I also hate. 7 Let anyone who has an ear listen to what the Spirit is saying to the churches. To everyone who conquers, I will give permission to eat from the tree of life that is in the paradise of God.

8 "And to the angel of the church in Smyrna write: These are the words of the first and the last, who was dead and came to life:

9 "I know your affliction and your poverty, even though you are rich. I know the slander on the part of those who say that they are Jews and are not, but are a synagogue of Satan. 10 Do not fear what

[a]Gk *slaves* [b]Gk *and he made* [c]Gk *slave* [d]Other ancient authorities read *washed* [e]Gk *priests to* [f]Or *testimony to Jesus* [g]Or *in the Spirit*

you are about to suffer. Beware, the devil is about to throw some of you into prison so that you may be tested, and for ten days you will have affliction. Be faithful until death, and I will give you the crown of life. 11 Let anyone who has an ear listen to what the Spirit is saying to the churches. Whoever conquers will not be harmed by the second death.

12 "And to the angel of the church in Pergamum write: These are the words of him who has the sharp two-edged sword:

13 "I know where you are living, where Satan's throne is. Yet you are holding fast to my name, and you did not deny your faith in me[h] even in the days of Antipas my witness, my faithful one, who was killed among you, where Satan lives. 14 But I have a few things against you: you have some there who hold to the teaching of Balaam, who taught Balak to put a stumbling block before the people of Israel, so that they would eat food sacrificed to idols and practice fornication. 15 So you also have some who hold to the teaching of the Nicolaitans. 16 Repent then. If not, I will come to you soon and make war against them with the sword of my mouth. 17 Let anyone who has an ear listen to what the Spirit is saying to the churches. To everyone who conquers I will give some of the hidden manna, and I will give a white stone, and on the white stone is written a new name that no one knows except the one who receives it.

18 "And to the angel of the church in Thyatira write: These are the words of the Son of God, who has eyes like a flame of fire, and whose feet are like burnished bronze:

19 "I know your works—your love, faith, service, and patient endurance. I know that your last works are greater than the first. 20 But I have this against you: you tolerate that woman Jezebel, who calls herself a prophet and is teaching and beguiling my servants[i] to practice fornication and to eat food sacrificed to idols. 21 I gave her time to repent, but she refuses to repent of her fornication. 22 Beware, I am throwing her on a bed, and those who commit adultery with her I am throwing into great distress, unless they repent of her doings; 23 and I will strike her children dead. And all the churches will know that I am the one who searches minds and hearts, and I will give to each of you

as your works deserve. 24 But to the rest of you in Thyatira, who do not hold this teaching, who have not learned what some call 'the deep things of Satan,' to you I say, I do not lay on you any other burden; 25 only hold fast to what you have until I come. 26 To everyone who conquers and continues to do my works to the end,

I will give authority over the
  nations;
27 to rule[j] them with an iron rod,
    as when clay pots are
      shattered—

28 even as I also received authority from my Father. To the one who conquers I will also give the morning star. 29 Let anyone who has an ear listen to what the Spirit is saying to the churches.

3 "And to the angel of the church in Sardis write: These are the words of him who has the seven spirits of God and the seven stars:

"I know your works; you have a name of being alive, but you are dead. 2 Wake up, and strengthen what remains and is on the point of death, for I have not found your works perfect in the sight of my God. 3 Remember then what you received and heard; obey it, and repent. If you do not wake up, I will come like a thief, and you will not know at what hour I will come to you. 4 Yet you have still a few persons in Sardis who have not soiled their clothes; they will walk with me, dressed in white, for they are worthy. 5 If you conquer, you will be clothed like them in white robes, and I will not blot your name out of the book of life; I will confess your name before my Father and before his angels. 6 Let anyone who has an ear listen to what the Spirit is saying to the churches.

7 "And to the angel of the church in Philadelphia write:

These are the words of the holy
  one, the true one,
  who has the key of David,
  who opens and no one will
    shut,
  who shuts and no one opens:
8 "I know your works. Look, I have set before you an open door, which no one is able to shut. I

[h]Or deny my faith [i]Gk slaves [j]Or to shepherd

know that you have but little power, and yet you have kept my word and have not denied my name. 9 I will make those of the synagogue of Satan who say that they are Jews and are not, but are lying— I will make them come and bow down before your feet, and they will learn that I have loved you. 10 Because you have kept my word of patient endurance, I will keep you from the hour of trial that is coming on the whole world to test the inhabitants of the earth. 11 I am coming soon; hold fast to what you have, so that no one may seize your crown. 12 If you conquer, I will make you a pillar in the temple of my God; you will never go out of it. I will write on you the name of my God, and the name of the city of my God, the new Jerusalem that comes down from my God out of heaven, and my own new name. 13 Let anyone who has an ear listen to what the Spirit is saying to the churches.

14 "And to the angel of the church in Laodicea write: The words of the Amen, the faithful and true witness, the origin[k] of God's creation:

15 "I know your works; you are neither cold nor hot. I wish that you were either cold or hot. 16 So, because you are lukewarm, and neither cold nor hot, I am about to spit you out of my mouth. 17 For you say, 'I am rich, I have prospered, and I need nothing.' You do not realize that you are wretched, pitiable, poor, blind, and naked. 18 Therefore I counsel you to buy from me gold refined by fire so that you may be rich; and white robes to clothe you and to keep the shame of your nakedness from being seen; and salve to anoint your eyes so that you may see. 19 I reprove and discipline those whom I love. Be earnest, therefore, and repent. 20 Listen! I am standing at the door, knocking; if you hear my voice and open the door, I will come in to you and eat with you, and you with me. 21 To the one who conquers I will give a place with me on my throne, just as I myself conquered and sat down with my Father on his throne. 22 Let anyone who has an ear listen to what the Spirit is saying to the churches."

4 After this I looked, and there in heaven a door stood open! And the first voice, which I had heard speaking to me like a trumpet, said, "Come up here, and I will show you what must take place after this." 2 At once I was in the spir-

it,[l] and there in heaven stood a throne, with one seated on the throne! 3 And the one seated there looks like jasper and carnelian, and around the throne is a rainbow that looks like an emerald. 4 Around the throne are twenty-four thrones, and seated on the thrones are twenty-four elders, dressed in white robes, with golden crowns on their heads. 5 Coming from the throne are flashes of lightning, and rumblings and peals of thunder, and in front of the throne burn seven flaming torches, which are the seven spirits of God; 6 and in front of the throne there is something like a sea of glass, like crystal.

Around the throne, and on each side of the throne, are four living creatures, full of eyes in front and behind: 7 the first living creature like a lion, the second living creature like an ox, the third living creature with a face like a human face, and the fourth living creature like a flying eagle. 8 And the four living creatures, each of them with six wings, are full of eyes all around and inside. Day and night without ceasing they sing,

"Holy, holy, holy,
    the Lord God the Almighty,
        who was and is and is to
            come."

9 And whenever the living creatures give glory and honor and thanks to the one who is seated on the throne, who lives forever and ever, 10 the twenty-four elders fall before the one who is seated on the throne and worship the one who lives forever and ever; they cast their crowns before the throne, singing,

11   "You are worthy, our Lord and
            God,
        to receive glory and honor and
            power,
    for you created all things,
        and by your will they existed
            and were created."

5 Then I saw in the right hand of the one seated on the throne a scroll written on the inside and on the back, sealed[m] with seven seals; 2 and I saw a mighty angel proclaiming with a loud voice, "Who is worthy to open the scroll and break its seals?" 3 And no one in heaven or on earth or under the earth was able to open the scroll or to

[k]Or *beginning*   [l]Or *in the Spirit*   [m]Or *written on the inside, and sealed on the back*

look into it. 4 And I began to weep bitterly because no one was found worthy to open the scroll or to look into it. 5 Then one of the elders said to me, "Do not weep. See, the Lion of the tribe of Judah, the Root of David, has conquered, so that he can open the scroll and its seven seals."

6 Then I saw between the throne and the four living creatures and among the elders a Lamb standing as if it had been slaughtered, having seven horns and seven eyes, which are the seven spirits of God sent out into all the earth. 7 He went and took the scroll from the right hand of the one who was seated on the throne. 8 When he had taken the scroll, the four living creatures and the twenty-four elders fell before the Lamb, each holding a harp and golden bowls full of incense, which are the prayers of the saints. 9 They sing a new song:

> "You are worthy to take the scroll
> and to open its seals,
> for you were slaughtered and by
> your blood you ransomed
> for God
> saints from[n] every tribe and
> language and people and
> nation;
10   you have made them to be a
> kingdom and priests
> serving[o] our God,
> and they will reign on earth."

11 Then I looked, and I heard the voice of many angels surrounding the throne and the living creatures and the elders; they numbered myriads of myriads and thousands of thousands, 12 singing with full voice,

> "Worthy is the Lamb that was
> slaughtered
> to receive power and wealth and
> wisdom and might
> and honor and glory and
> blessing!"

13 Then I heard every creature in heaven and on earth and under the earth and in the sea, and all that is in them, singing,

> "To the one seated on the throne
> and to the Lamb
> be blessing and honor and glory
> and might
> forever and ever!"

14 And the four living creatures said, "Amen!" And the elders fell down and worshiped.

6 Then I saw the Lamb open one of the seven seals, and I heard one of the four living creatures call out, as with a voice of thunder, "Come!"[p] 2 I looked, and there was a white horse! Its rider had a bow; a crown was given to him, and he came out conquering and to conquer.

3 When he opened the second seal, I heard the second living creature call out, "Come!"[p] 4 And out came[q] another horse, bright red; its rider was permitted to take peace from the earth, so that people would slaughter one another; and he was given a great sword.

5 When he opened the third seal, I heard the third living creature call out, "Come!"[p] I looked, and there was a black horse! Its rider held a pair of scales in his hand, 6 and I heard what seemed to be a voice in the midst of the four living creatures saying, "A quart of wheat for a day's pay,[r] and three quarts of barley for a day's pay,[r] but do not damage the olive oil and the wine!"

7 When he opened the fourth seal, I heard the voice of the fourth living creature call out, "Come!"[p] 8 I looked and there was a pale green horse! Its rider's name was Death, and Hades followed with him; they were given authority over a fourth of the earth, to kill with sword, famine, and pestilence, and by the wild animals of the earth.

9 When he opened the fifth seal, I saw under the altar the souls of those who had been slaughtered for the word of God and for the testimony they had given; 10 they cried out with a loud voice, "Sovereign Lord, holy and true, how long will it be before you judge and avenge our blood on the inhabitants of the earth?" 11 They were each given a white robe and told to rest a little longer, until the number would be complete both of their fellow servants[s] and of their brothers and sisters,[t] who were soon to be killed as they themselves had been killed.

12 When he opened the sixth seal, I looked, and there came a great earthquake; the sun became black as sackcloth, the full moon became like blood, 13 and the stars of the sky fell to the earth as the fig tree drops its winter fruit when shaken

---

[n]Gk ransomed for God from   [o]Gk priests to   [p]Or "Go!"   [q]Or went
[r]Gk a denarius   [s]Gk slaves   [t]Gk brothers

by a gale. 14 The sky vanished like a scroll rolling itself up, and every mountain and island was removed from its place. 15 Then the kings of the earth and the magnates and the generals and the rich and the powerful, and everyone, slave and free, hid in the caves and among the rocks of the mountains, 16 calling to the mountains and rocks, "Fall on us and hide us from the face of the one seated on the throne and from the wrath of the Lamb; 17 for the great day of their wrath has come, and who is able to stand?"

7 After this I saw four angels standing at the four corners of the earth, holding back the four winds of the earth so that no wind could blow on earth or sea or against any tree. 2 I saw another angel ascending from the rising of the sun, having the seal of the living God, and he called with a loud voice to the four angels who had been given power to damage earth and sea, 3 saying, "Do not damage the earth or the sea or the trees, until we have marked the servants[u] of our God with a seal on their foreheads."

4 And I heard the number of those who were sealed, one hundred forty-four thousand, sealed out of every tribe of the people of Israel:

5 From the tribe of Judah twelve thousand sealed,

from the tribe of Reuben twelve thousand,
from the tribe of Gad twelve thousand,

6 from the tribe of Asher twelve thousand,
from the tribe of Naphtali twelve thousand,
from the tribe of Manasseh twelve thousand,

7 from the tribe of Simeon twelve thousand,
from the tribe of Levi twelve thousand,
from the tribe of Issachar twelve thousand,

8 from the tribe of Zebulun twelve thousand,
from the tribe of Joseph twelve thousand,
from the tribe of Benjamin twelve thousand sealed.

9 After this I looked, and there was a great multitude that no one could count, from every nation, from all tribes and peoples and languages, standing before the throne and before the Lamb, robed in white, with palm branches in their hands. 10 They cried out in a loud voice, saying,

"Salvation belongs to our God
who is seated on the
throne, and to the Lamb!"

11 And all the angels stood around the throne and around the elders and the four living creatures, and they fell on their faces before the throne and worshiped God, 12 singing,

"Amen! Blessing and glory and wisdom
and thanksgiving and honor
and power and might
be to our God forever and ever! Amen."

13 Then one of the elders addressed me, saying, "Who are these, robed in white, and where have they come from?" 14 I said to him, "Sir, you are the one that knows." Then he said to me, "These are they who have come out of the great ordeal; they have washed their robes and made them white in the blood of the Lamb.

15 For this reason they are before the throne of God,
and worship him day and night within his temple,
and the one who is seated on the throne will shelter them.

16 They will hunger no more, and thirst no more;
the sun will not strike them, nor any scorching heat;

17 for the Lamb at the center of the throne will be their shepherd,
and he will guide them to springs of the water of life,
and God will wipe away every tear from their eyes."

8 When the Lamb opened the seventh seal, there was silence in heaven for about half an hour. 2 And I saw the seven angels who stand before God, and seven trumpets were given to them.

3 Another angel with a golden censer came and stood at the altar; he was given a great quantity of incense to offer with the prayers of all the saints on the golden altar that is before the throne. 4 And the smoke of the incense, with the prayers of the saints, rose before God from the hand of the angel. 5 Then the angel took the censer and filled it with fire from the altar and threw it on the earth; and there were peals of thunder, rumblings, flashes of lightning, and an earthquake.

[u]Gk *slaves*

6 Now the seven angels who had the seven trumpets made ready to blow them.

7 The first angel blew his trumpet, and there came hail and fire, mixed with blood, and they were hurled to the earth; and a third of the earth was burned up, and a third of the trees were burned up, and all green grass was burned up.

8 The second angel blew his trumpet, and something like a great mountain, burning with fire, was thrown into the sea. 9 A third of the sea became blood, a third of the living creatures in the sea died, and a third of the ships were destroyed.

10 The third angel blew his trumpet, and a great star fell from heaven, blazing like a torch, and it fell on a third of the rivers and on the springs of water. 11 The name of the star is Wormwood. A third of the waters became wormwood, and many died from the water, because it was made bitter.

12 The fourth angel blew his trumpet, and a third of the sun was struck, and a third of the moon, and a third of the stars, so that a third of their light was darkened; a third of the day was kept from shining, and likewise the night.

13 Then I looked, and I heard an eagle crying with a loud voice as it flew in midheaven, "Woe, woe, woe to the inhabitants of the earth, at the blasts of the other trumpets that the three angels are about to blow!"

9 And the fifth angel blew his trumpet, and I saw a star that had fallen from heaven to earth, and he was given the key to the shaft of the bottomless pit; 2 he opened the shaft of the bottomless pit, and from the shaft rose smoke like the smoke of a great furnace, and the sun and the air were darkened with the smoke from the shaft. 3 Then from the smoke came locusts on the earth, and they were given authority like the authority of scorpions of the earth. 4 They were told not to damage the grass of the earth or any green growth or any tree, but only those people who do not have the seal of God on their foreheads. 5 They were allowed to torture them for five months, but not to kill them, and their torture was like the torture of a scorpion when it stings someone. 6 And in those days people will seek death but will not find it; they will long to die, but death will flee from them.

7 In appearance the locusts were like horses equipped for battle. On their heads were what looked like crowns of gold; their faces were like human faces, 8 their hair like women's hair, and their teeth like lions' teeth; 9 they had scales like iron breastplates, and the noise of their wings was like the noise of many chariots with horses rushing into battle. 10 They have tails like scorpions, with stingers, and in their tails is their power to harm people for five months. 11 They have as king over them the angel of the bottomless pit; his name in Hebrew is Abaddon,^{v} and in Greek he is called Apollyon.^{w}

12 The first woe has passed. There are still two woes to come.

13 Then the sixth angel blew his trumpet, and I heard a voice from the four^x horns of the golden altar before God, 14 saying to the sixth angel who had the trumpet, "Release the four angels who are bound at the great river Euphrates." 15 So the four angels were released, who had been held ready for the hour, the day, the month, and the year, to kill a third of humankind. 16 The number of the troops of cavalry was two hundred million; I heard their number. 17 And this was how I saw the horses in my vision: the riders wore breastplates the color of fire and of sapphire^y and of sulfur; the heads of the horses were like lions' heads, and fire and smoke and sulfur came out of their mouths. 18 By these three plagues a third of humankind was killed, by the fire and smoke and sulfur coming out of their mouths. 19 For the power of the horses is in their mouths and in their tails; their tails are like serpents, having heads; and with them they inflict harm.

20 The rest of humankind, who were not killed by these plagues, did not repent of the works of their hands or give up worshiping demons and idols of gold and silver and bronze and stone and wood, which cannot see or hear or walk. 21 And they did not repent of their murders or their sorceries or their fornication or their thefts.

10 And I saw another mighty angel coming down from heaven, wrapped in a cloud, with a rainbow over his head; his face was like the sun, and his legs like pillars of fire. 2 He held a little scroll open in his hand. Setting his right foot on the sea and his left foot on the land, 3 he gave a great shout, like a lion roaring. And when he

---

^{v}That is, *Destruction* ^{w}That is, *Destroyer* ^{x}Other ancient authorities lack *four* ^{y}Gk *hyacinth*

Break between 6/7 trumpet

shouted, the seven thunders sounded. 4 And when the seven thunders had sounded, I was about to write, but I heard a voice from heaven saying, "Seal up what the seven thunders have said, and do not write it down." 5 Then the angel whom I saw standing on the sea and the land

> raised his right hand to heaven
6   and swore by him who lives
> forever and ever,

who created heaven and what is in it, the earth and what is in it, and the sea and what is in it: "There will be no more delay, 7 but in the days when the seventh angel is to blow his trumpet, the mystery of God will be fulfilled, as he announced to his servants[z] the prophets."

8 Then the voice that I had heard from heaven spoke to me again, saying, "Go, take the scroll that is open in the hand of the angel who is standing on the sea and on the land." 9 So I went to the angel and told him to give me the little scroll; and he said to me, "Take it, and eat; it will be bitter to your stomach, but sweet as honey in your mouth." 10 So I took the little scroll from the hand of the angel and ate it; it was sweet as honey in my mouth, but when I had eaten it, my stomach was made bitter.

11 Then they said to me, "You must prophesy again about many peoples and nations and languages and kings."

11 Then I was given a measuring rod like a staff, and I was told, "Come and measure the temple of God and the altar and those who worship there, 2 but do not measure the court outside the temple; leave that out, for it is given over to the nations, and they will trample over the holy city for forty-two months. 3 And I will grant my two witnesses authority to prophesy for one thousand two hundred sixty days, wearing sackcloth."

4 These are the two olive trees and the two lampstands that stand before the Lord of the earth. 5 And if anyone wants to harm them, fire pours from their mouth and consumes their foes; anyone who wants to harm them must be killed in this manner. 6 They have authority to shut the sky, so that no rain may fall during the days of their prophesying, and they have authority over the waters to turn them into blood, and to strike the earth with every kind of plague, as often as they desire.

7 When they have finished their testimony, the beast that comes up from the bottomless pit will make war on them and conquer them and kill them, 8 and their dead bodies will lie in the street of the great city that is prophetically[a] called Sodom and Egypt, where also their Lord was crucified. 9 For three and a half days members of the peoples and tribes and languages and nations will gaze at their dead bodies and refuse to let them be placed in a tomb; 10 and the inhabitants of the earth will gloat over them and celebrate and exchange presents, because these two prophets had been a torment to the inhabitants of the earth.

11 But after the three and a half days, the breath[b] of life from God entered them, and they stood on their feet, and those who saw them were terrified. 12 Then they[c] heard a loud voice from heaven saying to them, "Come up here!" And they went up to heaven in a cloud while their enemies watched them. 13 At that moment there was a great earthquake, and a tenth of the city fell; seven thousand people were killed in the earthquake, and the rest were terrified and gave glory to the God of heaven.

14 The second woe has passed. The third woe is coming very soon.

15 Then the seventh angel blew his trumpet, and there were loud voices in heaven, saying,

> "The kingdom of the world has
> become the kingdom of our
> Lord
> and of his Messiah,[d]
> and he will reign forever and
> ever."

16 Then the twenty-four elders who sit on their thrones before God fell on their faces and worshiped God, 17 singing,

> "We give you thanks, Lord God
> Almighty,
> who are and who were,
> for you have taken your great
> power
> and begun to reign.
18   The nations raged,
> but your wrath has come,
> and the time for judging the
> dead,

---

[z]Gk slaves   [a]Or allegorically; Gk spiritually   [b]Or the spirit   [c]Other ancient authorities read I   [d]Gk Christ

for rewarding your servants,[c] the
prophets
and saints and all who fear your
name,
both small and great,
and for destroying those who
destroy the earth."

19 Then God's temple in heaven was opened, and the ark of his covenant was seen within his temple; and there were flashes of lightning, rumblings, peals of thunder, an earthquake, and heavy hail.

↙ dualistic

12 A great portent appeared in heaven: a woman clothed with the sun, with the moon under her feet, and on her head a crown of twelve stars. 2 She was pregnant and was crying out in birth pangs, in the agony of giving birth. 3 Then another portent appeared in heaven: a great red dragon, with seven heads and ten horns, and seven diadems on his heads. 4 His tail swept down a third of the stars of heaven and threw them to the earth. Then the dragon stood before the woman who was about to bear a child, so that he might devour her child as soon as it was born. 5 And she gave birth to a son, a male child, who is to rule[f] all the nations with a rod of iron. But her child was snatched away and taken to God and to his throne; 6 and the woman fled into the wilderness, where she has a place prepared by God, so that there she can be nourished for one thousand two hundred sixty days.

7 And war broke out in heaven; Michael and his angels fought against the dragon. The dragon and his angels fought back, 8 but they were defeated, and there was no longer any place for them in heaven. 9 The great dragon was thrown down, that ancient serpent, who is called the Devil and Satan, the deceiver of the whole world—he was thrown down to the earth, and his angels were thrown down with him.

10 Then I heard a loud voice in heaven, proclaiming,

"Now have come the salvation
and the power
and the kingdom of our God
and the authority of his
Messiah,[g]
for the accuser of our comrades[h]

has been thrown down,
who accuses them day and night
before our God.

11   But they have conquered him by
the blood of the Lamb
and by the word of their
testimony,
for they did not cling to life even
in the face of death.

12   Rejoice then, you heavens
and those who dwell in them!
But woe to the earth and the sea,
for the devil has come down to
you
with great wrath,
because he knows that his time
is short!"

13 So when the dragon saw that he had been thrown down to the earth, he pursued[i] the woman who had given birth to the male child. 14 But the woman was given the two wings of the great eagle, so that she could fly from the serpent into the wilderness, to her place where she is nourished for a time, and times, and half a time. 15 Then from his mouth the serpent poured water like a river after the woman, to sweep her away with the flood. 16 But the earth came to the help of the woman; it opened its mouth and swallowed the river that the dragon had poured from his mouth. 17 Then the dragon was angry with the woman, and went off to make war on the rest of her children, those who keep the commandments of God and hold the testimony of Jesus.

18 Then the dragon[j] took his stand on the sand of the seashore.

13 And I saw a beast rising out of the sea, having ten horns and seven heads; and on its horns were ten diadems, and on its heads were blasphemous names. 2 And the beast that I saw was like a leopard, its feet were like a bear's, and its mouth was like a lion's mouth. And the dragon gave it his power and his throne and great authority. 3 One of its heads seemed to have received a death-blow, but its mortal wound[k] had been healed. In amazement the whole earth followed the beast. 4 They worshiped the dragon, for he

[c]Gk slaves [f]Or to shepherd [g]Gk Christ [h]Gk brothers
[i]Or persecuted [j]Gk Then he: other ancient authorities read Then I
stood [k]Gk the plague of its death

"polemical parallelism" → Demonic counterpart to Christ (5:6)

had given his authority to the beast, and they worshiped the beast, saying, "Who is like the beast, and who can fight against it?"

5 The beast was given a mouth uttering haughty and blasphemous words, and it was allowed to exercise authority for forty-two months. 6 It opened its mouth to utter blasphemies against God, blaspheming his name and his dwelling, that is, those who dwell in heaven. 7 Also it was allowed to make war on the saints and to conquer them.[l] It was given authority over every tribe and people and language and nation, 8 and all the inhabitants of the earth will worship it, everyone whose name has not been written from the foundation of the world in the book of life of the Lamb that was slaughtered.[m]

9 Let anyone who has an ear listen:

10   If you are to be taken captive,
          into captivity you go;
       if you kill with the sword,
          with the sword you must be
            killed.

Here is a call for the endurance and faith of the saints.

11 Then I saw another beast that rose out of the earth; it had two horns like a lamb and it spoke like a dragon. 12 It exercises all the authority of the first beast on its behalf, and it makes the earth and its inhabitants worship the first beast, whose mortal wound[n] had been healed. 13 It performs great signs, even making fire come down from heaven to earth in the sight of all; 14 and by the signs that it is allowed to perform on behalf of the beast, it deceives the inhabitants of earth, telling them to make an image for the beast that had been wounded by the sword[o] and yet lived; 15 and it was allowed to give breath[p] to the image of the beast so that the image of the beast could even speak and cause those who would not worship the image of the beast to be killed. 16 Also it causes all, both small and great, both rich and poor, both free and slave, to be marked on the right hand or the forehead, 17 so that no one can buy or sell who does not have the mark, that is, the name of the beast or the number of its name. 18 This calls for wisdom: let anyone with understanding calculate the number of the beast, for it is the number of a person. Its number is six hundred sixty-six.[q]

14 Then I looked, and there was the Lamb, standing on Mount Zion! And with him were one hundred forty-four thousand who had his name and his Father's name written on their foreheads. 2 And I heard a voice from heaven like the sound of many waters and like the sound of loud thunder; the voice I heard was like the sound of harpists playing on their harps, 3 and they sing a new song before the throne and before the four living creatures and before the elders. No one could learn that song except the one hundred forty-four thousand who have been redeemed from the earth. 4 It is these who have not defiled themselves with women, for they are virgins; these follow the Lamb wherever he goes. They have been redeemed from humankind as first fruits for God and the Lamb, 5 and in their mouth no lie was found; they are blameless.

6 Then I saw another angel flying in midheaven, with an eternal gospel to proclaim to those who live[r] on the earth—to every nation and tribe and language and people. 7 He said in a loud voice, "Fear God and give him glory, for the hour of his judgment has come; and worship him who made heaven and earth, the sea and the springs of water."

8 Then another angel, a second, followed, saying, "Fallen, fallen is Babylon the great! She has made all nations drink of the wine of the wrath of her fornication."

9 Then another angel, a third, followed them, crying with a loud voice, "Those who worship the beast and its image, and receive a mark on their foreheads or on their hands, 10 they will also drink the wine of God's wrath, poured unmixed into the cup of his anger, and they will be tormented with fire and sulfur in the presence of the holy angels and in the presence of the Lamb. 11 And the smoke of their torment goes up forever and ever. There is no rest day or night for those who worship the beast and its image and for anyone who receives the mark of its name."

12 Here is a call for the endurance of the saints, those who keep the commandments of God and hold fast to the faith of[s] Jesus.

---

[l]Other ancient authorities lack this sentence   [m]Or *written in the book of life of the Lamb that was slaughtered from the foundation of the world*   [n]Gk *whose plague of its death*   [o]Or *that had received the plague of the sword*   [p]Or *spirit*   [q]Other ancient authorities read *six hundred sixteen*   [r]Gk *sit*   [s]Or *to their faith in*

13 And I heard a voice from heaven saying, "Write this: Blessed are the dead who from now on die in the Lord." "Yes," says the Spirit, "they will rest from their labors, for their deeds follow them."

14 Then I looked, and there was a white cloud, and seated on the cloud was one like the Son of Man, with a golden crown on his head, and a sharp sickle in his hand! 15 Another angel came out of the temple, calling with a loud voice to the one who sat on the cloud, "Use your sickle and reap, for the hour to reap has come, because the harvest of the earth is fully ripe." 16 So the one who sat on the cloud swung his sickle over the earth, and the earth was reaped.

17 Then another angel came out of the temple in heaven, and he too had a sharp sickle. 18 Then another angel came out from the altar, the angel who has authority over fire, and he called with a loud voice to him who had the sharp sickle, "Use your sharp sickle and gather the clusters of the vine of the earth, for its grapes are ripe." 19 So the angel swung his sickle over the earth and gathered the vintage of the earth, and he threw it into the great wine press of the wrath of God. 20 And the wine press was trodden outside the city, and blood flowed from the wine press, as high as a horse's bridle, for a distance of about two hundred miles.[t]

15 Then I saw another portent in heaven, great and amazing: seven angels with seven plagues, which are the last, for with them the wrath of God is ended.

2 And I saw what appeared to be a sea of glass mixed with fire, and those who had conquered the beast and its image and the number of its name, standing beside the sea of glass with harps of God in their hands. 3 And they sing the song of Moses, the servant[u] of God, and the song of the Lamb:

> "Great and amazing are your deeds,
> Lord God the Almighty!
> Just and true are your ways,
> King of the nations![v]

4

> Lord, who will not fear
> and glorify your name?
> For you alone are holy.
> All nations will come
> and worship before you,
> for your judgments have been revealed."

5 After this I looked, and the temple of the tent[w] of witness in heaven was opened, 6 and out of the temple came the seven angels with the seven plagues, robed in pure bright linen,[x] with golden sashes across their chests. 7 Then one of the four living creatures gave the seven angels seven golden bowls full of the wrath of God, who lives forever and ever; 8 and the temple was filled with smoke from the glory of God and from his power, and no one could enter the temple until the seven plagues of the seven angels were ended.

16 Then I heard a loud voice from the temple telling the seven angels, "Go and pour out on the earth the seven bowls of the wrath of God."

2 So the first angel went and poured his bowl on the earth, and a foul and painful sore came on those who had the mark of the beast and who worshiped its image.

3 The second angel poured his bowl into the sea, and it became like the blood of a corpse, and every living thing in the sea died.

4 The third angel poured his bowl into the rivers and the springs of water, and they became blood. 5 And I heard the angel of the waters say,

> "You are just, O Holy One, who are and were,
> for you have judged these things;

6

> because they shed the blood of saints and prophets,
> you have given them blood to drink.
> It is what they deserve!"

7 And I heard the altar respond,

> "Yes, O Lord God, the Almighty,
> your judgments are true and just!"

8 The fourth angel poured his bowl on the sun, and it was allowed to scorch people with fire; 9 they were scorched by the fierce heat, but they cursed the name of God, who had authority over these plagues, and they did not repent and give him glory.

10 The fifth angel poured his bowl on the throne of the beast, and its kingdom was plunged into dark-

---

[t]Gk *one thousand six hundred stadia* [u]Gk *slave* [v]Other ancient authorities read *the ages* [w]Or *tabernacle* [x]Other ancient authorities read *stone*

ness; people gnawed their tongues in agony, 11 and cursed the God of heaven because of their pains and sores, and they did not repent of their deeds.

12 The sixth angel poured his bowl on the great river Euphrates, and its water was dried up in order to prepare the way for the kings from the east. 13 And I saw three foul spirits like frogs coming from the mouth of the dragon, from the mouth of the beast, and from the mouth of the false prophet. 14 These are demonic spirits, performing signs, who go abroad to the kings of the whole world, to assemble them for battle on the great day of God the Almighty. 15 ("See, I am coming like a thief! Blessed is the one who stays awake and is clothed,[y] not going about naked and exposed to shame.") 16 And they assembled them at the place that in Hebrew is called Harmagedon.

17 The seventh angel poured his bowl into the air, and a loud voice came out of the temple, from the throne, saying, "It is done!" 18 And there came flashes of lightning, rumblings, peals of thunder, and a violent earthquake, such as had not occurred since people were upon the earth, so violent was that earthquake. 19 The great city was split into three parts, and the cities of the nations fell. God remembered great Babylon and gave her the wine-cup of the fury of his wrath. 20 And every island fled away, and no mountains were to be found; 21 and huge hailstones, each weighing about a hundred pounds,[z] dropped from heaven on people, until they cursed God for the plague of the hail, so fearful was that plague.

17 Then one of the seven angels who had the seven bowls came and said to me, "Come, I will show you the judgment of the great whore who is seated on many waters, 2 with whom the kings of the earth have committed fornication, and with the wine of whose fornication the inhabitants of the earth have become drunk." 3 So he carried me away in the spirit[a] into a wilderness, and I saw a woman sitting on a scarlet beast that was full of blasphemous names, and it had seven heads and ten horns. 4 The woman was clothed in purple and scarlet, and adorned with gold and jewels and pearls, holding in her hand a golden cup full of abominations and the impurities of her fornication; 5 and on her forehead was writ-

ten a name, a mystery: "Babylon the great, mother of whores and of earth's abominations." 6 And I saw that the woman was drunk with the blood of the saints and the blood of the witnesses to Jesus.

When I saw her, I was greatly amazed. 7 But the angel said to me, "Why are you so amazed? I will tell you the mystery of the woman, and of the beast with seven heads and ten horns that carries her. 8 The beast that you saw was, and is not, and is about to ascend from the bottomless pit and go to destruction. And the inhabitants of the earth, whose names have not been written in the book of life from the foundation of the world, will be amazed when they see the beast, because it was and is not and is to come.

9 "This calls for a mind that has wisdom: the seven heads are seven mountains on which the woman is seated; also, they are seven kings, 10 of whom five have fallen, one is living, and the other has not yet come; and when he comes, he must remain only a little while. 11 As for the beast that was and is not, it is an eighth but it belongs to the seven, and it goes to destruction. 12 And the ten horns that you saw are ten kings who have not yet received a kingdom, but they are to receive authority as kings for one hour, together with the beast. 13 These are united in yielding their power and authority to the beast; 14 they will make war on the Lamb, and the Lamb will conquer them, for he is Lord of lords and King of kings, and those with him are called and chosen and faithful."

15 And he said to me, "The waters that you saw, where the whore is seated, are peoples and multitudes and nations and languages. 16 And the ten horns that you saw, they and the beast will hate the whore; they will make her desolate and naked; they will devour her flesh and burn her up with fire. 17 For God has put it into their hearts to carry out his purpose by agreeing to give their kingdom to the beast, until the words of God will be fulfilled. 18 The woman you saw is the great city that rules over the kings of the earth."

18 After this I saw another angel coming down from heaven, having great authority; and the earth was made bright with his splendor. 2 He called out with a mighty voice,

---

[y]Gk *and keeps his robes*   [z]Gk *weighing about a talent*   [a]Or *in the Spirit*

"Fallen, fallen is Babylon the great!
It has become a dwelling place
of demons,
a haunt of every foul spirit,
a haunt of every foul bird,
a haunt of every foul and hateful
beast.[b]
3 For all the nations have drunk[c]
of the wine of the wrath of her
fornication,
and the kings of the earth have
committed fornication with
her,
and the merchants of the earth
have grown rich from the
power[d] of her luxury."

4 Then I heard another voice from heaven saying,

"Come out of her, my people,
so that you do not take part in
her sins,
and so that you do not share
in her plagues;
5 for her sins are heaped high as
heaven,
and God has remembered her
iniquities.
6 Render to her as she herself has
rendered,
and repay her double for her
deeds;
mix a double draught for her in
the cup she mixed.
7 As she glorified herself and lived
luxuriously,
so give her a like measure of
torment and grief.
Since in her heart she says,
'I rule as a queen;
I am no widow,
and I will never see grief,'
8 therefore her plagues will come in
a single day—
pestilence and mourning and
famine—
and she will be burned with fire;
for mighty is the Lord God who
judges her."

9 And the kings of the earth, who committed fornication and lived in luxury with her, will weep and wail over her when they see the smoke of her burning; 10 they will stand far off, in fear of her torment, and say,

"Alas, alas, the great city,
Babylon, the mighty city!
For in one hour your judgment
has come."

11 And the merchants of the earth weep and mourn for her, since no one buys their cargo anymore, 12 cargo of gold, silver, jewels and pearls, fine linen, purple, silk and scarlet, all kinds of scented wood, all articles of ivory, all articles of costly wood, bronze, iron, and marble, 13 cinnamon, spice, incense, myrrh, frankincense, wine, olive oil, choice flour and wheat, cattle and sheep, horses and chariots, slaves—and human lives.[e]

14 "The fruit for which your soul
longed
has gone from you,
and all your dainties and your
splendor
are lost to you,
never to be found again!"

15 The merchants of these wares, who gained wealth from her, will stand far off, in fear of her torment, weeping and mourning aloud,

16 "Alas, alas, the great city,
clothed in fine linen,
in purple and scarlet,
adorned with gold,
with jewels, and with pearls!
17 For in one hour all this wealth has
been laid waste!"

And all shipmasters and seafarers, sailors and all whose trade is on the sea, stood far off 18 and cried out as they saw the smoke of her burning,

"What city was like the great
city?"

19 And they threw dust on their heads, as they wept and mourned, crying out,

"Alas, alas, the great city,
where all who had ships at sea
grew rich by her wealth!

---

[b]Other ancient authorities lack the words *a haunt of every foul beast* and attach the words *and hateful* to the previous line so as to read *a haunt of every foul and hateful bird* [c]Other ancient authorities read *She has made all nations drink* [d]Or *resources* [e]Or *chariots, and human bodies and souls*

For in one hour she has been laid
        waste."
20   Rejoice over her, O heaven,
          you saints and apostles and
              prophets!
      For God has given judgment for
          you against her.

21 Then a mighty angel took up a stone like a great millstone and threw it into the sea, saying,

      "With such violence Babylon the
          great city
        will be thrown down,
        and will be found no more;
22   and the sound of harpists and
              minstrels and of flutists and
              trumpeters
        will be heard in you no more;
      and an artisan of any trade
        will be found in you no more;
      and the sound of the millstone
        will be heard in you no more;
23   and the light of a lamp
        will shine in you no more;
      and the voice of bridegroom and
              bride
        will be heard in you no more;
      for your merchants were the
              magnates of the earth,
        and all nations were deceived by
              your sorcery.
24   And in you[f] was found the blood
              of prophets and of saints,
        and of all who have been
              slaughtered on earth."

19 After this I heard what seemed to be the loud voice of a great multitude in heaven, saying,

      "Hallelujah!
      Salvation and glory and power to
              our God,
2   for his judgments are true and
              just;
      he has judged the great whore
          who corrupted the earth with
              her fornication,
      and he has avenged on her the
          blood of his servants."[g]

3 Once more they said,
      "Hallelujah!

      The smoke goes up from her
          forever and ever."

4 And the twenty-four elders and the four living creatures fell down and worshiped God who is seated on the throne, saying,

          "Amen. Hallelujah!"

5 And from the throne came a voice saying,
      "Praise our God,
          all you his servants,[g]
      and all who fear him,
          small and great."

6 Then I heard what seemed to be the voice of a great multitude, like the sound of many waters and like the sound of mighty thunderpeals, crying out,

      "Hallelujah!
      For the Lord our God
          the Almighty reigns.
7   Let us rejoice and exult
          and give him the glory,
      for the marriage of the Lamb has
              come,
          and his bride has made herself
              ready;
8   to her it has been granted to be
              clothed
          with fine linen, bright and
              pure"—

for the fine linen is the righteous deeds of the saints.

9 And the angel said[h] to me, "Write this: Blessed are those who are invited to the marriage supper of the Lamb." And he said to me, "These are true words of God." 10 Then I fell down at his feet to worship him, but he said to me, "You must not do that! I am a fellow servant[i] with you and your comrades[j] who hold the testimony of Jesus.[k] Worship God! For the testimony of Jesus[k] is the spirit of prophecy."

11 Then I saw heaven opened, and there was a white horse! Its rider is called Faithful and True, and in righteousness he judges and makes war. 12 His eyes are like a flame of fire, and on his head are many diadems; and he has a name inscribed that no one knows but himself. 13 He is clothed in a robe dipped in[l] blood, and his name is called The

[f]Gk *her* [g]Gk *slaves* [h]Gk *he said* [i]Gk *slave* [j]Gk *brothers*
[k]Or *to Jesus* [l]Other ancient authorities read *sprinkled with*

Christ the Warrior

Word of God. 14 And the armies of heaven, wearing fine linen, white and pure, were following him on white horses. 15 From his mouth comes a sharp sword with which to strike down the nations, and he will rule[m] them with a rod of iron; he will tread the wine press of the fury of the wrath of God the Almighty. 16 On his robe and on his thigh he has a name inscribed, "King of kings and Lord of lords."

17 Then I saw an angel standing in the sun, and with a loud voice he called to all the birds that fly in midheaven, "Come, gather for the great supper of God, 18 to eat the flesh of kings, the flesh of captains, the flesh of the mighty, the flesh of horses and their riders—flesh of all, both free and slave, both small and great." 19 Then I saw the beast and the kings of the earth with their armies gathered to make war against the rider on the horse and against his army. 20 And the beast was captured, and with it the false prophet who had performed in its presence the signs by which he deceived those who had received the mark of the beast and those who worshiped its image. These two were thrown alive into the lake of fire that burns with sulfur. 21 And the rest were killed by the sword of the rider on the horse, the sword that came from his mouth; and all the birds were gorged with their flesh.

20 Then I saw an angel coming down from heaven, holding in his hand the key to the bottomless pit and a great chain. 2 He seized the dragon, that ancient serpent, who is the Devil and Satan, and bound him for a thousand years, 3 and threw him into the pit, and locked and sealed it over him, so that he would deceive the nations no more, until the thousand years were ended. After that he must be let out for a little while.

4 Then I saw thrones, and those seated on them were given authority to judge. I also saw the souls of those who had been beheaded for their testimony to Jesus[n] and for the word of God. They had not worshiped the beast or its image and had not received its mark on their foreheads or their hands. They came to life and reigned with Christ a thousand years. 5 (The rest of the dead did not come to life until the thousand years were ended.) This is the first resurrection. 6 Blessed and holy are those who share in the first resurrection. Over these the second death has no power, but they will

be priests of God and of Christ, and they will reign with him a thousand years.

7 When the thousand years are ended, Satan will be released from his prison 8 and will come out to deceive the nations at the four corners of the earth, Gog and Magog, in order to gather them for battle; they are as numerous as the sands of the sea. 9 They marched up over the breadth of the earth and surrounded the camp of the saints and the beloved city. And fire came down from heaven[o] and consumed them. 10 And the devil who had deceived them was thrown into the lake of fire and sulfur, where the beast and the false prophet were, and they will be tormented day and night forever and ever.

11 Then I saw a great white throne and the one who sat on it; the earth and the heaven fled from his presence, and no place was found for them. 12 And I saw the dead, great and small, standing before the throne, and books were opened. Also another book was opened, the book of life. And the dead were judged according to their works, as recorded in the books. 13 And the sea gave up the dead that were in it, Death and Hades gave up the dead that were in them, and all were judged according to what they had done. 14 Then Death and Hades were thrown into the lake of fire. This is the second death, the lake of fire; 15 and anyone whose name was not found written in the book of life was thrown into the lake of fire.

21 Then I saw a new heaven and a new earth; for the first heaven and the first earth had passed away, and the sea was no more. 2 And I saw the holy city, the new Jerusalem, coming down out of heaven from God, prepared as a bride adorned for her husband. 3 And I heard a loud voice from the throne saying,

"See, the home[p] of God is among
        mortals.
He will dwell[p] with them as their
        God;[q]
they will be his peoples,[r]
and God himself will be with
        them;[s]

[m]Or *will shepherd* [n]Or *for the testimony of Jesus* [o]Other ancient authorities read *from God, out of heaven*, or *out of heaven from God* [p]Gk *the tabernacle* [q]Other ancient authorities lack *as their God* [r]Other ancient authorities read *people* [s]Other ancient authorities add *and be their God*

4   he will wipe every tear from their
              eyes.
        Death will be no more;
        mourning and crying and pain will
              be no more,
        for the first things have passed
              away."

5 And the one who was seated on the throne said, "See, I am making all things new." Also he said, "Write this, for these words are trustworthy and true." 6 Then he said to me, "It is done! I am the Alpha and the Omega, the beginning and the end. To the thirsty I will give water as a gift from the spring of the water of life. 7 Those who conquer will inherit these things, and I will be their God and they will be my children. 8 But as for the cowardly, the faithless,[t] the polluted, the murderers, the fornicators, the sorcerers, the idolaters, and all liars, their place will be in the lake that burns with fire and sulfur, which is the second death."

9 Then one of the seven angels who had the seven bowls full of the seven last plagues came and said to me, "Come, I will show you the bride, the wife of the Lamb." 10 And in the spirit[u] he carried me away to a great, high mountain and showed me the holy city Jerusalem coming down out of heaven from God. 11 It has the glory of God and a radiance like a very rare jewel, like jasper, clear as crystal. 12 It has a great, high wall with twelve gates, and at the gates twelve angels, and on the gates are inscribed the names of the twelve tribes of the Israelites; 13 on the east three gates, on the north three gates, on the south three gates, and on the west three gates. 14 And the wall of the city has twelve foundations, and on them are the twelve names of the twelve apostles of the Lamb.

15 The angel[v] who talked to me had a measuring rod of gold to measure the city and its gates and walls. 16 The city lies foursquare, its length the same as its width; and he measured the city with his rod, fifteen hundred miles;[w] its length and width and height are equal. 17 He also measured its wall, one hundred forty-four cubits[x] by human measurement, which the angel was using. 18 The wall is built of jasper, while the city is pure gold, clear as glass. 19 The foundations of the wall of the city are adorned with every jewel; the first was jasper, the second sapphire, the third agate, the fourth emerald, 20 the fifth onyx, the sixth car-

nelian, the seventh chrysolite, the eighth beryl, the ninth topaz, the tenth chrysoprase, the eleventh jacinth, the twelfth amethyst. 21 And the twelve gates are twelve pearls, each of the gates is a single pearl, and the street of the city is pure gold, transparent as glass.

22 I saw no temple in the city, for its temple is the Lord God the Almighty and the Lamb. 23 And the city has no need of sun or moon to shine on it, for the glory of God is its light, and its lamp is the Lamb. 24 The nations will walk by its light, and the kings of the earth will bring their glory into it. 25 Its gates will never be shut by day—and there will be no night there. 26 People will bring into it the glory and the honor of the nations. 27 But nothing unclean will enter it, nor anyone who practices abomination or falsehood, but only those who are written in the Lamb's book of life.

22

Then the angel[y] showed me the river of the water of life, bright as crystal, flowing from the throne of God and of the Lamb 2 through the middle of the street of the city. On either side of the river is the tree of life[z] with its twelve kinds of fruit, producing its fruit each month; and the leaves of the tree are for the healing of the nations. 3 Nothing accursed will be found there any more. But the throne of God and of the Lamb will be in it, and his servants[a] will worship him; 4 they will see his face, and his name will be on their foreheads. 5 And there will be no more night; they need no light of lamp or sun, for the Lord God will be their light, and they will reign forever and ever.

6 And he said to me, "These words are trustworthy and true, for the Lord, the God of the spirits of the prophets, has sent his angel to show his servants[a] what must soon take place."

7 "See, I am coming soon! Blessed is the one who keeps the words of the prophecy of this book."

8 I, John, am the one who heard and saw these things. And when I heard and saw them, I fell down to worship at the feet of the angel who showed them to me; 9 but he said to me, "You

[t]Or the unbelieving   [u]Or in the Spirit   [v]Gk He   [w]Gk twelve thousand stadia   [x]That is, almost seventy-five yards   [y]Gk he [z]Or the Lamb. [2]In the middle of the street of the city, and on either side of the river, is the tree of life   [a]Gk slaves

must not do that! I am a fellow servant[b] with you and your comrades[c] the prophets, and with those who keep the words of this book. Worship God!"

10 And he said to me, "Do not seal up the words of the prophecy of this book, for the time is near. 11 Let the evildoer still do evil, and the filthy still be filthy, and the righteous still do right, and the holy still be holy."

12 "See, I am coming soon; my reward is with me, to repay according to everyone's work. 13 I am the Alpha and the Omega, the first and the last, the beginning and the end."

14 Blessed are those who wash their robes,[d] so that they will have the right to the tree of life and may enter the city by the gates. 15 Outside are the dogs and sorcerers and fornicators and murderers and idolaters, and everyone who loves and practices falsehood. (Jezebel / John's Enemies)

16 "It is I, Jesus, who sent my angel to you with this testimony for the churches. I am the root and the descendant of David, the bright morning star."

17   The Spirit and the bride say,

"Come."
And let everyone who hears say,
        "Come."
And let everyone who is thirsty
        come.
Let anyone who wishes take the
        water of life as a gift.

18 I warn everyone who hears the words of the prophecy of this book: if anyone adds to them, God will add to that person the plagues described in this book; 19 if anyone takes away from the words of the book of this prophecy, God will take away that person's share in the tree of life and in the holy city, which are described in this book.

20 The one who testifies to these things says, "Surely I am coming soon."

Amen. Come, Lord Jesus!

21 The grace of the Lord Jesus be with all the saints. Amen.[e]

---

[b]Gk slave [c]Gk brothers [d]Other ancient authorities read do his commandments [e]Other ancient authorities lack all; others lack the saints; others lack Amen

The Shepherd of Hermas

The Shepherd was a popular book among Christians of the first four centuries. Written by Hermas, brother of Pius, bishop of Rome, during the first half of the second century, the book was regarded by some churches as canonical Scripture, although it was eventually excluded from the New Testament, in part because it was known not to have been written by an apostle.

The book takes its name from an angelic mediator who appears to Hermas in the form of a shepherd. Other angelic beings appear here as well, in particular an old woman who identifies herself as the personification of the Christian church. These various figures communicate divine revelations to Hermas and, upon request (sometimes grudgingly), interpret their meaning to him.

The book is divided into a series of five visions, twelve sets of commandments (or "mandates"), and ten parables (or "similitudes"). The visions and similitudes are enigmatic and symbolic; they are usually explained to Hermas as having a spiritual significance for the Christian here on earth. The mandates are somewhat easier to interpret, consisting of direct exhortations to speak the truth, give alms, do good, and avoid sexual immorality, drunkenness, gluttony, and other vices.

Indeed, the entire book is driven by an ethical concern: what can Christians do if they have fallen into sin after being baptized? A number of early Christians had insisted that those who returned to lives of sin after joining the church had lost any hope of salvation. An alternative view is advanced by Hermas. This book maintains, on the basis of its divine revelations, that Christians who had fallen again into sin after their baptism had a second chance (but only *one* second chance) to repent and return to God's good graces. Those who refused to avail themselves of this opportunity, however, or who reverted to sin again thereafter, would be forced to face the judgment of God on the day of reckoning that was soon to come.

The book is the longest work to survive from the first hundred years of the Christian church. The following extracts are representative of the whole.

The Visions

Vision One

1 The one who raised me sold me to a certain woman named Rhoda, in Rome. After many years, I regained her acquaintance and began to love her as a sister. 2 When some time had passed, I saw her bathing in the Tiber river; and I gave her my hand to help her out of the river. When I observed her beauty I began reasoning in my heart, "I would be fortunate to have a wife of such beauty and character." This is all I had in mind, nothing else. 3 When some time had passed, I was

"The Shepherd of Hermas," from *The Apostolic Fathers,* translated by Bart D. Ehrman. Loeb Classical Library; © 2003. Reprinted by permission of Harvard University Press.

traveling to the countryside,[a] glorifying the creations of God and thinking how great, remarkable, and powerful they are. On the way I fell asleep and a spirit took me and carried me through a certain deserted place that was impassable, for the place was steep and split up by the courses of water. When I crossed the river I came to level ground and bowed my knees; and I began praying to the Lord and confessing my sins. 4 While I was praying the sky opened up and I saw the woman I had desired, addressing me from heaven: "Hermas, greeting!" I looked at her and said. "Lady, what are you doing here?" 5 She replied to me, "I have been taken up to accuse your sins before the Lord." 6 I said to her, "So now are you accusing me?" "No," she said, "but listen to what I have to say to you. The God who dwells in heaven and who, for the sake of his holy church, created, increased, and multiplied that which exists out of that which does not exist, is angry at you for sinning against me." 7 I answered her, "Have I sinned against you? In what way? When did I speak an inappropriate word to you? Have I not always thought of you as a goddess? Have I not always respected you as a sister? Why do you make such evil and foul accusations against me, O woman?" 8 But she laughed and said to me, "The desire for evil did rise up in your heart. Or do you not think it is evil for an evil desire to arise in the heart of an upright man? Indeed," she said, "it is a great sin. For the upright man intends to do what is right. And so, when he intends to do what is right his reputation is firmly established in heaven and he finds that the Lord looks favorably on everything he does. But those who intend in their hearts to do evil bring death and captivity on themselves—especially those who are invested in this age, who rejoice in their wealth and do not cling to the good things yet to come. 9 Those who have no hope but have already abandoned themselves and their lives will regret it. But pray to God, and he will heal your sins, along with those of your entire household and of all the saints."

2 After she had spoken these words, the skies were shut; I was trembling all over and upset. I began saying to myself, "If this sin is recorded against me, how can I be saved? Or how will I appease God for the sins I have recently committed?[b] What words can I use to ask the Lord for mercy?" 2 While I was mulling these things over in my heart and trying to reach a decision, I saw across from me a large white chair, made of wool, white as snow. And an elderly woman came, dressed in radiant clothes and holding a book in her hands. She sat down, alone, and addressed me, "Greetings, Hermas." And I said, still upset and weeping, "Greetings, Lady." 3 She said to me, "Why are you sad, Hermas—you who are patient, slow to anger, and always laughing? Why are you so downcast, and not cheerful?" I replied to her, "Because of a very good woman who has been telling me that I sinned against her." 4 And she said, "May such a thing never happen to a slave of God. But probably something did rise up in your heart about her. This kind of notion brings the slaves of God into sin. For when someone longs to do what is evil, it is an evil and shocking notion, directed against a fully reverend and tested spirit—especially for Hermas, the self-controlled, who abstains from every evil desire and is full of all simplicity and great innocence.

3 "Still, God is angry with you, not about this, but so that you may convert your household, which has acted lawlessly against the Lord and against you, their parents. But since you yourself are so fond of your children you do not admonish your household, and so you allow it to be terribly ruined. This is why the Lord is angry with you. But he will heal every evil your household formerly committed. For you yourself have been brought to ruin by the affairs of daily life—because of their sins and lawless acts. 2 But the Lord's compassion has granted you and your household mercy, and it will make you strong and establish you in its glory. But you must not relax; instead, take courage and strengthen your household. For as the coppersmith hammers his work to master the material as he wants, so also the upright word spoken every day masters all evil. Do not stop exhorting your children. For I know that if they repent from their whole heart, they will be recorded with the saints in the books of the living." 3 When she finished these words, she said to me, "Do you want to hear me read?" I replied to her, "Yes, Lady, I do." She said to me, "Be a hearer and hear the glories of God." I heard great and amazing matters

[a] Or to the villages [b] Or for the sins I am yet to commit

that I could not remember. For all the words were terrifying, more than a person can bear. But I have remembered the final words, for they were beneficial to us, and gentle: 4 "Behold, the powerful God, who with his invisible power, might, and great understanding created the world, and by his glorious plan encompassed his creation with beauty, and by his powerful word fixed the sky and founded the earth upon the waters, and by his unique wisdom and foreknowledge created his holy church, which he also blessed—behold, he transforms the skies and the mountains and the hills and the seas, and everything becomes level for his elect, that he may deliver over to them the promise he made, with great glory and joy, if they keep the ordinances of God, which they received in great faith."

4 Then, when she finished reading and rose up from the chair, four young men came and took the chair and went away to the east. 2 She called me over and touched my breast and said to me, "Did my reading please you?" I said to her, "Lady, these last words are pleasing to me, but the earlier ones were difficult and hard." She said to me, "These last words are for those who are upright, but the former are for the outsiders[c] and apostates." 3 While she was speaking with me, two other men appeared and took her by the arms and went away to the east, where the chair was. She went away cheerfully; and while she was going she said to me, "Be a man,[d] Hermas."

Vision Two

5 I was traveling to the countryside[e] at the same time as the previous year, and on the way I remembered the vision from the year before. And again a spirit took me and bore me to the same place I had been then. 2 And so, when I came to the place, I bowed my knees and began praying to the Lord and glorifying his name, because he considered me worthy and showed me my former sins. 3 When I arose from prayer I saw across from me the elderly woman I had seen the year before, walking and reading a little book. And she said to me, "Can you announce these things to the ones chosen by God?" I said to her, "Lady, I cannot remember so many things. Give me the book

to make a copy." "Take it," she said, "and then return it to me." 4 I took it and went away to another part of the field, where I copied the whole thing, letter by letter, for I could not distinguish between the syllables. And then, when I completed the letters of the book, it was suddenly seized from my hand; but I did not see by whom.

6 Fifteen days later, after I had fasted and asked the Lord many things, the meaning of the writing was revealed to me. These are the words that were written: 2 "Your offspring, Hermas, have rejected God, blasphemed the Lord, and betrayed their parents with a great evil. And even though they have been called betrayers of their parents, they have gained nothing from their betrayal. Yet they have added still more licentious acts to their sins and piled on more evil; and so their lawless acts have gone as far as they can go. 3 But make these words known to all your children and your wife, who is about to become your sister. For she also does not restrain her tongue, but uses it to perpetrate evil. But when she hears these words she will control it and receive mercy. 4 After you have made known to them these words that the Master has commanded me to reveal to you, then all the sins they formerly committed will be forgiven them, along with those of all the saints who have sinned till this day, if they repent from their whole heart and remove double-mindedness from it. 5 For the Master swore by his own glory to his chosen ones: 'If there is any more sinning once this day has been appointed, they will not find salvation. For there is a limit to repentance for those who are upright, and the days of repentance for all the saints are complete. But the outsiders[f] will be able to repent until the final day.' 6 And so, say to those who lead the church that they are to make their paths straight in righteousness, that they may fully receive the promises with great glory. 7 You who do what is righteous should stand firm and not be of two minds, that your path may lie with the holy angels. How fortunate are all you who endure the great affliction that is coming and do not deny your life. 8 For the Lord has sworn by his Son, that those who deny their Lord have lost their life—that is, those who are about to deny him

[c]Literally, *Gentiles*; or *nations*   [d]Or *be courageous*   [e]Or *to the villages*   [f]Literally, *Gentiles*; or *nations*

in the days that are coming. But through his great compassion, mercy has been given to those who denied the Lord previously.

7 "But you, Hermas, must no longer hold a grudge against your children nor leave your sister to her own devices,[g] that they may be cleansed from their former sins. For they will be disciplined with an upright discipline, if you bear no grudge against them. A grudge produces death. But you, Hermas, have experienced great afflictions of your own because of your family's transgressions, since you paid no attention to them. You neglected them and became enmeshed in your own evil deeds.[h] 2 But you are saved by not straying from the living God, and by your simplicity and great self-restraint. These things have saved you, if you continue; and they save all those who do them and who proceed in innocence and simplicity. Such people will overcome all evil and persist to eternal life. 3 How fortunate are all those who do righteousness. They will never perish. 4 Say to Maximus, 'See, affliction is coming. If it seems right to you, make another denial.'[i] The Lord is near to those who convert, as is written in the Book of Eldad and Modat,[j] who prophesied to the people in the wilderness."

8 While I was sleeping, brothers, I received a revelation from a very beautiful young man, who said to me, "The elderly woman from whom you received the little book—who do you think she is?" "The Sibyl," I replied. "You are wrong," he said; "it is not she." "Who then is it?" I asked. "The church," he said. I said to him, "Why then is she elderly?" "Because," he said, "she was created first, before anything else. That is why she is elderly, and for her sake the world was created." 2 And afterward I saw a vision in my house. The elderly woman came and asked if I had already given the book to the presbyters. I said that I had not. "You have done well," she said. "For I have some words to add. Then, when I complete all the words, they will be made known through you to all those who are chosen. 3 And so, you will write two little books, sending one to Clement and the other to Grapte. Clement will send his to the foreign cities, for that is his commission. But Grapte will admonish the widows and orphans. And you will read yours in this city, with the presbyters who lead the church."

Vision Three

9 What I saw, brothers, was this. 2 After I fasted a great deal and asked the Lord to show me the revelation that he promised to reveal through the elderly woman, that same night the elderly woman appeared and said to me, "Since you are so needy and eager to know everything, come to the field where you farm,[k] and around eleven in the morning I will be revealed to you and show you what you must see." 3 I asked her, "Lady, in what part of the field?" "Wherever you wish," she said. I chose a beautiful spot that was secluded. But before I could speak with her to tell her the place, she said to me, "I will come there, wherever you wish." 4 And so, brothers, I went into the field and counted the hours. I arrived at the place that I had directed her to come, and I saw an ivory couch set up. On the couch was placed a linen pillow, with a piece of fine linen cloth on top. 5 When I saw these things laid out with no one there, I was astounded and seized with trembling, and my hair stood on end—terrified, because I was alone. Then when I came to myself, I remembered the glory of God and took courage. I bowed my knees and confessed my sins again to the Lord, as I had done before. 6 And she came with six young men, whom I had seen before, and she stood beside me and listened closely while I prayed and confessed my sins to the Lord. She touched me and said, "Hermas, stop asking exclusively about your sins; ask also about righteousness, that you may receive some of it in your house." 7 She raised me by the hand and led me to the couch; and she said to the young men, "Go and build." 8 After the young men left and we were alone, she said to me, "Sit here." I said to her, "Lady, let the elders sit first." "Do what I tell you," she said. "Sit." 9 But then, when I wanted to sit on the right side, she did not let me, but signaled with her hand for me to sit on the left. As I was mulling this over and becoming upset that she did not allow me to sit on the right, she said to me, "Are you upset, Hermas? The place on the right is for others, who have already pleased God and suffered on behalf of the

---

[g]Or *nor avoid your sister*   [h]Or *business dealings*   [i]The quotation may continue to the end of the verse   [j]This was an apocryphal book written in the names of the two prophets mentioned in Num. 11:26; it no longer survives   [k]Meaning obscure

name. Many things must happen to you before you can sit with them. But continue in your simplicity, as you are doing, and you will sit with them, as will everyone who does what they have done and endures what they have endured."

10 "What have they endured?" I asked. "Listen," she said: "floggings, imprisonments, great afflictions, crucifixions, and wild beasts—for the sake of the name. For this reason, the right side of holiness belongs to them, and to anyone who suffers on account of the name. And the left side is for the others. The same gifts and promises belong to both, those seated on the right and those on the left. But they alone sit on the right and have a certain glory. 2 You want to sit on the right side with them, but you have many shortcomings. But you will be cleansed of your shortcomings. And all those who are not of two minds will be cleansed from all the sins they have committed up to this day." 3 After she said these things she wanted to leave. But I fell before her feet and pled with her by the Lord to show me the vision she had promised. 4 Again she took my hand, raised me up, and seated me on the couch on the left side. She herself sat on the right. And raising up a bright rod she said to me, "Do you see a great thing?" I said to her, "Lady, I see nothing." She said to me, "Look, do you not see a great tower being built upon the water across from you, with bright, squared stones?" 5 The tower was being built in a square by the six young men who had come with her. And thousands of other men were bringing stones, some of them from the depths of the sea and some from the land, and they were handing them over to the six young men, who were taking them and building. 6 Thus they placed all the stones drawn from the depths in the building; for they fit together and were straight at their joints with the other stones. And they were placed together so that their joints were invisible. The building of the tower seemed to have been made out of a single stone. 7 But they tossed aside some of the other stones that were brought from the dry land, while others they placed in the building. Others they broke up and cast far from the tower. 8 Many other stones were lying around the tower, and they did not use them in the building. For some of them had a rough surface,[l] others had cracks, others were broken off, and others were

white and round, and did not fit in the building. 9 I saw other stones cast far from the tower; these came onto the path, but did not remain there, but rolled from the path onto the rough terrain. Others fell into the fire and were burned. And others fell near the water, but could not be rolled into it, even though they wanted to be.

11 When she had shown me these things she wanted to hurry away. I said to her, "Lady, what good is it for me to see these things if I do not know what they mean?" She answered and said to me, "You, fellow, are a crafty one, wanting to know about the tower." "Yes, Lady," I said; "I want to announce it to the brothers that they can become more cheerful; for when they hear these things they will know the Lord in great glory." 2 She said, "Many will indeed hear; and some of those who hear will rejoice, but some will weep. But even these latter, if they hear and repent, will rejoice as well. Hear therefore the parables of the tower. For I will reveal everything to you. Then trouble me no further about the revelation. For these revelations are completed and fulfilled. But you will not stop asking about[m] revelations, because you are shameless. 3 The tower, which you see being built, is I, the church, who has appeared to you both now and previously. And so, ask whatever you wish about the tower and I will reveal it to you, that you may rejoice with the saints." 4 I said to her, "Lady, since you have on this one occasion considered me worthy to reveal all things to me, reveal them." She said to me, "Whatever can be revealed to you will be revealed. Only let your heart be set on God, and do not be of two minds, whatever you see." 5 I asked her, "Why, Lady, is the tower built upon water?" "I have told you already," she said, "and you keep seeking; it is by seeking, therefore, that you find the truth. As to why the tower is built upon water, listen: It is because your life was saved and will be saved through water. But the tower is founded on the word of the almighty and glorious name, and it is strengthened by the invisible power of the Master."

12 And I responded to her, "Lady, this is a great and amazing thing. But the six young men who are building, Lady—who are

[l] Or *were scaly*; meaning obscure   [m] Or *for*

they?" "These are the holy angels of God who were created first, to whom the Lord handed over his entire creation, so that they could increase, build up, and rule over it all. Thus, through these the building of the tower will be brought to completion." 2 "But the others—the ones bringing the stones—who are they?" "They also are holy angels of God; but these six are superior to them. And so the building of the tower will be completed, and then all of them will rejoice together around the tower and glorify God, because the building of the tower has been completed." 3 I asked her, "Lady, I want to know about the destination of the stones, and about what they mean."[n] And she answered me, "This will be revealed to you, but not because you are more worthy than everyone else. For others are ahead of you and better than you; and these visions should have been revealed to them. But that the name of God may be glorified, the matter has been revealed to you and will be revealed, for the sake of those who are of two minds, who debate in their hearts whether these things are so or not. Tell them that all these things are true, that none of them is outside the truth, but that everything is firm and certain and established.

13 "Hear now about the stones that go into the building. On the one hand, the squared and white stones that fit together at the joints are the apostles, bishops, teachers, and deacons who live reverently towards God and perform their duties as bishops, teachers, and deacons for the chosen ones of God in a holy and respectful way; some of these have fallen asleep, but others are still living. And they have always been harmonious with one another and at peace with one another, and they have listened to one another. For this reason their joints fit together in the building of the tower." 2 "But who are the ones drawn from the depths of the sea and placed into the building, who fit together at their joints with the other stones already built in it?" "These are those who have suffered on account of the name of the Lord." 3 "But I also want to know, Lady, who the other stones are, the ones brought from the dry land." She said, "Those that go into the building without being hewn are ones the Lord has approved, because they walk in the uprightness of

the Lord and carry out his commandments." 4 "And who are the ones brought and placed in the building?" "These are those who are new in the faith and faithful. They are admonished by the angels to do good; for this reason, no evil has been found in them." 5 "But who are the ones who were tossed aside and cast out?" "These are those who have sinned but wish to repent. For this reason they are not cast far away from the tower, because they will be useful for the building, if they repent. And so if those who are about to repent do so, they will be strong in faith—if they repent now while the tower is still under construction. But if the building is completed, they will no longer have a place, but will be outcasts. This alone is to their advantage, that they lie next to the tower.

14 "But do you want to know about the ones that are broken off and cast far from the tower? These are the children of lawlessness. For they came to faith hypocritically and no wickedness ever left them. And so they have no salvation, since, because of their wickedness, they are useless for the building. This is why they were broken off and cast far away, because of the Lord's anger, since they aggravated him. 2 But with respect to the many other stones you saw lying on the ground and not coming into the building: The ones that are rough[o] are those who know the truth but do not remain in it, nor cling to the saints. This is why they are of no use." 3 "But who are the ones with cracks?" "These are those who hold a grudge against one another in their hearts and have no peace among themselves. Even though they seem to be peace-loving, when they leave one another's presence, their wickedness remains in their hearts. These are the cracks the stones have. 4 But the ones that are broken off are those who have believed and live, for the most part, in righteousness, but also have a certain share of lawlessness. This is why they are broken off and not whole." 5 "But who are the white stones, Lady, which are rounded and do not fit into the building?" She replied to me, "How long will you be foolish and ignorant, asking everything and understanding nothing? These are the ones who have faith, but also are wealthy in this age. But when affliction comes, be-

[n]Literally, *about their power*; meaning obscure [o]Or *scaly*; meaning obscure

cause of their wealth and their business[p] affairs, they deny their Lord." 6 And I responded to her, "And so when, Lady, will they be useful for the building?" "When the wealth that beguiles them is cut off from them," she said, "then they will be useful to God. For just as a round stone cannot be made square unless it has something cut off and discarded, so also with those who are rich in this age: If their wealth is not cut off from them, they cannot be useful to the Lord. 7 You should know this above all from your own case. When you were wealthy, you were of no use; but now you are useful and helpful in life. All of you should be useful to God. For you yourself are also being taken from the same stones.[q]

15 "But the other stones that you saw cast far from the tower and falling on the path and rolling from the path onto the rough terrain, these are the ones who have believed, but have left their true path because they are of two minds. They are lost, thinking they can find a better path; and they are miserable, walking over the rough terrain. 2 But the ones that fell into the fire and were burned are those who completely abandoned the living God; and they no longer think about repenting because of their licentious desires and the wicked deeds they have performed." 3 "But who are the other ones, which fall near the water but cannot be rolled into it?" "These are the ones who have heard the word and wanted to be baptized in the name of the Lord. But then when they recall what the life of true purity involves,[r] they change their minds and return to pursue their evil desires." 4 And so she completed her interpretation of the tower. 5 But being completely shameless, I asked her yet another question, whether these stones that were tossed aside and not fit into the building of the tower could repent and have a place in the tower. "They can repent," she said, "but they cannot be fit into this tower. 6 They will be fit into a greatly inferior place—and then only after they have been tormented and have completed the days of their sins. That is why they will be removed from there, because they have taken part in the righteous word. And then they will be removed from the torments inflicted for the evil deeds they did. But if deep down they do not want to repent, they will not be saved, because of their hardened hearts."

16 And so, when I stopped asking her about all these things, she said to me, "Do you want to see something else?" Being so eager to observe, I was excited by the prospect. 2 She looked at me and smiled, and said to me, "Do you see seven women around the tower?" "I see them, Lady," I replied. "This tower," she said, "is supported by them according to the commandment of the Lord. 3 Hear now about the work they do. The first of them, the one clasping her hands, is called Faith. Those who are chosen by God are saved through her. 4 And the other one, the one wearing a belt and acting like a man,[s] is called Self-restraint. She is the daughter of Faith. Whoever follows her will be fortunate in his life, because he will abandon all his evil deeds, believing that if he abandons every evil desire, he will inherit eternal life." 5 "And the others, Lady, who are they?" "They are daughters of one another, called Simplicity, Knowledge, Innocence, Reverence, and Love. And so, when you perform all the works of their mother, you will be able to live." 6 I replied, "I wish to know, Lady, about the power[t] that each of them has." "Listen," she said, "to the powers they have. 7 Their powers[u] are connected and follow one another in the order of their birth. From Faith is born Self-restraint; from Self-restraint, Simplicity; from Simplicity, Innocence; from Innocence, Reverence; from Reverence, Knowledge; and from Knowledge, Love. And so their deeds are pure, reverent, and godly. 8 Whoever serves as their slave and is able to adhere to their deeds will have a place to reside in the tower, along with the saints of God." 9 I began to ask her about the times, about whether the end had already come, and she cried out with a great voice, "You fool! Do you not see that the tower is still under construction? Only when its construction is finished will the end arrive. But it will be built quickly. No longer ask me anything. This reminder is enough for you and the saints—along with the renewal of your spirits. 10 These things have not been revealed for your sake alone; for you are to show them to all the others, 11 in three days; first, however, you must

[p]Or *daily* [q]Meaning obscure [r]Literally, *recall the purity of truth* [s]Or *the one girded and courageous* [t]Or *the meaning* [u]Or *their meanings*

think. But I enjoin you first, Hermas, with these words I am about to say; you are to speak them all in the ears of the saints, that once they have heard and done them they may be cleansed from their wicked deeds, and you along with them.

17 "Listen to me, children. I raised you with great simplicity, innocence, and reverence because of the mercy of the Lord, who drizzled his righteousness upon you that you may be made upright and purified from all evil and perversity. Yet you do not wish to stop doing your wicked deeds. 2 And so, now, listen to me: be at peace with one another, take care of one another, help one another; and do not take an overabundance[v] of God's creations for yourselves, but share with those in need. 3 For those who enjoy many kinds of food make their flesh weak and harm it; but the flesh of those without enough food is harmed by lack of proper nourishment, and their body wastes away. 4 This disparity is harmful to you who have but do not share with those in need. 5 Consider the judgment that is coming. You who have an abundance should therefore seek out the hungry, before the tower is completed. For after the tower is completed you will long to do good but will have no opportunity. 6 And so, take heed, you who exult in your wealth, lest those in need complain and their complaint rises up to the Lord, and you be shut out from the gate of the tower, along with your goods. 7 And so now I say to you who lead the church and sit in its chief seats. Do not be like the sorcerers. For the sorcerers carry their potions in boxes, but you carry your potion and poison in the heart. 8 You have grown calloused and refuse to cleanse your hearts and to join your minds together in clean hearts, so as to receive mercy from the great king. 9 And so take heed, children, lest these dissensions deprive you of your life. 10 How can you want to discipline the Lord's chosen ones, when you yourselves have no discipline? And so, discipline one another and be at peace among yourselves, that I also may stand before the Father cheerfully and so render an account to our Lord for all of you."

18 Then, when she stopped speaking with me, the six young men who were building came and took her away to the tower. And four others came and took the couch and carried it off to the tower as well. I did not see their faces, because they were turned away. 2 But as she was leaving I began asking her to give me a revelation about the three forms in which she appeared to me. And she answered me, "You must ask someone else to reveal these things to you." 3 For in the first vision, brothers, the year before, she appeared to me as a very elderly woman, seated on a chair. 4 In the other vision she had a younger face, but her skin and hair were older, and she spoke to me while standing. But she was more cheerful than before. 5 And in the third vision she was very young and exceedingly beautiful in appearance; only her hair was older. But she was completely cheerful and seated on a couch. 6 I was very sad, wanting to know about this revelation. Then I saw the elderly woman in a night vision, saying to me, "Every request requires humility. And so fast, and you will receive from the Lord what you ask." 7 So I fasted one day, and in that night a young man appeared to me and said, "Why do you constantly ask for revelations in your prayer? Take care, or you will harm your flesh by asking so much. 8 These revelations are enough for you. How can you manage to see revelations even more powerful than the ones you have already seen?" 9 I replied to him, "Lord, I am asking only about the three forms of the elderly woman, that the revelation may be complete." He answered me, "How long will you people be ignorant? You have become ignorant from being of two minds, not having your hearts set on the Lord." 10 I said to him again, "But from you, Lord, we will learn all these things more accurately."

19 "Listen," he said, "concerning the forms you are inquiring after. 2 In the first vision, why did she appear to you as an elderly woman, seated on a chair? Because your spirit is elderly and already fading away, having no vigor because you are feeble and of two minds. 3 For just as elderly people who have no hope of being rejuvenated look forward to nothing but their sleep,[w] so also you, grown feeble because of your worldly affairs, have handed yourselves over to apathy, and you do not cast your anxieties upon the Lord. Your mind has been wounded and you have

[v]Or *the best*   [w]Or *death*

grown old in your sorrows." 4 "I also want to know, Lord, why she was seated in a chair." "Because anyone who is weak sits in a chair out of weakness, to support the weakness of the body. Now you have the meaning[x] of the first vision.

20 "And in the second vision you saw her standing, and she had a younger face and was more cheerful than before, even though her skin and hair looked older. Listen," he said, "to this parable as well. 2 Someone who is older and has already given up all hope because of his bodily weakness and poverty looks forward to nothing except the last day of his life. Then suddenly an inheritance is left to him. And when he hears about it he rises up and in his excitement grows strong. No longer does he recline, but he stands and his spirit becomes rejuvenated even though it has been wasting away because of his daily life from before; and he no longer sits, but becomes manly.[y] You are like this as well, when you hear what the Lord has revealed to you. 3 For he showed you compassion and rejuvenated your spirits; and you laid your feebleness to the side and strength seized you and you were empowered with faith. And when the Lord saw your renewed strength he was glad. For this reason he showed you the building of the tower, just as he will show you other things as well, if you are at peace with one another from your whole heart.

21 "But in the third vision you saw her younger and beautiful and cheerful, and her form was beautiful. 2 For it is as when some good news comes to a person who is grieving: Immediately he forgets his former griefs and thinks about nothing but the news he has heard. And he is strengthened from that time on to do what is good, and his spirit is rejuvenated because of the exciting news he has received. So also your spirits have been rejuvenated from seeing these good things. 3 And you saw her seated on a couch because that is a strong position, since the couch has four legs and stands firmly. For the world is also held firm through the four elements. 4 And so, those who fully repent will become new and firmly established—those who have repented from their whole heart. Now you have the revelation complete. No longer ask anything about it; if anything is still needed, it will be revealed to you."

Vision Four

22 This is what I saw, brothers, twenty days after the earlier vision, as a foreshadowing[z] of the coming affliction. 2 I was going into the country[a] on the Via Campania. This is just over a mile off the public road; the place is easily reached. 3 While walking alone, I was asking the Lord to complete the revelations and visions he had shown me through his holy church, that he might strengthen me and give repentance to his slaves who had stumbled, so that his great and glorious name might be glorified, since he had considered me worthy to see his marvelous acts. 4 And while I was giving him glory and thanks, something like the sound of a voice answered me, "Do not be of two minds, Hermas." I began to debate with myself, "How can I be of two minds, when I have been firmly established by the Lord and seen his glorious deeds?" 5 I passed on a bit, brothers, and suddenly saw a cloud of dust, reaching up to the sky. And I began saying to myself, "Is that a herd of cattle coming, raising the dust?" But it was still about two hundred yards away from me. 6 And as the dust cloud grew larger and larger, I realized that it was something supernatural. The sun began to shine a bit and suddenly I saw an enormous wild beast, something like a sea monster, with fiery locusts spewing from its mouth. The beast was nearly a hundred feet long, and its head looked like a ceramic jar.[b] 7 And I began to weep and ask the Lord to save me from it. Then I remembered the word I had heard: "Do not be of two minds, Hermas." 8 And so, putting on the faith of the Lord, brothers, and remembering the great things he had taught me, I courageously gave myself over to the beast. And so it came on with a roar, enough to lay waste a city. 9 But when I approached it, the enormous sea monster stretched itself out on the ground and did nothing but stick out its tongue; otherwise it did not move at all until I had passed it by. 10 And the beast had four colors on its head: black, fire-and-blood red, gold, and white.

---

[x]Literally, *type* [y]Or *courageous* [z]Literally, *type* [a]Or *passing through a field* [b]Meaning obscure

23 After I passed by the beast and went about thirty feet ahead, a young woman suddenly met me, clothed as if coming from a bridal chamber, dressed all in white and with white sandals, veiled down to her forehead. Her veil was a headband and her hair was white. 2 From my earlier visions I knew that she was the church, and I became cheerful. She welcomed me, "Greetings, my man." And I welcomed her in return, "Greetings, Lady." 3 She said to me, "Did anything meet you?" I responded, "An enormous wild beast, Lady, able to destroy entire peoples. But by the power of the Lord and his great compassion, I escaped it." 4 "You escaped well," she said, "because you cast your anxiety upon God and opened your heart to the Lord, believing that you could not be saved except through his great and glorious name. For this reason the Lord sent his angel, named Thegri, who is in charge of the wild beasts; and he shut the beast's mouth, so that it could not harm you. You have escaped a great affliction because of your faith, and because you were not of two minds even though you saw such an enormous wild beast. 5 And so, go and explain the great acts of the Lord to his chosen ones, and tell them that this wild beast is a foreshadowing[c] of the great affliction that is coming. If then all of you prepare and repent before the Lord from your whole heart, you will be able to escape it—if your heart becomes clean and blameless and you serve the Lord blamelessly the rest of your days. Cast your anxieties upon the Lord and he will take care of them. 6 Trust in the Lord, you who are of two minds, because he can do all things; he both diverts his anger from you and sends punishments to you who are double-minded. Woe to those who hear these words and disobey. It would be better for them not to have been born."

24 I then asked her about the four colors the beast had on its head. And she answered me, "Once again you are being overly inquisitive about these matters." "Yes Lady," I said, "explain these things to me." 2 "Listen," she said. "The black is this world, in which all of you live. 3 The fire-and-blood red shows that this world must be destroyed through blood and fire. 4 But you who escape this world are the part that is gold. For just as gold is tested through fire and thus becomes

useful, so also you who dwell among them[d] are put to the test. Those who endure and are burned by them will be made pure. For just as gold casts off its dross, so also you will cast off every grief and tribulation, and be cleansed and made useful for the building of the tower. 5 But the part that is white is the age that is coming, in which the chosen ones of God will dwell. For those who have been chosen by God for eternal life will be spotless and pure. 6 And so, do not stop speaking in the ears of the saints. You now have the foreshadowing[e] of the great affliction that is coming. But if you wish, it will come to nothing. Remember the things written before." 7 When she said these things she departed; but I did not see where she went. For there was a noise, and I turned around out of fear, thinking that the beast was coming.

Vision Five

25 After I prayed in my house, sitting on my bed, an eminent looking man came to me, dressed in shepherd's clothing—wrapped with a white goat skin around his waist, with a bag on his shoulder and a staff in his hand. He greeted me, and I greeted him in return. 2 He immediately sat next to me and said, "I have been sent from the most reverend angel to live with you for the rest of your life." 3 I thought he had come to put me to the test, and I said to him, "Who are you? For I know the one to whom I have been entrusted." He said to me, "Do you not recognize me?" "No," I replied. He said, "I am the shepherd to whom you have been entrusted." 4 While he was speaking his appearance changed, and I recognized him, since he was in fact the one to whom I had been entrusted. And I was suddenly thrown into confusion, seized with fear, and entirely broken up by grief, because I had given him such a wicked and foolish response. 5 But he said to me, "Do not be confused, but become strong in my commandments, which I am about to give you. For I was sent," he said, "to show you yet again all the things that you saw before, since these are what will

[c]Literally, *type* [d]I.e., *either among the inhabitants of the world or among the fire and the blood* [e]Literally, *type*

chiefly benefit you. First, however, write my commandments and parables; but write the other things just as I show them to you. This is why," he said, "I am commanding you first to write the commandments and parables—that you may read them regularly and so be able to keep them." 6 And so I wrote the commandments and parables, just as he commanded me. 7 If then, after you hear

them, you keep them and walk in them and accomplish them with a pure heart, you will receive from the Lord everything he promised you. But if you do not repent once you have heard them, but increase your sins still further, you will receive the opposite from the Lord. The shepherd, the angel of repentance, thus commanded me to write all these things.

The Commandments

First Commandment

26 "First of all, believe that God is one, who created and completed all things, and made everything that exists out of that which did not, who contains all things but is himself, alone, uncontained. 2 And so believe in him and fear him, and in your fear be self-restrained. Guard these matters and you will cast all wickedness from yourselves and clothe yourselves with every righteous virtue, and you will live to God—if you guard this commandment."

Second Commandment

27 He said to me, "Hold on to simplicity and be innocent, and you will be like young children who do not know the wickedness that destroys human life. 2 First, of all, do not slander anyone. Nor listen gladly to anyone else who slanders. Otherwise, you the hearer will share the sin of the slanderer—if you believe the slander you hear. For when you believe it you also will hold something against your brother. And so you will share the sin of the one who slanders. 3 Slander is evil, a restless demon, never at peace but always living in dissension. And so, abstain from it and you will always be in good standing with all. 4 Clothe yourself with reverence, in which there is no wicked stumbling block, but everything is smooth and cheerful. Do what is good, and take what you have earned through the toils God has given you and give simply to those in need, not wavering about to whom you should give something and to whom not. Give to everyone. For God wishes everyone to be given something from his

own gifts. 5 And so, those who receive something will render an account to God, about why they received something and to what end. For those who received because of hardship will not face condemnation; but those who received out of hypocrisy will pay a penalty. 6 And so the one who gives is innocent. For as he was given a ministry from the Lord to complete, he has completed it in a simple way, having no doubts about to whom he should give or not give something. This ministry that is completed in a simple way becomes glorious before God, so that the one who ministers thus, in a simple way, will live to God. 7 And so guard this commandment as I have spoken it to you, that your repentance and that of your household may be found to be in simplicity—and pure, innocent, and blameless."

Third Commandment

28 Then he spoke to me again, "Love the truth and let all truth come from your mouth, so that the spirit that God made to live in this flesh may be recognized as true by everyone; in this way the Lord who dwells in you will be glorified. For the Lord is true in his every word, and there is no lie in him. 2 And so, those who lie reject the Lord and defraud him, not handing over to him the down payment they received. For they received from him a spirit that does not lie; if they return it to him as a liar, they defile the commandment of the Lord and become defrauders." 3 When I heard these things, I wept bitterly. When he saw me weeping he asked, "Why are you weeping?" "Because, Lord," I said, "I do not know if I can be saved." "Why?" he asked. "Because, Lord"

I said, "I have never in my entire life spoken a true word, but have always lived craftily with everyone, and have portrayed my lie as truth to all. And no one has ever contradicted me, but has trusted my word. How then, Lord," I asked, "can I live, having done such things?" 4 "Your thoughts are good and true," he said. "For you should have been conducting yourself as a slave of God; and a wicked conscience should not have dwelt with the spirit of truth or brought grief to the reverend and true spirit." "Never," I replied, "have I heard such words so accurately." 5 "You are hearing them now," he said. "Guard these matters so that the lies you spoke before in your daily life[f] may themselves become trustworthy when these other words are found to be true. For even those other ones can become trustworthy. If you guard these matters and from now on speak only the truth, you will be able to give yourself life. And whoever hears this commandment and avoids lying most wickedly will live to God."

Fourth Commandment

29 "I command you," he said, "to guard your holiness, and do not allow any thought to rise up in your heart about someone else's wife, or sexual immorality, or any other similarly wicked things. Otherwise you commit a great sin. But if you always keep thinking about your own wife, you will never sin. 2 For if this notion should rise up in your heart you will sin, and if another such wicked idea should arise, you commit a sin. For this notion is a great sin for the slave of God. And anyone who does such an evil deed brings death upon himself. 3 So be on the alert and avoid this notion. For where reverence dwells, lawlessness should not rise up in the heart of an upright man." 4 I said to him, "Lord, allow me to ask you a few questions." "Go ahead," he replied. "Lord," I said, "if someone is married to a woman who believes in the Lord, but he discovers that she is having an adulterous relationship, does the man then sin if he continues to live with her?" 5 "As long as he is ignorant of the affair," he replied, "he does not sin. But if the husband knows about her sin, and the wife does not repent, but remains in

her sexual immorality, and the husband continues to live with her, he becomes guilty of her sin and a partner in her immorality." 6 "What then should the husband do, Lord" I said, "if the wife continues in her passion?" "He should divorce her," he replied, "and live alone. But if he marries someone else after the divorce, he also commits adultery." 7 "But, Lord," I said, "if after the wife is divorced she repents and wants to return to her husband, should she not be taken back?" 8 "Yes indeed," he replied. "If her husband does not take her back, he sins, and drags a great sin upon himself; for the one who sins and repents must be accepted back. But not many times. For there is but one repentance given to the slaves of God. Because of repentance, therefore, the husband ought not to marry. The same applies to both wife and husband. 9 Not only is it adultery," he continued, "if a person defiles his flesh; but also, whoever behaves like the outsiders[g] commits adultery. And so, if anyone continues doing such deeds and does not repent, you should avoid him and not allow him to live in your midst. Otherwise you also share in his sin. 10 This is why you have been ordered to remain by yourselves, whether a husband or wife; for repentance is possible in such cases. 11 And so," he said, "I am not giving an occasion for things to turn out this way; I am saying that the sinner should sin no more. But with respect to his former sin, there is one who can provide healing. For he has the authority over all things."

30 I asked him again, "Since the Lord has considered me worthy to have you live with me always, bear with me for a few more words, since I understand nothing and my heart has been hardened because of my former actions. Give me insight, for I am extremely senseless and comprehend nothing at all." 2 He answered me, "I am in charge of repentance and give understanding to all those who repent. Or do you not realize," he said, "that repentance is itself a form of understanding? Repentance," he said, "is indeed a great understanding. For the one who sins understands that he has done something evil before the Lord, and what he has done rises up in his heart; then he repents and no longer does what is evil, but lavishly does what is good; and he humbles and tor-

---

[f]Or *business affairs* [g]Literally, *Gentiles*; or *nations*

ments himself, because he has sinned. So you see that repentance is a great understanding." 3 I replied, "This, Lord, is why I am carefully inquiring about everything from you—chiefly because I am a sinner, and I need to know what sorts of things I must do to live; for my sins are many and various." 4 "You will live," he said, "if you guard my commandments and proceed in them. Whoever guards these commandments, once he has heard them, will live to God."

31 "I still have some things to ask, Lord," I said. "Go ahead," he replied. "I have heard from some teachers, Lord," I said, "that there is no repentance apart from the one that came when we descended into the water and received forgiveness for the sins we formerly committed." 2 He said to me, "You have heard well, for that is so. For the one who has received forgiveness of sins must sin no more, but live in holiness. 3 And since you are carefully inquiring about all things, I will show this to you as well—not, however, to give an occasion for those who are about to believe in the Lord or who have already come to believe. For those who now believe or who are about to believe have no further repentance for their sins, but have received forgiveness for the sins they previously committed. 4 And so the Lord has given those who were called before these days an opportunity to repent. For the Lord knows the heart, and knowing all things in advance he recognized the weakness of humans and the intricate plots of the devil—that he will do some harm to the slaves of God and will wreck havoc among them. 5 And so, since the Lord is full of compassion, he had mercy on his creation and provided this opportunity to repent; and the authority for this repentance was given to me. 6 But this also I say to you," he said. "Whoever is tempted by the devil and sins after that great and reverent calling has one repentance. But if he should sin and repent repeatedly it is of no benefit to him. For he will find it difficult to live." 7 I said to him, "I have been made alive by hearing these things from you so accurately. For I know that if I no longer increase my sins, I will be saved." "You will be saved," he replied, "as will everyone else who does these things."

32 I asked him again, "Lord, since you have borne with me once, reveal this to me as well." "Speak," he said. "Lord," I said, "if a wife

or, again, a husband, should die and the survivor marry, does the one who marries commit a sin?" 2 "That one does not sin," he said, "but anyone who remains alone has provided a superior honor for himself and a great glory to the Lord. But if such a one does marry, it is not a sin. 3 And so, maintain your purity and reverence, and you will live to God. From now on, from this day in which you have been entrusted to me, guard all these things that I say and am about to say to you, and I will reside in your house. 4 For your former transgressions will be forgiven if you guard my commandments. And everyone will be forgiven, if they guard these my commandments and proceed in this purity."

Fifth Commandment

33 "Be patient," he said, "and understanding, and you will rule over every evil work and do all that is righteous. 2 For if you are patient, the holy spirit that dwells in you will be pure and will not be overshadowed by another, evil spirit; but dwelling in a broad place it will rejoice and be glad with the vessel it inhabits, and it will serve God with great cheerfulness, flourishing in itself. 3 But if any irascibility should enter in, immediately the holy spirit, which is sensitive, feels cramped; and not having a pure place it seeks to leave. For it is suffocated by the evil spirit, not having a place to serve the Lord as it wishes, being polluted by the irascibility. For the Lord dwells in patience, but the devil in irascibility. 4 And so, when both spirits dwell in the same place, it is unprofitable and evil for that person in whom they dwell. 5 For if you take a very small portion of wormwood and pour it into a jar of honey, is not all the honey spoiled? A great deal of honey is ruined by the least bit of wormwood. It destroys the sweetness of the honey, which is no longer pleasing to the master, because it has become bitter and lost its value. But if the wormwood is not put into the honey, the honey is found to be sweet and is valuable to the master. 6 You see that patience is sweeter than honey and is valuable to the Lord, and he dwells in it. But irascibility is bitter and useless. And so, if irascibility is mixed with patience, the patience is defiled and its prayer is of no use to God." 7 "I wish to know, Lord," I said, "the inner workings of irascibility, that I may guard against it." "Yes indeed," he replied, "if you and your household do not guard against it, you destroy your entire hope. But guard against it, for I am with you. And all those who repent from their whole heart will abstain from it; for I will be with them and protect them. For all have been made upright by the most reverend angel.

34 "Hear, now," he said, "the inner workings of irascibility, how it is evil and brings ruin on the slaves of God by the way it works, and misleads them away from righteousness. It does not mislead those who are full of faith, nor is it able to work against them, because the power of God is with them. But it misleads those who are empty and of two minds. 2 For when it sees such people at rest it inserts itself into their hearts, and with no warning the woman or man becomes embittered on account of some business deals, or because of food or something trivial, or because of a friend or something received or given, or because of other such foolish matters. For all these things are foolish, empty, senseless, and unprofitable for the slaves of God. 3 But patience is great and mighty; it has a forceful power that flourishes in a spacious arena; it is cheerful, glad, and free of anxiety, glorifying the Lord at all times, having no bitterness in itself but remaining always meek and mild. This patience,

therefore, dwells with all those who hold on to faith intact. 4 But irascibility is first of all foolish, fickle, and senseless. And then, from senselessness comes bitterness; from bitterness, anger; from anger, wrath; and from wrath, rage. Then this rage, which is compounded of such evil things, becomes a great and incurable sin. 5 For when these spirits dwell in one and the same vessel with the holy spirit, the vessel no longer has sufficient space but is stuffed to the brim. 6 And so the sensitive spirit, which is not accustomed to dwelling with an evil spirit nor with harshness, leaves the person and seeks to live with meekness and mildness. 7 Then when it leaves the one it had inhabited, the person becomes devoid of the upright spirit and at last, being filled with evil spirits, vacillates in everything he does, being dragged back and forth by the evil spirits, entirely blinded from any good understanding. This then is what happens to everyone who is irascible. 8 And so, avoid irascibility, which is the most wicked spirit. Clothe yourself with patience and stand against irascibility and bitterness, and you will be found with the reverence that is loved by the Lord. Take care that you never neglect this commandment. For if you master it, you will be able to guard the other commandments, which I am about to give you. And so, be strong and empowered in them, and may everyone who wishes to proceed in them be so empowered." . . .

The Parables That He Spoke with Me

Parable One

50 He said to me, "You know that you slaves of God are living in a foreign land. For your own city is a long way from this one. If, then," he said, "you know your own city, where you are about to live, why are you preparing fields, expensive furnishings, buildings, and pointless rooms for yourselves here? 2 Anyone who prepares these things in this city, therefore, cannot return to his own city. 3 You foolish, double-minded, and miserable person! Do you not understand that all these things belong to another and are under someone else's control? For the ruler of this city will say, 'I do not want you living in my city;

leave it, because you are not living by my laws.' 4 And so, you who have fields and houses and many other possessions—when he casts you out, what will you do with your field and house and whatever else you have prepared for yourself? For the ruler of this country rightly says to you, 'Either live by my laws or leave my country.' 5 And so what will you do, you who have a law from your own city? Will you completely renounce your own law for the sake of your fields and whatever else you own, and follow the law of the city you are in now? Take care, because renouncing your law may be against your own interests. For if you want to return to your own city, you will not be welcomed, because you have renounced its law; and you will be shut out of it. 6 And so take care. Since you are dwelling in a foreign land, fix nothing up for yourself except what is absolutely necessary; and be ready, so that when the master of this city wants to banish you for not adhering to his law, you can leave his city and go to your own, and live according to your own law gladly, suffering no mistreatment. 7 Take care, then, you who are enslaved to the Lord and have him in your heart. Do the works of God, remembering his commandments and the promises he made; and trust in him, because he will do these things, if his commandments are guarded. 8 Instead of fields, then, purchase souls that have been afflicted, insofar as you can, and take care of widows and orphans and do not neglect them; spend your wealth and all your furnishings for such fields and houses as you have received from God. 9 For this is why the Master made you rich, that you may carry out these ministries for him. It is much better to purchase the fields, goods, and houses you will find in your own city when you return to it. 10 This kind of extravagance is good and makes one glad; it has no grief or fear, but joy instead. And so, do not participate in the extravagance sought by outsiders;[h] for it is of no profit for you who are slaves of God. 11 But participate in your own extravagance in which you can rejoice. And do not counterfeit or touch what belongs to another, or desire it. For it is evil to desire someone else's goods. But do your own work, and you will be saved."

Parable Two

51 While I was walking in the field and considering an elm tree and a vine, reflecting on them and their fruits, the shepherd appeared to me and said, "Why are you asking yourself about the elm tree and the vine?" "I am thinking, Lord," I replied, "that they are extremely well suited for one another." 2 "These two trees," he replied, "symbolize the slaves of God." "I would like to know," I said, "what these two trees you are speaking about symbolize. " "You see," he said, "the elm and the vine?" "I see them, Lord," I replied. 3 "This vine," he said, "bears fruit; but the elm is a tree that does not. Yet if this vine did not grow up onto the elm, it could not bear much fruit, since

it would be lying on the ground, and the fruit it bore would be rotten, since it would not be clinging to the elm. And so, when the vine attaches to the elm, it bears fruit both of itself and because of the elm. 4 And so you see that the elm also gives much fruit—no less than the vine, but rather more." "How does it bear more, Lord" I asked. "Because," he said, "it is by clinging to the elm that the vine gives an abundance of good fruit; but when it is lying on the ground it bears just a little rotten fruit. And so this parable applies to the slaves of God, the poor and the rich." 5 "How so, Lord?" I asked. "Explain it to me." "Listen," he said. "The rich person has money, but is poor toward the Lord, since he is distracted by his wealth. The prayer and confession he makes to the Lord are very small—weak, small, and of no real effect. And so, when the rich person depends upon the one who is poor and supplies him with what he needs, he believes that by helping the one who is poor he will find his recompense before God. For the poor person is rich in his petition and confession, and his petition has a great effect before God. And so the rich person supplies everything to the one who is poor, without hesitation. 6 And then the poor person, having his needs supplied by the one who is rich, prays to God and thanks him for the one who has given him what he needs. And that one becomes even more eager to help out the poor person, so that he may lack nothing in his life. For he knows that the petition of the poor person is acceptable and rich before the Lord. 7 And so both accomplish their work. The poor person works at his prayer in which he is rich and which he received from the Lord; and he gives it back to the Lord who supplied it to him in the first place. So too the rich person does not hesitate to supply his wealth to the poor person, since he received it from the Lord. And this is a great and acceptable thing to do before God, because the rich person has gained understanding by his wealth and has worked for the poor person out of the gifts provided by the Lord, and he has accomplished his ministry well. 8 And so, people may think that the elm tree bears no fruit; but they neither know nor understand that when a drought comes, the elm nourishes the vine by holding water; and the vine,

[h]Literally, *Gentiles*; or *nations*

since it has an undiminished supply of water, produces fruit for two, both for itself and for the elm. Thus also those who are poor who pray to the Lord on behalf of the rich bring their own wealth to completion; and again those who are rich and supply the poor with what they need bring their souls to completion. 9 Both then share in an upright work. And so the one who does these things will not be abandoned by God, but will be recorded in the books of the living. 10 Happy are those who have possessions and understand that their riches have come from the Lord; for the one who understands this will also be able to perform a good ministry."

Parable Three

52 He showed me many trees that did not have leaves but appeared to me to be withered. And they were all alike. He said to me, "Do you see these trees?" "I see them, Lord," I replied. "They are like one another and withered." He said, "These trees you see are the people who dwell in this age." 2 "Why, then, Lord," I asked, "do they seem withered and like one another?" "Because," he said, neither the upright nor the sinners stand out clearly in this age, but they are like one another. For this age is a winter for those who are upright: They do not stand out clearly while dwelling with the sinners. 3 For just as the trees that shed their leaves in the winter all look alike, with the withered indistinguishable from the living, so too in this age it is not clear who the upright are and who the sinners, but they all appear alike."

Parable Four

53 He showed me again a number of trees, some of them budding, others withered. And he said to me, "Do you see these trees?" "I see them, Lord," I replied. "Some of them are budding and others are withered." 2 "These trees that are budding," he said, "are the upright who are about to dwell in the age that is coming. For the coming age is a summer for the upright, but a winter for sinners. And so, when the mercy of the Lord

shines forth, those who serve as slaves to God will stand out clearly, and everyone will be able to recognize them. 3 For just as the fruits of each individual tree appear in the summer and their species are recognized, so too the fruits of the upright will appear, and they will all be known in that age because they will be blossoming. 4 But the outsiders[i] and sinners—who are the withered trees you saw—will be found withered and fruitless in that age, and they will be burned like withered trees and shown for what they are, because they did what was evil in their lifetimes. The sinners will be burned for sinning and not repenting. But the outsiders will be burned for not knowing the one who created them. 5 You, therefore, bear fruit in yourself, that your fruit may appear in that summer. But avoid many business activities and you will not sin at all. For those involved with numerous business dealings are also involved in numerous sins, since they are distracted by their affairs and do not serve as the Lord's slaves. 6 How then," he continued, "can someone like this receive anything he asks from the Lord, if he does not serve as the Lord's slave? For his slaves will receive what they request, but those who are not his slaves will receive nothing. 7 But if someone should engage in just one kind of business,[j] he will also be able to serve as the Lord's slave. For his thoughts will in no way be corrupted away from the Lord, but he will be enslaved to him, keeping his thoughts pure. 8 So then, if you do these things you will be able to bear fruit in the age that is coming. And whoever else does these things will bear fruit."

Parable Five

54 While I was fasting and sitting on a certain mountain, thanking the Lord for everything he had done for me, I saw the shepherd sitting next to me. And he said to me, "Why have you come here so early?" "Because, Lord," I said, "I have a duty to perform."[k] 2 "What is the duty?"[l] he asked. "I am fasting, Lord," I replied.

---

[i]Literally, *Gentiles; or nations*　　[j]Or *one business transaction*
[k]Literally, *I have a station*

---

[l]Or *What is a station?*

"But what is this fast you people are keeping?" he asked. "I am fasting according to my custom, Lord," I said. 3 "You people do not know how to fast for God," he said, "and this worthless fast you are keeping for him is not a fast." "Why do you say this, Lord," I asked. "I say this," he said, "because what you think you are keeping is not a fast. But I will teach you a fast that is acceptable and complete to the Lord." "Yes, Lord," I said, "you will make me blessed if you show me the fast acceptable to God." "Listen," he said. 4 "God does not want this kind of vain fast. For when you fast like this to God you do nothing at all righteous. But fast to God as follows: 5 Do no evil in your life, but serve as the Lord's slave with a pure heart, keeping his commandments and proceeding in his injunctions; and let no evil desire rise up in your heart. Trust in God, because if you do these things and fear him and are self-restrained from every evil deed, you will live to God. If you do these things, you will accomplish a fast that is great and acceptable to the Lord.

55 "Listen to this parable I am about to tell you; for it relates to fasting. 2 There was a person who owned a field and many slaves, and he planted a vineyard in part of the field. And he chose a certain slave who was most trustworthy and pleasing to him. And he was about to go on a journey, he called him in and said to him, 'Take this vineyard that I have planted and build a fence around it before I return, and do nothing else to the vineyard. Do what I have commanded and I will set you free.' And the master of the slave went away on his journey. 3 When he had gone, his slave took the vineyard and built a fence around it. When he finished the fence he saw that the vineyard was full of weeds. 4 And so he reasoned to himself, 'I have finished what the lord commanded; so now I will dig in this vineyard. Once it is dug it will be more attractive, and without the weeds it will give more fruit, since it will not be choked by the weeds.' So he dug the vineyard and removed all the weeds that were in it. And that vineyard became more attractive and flourishing, since there were no weeds that could choke it. 5 After some time the master of both field and slave returned and came into the vineyard. When he saw that the vineyard was attractively fenced and even more that it was dug, with all the weeds

removed, and that the vines were flourishing, he was extremely pleased with what the slave had done. 6 So he called his beloved son, who was to be his heir, and his friends, who served as his advisors, and he told them everything he had commanded his slave and everything he found accomplished. And they congratulated the slave for the good testimony that the master had given him. 7 He said to them, 'I promised to free this slave if he did what I commanded him. And he did what I commanded and an additional good work in my vineyard besides. He has pleased me greatly. In exchange for the work he has done I want to make him a fellow heir with my son; for when he thought of the good deed, he did not leave it alone, but he accomplished it.' 8 The master's son approved of the idea that the slave should become his fellow heir. 9 After some days the master of the house gave a dinner and sent a number of foods to the slave from his table. When the slave received the food his master sent, he took what he needed and distributed the rest to his fellow slaves. 10 His fellow slaves took the food gladly, and began also to pray for him, that he might find even greater favor with the master, since he had treated them so well. 11 The master heard everything that happened and was again extremely pleased at what the slave had done. So he once more assembled his friends and his son, and he reported to them what the slave had done with the foods he had received. And they approved even more heartily his plan to make the slave his son's fellow heir."

56 I said to him, "Lord, I do not know what these parables mean and cannot understand them, unless you explain them to me." 2 "I will explain everything to you," he said, "and show you the meaning of everything I tell you. Guard what the Lord commands and you will be acceptable to him and enrolled among those who keep his commandments. 3 But if you do anything good beyond what God commands, you will be glorified even more and even more highly honored before God than you were bound to be. If, then, you do what God commands and perform any of these services in addition, you will be filled with joy—if you keep them according to my commandment." 4 I said to him, "Lord, I will guard whatever you command me. For I know you are with me." "I will be with you," he said, "because you are so eager to do good; and I will be with everyone who is just as eager. 5 This fast that consists of keeping the Lord's commandments," he said, "is very good. And so guard the fast. 6 First of all, be on your guard against every evil word and desire, and cleanse your heart from all the vain affairs of this age. If you guard these things, this fast will be complete. 7 And act as follows: When you have completed the things that have already been written, taste nothing but bread and water on the day you fast. Then estimate the cost of the food you would have eaten on that day and give that amount to a widow or orphan or someone in need. Be humble in this way, that the one who receives something because of your humility may fill his own soul and pray to the Lord for you. 8 If then you complete your fast like this, as I have commanded you, your sacrifice will be acceptable before God and the fast will be recorded. The service done in this way will be good and cheerful and pleasing to the Lord. 9 Thus you should keep these things, as should your children and your entire household. When you do so, you will be blessed. Everyone who hears these things and keeps them will be blessed, and they will receive whatever they ask from the Lord."

57 I begged him fervently to explain to me the parable of the field, the master, the vineyard, the slave who built a fence around the vineyard, the fence posts, the weeds that were removed from the vineyard, the son, and the friends who were advisors. For I understood that all these things were a parable. 2 He answered me, "You are extremely brazen in your requests. You should ask nothing at all, for if anything needs to be explained to you, it will be." I said to him, "Lord, there is no point in showing me something that you do not explain, when I do not know what it is. If you tell me parables without explaining them to me, there is no point in my hearing them from you." 3 Again he said to me, "Whoever is a slave of God and has the Lord in his heart asks him for understanding and receives it. And he interprets every parable; and the words of the Lord spoken in parables are made known to him. But all those who are weak and lazy in prayer hesitate to ask anything from the Lord. 4 The Lord has great compassion and gives without hesitation to every-

one who asks of him. But you have been empowered by the glorious angel and have received from him this petition; since you are not lazy, why do you not ask for understanding from the Lord and receive it directly from him?" 5 I said to him, "Lord, since I have you with me I need to ask and inquire of you. For you are the one showing everything to me and speaking with me. If I had seen or heard these things without you, I would ask the Lord to clarify them for me."

58 "I told you just now," he said, "that you are crafty and brazen, asking for the interpretations of the parables. But since you are so persistent, I will interpret for you the parable of the field and everything that follows it, that you may make these things known to all. Listen, now," he said, "and understand these things. 2 The field is this world. And the lord of the field is the one who created all things and completed them and empowered them. The son is the Holy Spirit and the slave is the Son of God. The vines are this people, which he has planted. 3 The fence posts are the Lord's holy angels who surround his people. The weeds that were removed from the vineyard are the lawless deeds of the slaves of God. The foods that he sent to him from his dinner are the commandments he has given his people through his Son. The friends and advisors are the holy angels who were created first. And the absence of the master is the time that remains until his coming." 4 I said to him, "Lord, all these things are great, marvelous, and glorious. How could I have understood them? No one else could have understood them either, even if he were extremely insightful. Yet, Lord," I said, "explain to me what I am about to ask you." 5 "Say what you wish," he said. "Why, Lord," I asked, "is the Son of God represented as a slave in the parable?"

59 "Listen," he said; "the Son of God is not represented as a slave, but as one who has great authority and lordship." "I don't see how, Lord," I replied. 2 "Because," he said, "God planted the vineyard—that is, he created the people and handed them over to his Son. And the Son appointed the angels over them, to protect each one. And he cleansed their sins through great labor, bearing up under his many labors. For a vine cannot be dug around without labor or toil. 3 And so, when he had cleansed the sins of the people he

showed them the paths of life, giving them the law, which he received from his Father. 4 You see, then," he said, "that he is the Lord of the people, having received all authority from his Father. But listen to what it means that the Lord took his Son, along with the glorious angels, as a counselor about the slave's inheritance. 5 God made the Holy Spirit dwell in the flesh that he desired,[m] even though it pre-existed and created all things. This flesh, then, in which the Holy Spirit dwelled, served well as the Spirit's slave, for it conducted itself in reverence and purity, not defiling the Spirit at all. 6 Since it lived in a good and pure way, cooperating with the Spirit and working with it in everything it did, behaving in a strong and manly way, God chose it to be a partner with the Holy Spirit. For the conduct of this flesh was pleasing, because it was not defiled on earth while bearing the Holy Spirit. 7 Thus he took his Son and the glorious angels as counselors, so that this flesh, which served blamelessly as the Spirit's slave, might have a place of residence and not appear to have lost the reward for serving as a slave. For all flesh in which the Holy Spirit has dwelled—and which has been found undefiled and spotless— will receive a reward. 8 Now you have the interpretation of this parable."

60 "I am very glad to have heard this interpretation, Lord," I said. "And now listen," he replied. "Guard this flesh of yours to keep it clean and undefiled, so that the spirit dwelling in it may bear a good testimony to it, and your flesh may be made upright. 2 Take care that the thought never occur to you that this flesh of yours is corrupt, and never misuse it in a defiling way. If you defile your flesh, you defile the Holy Spirit as well. And if you defile your flesh, you will not live." 3 "But Lord," I said, "if anyone was ignorant earlier—before having heard these words— and defiled his flesh, how will he be saved?" "God alone," he replied, "can bring healing to those who were ignorant earlier. For all authority is his. 4 But guard these things for now, and the Lord who has great compassion will provide healing for these things,[n] if here at the end you defile neither your flesh nor your spirit. For these two go together, and one cannot be defiled without the other. Keep both of them pure, therefore, and you will live to God."

Parable Six

61 While I was sitting in my house and giving glory to the Lord for all the things I had seen, and reflecting that his commandments are good, powerful, cheerful, glorious, and able to save a person's soul, I was telling myself, "I will be fortunate if I proceed in these commandments; for whoever proceeds in them is fortunate." 2 While I was telling myself these things, I suddenly saw him sitting next to me and saying, "Why are you of two minds about the commandments I have given you? They are good. Do not be at all of two minds, but clothe yourself with the faith of the Lord and proceed in them. For I will empower you to do them. 3 These commandments are profitable to those who are about to repent. If they do not proceed in them, their repentance is in vain. 4 And so, you who repent should cast aside the evil affairs of this age, which wear you down. For when you are clothed with every righteous virtue, you will be able to keep these commandments and no longer increase your sins. And so, by not increasing them, you will greatly cut off your former sins. Proceed therefore in my commandments, and you will live to God, for I have spoken these things to all of you." 5 After he spoke these things to me, he said, "Let us go into the country, and I will show you the shepherds of the sheep." "Yes, Lord," I said, "let's go." We came to a certain plain and he showed me a young shepherd, wearing a bright yellow suit of clothes. 6 He was tending a large flock of sheep. These sheep were luxuriously fed and extremely frisky and cheerful, leaping about here and there; and the shepherd also was cheerful with his flock. The shepherd's appearance was very cheerful, and he was running about among the sheep.

62 He said to me, "Do you see this shepherd?" "I see him, Lord," I replied. "This," he said, "is the angel of luxury and deceit. He, then, is the one who wears down the souls of the vacuous slaves of God and turns them away from the truth, deceiving them with evil desires that destroy them. 2 For they forget the commandments of the living God and proceed in vain deceits and luxuries and are destroyed by this an-

---

[m]Meaning obscure　　[n]Meaning obscure

gel—some to death and others to ruin." 3 I said to him, "Lord, I do not know what you mean that some are destroyed to death and others to ruin." "Listen," he said. "All the sheep you saw that were extremely cheerful and leaping about are the ones who have finally fallen away from God and have delivered themselves over to the desires of this age. Among these there is no repentance that leads to life, because they have also committed blasphemy against the name of the Lord. Death therefore belongs to them. 4 But the ones you saw that were not leaping about but were grazing in one place, these are the ones who have delivered themselves over to luxuries and deceits, without committing blasphemy against the Lord. They have been ruined by falling from the truth. For these there is a hope of repentance, and it can make them live. And so, those who have experienced this kind of ruin have some hope of new life, but death brings eternal destruction." 5 Then we went a little way ahead, and he showed me a large shepherd with a wild kind of appearance, clothed in the skin of a white goat, with a bag on his shoulder, a very hard and knotty staff, and a great whip. He had an extremely bitter look about him. I was afraid of him, he had such a look. 6 This shepherd was taking the sheep from the young shepherd—those that were frisky and luxuriously fed, but not leaping—and driving them into an area that was steep and filled with thorns and thistles. And the sheep could not extricate themselves from the thorns and thistles but became entangled in them. 7 And so they had to graze while being entangled among the thorns and thistles; and they were being miserably beaten by the shepherd. He was forcing them to move here and there, giving them no rest at all, so that those sheep were not at all tranquil.

63 When I saw them flogged like this and made so miserable, I started to grieve for them, because they were tormented in this way and had no respite. 2 I said to the shepherd who was speaking with me, "Lord," I said, "who is this merciless and bitter shepherd, who is showing no compassion at all for these sheep?" "This," he replied, "is the angel of punishment. He is one of the upright angels, but he has been appointed to mete out punishment. 3 And so he takes those who have strayed from God and proceeded in the desires of this age, and he punishes them with the

various terrifying punishments that each of them deserves." 4 "I want to know, Lord," I said, "what sorts of punishments there are." "Listen," he said, "to the various torments and punishments. For the torments come in the present life. Some people are punished with financial losses, others with deprivations, various diseases, or every kind of disruption, or by being abused by miscreants, and with many other kinds of suffering. 5 For many people undertake numerous projects but go back and forth in their minds, and nothing at all goes well for them. And they say that they do not prosper in what they do, but it never occurs to them that they have done what is evil; instead, they blame the Lord. 6 And so, when they have suffered every affliction, they are handed over to me for good discipline, and they are made strong in the faith of the Lord, and they serve as the Lord's slaves the remaining days of their lives, with pure hearts. When they repent, they think about the evil deeds they have done, and then they give glory to God, because he is an upright judge and each one has rightly suffered everything in light of what he has done. For the rest of their lives they will serve as the Lord's slaves with pure hearts, and they will prosper in their every deed, receiving everything they ask from the Lord. Then they glorify the Lord, because they have been delivered over to me, and they no longer suffer any evil."

64 I said to him, "Lord, explain something else to me." "What do you want to know?" he asked. "Are those who live in luxury and deceit," I asked, "tormented for the same amount of time that they lived in luxury and deceit?" He replied to me, "They are tormented the same amount of time." 2 "Then they are tormented very little, Lord," I said. "For those who have lived in luxury like this and forgotten God should be tormented seven times as long." 3 He said to me, "You are a fool and do not understand the force of the torment." "If I had understood it, Lord," I replied, "I would not have asked you to explain it to me." "Listen," he said, "and I will tell you the force of both things. 4 The time of luxury and deceit is a single hour. But an hour's worth of torment has the force of thirty days. And so, if someone lives in luxury and deceit for a single day, and is then tormented for a single day, that day of torment has the force of an entire year. Thus, a person is tormented for the same number of years as the days he has lived in luxury.° You see," he said, "that the time of luxury and deceit is very brief, but that of punishment and torment is long."

65 I said, "Lord, since I have not completely understood about the times of deceit and luxury and torment, explain them to me more clearly." 2 He answered me, "You are persistently foolish and do not wish to cleanse your heart and serve God. Take care," he said, "lest the time be fulfilled and you be found foolish. Listen, now," he said, "to what you want to know, so that you may understand these things. 3 The one who lives in luxury and deceit for a single day, doing whatever he wants, is clothed with great foolishness and does not understand what he is doing. The next day he forgets what he did the day before. For luxury and deceit have no memories, because the person is clothed in foolishness. But when punishment and torment cling to a person for a single day, he is punished and tormented for a year, because punishment and torment have great memories, 4 And so, when he is tormented and punished over the course of the entire year, then he remembers his luxury and deceit and he knows that he is suffering because of these evil deeds. All those who live in luxury and deceit are tormented in this way, because even though they are alive they have handed themselves over to death." 5 "What sorts of luxuries, Lord," I asked, "are harmful?" He replied, "Everything that brings a person pleasure is a luxury. For even the foul-tempered person who acts as he desires enjoys a luxury. So too does the adulterer, the drunkard, the slanderer, the liar, the greedy, the defrauder, and anyone who does anything similar, as he desires, in his own diseased way. Such a person, then, enjoys a luxury in what he does. 6 All these luxuries are harmful to the slaves of God. Those who are punished and tormented, therefore, suffer because of these deceitful practices. 7 But there are also luxuries that save people. For many people who do what is good enjoy luxury by being borne along by their own pleasure. And so this kind of luxury can be profitable for the slaves of God, and provides life to such a person. But the harmful luxuries that I mentioned before provide torments and punishments. If people remain in them without repenting, they provide death for themselves."

Parable Seven

66 After a few days I saw him in the same plain where I had seen the shepherds, and he said to me, "What are you looking for?" "I have come here, Lord," I said, "to ask you to order the punishing angel to leave my house, because he is afflicting me terribly." "You need to be afflicted," he replied, "because this is what the glorious angel commanded for you. For he wants you to be put to the test." "What evil thing have I done, Lord, to be handed over to this angel?" I asked. 2 "Listen," he said, "your sins are many, but not enough for you to be handed over to this angel. But your household has committed great sins and lawless acts, and the glorious angel is embittered by their deeds. This is why he commanded you to be afflicted for a time, to lead them to repent and cleanse themselves from all worldly desires. When they repent and are cleansed, then the punishing angel will leave." 3 I said to him, "Lord, even if they are acting in ways that embitter the glorious angel, what have I done?" "It cannot be otherwise," he said. "They cannot be afflicted unless you are as well, since you are the head of the household. For if you are afflicted, of necessity they are too; but if you are flourishing, they can experience no affliction." 4 "But look, Lord," I said, "they have in fact repented from their whole heart." "I myself know they have repented from their whole heart," he replied. "But do you think," he said, "that the sins of those who repent are forgiven on the spot? Not at all! But the one who repents must torment his own soul and become mightily humble in his every deed and be afflicted with many and various afflictions. And if he should endure the afflictions that come upon him, the one who created and empowered all things will be fully compassionate and bring him some healing. 5 This will certainly happen if he sees that the heart of the one who repents is pure from every evil deed. And it is to your advantage, and to your household's, to be afflicted now. But why am I telling you so much? You must be afflicted, just as that angel of the Lord commanded, the one who delivered you over to me. Give the Lord thanks for this—for he considered you worthy to have the af-

°Note: the calculations are based on a twelve-hour day

fliction explained in advance, that by knowing about it in advance you could endure it strongly." 6 I said to him, "Lord, be with me and I will be able to endure every affliction." "I will be with you," he said. "And I will also ask the punishing angel to afflict you less severely. You will be afflicted for a brief time, and you will again be restored to your place. But continue by being humble, serving the Lord with a pure heart—you, your children, and your household—and proceed in my commandments, which I have given you, and your repentance will be able to be strong and pure. 7 If you guard these matters, along with your household, every affliction will leave you. And affliction will leave everyone who proceeds in these my commandments."

The Apocalypse of Peter

Three different apocalypses surviving from ancient Christianity claim to have been written by Peter. The one presented here was discovered in 1887 in the tomb of a Christian monk, along with the *Gospel of Peter* (see that Introduction), and subsequently found in a fuller Ethiopic translation. This apocalypse was well known in early Christianity; some churches counted it among the New Testament Scriptures. Even when it came to be excluded from the canon (in part because Christians realized that it was pseudonymous), the book continued to exercise a significant influence on Christian thought. This is the first Christian writing to describe a journey through hell and heaven, an account that inspired a large number of successors, including, ultimately, Dante's *Divine Comedy.*

The book begins with Peter and the other disciples on the Mount of Olives listening to Jesus deliver his "apocalyptic discourse" (see Mark 13). Peter asks about the end of the world. Jesus responds by describing the terrifying events that will occur when the world is destroyed by fire at the last judgment. He then details the eternal terrors that await those destined for hell and, more briefly (possibly because they are somewhat less interesting, and certainly less graphic), the perpetual blessings of those bound for heaven.

There is some ambiguity over whether Jesus actually takes Peter on a journey through these two abodes of the dead or simply describes them in such vivid detail that it *feels* as if Peter is actually seeing them. There is no ambiguity, however, concerning the respective fates of those destined for one place or the other. In an unsettling way, the horrific punishments of the damned are made to fit their crimes (chaps. 7–12). Those who have followed Christ and kept the commandments of God, however, will be brought into the eternal kingdom, where they will enjoy the blissful life of heaven forever. The book ends with Peter describing firsthand what he saw on the Mount of Transfiguration, possibly in order to validate the legitimacy of the rest of his vision (cf. 2 Pet 1:17–18).

The ultimate goal of this first-hand description of hellish and heavenly realities is reasonably clear. There is one way to escape eternal torment: avoid sin. This message no doubt made a considerable impact on its Christian readers—it was, after all, written by "Peter," the closest disciple to Jesus, who could therefore be expected to know about such things. Moreover, it became an essential element in the Christian missionary proclamation, providing an incentive for pagans and Jews to turn from their false ways to worship the one true God who would reward those who came to accept his truth, but punish for all eternity those who did not.

The following translation follows the more complete and, probably, more accurate Ethiopic version of the text.

1 The Second Coming of Christ and Resurrection of the Dead which Christ revealed through Peter to those who died for their sins, because they did not keep the commandment of God, their creator.

And he (Peter) pondered thereon. that he might perceive the mystery of the Son of God, the merciful and lover of mercy.

And when the Lord was seated upon the Mount of Olives, his disciples came to him.

And we besought and entreated him severally and implored him, saying to him, "Declare to us what are the signs of your coming and of the end of the world, that we may perceive and mark the time of your coming and instruct those who come after us, to whom we preach the word of your gospel, and whom we install in your church, that they, when they hear it, may take heed to themselves and mark the time of your coming."

And our Lord answered us saying, "Take heed that no one deceive you and that you be not doubters and serve other gods. Many shall come in my name saying, 'I am the Christ.' Believe them not, neither draw near to them. For the coming of the Son of God shall not be plain: but as the lightning that shines from the east to the west, so will I come upon the clouds of heaven with a great host in my majesty; with my cross going before my face will I come in my majesty; shining seven times brighter than the sun will I come in my majesty with all my saints, my angels. And my Father shall set a crown upon my head, that I may judge the quick and the dead and recompense every one according to his works.

2 "And you learn a parable from the fig-tree: as soon as its shoots have come forth and the twigs grown, the end of the world shall come."

And I, Peter, answered and said to him, "Interpret the fig-tree to me: how can we understand it? For throughout all its days the fig-tree sends forth shoots and every year it brings forth its fruit for its master? What then does the parable of the fig-tree mean? We do not know."

And the Master answered and said to me, "Do you not understand that the fig-tree is the house of Israel? It is like a man who planted a fig-tree in his garden and it brought forth no fruit. And he sought the fruit many years, and when he did not find it he said to the keeper of his garden, 'Uproot this fig-tree so that it does not make our ground un-

fruitful.' And the gardener said to his master, 'Let us rid it of weeds and dig the ground round about it and water it. If then it does not bear fruit, we will straightway uproot it from the garden and plant another in place of it.' Have you not understood that the fig-tree is the house of Israel? Verily I say to you, when its twigs have sprouted forth in the last days, then shall false Christs come and awake expectation, saying 'I am the Christ who has now come into the world.' And when they perceive the wickedness of their deeds they shall turn away and deny him whom our fathers praised, the first Christ whom they crucified and therein sinned a great sin. But this deceiver is not the Christ. And when they reject him, he shall slay them with the sword, and there shall be many martyrs. Then shall the twigs of the fig-tree, that is, the house of Israel, shoot forth: many shall become martyrs at his hand. Enoch and Elijah shall be sent to teach them that this is the deceiver who must come into the world and do signs and wonders in order to deceive. And therefore those who die by his hand shall be martyrs, and shall be reckoned among the good and righteous martyrs who have pleased God in their life."

3 And he showed me in his right hand the souls of all people. And on the palm of his right hand the image of that which shall be accomplished at the last day; and how the righteous and the sinners shall be separated, and how those who are upright in heart will fare, and how the evil-doers shall be rooted out to all eternity. We beheld how the sinners wept in great affliction and sorrow, until all who saw it with their eyes wept, whether righteous or angels, and he himself also.

And I asked him and said to him, "Lord, allow me to speak your word concerning the sinners, 'It were better for them if they had not been created.'" And the Saviour answered and said to me, "Peter, why do you say that not to have been created were better for them? You resist God. You would not have more compassion than he for his image: for he has created them and brought them forth out of not-being. Now because you have seen the lamentation which shall come upon the sinners in the last days, therefore your heart is troubled; but I will show you their works, whereby they have sinned against the Most High.

4 "Behold now what shall come upon them in

the last days, when the day of God and the day of the decision of the judgment of God comes. From the east to the west shall all the children of men be gathered together before my Father who lives for ever. And he shall command hell to open its bars of adamant and give up all that is therein.

"And the wild beasts and the fowls shall he command to restore all the flesh that they have devoured, because he wills that people should appear; for nothing perishes before God and nothing is impossible with him, because all things are his.

"For all things come to pass on the day of decision, on the day of judgment, at the word of God: and as all things were done when he created the world and commanded all that is therein and it was done, even so shall it be in the last days; for all things are possible with God. And therefore he said in the scripture, 'Son of man, prophesy upon the several bones and say to the bones: bone unto bone in joints, sinew, nerves, flesh, and skin and hair thereon.'[1]

"And soul and spirit shall the great Uriel give them at the commandment of God; for God has set him over the resurrection of the dead at the day of judgment.

"Behold and consider the corns of wheat that are sown in the earth. As something dry and without soul do men sow them in the earth: and they live again and bear fruit, and the earth restores them as a pledge entrusted to it.

"And this which dies, that is sown as seed in the earth, and shall become alive and be restored to life, is man.

"How much more shall God raise up on the day of decision those who believe in him and are chosen of him, for whose sake he made the world? And all things shall the earth restore on the day of decision, for it also shall be judged with them, and the heaven with it.

5 "And this shall come at the day of judgment upon those who have fallen away from faith in God and have committed sin. Cataracts of fire shall be let loose; and darkness and obscurity shall come up and clothe and veil the whole world; and the waters shall be changed and turned into coals of fire, and all that is in them shall burn, and the sea shall become fire. Under the heaven there shall be a sharp fire that cannot be quenched, and it flows to fulfil the judgment of wrath. And the stars shall be melted by flames of fire, as if they had not been created, and the firmaments of the heaven shall pass away for lack of water and shall be as though they had not been. And the lightnings of heaven shall be no more, and by their enchantment they shall affright the world. The spirits of the dead bodies shall be like them and shall become fire at the commandment of God.

"And as soon as the whole creation dissolves, the people who are in the east shall flee to the west, [and those who are in the west] to the east; those in the south shall flee to the north, and those who are in the north to the south. And in all places shall the wrath of a fearful fire overtake them; and an unquenchable flame driving them shall bring them to the judgment of wrath, to the stream of unquenchable fire which flows, flaming with fire, and when the waves thereof part themselves one from another, burning, there shall be a great gnashing of teeth among the children of men.

6 "Then shall they all behold me coming upon an eternal cloud of brightness; and the angels of God who are with me shall sit upon the throne of my glory at the right hand of my heavenly Father; and he shall set a crown upon my head. And when the nations behold it, they shall weep, every nation for itself.

"Then shall he command them to enter into the river of fire while the works of every one of them shall stand before them. [Rewards shall be given] to everyone according to his deeds. As for the elect who have done good, they shall come to me and not see death by the devouring fire. But the unrighteous, the sinners, and the hypocrites shall stand in the depths of darkness that shall not pass away, and their chastisement is the fire, and angels bring forward their sins and prepare for them a place wherein they shall be punished for ever, every one according to his transgression.

"Uriel the angel of God shall bring forth the souls of those sinners who perished in the flood, and of all who dwelt in all idols, in every molten image, in every object of love, and in pictures, and of those who dwelt on all hills and in stones and by the wayside, whom people called gods: they shall be burned with them in everlasting fire; and after all of them with their dwelling-

---

[1] Ezek 37:4–6

places are destroyed, they shall be punished eternally.

7 "Then shall men and women come to the place prepared for them. By their tongues wherewith they have blasphemed the way of righteousness shall they be hanged up. There is spread under them unquenchable fire so that they do not escape it.

"Behold another place: there is a pit, great and full. In it are those who have denied righteousness: and angels of punishment chastise them and there they kindle upon them the fire of their torment.

"And again behold two women: they hang them up by their neck and by their hair; they shall cast them into the pit. These are those who plaited their hair, not to make themselves beautiful but to turn them to fornication, that they might ensnare the souls of men to perdition. And the men who lay with them in fornication shall be hung by their loins in that place of fire; and they shall say one to another, 'We did not know that we should come to everlasting punishment.'

"And the murderers and those who have made common cause with them shall they cast into the fire, in a place full of venomous beasts, and they shall be tormented without rest, feeling their pains; and their worms shall be as many in number as a dark cloud. And the angel Ezrael shall bring forth the souls of those who have been slain, and they shall behold the torment of those who slew them and say one to another, 'Righteousness and justice is the judgment of God. For we heard, but we believed not, that we should come into this place of eternal judgment.'

8 "And near this flame there is a pit, great and very deep, and into it flows from above all manner of torment, foulness, and excrement. And women are swallowed up therein up to their necks and tormented with great pain. These are they who have caused their children to be born untimely and have corrupted the work of God who created them. Opposite them shall be another place where children sit alive and cry to God. And flashes of lightning go forth from those children and pierce the eyes of those who for fornication's sake have caused their destruction.

"Other men and women shall stand above them, naked; and their children stand opposite them in a place of delight, and sigh and cry to God because

of their parents saying, 'These are they who despised and cursed and transgressed your commandments and delivered us to death: they have cursed the angel that formed us and have hanged us up and begrudged us the light which you have given to all creatures. And the milk of their mothers flowing from their breasts shall congeal and from it shall come beasts devouring flesh, which shall come forth and turn and torment them for ever with their husbands because they forsook the commandments of God and slew their children. As for their children, they shall be delivered to the angel Temlakos. And those who slew them shall be tormented eternally, for God wills it so.

9 "Ezrael the angel of wrath shall bring men and women, with half of their bodies burning, and cast them into a place of darkness, the hell of men; and a spirit of wrath shall chastise them with all manner of torment, and a worm that never sleeps shall devour their entrails; and these are the persecutors and betrayers of my righteous ones.

"And beside those who are there, shall be other men and women, gnawing their tongues; and they shall torment them with red-hot irons and burn their eyes. These are they who slander and doubt my righteousness.

"Other men and women whose works were done in deceitfulness shall have their lips cut off; and fire enters into their mouth and their entrails. These are they who caused the martyrs to die by their lying.

"And beside them, in a place near at hand, upon the stone shall be a pillar of fire, and the pillar is sharper than swords. And there shall be men and women clad in rags and filthy garments, and they shall be cast thereon to suffer the judgment of an unceasing torment; these are the ones who trusted in their riches and despised the widows and the women with fatherless children . . . before God.

10 "And into another place nearby, full of filth, they cast men and women up to the knees. These are they who lent money and took usury.

"And other men and women cast themselves down from a high place and return again and run, and devils drive them. These are the worshippers of idols, and they drive them up to the top of the height and they cast themselves down. And this they do continually and are tormented for ever. These are they who have cut their flesh as apostles of a man: and the women with them . . . and these are the men who defiled themselves together as women.

"And beside them . . . and beneath them shall the angel Ezrael prepare a place of much fire: and all the idols of gold and silver, all idols, the work of human hands, and the semblances of images of cats and lions, of creeping things and wild beasts, and the men and women that have prepared the images thereof, shall be in chains of fire and shall be chastised because of their error before the idols, and this is their judgment for ever.

"And beside them shall be other men and women, burning in the fire of the judgment, and their torment is everlasting. These are they who have forsaken the commandment of God and followed the (persuasions?) of devils.

11 "And there shall be another place, very high . . . The men and women whose feet slip shall go rolling down into a place where is fear. And again while the fire that is prepared flows, they mount up and fall down again and continue to roll down. Thus shall they be tormented for ever. These are they who honored not their father and mother and of their own accord withheld themselves from them. Therefore shall they be chastised eternally.

"Furthermore the angel Ezrael shall bring children and maidens, to show them those who are tormented. They shall be chastised with pains, with hanging up(?) and with a multitude of wounds which flesh-devouring birds shall inflict upon them. These are they who trust in their sins and do not obey their parents and do not follow the instruction of their fathers and do not honor those more aged than they.

"Beside them shall be girls clad in darkness for a garment, and they shall be seriously punished and their flesh shall be torn in pieces. These are they who did not preserve their virginity until they were given in marriage and with these torments shall they be punished and shall feel them.

"And again, other men and women, gnawing their tongues without ceasing, and being tormented with everlasting fire. These are the servants who were not obedient to their masters; and this then is their judgment for ever.

12 "And near by this place of torment shall be men and women who are dumb and blind and whose raiment is white. They shall crowd one upon another, and fall upon coals of unquenchable fire. These are they who give alms and say, 'We are righteous before God', whereas they have not sought after righteousness.

"Ezrael the angel of God shall bring them forth out of this fire and establish a judgment of decision(?). This then is their judgment. A river of fire shall flow, and all those judged shall be drawn down into the middle of the river. And Uriel shall set them there.

"And there are wheels of fire, and men and women hung thereon by the force of the whirling. And those in the pit shall burn; now these are the sorcerers and sorceresses. Those wheels shall be in all decision by fire without number.

13 "Thereafter shall the angels bring my elect and righteous who are perfect in all uprightness and bear them in their hands and clothe them with the raiment of the life that is above. They shall see their desire on those who hated them, when he punishes them and the torment of every one shall be for ever according to his works.

"And all those in torment shall say with one voice, 'Have mercy upon us, for now we know the judgment of God, which he declared to us beforetime and we did not believe.' And the angel Tatirokos shall come and chastise them with even greater torment, and say to them, 'Now do you repent, when it is no longer the time for repentance, and nothing of life remains.' And they shall say, 'Righteous is the judgment of God, for we have heard and perceived that his judgment is good, for we are recompensed according to our deeds.'

14 "Then will I give to my elect and righteous the baptism and the salvation for which they have besought me, in the field of Akrosja (Acherusia) which is called Aneslasleja (Elysium). They shall adorn with flowers the portion of the righteous, and I shall go . . . I shall rejoice with them. I will cause the peoples to enter into my everlasting kingdom, and show them eternal good things to which I have made them set their hope, I and my Father in heaven.

"I have spoke this to you, Peter, and declared it to you. Go forth therefore and go to the city of the west and enter into the vineyard which I shall tell you of, in order that by the sufferings of the Son who is without sin the deeds of corruption may be sanctified. As for you, you are chosen according to the promise which I have given you. Spread my gospel throughout all the world in peace. Verily people shall rejoice; my words shall be the source of hope and of life, and suddenly shall the world be ravished.

15 And my Lord Jesus Christ, our King, said to me, "Let us go to the holy mountain." And his disciples went with him, praying.

And behold there were two men there, and we could not look upon their faces, for a light came from them, shining more than the sun and their raiment also was shining and cannot be described and nothing is sufficient to be compared to them in this world. And the sweetness of them . . . that no mouth is able to utter the beauty of their appearance, for their aspect was astonishing and wonderful. And the other, great, I say, shines in his aspect above crystal. Like the flower of roses is the appearance of the color of his aspect and of his body . . . his head. And upon his shoulders . . . and on their foreheads was a crown of nard woven from fair flowers. As the rainbow in the water, so was their hair. And such was the comeliness of their countenance, adorned with all manner of ornament.

16 And when we suddenly saw them, we marvelled. And I drew near to God, Jesus Christ, and said to him, "O my Lord, who are these?" And he said to me, "They are Moses and Elijah." And I said to him, "Where then are Abraham and Isaac and Jacob and the rest of the righteous fathers?" And he showed us a great garden, open, full of fair trees and blessed fruits and of the odor of perfumes. The fragrance was pleasant and reached us. And of that tree . . . I saw many fruits. And my Lord and God Jesus Christ said to me, "Have you seen the companies of the fathers?"

"As is their rest, such also is the honor and the glory of those who are persecuted for my righteousness' sake." And I rejoiced and believed and understood that which is written in the book of my Lord Jesus Christ. And I said to him, "O my Lord, do you wish that I make here three tabernacles, one for you, and one for Moses, and one for Elijah?".[2] And he said to me in wrath, "Satan makes war against you, and has veiled your understanding; and the good things of this world prevail against you. Your eyes therefore must be opened and your ears unstopped that you may see a tabernacle, not made with human hands, which my heavenly Father has made for me and for the elect." And we beheld it and were full of gladness.

17 And behold, suddenly there came a voice from heaven, saying, "This is my beloved Son in whom I am well pleased:[3] [he has kept] my commandments." And then came a great and exceedingly white cloud over our heads and bore away our Lord and Moses and Elijah. And I trembled and was afraid; and we looked up, and the heaven opened and we beheld men in the flesh and they came and greeted our Lord and Moses and Elijah and went to another heaven. And the word of the scripture was fulfilled: "This is the generation that seeks him and seeks the face of the God of Jacob."[4] And great fear and commotion took place in heaven, and the angels pressed one upon another that the word of the scripture might be fulfilled which says, "Open the gates, you princes."[5]

Thereafter was the heaven shut, that had been open.

And we prayed and went down from the mountain, glorifying God, who has written the names of the righteous in heaven in the book of life.

---

[2]Matt 17:4; Mark 9:5; Luke 9:33   [3]Matt 17:5   [4]Ps 24:6   [5]Ps 24:7, 9

CPSIA information can be obtained at www.ICGtesting.com
Printed in the USA
BVOW05s1515131213

338998BV00007B/126/P